THE
ARCHITECT'S
HOME

GENERAL EDITOR
GENNARO POSTIGLIONE

WITH FRANCESCA ACERBONI,
ANDREA CANZIANI,
LORENZA COMINO,
CLAUDIA ZANLUNGO

THE
ARCHITECT'S
HOME

TASCHEN

Contents

Architects' Houses

DOMESTIC INTERIORS AND CULTURAL PRAXIS

Because of its private and intimate character, the interior has never attracted much attention. This low level of interest can perhaps be accounted for in terms of the short-lived nature of interiors. Private fittings and furnishings are tied to the necessity of meeting the current, subjective, specific and thus fugitive and changeable needs of the occupants. Criticism of architecture, by contrast, seeks to identify permanent manifestations of general and collective values, of a kind such as architecture can comprehensively include and harmonise[1], and does not recognise in the private space any values specific to the field. This criticism does not count the peculiar features of the interior, its constituent features, or its compositional principles – in short, everything that distinguishes the interior from other spaces and lends it an autonomous nature.

If, however, we examine the issues involved in the establishment of domestic space, the questions that arise time and again are those concerning relations between the public and the private, the collective and the individual, the spectacular and the intimate. There is no doubt that the private has always existed, since in every age there has been at least one zone protected from the intrusive gaze of strangers, an area reserved for more personal and intimate activities, even if its boundaries have been variously demarcated according to period and culture. It is this circumstance that constitutes the true foundation for inquiry into the nature of domestic space.[2] What follows in the present book is not an exhaustive presentation of individual works by a certain number of architects, but it does afford a hitherto unpublished, "transnational" panorama that differs substantially from what readers will encounter when leafing through the usual histories of architecture.[3]

This project, which showcases the residences of some of the most significant twentieth century European architects, aims not only to make visible an aspect of our culture that has hitherto been neglected by scholars, and to promote a public esteem and valuation of this cultural property, but also, ambitiously, to help assure the preservation of this shared international heritage.

The fact that it is indeed a shared international heritage, despite the location of the houses in specific places and thus their positions in specific national identities, is impressively documented in the present publication. The residences selected here reflect a new, transnational, intercultural dimension, in which mutual influences and thematic absorptions can be seen clearly prevailing over national traditions. The manifold network of connections linking the lives of these architects enriches their homes and affords concrete proof of the impossibility of confining a cultural praxis such as interior architecture within fixed geographic boundaries.

A further concern of this book is to liberate architecture from its function as a utility and to highlight its quality as a "hybrid cultural praxis". Its argument, presented to a wide public not consisting only of specialists, is that the private space is distinctly capable of absorbing cultural development. If we are better to understand the cultural and political frame of influence around the history of architecture, and to comprehend the ongoing interchange of thoughts, ideas and values that has been the hallmark of the modern era, we must of necessity take a close look at the houses architects have created for themselves. This is no act of voyeurism, nor any kind of intrusion into the private sphere.

Private spaces not only reflect the manifold living requirements of a particular time, they are also invariably both the transmitter and receiver of influences, styles and crossovers. In examining them, we are able to place the fashioning of interior spaces in a larger context, one that transcends the national boundaries within which that context has

1 Cf. P. Thornton, *Authentic Décor. The Domestic Interior: 1620–1920*, London, 1985

2 Cf. N. Flora, P. Giardiello, G. Postiglione, 'L'Impianto spaziale', in M. Vaudetti (ed.), *Manuale di ristrutturazione e rinnovo degli ambienti*, UTET, 1999

3 The present publication includes the work done by the MEAM Net research group at the Politecnico di Milano in collaboration with 27 institutions Europe-wide. This work, titled 'One Hundred Houses for One Hundred European Architects of the 20th Century', bore fruit in a travelling exhibition and a website (http://www.meamnet.polimi.it).

"A GOOD HOUSE IS A HOUSE IN WHICH ONE CAN LIVE WELL."

ADRIANO CORNOLDI

taken on concrete form. Our argument does not merely propose rolling back the borders (from the national to the European), however; it questions the very concept of borders and confines. If discourse is thus shifted from the political to the cultural level, the border becomes of necessity a fluid zone incapable of clear definition. What results is a hybrid space full of combinations, a space that allows for the emergence of a network of relations, processes of exchange, borrowing and mutation, which is not always recognised for what it is.[4]

To reflect upon the transnational dimension of cultural practices, especially in architecture, implies opening up private space to the unfamiliar. This brings consequences with it. As Iain Chambers has emphasised, the house is located "in traffic" in a twofold sense: doors and windows not only afford points of contact with the outside world, but also constitute those routes of communication by which what is alien, other, or different, can come in and people the domestic scene[5]. The irruption of the alien into the familiar area signifies the meeting of "what is of the home and what is not, what is familiar and what is not"[6]. This disrupts that positivist trust that is founded on the dialectic of opposites, and the concepts of authenticity and of unspoilt communities, on which occidental civilisation has built the organisation of its knowledge and its traditions, are undermined.

The transnational character of interior architecture, and its significance as a hybrid cultural praxis, has been expounded by Chambers as follows: "The journey back into one's tradition, just as the journey outwards towards another, is perhaps an altogether more fragile and fractured operation than our history and culture would have us believe. ... No tradition exists in isolation, it invariably cites/sites others."[7] This statement invites a new scrutiny of the interior of the house, the seemingly inviolable threshold of the private sphere[8], and demands that assessments of the built product be revised. The status of the domestic interior needs liberating from the subordinate role it has been assigned by a dominant architectural culture that has always been chiefly interested in the design of cities and of the principal buildings in them. For it is precisely the house, as a privileged place of action and exposure, that constitutes the "instrument" by means of which, as Christian Norberg-Schulz holds[9], man perceives and orders the world around him.

The private apartment as an object of reflection and design cannot, however, be considered in direct relation to the question of the "house and apartment for everyone" which governed the debate in European architecture in the first half of the twentieth century. Despite the thematic parallel, there are substantial differences owing to the different methodological approaches and aims. On the one hand, a process of definition, dimensioning and standardisation of requirements produced goals (in terms of rooms, fittings and furnishings) that aimed at the democratic distribution of resources (the house for everyone). On the other hand, interest in the apartment interior was always determined by the quest for comprehensive criteria which, regardless of forms and architectural idioms that had already been codified, would give to interior spaces that warm quality of comfort that renders a house a place of snug security, indeed makes a house a home.[10]

Moreover, the culture of interior spaces has all too often been equated with the history of architecture or of interior architecture. This involves a failure to grasp that the distinctive characteristic of domestic space consists precisely in transcending the historical facts of both, without being the product of their conjunction.

Although the evolution of the interior is intimately connected with the history of architecture – and with that of interior architecture, to which the interior belongs – it also has a distinctive individual character of its own. This individuality is manifested in the combination of forms and gestalts in the constituent elements that determine the nature of the

4   H. K. Bhabha, 'The Third Space' in J. Rutherford (ed.), *Identity, Community, Culture, Difference*, London, 1990, pp. 211–215.

5   Cf. I. Chambers, 'Le fondamenta disturbate e il linguaggio degli habitat infestati dai fantasmi', paper presented to the international conference 'One Hundred Houses for One Hundred European Architects of the 20th Century', October 2001, Milan Triennale

6   Cf. S. Freud, 'The Uncanny', in The Standard Edition of the Complete Psychological Works of Sigmund Freud, ed. and trs. James Strachey, vol. XVII, London, 1953, pp. 219–252

7   I. Chambers, 'Tradition, Transcription, Translation and Transit', in *AREA* 51, July/August 2000, p. 3

8   Cf. W. Rybczynski, *Home. A Short History of an Idea*, New York, 1987

9   Cf. C. Norberg-Schulz, *Dwelling*, London, 1986

10 Cf. F. Alison, F. Ll. Wright, *Designer of Furniture*, Naples, 1997

living place, including essential fittings and furnishings. The spaces are bound up with the lives, requirements and wishes of the people who have conceived and then realised them.[11] This relation of the form of the interior space to the life conducted in it is a fundamental feature. And for this reason it is impossible to assess the significance of the forms without taking the occupants, and their needs and sensibilities, into account.[12] An architect who designs a house or even simply its interior is taking on a delicate assignment that requires him to relate various kinds of information one to another, and to harmonise them. He translates them into a constructed form, in the hope of establishing the subtle and difficult synthesis of form and life.[13]

In the specific case of architects' houses, we can furthermore identify a "more sturdy relation between occupant and dwelling ... which allows us to determine the real, actual intention prevailing in the organisation of the daily living space and the private work space. That this applies not only in the case of architects, however, is evidenced by examples such as Pablo Neruda's apartments in Santiago and Valparaiso, Gabriele d'Annunzio's Villa Vittoriale in Gardone Riviera, Hearst Castle in San Simeon, or the Isabella Stewart Gardner Museum in Boston."[14]

As sites, architects' houses always engage two lines of interest: they are works, and they afford biographical testimony to their creators.[15] Insofar as this is so, the anthropological interest taken in cultural products in architects' houses is a fit area of research. One must concur with Adriano Cornoldi: "The study of residences designed by architects for themselves shows that, from the very core, the designs pursue an aim that ranges across a richly nuanced spectrum from a condition of absolute involvement to one of the utmost detachment. That aim may be to do with making a statement, one that leads to the building of a residence of one's own, free of anyone else's intentions, much in the spirit of a poetic manifesto. For Eliel Saarinen, Gerrit Rietveld, Robert Mallet-Stevens, Günther Domenig it is the statement of a new idiom; many use it to bring word of a new life style, be it one that prompts enthusiasm, as in Joseph Maria Olbrich or Konstantin Melnikov; be it one at once more free and more composed, as in Luigi Figini or André Lurçat; or be it a more down-to-basics style, as in Clemens Holzmeister or Ralph Erskine. For Jean Prouvé, Angelo Invernizzi and Arne Korsmo it is the 'unique' opportunity for a technological experiment. Auguste Perret's venture is a demonstration of entrepreneurial daring. The sheer pleasure of dwelling is particularly expressed in the apartments of Erik Willem Bryggman,

Umberto Riva and Enric Miralles and in the houses of Gunnar Asplund, Daniele Calabi, Alvar Aalto, Juan Navarro Baldeweg and Marie José Van Hee."[16]

One can add that in houses of such uniqueness, the architectural achievement is by no means at odds with the occupants. Unlike cases of cautious quest or of free experimentation, architecture is here invariably deployed as a means, not an end. The resolve to place praxis and theoretical speculation at the service of man and his requirements by no means issues in banality of the form or content of the architectural work, but rather in its further evolution. The needs and expectations of the occupants are satisfied without robbing innovative drive of its verve.

Alas, this happy union of private requirement and architectural ambition is increasingly being forfeited, as we see in publications where the visual realm of the interiors coincides with the will of the designers. They confirm the hegemony of objects over people, presenting to the public vacuous models of living bereft of meaning.

The present compilation intends, with resolve and perhaps just a little presumption as well, to supply the legitimation for the very existence of a theory and poetics of interior design that proposes practicable solutions. The object is to promote understanding of architecture that pays regard both to the occupants and to the ideas of the designers.

11 Cf. G. Teyssot (ed.), *Il progetto domestico. La casa dell'uomo: archetipi e prototipi*, catalogue of the XVII. Milan Triennale, Milan,1986
12 Cf. A. Cornoldi, *L'architettura dei luoghi domestici*, Milan, 1994, p. 20
13 Cf. G. Ottolini (ed.), *Civiltà dell'abitare*, Cantú, 1997
14 Cf. M. Boriani, 'Le case degli architetti. Conservazione, restauro e ricostruzione?', paper presented to the international conference 'One Hundred Houses for One Hundred European Architects of the 20th Century', October 2001, Milan Triennale
15 Cf. W. Rybczynski, *The Most Beautiful House in the World,* New York and London, 1989
16 A. Cornoldi, 'Le case degli architetti', paper presented to the international conference 'One Hundred Houses for One Hundred European Architects of the 20th Century', October 2001, Milan Triennale

The landscape of the interior is determined and characterised by objects that satisfy the needs and expectations of the occupants. It is these objects that make a space into a room.[17] A house without objects is an empty house, incapable of accommodating life. "That is the message conveyed by the interiors of the houses of Peter Behrens or Josef Plečnik, of Vittoriano Viganò or Franco Albini, of Carlo Mollino or Ignazio Gardella. The 'beauty' of the furnishings and objects may be relative, and subjective, but they are no less significant for that: it is precisely the absence of these things that is the hallmark of a prison cell."[18] Maurizio Boriani observes: "The sturdy relation that obtains between the spaces, the objects, and their meanings, is known only to the occupants and frequently not even by them, since a part is played by psychological considerations that are not always clear but indeed must sometimes be unconsciously sidelined."[19]

The fittings and furnishings bear silent witness to the act of living, and it is thanks to them that the occupants are able to enjoy rooms that were empty when the house was as yet uninhabited. The fittings and furnishings are true settlers: together with the objects that enter the interior of a dwelling when one takes possession of it, they transform spaces into locations that are in readiness for life.[20] "The distinctive character of the objects and furnishings in a house, their disposition in the rooms, their associations with each other, strong or less so, the order (or dis-order) in which people live in a house, can express a person's personality as well as a letter, a work of art, or social behaviour."[21]

To a particular degree, houses or apartments designed by architects for themselves are places of exchange and of cultural production. They not only afford an opportunity to observe how the relation between built form and the act of living has been established; they additionally elucidate a historical legacy that has hitherto remained almost entirely in the dark. Seen thus, the architect is not only a man of technology, professionally deploying a specialised form of expression within a defined field of operation, but is an intellectual who, like a writer, musician or any other artist, interprets communicable cultural values.[22]

If we are successfully persuasive in arguing that the significance of architects' houses lies in their high cultural value, and thus helping them toward the recognition they merit, the fraught question of how they can possibly be preserved immediately arises. The notion of some sort of museum preservation does indeed seem the only option for a heritage subject to constant wear and tear.[23] Boriani is thinking along similar lines when he writes: "In this case, preservation must be understood as the attempt to forestall dereliction and the associated loss of memory, by eliminating the factors that cause or accelerate it; in the full knowledge that any and every object we preserve for posterity can be nothing but an approximation to the original, even if it is our task to assure for the future the greatest possible use of the object (and hence also the greatest possible understanding of it)."[24]

Though the processes of preservation and restoration involved in architects' houses do not fundamentally differ from those other buildings require, the buildings do pose additional problems. The technical and structural aspects need to be taken adequately into consideration. Boriani comments: "Among the questions raised by the preservation of modern architecture, that of the materials and the experimental building techniques is one that occasions considerable problems. ... The 'test houses' in particular (frequently the residences of the architects and artists) merit preserving in their original state, in order to document the structural ventures, whether successful or not, even if this involves a lower level of functionality measured by today's standards."[25]

A further consideration is that architects' houses and apartments, as privileged locations of the private sphere, are not necessarily capable of transformation into public spaces. Even so, the number of houses adapted to a new museum role is growing constantly, and some already

17 G. Ottolini, V. del Prizio, *La casa attrezzata*, Naples, 1993
18 A. Cornoldi, 'Le case degli architetti', ebd.
19 Cf. M. Boriani, 'Le case degli architetti. Conservazione, restauro e ricostruzione?', ebd.
    Cf. J. Baudrillard, *Le système des objets*, Paris, 1968
21 Cf. M. Boriani, 'Le case degli architetti. Conservazione, restauro e ricostruzione?', ebd.
22 Cf. G. Bachelard, *La poétique de l'espace*, Paris, 1970
23 F. Drugman, 'Imparare dalla case', in F. di Valerio (ed.), *Contesto e identità*, Bologna, 2001
24 Cf. M. Boriani, 'Le case degli architetti. Conservazione, restauro e ricostruzione?', ebd.
25 Ebd.

serve as benchmarks, such as Pierre Chareau's Maison de Verre in Paris or Frank Lloyd Wright's house in Chicago[26]. These examples point up a difficult compromise, in the attempt to pursue restoration within existing parameters and regulations whilst at the same time following the unusual desire not to transform the dwelling into a "museum", in so far as the domestic character that sets it apart from other objects and defines it as a place of living and culture is to be preserved[27].

In raising the question of the museum character of dwellings, we are again foregrounding cultural discourse. In the course of history, the endeavour to give rhetorical embodiment to the power of knowledge has led the design of museums into an ongoing process by which frontiers are transgressed and purposes modified. This has gone hand in hand with that other process by which, over centuries, access has been extended from a privileged group of users to the broad masses.[28] Despite the greater permeability of their boundaries, and the change in their roles, museums still adhere to architecture as a display of public power. They have become places where a governance obtains that does not exclude but, rather, is based on a national identity in which any individual can recognise himself.[29] In this sense, the museum is indeed the institutional location where the occidental memory is given representative display, especially the memory of the social group that produced it — affording a precise image of the dominant culture.

The present publication wishes to endorse a different identity for museums. Our approach adopts a spirit cognate with that of Marie Louise Pratt's[30] idea of the "contact zone", that place where people separate from each other geographically and historically make contact by entering into mutual, interactive relations. In this spirit, realising an architectural network by transforming twentieth century European architects' houses into museums constitutes a true challenge for the future.

GENNARO POSTIGLIONE

26   Ebd.
27   Cf. A. Cornoldi, *Le case degli architetti. Dizionario privato dal Rinascimento ad oggi,* Venice, 2001
28   Cf. T. Bennett, *The Birth of the Museum*, London and New York, 1995
29   Cf. J. Karp, D. Lavine (eds.), *Exhibiting Cultures*, Washington, 1992
30   Cf. M. L. Pratt, *Imperial Eyes. Travel Writing and Transculturation*, London and New York, 1991

Alvar Aalto
1898–1976

1936, NEW CONSTRUCTION, NOW MUSEUM OWNED BY THE ALVAR AALTO FOUNDATION
RIIHITIE 20, MUNKKINIEMI, HELSINKI (FIN)

MAIN WORKS AND PROJECTS

1927–29	Editorial offices of Turun Sanomat, Turku (FIN)
1927–35	Viipuri City Library (FIN)
1928–33	Paimio Sanatorium (FIN)
1938–39	Mairea villa, Noormarkku (FIN)
1949–52	Säynätsalo municipal offices (FIN)
1949–64	University of Technology, main building, Otaniemi, Espoo (FIN)
1951–55	Rautatalo, office and commercial building, Keskuskatu 3, Helsinki (FIN)

1955–58	House of Culture, Sturenkatu 4, Helsinki (FIN)
	Church of the Three Crosses, Vuoksenniska Imatra (FIN)
1962–71	Finlandia Hall, concert and congress building, Mannerheimintie 13e, Helsinki (FIN)

ALVAR AALTO was born in Kuortane in 1898. When he was 5 years old, his family moved to Jyväskylä, which became Alvar Aalto's home town. His father, J. H. Aalto, was a surveyor, and the ordnance survey maps and outdoor fieldwork of the father affected the young Alvar's understanding of terrain and the location of buildings in the outdoors. These points were to become central to Aalto's design work.

In 1916 Aalto enrolled in the University of Technology, Helsinki, where he began to study architecture. While he was studying, important social events unfolded around him. Finland gained independence in 1917, but the country drifted into a civil war, in which young students, including Aalto, took part. After graduating from Helsinki University of Technology in 1921, he tried for a while to make a career for himself in Helsinki, but in 1923 moved back to his home town, Jyväskylä, where he opened an architectural practice. In this initial period Aalto's designs included church restorations and buildings in Jyväskylä. During the 1920s his output had a classical stamp. In 1924 he married Aino Marsio, also an architect, who had come to work as an assistant in his office. Aino Aalto became an important partner, whose rational thinking counterbalanced Aalto's exuberant bubbling ideas. Aino died in 1949, and Aalto remarried in 1952. His new wife, Elissa Mäkiniemi, also participated closely in her husband's design work.

In 1927, Aalto moved from Jyväskylä to Turku, where victory in a competition gave him a foothold in western Finland. The change in location marked the start of the architect's functionalist period. He now moved towards a rational architectural language, inspired by Le Corbusier's ideas. In Turku, he found a kindred spirit in the architect Erik Bryggman, with whom he made some joint designs. The most important works of Aalto's Turku period are his Paimio Sanatorium and Turun Sanomat office building, which laid the foundations of his international reputation.

In 1933 Aalto moved to Helsinki. During his early years in the Finnish capital, the architect distanced himself from strict theoretical rationalism and moved towards a human architecture that comprehensively embraced people. Aalto was in contact with the international avant-garde of both architecture and art, and his friends included Sigfried Giedion, László Moholy-Nagy and Fernand Léger. Aalto made a major contribution not just to modern architecture, but also – as a designer of furniture and art glass – to 20th-century industrial or applied art. The architect received various awards, among the RIBA Royal Gold Medal for Architecture (1957), the AIA Gold Medal (1963) and the Médaille d'Or of the Académie d'Architecture in Paris (1972).

A few years after his move to Helsinki, Alvar Aalto designed and built a house for himself and his family at Riihitie 20, Munkkiniemi, Helsinki (1936). A new construction, the building would be the architect's home for 40 years, until his death. Initially Aalto had his office in his private Riihitie house, but as his practice grew, he built a new separate studio elsewhere in Munkkiniemi, where his archives are still located today. Aalto's own home perfectly illustrates the turning point in his career in the mid-1930s, when he moved away from the restrictions of functionalism to a freer human architecture, close to nature.

In August 1937, the architect presented his new house in *Arkkitehti* (Finnish Architectural Review), describing it as follows: "The building is situated in Munkkiniemi, on a fairly steeply rising hillside site, Riihitie 10. It is built as a single-family house combined with the office and studio

EXTERIOR VIEW

VIEW FROM THE GARDEN

THE OFFICE

PAGES 16–17: VIEW FROM THE SOUTH

DAUGHTER'S ROOM

DINING ROOM

THE LIVING AREA

rooms needed for normal architectural work. Internally, the building is divided into three parts: a two-storey volume containing the workrooms, which are separated by a roof terrace from a group of rooms intended for private use (bedrooms and a hall), and a living room on the ground floor, complete with kitchen and patio for meals alfresco. The workroom can be combined with the living room by opening a sliding wall." Aalto also mentions the structure: "The vertical load-bearing structure is partly brick, but mostly steel columns, both I-section and circular. Horizontal components are reinforced concrete, while the eastern and south-facing external walls are timber, wedged into special grooves in the concrete." The furnishing includes armchairs, chairs, tables and vases designed by Aalto himself, but also Renaissance-style chairs purchased during his and Aino's honeymoon in Italy in 1924.

Aalto's own house in Munkkiniemi resembles in some respects the houses that Walter Gropius designed for the 'old masters' of the Bauhaus in Dessau. However, his use of wood with a pale, plastered brick surface, as well as the seamless union of living and work spaces, indicate the new direction he was taking. If his own house at Riihitie 10 shows Aalto beginning to incorporate his new ideas, his Villa Mairea of a couple of years later (1938–39) is the consummate embodiment of them.

TIMO KEINÄNEN

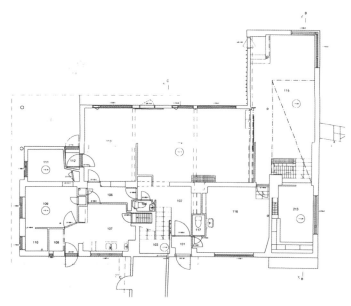

PLAN OF THE GROUND FLOOR

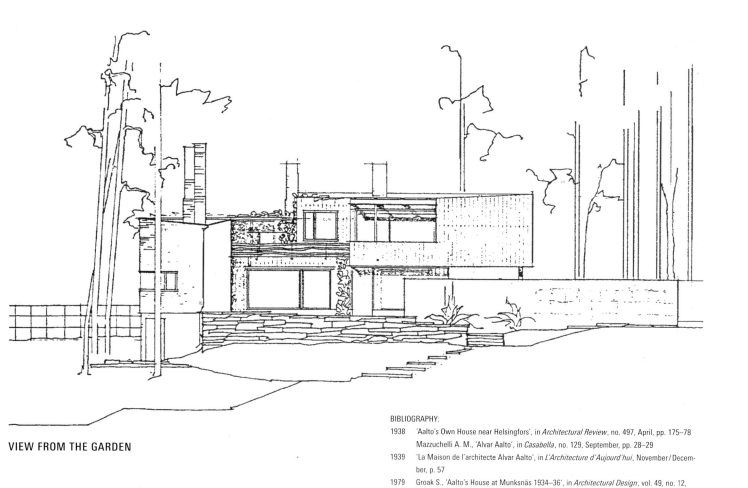

VIEW FROM THE GARDEN

BIBLIOGRAPHY:

1938 'Aalto's Own House near Helsingfors', in *Architectural Review*, no. 497, April, pp. 175–78

Mazzuchelli A. M., 'Alvar Aalto', in *Casabella*, no. 129, September, pp. 28–29

1939 'La Maison de l'architecte Alvar Aalto', in *L'Architecture d'Aujourd'hui*, November / December, p. 57

1979 Groak S., 'Aalto's House at Munksnäs 1934–36', in *Architectural Design*, vol. 49, no. 12, pp. 14–15

1994 Schildt G., *Alvar Aalto, The Complete Catalogue of Architecture, Design and Art*, Keruu

Franco Albini
1905 – 1977

1940, FURNISHING, NOW DEMOLISHED
VIA DE TOGNI, MILAN (I)

MAIN WORKS AND PROJECTS

1934	Italian Aeronautical Exhibition, Milan (I)	**1952–62**	Restoration and design of Palazzo Rosso museum, Genoa (I)
1938	Own house, via De Alessandri, Milan (I)	**1953**	Modern Italian Art, travelling exhibition
1949	Pirovano chalet, Cervinia (I)	**1962**	Milan underground, Linea 1 (I)
1949–51	Design of municipal galleries in the Palazzo Bianco, Genoa (I)	**1976**	Project for restoration of Masmak, Riyadh (Saudi Arabia)
1952–56	Museum of San Lorenzo Tesoro, Genoa (I)		

FRANCO ALBINI was one of the principal exponents of the second generation of modern architects who played a leading role in the Italian architectural debate for over 40 years, from the 1930s to the 1960s. A versatile artist, whose output ranged from design to furnishing objects and low-cost popular housing, Albini first came to the attention of critics – together with other architects – with several museum design projects, especially his contribution to the Aeronautical Exhibition of 1934, curated by Edoardo Persico.

The innumerable exhibitions and fairs held in the 20-year period between the wars, in which Albini often took part, were a great opportunity for experimentation, combining the various languages of the avant-garde with the communication strategies necessary for both propaganda and marketing. In his exhibition designs at the Milan Triennale in 1933, 1936 and 1940, Albini demonstrated his ability to break with the rhetoric of the academy and to assimilate the modern principles of New Objectivity. The exhibitions and fairs of this period laid down the foundations of modern museum design in Italy and saw the emergence of the great artists who gave rise to the Italian school of museum and exhibition design. Together with Luciano Baldessari, Ignazio Gardella, Marcello Nizzoli and Carlo Scarpa, Albini was undoubtedly one of the fathers of this tradition.

It was not only in the sphere of exhibition design that Albini was able to develop his experiments, as is shown by his two private houses in Milan, designed in 1938 and 1940, where his own home becomes the place of even more radical reflection and research. These houses present a whole series of design solutions that he would later adopt in important exhibition designs, like that of the Scipione and Bianco e Nero exhibitions at the Brera Art Gallery in Milan in 1941, or the renovation of the municipal galleries in the Palazzo Bianco, Genoa, in 1950. Especially the latter features the same display solutions that he used for the paint-ings in both his houses. Departing from 19th-century traditional practice, the paintings are shown without frames and placed in the middle of the rooms, rather than along the walls. The pictures are simply attached to metal structures, which stretch from the floor to the ceiling, and which are arranged along a path, thus creating an optimal view of the works displayed, and serving to divide up the living space.

In his via De Alessandri house (1938), Albini introduces elements that break up the space and block off the view. He deploys vertical panels made of cloth, which allow him to divide up the continuous space of the house into different areas. Thus "…the division between the living room and the dining room", as he wrote in the project outline, "is obtained with straw hanging to a rod sliding on metal rails… [while] the bedroom is separated from the living room by a double dividing curtain, one in white rubber, one in blue stitch with black threads". These partitions demonstrate his interest in the material aspect of objects, which some elements of Central European culture found so objectionable.

Albini resolutely publicised this attitude at the VII Triennale of 1940, where he showed his Living Room for a Villa designs. In this work he produced a sensitive although abstract domestic environment, ambiguously divided between an exterior and an interior, between an above and a below, where he juxtaposed furnishing objects designed by himself and products of contemporary culture, creating a harmonious unity that has much in common with the terrace of his 1938 house in Milan. An awareness of the value of tradition and of the lessons of the past allows him to avoid the indiscriminate adoption of the rationalist style which characterised much of Italy's architectonic output between the wars. In this sense we can clearly see Albini's affinity with and admiration for Giuseppe Pagano, whose important study on rural homes was undoubtedly known to the young architect.

THE LIVING ROOM

THE FIREPLACE AREA

DETAIL OF THE LIVING ROOM WITH RADIO

DETAIL OF THE FURNITURE IN THE LIVING ROOM

VIEW OF THE LIVING ROOM TOWARDS THE FIREPLACE AREA

Albini's other second private Milan house, in via De Togni (1940), continues to use free spaces in which the rooms are divided by complementary elements, such as fixed and mobile furnishings. Here, too, ancient and modern objects likewise contribute to the definition of internal space, with a blue curtain in the living room, for example, serving to separate the dining and living areas. The design of the master bedroom, which is dominated by a feeling of lightness and transparency, is particularly significant. Most of the furniture is made of white-painted metal tubes, and an old canvas is used to divide off the part of the room used for the lady's toilet.

Steel, wood and glass, but also cloth and light, are the materials used by Albini to build the spatial network of his domestic environments.

The resulting geometric and compositional order is both perfectly legible, like the finest Renaissance architecture, and conceived in the service of man.

In the post-war years Albini achieved growing professional success with his great urban plans and important museum designs, of which the Milan town plan (1945) and the Museum of S. Lorenzo in Genoa (1952) are only two of the most famous. In the mid-1950s he continued his architectural activity (1951–60 in partnership with Franca Helg, from 1962 with Antonio Piva and from 165 with his son Marco Albini) and his editorial work for Casabella. In 1955, 1958 and 1964 he received the Compasso d'Oro. In addition to that he continued his teaching career in Turin. He was an important academic figure at the IUAV (Istituto Universitario di Architettura di Venezia), where he taught until 1964, when the new political situation within the Polytechnic in Milan allowed him to move to the institute from which he had graduated in 1929. In his courses on furnishing, and later on architectonic composition, Albini based his teaching on a professional methodology that fully reflected the moral and theoretical assumptions of his own practice, maintaining a continuous focus over the years on the problems posed by design in various scales, from urban design to furnishing design. It was the same variety that had distinguished his poetics right from the beginning, when in the 1930s he tackled with equally confident ability the social theme of working-class housing and the close detail of exhibition design.   GENNARO POSTIGLIONE

BIBLIOGRAPHY:

1939   'Arredamenti in casa', in *Domus*, no. 134, pp. 60, 63
1941   Romano G., 'La casa dell'architetto Albini', in *Domus*, no. 163, pp. 9–17
1997   Piva A. and Prina V., Franco Albini. *Opera Completa*, Milan
2001   Cornoldi A., *Le case degli architetti. Dizionario privato dal Rinascimento ad oggi*, Venice, pp. 52–54

PLAN OF THE GROUND FLOOR

Reinhold Andris
*1958

1998, NEW CONSTRUCTION, STILL INHABITED BY THE ARCHITECT WALDDORFHÄSLACH (D)

MAIN WORKS AND PROJECTS

1992	One-family house, Iggingen (D)	1997	One-family house, Horn, Lake Constance (D)
	Semi-detached house, Esslingen-Berkheim (D)	1998	Terraced house, Stuttgart-Cannstatt (D)
1993	Atrium House, Holzgerlingen (D)	1999	One-family house, Weilheim / Teck (D)
	6-family house, Sindelfingen-Maichingen (D)	2000	One-family house in Niedrigenergiebauweise,
1994	One-family house, Villingen-Schwenningen (D)		Unterkirnach, Black Forest (D)
1996	Extension of school complex, Müllheim, Baden (D)	2001	Schank House, Walddorfhäslach (D)
	Semi-detached houses in Nürtingen-Neckarshausen (D)		
	and in Wolfschlungen (D)		

REINHOLD ANDRIS, born in 1958, studied at the University of Stuttgart from 1979–87. He interrupted his university course to study for a year in Phoenix, Arizona. He has run an architectural practice with two partners in Stuttgart-Botnang for several years.

In 1996, Andris and his wife Ingrid purchased a site in Walddorf-häslach to the south-east of Stuttgart on which to build their own home. The site appealed to them because of the beautiful landscape, for which Andris was even prepared to accept a half-hour commute to his office. To the south and east the site affords magnificent views over the hills of the Swabian Jura, and is bounded to the north by arable farmland which cannot be developed.

Completed in 1998, the house stands on a corner site in the vicinity of a number of other newly built one-family homes. Planning office regulations dictated a two-storey building with a saddleback roof and also prescribed the eave height and the use of red rooftiles. In spite of these restrictions, the result is a building that brings a breath of fresh air to an otherwise thoroughly conventional suburban environment. The extensive use of wood, as in the wall cladding, and the covered walkways at the sides, are reminiscent of Scandinavian country houses. Yet this rustic look is countered by the use of large swathes of glass around the corners and ribbon glazing below the eaves, which are anything but traditional. The red-tiled roof has also been "deconstructed" in similar vein: the line of the eaves is formed by an uninterrupted band of glass, lending the overall building the air of a synthesis of traditional house and glass house.

The large expanses of glass make the underlying structure of the house easily legible from the outside. Unusually for a family home, this takes the form of a steel frame structure. The simple building unit is based on six load-bearing frames set at intervals of 1.20 m and 2.40 m, respectively, reinforced at the sides by diagonal masonry bonds. The wooden structures for the ceilings, walls and roof are affixed by butt straps and dowels so that the interior load-bearing structure of steel girders remains visible. The girders are painted blue. Blue, red and yellow are the predominant interior colours, vaguely evoking associations of De Stijl – an impression already suggested by the red of the roof and the bright yellow of the timber cladding. The alternation between open and closed areas, indicated on the exterior of the building by alternating closed wall sections and expanses of glass, clearly reflects the interior with its private and reception areas.

The hillside situation and the alignment of the floors has created two superimposed sleeping areas. The lower one is on the right next to the central entrance area and is intended as a guest room, but could also be converted into a separate self-contained apartment. From the entrance, four steps lead down into the cellar and a longer stairway leads to the open-plan kitchen and dining area that takes up the entire north-west half of this floor. A large swathe of glass wrapping around the corner creates a link to the terrace on top of the equipment room which is situated to the side of the building. A short stairway links the dining area to the second bedroom. The overall sense of space is heightened by a central light shaft that creates an optical link between the dining area and the spacious living area under the roof. This high-ceiling room without pillars reiterates the form of the lower storeys and is undoubtedly the highlight of the house: a thoroughly flexible open-plan space that can be divided into a gallery and living room with many possible uses. The many different windows, glass walls and ribbon windows create an exhilarating play of light and shadow that changes constantly

NIGHT VIEW >

GROUND FLOOR

STAIRCASE

UPPER FLOOR

LIVING ROOM WITH DINING ROOM

throughout the day and with the changing seasons. Walking through the room, one finds ever new and exciting views and vistas – including a diagonal view into the lower storeys. The fact that the main living area in this house is not adjoined to the garden, as in most conventional designs, is mainly in deference to the breathtaking views over undeveloped countryside, which can be enjoyed to the full from this raised vantage point. All in all, the fluid handling of space in the interior of the house is more satisfactory than the exterior design, whose alternation between modern glass house and traditional style might have been a little bolder.

EBERHARD SYRING

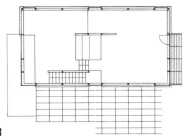

PLAN OF THE UPPER FLOOR

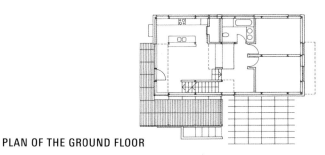

PLAN OF THE GROUND FLOOR

BIBLIOGRAPHY:
2000   'Experiment klares Wohnen', in *Häuser*, no. 5, pp. 38–44
2001   Stahl-Informations-Zentrum (ed.), *Wohnungsbau mit Stahl 077. Wohnhaus in Walddorfhäslach*, Düsseldorf
       Reiner H., *Bauen mit Holz. Die besten Einfamilienhäuser*, Munich, pp. 42–47

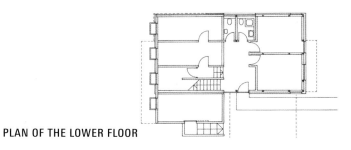

PLAN OF THE LOWER FLOOR

Erik Gunnar Asplund
1885 – 1940

1937, NEW CONSTRUCTION
STENNÄS, HÄSTNÄSVIKEN, LISÖN (S)

MAIN WORKS AND PROJECTS

1917 – 18	Snellman villa, Djursholm (S)		1928 – 30	Stockholm Exhibition, 1930 (S)
1918 – 20	Woodland Chapel, Woodland Cemetery, Stockholm (S)		1933 – 35	Bredenberg storehouse, Stockholm (S)
1918 – 27	Stockholm Public Library, Stockholm (S)		1934 – 37	Extension to Gothenburg Law Court, Gothenburg (S)
1919 – 21	Lister Courthouse, Sölvesborg (S)		1935 – 40	Woodland Crematorium, Woodland Cemetery, Stockholm (S)
1922 – 23	Skandia Cinema, Stockholm (S)			

ERIK GUNNAR ASPLUND was born in Stockholm on 22 September 1885. He took his school-leaving examinations at Norra Latin in Stockholm in 1904 and in 1905 enrolled as a student of architecture in the Royal Institute of Technology, Stockholm, from which he graduated in 1909. At that time prospective architects were not considered fully trained unless they studied two further years at Stockholm's Royal Academy of Art. Asplund enrolled instead in the Klara Skolan or 'Liberated Academy', which was a private institution in Stockholm directed by four well-known architects: Ragnar Östberg, Carl Westman, Ivar Tengbom and Carl Bergsten. His fellow students there included Oswald Almqvist and Sigurd Lewerentz. During this period Asplund also started to enter competitions. In 1913 he won First Prize in a competition to design the Gothenburg Law Court extension, and in 1915 – together with Lewerentz – he won an international competition for the Woodland Cemetery. It is characteristic of Asplund that he worked on both these projects for more than 30 years, and in each of them it is possible to follow his individual development as well as the changing times.

In 1914, after completing his studies, Asplund did his 'grand tour', visiting France and Italy. A few years later, in 1918, he married Gerda Sellman, with whom he had four children. They lived in an apartment near Mossebacke, in Stockholm. For a while, from 1917 to 1920, he also worked as an editor of the Swedish architectural review *Arkitektur*. In 1934 Asplund got remarried to Ingrid Kling, who had previously been the wife of the architect Lars Israel Wahlman. They lived in an apartment at Stureplan, directly connected to his office. In 1931 Asplund was appointed to a professorship in architecture at his Alma Mater, the Royal Institute of Technology. He died in Stockholm on 20 October 1940, aged 55.

Asplund now enjoys an international reputation as one of Sweden's foremost architects. This is despite the fact that he always worked only in Sweden and in a Swedish cultural context. He belonged to the generation that also numbered the great pioneering modern architects Walter Gropius, Ludwig Mies van der Rohe and Le Corbusier, but he was never a trailblazer like them. Asplund was not a man of revolutionary thoughts, oppositional programs or avant-garde innovations. The greatness of his work is to be found elsewhere. One of his qualities is authenticity, which can be found throughout his oeuvre. During his architectural development, which started early during his studies at the Royal Institute of Technology, Asplund moved from Romanticism and Classicism to Modernism, but without losing a pragmatic, humanistic and sensible way of working with architecture. Pervading all his designs is a solid ground of personal values, continuously evolving.

Asplund may not have been a groundbreaking architect, but he was nevertheless an artist who completed and interpreted the intentional and accidental programmatic ideas and projects of his time, transforming his experiences into durable architectural masterpieces, which can be returned to time after time. The impact of many other architects, from Palladio to Le Corbusier, can be seen in his work, but the most important influences came from his teachers Östberg, Westman, and och Bergsten. After graduating, Asplund – like many another northern architect – travelled to Italy and France. His experiences there, especially in Italy, when in 1914 he visited the temples of Paestum, the town of Pompeii, and the pastoral landscapes of southern Italy, left a mark on most of his work and are skilfully combined with northern conditions and Swedish culture. They are even clearly recognisable in one of his last works, the Woodland Cemetery and the Woodland Crematorium.

When we arrive at Asplund's private summer house (1937), a new construction at Stennäs, Hästnäsviken, Lisön, some 50 km south of Stockholm, we are struck most by the intimate scale and welcoming view of the house and its site. Even from a distance we experience a sense of cosiness and an unpretentious simplicity. To the north the building seems to be docked into the cliff, while to the west it opens up towards the en-

VIEW OF THE HOUSE WITH HÄSTNÄSVIKEN IN THE BACKGROUND >

VIEW OF THE TERRACE ON THE WESTERN SIDE

trance road and the lawn, more than to the bay in the south. This exterior space, with the entrance and roofed deck directed to the west, immediately recalls vibrant summer life with a large family and many visiting friends.

The façade is covered with narrow matched boards that have a sharp elegant profile. The boards are planed, smoothed off and painted white. The flat angled roof is made of wooden tiles. The difference between the delicate smooth surface of the façade and the raw tough materiality of the roof gives the exterior a poetic quality. The house seems to approximate to the traditional rural houses of Sweden, despite being at the same time a highly refined and sophisticated piece of architecture.

The main entrance door, facing west, opens from the deck, which is made of smooth wooden battens. Together with the smooth panelled façade, the deck creates an almost interior atmosphere. The door leads into a space that connects the dining room and a large combined drawing, sleeping and study room. In this way the exterior and interior public and 'social' parts are combined for meaningful use.

In plan, the large room facing south is drawn towards the west and turned in order to make a wide angle by the entrance terrace. This subtle

ENTRANCE ON THE EASTERN SIDE

arrangement is hardly noticeable. We 'read' the house as if it were right-angled. However, if it had been a right angle, the entrance would not have been so clear and welcoming, located as it is in the very corner.

The drawing room, with its view over the water, is the largest room in the house, however small in scale. The complexity of space and function is quite astonishing. The room seems to be divided into several smaller ones. The most obvious of these is the wide tiled staircase in connection with the fireplace. The composition is very intimate, and it is not difficult to imagine the comfortable feeling of sitting in the staircase looking out onto the meadows and the bay, with a lit fire. This is a perfect vision of Swedish summers, which can be wet and chilly as well as gentle and warm. At the southern window, there is a space for a sofa and armchairs, while by the windows looking west we find a place for study and work, with fine fitted desks and surfaces for sketching and writing. The master bed, used as a sofa during the day, stands beside one of the desks. The blankets and sheets are kept in the desk arrangement, hidden during the day in Japanese manner. Behind the fireplace is the basin, and originally the whole eastern part of the room was separated by a curtain and used as a wardrobe. The room is a multi-purpose place with rooms within the room, yet it nevertheless adds up to a powerful whole.

THE LIVING ROOM

34

In a more hidden part of the house, north of the dining room, is the children's bedroom and maid's room, while at the northernmost end lies the kitchen, with an outdoor part for cooking and working in the open air. The original wooden cupboards are still in use. The organisation of the house, with the kitchen concealed from the more public parts, shows that it was designed at a time when work and leisure were still separate.

A peculiar fact about the connection between the indoor and outdoor spaces is that the house is very much oriented to the west and the evening light. The northern side of the house is treated as the back, as is the east side, even though the contact with the sea is stronger on that side. It may be that the architectonic organisation is related to the pace of the family – or of the architect himself.

The inside walls and ceilings are made of rather rough, unmatched panels, whose wood is unplaned. Ironically, therefore, the exterior is far

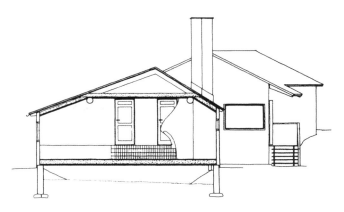

CROSS-SECTION

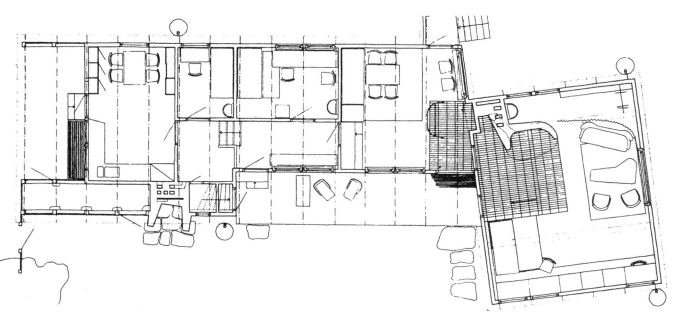

PLAN OF THE GROUND FLOOR

more elegant and in a sense more interior than the inside. This is an exceptional choice, and traditionally it would have been the other way round. One interpretation could be that the interior should be more generous and more flexible. The inhabitants should be allowed to put up hooks and nails for paintings, summer things, clothes etc. But the façade should be elegant and have a smooth finish, creating the paradoxically intimate and interior outdoor places, like a drawing room in the summer landscape.

The whole site, in terms of both organisation of space and treatment of materials and details, has an air of delicacy and grace. One possible influence could be that of the Arts and Crafts movement in England, which at the time was more than half a century old. Lars Israel Wahlman made the movement popular in Sweden, while it was also related to the ideas of the author Ellen Key, who created a debate about domestic aesthetics in Sweden at the beginning of the 20th century. Other important figures in this context were the painters Carl and Karin Larsson, who created a famous home with numerous qualities of daily life, of beauty and of convenience. This was a discussion of great importance for many

architects at the start of the 20th century, and it created a tradition that Asplund never abandoned.

Both the house and its site in Stennäs communicate a vivid image of the good life, with private and social goings-on, with cosy evenings by the fire, and with outdoor dinners in the light summer evenings.

GUNILLA SVENSSON, FINN WERNE

BIBLIOGRAPHY:

1943 Holmdahl G., Lind S. I. and Ödeen K. (eds), *Gunnar Asplund Arkitekt 1885–1940, Ritningar skisser och fotografier*, with an essay by H. Ahlberg, Stockholm, (English version published in 1950: *Gunnar Asplund Architect 1885–1940. Drawings, sketches and pictures*, Stockholm)
1980 Wrede S., *The Architecture of Erik Gunnar Asplund*, MIT Press, Cambridge, Mass.
1983 *Quaderns*, no. 157, special issue on Erik Gunnar Asplund
1985 Caldenby C. and Hultin O. (eds), *Asplund*, Arkitektur Förlag, Stockholm
2001 Cornoldi A., *Le case degli architetti. Dizionario privato dal Rinascimento ad oggi*, Venice, pp. 52–54

Ernesto Basile
1857 – 1932

1903–04, NEW CONSTRUCTION, NOW BRANCH OFFICE OF THE LOCAL DEPARTMENT OF CULTURAL HERITAGE FOR THE PROVINCE OF PALERMO VIA SIRACUSA, PALERMO (I)

MAIN WORKS AND PROJECTS

1891–97	Completion of Teatro Massimo, Palermo (I)
1899	Florio Vincenzo house, Olivuzza, Palermo (I)
1899–1900	Grand Hôtel Villa Igiea all'Acquasanta, Palermo (I)
1902–27	Extension of the Palazzo di Montecitorio and construction of the new hall in the Chamber of Deputies, Rome (I)
1903–04	Own house (Villino Ida), via Siracusa, Palermo (I)
	Fassini house, Palermo (I), destroyed

1907–12	New building for the Cassa Centrale di Risparmio Vittorio Emanuele, Palermo (I)
1911	New town hall, Reggio Calabria (I)
1913–14	Kursaal Biondo, Palermo (I)
1916	Chiosco Ribaldo in Piazza Castelnuovo, Palermo (I)
1923	Social housing in via A. Volta, Palermo (I)

ERNESTO BASILE was born in 1857 in Palermo, the capital of Sicily, the son of Giovanni Battista Filippo and Benedetta Vasari. His cultural and professional education took place under the guidance of his father, a renowned and versatile artist and scientist. Basile studied at Palermo's Regia Scuola di Applicazione per Ingegneri e Architetti (Royal School of Engineering and Architecture), graduating in 1878 as a qualified architect. During the 1880s he lived in Rome, where he married Ida Negrini (1887) and became an assistant professor with Enrico Guy at the University of Rome. He was later appointed professor of technical architecture there. At this time he travelled widely in the north of Italy and abroad (Brazil, Barcelona), often returning to Sicily. He also entered many architectural competitions. Following the death of his father in 1891, Basile moved back to Palermo to take over his position at the Academy of Fine Arts and at the School of Engineering and Architecture, which he led to prominence as a modern institution every bit as prestigious as the schools of Fischer and Wagner.

His father's passionate interest in botany led Basile to study the forms of nature, just as his father's scientific surveys helped Ernesto to acquire a knowledge of Sicilian architecture through the ages. Constant references to Arab-Norman, Gothic and Renaissance architecture would form the basis of Ernesto Basile's creative output, although his highly personal style was never limited to the confines of Sicily, but was always open to new cultural developments across Europe. He spoke several languages, and in his writings there are references to, among others, Eugène-Emmanuel Viollet-le-Duc and Gottfried Semper. Among his many journeys, his trip to Vienna in 1898 was particularly fruitful, as he came into contact with the school of Riegl and frequented Austrian Secessionist circles. From 1899 to 1909, Basile worked with the Ducrot furniture factory, for which he created elegant but economical pieces for mass production, alluding frequently to the low-cost furniture of Richard Riemerschmid and to the Glasgow school. The collaboration was the first of its kind in Italy and was compared by European furnishing journals such as *The Studio* and *Der Architekt* to Peter Behrens' experience with AEG.

Basile built his own house-cum-studio, the Villino Basile, which is widely known as the Villino Ida (Ida villa or house, so named after his wife), between 1903 and 1904. He chose to site the building, which was a new construction, on Palermo's via Siracusa (the house also has a façade on via Villafranca). In locating his home in a Liberty district of bourgeois residences, and in setting it on the road front, Basile renounced the traditional concept of the secluded villa and gave the house a markedly urban character. Nevertheless a sense of privacy is achieved because, externally, Basile extended the horizontal, ashlar and brick footing to form a true enclosing wall for the garden. On the house's public side, the living spaces are more closed, while on the private sides they are more open. Diverging from the practice of other studio-houses of the time, the architect did not place his studio at the front of the building, but positioned it stretching towards the garden, creating a further link between the public and the private.

In his 1981 book on Basile's private home, Gianni Pirrone wrote that "if the villa is a self-portrait, the care taken over the entrance makes it a sort of 'visiting card'". The nameplate by the main door makes use of the design on the architect's writing paper, thus acting as an invitation. But the door not only fulfils a representative and symbolic function, it also constitutes the threshold between the public and the private worlds. It does not lead directly into the house, but to a passage which, thanks to plays of light, is at once a place of transition from one area to another, a place to pause, and a 'crossroad'. Inside, the dining room forms the heart

STREET VIEW

THE MAIN ENTRANCE HALL

SKETCH OF THE MAIN ENTRANCE

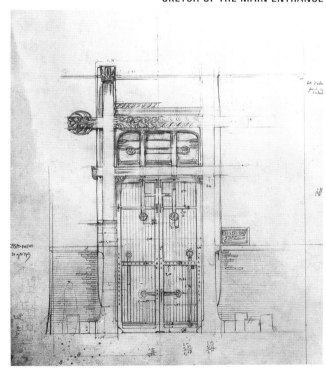

THE DINING ROOM

of the house, both in terms of distribution and in terms of its symbolic value, representing the family nucleus. Basile's search for cosiness and warmth is also underlined by the presence of the stove – the architect's pupils remember him as a man who hated the cold.

The villa's furnishings present details of ancient Mediterranean iconography, both marine (such as the octopuses and crabs in the carvings) and solar (the augural swastika, used in Hellenic times, on the dining-room floor). Every detail bears witness both to the lively personal involvement of the architect and the high level of domesticity, not found

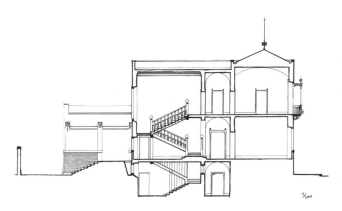

in the villas he designed for clients. "I planned my house thinking first of all of the interior distribution for the purpose of convenience, then of the construction, and finally of the decoration, which must be the logical consequence of the ground plan and the structure... The modern villa allows the house to be distributed over more than one floor, with one partly underground floor for bathroom and kitchen, with the ground floor for the studio, reception and dining rooms, with the first floor for the bedrooms and their annexes, and with the mezzanines for the domestic staff. This is the way my house is arranged." (*Skema*, nos. 8/9, 1972, p. 31)

Outside, the system of volumes is very simple. The prospects recall Mediterranean architecture and are extremely regular, with rhythmic openings and decorative motifs, slightly projecting, whose sculptural form is enhanced by the strong Sicilian light. Inside, the entrance hall, clad in ceramic tiles, is a hub from which three alternative routes depart. The first, up the stairs on the left, leads to the family accommodation. The second, down to the right, leads to the studio, while the third leads through a gate straight into the garden. On the raised floor, the ante-chamber leads to the true centre of the living area, formed by a square central block that contains the dining room, the stairs and the hall. Around this central block are a series of perimetric rooms linked to one another (the rooms of the studio are more isolated in the right-hand

FAÇADE ALONG VIA SIRACUSA

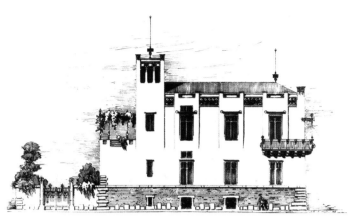

FAÇADE ALONG VIA VILLAFRANCA

wing, which stretches out to the garden; those of the living and reception area are situated to the left on via Siracusa; while the bathroom and kitchen are on via Villafranca).

Basile's own Ida house was designed during his most productive period, when he was also working on the Fassini and Monroy villas. These three houses, together known as the 'white villas', are distinguished by the abandonment of stone-clad façades in favour of plaster cladding, and show the influence of the architect's journeys in the Mediterranean area (Catalonia, Greece and Egypt). The themes shared by the three projects are developed in his own house in a coherent original way, and the fact that the architect was working for himself, unconstrained by the demands of clients, allowed him to go beyond the usual formal patterns and to achieve completely innovative results – the furnishings themselves can be considered prototypes of those he would create for Ducrot.

Basile's *esprit nouveau* is achieved by means of a simple harmony that represents the "plastic model of his style of life, the architectural

equivalent of a self-portrait" (Pirrone 1981). But it is also the expression of the architect's familiarity with the latest cultural trends. At a time when the main exponents of modern architecture were tackling the same theme, Basile combined the influences of the cultural production of contemporary Europe (Olbrich, Horta, Hoffmann, Mackintosh, Van de Velde) with the local Sicilian tradition. The Islamic style of the entrance, the little tower, the majolica, the mosaics, the stucco and the use as well as colour of the shutters are all quotations from and reworkings of Sicilian architecture and traditions. The Mediterranean myth was, in fact, also growing in Central Europe, for Byzantine and Islamic features were to be found in the works of Gustav Klimt and Alfons Mucha, in the Wagner school, and in the 1903 Universal Exhibition of Islamic Art in Paris.

CLAUDIA ZANLUNGO

PLAN OF THE GROUND FLOOR

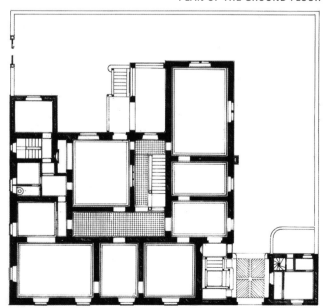

BIBLIOGRAPHY:

1976   Pirrone G. (ed.), *Studi e schizzi di Ernesto Basile*, Sellerio, Palermo
1980   Portoghesi P. and De Bonis A. (eds), *Ernesto Basile architetto, La Biennale di Venezia*, Electa, Milan
1980   Sessa E. (ed.), *Mobili e arredi di Ernesto Basile nella produzione Ducrot*, Novecento, Palermo
1981   Basile E., *Architettura dei suoi principi e del suo rinnovamento*, Novecento, Palermo
1981   Pirrone G., *Villino Basile: Palermo*, Officina, Rome
1987   Ingria A. M. (ed.), *Ernesto Basile e il Liberty a Palermo*, Herbita, Palermo
2001   Cornoldi A., *Le case degli architetti. Dizionario privato dal Rinascimento ad oggi*, Venice, pp. 62–64

Peter Behrens
1868 – 1940

1901, NEW CONSTRUCTION, INTERIOR DESTROYED BY A FIRE IN 1944, EXTERIOR REBUILT BY THE OWNER
MATHILDENHÖHE, ALEXANDRAWEG, DARMSTADT (D)

MAIN WORKS AND PROJECTS

1905 – 06	Gustav Obenauer house, Saarbrücken (D)
1908 – 09	Turbine factory for AEG, Berlin (D)
1910	Housing for AEG workers, Hennigsdorf (D)
1912	Gasworks, Frankfurt/Main (D)
	Offices for Mannesmann company, Düsseldorf (D)
1915	Housing developments at Berlin-Lichtenberg and Berlin-Oberschöneweide (D)
1920 – 24	Offices for Hoechster Farbwerke, Frankfurt-Höchst (D)
1921 – 25	HOAG steelworks, Oberhausen (D)
1924 – 26	Residential block (part of a social housing project), Vienna (A)
1926 – 27	Houses in the Weissenhof development, Stuttgart (D)
1930	Tobacco factory, Linz (A), with A. Popp

BORN IN HAMBURG in 1868, Peter Behrens studied painting between 1886 and 1889 at the Academy in Karlsruhe and also in Düsseldorf. In 1890, influenced by the teaching of William Morris and attracted by design and applied art, he moved to Munich, where he worked as a painter and typographer. Here, in 1892, he was one of the founding members of the Munich Sezession, and in 1897 he co-founded the Vereinigte Werkstätten für Kunst und Handwerk (United Workshops for Art and Craft).

In 1900, at the invitation of Grand Duke Ernst Ludwig von Hessen, Behrens moved to Darmstadt, where as a founder member he joined the Künstlerkolonie (Artists' Colony), a group that aspired to the integration of all the arts. The Colony had its first exhibition in 1901, and Behrens marked the occasion by building a home for himself. Constructed on Darmstadt's Mathildenhöhe, this 'manifesto of art nouveau' was his first architectural work. In 1902 Behrens took part in the International Exhibition of Applied Arts in Turin, and in 1903 he designed a dining room for an exhibition of the Dresdner Werkstätten für Handwerkskunst (Dresden Workshops for Applied Art). During these two years he taught at the Bayerisches Gewerbemuseum (Bavarian Trade Museum) in Nuremberg.

In 1903 Behrens moved on from Darmstadt to Düsseldorf, where in 1902 he had been appointed director of the Kunstgewerbeschule (School of Applied Arts), a post that he held until 1907. In the latter year he was offered by Emil Rathenau the position of artistic consultant with AEG (Allgemeine Elektrizitäts-Gesellschaft or General Electric Company) in Berlin, an offer which he accepted. At AEG Behrens was responsible for industrial design, overseeing the design of every product, from lamps to radiators, from industrial buildings to workers' housing, from the furnishing in local branches to advertising graphics. His work with the company helped to create a new figure: the industrial designer. Behrens' designs were a clear application of the ideas of Hermann Muthesius on the role of the artist in the context of mass production. From 1909 Behrens began to work in the industrial building sector. Around this time (1908–11) he employed in his studio architects who would become key exponents of modern architecture, including Walter Gropius, Ludwig Mies van der Rohe and Le Corbusier.

After Berlin, Behrens moved to Vienna, where in 1922 he was appointed to a professorship in the Academy of Fine Arts, taking over Otto Wagner's chair in the School of Architecture. He was involved 1925–26 in the experimental social housing developments and town planning being undertaken by Vienna's Socialist city council (the construction of the famous Höfe). Subsequently (1929–35) Behrens worked on similar town-planning projects for large-scale buildings in Berlin. Moving back from Vienna to Berlin, he was appointed to the chair of architecture at the Academy of Fine Arts there in 1936, directing the master studio for architecture. Peter Behrens died in Berlin in 1940.

The home that Peter Behrens built for himself was part of the Artists' Colony at Alexandraweg in Darmstadt. A single-family house, constructed new in 1901 on the occasion of the Colony's first exhibition, it formed part of the exhibition of that same year, indeed, may be said to have constituted the *pièce de résistance* of the Künstlerkolonie show. Despite this, and despite the fact that the architect designed the building down to the last detail, even the china plates, the home, which was Behrens' first architectural design, was lived in by himself and his wife Lilli for only two years (1901–03). Behrens once said that the principles underlying the design of the house were explained in the phrase "Everything that belongs to life must attain beauty." The dwelling provides an exhaustive interpretation of the concept of 'living'. In his own house Behrens man-

VIEW FROM THE GARDEN

aged to unite the vitalistic features of the 'new style' with a certain rational order that tends to anticipate the advent of Functionalism.

The building is both castle and sanctuary, place of action and intimate shelter. The bay windows project, the gables climb, and the niches in the music room and the studio enclose the treasure of the hearth (Christian Norberg-Schulz). The sober form of the exterior encloses the spaces of domestic life, characterised by the functions that take place within them, and the wall thus becomes a frontier between two distinct areas. The dining room is not only a place in which meals are taken, for a special atmosphere is created by the careful use of light, colour, decoration and openings.

Compact and tall, with a steep pavilion roof, Behrens' house stands on the Mathildenhöhe reminding the viewer of a small castle. The footing of red bricks, a continuous element that marks the basement floor used for services, contrasts with the dynamic arrangement of the upper floors.

The volume of the house-cum-studio is enlivened through the use of bay windows and recesses in the walls or of the lively outlines of the dormer windows and the gables, or by the use of the bands of red bricks and green tiles (in zigzag form) that mark the corners, cornices, gables and windows. The exterior can be understood as a highly sophisticated interaction between vertical and horizontal movements, which defines the various relations between earth and sky (Christian Norberg-Schulz).

The arrangement of the interior spaces is rather conventional. The main door, marked by an ornament in bronze aluminium, opens into the hall, which leads on the mezzanine floor to adjacent rooms, including the music room, the dining room and the parlour. On the first floor are the bedrooms and the library. The richness of the project is a result of the careful control over every room, in which every last detail has been designed by the architect – from the furnishing and the decoration of the walls, floors and ceilings, to the design of handles, chandeliers, curtains, crockery and cutlery. The severity of the music room, lined with sheets of blue glass, contrasts with the more festive appearance of the dining room, with its white walls and furniture, which opens onto the garden through the wide bay window. The same decorative motif is found in the lines of the ceiling and of the sideboards, in the decorations of plates and bowls, on the handles of knives and spoons, in the crystals of the chandeliers and even woven on the precious tablecloths. Behrens even designed the geometric inlay pattern on the Schiedmayer piano and on the wooden floor in the music room.

GROUND FLOOR DINING ROOM

LADY'S DRAWING ROOM, GROUND FLOOR

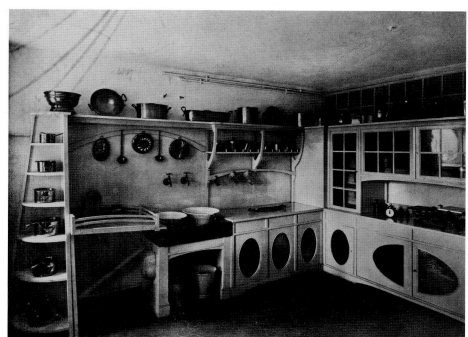

KITCHEN

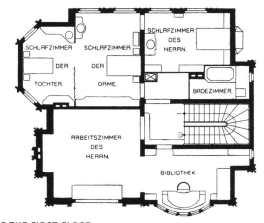

PLAN OF THE FIRST FLOOR

The more intimate spaces of the parlour and the bedrooms, on the other hand, are characterised by a warm atmosphere, created through the clever use of wood and fabrics. The library is a significant example of harmony between furnishing and space – the curve of the upright of the shelves and the organic forms heighten the elegance of the room.

LUISA GATTI

CROSS-SECTION

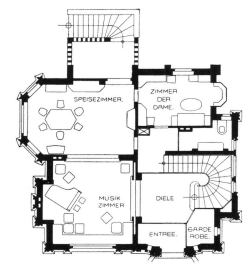

PLAN OF THE GROUND FLOOR

BIBLIOGRAPHY:

1913   Hoeber F., *Peter Behrens*, Munich
1981   Windsor A., *Peter Behrens: Architect and Designer*, London
1981   Bilancioni G., *Il primo Behrens: origini del moderno in architettura*, Florence
1986   Norberg-Schulz C. (ed.), *Casa Behrens: Darmstadt*, Rome
2000   Anderson S., *Peter Behrens and a New Architecture for the 20th Century*, Cambridge

Jan Benthem
*1952

1982–84, NEW CONSTRUCTION, IN COLLABORATION WITH
MELS CROUWEL, STILL INHABITED BY THE ARCHITECT
DE FANTASIE, ALMERE (NL)

MAIN WORKS AND PROJECTS

1985–86   Sculpture pavilion, Sonsbeek (NL)
1989–93   De Pont Museum, Tilburg (NL)
1991–94   Nieuw Land Poldermuseum, Lelystad (NL)
1991–95   Schiphol railway station and plaza, Schiphol Airport,
          Amsterdam (NL)
1993–99   Anne Frank House and Museum, Amsterdam (NL)

1994–98   Popcluster 013, Tilburg (NL)
1998–2002 IJburg bridges, Amsterdam (NL)
2000–03   GEM Museum of Contemporary Art, The Hague (NL)

JAN BENTHEM and Mels Crouwel were both born in Amsterdam, in 1952 and 1953 respectively. They studied together in the school of architecture at the Technical University of Delft, graduating in 1978. The following year Benthem and Crouwel founded a joint architectural practice in Amsterdam, which has now been running for some 25 years. Their office comprises five task areas, which they themselves label as: living, working, shopping, travelling, and visiting. The categorisation reveals an important aspect of Benthem and Crouwel's conception of architecture. They describe the products of their studio in terms of uses. The accent is not on outward appearances but on human beings, and hence on a building's functionality.

Between 1987 and 1992 the two architects realised the Ibis Hotel and, next door, the Wagons Lits office building, both in Amsterdam. Constructed of concrete and steel, and clad with aluminium and glass, the office tower with its rounded façades stands partially freely on pilotis. An external zigzag staircase descends from the roof, leading on each floor into a narrow encircling balcony with a grille floor. Another work of theirs is the Nieuw Land Poldermuseum in Lelystad (1991–94), a tube resting on oblique supports, clad with steel and combined with a rectangular substructure, whose façade is reminiscent of the cross section of the great dyke.

Commissioned to produce an extension for Amsterdam's Schiphol Airport (1991–95), Benthem and Crouwel designed a projecting structure with a vaulted steel roof, a terminal building, and a railway station. More recently they have realised a concert hall in Tilburg (1994–98), where they screwed CDs in staggered rows onto the dark rubber cladding of the building, making its façade look like a quilt.

Their extension to the Anne Frank House in Amsterdam, intended to accommodate infrastructural and exhibition areas of the museum (1993–99), managed skilfully to do justice to the demands of a mass op-

eration while remaining sensitive to the requirements of an old, small-scale, listed monument.

An important consideration for Benthem and Crouwel is materials. While glass, steel and aluminium predominate, they also make use of untypical or new building materials and products. This deployment of materials has crucially affected the reputation of the architects – as building materials develop, so also does their formal vocabulary. "We expressly abstain from including historical stylistic features in modern buildings as well as from using outdated materials and building techniques. In our view, it must be possible to see when buildings were erected by looking at them, moreover both in terms of how life was lived in them and in terms of the technical possibilities available at the time of their construction." Now and then Benthem and Crouwel come up against the bounds of what is possible. Their free and unprejudiced handling of materials gives their buildings a playful, fun character.

The design of Jan Benthem's home, a new construction executed 1982–84 in collaboration with Mels Crouwel at De Fantasie, Almere, arose in special circumstances. A competition, entitled 'Unusual Homes', had been announced for the construction of houses on a series of plots in Almere. The winners were promised rent-free use of a 450-m²-large polder site on which they could realise the designs they had submitted. A proviso was that after five years the plot should be given back, cleared of whatever had been built on it.

Except for the usual fire and other essential building regulations, the competitors could disregard all the building regulations currently in force. Thus, on the one hand, they were freed from the customary restrictions, and were even encouraged to come up with an 'unusual' design, and, on the other, they were required to build a 'non-permanent house', meaning that they had to plan for a structure that could easily be dis-

SOUTH FAÇADE WITH BALCONY

LIVING ROOM WITH VIEW

PAGES 46–47: LIVING ROOM WITH DOORS TO KITCHEN, BATHROOM AND BEDROOM

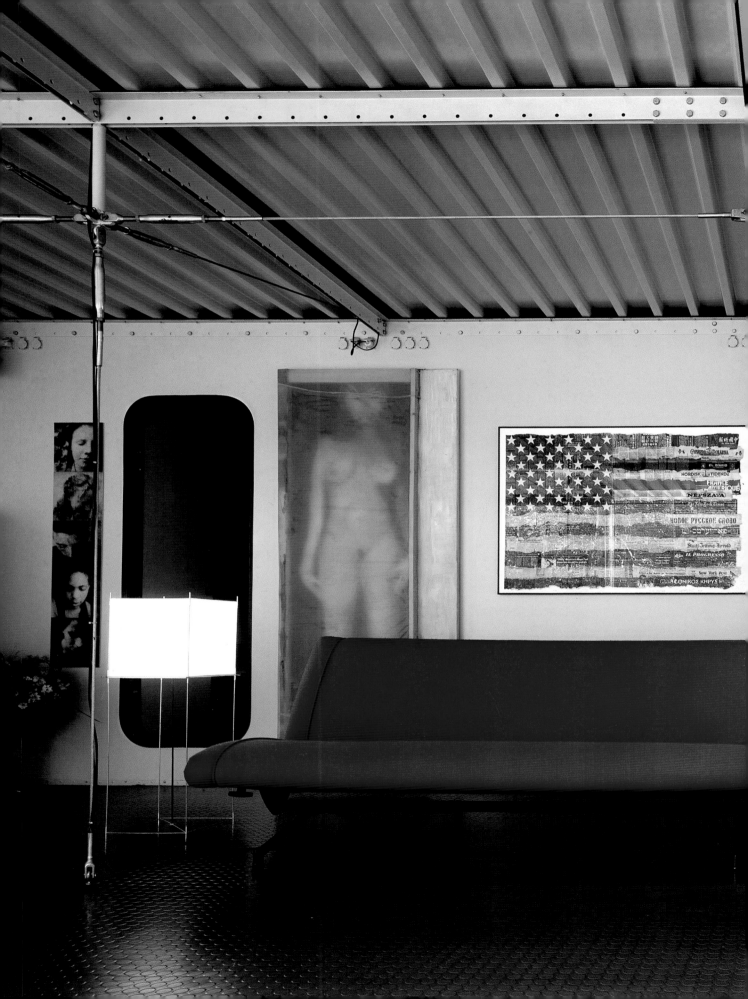

EAST FAÇADE

mantled. Benthem and Crouwel decided to design the temporary property inexpensively and to use building materials and elements that could be recycled after disassembly.

When viewed from a distance, the property does not immediately give the impression of being a dwelling house. Rather, its green-painted street façade with incised doors, whose black rubber draught-proofing stands out, reminds one of some technical installation. The garden façade, by contrast, consists only of glass, which is used here as a bearing structural element. When the venetian blinds are open, there is a clear view into the living room, which extends the whole width of the cube. The necessary strength is ensured through 12-mm-thick, toughened safety glass, which is braced against wind pressure through stabilising glass strips placed vertically to the façade, which themselves are stuck together with silicon glue, just like the external surface. Both for the closed walls and for the floor a sandwich of PU foam and plywood was used. The ceiling consists of a steel construction resting simply on the glass and plywood walls.

The thinness of the walls in the structural elements is further accentuated by the way the building is supported on a three-dimensional framework made of steel-tube elements. They emphasise the provisionality of the project, which could just as easily be installed somewhere else. But the elevation off the ground also supports the idea of a resident who does not want to come into direct contact with the outside world. Inside, this impression is reversed through the glazing of the living area. Only the bedrooms as well as kitchen and bathroom are completely cut off from the outside world. These rooms are arranged side by side on the street side of the house. While their combined area is only 16 m^2, the living room has a surface of c. 48 m^2.

Benthem's unusual home is seen by many as an attractive alternative to the conventional single-family house. To others it looks impractical, for in everyday life you would have to get used not only to a lack of available space but also to the way the house heats up during sunny weather. The 'service rooms' are tiny, especially the kitchen, and in the parents' bedroom there is only space for a bunk bed. The biggest storage space is in a container next to the house. Jan Benthem, who lives the experiment, is aware of all this. Nevertheless, he finds the home a nice place in which to live.

At the time of writing, in 2003, the Benthem house is still standing. Because the whole project was such a triumph, the competition entries did not have to be dismantled, after all. The fact that Jan Benthem continues to live here testifies to the success of the experiment in designing an unusual home.

KATJA GAZEY

BIBLIOGRAPHY:
1985   'High Tech and High Style', in *Architectural Review*, no. 1, pp. 58–59
1989   'Glashaus in Almere', in *Arch+*, nos. 100/101, p. 103
1991   'Benthem/Crouwel', in *Der Architekt*, no. 9, pp. 433–35
1991   'Glashaus auf Zeit in Almere', in *Detail*, no. 1, pp. 51–52
1992   Kloos M., Thackera J. et al., *Benthem Crouwel 1980–2000*, Rotterdam

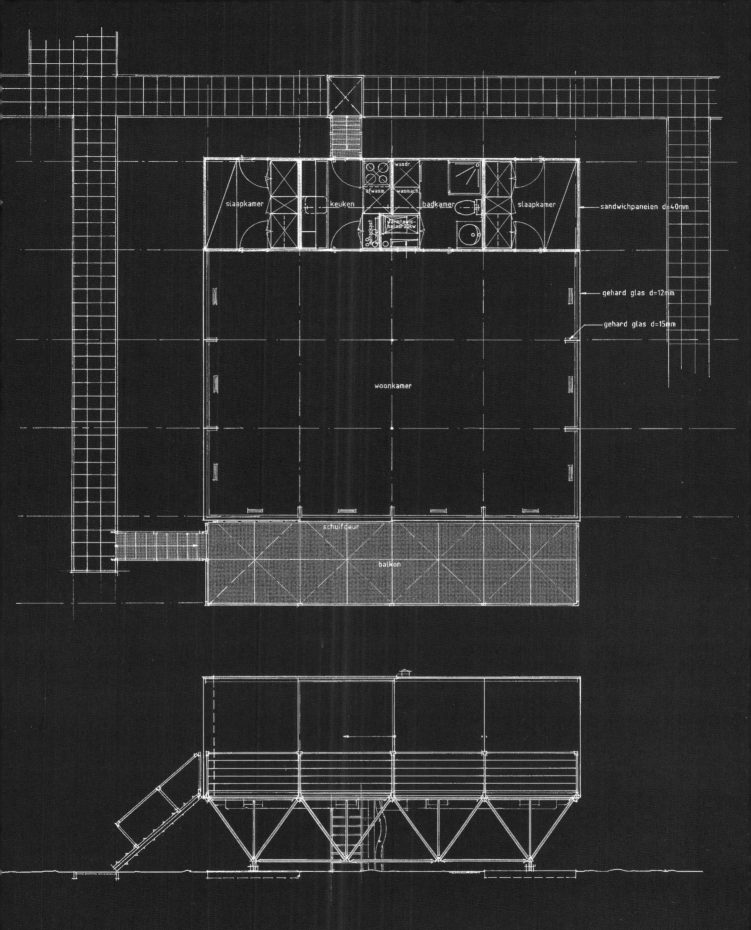

slaapkamer

keuken

wasdr.

afwasm   wasmach.

badkamer

slaapkamer

sandwichpanelen d=40mm

gehard glas d=12mm

gehard glas d=15mm

woonkamer

schuifdeur

balkon

Hendrik Petrus Berlage
1856 – 1934

1914, NEW CONSTRUCTION, NOW DEMOLISHED
VIOLENWEG 14, THE HAGUE (NL)

MAIN WORKS AND PROJECTS

1894	De Algemeene office building, Amsterdam (NL)
1897 – 1903	International competition project for the Exchange, Amsterdam (NL)
1898	Henny villa, The Hague (NL)
1914 – 20	Kröller-Müller hunting lodge, Otterlo (NL)
1919 – 35	Community Museum, The Hague (NL)
1924 – 27	Housing, Mercatoplein, Amsterdam (NL)
1926	Christian Science Church, The Hague (NL)
1926 – 32	Bridge over Amstel, Amsterdam (NL)
1928 – 30	Town Hall, Usquert (NL)

HENDRIK PETRUS BERLAGE was born in Amsterdam in 1856 the son of Nicolaas Willem Berlage, who was director of the municipal registry office, and Anna Catharina Bosscha, who was of Frisian farming stock. There does not appear to have been any artistic background or talent on his father's side, but his mother's family were moderately artistic. Johannes Bosscha, Berlage's maternal grandfather, had been a talented writer, historian, professor and politician, whose brothers had been professors of classical literature and anatomy.

From childhood onwards, Berlage possessed great energy, a sense of duty, the conviction that he had a task to fulfil, literary ability, historical insight, a somewhat melancholic philosophical disposition, and an aversion to vacuity in the established order of things. In 1868 his mother died of tuberculosis, aged only 35. Two years later his father remarried Gesina Catherina Keer, who proved to be a caring stepmother. After secondary school Berlage entered the Academy of Fine Arts in Amsterdam to train as a painter, but a year later, in 1875, he decided to change to architecture and enrolled in the School of Architecture of the Federal Polytechnic (now the Swiss Federal Institute of Technology or ETH) in Zurich. At that time, this school was a very young institution, founded only in 1855, but architecture training in the Netherlands had only a poor reputation, so it was considered normal for prospective Dutch architects to study abroad.

After three years of study, Berlage started three years of travel, recording most of his impressions in sketchbooks. In the spring and summer of 1879 he toured Germany, where he also worked for a few months on the construction of the Panoptikum in Frankfurt. He then went to Holland for a short time, and in September 1880 started a two-year journey around Italy.

In 1881 he returned to Amsterdam, where he worked in the office of Theodorus Sanders, a civil engineer. Three years later they became part-

ners, an association that would last five years. In 1887 Berlage married Marie Bienfait, and in 1889 he set up as an independent architect. In the same year Berlage gave his notorious unpublished lecture *De Menselijke Woning* (The Human Habitation), in which he accused his colleagues of merely copying for the last 50 years, but concluded with the far-sighted observation that a regeneration would arise from this crisis.

The first years of independent practice must have been difficult, for he had only one commission. In October 1895 he won an international competition to build the Exchange Hall in Amsterdam, which totally preoccupied him for several years (1897 – 1903). The Exchange commission enabled him to mature as an architect, and in the period from 1903 until his death he mostly perfected what he had developed before. He took part in exhibitions, and very often won awards. In 1911 he visited the United States, where he gave lectures and encountered the work of Louis Sullivan and Frank Lloyd Wright.

In 1913 Berlage started working for the Kröller-Müller family, and moved to The Hague. His own house in Violenweg was finished a year later. At this time Ludwig Mies van der Rohe was also living in The Hague, and the two became friends. However, his relation with the Kröller-Müllers deteriorated, who some years later turned away from Berlage to Henry van de Velde. Berlage's last main project was The Hague Community Museum. He started the first drawings in 1919, but never lived to see the building finished, for the Museum was only finally opened to the public in 1935, one year after his death in 1934.

Berlage's aspiration in his own home, a new construction built in 1914 at Violenweg 14, The Hague, can be understood by considering two of his lectures: *De Menselijke Woning* (The Human Habitation), given in 1889, and *De Moderne Woning* (The Modern House), held in 1910. In the first lecture Berlage explained his position on light and heating, hygienics

VIEW FROM THE STREET

THE LIVING ROOM

THE HALL

and a 'useful' style, a kind of industrial design *avant la lettre*. In the second lecture he pleaded for architectural efficiency, structural accuracy, simplicity and clear organisation, qualities that were constant throughout his entire career. His own house was, in fact, proof of a rare efficiency, with its light, sober and slender quality. For a family with growing children, it was a modest house. Berlage did not come up with any manifesto or prototype – at the age of nearly 60 he no longer had anything to prove. For Berlage, a very important aspect of the house was the bond between fire, smoke and light. Fire and light were among the greatest and oldest forces, and smoking chimneys were a very important part of his projects. Berlage argued against the individual domestic hearth, but his defence of central heating had a much greater significance than a mere practical solution. He considered central heating as one great domestic hearth. For that same reason, he totally rejected a fireplace in addition to central heating. Berlage wanted open space and light in his house. He positioned the staircase in the bright open central hall, and combined the dining room and the living room in one modest but ample luminous space, a highly unusual decision at the time.

The Berlage house had a strong simple form. It consisted of a cube with a pyramidal roof and a small prism on the street side, following the golden section. The roof of the small volume was inserted into the main roof. This simple form was the functional consequence of the efficient floor plans. At ground level, Berlage located all minor rooms in the prism, outside the main volume of the house. On the garden side, in the living room, there was a small bay. This bay returned in a slightly different form

on the first floor in the sitting room, next to the main bedroom, directly connected to a large terrace. The house had two entrances, a main entrance for visitors on the front right of the house, and a tradesmen's entrance on the street front. The main entrance gave access through an enclosed porch to a large hall, which was in open connection with the staircase. All the rooms of the house were directly linked with this central hall.

The detailing of the house was strictly functional. Berlage was very concerned with the hygiene aspect of the house. He searched for new building techniques, looking for solutions that gathered less dust. The interior walls and the ceilings were stuccoed and the floors were covered with linoleum, a cheap and clean material that was to become a feature of Dutch New Realism some years later. The curtains were as light as possible. The slender chimney played an important role in the rhythm of surfaces and colours. In the central hall, Berlage used a white ceramic wainscoting. Thanks to the regular organisation of the floor plans and the stable form, the house made a perfect balanced impression.

Berlage's private houses were the least known part of his work. He became famous, in fact, for the Exchange, offices and popular housing. Nevertheless, between 1892 and 1914 he built about 20 villas, of which his own home was the last in the series and for that reason significant. Berlage was very much influenced by English architects such as Norman Shaw. With the central location of the hall, he deviated from the usual Dutch 'en suite' organisation of rooms, parallel to a long corridor, with the kitchen at the end. This freed the house from its structural symmetry and aristocratic ceremony. The first time he used this typical floor plan was in 1892, in his house for the writer Frederik van Eeden. Berlage was even more influenced by the English after the publication of Muthesius' *Das Englische Haus* in 1904. He was also indebted to Muthesius in the sphere of hygienics.

Berlage tested his idea on architecture in private housing for the first time with the Henny villa (1898), which was extremely provocative and innovative, aiming to cleanse architecture of all its impurity. While his Heymans house (1893–95) was still rather stylish, the Henny house was so complex and dramatic that it resulted in uneasiness. For this reason his own house is the best example of his principles in their purest form. All architectural decoration, still evident in the 1890s, was absent. The house was, in a different way, as rational, functional and efficient as the white cubes of the modernists. It was exactly this purity that gave Berlage's own house its strength and timelessness.   SILVIA DE NOLF

BIBLIOGRAPHY:
1969   Singelenberg P., *H.P. Berlage*, Amsterdam
1987   Polano S., *Hendrik Petrus Berlage, Opera Completa*, Milan
1996   Berlage H. P., *Hendrik Petrus Berlage, Thoughts on Style 1886–1909, texts and documents*, Santa Monica
1999   Krabbe C. P., Smit J., Smit E. and Van der Werf J., *Het huis van de architect*, Arnhem
2001   Cornoldi A., *Le case degli architetti. Dizionario privato dal Rinascimento ad oggi*, Venice, pp. 70–72

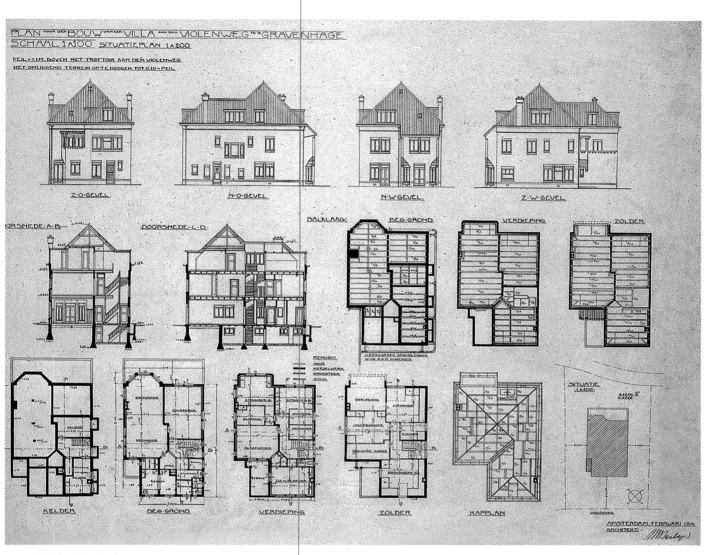

ELEVATIONS, SECTIONS AND PLANS

SKETCH OF THE FIRST SOLUTION

SKETCH OF THE MAIN ENTRANCE

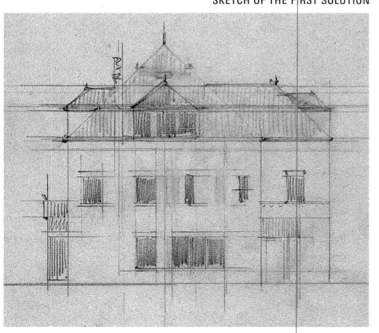

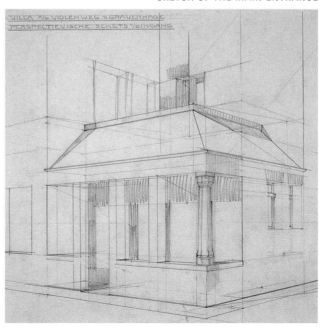

Antonio Bonet i Castellana
1913 – 1989

1972 – 76, NEW CONSTRUCTION, NOW DEMOLISHED
CARRER CAVALLERS 76, BARCELONA (E)

MAIN WORKS AND PROJECTS

1938 – 39   Building on corners of avenidas Paraguay and Suipacha, Buenos Aires (Argentina)

1942 – 43   Houses, avenida Martinez, Buenos Aires (Argentina)

1945 – 48   Punta Ballena development, Maldonado (Uruguay)

1947 – 48   La Solana del Mar, Berlingieri house and La Rinconada house, Maldonado (Uruguay)

1953 – 56   Oks house, Buenos Aires (Argentina)

1953 – 63   La Ricarda house, Barcelona (E)

1960 – 63   Mediterráneo building, Barcelona (E)

1962 – 63   Meridiana greyhound track, Barcelona (E)

1964 – 69   Castanera house and Cruylles house, Catalonia (E)

1970 – 76   Mutua Metalúrgica, Ribera house, Raventós house and Balañá house, Catalonia (E)

ANTONIO BONET was born on 13 August 1913 in Barcelona the son of Magí Bonet and Teresa Castellana, who originally came from the province of Tarragona. He spent his childhood in Barcelona's Ronda Sant Antoni district and in 1919, at the age of 6 started to attend the Escoles Pies, where on the basis of his scholastic performance he won a scholarship, allowing him to complete his secondary studies.

In 1929 Bonet enrolled in the School of Architecture in Barcelona, which was characterised at the time by classical and regionalist teaching. In 1932, while still a student, he joined – on the recommendation of his friend Guillermo Diaz Plaja – the practice of Josep Lluís Sert and José Torres Clavé, and participated in their projects for Roca Jeweller's and houses in El Garraf. In 1933 Bonet attended the IV CIAM, where he met the leading figures of the modern movement, and in 1934 he became a student member of GATEPAC (Grupo de arquitectos y técnicos españoles para el Progreso de la Arquitectura Contemporánea – Group of Spanish Architects and Technicians for the Progress of Contemporary Architecture), participating in projects for the Ciutat de Repòs i Vacances (workers' holiday development) and the Pla Macià (Macià plan).

In the same year, 1934, Bonet was called to the first Summer University in Santander, organised as part of the Republic's programme by the Institución Libre de Enseñanza (Free Teaching Institution) for the "creation of an aristocracy of the spirit". In 1935, with Sert and Torres Clavé, he formed the firm MIDVA (Muebles y decoración para la vivienda actual – Furnishings and decoration for today's living), and in the following year, 1936, he graduated from the School of Architecture, Barcelona.

These early experiences left their mark on Bonet's training, which departed from the calvary of the previous generation, as from the very

beginning his technical apprenticeship developed against the backdrop of rationalism and his role as a Republican intellectual, integrated in the search for new ways of life and new social situations. The culmination of this first phase of Bonet's career came immediately after his graduation, when he moved to Paris.

Here he worked with Josep Lluís Sert and Luis Lacasa on the Spanish Republic's pavilion for the 1937 Paris International Exhibition, which was also the context for the first public appearance of Pablo Picasso's *Guernica* and Alexander Calder's *Mercury Fountain*. In the same year Bonet joined Le Corbusier's practice, which was the occasion for some key meetings. First, he came into contact with the Chilean surrealist Roberto Matta, with whom he developed the project for the Maison de Weekend Jaoul, and then he met the Argentinians Enrique Ferrari Hardoy and Juan Kurchan, who – given the circumstances of the Spanish Civil War (1936 – 39) – encouraged him to go into exile in Buenos Aires, which he did.

In Argentina Bonet co-founded the Grupo Austral, acting as a disseminator of Corbusian imagery in the climate of intense urban-planning debate that was generated by the spectacular growth of the Argentine capital, from where he extended his activity to Uruguay. In 1958 he opened a studio in Barcelona with Josep Puig Torné, and a second practice in Madrid with Manuel Jaén, which produced numerous projects for the Catalonia and Murcia coastlines. In 1963 he returned to settle in Barcelona, seperated from Puig Torné and centred intense architectural and urban-planning activity in Madrid and Catalonia. Bonet designed and built a great many buildings of interest, and also designed prefabrication and furnishing systems, including his famous BKF easy chair (1938).

THE LIVING AREA

DETAIL OF THE FAÇADE

VIEW FROM THE STREET

WORK SPACE

Like Berthold Lubetkin or Richard Neutra, who travelled the world out of necessity or choice, it took Antonio Bonet quite some time to find a definitive home. It is difficult to say whether his penthouse home at Carrer Cavallers 76, which is part of a building that he constructed new (1972–76) in the district of Pedralbes, in the north of Barcelona, was just one more stop, perhaps a longer enforced stay that was less short-lived than others, as the architect designed it when he was over 60 years old. Whatever the case, curiously there are almost no photographs of Bonet in his Carrer Cavallers home, just as there are very few of him in all the other places in which he lived, mostly rented apartments and houses in

Buenos Aires, Argentina, in Uruguay, in Madrid and in Barcelona. Nevertheless, the fact that the architect set up his studio in the basement of the building that contained his new home would seem to confirm the hypothesis of a detente, of a desire to establish physical routines between his house and office, replacing the wide range of experiences provided by movement around the city with the memory of what he had once experienced.

We know that this house was the scene for the family and social rituals of a Bonet who was by then established, was the setting for the works of art he had collected, along with the keepsakes he loved, and was a place where he could evoke the years he had lived with Ana Maria in Buenos Aires or look out, as if from a watchtower, at the skyline of 1970s Barcelona and imagine it improved by a rather more generous vision than the prevailing one. If there is a common factor in Bonet's houses, it is exactly this need to be able to look into the distance – they all overlook broad avenues, street corners or wide natural spaces.

The outer volume of Bonet's building is determined by the new urban-planning regulations that were just coming into force for this sector in the early 1970s. It is a construction with a free perimeter, standing five storeys high, executed exclusively in bare concrete. The idea of continuity suggested by the use of a single material in this building in the Pedralbes district is tempered by a series of expressive variations which, in spite of the limitations of the programme, Bonet incorporated into the design. These include a series of structural elements, facing and sun-shading organised according to a single axis of symmetry which affects the façades facing south (garden and tennis court) and north (street).

The joinery is subordinated to the general composition in the form of continuous windows with regularly distributed uprights, in keeping with the overall modulation. Each floor is divided according to the general axis of symmetry and houses two half-apartments. Bonet set aside a large surface area for the living-cum-dining room, a space which he organised virtually by means of a false ceiling, which is perfectly defined as a plane that is turned around, marking out the various parts of the home with different forms: a space for resting and reading beside the fireplace and study, and an area for conversation and observation next to the clerestory and the dining area. Starting out from the limestone floor and a virtual 'height scale' indicated by the horizontal planes forming the fireplace, Bonet completed his architecture by installing fitted and moveable pieces of furniture, whose ochres, olive greens and Pompeii

reds contrast with the white walls, floor and ceilings. His works of art and other favourite objects were arranged in these different spaces. On the walls hung a painting by his master, Le Corbusier, and works by friends such as Augusto Torres and Maruja Mallo.

One characteristic that the building housing Bonet's home shares with other houses he produced is the predominance of a single material in the façade (bare concrete or sandstone) accompanied by the endeavour to create the effect of dynamic equilibrium with clearly sculptural influences. To some extent this attitude expresses the need to find his own model for a high-rise building, as shown in contemporaneous buildings in the Parc Cervantes and Plaça Urquinaona (Barcelona) and the project for Plaza Castilla (Madrid), at a time when 'singular buildings' were beginning to change the city skyline in keeping with property development operations. We can see his attempt to distinguish himself from the models of what was called 'international architecture' of Anglo-Saxon origin (Jacobsen, for instance), which, taking Le Corbusier and the post-war CIAM debates as a starting point, seems to coincide with Italian explorations prior to Aldo Rossi.

In Bonet's final years, the precise demarcation of the functional spaces of the home and of the sub-spaces he created in the living-cum-dining room by means of an interplay of false ceilings, horizontal planes, partition walls and pivoting doors, combined with the active use of his own furnishing designs, confirm a constant that dates back to his early works in Buenos Aires, substantiating an architect for whom urban planning, architecture and design were inseparable.

FERNANDO ALVAREZ, JORDI ROIG

FLOOR PLAN

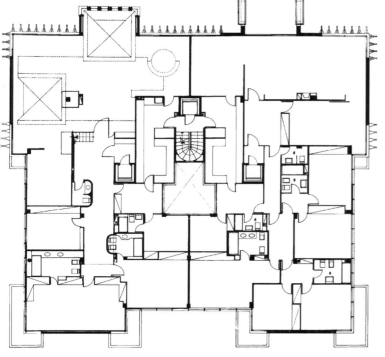

BIBLIOGRAPHY:

1978 Ortiz F. and Balldellou M. A., *La obra de Antonio Bonet*, Buenos Aires
1985 Katzenstein H., Natanson E. and Schwartzman G., *Antonio Bonet, Arquitectura y urbanismo en el Rio de la Plata y España*, Buenos Aires
1987 Alvarez F., Roig J. et al., *Antonio Bonet y el Rio de la Plata*, Barcelona
1996 Alvarez F. and Roig J. (eds), *Bonet 1913–1989*, Ministerio de Fomento/Collegi d'Arquitectes de Catalunya, Barcelona
1999 Alvarez F. and Roig J., *Antoni Bonet Castellana*, Barcelona

Piero Bottoni
1903–1973

**1945, NEW CONSTRUCTION
RONCHI, MARINA DI MASSA (I)**

MAIN WORKS AND PROJECTS

1934–35	House, via Mercadante, corner of via Gomes, Milan (I)
	Dello Strologo villa, via Calzabigi, Livorno (I)
1936–37	Muggia villa and annexes at the Bel Poggio Farm, Imola (I), with Mario Pucci
1937–40	Horse-riding club, via Siepelunga, Bologna (I), with Mario Pucci
1946–51	Multi-purpose building, corso Buenos Aires, Milan (I), with Mario Pucci and Guglielmo Ulrich
1951–53	INA housing, Harrar district, Milan (I), with Mario Morini and Carlo Villa
1953–58	INA building, corso Sempione, Milan (I)
1956–57	Two INA housing blocks, Comasina district, Milan (I), with P. Lingeri
1960–64	Restoration of Palazzo di Renata di Francia, new seat of Ferrara University (I)
1961–71	Sesto San Giovanni Town Hall (I), with Antonio Didoni

PIERO BOTTONI'S architecture has an artistic quality about it. His tendency to yoke together architectural design and artistic experience undoubtedly derives from a number of factors: the rich and diverse education he received at Brera Academy and Milan Polytechnic; his familiarity from early on with the techniques and languages of a wide range of arts (painting, sculpture, drawing, set design, photography, film, and fashion); his friendship with leading exponents of various avant-garde movements; and his interest in the history of both art and architecture.

Numerous early study trips soon brought Bottoni into contact with some of the most significant strands of European Modernism. Le Corbusier wrote him a long letter to express his appreciation of the Italian architect's *Cromatismi architettonici* (1927). Bottoni was among the leading exponents of Italian Rationalism. As Italian delegate to the CIAM international architecture conferences (1929–49), he played – like Maurizio Pollini – an important role in relations between Italy and Europe.

Bottoni left significant works in several fields: not just architecture, but also town planning, restoration, museum design, and furnishing design. Between 1927 and 1954 he participated in all the Milan Triennale exhibitions, showing works of his at them. He contributed to some of the most important Italian town-planning projects of the 20th century, including the Valle d'Aosta Urban Development Plan (1936–37), the A.R. Plan for Milan and Lombardy (1944–45), and the experimental QT8 plan for a district of Milan (1946–54). Other projects comprised factories, a horse-riding club, shops and offices, an insurance company building, rural buildings, a university, and a town hall.

Despite these wide-ranging interests and diverse implementations, Bottoni's primary concern, however, was with residential quarters and housing. In both his designs and his theoretical writings, he continually explored a variety of aspects of these themes: the invention of new forms, the standardisation of building methods and furnishings, interior design, and housing policy. Of great interest, for example, are his ideas about providing housing for all workers. Within the context of housing and residential districts, Bottoni focussed always on the relationship between architecture and context, concentrating especially on the urban quality of housing areas and the quality of places and landscapes. An exemplary result of this eclectic exploration was his proposal in the mid-1950s for the 'living street', a proposal that was enhanced by significant reflections on landscape architecture.

Bottoni's manifesto in this respect was the Monte Stella, the hill realised in Milan's QT8 district with rubble from bombing raids, which Aldo Rossi described as one of the two "monuments of modern architecture" in the city whose "significance goes beyond their technical quality". Piero Bottoni himself once said, to Giulia Veronesi in 1959, that "I am not interested in building just a house, but that particular house which, at least in my aspirations, can be a social as well as an aesthetic event – that particular house which, in its structural and figurative design, clearly interprets a given moment of life and culture." The thought illuminates many aspects of Bottoni's work as a designer and also the ideas and sensibility that inspired it.

To see the construction of a house as a 'social event' means to be aware of the fundamental importance that this act always assumes. The construction of a house marks the conquest of a place in the world, a 'station' from which the inhabitant will establish a horizon made up of relations with other human beings, with the needs and the opportunities of life, with the landscape and the universe. *To go to live in a house –* even when it depends on obligatory choices, and all the more so when it

VIEW FROM SOUTH-EAST

VIEW FROM THE SOUTH

VIEW FROM THE PINE-WOOD

is the result of a voluntary decision – brings with it an expectation: the hope of bringing vital sap to and drawing vital sap from the place, in the sense of energy and care capable of turning the site into a place and setting off processes of identification. Living involves *placing one's self*, and architecture can influence this process. It can open it up or force it in a negative sense. It can allow or prevent the rediscovery of a balance between refuge and relations. Bottoni's houses, with varying results, always face up to this kind of question.

No less significant is Bottoni's insistence on *'that particular house'*. Here there is a clear self-critical reference to the simplifications of the rationalist proclamations. Bottoni had now developed the awareness that meaning cannot be tied down to any classification, and that the task of the project is actually to preserve the mystery that accompanies the *individuality* of things, people, buildings or landscapes. Since he had practised and gone beyond it, he knew what deadly thought is hidden in the attempt to place under lock and key the secrets of beauty and of human life itself, and the role that places and living have in all this.

The thoughts confided to Giulia Veronesi also highlight the link between the 'structural design' and the figurative choice. Bottoni is well aware that the ability of architecture to attain a moment of truth, to interpret 'a given moment of life and culture', depends on the combination of the two aspects.

These principles are brilliantly transfused into architecture in Bottoni's Casetta nella pineta (little house in the pine wood), the holiday home that he built new for himself and his wife in 1945, in Ronchi at Marina di Massa. From the late 1920s to the war period, the architect had taken a

constant interest in the theme of the holiday home. The Villa Latina project at the Milan Triennale of 1930, the four holiday homes (with Eugenio Faludi and Enrico A. Griffini) at the Triennale of 1933, and the many villas and houses which he designed for holiday resorts had formed a substantial repertoire of solutions for spaces created for the leisure of the middle classes. Bottoni's Casetta nella pineta was the mature result of this long path.

The little building was, however, also the direct offspring of another of his works: the unrealised plan for an 'ideal house on piles' drawn up three years earlier, probably for the competition for the ideal house organised by the journal *Domus*. In that project we find a condensation of the space-saving exercises inspired by Taylor that Bottoni had conducted up to then with all his characteristic irony and poetry. But, above all, what emerges in the work is the need to give meaning to living and figurative form to the *having a place in the world* at that dramatic moment in history. Defined in just a few drawings and conceived entirely in wood (apart from the steel supports), the 'ideal house' was a way for Bottoni to come to terms with the tragedy of the Second World War. It is perhaps for this reason, too, that the sketches remained a very private record, almost like the pages of a diary.

The little house in the pine wood, by contrast, which transposed the 'ideal house' to an entirely different environment, was the expression of a new hope of rebirth. The dimensions of the overall volume changed – 4.09 x 3.51 metres for the wooden ideal house on piles compared to 6.60 x 5.00 for the Casetta in stone – but the arrangement of the interior space is similar in the centrality of the multifunctional living room / bedroom, with one side only open to the outside through wide windows –

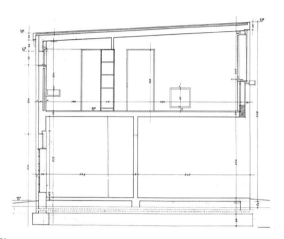

SECTION

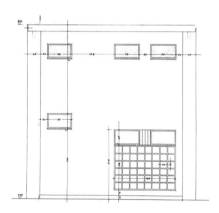

NORTH FAÇADE

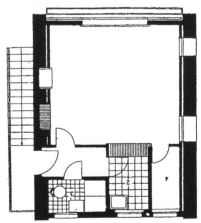

PLAN OF THE UPPER FLOOR

VIEW OF THE INTERIOR

almost a 'place to think', a place of isolation and contemplation. The materials are different. In keeping with the pine wood, two walls in river stones support the 'cabin' on the first floor, which is reached by an external staircase with uneven steps – a reinterpretation of a Mediterranean model that aims to have as little effect as possible on the opus incertum of the wall. On the ground floor there is a shelter for a small car (the legendary Fiat 500 Topolino) and a bathroom lit by an elegant wall in reinforced concrete and glass blocks, surmounted by windows.

Bottoni did not want to live in the house for long, and he was already planning to sell it as early as 1949 (offering it to Adriano Olivetti, no less). In the event, however, he ended up using the dwelling until 1956, when his wife Stella died. To convince prospective purchasers of the little house in the pine wood, the architect provided an extension plan, thus betraying the original monastic spirit of a work which in its minimalism was already out of time, on the eve of the economic boom.

GIANCARLO CONSONNI

BIBLIOGRAPHY:

1973   Consonni G., Meneghetti L. and Patetta L., 'Bottoni: 40 anni di battaglie per l'architettura', monographic issue of *Controspazio*, no. 4, October

1990   Consonni G., Meneghetti L. and Tonon G. (eds), *Piero Bottoni Opera Completa*, Milan

1995   Tonon G., *Introduzione a Piero Bottoni, Una Nuova Antichissima Bellezza*, Rome/Bari

1998   Portoghesi P., *I grandi architetti del Novecento. Una nuova storia dell'architettura contemporanea attraverso le personalità e le opere dei protagonisti*, ed. C. Di Stefano and M. Pisani, Rome, pp. 336–341

2000   Tonon G., 'Bottoni Piero. 1903–1973', in *Dizionario dell'architettura del XX secolo*, ed. C. Olmo, Turin/London, pp. 296–300

Johannes Hendrik van den Broek
1898–1978

1948–52, NEW CONSTRUCTION
KRALINGSEWEG, ROTTERDAM (NL)

MAIN WORKS AND PROJECTS

1930	Blijdorp and Bergpolder housing projects, Rotterdam (NL)
1931–34	Eendracht housing project, Vroesenlaan, Rotterdam (NL)
1937	Dutch pavilion at the Universal Exhibition, Paris (F)
1942–43	Van Nelle Company, warehouse extension, Rotterdam (NL)
1945–49	Ardath Tobacco Company, building extension, Dordrecht (NL)

1949–53	Lijnbaan shopping centre, Rotterdam (NL),
1957	Housing project, Hansa district, Berlin (D)
1957–61	Laboratory for metallurgy, Technical University, Delft (NL)
1965–76	Town Hall, Ede (NL)
1968–73	Cultural and Community Centre, Winschoten (NL)

JOHANNES HENDRIK van den Broek was born in Rotterdam in 1898. His father was a timber dealer, and years later his connections with the building industry would be a great help for van den Broek's career. At the age of fifteen he went to a Teachers' College in Nijmegen. He got his degree in 1917, and was called up the same year. In 1919 he started to study architecture at the Technische Hogeschool in Delft, working in the evenings as a teacher in Vlaardingen. Five years later he obtained his diploma as an engineer. The young van de Broek was greatly influenced by the architect J.J.P. Oud. He met him at a lecture in 1927, and for many years after Oud would be his guiding light.

After his architecture degree, van den Broek worked for three years in the office of B.J. Ouëndag. He then started his own office in Rotterdam in the Mathenesserlaan. Thanks to his father he succeeded in having a successful business even in the years of crisis. In 1937, J.A. Brinkman offered the 29-year-old van den Broek a partnership. Brinkman and van der Vlugt were the architects of the exemplary Van Nelle factory in Rotterdam, which brought fame to their office. In 1947 van den Broek obtained a tutorship at the T.H. in Delft, where he taught for many years. After Brinkman's death he started a partnership with the much younger architect Bakema.

Van den Broek's architecture was influenced by two important study trips. In 1928 he visited several housing projects in Frankfurt together with W. Van Tijen and Ernst May. Van Tijen was his closest friend and conversation partner for many years. The influence of this study trip was clearly recognisable in the "Eendracht" housing project in the Vroesenlaan, Rotterdam. This trip marked the first period of his maturation. In 1948 he went with Van Tijen on a second study trip to the United States. In the same year he started to collaborate with Bakema. They analysed the skyscrapers of Chicago and Detroit and used this experience for the masterplan of the Lijnbaan in Rotterdam.

Van den Broek dedicated the war years to the development of new structures, building techniques and typologies for popular housing. He was one of the few architects who didn't employ his staff on short-term contracts, as a result of which he was able to gather together a close team of high qualified people. After the war this gave him a much quicker start than all the other offices, with the fresh ideas developed beforehand. In those post-war years van den Broek achieved fame because of his participation in Dutch New Realism. He had a very busy social life, and joined many architectural associations and commissions for popular housing and building techniques. The most important was the Union Internationale des Architectes, which was less militant than organisations such as CIAM and TEAM X.

Van den Broek considered himself an important example for younger architects and assumed a clear social and political responsibility in the Dutch architecture debate.

In 1948 van den Broek discovered the former cottage "Ypenhof" at the Kralingse Plas. A few years later Herman Haan decided to live a few houses further on in the same street. Van den Broek aimed to give economic importance to the formal rules of modernism, such as *fenêtres à longueur*, flat roofs, the aesthetic use of concrete and free-standing columns, leading to a social and productive structure for the building industry. This ambition was the only real continuity in his work from start to finish, before and after the war, and was also apparent in his own house. The suggestions he made were economical and constructive proposals that were fully reproducible. There was no difference between his ideological and aesthetic point of view. In his own villa he experimented with the strategy of separation of day and night areas of the house, creating a more efficient double use of the floorplan. The house had a radical New Realist character, but on the other hand van den Broek felt a need for home comfort. Every detail of the house, including all the furni-

VIEW FROM THE GARDEN

THE LIVING ROOM WITH THE MEZZANINE

ture, was designed by van den Broek himself. The floorplan was so simple that it resulted in one open space with a huge void, every room flowing into another without any obvious separation. Bakema identified van den Broek's house as an experiment for "sleeping on a balcony in the living room". Peter Smithson declared that the house was "the only post-war house in which he had felt anything more than despair", and that "there architecture lived".

Ypenhof was introduced by a large entrance flanked by two small guardhouses. The environment made van den Broek decide for a glass front on the beautiful landscape of the south side, and a totally closed front to the busy street on the north side. The house had a rectangular floorplan, with a square annex on ground level. The main entrance was located in the annex next to the serving rooms, such as the cloakroom, the reception room, the kitchen and a large hall. The annex had a traditional division in rooms with supporting walls. The main volume, on the contrary, was designed as a flexible floorplan with interlocking areas for living and sleeping. The huge glass wall opened the interior to the garden and to the landscape behind. The house mainly rested on structural steelwork. This resulted in a wide open space and made the five-metre high glass front possible. Between the two levels a huge void symbolised the Modernist aspiration of one open volume. Van den Broek didn't use any superficial decoration in the house. The detailing was sober: steel columns, nude brick walls, glass walls in the interior, and marble floors created a clean environment and a certain natural monumentality. On

the other hand van den Broek designed a fireplace and put carpets on the floors to give the interior a more intimate aspect. Beside the radiators, the house was also heated through fissures in the floor. Van den Broek also designed steel furniture such as cupboards, wardrobes, closets, tables and shelves. On the first level the sleeping area of the couple had a panoramic view over the living room and the garden, and was in fluent connection with a dressing room, a bathroom and a shower. A long terrace with staircase created a direct connection with the garden.

Van den Broek used his own house as an experiment to serve as a model for his later housing projects. The structural concrete and steelwork, the sliding walls and the orientation of the house were several aspects experimented beforehand in housing projects such as Vroesenlaan in Rotterdam in 1934. These elements were, in fact, inherited from his study trip to Frankfurt, and originated from the pre-war experiments of Dutch New Realism and French Modernism. However, the use of split-levels and the spatial unity of the house created a totally new typology in floorplan and section. After his own house, together with Bakema van den Broek designed several split-level houses. The day and night use of the plan was an economical solution for popular housing and could lead to standardisation. It created huge possibilities, mostly in high-rise blocks and large-scale housing programs such as the project in the Berlin Hansa district of 1957.

Van den Broek's house was, in fact, the result of many years of research on housing typology, almost an entire life's work. After the bom-

AERIAL PERSPECTIVE OF THE FIRST SOLUTION, 1949

DETAIL OF THE LIVING ROOM WITH FIREPLACE

THE LIVING ROOM SEEN FROM THE BALCONY

bing of Rotterdam in 1940, Brinkman and van den Broek developed three housing typologies to be realised after the war. House Ypenhof can for that reason be considered as the emphasis of these experiments, a house that aimed to be an example.
SILVIA DE NOLF

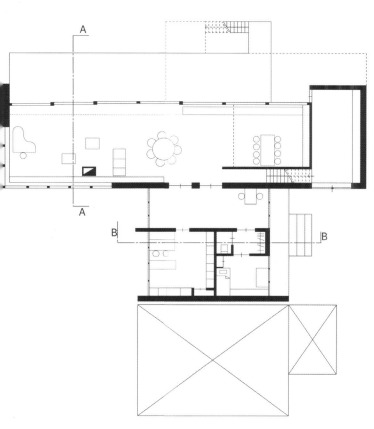

PLAN OF THE GROUND FLOOR

BIBLIOGRAPHY:

1958   'Woonhuis van prof. ir. J. H. van den Broek', in *Bouw*, no. 13, pp. 494–95

1976   Andreas E., Architektur und Städtebau, *Das Werk von van den Broek und Bakema*, Stuttgart

1981   Schrofer J., *bouwen voor een open samenleving, Brinkman–van der Vlugt–van den Broek–Bakema*, Museum Boymans van Beuningen, Rotterdam

1999   Krabbe C. P., Smit J., Smit E. and Van der Werf J., *Het huis van de architect*, Arnhem

Francisco de Asís Cabrero Torres-Quevedo
1912 – 2005

1961 – 62, NEW CONSTRUCTION
AVENIDA DE MIRAFLORES 14, PUERTA DE HIERRO, MADRID (E)

MAIN WORKS AND PROJECTS

1948 Virgen del Pilar apartment block, Madrid (E)

1949 – 53 Competition project for and realisation of Trade Union Headquarters Madrid (E), with Rafael Aburto

1952 – 53 Own house, Avenida de Miraflores 14, Puerta de Hierro, Madrid (E)

1956 Duplex apartment, Plaza de los Reyes Magos, Madrid (E)

1956 – 57 National School of Catering, Madrid (E)

1956 – 58 Swimming pool for the Madrid Trade Union, Madrid (E)

1961 Head office of Arriba newspaper, Paseo de la Castellana, Madrid (E)

1964 Glass Pavilion, in the Casa de Campo exhibition park, Madrid (E), with José Ruiz and Luis Labiano

1971 Service station on A6 motorway, Villalba, Madrid (E)

1973 Competition project for (wins First Prize) and realisation of Alcorcón town hall, Madrid (E)

1988 El Pastor apartment block, Madrid (E)

FRANCISCO DE ASÍS CABRERO TORRES-QUEVEDO was born in Santander on 4 October 1912 into a traditional middle-class Spanish family, which had strong connections with the worlds of the arts and sciences. His father, José Cabrero Pons, a leading figure in Madrid's cultural life, had studied engineering in Leuven and painting at the La Palette school in Paris, and was friends with the sculptor Francisco Durrio and the writer Ramón Gómez de la Serna. His maternal grandfather, Leonardo Torres Quevedo, had been an engineer, mathematician and inventor, familiar with the latest advances of his day in the fields of aviation, telecommunications and civil engineering. Cabrero grew up against this background of artistic debate and technological innovation, which also helped shape his early education.

Before he embarked on his architectural vocation, the young Cabrero first studied art, enrolling in 1932 in the Royal Academy of Fine Arts in San Fernando. But two years later, in 1934, he switched to the School of Architecture in Madrid. During his student days, Cabrero lived with his maternal grandfather, with whom he had a close relationship. From Leonardo Torres Quevedo he learned the need for objectivity, discipline and perseverance when tackling professional problems, as well as a familiarity with and commitment to new materials and technologies – all valuable lessons for a budding architect.

Cabrero's studies at the Madrid School of Architecture, where he met Miguel Fisac and Alejandro de la Sota, were interrupted by the Spanish Civil War (1936 – 39), during which he served in the military. When the conflict was over, he was able to continue his studies, finally graduating from the School as a qualified architect in 1942, in the midst of the

Second World War. During these dark years Cabrero explored Italian architecture with José Antonio Coderch and even travelled to Italy, where he met Adalberto Libera and the painter Giorgio De Chirico, also encountering the architecture of Giuseppe Terragni.

For Cabrero, the study trip marked the start of a critical review of 1940s Spanish architecture. "I have seen something very different in Italy," he said, immediately translating his new insights into designs, witness his project for the Cross of The Fallen competition. His Italian journey ushered in a period in which he travelled more widely, visiting Alvar Aalto and Max Bill, and making study trips to Moscow and New York, even to the Polynesian islands of Samoa. Cabrero's somewhat solitary travels and meditations on architecture during this period of his life eventually culminated in his *Cuatro libros de arquitectura* (Four Books of Architecture).

Following graduation in 1942, Cabrero joined the "Obra Social del Hogar" (Trade Union Organization for low cost housing) as an architect, later opening an architectural practice of his own in Madrid, although he still worked on some projects in collaboration with other architects. In 1949, for example, he won First Prize together with Rafael Aburto in a competition to design the Trade Union Headquarters in Madrid, which was realised 1950 – 53. The building virtually launched modern architecture in Spain and even gave rise to the so-called 'Madrid school', although this was never an organised or structured group. In the mid-20th century, the situation in Spain was such that, far from inheriting and continuing the adventure of architectural Modernism, young architects like Cabrero and his colleagues had first to institute it, even invent it.

NIGHT VIEW FROM THE SOUTHERN GARDEN

The roots of Cabrero's architecture lie in the controlled, orderly, strict and completely rational aspects of the discipline. However, far from simply translating these aspects into built projects, he adapted or supplemented them, converting them into a flexible system that both afforded constructive and formal control, and permitted the adjustments and variations necessary for an adequate response. In this way he arrived at a personal arcane architecture that drew on the creative heterodoxy of the 1950s, structural sincerity, classic 19th-century rationalism, geometric precision learnt from Max Bill, and the atmospheric pre-existences developed by Ernesto Rogers.

In the early 1950s, Cabrero purchased a plot of land in La Colonia Puerta de Hierro, a growing area to the north of Madrid. The sloping site is bound to the north and south by two avenues. On one of these, the Avenida de Miraflores, he built his first private house-cum-studio between 1952 and 1953. The building has two wings each orientated in different directions, using a small angle variation, in order to make subtle use of the lie of the land, into which it is organically integrated. Its roof as well as the articulations of its surfaces are reminiscent of the Scandinavian styles of the period.

A decade later (1961–62), Cabrero constructed a second private studio-house at Avenida de Miraflores 14, Puerta de Hierro, at the southern end of the same plot. Again, the building had two perfectly differentiated wings, but this time they were orthogonally placed to form an L-shape. And where the first house was adapted to the topography, the second one made a hard intervention in the site with a pre-horizontal platform and a containment wall, which divided the land into two parts. This second house is totally supported on the concrete containment wall, on top of which lies a metal structure with wooden joists. The larger of the two wings opens onto the garden. All the public areas of the house are found in this wing, with the living room and dining room located on the ground floor and the studio in the semi-basement. The second smaller wing houses the bedrooms and service areas.

The perfect modulation of the house ensures the compatibility of the different materials used inside (steel, brick, cement, aluminium and wood), while the outside has a free rhythm. Thus, the precise articulation of the concrete wall allows to contain inside it a cupboard or a chimney, and even act as a limit of the staircase that joins the studio and the hall. The constructive design of the light façade is directly related to the furniture made for the house. For instance, a rigid steel or wooden structure is adapted in such a way that it can be used as a seat or table.

The materials that Cabrero used for his second house at Avenida de Miraflores 14 were consistent with the steel, glass and brick architecture of the time. He employed the same materials in the construction of many of his most notable buildings, such as the head office of the Arriba newspaper (1961) and his Glass Pavilion in the Casa de Campo exhibition park, Madrid (1964).

ALBERTO GRIJALBA BENGOETXEA

THE LIVING ROOM **STAIRS LEADING DOWN TO THE OFFICE**

THE ARCHITECT´S OFFICE IN THE BASEMENT

SITE PLAN

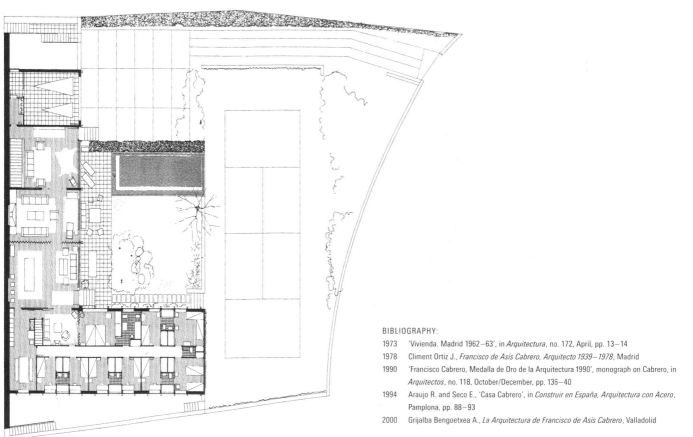

BIBLIOGRAPHY:

1973   'Vivienda. Madrid 1962–63', in *Arquitectura*, no. 172, April, pp. 13–14

1978   Climent Ortiz J., *Francisco de Asís Cabrero, Arquitecto 1939–1978*, Madrid

1990   'Francisco Cabrero, Medalla de Oro de la Arquitectura 1990', monograph on Cabrero, in *Arquitectos*, no. 118, October/December, pp. 136–40

1994   Araujo R. and Seco E., 'Casa Cabrero', in *Construir en España, Arquitectura con Acero*, Pamplona, pp. 88–93

2000   Grijalba Bengoetxea A., *La Arquitectura de Francisco de Asís Cabrero*, Valladolid

Peter Andrew Campbell Callebout
1916 – 1970

1954 – 56, NEW CONSTRUCTION
MOSWEG 7, NIEUWPOORT-BAD (B)

MAIN WORKS AND PROJECTS

1949	Gérard house, Namur (B)
1952 – 57	De Saedeleer two-family house, Nieuwpoort-Bad (B)
1954	Pauwels house, Blankenberge (B)
1954 – 61	Surgical wing of Wante Foundation Maternity Hospital, Ostend (B), with Fernand Sohier
1956	Holiday pavilion at the International Wood Salon of the Annual Trade Fair in Ghent (B)

1957 – 58	Exhibition design '50 ans d'art moderne' in Palace 2 at Expo 58, Brussels (B), with Marc Mendelson
1960 – 62	Van Hoorebeke holiday cottage, Zeebrugge (B), (Atelier CS)
1964	Salkin house, Coignac-Var, Provence (F)
1968 – 70	Valerius De Saedeleer Arts and Crafts Centre, Etikhove (B), with Paul Viérin

PETER ANDREW CAMPBELL CALLEBOUT was born in London on 20 June 1916, the only child of the Belgian architect and sculptor Ernest Callebout and the English carpet weaver May Wilson. His father had achieved a solid reputation as the chairman of the Belgian Association of Architects, and had implemented medium-sized projects in the Congo as well as private briefs in Belgium.

After the First World War the family returned from Britain to Bruges. Here, Peter Callebout went through secondary education at the Koninklijk Atheneum (Royal Athenaeum) and a classical higher education at the Academie voor Schone Kunsten (Academy of Fine Arts). When he graduated in 1937, he won First Prize in the Delacencerie competition with a design for a stock-exchange building. This was the first, and also the last, academic work he did. Even so, it already displayed qualities that were to be found in his later work: simplicity, discretion and refinement.

In 1938 Callebout married Simone Roose, and a year later he was registered as an architect, having passed the necessary exams. After the Second World War he worked with his father until 1952. In his father's studio he mastered the skills in an intuitive and non-academic way. In addition to this pragmatic approach, he also embarked on intensive studies of his own. On the basis of the craft taught him by his father, Callebout probed the no man's land between tradition and modernity. He transposed the modernist idiom from the regional and international architectural cultures he had encountered on his patient quest into an architectural vocabulary of his own.

Peter Callebout's highly individual approach to architecture brought him gradual but definite success. He won several architectural prizes, was a member of major juries, and in 1959 was invited to the CIAM congress in Otterlo. He was also on friendly terms with several artists and designers, including Marc Mendelson and Michel Olyff, as well as with

a number of renowned architects. In 1964, in the book *Gewetensonderzoek bij een whisky* (Soul-Searching with a Whisky), which is a conversation with Willy Van Der Meeren, Renaat Braem, Georges Baines and K. N. Elno, Callebout asks himself: "Is there still any point to architecture? ...we should go back to zero and do research and for the time being not think about architecture at all. ...we should first become constructors and not architects, who just build self-portraits."

In 1967 Callebout was appointed a professor by the Commission de Surveillance at La Cambre, Brussels. His independent spirit, feeling for dialogue and sense of justice made him an essential link in the changes the art school was undergoing. Together with his colleague Maxime Wynants, he stood on the side of the students in an attempt to break down the established order and paralysing routine into which the institution had lapsed. But he did not revolt purely in the name of revolution. He tried to set architectural education in a broader context and to make the students aware of the human and social tasks they had to fulfil. The most pressing and controversial studies were the proposals for the revaluation of the Marolles district in Brussels and the rue des Brasseurs in Namur, one of Belgium's first urban development renovations.

Although Peter Callebout stayed in Belgium, he had always retained his British nationality. The dandyish aspect of his character had already developed during his youth. He grew up in a very wealthy environment, received a highly cultivated education and adopted the habits of the British upper class. With his English origins and cultivation he developed into a true gentleman. Despite his connections in the beau monde, he received virtually no large-scale briefs or public commissions. Moreover, as a freemason, he could not expect anything from the clerical world. In this respect, his professional mentality worked against him, in addition to his British nationality and lack of interest in politics.

NORTH-WEST FAÇADE

NORTH-EAST FAÇADE   SOUTH-EAST FAÇADE

THE STUDIO

He saw a close relationship between the architect, client and building contractor as the most essential factor. When no open dialogue was possible with the client, his pride prevented him from continuing with the project. When his ideas were well received, it often led to a sincere friendship with the client. Put the other way round, he built his most successful works for friends. What is more, Callebout did not see his architectural briefs as a way of earning a living. He only drew up his contracts after the design stage and was not averse to cancelling an uninteresting job without payment. Nor was he at ease with the complexity of large-scale briefs, even considering them to be a hindrance to his creativity. This is why he remained primarily an architect of single-family homes. Despite what, in terms of quantity, was only a marginal production in the post-war construction frenzy, Callebout set up partnerships with Fernand Sohier and Paul Viérin, two former assistants.

After his father died, Callebout started a series of notable houses in Nieuwpoort-Bad, including his own home at Mosweg 7, a new construction designed and built 1954—56. In 1956 he left Bruges and liberated himself from everything the medium-sized town had to offer. He withdrew into an area of unspoiled polder land and tried to rediscover the landscape through the simplicity and discretion of his own house. His

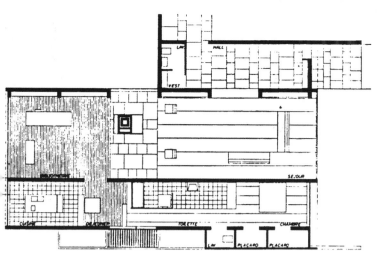

FLOOR PLAN

home was the result of a quest that lasted at least a year and a half. He never fully completed the building, however, since he used it as a laboratory for his ideas. The interior and the careful placing of the house in its natural surroundings reveal Callebout's feeling for detail. The building has only a single storey and follows the natural slope. The ceiling is in wood. The long walls are in brick, painted white. The furnishings are modest and minimal. On the floor were cherished vases and paintings by artist friends, with their backs facing the room. The landscape was the only form of decoration. Callebout withdrew like an ascetic into the visual stillness of his home. He was not without a touch of conceit, regularly having his house photographed, often with himself in the foreground. A painful, almost deadly anecdote demonstrates just how deep-rooted Callebout's respect for the dune landscape was. When a contractor levelled the slope of the dune on an adjacent lot, Callebout was shattered, and that same evening had his first heart attack. Because of his appointment at La Cambre, his doctor ordered him to move to Brussels, which he did shortly afterwards. He handed over his house in Nieuwpoort to the sculptor Roel d'Haese.

In the final design, the house was reduced to essentials. Four parallel brick walls support the aluminium roof and divide the house into three zones: one broad zone for the living area, and two narrower ones for the utility rooms and the hall. The long walls and the open side walls create powerful perspective views of the natural surroundings. But this simplicity does not create a sterile impression. The living area merges smoothly into the utility rooms and hall. The solid chimney over the hearth breaks the 'emptiness' of the enormous space. The window in the transverse wall makes the sidelong framing acceptable and provides for sufficient light in the middle section. Although the division of the house is largely undefined, the floor covering subtly indicates a functional purpose. The hearth stands on a floor of bluestone, the kitchen and generous hall are tiled, and the floor in the breakfast, working and sitting areas is in parquet. The bathroom is integrated into the bedroom space.

The façades also balance nimbly on the boundary between simplicity and complexity. At first sight a horizontal silhouette stands out against the gentle undulation of the dune landscape and the distant horizon. It is only when we go closer that we notice the subtle gradations of material. It seems complex in its simplicity: simple as an expression of the logical floor plan, complex as a composition of various elements and

surfaces. It is only the horizontal articulated edge of the roof that brings unity to the fragmentation of the different façades.

Peter Callebout's house fits into a modern quarter of Nieuwpoort-Bad. Of the twelve houses the architect designed, ten were built. These little masterpieces lend themselves particularly well to an examination of his architectural idiom, which clearly bears the traces of Ludwig Mies van der Rohe's adage that less is more. The floor plan of his house is no more than a minimal composition of lines. Although the line drawings themselves are already fascinating, they express in the first instance a maximal spatiality. After all, Callebout considered architecture to be essentially an art of space. The district not only makes reference to van der Rohe's minimalist architecture, but also to the work of Frank Lloyd Wright. In Callebout's home, the open floor plan in the horizontal white body of the building and the partly projecting roof contrast with the solid black chimney. Continuous low exterior walls confirm the dialogue with the surroundings. The regional character of the houses in Nieuwpoort-Bad originates equally in traditional Japanese architecture and post-war Scandinavian architecture. Conforming to the Japanese creed that nature comes first, he leaves the landscape around the houses untouched.

In this group of houses Peter Callebout offered a worthy alternative to the cacophony or monotony we often encounter in suburban and social housing estates. These houses resonate in polyphony with each other and their surroundings. The district has drawn considerable response. Belgian and international periodicals have devoted articles to it. In 1970 Jacques Meuris described the neighbourhood as a "place of pilgrimage for young architects". A year later Geert Bekaert called it "an exceptionally praiseworthy ensemble". GERT VAN CONKELBERGEA

BIBLIOGRAPHY:

1956   Henselmans J., *Landhuizen en Bungalows*, Amsterdam

1963   Bontridder A., *Hedendaagse Bouwkunst in België. Dialoog tussen licht en stilte*, Antwerp

1985   Burniat P. and Chantrenne D. (eds), *Ces Architectes qui ont fait La Cambre*, exhibition catalogue, Brussels

1991   Bekaert G., 'Het einde van de architectuur', in 1951–1991. *Een Tijdsbeeld*, exhibition catalogue, Paleis voor Schone Kunsten, Brussels, pp. 197–207

1998   Van Conkelberge G. and Speliers H., 'Peter Callebout', in De Kooning M. and Vanackere L. (eds), *Viees en Beton*, Mechelen, pp 35–36

Adam Caruso
*1962

**1993 – 94, CONVERSION, DESIGNED AND BUILT BY CARUSO ST JOHN
HIGHBURY, LONDON (GB)**

MAIN WORKS AND PROJECTS

1994	House Fishtoft, Lincolnshire (GB)	2002	Coate House, Office refurbishment, London (GB)
1998	Bankside Signage, London (GB)	2003	Stortorget, Kalmar (Sweden), with artist Eva Löfdahl
	Mews house, Islington, London (GB)		Bethnal Green Museum of Childhood, London (GB)
2000	New Art Gallery, Walsall (GB)		*Medicine Man* Exhibition at the British Museum, London (GB)
2001	Renovation of Barbican Concert Hall, London (GB)		
	Gagosian Gallery, London (GB)		

ADAM CARUSO was born in 1962 and studied architecture at McGill University in Montreal. In 1990, he founded, together with Peter St John (born 1959) from England, his own office. Both Caruso and St John gained practical architectural experience working in the London offices of Florian Beigel and Arup Associates and with their Studio Caruso, completed in 1993, already began to receive international notice. They owe their reputation as whiz kids in the young architectural scene, however, to the New Art Gallery, a building in the industrial city of Walsall north of Birmingham that opened in 2000. With their buildings and projects, both Caruso and St John demonstrate an individual architectural approach which is clearly differentiated from the reigning English architectural positions of high-tech, late Postmodernism or Minimalism. Searching for possible influences or role models, one could note Peter Smithson or the earlier work of Herzog and de Meuron, however, the visual arts, chiefly through photography, video and installation, also play an important role.

The core of Caruso St John's concept can be encapsulated by the term "realism". In this context, the contradictory appearance of the post-industrial cityscape provides the best conditions for the team's strategies: to reflect on the urban context through architectonic interventions, to make this context perceivable and to transform it, in the sense of a revaluation. Caruso St John's buildings synthesize the characteristic elements of their surroundings and enter into a dialogue with them. The complex and contradictory nature of the surroundings becomes so much part of the building that it often takes on an oscillating appearance. At first glance the hulking structure of the New Art Gallery in Walsall suggests the relic of an industrial-age building in which window openings were randomly inserted. From another perspective, however, it seems to be an abstract version of a city palace and from yet another, reminds one of an unfinished high rise. These facets, carefully attained by the architects from the context, anchor the structure in its surround-

ings, while its sphinx-like aura captures our attention in a subtle and suggestive manner.

Despite certain historical references, the relinquishing of surface level nostalgic effects enables the building to display an uncompromising modern quality; a quality whose association with the Modernist tradition is present less in social utopianism than in the careful choreography of spatial experience. This is demonstrated in Walsall not least through the interior design. Here, the numerous windows guarantee that the art is confronted with the view towards the outside, with the city presented in various perspectives as an aesthetic object open to perception. Along with the careful analysis of the surroundings, Caruso St John evidence an almost obsessive type of exactness in their approach to materials and their aesthetic effect; an approach which reminds one of Swiss Minimalist architecture. Based not least on their success in Walsall, the architects are currently working on various projects in Europe, among others in Rome, Zurich, Berlin and in the southern Swedish city of Kalmar, where the architect team uses its typical approach of contextual sensibility combined with contemporary forms of expression, in the new design of a baroque city square.

The formal and conceptual characteristics of Caruso St John's work are already fully formulated in their London-based Studio Caruso, completed in 1993. Only renovations absolutely necessary for new use have been made in Adam Caruso's house and studio, located on a side street in a former small warehouse in the city district of Highbury. Otherwise, the original building is still visible in its basic substance with all traces of its former use.

In the sparsely furnished work room on the ground floor, the bare brick wall, partly plastered, partly raw, often spackled over, creates a conflicting atmospheric quality: on the one hand, the feeling of an artist's

KITCHEN

SITTING AREA

STUDIO

SLEEPING AREA

studio and on the other, a work of art itself, such as a stage design or Arte Povera installation. The street front is the only wall that was not preserved in its original materiality. Here, the architects have inserted a large structure made of glass elements with semi-transparent insulation, which allows daylight to come in without permitting anyone to look in or out. In the evening, the indoor lighting makes the space appear from the outside like a paper lantern. On the first floor, where the living room and bedrooms are located, the walls and ceilings are covered in gypsum board in order to create a cozier atmosphere. Yet, even here the architects experiment with the aesthetic of the material's basic substance: the boards are left raw so that the room is characterized by the frayed network of the filled-in gaps. With such experimental use of materials, a wild collage of diverse possibilities could happen that might appear completely arbitrary. Such an effect, however, does not occur since the central interest of Caruso St John is clearly directed by the overall spatial composition.

In the studio house, the decisive spatial element is a light well in the back connected to a roof extension that houses a work and guest room. In interaction with the staircase, the spatial experience of the light well offers not only a surprising depth in the vertical direction but also a complex structure of visually overlapping surfaces and changing lighting moods.

The house which at first glance appears like a randomly assembled work of everyday architecture, on second sight proves itself to be a sophisticated composition of materials and space: a quality which does not necessarily conform to general concepts of "coziness". Architectonic

ELEVATION AND SECTIONS

REAR VIEW

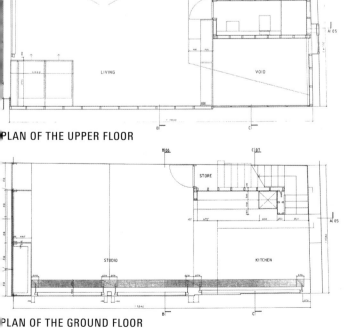

quests for form and everyday use are not always congruent. Didn't Goethe remark after his visit to Palladio's Villa Rotonda that the house was "livable but not comfortable?" An architect living in the house, however, may have other criteria.   EBERHARD SYRING

PLAN OF THE UPPER FLOOR

PLAN OF THE GROUND FLOOR

BIBLIOGRAPHY:
1995   'Studio Caruso in London', in *Bauwelt*, 17/1995, pp. 970–971
2000   Cerver F. A., *Häuser der Welt*, Cologne, pp. 56–59
        Keller T. K., 'Realistisches Spiel mit Gefühlswelten', in *Neue Zürcher Zeitung*, March 5, p. 27
        'Caruso, Adam; St John, Peter: London zum Beispiel', in *Daidalos*, 75, pp. 18–21
2002   Haeflinger T. (ed.), Deon L. (ed.), *Knitting weaving wrapping pressing – Caruso St John Architects*, Basle
        Caruso St John Architects, exhibition catalogue, Architekturgalerie Luzern, Basle

José Antonio Coderch de Sentmenat
1913–1984

1964, RENOVATION AND CONVERSION, NOW ALTERED
ESPOLLA, GIRONA (E)

MAIN WORKS AND PROJECTS

1946 Own house-cum-studio, Plaça Calvó 4, Barcelona (E)

1951–52 Ugalde house, Caldes d'Estrac, Caldetes, Barcelona (E)

1951–55 Barceloneta apartment building (Edificio de viviendas para el Instituto Social de la Marina en la Barceloneta), Passeig Joan de Borbó 43, Barcelona (E)

1956–58 Catasús house, Carrer Josep Carner, Sitges, Barcelona (E)

1958 Own Milà holiday house, Cadaqués, Girona (E)

1958–59 Torre Valentina urban development project, Sant Antoni de Calonge, Girona (E)

1960–63 Tàpies house, Carrer de Saragossa 57, Barcelona (E)

1961–62 Rozes house, Avinguda Díaz Pacheco 184, Cala Canyelles, Roses, Girona (E)

1964–66 Girasol apartment building (Edificio Girasol), Calle Ortega y Gasset 23, Madrid (E)

1965–69 Trade buildings (Edificios Trade), Gran Vía de Carles III 86–94, Barcelona (E)

1967 Urquijo apartment buildings (Viviendas para el Banco Urquijo), Carrer de Raset 21–31, Barcelona (E)

1972–75 French Institute (Instituto francés), Carrer de Moià 8, Barcelona (E)

JOSÉ ANTONIO CODERCH DE SENTMENAT is one of the foremost figures of post-war Spanish architecture, not only because of the quality of his works, but also because of his defence of a moral integrity applied both to the field of architecture and to his private life. His aristocratic background played a decisive role in the formation of these convictions, leading him to construct an etymological interpretation of his social condition – of the individual who derives his power from a commitment to being best, which in his case was associated with a confident defence of attitudes that were often controversial, and soon helped to set him apart as a 'master'.

Coderch was born in Barcelona on 26 November 1913, the eldest of eight children of José Coderch, chief engineer of the port of Barcelona, and María Luisa de Sentmenat. Originally he wanted to be a naval engineer, but his parents' convinced him that he should take up architecture instead, so in 1931 he enrolled in the School of Architecture, Barcelona. In 1936 he travelled to Germany briefly, after which his studies were interrupted by the Spanish Civil War (1936–39), during which he served on the nationalist side as a reserve officer. Coderch graduated from the School of Architecture in 1940. In 1943 he married Ana María Giménez, whom he had met in Malaga during the Second World War, and with whom he subsequently had four children.

It was at architecture school that he met Manuel Valls Vergés, with whom he joined forces in 1942, when the two young architects decided to set up an office together. He combined his professional practice with the post of municipal architect of Sitges (until 1945) and collaborated with central Spanish bodies responsible for the development of social housing and reconstruction.

From this time in the early 1940s onwards, the theme of the individual dwelling and the recovery of the most inherent elements of habitation became the greatest concern of Coderch, who was particularly influenced by the proposals made by the Italian architect Gio Ponti in *Domus* and by the return to modernity in popular Mediterranean architecture. Ponti altogether played a decisive role in Coderch's professional life, both making him definitively aware of the need for new interpretations of the legacy of modern architecture and introducing Coderch onto the international scene, where he was welcomed as a master of emerging Spanish architecture.

In 1946 Coderch designed a first studio-home for himself, his wife and their children at Plaça de Calvó 4, in the Sant Gervasi district of Barcelona, moving his practice into the building. Another home that he built around this time, the Garriga Nogués house (1949), attracted the interest both of his mentor Gio Ponti and of Alberto Sartoris. From the late 1940s onwards the influential architectural review *Domus*, founded and edited by Ponti, began to publish Coderch's work regularly. Three works dating to the early 1950s consolidated Coderch's position as one of the young masters of Spanish architecture and projected him onto the international scene: his Barceloneta apartment building (Edificio de viviendas para el Instituto Social de la Marina en la Barceloneta) in Barcelona (1951–55),

DINING TABLE IN THE LARGE LIVING ROOM

THE LIVING ROOM

ONE OF THE BEDROOMS

his Ugalde house (1951–52) likewise in Barcelona, and his Spanish pavilion (1951) for the IX Triennale in Milan.

Also in 1951 Coderch co-founded on 21 August (with Josep Prat-
marsó Parera, Oriol Bohigas, Joaquim Gili Moros, Antoní de Maragas
Gallíssà, José M. Sostres Maluquer, Josep Martorell und Manuel Valls
Veges) the Grupo R, whose programme centred on a resumption of contacts with modern architecture in a country which was still very much
isolated and out of touch with the contemporary debate. A decade later,
in 1960, he also became a member of Team X. However, Coderch's participation in both groups was only brief, which is perhaps explained by his
misgivings in the face of architectural discourses that were moving away
from the verification of design and by his disappointment at discovering
how difficult it was to put notably experimental proposals into practice.
Altogether the architect's involvement mid-century in contemporary cultural and theoretical debate was problematic – despite the excellent
position he was carving out for himself, the important friendships he was
forging at international level, and the many opportunities these contacts
afforded him.

In 1958 Coderch built a holiday house for himself and his family at
Cadaqués, Girona. Also in Girona he worked wholeheartedly on his Torre
Valentina urban development project (1958–59), experimenting with
new residential solutions for holiday homes, which unfortunately met
with incomprehension on the part of the owners. In the same year, 1958,
Coderch became a member of the CIAM on the recommendation of
Josep Lluís Sert, who invited him to take part in the CIAM congress of
that year in Otterlo and present his Torre Valentina project.

Coderch's disappointment with the lukewarm response to his Torre
Valentina project, combined with a lack of briefs coming to his practice,
led in 1960 to a moment of crisis for the architect, which was alleviated

somewhat when the painter Antoni Tàpies commissioned from him a studio-cum-house in Barcelona (1960–63). Nevertheless, partly because of
these downturns in his fortune, Coderch became disillusioned in the mid-
1960s and withdrew somewhat, a malaise that was compounded by his
entry into the urban context, a field in which he never felt truly at ease,
despite the quality of works such as his Girasol apartment building,
Madrid (1964–66), in which he strove to produce an original reworking of
his proposals for the individual dwelling in collective terms.

In 1961, in response to a questionnaire sent by Jacob Berend
Bakema, Coderch wrote his best-known text, *No son genios lo que nece-
sitamos ahora* (It is not genius that we need now). In 1964 he purchased
and renovated the old Coderch family house at Espolla, and in the mid-
1960s started lecturing at his old college, the School of Architecture in
Barcelona. In the second half of the decade, projects for residential and
commercial buildings in urban contexts began to account for much of
Coderch's professional activity – besides the Girasol apartment block in
Madrid, there was in Barcelona his Trade buildings (1965–69), his Banco
Urquijo project (1967) and his Las Cocheras development (1968).

Throughout the 1970s the Coderch's work continued to win prizes
and gain recognition, although in 1972 Manuel Valls left their joint practice to set up with his son. In 1978 the architect won the competition for
an extension to the Barcelona School of Architecture, which turned out
to be his last work. Following this, in the last six years of his life, a selection of Coderch's designs was shown in the group exhibition *Catalan
Architecture 1950–1977* at the Centre Pompidou in Paris, after which his
work was the subject of solo exhibitions at the II Architecture Biennial in
Santiago de Chile (1979), in Madrid (1980) and in Barcelona (1981).
Coderch died in Barcelona on 6 November 1984, and his remains are
buried in the cemetery of Espolla.

BEDROOM WITH DESK

Even more than the construction of his studio-home in Plaça de Calvó (1946), Barcelona, the project which for Coderch truly represented his own domestic values was the purchase and renovation of the old family home in the village of Espolla, Girona (1964). This symbolic return to his origins came about as the result of an intense period of public commitment for Coderch, an effort which, however, ultimately acted as a discouragement for a man who was already unsure of the possibility of defending architecture and teaching on the basis of theory in such an unreceptive environment. It was, therefore, with great joy and the realisation of enacting what was almost a rite which would reunite him with his predecessors that in 1964 Coderch undertook the remodelling of the Mas del Puig, a building dating from the 18th century which had been sold in the early 20th century by the brother of his great-grandfather.

Coderch himself loved to recall the fortuitous circumstances of the discovery of the house, explaining how a friend who was passing through Espolla saw an inscription on the lintel of one of the doors, referring to a renovation which had been carried out just before the French Revolution by Coderch's great-great-grandfather, Narciso. For the architect, the recovery of the Coderch family house was a definite opportunity to recovery historical memory, an act of bonding with his land, in the place which was the repository of the most deeply felt family memories. "My family said that I was crazy. But it was our motherhouse, and the one that I was most interested in," he declared in his *Conversations with Enric Soria*.

For Coderch, then, the importance of the project lay in the evocative capacity of these domestic spaces, more even than in the actual architectural solutions, which were guided by the discoveries made during work in progress or during the excavation of the bowels of the house in search of the secrets it concealed. In an interview with Baltasar Porcel, published in 1967 in *Destino*, Coderch clearly explained the reason

for his interest: "It is like going back to my roots, linking up with the past, with my grandmother, full of fantastic stories that thrilled me, and her cats; with my father, who used to say 'There are things a Coderch cannot do'; with the farm people." The project was, therefore, another manifestation of the attitude of consistency which Coderch upheld, of the need to conserve the fragments of a dying world and keep them alive by giving them new meanings. And it was in this spirit that Coderch undertook the renovation and conversion of the Can Coderch, which had been damaged by years of transformations and additions. Situated in a village in the Alt Empordà, the building presents the typical characteristics of the rural constructions of the area, comprising a porch, a ground floor originally intended as stables, and a first floor with an attic as the living quarters.

The rehabilitation, which only affected the ground floor, took the form of an intense dialogue between the architect and the building with a view to recovering, as far as possible, the integrity of the original structure with its stone-built walls and vaults, and carefully incorporating new elements which were charged with giving contemporary significance to this space of memory. The central part of this comfortable refuge, where the architect was to spend long periods of time, was the living-cum-dining room, which also leads into the other rooms: the master bedroom, another cosier living room that communicates directly with the children's bedroom, a third bedroom, and the kitchen. Despite the limitations imposed by the existing structure, the architect was able to adapt the spaces to the complexity of a contemporary domestic programme, as in the best examples of his own work. The most characteristic elements of Coderch's architecture are in this way combined with the essential nature of the original spaces. The few items of furniture are specially designed to make the most of space; and the fireplaces and lamps, also designed by the architect, confer intimacy and quiet seclusion to a house which is the quintessence of the home.   PABLO SUSTERSIC

FLOOR PLAN

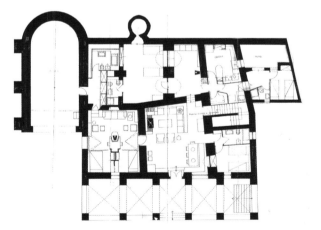

BIBLIOGRAPHY:
1966   'Dentro un'antica struttura, a Espolla, Catalogna', in *Domus*, no. 445, December, pp. 26–30
1968   'Mas del Puig en Espolla', in *Hogar y Arquitectura*, no. 78, September/October, pp. 99–104
1989   Fochs C. (ed.), *Coderch 1913–1984*, Barcelona
2000   Pizza A. and Rovira J. M. (eds.), *Coderch 1940–1964. En busca del hogar*, Barcelona
2001   Cornoldi A., *Le case degli architetti. Dizionario privato dal Rinascimento ad oggi*, Venice, pp.108–109

José Antonio Corrales Gutiérrez
1921–2010

1976–79, NEW CONSTRUCTION
FUENTE DEL REY 13B, ARAVACA, MADRID (E)

MAIN WORKS AND PROJECTS

1954–56	Centre for professional study, Herrera de Pisuerga, Valladolid (E), with R. V. Molezún
1957–58	Spanish pavilion at the Brussels International EXPO, Brussels (B), with R. V. Molezún
1961–62	Camilo José Cela house, Palma de Mallorca (E), with R. V. Molezún
1965–67	Social housing in the Unidad Vecinal Elviña, La Coruña (E)
1966	Huarte house, Madrid (E), with R. V. Molezún
1968	Tabanera house, Sangenjo, Pontevedra (E)
1970–75	Bankunión building, Madrid (E), with R. V. Molezún
1973	Banco Pastor building, Madrid (E), with R. V. Molezún
1976–78	Apartments on Conde de Orgaz, Madrid (E), with A. Cavero
1980	Apartment block on M30 motorway, Madrid (E), with R. V. Molezún

JOSÉ ANTONIO CORRALES was born in Madrid in 1921 and graduated from the city's School of Architecture in 1948, at a time when there were still only two such schools in Spain, the one in the capital and a second in Barcelona. Perhaps a sign of this was that when Corrales started out as a qualified fledgling architect there was a distinct lack of practitioners and hence excellent work prospects. Initially he collaborated with his uncle, Luis Gutiérrez Soto, who was one of Madrid's most prominent architects, but, disliking the idea of picking up easy commissions in the wake of his illustrious relative, he soon decided to open a practice of his own. He did so in 1952, joining forces with Ramón Vázquez Molezún, one of Corrales' fellow graduates from the School of Architecture. It was the start of a professional partnership that was to last until Molezún's death 40 years later.

The long-standing cooperation of Corrales and Molezún explains why in the literature the two are almost always mentioned in one and the same breath. But this does not in any way diminish the stature of either architect or, indeed, of both. At a time when Spanish architecture, relatively isolated from developments in the wider world, was languishing in an official historical design idiom, the duo became for decades a byword for Spanish architectural modernity, starting with their Spanish pavilion for the 1958 Brussels international exhibition. It is largely to Corrales and Molezún that the country owes the development of its architectural Modernism and to a whole series of remarkable fascinating modern architectonic projects.

Corrales and Molezún's partnership was untypical in some respects, for although they collaborated on many joint works, they also always maintained their own independent studios, implementing briefs separately when circumstances required. Thus each alternated between collaborative and individual work. The flexible arrangement also had the virtue that both Corrales and Molezún were able to cooperate with other important architects of their generation, including Francisco Javier Sáenz de Oíza, Alejandro de la Sota and José María García de Paredes.

During his career Corrales has dedicated himself wholeheartedly to his architecture, also entering numerous competitions, an industriousness that continues unabated today. This has sometimes been at the expense, as he himself recognises, of his personal life. It comes as no surprise, therefore, that when he decided to build a private home for himself in Aravaca, he incorporated a studio in it.

Corrales built his own studio-house at Fuente del Rey 13b, in Aravaca, Madrid, between 1976 and 1979. A new construction, it is located in a residential area of detached houses to the north-west of Madrid, an area separated from the urban centre by an extensive empty green space. The building combines a complex home for Corrales' large family and a studio for the architect. Although the studio can be entered independently, the emphasis overall is not on separation, isolation and the closing off of discrete spaces, but on integration, transparency and fusion, both between the home and studio, and between the private and public areas. Striking features of the house are its space, its long perspectives, the richness of the space, and the superimposition of heights and levels, objects and rooms, all resulting in a complex and eternal multiple.

The house is sited in a triangular plot of land, amid other lots, on a slope with southerly views. The lie of the land and siting is such that the dwelling has no showy front façade, but is a hidden enclave. On each side of the building, as is the case with the other neighbouring houses, there is a separating space which complies with local planning regula-

VIEW OF THE OUTSIDE CANOPY FROM THE GARDEN

VIEW OF THE OUTSIDE CANOPY FROM THE WINDOW OF THE BEDROOM

VIEW FROM THE LIVING ROOM

DETAIL OF THE LIVING ROOM

PLAN OF THE GROUND FLOOR

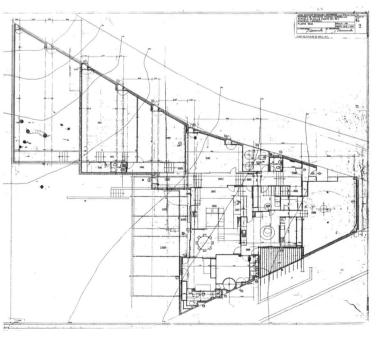

tions that new dwellings must have such a gap at least 5 m wide. Corrales has not simply left this space as a 'dead' area, but has fully factored it into the overall design, creating not just a home 'placed' on the plot, but a total architectural unity of building and land.

Consistent with the sloping terrain, the building is entered at its uppermost level, from which the house descends in steps. The 'terracing' is reflected in the movement of the roof, through which the house is lit up by the sun, creating a wonderful continuity in the interior. The southern wing extends towards the garden, protecting and defining this exterior area in such a way that it is not, once again, merely something empty, but is space beyond the house magnetised by the building. Nor is the house itself, like many of the finest modern homes, merely a 'box to be furnished', with walls that need 'camouflaging' with items of furniture that 'blend in', but is an architectural statement conveying intentions and integrity that defies easy categorisation.

This can be seen, for example, in the way that the house climbs up to the second floor and to the entrance at half level. It does so not by what we commonly and lazily call a staircase, but by a wooden board (okumen), which resembles a rising pavement and, refusing to be strait-jacketed, reaches hard-to-define intermediate spaces and the ambiguous limit of the upper floor. It can be seen also in the way that the architect chose to open the house towards the sides, even though this meant looking out uncomfortably onto the neighbours and that the neighbours might be discomforted by the presence of the Corrales. Further, there are no more or less sophisticated models of windows, but just pieces of laminated boarding, equipped with minimal mechanisms to allow them to move.

The house features metallic profiles, boards screwed to the floor and walls, mobile moulded boards, and neutral colours. It evidences perpetual invention and a reinvigorated criticism of terms such as façade, border, patio, window and parasol. Following his characteristically modernist and constructively rigorous line, Corrales finds new architectural possibilities through novel ways of manipulating materials.

Corrales lived in his Aravaca house-cum-studio for a few years, but then for personal reasons moved out, leaving it empty. However, he did not abandon the building, allowing it to become derelict. Today, a quarter of a century later, the house is in impeccable condition, despite its experimental nature and the inventiveness of many of its solutions, and was recently sold to a member of the family.   JOSÉ MARÍA G. DEL MONTE

BIBLIOGRAPHY:

1980 Junquera J. et al., 'Casa en Aravaca, Madrid', in *Quaderns*, no. 160, January/March, p. 24
1981 Corrales J. A., 'Casa Corrales', in *Arquitectura*, no. 229, March/April, pp. 60–64
1983 Corrales J. A and Molezún, R.V., *Corrales y Molezún*, *Arquitectura*, Madrid
1985 'Casa en Aravaca, Madrid', in *Process: Architecture*, no. 57, April
1993 *Corrales y Molezún, Medalla de Oro de la Arquitectura 1992*, Consejo Superior de Colegios de Arquitectos de España, Madrid
1996 Corrales J. A and Molezún, R.V., *José Antonio Corrales, Ramón Vázquez Molezún*, Colegio Oficial de Arquitectos de Andalucía Oriental, Almería
      Pieltain A., 'José Antonio Corrales: Casa Corrales en Aravaca', in *AV monografías*, no. 60, July/August, pp. 38–39
1997 Buchanan P., 'La Casa Corrales', in *Arquitectura*, no. 309, pp. 54–57

Günther Domenig

1934 – 2012

1986, NEW CONSTRUCTION
STEINDORF AM OSSIACHER SEE, CARINTHIA (A)

MAIN WORKS AND PROJECTS

1963 – 69	Pädagogische Akademie (College of Education), Graz (A), with Eilfried Huth
1970 – 72	Pavilion indoor swimming pool, Munich (D), with Eilfried Huth
1972 – 77	Convent dining hall, Graz-Eggenberg (A), with Eilfried Huth
1975 – 79	Z-Bank, Favoritenstrasse, Vienna (A)
1986 – 88	Neufeldweg housing development, Graz (A)
1990 – 92	Institute building, Technical University, Steyrergasse, Graz (A)

1991 – 94	Bruck an der Mur Hospital (A), with Hermann Eisenköck and Peter Zinganel
1994 – 96	Institutes of Jurisprudence, Social Sciences and Economics of the Karl Franzens University, RESOWI-Zentrum, Graz (A), with Hermann Eisenköck
	Secondary school, Essling, Vienna (A)
1995	Hüttenberg Exhibition, Carinthia (A)
1999 – 2001	Documentation Center, Nazi Party Rally Grounds, Nuremberg (D)

GÜNTHER DOMENIG was born in Klagenfurt in 1934. His father was a judge, while his mother, originally from a wealthy patrician family, was a housewife. He had a twin brother, Herbert, who became a merchant. Domenig was raised in Obervellach, a small village near Klagenfurt, where he went to primary school. He then attended an arts-oriented Gymnasium or 'grammar school' in Klagenfurt for four years. As he was good at drawing, he transferred to Villach Höhere Technische Lehranstalt (Technical School), which he successfully completed in 1953. Today Domenig considers this change of school as "a lucky misunderstanding of the real significance of drawing". In the same year he started to study architecture at the Technical University in Graz. After graduating in 1959, he worked in a number of architecture offices in Austria and abroad.

In 1963 Domenig established a working partnership with his friend and colleague Eilfried Huth, which lasted until 1973. Together they realised some exemplary projects that have had a major impact on the evolution of post-war Austrian architecture. "Günther Domenig and Eilfried Huth are undoubtedly the key figures of the new Graz School. Their architecture is not based on tradition, as is the case in Vienna, but on invention, experiment and the process of construction itself," wrote Johann Kräftner in 1983. Since 1973 Domenig has run architecture offices in Vienna, Klagenfurt, and above all Graz. In 1980 he was appointed to a chair at the Technical University in Graz, where he taught until recently.

Although the National Socialist era was relatively short in Austria (1938 – 45), the consequences were no less disastrous. Austrian Modernism, which was in any case not particularly strong, was totally eliminated, together with the more important tradition of building culture. The bleak atmosphere of Nazi anti-modernism continued until after the liber-

ation in 1945. Like Gustav Peichl, Hans Hollein and Wilhelm Holzbauer, Domenig belongs to the generation of Austrian architects of the post-war period who had the unique historical task of dismantling moribund Nazi structures and founding a new cosmopolitan building culture. In Austria, the cities of Vienna and Graz assumed a leading role in this process. Whereas Vienna, the federal capital and the country's only large city, was able to take up the glorious tradition of one of the most important metropolises of Modernism, Graz was a relatively small provincial town that had hardly appeared on Europe's cultural map. Moreover, due to its border situation, the town was inhabited by an ultraconservative population. It was thus all the more surprising that in the 1960s Graz suddenly had the deserved reputation of being the most avant-garde city in Austria. The new architectural conception developed and supported by graduates of the Technical University was characterised by an impatient vehemence and focussed power, as well as by a formal originality, a situation that was totally different from that in Vienna and in many other European cities.

The phenomenon of avant-garde architecture in Graz created out of nothing was called the Grazer Schule or Graz School. Under this name it became a remarkable example of a regional evolution in architecture that had a significant international impact. Friedrich Achleitner, the renowned Austrian architectural theorist, has stated: "If Styria has become a province with a vigorous architectural 'scene' and with several personalities whose influence extends beyond Austria's borders, it is due to the 'drawing-room revolution' that took place at the Technical University in the 1960s and to the general cultural atmosphere that resulted in brands such as 'trigon', 'Forum Stadtpark' and 'Steirischer Herbst'. Styrian artists are still

THE ENTRANCE SIDE WITH THE GARAGE

VIEW FROM THE LAKE

THE OFFICE

THE MAIN STAIRCASES >

THE GUEST TOILETS

a genius. Then, when Herbert injured himself on the surreal wooden bathing bridge that Günther had designed as a first construction on the beautiful plot, the merchant realised that he was faced with a dilemma. He would never be able to live under the roof that his brother had planned to build, but he did not want to have the house built in the local style by another architect, as he did not want to offend his beloved brother. He therefore gave his brother Günther the entire plot for building. It turned out to be a wise decision, for Domenig continued to work on the house for 20 years.

After all that time, the house was only two-thirds complete, and only one third is usable. But for Domenig what mattered was neither usability nor the time needed for completion. He said that he was building the Stonehouse with three premises in mind, and these differed from the starting point of conventional building practice. First, there was no deadline, no pressure of time. Domenig continued the construction as and when more money came in from his other architectural activities. Second, he couldn't make any mistakes – the building had to be technically

rooted in the province's industrial and rural basis, but, faced with international trends, they have also found new resources." The Graz School might be categorised as Neo-Expressionist in character and related to the tradition of Bruno Taut and Erich Mendelsohn.

Although Eilfried Huth and Günther Domenig dissolved their partnership in 1973, they nevertheless continued to work together on projects. A building realised during this period by Domenig in collaboration with Huth, one that is a key example of Domenig's characteristic architectural style, is the multi-purpose hall in Graz-Eggenberg. In general, Huth underlined the political aspects of architecture, whereas Domenig tended increasingly towards an architecture that viewed the building as a sculpture or work of art. Domenig's high-quality buildings did not spring complete solely from his head, but were based on a discourse he had with his team about the realisability of his sculptural ideas. Most of Domenig's buildings look as if they are built from the inside out, so that the outside looks like the inside and vice versa. The effect thus achieved is dramatic, expressive and deconstructive.

Around 1986 Domenig started to build his own 'Steinhaus' or 'Stonehouse' in line with his theories. In the Carinthian village of Steindorf on Lake Ossiach, he and his twin brother Herbert owned a plot of land measuring approximately 4,000 m², which was situated on the shore of the lake, and which was a gift from their wealthy grandmother. Herbert Domenig, the merchant, expected his famous architect brother to build a respectable summer house. But he overlooked the fact that Günther was

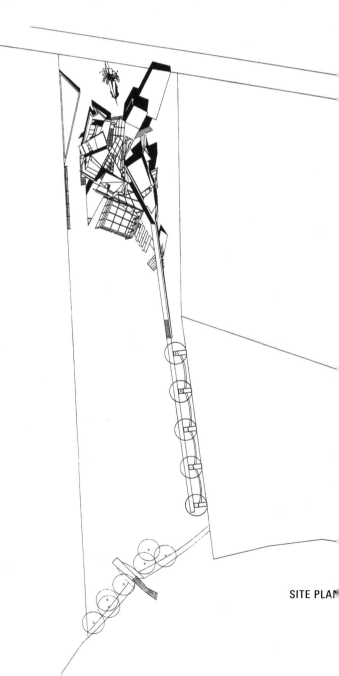

SITE PLAN

LONGITUDINAL SECTION

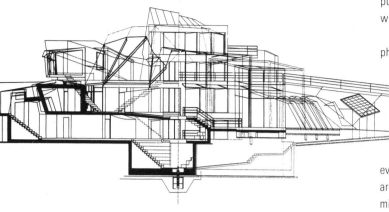

and artistically flawless. And third, the house couldn't be something purely functional. Meanwhile the Stonehouse looked like a stranded wreck.

Domenig's Stonehouse is a built metaphor, an architectural metaphor, which can be interpreted in any number of ways. It is an artefact, the expression of a pharaoh's complex, the expression of a building instinct, an ancient hut, a 20th-century Stonehenge, an experiment, a research project, a homage to his mother and grandmother, his own profile, a protest against everyday life, an axiom, and a missing link both between nature and architecture and between art and building. Or it is the countryside hermitage of a building sect, of which Domenig was the high priest – the Stonehouse rather resembles a seminary with space for 30 participants. Or it is a one-man single-family house perfectly adapted to the psychic needs of the only real resident, a psychograph of Domenig's life and a reaction to Nazism and its architecture. There is just one interpretation that Günther Domenig considered unpalatable: that in building the Stonehouse the architect was constructing a monument to himself and his life, his own obituary. Meanwhile, a photo shown Domenig leaning against the rail at the edge of the Stonehouse's roof, gazing into the distance as if from the bridge of a ship, looking for all the world like some new Noah on a new Stonehouse ark.

JAN TABOR

BIBLIOGRAPHY:
1989   Domenig G., *Das Steinhaus*, Exhibition Catalogue, Museum for Applied Arts, Vienna
1993   *Künstlerhäuser*, Exhibition Catalogue, Deutsches Architekturmuseum, Frankfurt/Main
2002   Domenig G., *Steinhaus in Steindorf, Skizzen, Zeichnungen, Modelle, Objekte*, Klagenfurt
       Amann E.-M., *Domenigs steinernes Ich: das Steinhaus*, Vienna
       Steixner G. and Welzig M. (eds.), *Die Architektur und ich*, Vienna

VIEW INTO THE OFFICE

BEDROOM

BEDROOM LOOKING OUTSIDE

Egon Eiermann
1904–1970

1959–62, NEW CONSTRUCTION, NOW LISTED
KRIPPENHOF 16–18, BADEN-BADEN (D)

MAIN WORKS AND PROJECTS

1929–30	Transformer station for Berlin Electricity Works (BEWAG), Berlin (D)
1938	Factory and boilerhouse for Degea AG (D)
1949–51	Blumberg handkerchief weaving mill and boilerhouse, Blumberg, Black Forest (D)
1951	Merkur department store, Heilbronn (D)
1956–58	German pavilion at the World Exhibition in Brussels (B), with Sep Ruf

1957–63	Kaiser Wilhelm Memorial Church, Berlin (D)
1958–60	Count Hardenberg house, Baden-Baden (D)
1958–61	Mail-order offices for Josef Neckermann KG, Frankfurt (D)
1958–64	German Embassy offices, Washington DC (USA)
1968–72	Head office for IBM Germany, Stuttgart (D)

EGON EIERMANN was born in 1904 in Neuendorf, the son of Wilhelm Eiermann, a locomotive engineer, and his wife Emma Gellhorn. After gaining some experience as a building worker, he studied architecture from 1923 to 1927 at the Technical University in Charlottenburg, Berlin. In 1925 he designed film sets for the UFA (Universum Film AG) film *Der Rosa Diamant*. Between 1925 and 1928 he took part in Hans Poelzig's masterclass. From 1928 to 1929 Eiermann worked in the architects' department of Karstadt Ltd in Hamburg, and from 1929 to 1930 in the architects' department of Berlin Electricity Works Ltd (BEWAG). During this time he also made study trips to Paris and London.

In 1931 Eiermann opened his own practice in Berlin, which ran – for the first five years in partnership with Fritz Jaenecke – until 1945. From 1931 he was a member of both the Deutscher Werkbund and the BDA or Bund Deutscher Architekten (Association of German Architects). In 1936 he made his first visit to the USA. From 1940 to 1952 he was married to Charlotte Friedheim, with whom he had a son, Andreas, born in 1942. During this period Eiermann designed the stage sets for the play *Alexander*, directed by Gustav Gründgens and performed at the State Theatre on Berlin's Gendarmenmarkt.

In 1943, owing to the bombing of Berlin, Eiermann relocated his office to Beelitz, and when in 1945 his office was destroyed, he fled to Buchen, his father's home town. He opened a new practice a year later, which operated first for two years in Mosbach in the Odenwald, and then in Karlsruhe. Between 1946 and 1965 Eiermann worked in partnership with Robert Hilgers. In 1947 he was appointed to a professorship at Karlsruhe Institute of Technology, and in the same year he collaborated with editor Alfons Leitl on the journal *Baukunst und Werkform*. In 1950, Eiermann travelled to the USA, where in Boston he met Walter Gropius, Mar-

cel Breuer and Konrad Wachsmann. He was responsible for the German section of the X Milan Triennale in 1954, and in the same year he remarried to Brigitte Feyerabendt, with whom he had a daughter, Anna, born in 1956. In 1955 Eiermann was invited to become a fellow of the Berlin Academy of Arts.

In 1956, on behalf of the steel manufacturing company Mannesman, Eiermann made a second trip to the USA, during which he visited Ludwig Mies van der Rohe. In 1962, together with Paul Baumgarten and Sep Ruf, he acted as member of the Planning Council for New Buildings for the Upper and Lower Chambers of the German Parliament in Bonn, and in the same year he was awarded the Berlin Art Prize for Architecture. From 1963 on, Eiermann was an Honorary Corresponding Member of the Royal Institute of British Architects (RIBA). In 1968 he won the BDA's Grand Prize and was also awarded the German Federal Cross of Merit. In 1969 and 1974 he won the Hugo Häring Prize for his project for the Blumberg handkerchief weaving mill and boilerhouse. Until 1970, the year of his death, Eiermann was a member of the Federal Republic of Germany's Order of Merit for the Arts and Sciences.

Of the home that he planned for his family at Krippenhof 16–18, in Baden-Baden (1959–62), Egon Eiermann wrote: "I really just want to put up the kind of brick house that country peasants used to build, very primitive, perhaps containing a big tiled stove, and with a large terrace." And Immo Beuken adds: "Eiermann's original idea was that each member of the family – then ranging in age from 3 to 83 – would have their own house, however small." This latter idea eventually became the "house with a secondary house", the main one being the residence, the other a studio, with a fall of about 7 m in the street level in front of the two buildings.

STREET VIEW

GARDEN FRONT

PAGES 96–97: NIGHT VIEW FROM THE GARDEN

THE LIVING ROOM

THE STUDIO SEEN FROM THE LIVING UNIT

The residential house is a two-storey cross-wall structure, with load-bearing cross walls set 4 m apart. A staircase divides the residence into two parts. The floors of each of these parts form split levels, linked by the stairs and set half a storey apart. The studio building stands at right angles to the residence, and has three storeys to the street and two storeys to the garden side. The building is of fairfaced brickwork, was painted charcoal grey inside and out (unfortunately, it has been repainted white by the present owners, although both the house and the garden are listed for preservation). The roof is of corrugated asbestos-cement with wide overhanging eaves and no gutters. The roof timbers, windows, ceiling boarding and furnishings are made of bright red-brown Oregon pine. The floors are covered with round, partially glazed fireclay tiles in various colours.

JUDITH WEINSTOCK-MONTAG

PLAN OF THE GROUND FLOOR

PLAN OF THE FIRST FLOOR

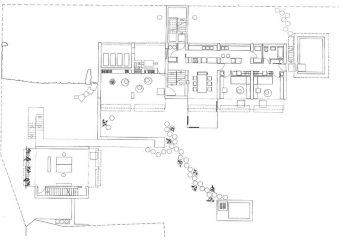

ELEVATION OF THE OFFICE AND SECTION OF THE HOUSE

BIBLIOGRAPHY:

1961 Jaenecke F., 'Mein Freund Eiermann', in *Baukunst und Werkform*, no. 12, p. 687
1963 Eiermann B., 'Haus und Nebenhaus in Baden-Baden', in *Architektur und Werkform* no. 7, p. 291
1965 Joedicke J., *Für eine Lebendige Baukunst*, Stuttgart / Berne
1984 Schirmer W. (ed.), *Egon Eiermann 1904–1970. Bauten und Projekte*, Stuttgart
2001 Cornoldi A., *Le case degli architetti. Dizionario privato dal Rinascimento ad oggi*, Venice, p. 132

Kaj & Dag Englund
1905–1976, 1906–1979

1936–38, NEW CONSTRUCTION, EXTENSIONS IN 1949 AND 1959, NOW DEMOLISHED
KOILLISVÄYLÄ 13, LAUTTASAARI, HELSINKI (FIN)

MAIN WORKS AND PROJECTS

1929–31	Accommodation for technology students, Lönnrotinkatu 27 Helsinki (FIN)	1933	Competition project (wins First Prize) for Temppeliaukio Church, Helsinki (FIN), with Kaj Englund
1937	Lucander villa, Westend, Helsinki (FIN), with Dag Englund	1935–38	Malmi Airport, Helsinki (FIN)
1939	Granroth villa, Kulosaarentie 5, Helsinki (FIN)	1948	Järvenpää Parish Institute (FIN), with Toivo Pelli
1944–45	Mäntylä housing development, Kemi (FIN)	1956–60	Kalevankartano housing development, Tampere (FIN), with Lauri Silvennoinen
1954–56	Sieppijärvi Church (FIN)	1958	Liljeqvist villa, Porkkala (FIN)
1959	Apartment block, Männikkötie 5, Maunula, Helsinki (FIN)	1959–64	School of Veterinary Medicine, Hämeentie 57, Helsinki (FIN)

KAJ AND DAG ENGLUND, born in 1905 and in 1906 in Oulu, were two of five artistically gifted brothers, together with Göran (a successful advertising artist), the youngest brother Einar (a renowned composer), and Bengt (who was a "Master of Arts"). Their father, Gösta Englund, taught gymnastics at the Swedish teacher-training school in Helsinki. He passed on his love of sports to his sons, who won championships in orienteering. Kaj Englund graduated from Helsinki University of Technology in 1931, his younger brother Dag two years later. They started their careers in a joint office and carried out several collaborative projects, also successfully entering competitions together. From the mid-1940s each had his own separate practice in Helsinki.

Kaj Englund's career got off to an auspicious start when he won a student competition for a dormitory for technology students organised in 1929. The building was completed at the time of his graduation in 1931. In that early competition project he was already exploring housing design, which was to become the main theme of his whole career. Kaj designed both private houses and apartment buildings. Besides design work, he also advanced housing culture in other ways. As Commissioner of the 1939 Helsinki Housing Exhibition, he had an opportunity to introduce good housing design and functional furnishing to the general public. He also wrote frequent articles in the press on the issue of housing. Kaj Englund's career coincided with a period of remarkable progress in housing architecture. In the 1930s, like other young colleagues, he was very interested in solving problems related to small apartments and in rationalising housing production. During the extensive reconstruction carried out after the Second World War, it was possible to put these ideas into practice. Kaj Englund's work in 1945–50 as Director of the Standardization Institute of the Finnish Association of Architects was

connected with these undertakings. He designed apartment blocks for Helsinki's suburbs, such as Herttoniemi, Pohjois-Haaga and Maunula, and also for other Finnish towns, especially Vaasa and Pietarsaari in Ostrobothnia. In the office he was assisted by his wife Li (Inkeri) Englund, whose handiwork can be seen in the finished details of the drawings. Li Englund became famous for her printed furnishing fabrics and wallpaper designs, while the dresses and hats she designed for herself once represented the most distinguished *haute couture* in Helsinki. 1954–67 Kaj Englund lectures in the School of Architecture at Helsinki University of Technology.

Dag Englund achieved success in the 1930s for several elegant functionalist church designs which he entered in competitions. His prize-winning submissions were, however, never realised. His most remarkable completed building from that decade is Helsinki's Malmi Airport, once a super-modern example of functionalist architecture. He also found success in competitions for various institutional buildings. His Järvenpää Parish Institute, for example, was built in 1950 following a competition. Dag Englund designed numerous industrial and apartment buildings in various parts of Finland. His wife Doris was a fashion designer.

In 1936 father Gösta Englund and his sons bought a rocky plot at Koillis-väylä 13 in Lauttasaari, west of the urban area of Helsinki. The transformation of Lauttasaari from a summer cottage district into an urban community had just begun at that time. Kaj Englund later said that he had been inspired to buy the site by Alvar Aalto's recently completed house in Munkkiniemi, Helsinki. Together Kaj and Dag Englund designed for the plot a two-storey building ("Bjerges") containing four separate apartment-homes for four families. However, within the overall building,

OVERVIEW OF THE PROPERTY

VIEW FROM THE GARDEN

VIEW FROM THE GARDEN

DETAIL OF THE LIVING ROOM IN DAG ENGLUND'S APARTMENT

THE LIVING ROOM IN KAJ ENGLUND'S APARTMENT

Kaj and Dag designed their own apartments independently. The homes of the architect brothers were on the first floor, while the second floor comprised the apartment of their brother Bengt and the apartment of their parents, with whom the two youngest brothers lived. The size of the four apartments in the Englund family building were regulated by the strict Finnish housing regulations of the time. Thus, in their home Kaj Englund and his family of five had 121.4 m² of space, while Dag Englund and his smaller family had 86.9 m².

The building is made of brick and plastered white. Its flat roof, narrow eaves and ribbon windows in the attic reflect the designers' adoption of Le Corbusier's doctrine. The overall impression is lightened by the timber-structured attic, whose material connects the building with the surrounding nature. The natural landscape was an important consideration even at the time the site was being purchased. The original vegetation was carefully protected in the design and construction of the building, and was also the basis of the garden design. The rocky garden became Kaj and Li Englund's permanent hobby, and was often featured in Finnish magazines. The possibility of extension was observed from the outset, and accordingly the whole south-western end was made of wood.

THE FIREPLACE AREA IN KAJ ENGLUND'S APARTMENT

Kaj Englund's apartment was extended in 1949, and ten years later Dag Englund got some extra space when a new wing was built.

When Kaj Englund was young, he took part in competitions for furniture designs, but his own home was furnished with inherited pieces and new ready-made furnishings. According to him, the home was a living organism, changing from day to day, and its interior decoration should not be predetermined or fixed. Pieces of furniture and textiles were replaced whenever the current dwelling situation required. Kaj and Li Englund's home was repeatedly featured in Finnish interior design magazines. In the late 1930s Dag Englund equipped his home with Alvar Aalto furniture, which was not yet widely known. TIMO KEINÄNEN

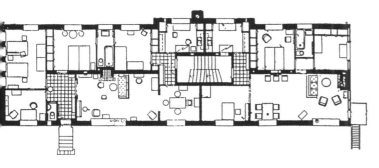

PLAN OF THE FIRST FLOOR

BIBLIOGRAPHY:

1938 Englund, Dag and Kaj, 'Asuintalo Lauttasaaressa Helsingissä', in *Arkkitehti*, no. 7, pp. 109–112

1946 Englund, K., 'Kalliopuutarha Lauttasaaressa. Asunto-osakeyhtiö Bjerges', in *Arkkitehti*, nos. 9/10, pp. 143–152

1948 Englund, K., '4-familjsbolag för hus och trädgård', in *Hem i Sverige*, no. 2, pp. 124–128

Ralph Erskine
1914 – 2005

1963, NEW CONSTRUCTION
GUSTAV III VÄG 4, DROTTNINGHOLM, STOCKHOLM (S)

MAIN WORKS AND PROJECTS

1941 – 42	Own house ('The Box'), Lissma, near Djupdalen, outside Stockholm (S), with his wife and Aage Rosenvold
1945 – 55 and 1961	Housing and school, Gyttorp (S)
1948 – 50	Ski Hotel, Borgafjäll (S)
1954 – 56	Shopping centre, Luleå (S)
1959	Housing, Brittgården, Tibro (S)
1961 – 66	Housing, offices, shops and church, Kiruna, Lapland (S)

1963 – 64	Housing and community plan, Svappavara, Lapland (S)
1968 – 71	Housing, Esperanza, Landskrona (S)
1969 – 81	Housing at Byker, Newcastle-upon-Tyne (GB)
1974 – 82 and 1997	Library, students' centre and Aula Magna, Frescati, Stockholm (S)

RALPH ERSKINE was born in 1914 and grew up in Mill Hill, on the northern fringe of London. His parents were drawn to the socialist ideals of the Fabian Society, an association of intellectuals devoted to the promotion of a socialist society through evolution, enlightenment and public debate, rather than through revolution. In 1925 they sent him to The Friends' School, a Quaker school near Cambridge, where he stayed for six years. Ever since that time, the Quakers' beliefs have been fundamental to him and to his views on society, democracy, town planning and architecture.

In 1932 Erskine began to study architecture at London's Regent Street Polytechnic. At that time the Polytechnic's school of architecture was run by Thornton White, who based his teaching on studies of classical architecture. One of Erskine's fellow students was Gordon Cullen. Erskine studied for five years and, after qualifying in 1937 as a RIBA architect, started to work in the office of Louis de Soisson, where he became involved in the Welwyn Garden City project. In the evenings he also studied town planning and neighbourhood planning.

In 1938 Erskine moved to Sweden, where he joined the practice of Weijke and Odeen, and also married Ruth Francis, whom he had previously met at his old Quaker school. When the Second World War broke out in 1939, he was unable to return to England for various reasons, and he started his own practise. In the winter of 1941–42 Erskine built his first private home, known as 'The Box', on a hillside in a wood at Lissma, near Djupdalen, outside Stockholm. He constructed the little house himself with the aid of his wife and a Danish architect, Aage Rosenvold, who later joined Erskine's office.

After four years, however, the Erskines moved to Drottningholm (in Stockholm), where they rented a traditional house and opened a new office. In the mid-1940s Erskine studied at the Royal Academy of Arts in Stockholm, and in 1955 he bought an old Thames barge in London, sailing it to Sweden, where it became an extension of his office. During the summer the whole practice embarked and sailed out to an island in the archipelagos outside Stockholm. In 1963 Erskine built a second private house with a studio at Drottningholm. His Stockholm practice expanded continually, as did his administrative duties, and in 1982 he decided to reorganise it to allow more time for creative work on his own. The main group started a new cooperative office under the name of Arken-Erskine-arkitekterna A.B. in Stockholm city, while Erskine set up a separate small office, which he housed in the studio next to his own Drottningholm house.

Since the 1940s Erskine was one of the most important regenerators of the modern movement. Ever since the Enlightenment, the modern project has been characterised by two more or less contradictory tendencies, one towards rationality and the other towards liberation and emancipation. During a period dominated by rational thinking, Erskine's greatness was always to strive for liberation and emancipation at all levels, in architectural form as well as in the creative processes. Even if he was unable to carry everyone on board with him in this orientation, nevertheless he tried to attain it, as in the Byker project for example (1969–81), and his architecture always resulted from empathy with users' everyday lives. Erskine was also one of the few practitioners during the mid–20th century who paid attention to the importance of adapting to local conditions. He developed the architectural knowledge of building and living in an Arctic climate like no one before him, and applied it in outstanding projects, such as at Kiruna and Svappavaara in northern Sweden and Resolute Bay in Canada. Beginning in the early 1960s

FRONT VIEW

DETAIL OF THE FAÇADE WITH PANORAMIC WINDOWS

Erskine wrote a number of articles, mainly about building in Arctic and sub-Arctic climates, which were published in internationally renowned architectural journals and reviews.

Erskine lectured at architectural schools and other institutions all over the world. He was awarded many honours: Commander of the British Empire, an honorary doctorate in technology by Lund University, an honorary doctorate of letters by Edinburgh's Heriot Watt University, and an honorary doctorate in civil law by Newcastle-upon-Tyne University. He also won many prizes and medals, including the RIBA Royal Gold Medal.

Ralph Erskine's own house-cum-studio at Gustav III väg 4, Drottningholm, is situated in a special area on the outskirts of Stockholm. Lake Mälaren lies nearby, as also does Drottningholm royal summer palace, with its houses – related to the royal court – dating back to the 18th century. The existing houses in the vicinity create an almost urban character. Given the special nature of the area, it is not surprising that the architect paid attention not just to the design of the house itself, a new construction (1963) in which he continued to live, but also to that of the garden. Everything within the borders of the site is well organised, with different spaces, materials, walls and gangways. The natural cliffs become an integral part of the whole, creating an extended working and living place. The studio was also situated on the site, placed parallel to the dwelling house and creating a courtyard between the two buildings. The boundary between work and family life was non-existent.

Erskine's interest in vernacular architecture, his reinterpretation of Modernism and above all his anti-authoritarian view of life led, in the house, to an architectural form that relates more to usefulness and feelings than to formal rules. The window settings are made according to the inside, and seem to be free from strict order. His contact with Team X and the Brutalist way of dealing with architecture inspired an authentic expression, with carefully designed, prefabricated porous concrete. The concrete elements were given different patterns and different colours in order to reduce the scale and to give the surface life, different character, understanding of the material, and a sensuous quality. Comparisons can be made to vernacular architecture from the Mediterranean countries and to rural houses in the British Isles.

Erskine's profound interest in solutions appropriate to the prevailing climate gave his house a specific form. The cold roof, made of corrugated sheeting, is an adjustment to the climate in order to avoid damage from icicles. The snow can remain on the roof. The inner roof is vaulted with pre-cast insulating concrete panels and forms an independent volume. It has the rounded corners that are significant for the house and for his other Arctic buildings.

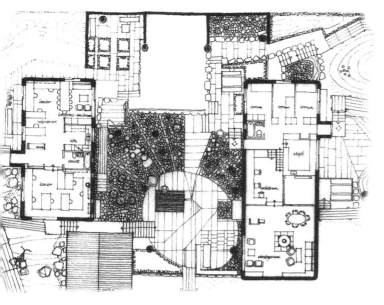

The section is extremely refined and subtle, creating rooms within the room in a highly useful and sophisticated way. Like the plan, it relates to the exterior, to the terraces, and to the wooden gangways, which sometimes work as staircases. The possibility of reaching and using the exterior is carefully treated. The cliff-top site becomes a place in which one can move around and sit in many ways. The treatment of levels inside and out is intricate, creating many useful areas. The authenticity and straightforwardness of the house is also seen in the immediate correspondence between interior and exterior. Altogether the house unites all Erskine's principal passions, such as freedom, social integration, an anti-authoritarian way of life, complexity and simplicity, combined with his interest in site and climate.

GUNILLA SVENSSON, FINN WERNE

GROUND PLAN

The interior could be regarded as one huge single room, like a hay barn with different lofts and volumes. If the plan is open and free, so too is the section. It creates a feeling of freedom and spatial diversity, and allows a complex integration of activities and functions. If the general plan reveals an integration of domestic life and work, so too does the organisation of the house. A study is situated close to the big drawing room, and Ruth Erskine's studio is in open connection with the rest of the house, above the kitchen.

BIBLIOGRAPHY:
1981   *Arkitektur*, no. 7 (Ralph Erskine monographic issue)
1982   Collymore P., *The Architecture of Ralph Erskine*, London (new ed.: 1994)
1990   Egelius M., *Ralph Erskine, Architect*, Stockholm
1990   Winter K., *Ralph Erskine Architect*, Stockholm
2001   Cornoldi A., *Le case degli architetti. Dizionario privato dal Rinascimento ad oggi*, Venice, pp. 132–135

KITCHEN AND LIVING ROOM

THE LIVING ROOM

Aarne Ervi
1910 – 1977

1949 – 50, NEW CONSTRUCTION, STUDIO EXTENSION ADDED IN 1961
KUUSINIEMENTIE 5, KUUSISAARI, HELSINKI (FIN)

MAIN WORKS AND PROJECTS

1939	Apartment and commercial building, Lauttasaarentie 9, Helsinki (FIN)		1954	Mäntytorni apartment block, Tapiola, Espoo (FIN)
1942 – 51	Pyhäkoski power station and residential development (FIN)		1956 – 61	Tapiola tower, Tapiontori, Espoo (FIN)
1950 – 57	Porthania building, University of Helsinki, Yliopistonkatu, Helsinki (FIN)		1961	Apartment block, Myllytie 3, Helsinki (FIN)
			1965	Tapiola swimming pool, Kirkkopolku 3, Espoo (FIN)
1951	Voimatalo commercial office building, Malminkatu 16, Helsinki (FIN)		1968 – 70	Töölö library, Topeliuksenkatu 6, Helsinki (FIN)

AARNE ERVI, one of the most remarkable and versatile architects of his time in Finland, is especially known for his designs for the garden city of Tapiola. All his works reflect the notion of architecture forming an integral part of the natural environment.

Ervi graduated from Helsinki University of Technology in 1935. In 1935 – 36 he worked in Alvar Aalto's architectural practice, participating among other things in the design of Viipuri library. In 1938 he opened an office of his own. During a career spanning over 40 years, he entered numerous competitions, and some of his most important works, such as the Tapiola centre and Helsinki University's Porthania building, were commissioned as the result of his winning them.

Although Ervi was keen on observing nature in his design work, he was not a romanticist. He was especially interested in the new possibilities of construction technology. In 1943 – 45 he was Director of the Standardization Institute of the Finnish Association of Architects, succeeded by Kaj Englund. Journeys to the United States made Ervi familiar with new building methods, and he had a positive attitude to industrialisation. His Porthania building was the first in Finland to be made of prefabricated elements. Ervi's wife from 1957 was Rauni Luoma, a highly regarded actress in the Finnish National Theatre. 1965 – 69 he worked as director of Helsinki City Planning Department.

In *Arkkitehti* (the Finnish Architectural Review), Aarne Ervi began a presentation in 1951 of his self-designed home at Kuusiniementie 5, Kuusisaari, Helsinki (new construction, 1949 – 50), as follows: "The design of a single-family house has always fascinated architects, but this is an especially interesting task when the client and the architect are one and same person, for in that case one has, in addition to construction experience, the chance to continuously observe the effects of the design on living

and on the wallet. This kind of building provides many new influences and perspectives." The house evolved over a long period of rumination. Ervi had bought the site in the residential suburb of Kuusisaari in northwest Helsinki in the late 1930s. In the spring of 1939 he had a set of drawings ready for a two-storey house and a separate office wing for five employees. The ground floor included a large living room opening onto the garden through big windows. Two steps separated the fireplace room with a curving wall from the higher-level dining room. There was a courtyard covered with slate stones and a small pond between the house and the office wing. The sketches show a careful study of garden details. These early designs reveal the influence of Alvar Aalto, in whose office Ervi worked at the time of the construction of Aalto's house. The relationship between house and surroundings and a natural link between rooms are characteristic features of Aalto's own house from 1936, and especially of his Mairea villa, which was under construction during the first design phase of Ervi's house.

However, the outbreak of the Second World War in 1939 prevented Ervi from realising this early design, and it was only after the war, in 1946, that he could once again think of building his private home. The first structure to be built on the site was the sauna.

Then, in 1949, the house was redesigned. It was essentially the same as in the earlier design, but significantly larger. The rectangular building is narrow. "The aim has been to make it possible for the afternoon sun to penetrate into the rooms, which is why the building has been made rather narrow and 'transparent'", was Ervi's argument. Large windows stretching from floor to ceiling on both sides of the living room connect it naturally with the garden. The whole ground floor forms a continuous spacious sequence of rooms. The outdoor spaces, with pavements and green areas, give a sheltered impression, as if they were

VIEW FROM THE GARDEN

THE GARDEN   THE STAIRCASE

interior rooms, and the living room opens onto the garden incon-spicuously.

In building his own home, Ervi was able to experiment with new technical solutions and methods inspired by his experience in the United States. The building frame is based on steel tube pillars. Prefabricated units were used as effectively as possible, employing innovative solutions. The experiments include electric floor-heating and extensive mechanisation, which was still rare in Finland in the early 1950s. Ervi's home is characterised by sophisticated detailing. The steel pillars are clad with rattan braiding, and the walls are partly covered with elm. Green plants and rattan furniture produce a garden-like atmosphere. For the Merivaara factory, Ervi designed tube-structured pieces of furniture, but for his own home he designed soft comfortable armchairs and sofas with the assistance of interior architect Lasse Ollinkari.

Ervi described the impressions of his 1948 journey to the United States in *Arkkitehti* in that same year. His own house shows American influence in the use of the steel frame and prefabricated units and in the experimentation with electric heating. The soft armchairs, leopard skins and plant groupings of the interiors are probably also drawn from the States. In 1961 a studio extension was designed to house Ervi's architectural office.

TIMO KEINÄNEN

DETAIL OF THE LIVING AREA

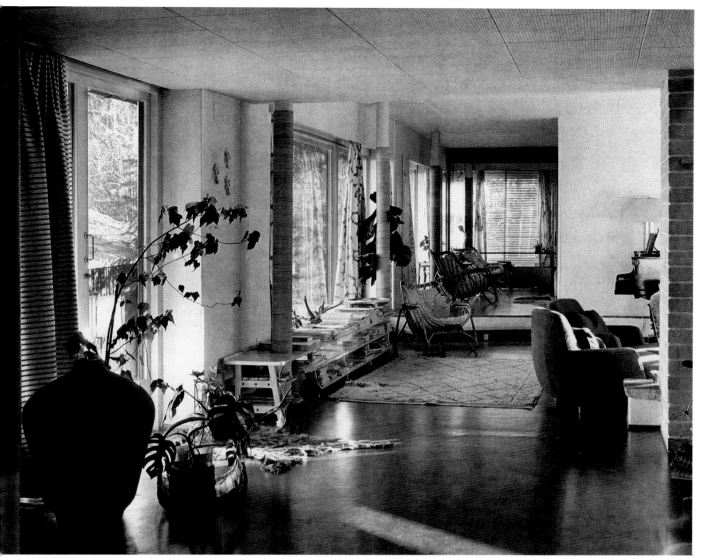

THE LIVING AREA

PLAN OF THE GROUND FLOOR

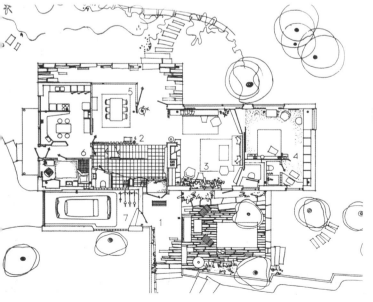

ELEVATION

BIBLIOGRAPHY:

1951   Ervi A., 'Yksityistalo Ervi' (Ervi private house), in *Arkkitehti*, nos. 11/12, pp. 145–162

1953   'Wohnhäuser in aller Welt, 2. Ein Wohnhaus in Finnland', in *Bauwelt*, 31, 3 August, pp. 608–609

1955   Winkler R., *Das Haus des Architekten, Architect's Home, La Maison de l'Architecte*, Zurich, pp. 144–149

1970   Solla P. (ed.), *Raportti rakennetusta ympäristöstä* (Report on the built environment), Helsinki

2001   Cornoldi A., *Le case degli architetti. Dizionario privato dal Rinascimento ad oggi*, Venice, p. 135

Aldo van Eyck
1918–1999

**1948, CONVERSION, NOW DEMOLISHED
BINNENKANT 32, AMSTERDAM (NL)**

MAIN WORKS AND PROJECTS

1948	Own apartment, Binnenkant 32, Amsterdam (NL)
1954–56	Three schools in Nagele, Noordoostpolder (NL), with Hans P. D. van Ginkel
1955–60	Municipal orphanage, Amstelveenseweg, Amsterdam (NL)
1958–60	Own Four Towers house, Baanbrugge (NL), project only, never built
1963–64	Winning design in limited competition for Protestant Church, Driebergen (NL)
1963–69	Roman Catholic church, Loosduinen, the Hague (NL)
1965–66	Sculpture pavilion for Sonsbeek Exhibition, Arnhem (NL)
1967–71	Alfred Schmela house and art gallery, Mutter-Ey-Strasse, Düsseldorf (D)
1973–78	House for single parents and their children, Plantage Middenlaan, Amsterdam (NL)
1983–92	Protestant church for Moluccan community, Deventer (NL)
1984–89	Conference centre and offices for the European Space Agency (ESTEC), Noordwijk (NL)
1992–97	Auditor's office building, Lange Voorhout, the Hague (NL)

ALDO VAN EYCK was born in Holland but grew up in Golders Green, north-west London, where his father, the poet Pieter Nicolaas van Eyck, was foreign correspondent for a Dutch newspaper. He received a classical yet unconventional education at King Alfred School, Hampstead (1924–32), and Sidcot School, Somerset (1932–35). From his early youth he was actively concerned with art and literature, and he nurtured a particular interest in symbolist poetry from Blake to Yeats. He studied architecture at the Royal Academy of The Hague (1935–38), and at the Eidgenössische Technische Hochschule or ETH (Swiss Federal Institute of Technology) in Zurich (1938–42). At the ETH, where architectural design was largely dominated by the functionalism of Rudolf Salvisberg, van Eyck attended the classical design course of the Beaux-Arts veteran Alphonse Laverrière. During his Zurich studies he also met Hannie van Roojen, whom he married in 1943. They became friends with Carola Giedion-Welcker, who introduced them to the world of the 20th-century avant-garde and put them in touch with Hans Arp, Richard Paul Lohse, Georges Vantongerloo, Alberto Giacometti, Tristan Tzara and Constantin Brancusi. Van Eyck's personal contact with these artists and their work led to a close acquaintance with the world view of modern art, which he set out to implement in the field of architecture.

After the war, van Eyck settled in Amsterdam, where Cor van Eesteren engaged him as a designer in the Municipal Department of Public Works (1946–51). This position involved the design of a large number of children's playgrounds, a project that enabled him to start the experimental development of his formal vocabulary. At the same time he became involved in the Cobra movement (1948–51). He actively defended young rebellious artists, and designed the layout of their major ex-

hibitions. In 1947 he also became a member of the Dutch CIAM group 'de 8 en Opbouw', which appointed him as a delegate to international CIAM congresses. Within CIAM he immediately adopted a critical stance towards post-war Functionalism. He strongly opposed its reductive rationalism and its mechanistic conception of progress, and at the same time championed the development of an authentically modern and humane architecture. He was one of the first CIAM members to manifest dissident views of this kind, and in 1954 he was one of the founders – together with Jacob Berend Bakema, Georges Candilis, Robert Gutmann, Alison and Peter Smithson and John Voelcker – of Team X, the group of angry young architects who rejected the established analytical method of the CIAM, and generated a new design approach, based on 'patterns of human association'.

Van Eyck's early work shows an attentive exploration of the basic components of architectonic form. Inspired by both Piet Mondrian and Constantin Brancusi, he developed an elementary idiom characterised by geometrical clarity and archetypal simplicity. One of his first achievements in this idiom was the interior design of his own apartment at Binnenkant 32 in Amsterdam's Lastage district. This did not involve constructing either the building or the flat, but merely of converting the third floor of an old canal house at that address, work that was carried out in 1948 (the building was demolished in 1965). Van Eyck had the transverse partitions removed to produce a continuous space from the front to the rear, and then divided this into three zones, using simple flexible means: two curtains on rails suspended beneath the ceiling, and a free-standing cupboard unit. The rear portion of the apartment, which contained his

THE CHILDREN'S ROOM

DETAIL OF THE LIVING ROOM

THE STUDIO

work table, could be screened off by a dark grey, slightly purplish curtain. Parallel to this, at a distance of 2.5 metres, he hung a second curtain of transparent material, thereby creating a kind of optional miniature drawing room between the living area proper, the work area and the entrance.

Above the curtains the ceiling could be seen continuing into the next space, changing colour precisely at the suspension of the rails. The walls and ceilings were largely painted white, but the ceiling above the middle zone and the adjoining living room wall were both finished in a matt metallic tint. The plank floor was varnished entirely in black. The furniture and household accessories were basic in the extreme. The most conspicuous object was the stove, a black cylinder of iron surrounded by a circular iron rail on six legs to keep the children at bay. The rail loosely supported a plank, which served as a small table or a seat. There was not much else in the way of seating apart from a few round stools, a few raffia chairs and a small, dark red bench of South-American Indian origin. The iron circle, however thin, formed a substantial focus, mediating between the surrounding paintings and objects: on the metallic grey wall a *Composition with Coloured Rectangles* (1917) by Mondrian, on the opposite white wall a large Miró from 1927, and facing the window overlooking the old city centre, against the dark curtain, *Mittelalterliche Stadt*, a pen drawing by Paul Klee from 1924.

In his private Binnenkant 32 apartment, which became a meeting place for Cobra, Aldo van Eyck designed numerous playgrounds for Amsterdam city centre, which displayed an elementary formal language. His interest in the basics of form and the origins of urban society caused him to undertake several expeditions into archaic habitations, notably the oasis settlements of the Sahara (1947–51), the villages of the Dogon (1960), and the pueblos of New Mexico (1961).

After the realisation of some minor projects, including houses, schools and exhibitions, van Eyck gave his ideas a fully elaborated form in his Amsterdam Children's Home (1955–60), a house he conceived as a tiny city, a dynamic fabric of various places, individual and collective, inside and outside, open and closed, a complex yet clear geometrical struc-

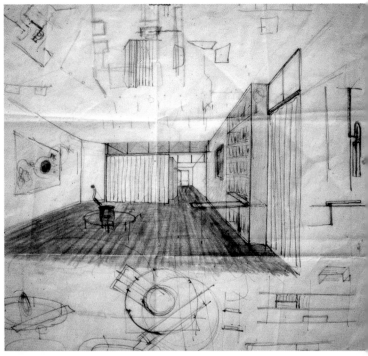

SKETCH OF THE LIVING ROOM

ture shaped in archetypal forms. In an analogous way, the country home he designed (1958–60) for himself and his family, after living for ten years in their Amsterdam apartment, was again conceived as a tiny city.

This was van Eyck's Four Towers house at Baanbrugge, a compact building based on a symmetrical, almost Palladian plan. But in spite of its axial symmetry, it did not constitute a subordination of secondary spaces to a dominant centre. The core of the house expanded in a cross shape into four walled-in exterior spaces within the building perimeter. These four patios strongly determined the ground plan. They shaped the four rooms situated at the corners of the rectangle, making them look like four small houses grouped around a public square. This 'urban' concept

FLOOR PLAN

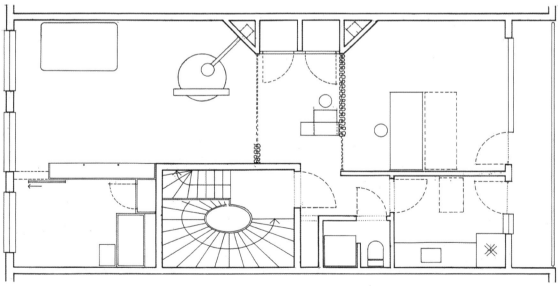

THE LIVING ROOM

was sustained in the further detailing of the design. Each of the four small 'houses' had an upper floor looking out through a window onto the central living space. They also projected above the main volume like small towers with outward-facing windows. The city square character of the central living area was enhanced by a large metal framework, which extended out through the glass walls, paradoxically bringing the two patios into the interior. Moreover, it was lit by fittings attached to the horizontal bars of the framework – a 'street lighting' which extended from interior to exterior, thereby making the living room and patios appear at night as a unified space, even more than during the day. It was like a small square marked by eight street lamps and surrounded by houses, houses from which one could see the windows opposite light up as dusk fell.

The formal vocabulary of the house was modest: an elementary volume constructed of large concrete blocks and covered by a flat concrete roof, whose shorter sides were articulated by the extremities of the supporting beams, the whole topped by the four small tower volumes and a cylindrical wooden solarium.

Unfortunately, van Eyck's Four Towers Baanbrugge house never got off the drawing board. The design failed to gain the approval of the Utrecht provincial planning authority. Building permission was withheld, the house remained only a project, and Aldo van Eyck found himself obliged to look elsewhere to set up his new home. Some time afterwards he bought a modest 18th-century terraced house in Loenen aan de Vecht and converted the interior, leaving the outside almost untouched.

FRANCIS STRAUVEN

BIBLIOGRAPHY:
1951   Salomonson H., 'Bij het interieur van Aldo van Eyck', in *Goed Wonen*, February, no. 2, pp. 25–27
1982   Hertzberger H., Wortmann A., and Strauven F., *Aldo van Eyck*, Amsterdam
1998   Strauven F., *Aldo van Eyck – the Shape of Relativity*, Amsterdam
1999   Ligtelijn V. (ed.), *Aldo van Eyck – Works*, Basle
2001   Cornoldi A., *Le case degli architetti. Dizionario privato dal Rinascimento ad oggi*, Venice, pp. 135–36

Gaston Eysselinck
1907–1953

1930–32, NEW CONSTRUCTION, NOW DEMOLISHED
CORNER OF VADERLANDSTRAAT AND FLEURUSSTRAAT, GHENT (B)

MAIN WORKS AND PROJECTS

1931	Serbruyns house, Ghent (B)
1932	Peeters house, Deurne (B)
1933	De Waele house, Ghent (B)
1934	Van Hoogenbemt and Contrijn houses, Mechelen (B)
1936	Defauw shop, Ghent (B)
1937–38	Vermaercke house, Ghent (Gentbrugge) (B)

1945–52	Post & Telephone company building, Ostend (B)
1947	SEO (Spaarzaamheid, Economie, Oostende) building, Ostend (B)
1952–53	De Wispelaere house, Ostend (B)

GASTON EYSSELINCK, a radical character with socialist convictions, belongs to the second generation of modernist Belgian architects, who launched their careers around 1930. He was born in 1907 in Tienen and studied at the Koninklijke Academie (Royal Academy) of Ghent, graduating in 1928. In 1927 and 1929 he made study trips to the Netherlands, where he came into contact with the work of Amsterdam School architects and avant-garde designers, including W. M. Dudok, J. J. P. Oud and Gerrit Rietveld. Through his reading he also became acquainted with the work of the European avant-garde, especially with that of Le Corbusier. He quickly assimilated this influence and applied it in an amazing way to his own home, one of the most fascinating houses built in Belgium during the 1930s. In 1935 Alberto Sartoris incorporated Eysselinck's house in his book *Gli Elementi dell'Architettura Funzionale*, together with the Peeters house in Deurne, which dates back to 1932.

From 1933 Eysselinck lectured at Ghent Royal Academy and a year later joined the editorial staff of the leading Belgian magazine *La Cité*. He realised a number of small urban terraced houses with innovative ground plans, making a significant contribution to the development of this type of housing. Around 1935 he dissociated himself from plastered whitewashed architecture and showed a preference for natural stone and bricks, a development towards a direct experience of materials reminiscent of Le Corbusier. In 1937 Eysselinck won the Van de Ven prize, Belgium's most prestigious architecture award, for his Verplancken terraced house. The De Wispelaere house in Ostend (1952–53) was the last in his series of terraced houses. Eysselinck also played an active role as an urbanist. In 1939 he worked on an urban development study for Ghent, which served as a contribution to the (disbanded) CIAM meeting in Liège in 1939. He did not realise any large projects prior to 1940.

Eysselinck's masterpiece was indisputably the Post and Telephone building in Ostend (1945–52), his first major commission. It is a work of crucial importance in post-1945 Belgian architecture, and a building still underrated in the history of European architecture. In his design Eysselinck hearkened to the pleas of Sigfried Giedion's and other CIAM members for a return to a new monumentality and a direct cooperation with artists. His choice of bronze window profiles and blue stone façade cladding was determined by his search for durability after the numerous problems he had been facing with houses with whitewashed plastering. The building was of crucial importance for the stylistic development of a number of architects, including Willy Van Der Meeren.

As a result of substantial protest against the realisation of the Post and Telephone building and of the sudden death of his girlfriend, Eysselinck committed suicide in 1953. In his slim oeuvre the individual dwelling house remains pivotal.

When he had only just turned 23, Eysselinck decided to build his own studio-house. He was able to buy an inexpensive plot on the corner of Vaderlandstraat and Fleurusstraat in Ghent, a site with a disadvantageous orientation towards the north, no garden, and two high side walls. He succeeded in neutralising all these negative factors by taking advantage of the young heritage of new architecture, obtaining an unexpected spaciousness through a number of interventions.

The first application for planning permission, made in February 1930, envisaged two houses – one for Eysselinck himself and one for his brother. The project was rejected, as was a second proposal lodged in November 1930 with only one house. The design that was finally approved dates back to April 1931. The cost of the house grew considerably as a result of building height requirements. An obligation to continue the plane of the dwelling's façade on the right as well as Eysselinck's own desire to obtain a right angle in the interior led to the house's closed tower volume.

STREET VIEW

VIEW FROM VADERLANDSTRAAT

In a commentary on his private house, Eysselinck referred to it in terms of the Corbusian notion of a home being a "machine à habiter". He was also able to apply undogmatically Le Corbusier's five points for new architecture. Eysselinck created the illusion that the building volume was floating by putting a pilotis at the corner and by painting the plinth in a dark colour. At ground level there is the garage, the architect's small office and an open staircase. The staircase up to first-floor level is within the building's volume while not being part of the interior. Eysselinck enabled sufficient daylight to penetrate the interior by means of a void. Thanks to this solution, the living room on the first floor was enhanced by a window on three sides – a remarkable solution for a corner house. In this living room there is one wall for one painting. The other paintings have been put away in a 'painting cabinet'. The concept that every function should be given a place of its own is accentuated by the introduction of a concrete dining table. Next to the kitchen there is a small maid's room. On the second floor there are two 'sleeping cabins' for the children and a large bedroom, separated into two zones. Alongside the bedroom there is a spacious terrace with a large plant trough. A small spiral staircase, integrated into the tower volume, provided access to a solarium, where one could sunbathe naked. The compulsory building height resulted in a separation between the terrace and the solarium.

PLAN OF THE GROUND FLOOR

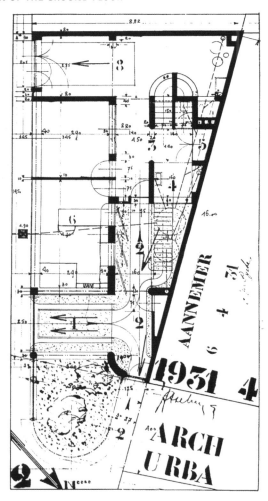

NEW CLADDING, 1948, DRAWING ON A PHOTO OF 1931

As Eysselinck's financial means were limited, he designed his own tubular metal furniture, a collection he hoped later to put into production under the name of FRATSTA. These designs can certainly be considered among Belgium's most significant contribution to the international movement for metal furniture. Eysselinck's chaise longue with its asymmetrical armrest, his stackable chair, and the elegant serving table are particularly fascinating creations. The unity between architecture and its own furniture makes the house in Ghent a unique example of Modernism in Belgium, even in Europe. All its metal furniture now belongs the collection of the Museum voor Sierkunst en Vormgeving (Museum of Decoration and Design) in Ghent. All the fitted cupboards formed an integral part of the architecture.

The presentation drawings also show that Eysselinck's house represents an important revolution. He turned the first design into a perspective with vanishing points: the definitive project into an axonometric perspective like other avant-garde architects. Thus he underscored the roof as an 'outside room'. Just like Le Corbusier and others, he used stencil letter type in his drawings.

The house's plastering soon revealed serious technical problems. In 1948 Eysselinck had the façade covered with thin bluestone tiles. A photograph taken in 1931 illustrates the situation and shows the architect marking off the tile size on the wall. He used this experience to further develop the façade decoration in his masterpiece, the Post and Telephone building in Ostend (1945–52). His own house thus served as a laboratory in his quest for durability and the design of thin façades made

PERSPECTIVE OF THE FIRST PROJECT, 1930

of natural stone. After Eysselinck's death some alterations were carried out, such as the transformation of the plinth and the closing of the void.

Whereas most individual houses in the international style are autonomous building volumes, Eysselinck's corner house is part of a classical urban building block. The photographs published by the architect do not show evidence of this – in order to reveal the new architecture, he eliminated all adjacent buildings. The unique thing about Eysselinck's Ghent house is that its exterior can be shown in just one photograph – it is a house with no rear elevation.

MARC DUBOIS

FAÇADE ON FLEURUSSTRAAT

LONGITUDINAL SECTION

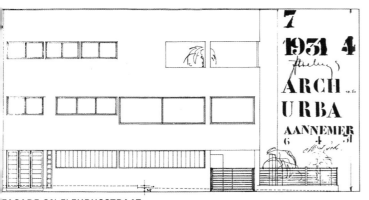

BIBLIOGRAPHY:

1986   Dubois M., *Architect Gaston Eysselinck: De fatale ontgoocheling – Zijn werk te Oostende 1945–1953*, Ostend
1987   Dubois M., *Buismeubelen in België tijdens het Interbellum*, catalogue, Museum voor Sierkunst en Vormgeving, Ghent
1993   Dubois M., 'A White Box in a Classical City Block / Gaston Eysselinck House in Ghent (1930–1931)', in *Archis*, no. 8, pp. 47–52
1996   Vandenbreeden J. and Vanlaethem F., *Art Deco en Modernisme in België – Architectuur in het Interbellum*, Tielt

Sverre Fehn
1924–2009

1986, RENOVATION AND FURNISHING OF THE DAMMAN VILLA, ORIGINALLY DESIGNED BY ARNE KORSMO
HAVNA ALLÉ 15, OSLO (N)

MAIN WORKS AND PROJECTS

1956–58	Competition project for the Norwegian pavilion, Brussels World Fair (B), wins First Prize
1958–62	Competition project for the Scandinavian pavilion in the Biennale Gardens, Venice (I), wins First Prize
1959–63	Schreiner house, Oslo (N)
1961–65	A. Bødtker house, Oslo (N)
1963–64	Villa, Norrköping (S)
1967–79	Archbishopric Museum, Hamar (N)

1971–77	School for deaf children, Skådalen, Oslo (N)
1987–90	Busk villa, Bamble (N)
1989–91	Glacier Museum, Fjærland (N)
1993–96	Aukrust Museum, Alvdal (N)

SVERRE FEHN was born in Kongsberg, Norway, on 14 August 1924, thus sharing his birthday with his future master Arne Korsmo, who was born 24 years before him. This circumstance, together with the fact that Fehn chose to live in a house built by Korsmo many years earlier (the Damman villa) rather than design one for himself, underlines a continuity of ideas between two architects who – within the conservative tradition of Norwegian architecture – were responsible for the birth and consolidation of a movement more open to international developments, so-called 'Poetic Modernism'. This trend was begun by the older of the two men, an architect who remained true to Modernism until his dying day, but found its main exponent in Fehn, the pupil and subsequently friend of the master, Korsmo. In the post-war years Fehn led Norwegian architecture to such heights that it could rival the greatest international schools, thanks to the stubborn determination with which he remained bound to the teachings of Modernism, as shown by his Scandinavian pavilion at the 1962 Venice Biennale and by his restoration of the Archbishopric Museum in Hamar (1967–79).

Christian Norberg-Schulz has written of Sverre Fehn and his architecture (1993, pp. 20–22): "Since the start of his career, Fehn has been concerned to seek out the origins of architecture, i.e. he has wanted to revive its basic forms. This does not imply, however, a nostalgic attitude, such as that of Historicism and Postmodernism, but rather a return to the true modern approach.

"In 1952, during his visit to Morocco, Fehn reported: 'I discover, and I *am* what I discover. Today, when you visit French Morocco to study primitive architecture, you do not go to discover new things.' What Fehn discovered in Morocco were not abstract forms, but built *realities*. Architecture is essentially the 'art of building' and implies *construction*. But the

construction may be more or less evident in the finished work. In some building traditions it is only present as a general substance which 'carries' the expressive forms. In other traditions the structure 'speaks' more directly. Norwegian architecture belongs to this latter kind.

"Norwegian structures are distinguished by 'sculptural' figuration. In several works Fehn has revived this complex quality, thereby realising an architecture that is simultaneously new and old as well as 'Norwegian'. He himself says that 'you can only enter into a dialogue with the past when you build the present', a dictum that implies that what is truly *present* consists in a new interpretation of the timeless.

"Three main phases can be distinguished in the architect's development. His first projects and executed buildings from the 1950s and 60s appear as orthogonal organised entities, distinguished by a certain uniformity. The second phase, comprising works from the late 1960s and 70s, shows a much more varied approach, without, however, giving up the stringency which distinguishes all Fehn's work. In the third phase, comprising works from the 1980s and early 90s, the architect arrives at a synthesis of what had been done before, i.e. space and built form now unify in buildings that possess true figural identity. At the same time the details become more articulated.

"With the works of Sverre Fehn, modern Norwegian architecture has gained true artistic status. Whereas Asplund brought Swedish modernism to an early perfection, and Aalto gave its Finnish equivalent a regional foothold, the Norwegians have been less able to relate their past to the aims of our time. This is probably due to the inherent 'complexity' of the Norwegian tradition. As a result, Norwegian modernism has more easily been subjected to the current fashion, such as Structuralism and Postmodernism. Fehn, however, has remained faithful to the

NORTH FAÇADE

THE NORTH AND EAST FAÇADES

THE STUDIO

THE LIVING ROOM

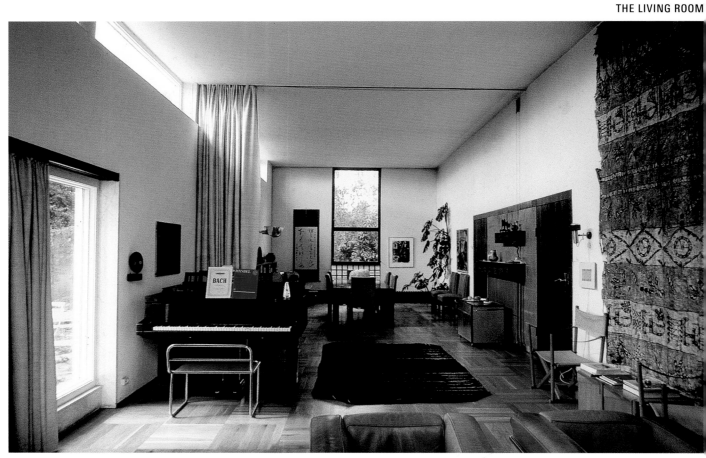

true modern approach and – together with Utzon in Denmark and Pietilä in Finland – has shown that Giedion's idea of a 'new regionalism' represents the way ahead, a way that shuns superficial nostalgia in favour of a true understanding of the here and now."

Sverre Fehn's own home, the so-called Damman villa, was situated in Havna Allé, Oslo. Fehn did not design and build the house himself. The luxury residence was created by Arne Korsmo in 1930 for a rich businessman with the name of Damman. Half a century later, in 1986, Fehn acquired the property and moved into it with his family. When he bought the house, it had lain abandoned for years and was even threatened with demolition. Fehn's contribution to the Damman villa was to restore it to its original splendour. This was no hardship for the architect both because it had been designed by his 'hero', Arne Korsmo, and because he much admired the building. These were the reasons, too, why Fehn purchased the villa and moved into it. "I have always thought that Arne Korsmo's Damman villa was a very beautiful house", he wrote. "It is a place I have often come to visit in the past, long before it became possible for my wife Ingrid and I to acquire the property." The house was also congenial to and a reflection of Fehn's professional and moral ethics, and moreover perfectly suited the Fehn family's lifestyle.

In 1932 Korsmo wrote of his Damman villa: "…The focal point of the composition of the house is the dining room, which – together with the living room – had to provide sufficient space for the owner's collection of paintings. …The small semicircular study and the terrace, both south-

GROUND PLAN

ISOMETRIC VIEW OF THE VILLA

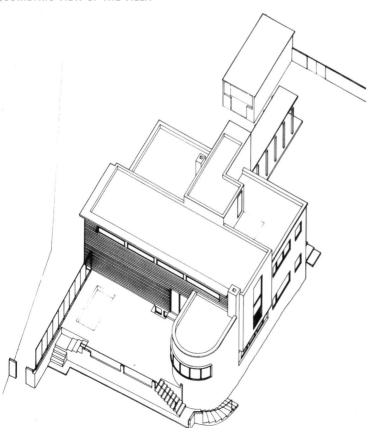

facing, overlook the fjord. Moreover, as can be seen in the ground plan, the design tends to create a unity between the garage, the entrance pergola and the entrance to the kitchen with its attached garden…" And Fehn recalled: "…Together with the Committee for the Preservation of Antiquities, we discovered the importance of restoring the original colours of buildings. I thus discovered that the battle between the Damman house and the light was linked to the architect's [Korsmo's] interpretation of the relation between the intensity of the building's materials and the colours. …The most important dialogue, however, is that between the snow and the colour of the winter sky. The black clinker cladding of the south wall also belongs to the winter light. …Restoring the house, I began to feel that through its original colours it was also recovering its dimension."

GENNARO POSTIGLIONE

BIBLIOGRAPHY:
1986   Norberg-Schulz C., *The Functionalist Arne Korsmo*, Oslo
1988   Fjeld P. O., *The Thought of Construction*, New York
1993   *Sverre Fehn: Architetto del paese delle ombre lunghe*, Naples
1996   'Villa Damman' in *Norwegian Functionalism*, Oslo 1927–1940, ed. G. Postiglione, Rome, pp. 155–159
1997   Norberg-Schulz C. and Postiglione G., *Sverre Fehn. Opera completa*, Milan

Luigi Figini
1903–1984

1933–35, NEW CONSTRUCTION
VILLAGGIO DEI GIORNALISTI, VIA PERRONE DI SAN MARTINO, MILAN (I)

MAIN WORKS AND PROJECTS

1930	Casa Elettrica (Electric House) at the 4th International Fair of Decorative Arts, Monza (I), with Gino Pollini
1932	Building with villas, via Annunciata, Milan (I)
1934–42	Olivetti workshop, Ivrea (I)
1938	Competition project for the Armed Forces buildings at E42, Rome (I)

1939–42	Nursery school and council housing at Borgo Olivetti, Ivrea (I)
1952	Church of Madonna dei Poveri, Milan (I)
1955	Office building, via Hoepli, Milan (I)
1960–63	Pozzi ceramics factory, Sparanise (I)
1967–69	Flat in an apartment block in via Morigi, Milan (I)

LUIGI FIGINI was born on 27 January 1903 in Milan the son of Alessandro Figini, an accountant, and Pia Jardini. He grew up with his younger brother, Paolo, playing on a big terrace on the top floor of a Liberty building in Milan, which his father had turned into a garden with fruit trees and sports facilities. His classical studies as a schoolboy at the Liceo Parini were a great influence on his future work and life. Figini's interest in painting also stemmed from that formative period, when he started to paint during the school summer holidays. However, painting would always be limited to his private life. In 1921 he enrolled in the School of Architecture at the Polytechnic of Milan, from which he graduated in 1926. In the same year Figini was able to study ancient monuments during a study trip to Naples and Pompeii. In such a stimulating cultural milieu, he founded Gruppo 7 together with six other students: Ubaldo Castagnoli, Guido Frette, Sebastiano Larco, Gino Pollini, Carlo Enrico Rava and Giuseppe Terragni. Gruppo 7 would be involved in many contemporary projects, for example the Casa Elettrica.

In 1929, in partnership with Gino Pollini, Figini opened an architectural office in Milan, in which the two would work together for over 50 years. In the early 1930s he met Gege Bottinelli, with whom he shared an interest in photography, and whom he married in 1935. Through the work of artists and writers from Giorgio De Chirico and Henri Rousseau to Charles Baudelaire, Alexander Archipenko, Jean Cocteau and Man Ray, Figini developed his own ideas about the mutual relationship between man and nature, as well as between inside and outside. His love of mountain hikes influenced his ideas about the natural environment. A later trip in the Mediterranean islands led to reflections on spontaneous architecture. Figini began a long correspondence with the writer Carlo Belli, in which they discussed the cultural fields that interested them (music, literature, cinema, and painting). 1934 saw the beginning of Figini's long professional relationship with the enlightened industrialist

Adriano Olivetti, who was to commission several works from Figini and Pollini.

In a notebook started in the summer of 1933, Figini defined the idea of his house-cum-studio, designed and constructed 1933–35 at the Villaggio dei Giornalisti, in via Perrone di san Martino, Milan, as a 'casa che cresce' or 'growing house' and as a 'casa thermos' or 'thermos house'. The first term indicates a house that will be flexible and grow as the composition of his family changes, while the second refers to a natural system designed by the architect to optimise ventilation and heating. Figini tried to give his own house a very personal character and make it place in which life is organised in harmony with nature and the outside world in general. The garden around the house and especially the terraces on top confirm this idea.

The bedroom is designed in close relationship with a terrace below it, which, although it is not a huge space, is well equipped with a pool, a small garden, and sports facilities. The bedroom thus overlooks the terrace, which actually leads into the dining room. Here the wall is cut in an open window to frame the mountains on the horizon and to underline the importance for the architect of open-air life. Inside, an aquarium is designed to provide a kind of living still-life. As a painter and photographer, Figini was interested in the contemporary experience of Surrealism, and realised the so-called 'quadro vivente' or 'living painting'. Photographs are treated like paintings, in which the living subject – often his wife Gege – is as much a part of the composition as the inanimate objects and the classical references of the whole.

The composition of Figini's private house is based on the golden section, a rectangle of 18 x 5.5 m (= 99 m^2) and is oriented, following the heliothermic rules of rationalism, on the north-north-east and south-south-west axis so as to exploit as far as possible the weather, in order

VIEW FROM THE TERRACE

FAÇADE

DINING TABLE IN THE LIVING ROOM

to obtain comfortable conditions inside. The logic of the 'thermos house' is that fresh air is brought from outside, on the north side, in the morning, after which the windows are closed hermetically to keep the inside temperature lower than outside. Figini designed other – only partially implemented – technical solutions in a similar vein, such as the 'isothermic terrace' with natural ventilation, or the positioning of inside rooms at different levels to encourage the flow of the air mass.

The volume of the house is suspended ship-style on six pairs of pillars and a narrow staircase, linking the garden to the entrance. On the first floor (3 m high) is a kitchen, an office, the maid's room, a wardrobe, the living room and the terrace, while on the second floor are the owner's bedroom and bathroom, both of which open onto the two terraces of the flat roof. The white compact Corbusian block is designed inside with a more complex composition of levels, voids and views. The structure is a grid of reinforced concrete, filled with light insulated walls made of pumice stone. Inside, artificial lighting is designed to control the effects of light and its direct and indirect impact on the space and also on the natural element present inside – the water in the bathtub is lit up like a blue grotto. Moveable spotlights are used in order to create a great variety of effects.

In 1933 Figini described his own house in the architecture magazine Quadrante as a "memo of the minimum of material and spiritual needs" of contemporary man that must (or rather should) be satisfied in any standard apartment in a 10/15-floor building. His aim was to realise a sort of 'anti-city' in the city, to guarantee the quality of life afforded by his

THE MAIN BEDROOM

own house to people living in apartment blocks. Seen in these terms, Figini's villa at the Villaggio dei Giornalist is a manifesto or memo reminding us of the amount of sun, greenery and sky that is necessary for a good quality of life. It is clearly influenced by Le Corbusier's five points (flat roof, pilotis, long windows, etc.) and by his Villa Savoye in Poissy (1929–31), the first example of a building on free pilotis. Figini's private house is designed in the way that the upper floors of typical bourgeois apartment blocks in Milan were conceived at the time, as a so-called 'villa sul tetto' or 'villa on the roof'. All the technical answers that Figini studied and applied reveal his technological competence and control in the design of the house, as well as his ability to transform solutions into aesthetic factors.

FRANCESCA ACERBONI

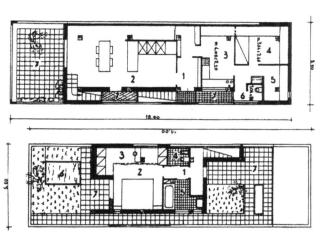

FLOOR PLANS

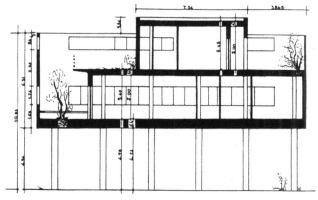

CROSS SECTION

BIBLIOGRAPHY:
1935   Figini L., 'Una casa di Luigi Figini', in Quadrante, nos. 31/32, November, pp. 20–24
1937   'Villa de l'architecte Luigi Figini', in L'Architecture d'Aujourd'hui, no. 1, January, pp. 42–47
1978   '1935. L'abitazione di un architetto', in Abitare, no. 167, September, pp. 32–39
1996   Gregotti V. (ed.), Figini Pollini. Opera Completa, Milan
2001   Cornoldi A., Le case degli architetti. Dizionario privato dal Rinascimento ad oggi, Venice, pp. 141–143

Hans Fischli
1909 – 1989

1933, NEW CONSTRUCTION, NOW ALTERED
SCHUMBELSTRASSE, MEILEN (CH)

MAIN WORKS AND PROJECTS

1934	Blattmann metal factory, Wädenswil (CH)
1939	Children's paradise and amusement pavilion at the Swiss National Exhibition in Zurich (CH)
1940 – 73	Adolf Feller AG factory, Horgen (CH)
1943	Gwad housing development, Wädenswil (CH)
1945 – 49	Pestalozzi village, Trogen (CH)
1947	ZÜKA Agriculture and Trade Exhibition, Zurich (CH)
1956 – 57	Offices and shop for the Möbelgenossenschaft Basel, Basle (CH)
1960 – 62	Gulmenmatt development, Wädenswil (CH)
1961 – 62	Guggenbühl villa, Herrliberg (CH)
1968 – 78	Fellergut development, Bern-Bümpliz (CH)

HANS FISCHLI was born and grew up in Zurich, the son of a surveyor. Between 1925 and 1928 he served an apprenticeship as a draughtsman in a small architect's office run by Robert Ruggli, a pupil of Bonatz. This practical craftsmanship-oriented traineeship, during which Fischli was also entrusted with building supervision and the design of details, stood him in good stead later on and was reflected in the meticulous work that is evident in his own architecture. His first experience of Neues Bauen during a visit to the Weissenhof housing development in Stuttgart made such a deep impression on the young Fischli that in 1928 he decided – against his parents' will – to enrol as a student of architecture in the Bauhaus at Dessau. After the preparatory course and one semester at the workshop for wall painting, however, he terminated his studies for financial reasons after barely one year.

Back in Zurich, Fischli worked as a draughtsman and assistant building supervisor with Hubacher + Steiger on some of the most important buildings of modern Swiss architecture, for example the Neubühl housing development, the Bella-Lui Sanatorium, and the Z House. During this practical work, he acquired a knowledge of the formal language of Neues Bauen. His first solo commission, the Ländli bathing facilities, constructed entirely of wood, is distinguished by its clear simple forms, transparency, economic building techniques, straight strips of windows, and flat roof. The project for the Schlehstud house, which was commissioned in 1933 by Fischli's parents, enabled the architect to open his own office in Zurich. During the 1930s and 40s he realised numerous single-family houses, two larger terraced housing developments and a kindergarten, most of these buildings in the form of simple low-cost timber constructions. Stylistically, Fischli's designs range from Neues Bauen (Schlehstud house) to the regionalist farmhouse-type formal language of the Pestalozzi children's village constructed between 1945 and 1949.

In 1934 Fischli designed a complex for the Blattmann metal factory, which represented a transparent architectural interpretation of the factory's activities, and between 1940 and 1973 he designed and realised a whole series of factory extensions for the firm of Feller AG. In 1937 he became assistant to Hans Hofmann, the chief architect of the 1939 National Exhibition in Zurich. Responsible for the development plans, construction, interior decoration and timberwork, Fischli made a significant contribution to what came to be called the 'Landi style'.

During the 1950s and 60s, Fischli was primarily concerned with theoretical and practical work on housing developments and residential buildings, receiving commissions for numerous multiple family houses and large-scale housing estates. As he carried out this work, he developed standardised floor plans. From 1954 – 61 he was the director of both the Kunstgewerbeschule (School of Applied Arts) and the Kunstgewerbemuseum (Crafts Museum) in Zurich. He closed his office in Zurich in 1976.

Fischli's brief period of study at the Bauhaus, during which he attended classes by personalities such as Klee, Kandinsky and Schlemmer, inspired him not only as an architect, but also as an artist. Fischli became renowned not only as a successful and original architect, but also as an organic-abstract painter and sculptor. Even before he realised his first self-designed building, he had presented drawings at a solo exhibition in 1931. Over the years he was a member of, among other things, the Swiss Werkbund and the artists' group Allianz. In 1968 the Zurich Kunsthaus dedicated a large-scale retrospective exhibition to Fischli's lyrical geometrical work, and in 1974 the draughtsman, painter and sculptor was awarded the Art Prize of the City of Zurich.

The three-family house 'In der Schlehstud' or Schlehstud house, which Hans Fischli built in 1933 for his parents, is regarded as the architect's

THE ROOF TERRACE

THE SOUTH FAÇADE

THE WEST FAÇADE

THE NORTH AND EAST FAÇADES

masterpiece. A new construction, it is situated in open countryside, far from Meilen, the nearest town. The building's location on a hillside high above Lake Zurich affords a splendid panorama of the Swiss Alps. Fischli lived in the house with his family in an apartment-cum-studio on the top floor. This apartment is an almost exemplary implementation of Giedion's postulate of 'befreites Wohnen' or 'liberated living', according to which a house should be light, light-permeable and flexible, and liberated from rigidity and thick walls.

The Schlehstud house reflects this guiding principle. It is not an imposing prestigious building, but is – as Fischli wanted – characterised by a closeness to nature and by its fulfilment of the requirements of its inhabitants. For Fischli, achieving this proximity to nature and meeting these requirements meant reducing the bedrooms to 'sleeping cabins', and diminishing the kitchen to a 'kitchen recess'. The corridor and bathroom areas are likewise minimised. By contrast, the multi-functional studio-living room covers two thirds of the ground plan and on three sides opens onto the terrace, balcony and countryside, which are an integral part of the house. The arrangement reflected Fischli's belief that dwelling was not a retreat, but an active cultural pursuit. In his view, work, leisure and relaxation interpenetrated one another and were orientated towards light, air, movement and openness.

The house's long narrow ground plan made it possible to orient all the living and sleeping areas towards the south so as to achieve this light airy openness. Whereas the south side of the building is characterised by large windows, the north side has only high strip windows to provide light. The timber building volume of the upper floors rests lightly and dynamically on a half-open brick base. Strip windows and projecting roofs and terraces create horizontal accents. The outdoor flight of steps on the northern side and the virtuoso play with closed façade surfaces and strongly differentiated window openings give the building a sculptural look. Each aspect reveals a completely different character.

Constructionwise, Fischli decided on a wide steel skeleton structure bearing the timber supports and beams of the walls and ceilings. On the outside, the building is clad with untreated larch panels, while on the inside undisguised wood fibreboards are used for the ceilings, and maple panels for the walls. The prefabrication of most of the timber elements resulted not only in savings in cost, but also in an extremely short construction period. After a two-month planning stage, the whole Schlehstud house was completed in just five months.

On the subject of timber as a building material, Fischli made it clear that what motivated him and other architects to use this medium was not sentiment, but the constructive and economic advantages that wood

THE STUDIO

offered. The fact that the Schlehstud villa in particular and some of Fischli's later single houses and housing developments in general were constantly discussed in detail in publications on Swiss timber construction, made Hans Fischli into something of a timber specialist. His buildings are distinguished by careful attention to detail and highly skilled craftsmanship. He believed that: "Timber as a building material is exacting. It demands from those who use it a knowledge of and feeling for its qualities. Without enthusiasm and love for timber, it is impossible to get to know the material."

The 'liberated living' design of the Schlehstud house and its use of timber make the building, more widely, a product of its time. For the period during which it was constructed was a time that emphasised exercise outdoors, weekend hiking in the mountains, holidays in wooden chalets, healthy living and hygiene, an ethos pursued by wide sections of the public. This is reflected in the subtitling of a Werkbund exhibition on modern country and holiday houses held in Basle in 1935: 'Simple Building for Weekends, Holidays and Everyday Living'. It is no coincidence that the most frequent commissions for young Swiss architects around 1930 were — besides bathing facilities, sanatoriums, open-air swimming baths and hospitals — holiday homes, weekend houses and simple low-cost bathing houses. Many of these commissions, executed — like the

Schlehstud house — as examples of Neues Bauen, were built using the simple, expedient and appropriate material of timber. They marked a renaissance of timber, long rejected by modern architects, as a building material.

DANIEL WEISS

PLAN OF THE UPPER FLOOR

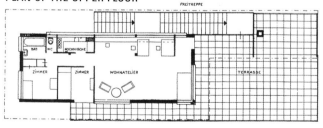

BIBLIOGRAPHY:
1936 Schmidt C.A., *Schweizer Holzbau*, Zurich / Leipzig, pp. 68–72
1968 *Hans Fischli. Malerei, Plastik, Architektur*, exhibition catalogue, Kunsthaus Zürich, Zurich
1971 *Hans Fischli. Skulpturen, Öl- und Acrylbilder, Graphik*, exhibition catalogue, Kunsthaus Zürich, Zurich
1986 *Haus Fischli. Bilder, Zeichnungen und Skulpturen*, exhibition catalogue, Kunsthaus Zug, Zug
1998 Rucki I. and Huber D. (eds.), *Architektenlexikon der Schweiz 19./20. Jahrhundert*, Basle / Boston / Berlin, pp. 177–179

Aurelio Galfetti
*1936

1986, NEW CONSTRUCTION, STILL INHABITED BY THE ARCHITECT
VIA D'ALBERTI, BELLINZONA (CH)

MAIN WORKS AND PROJECTS

1960–61	Rotalinti house, Bellinzona (CH)
1968–69	Nursery school, Riva San Vitale (CH), with I. Trümpy and F. Ruchat-Roncati
1976–77	Galli house, Caslano (CH)
1977–85	General Post Office, Bellinzona (CH)
1982–83	Projects for the Della Valle Theatre, Bellinzona (CH) and a multi-purpose centre, Lausanne (CH)

1985–86	Tennis Club and Sports Ground, Bellinzona (CH), with G. Cattaneo
1985–91	Castle of Uri, restauration, Bellinzona (CH)
1988	Indoor swimming pool and skating rink, Bellinzona (CH)
1989–92	Public Library, Chambéry (F)
1998	Civic Centre, Gorduno (CH)

AURELIO GALFETTI was born in Biasca on 2 April 1936, the son of Alda and Ugo Galfetti. He attended the cantonal 'grammar school' in Lugano, passing his school-leaving examinations in 1954. Even as a schoolboy he was keen to be an architect, and had his first architectural work experience with Tita Carloni. He enrolled in the School of Architecture of the Federal Polytechnic in Zurich (now the renowned Swiss Federal Institute of Technology or ETH), from which he graduated as a qualified architect in 1960. At the institute, where he was supervised and encouraged by Paul Waltenspühl, Galfetti 'discovered' Le Corbusier, who was to become his primary influence, marking him even more than Frank Lloyd Wright (his earliest love), Louis Kahn, Otto Wagner and Ludwig Mies van der Rohe. In 1960–61 Galfetti designed "what can be considered the true architectural incipit of the new developments in Ticino, the Rotalinti house". His formation was completed through numerous pilgrimages, first on the trail of Le Corbusier, then in quest of other 20th-century masters, and even of newcomers when they inspired debate.

Armed with a degree in architecture, Galfetti opened his own practice in Lugano in 1960. At first he collaborated with Flora Ruchat-Roncati and Ivo Trümpy. Then, in 1970, he began a fruitful four-year partnership with Livio Vacchini, who designed – together with Alberto Tibiletti – the Macconi building in Lugano, an architectural jewel. This was followed by a collaboration which brought together Rino Tami (a pioneer in Ticino of the rationalist use of reinforced concrete), Luigi Snozzi (who from the outset had been engaged on a dual front, practical and theoretical), and the tireless young Mario Botta (who had already achieved international fame and was destined to play a leading role in Switzerland). It was this team, augmented by Livio Vacchini, Dolf Schnebli, Flora Ruchat-Roncati, Ivo Trümpy, Ivano Gianola, Mario Campi, Franco Pessina, Elio Ostinelli, Fabio Muttoni and others, which gave rise to the legendary 'Ticino

School'. The 'school', which flourished in the second half of the 20th century in the Swiss canton of Ticino, and of which Galfetti is a leading protagonist, was responsible for numerous innovative architectural developments in the canton, and was confirmed in a now legendary exhibition *Tendenzen*, mounted in 1975 in Zurich, which stimulated an international debate on the Ticinese developments. It was a movement which, in Kenneth Frampton's words (1999), demonstrated "great sensibility towards the poetics of structure, right from the neo-Wrightian motorway bridges designed by Rino Tami in the early 1960s".

In 1976 Galfetti moved from Lugano to Bellinzona. Here, developing a theme that was particularly dear to him and on which he had been working for some time, he experimented with and perfected a new and original conception of town planning and architecture, a territorialistic one. His perception of territory derived on the one hand from a sensitivity to orographic aspects and to the development of the infrastructures and the very life of the city, and on the other hand from his attention to history. The result was a complex morphological conception, in which architecture, city and territory came to form a unique whole, an innovative holistic vision that was destined to stir up heated debate (Aldo Rossi would call it the 'analogous city'). Galfetti's conception was put into practice in a series of interventions that became 'nerve centres' of expanding Bellinzona, beginning with the public baths in 1967.

In 1984 Galfetti was a guest lecturer at the Federal Polytechnic School of Lausanne, and in 1987 at the Ecole d'Architecture of Paris (Belleville UP8). With Athanase Spitsas and Thierry Estoppey he opened a new office in Geneva in 1991. In 1996, together with Mario Botta and with the support of Giuseppe Buffi and others, he founded the Mendrisio Academy of Architecture at the University of Italian Switzerland, becoming the Academy's first director.

SIDE FAÇADE

STREET VIEW

BACK FAÇADE

THE LIVING AREA

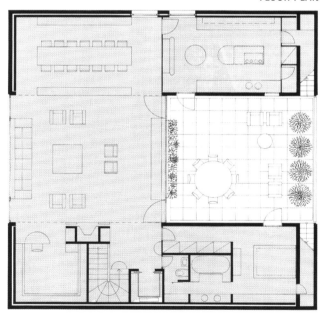

Galfetti's own private residence in the via D'Alberti, Bellinzona, Switzerland, designed and built in 1986, is actually part of two twin blocks. These are the Casa Bianca (White House) and the Casa Nera (Black House), so named because of the colours used on their exteriors to distinguish between them. Galfetti's home is an apartment that occupies the top three floors of the Black House. "The attic of the Casa Nera is my home. The apartment has a summer living room and also a winter living room, like the villas of long ago. There is a covered courtyard on the third floor, which must be crossed to get from the bedroom to the kitchen. The space is for passage and is highly transparent. The curtains that close off the terrace rustle in the wind rather like the sails of a boat that is coming, as it were, down to the valley, from the mountains to the lake". (The house is oriented along the longitudinal axis of the valley.)

Initially the two blocks were to be similar internally, both built around an open void and divided vertically between a studio (below) and an apartment (above). In the end they turned out to be very different, for the Casa Nera had a series of small flats for rent on the lower floors. The black block, therefore, came to have a more rarefied upper level and a denser lower level, making the overall project both complex and problematic. Galfetti discussed every choice with his wife Lola, and what emerged was a "living structure that first of all I had to like, and which then had to be pleasant to live in". It was a house to live in, designed around autobiographical and affective elements, and based on extreme symmetry, sobriety and comfort. The subsequent elaboration became a sort of introspective reflection that led Galfetti to question his own language, even the very idea of designing projects. The project for his own home thus became the pretext for a highly lucid, albeit tormented self-criticism, a maturing and a fruitful reflection on his own creative path.

THE KITCHEN

The visual impact from the top of the block, as we gaze from the terrace overlooking the side of the valley where Castelgrande lies, is described by Galfetti in the following Leonardesque terms: "There is a close link between Castelgrande and the Casa Nera, the three levels and the three walls. In the foreground is my wall, in reinforced concrete – the present time. Then, following on without interruption, come the walls and the towers of Castelgrande – the time of history. Beyond them, finally, is the barrier of mountains, which corresponds to ancient geological time. History and the contemporary era, nature and the work of man meet and enter into dialogue in this tight tectonic arrangement. ... I always like to have two opposite poles: opening–closure, mountain–lake, forest–plain, which also counter and enter into dialogue with the two architectures, external and internal, like the ever enlivening conflict between history and the contemporary era."

The peculiarity of the project lies in the 'pulverisation' of materiality, always so clearly present in architecture. This is brought about also by the symmetry of distribution and the unusual geometry of the colours, in the contrast between exterior and interior: black concrete outside right up to the corners, white inside. There is a clear sense of abstraction, which reaches its height on the roof-terrace, which offers itself as a symbolic opening towards the sky. "The universe is no longer unknown, and you no longer have to escape from its sight or protect yourself. You must be free to see your sky." The challenge taken on by Galfetti may be precisely that of a liberating architecture, a challenge that his own home meets in an exemplary manner, just as it expresses a growing attention towards territory that makes Galfetti one of the pioneers of a new commitment, more complex than in the past – the territorialist architect, who investigates and dissects reality and verifies its vitality, the synonym of livability for man.

In his own house and, more generally, in the twin complementary blocks, Galfetti creates a unique entity compared with the other houses round about, oriented orthogonally relative to his. The project was thus born first and foremost in terms of town planning, or rather of territorialistic aspects, measuring itself constantly against the territory seen both as an artistic entity and, even more importantly, as a living being.

ROLANDO BELLINI

BIBLIOGRAPHY:

1986   Lucan J., 'Aurelio Galfetti a Bellinzona', in *AMC*, no. 12, June, pp. 32–[43]
1988   Galfetti A., 'Quattro palazzine in Canton Ticino', in *Casabella*, no. 550, October, pp. 4–13
1989   Botta M. (intr. Cardini M.), *Aurelio Galfetti*, Barcelona
1994   Gubler J. and Galfetti A., *Aurelio Galfetti. Projets 1987–1993*, monographic catalogue published on the occasion of the exhibition at the Uni-Dufur of Geneva, 16 June – 8 July 1994, Geneva
2001   Cornoldi A., *Le case degli architetti. Dizionario privato dal Rinascimento ad oggi*, Venice, pp. 154, 155

Edoardo Gellner
1909 – 2004

1951 – 53, ALTERATION
VIA MENARDI 6, CORTINA D'AMPEZZO, BELLUNO (I)

MAIN WORKS AND PROJECTS

1945 – 48 Torre Rossa villa (partially transformed 1948 – 53 into the Villa Alta dance hall), Misano Adriatico, near Riccione, Forlì (I)

1947 – 48 Renovation and furnishing of La Genzianella pastry bar, Cortina d'Ampezzo, Belluno (I)

1950 – 55 General urban development plan for Cortina d'Ampezzo, Belluno (I)

1951 – 53 Detailed urban development plan for Cortina d'Ampezzo town centre, Belluno (I)

1953 – 55 Palazzo della Telve, and post office and telecommunications building, Cortina d'Ampezzo, Belluno (I)

1954 – 63 Holiday village for the employees of the ENI companies (urban plan, 263 single-family units, children's accommodation, general amenities building, campsite, two hotels and a church), Borca di Cadore, Belluno (I)

1960 – 62 Old people's home, Matelica, Macerata (I)

1963 – 65 Talamini house and ice-cream shop, Deventer (NL)

1972 – 79 Town hall and tourism office, Auronzo di Cadore, Belluno (I)

1973 – 80 Ca' Novella apartment block, Marina di Aurisina, Gorizia (I)

EDOARDO GELLNER was born on 20 January 1909 in Abbazia, a small town on the Adriatic coast near Fiume (now the Croatian port of Rijeka). The beauty of the region was to be a major factor in the development of his marked sensibility for landscape. His father, who had moved to Abbazia from Vienna, had set up a building firm, in which the 15-year-old Edoardo was employed as an apprentice. While gaining experience of the world of building techniques and materials, the young Gellner also pursued his interest in art under the guidance of the painter and family friend Robert Schober.

In 1927, at the end of his three-year apprenticeship, Gellner enrolled in the Kunstgewerbeschule (School of Applied Arts) in Vienna, where he came into contact with the continuing art déco inclinations of the academic world, the outside influence of Secessionist experimentation, and the new functionalist tendencies, which through the works of Loos reached the architecture of the Werkbundsiedlung (housing development) in 1932. During his studies in Vienna, Gellner began to work again in his father's firm, now as a design engineer. But he also started to practise independently, mainly carrying out small projects such as decorating kiosks, cafés, shops and shop windows. It was only later, after a second period of study, this time in Venice, that Gellner's professional horizons were to widen considerably.

After his studies, Gellner went to Venice, where he enrolled in 1941 in the Institute of Architecture, graduating from it in 1946. Following his solid technical training at home, his experience gained in his own studio, his studies in Vienna, and the many architectural insights that he had meanwhile acquired during trips to Paris, Stuttgart, Nuremberg and

Switzerland, Gellner came to Venice already in possession of a considerable knowledge of architecture. Among his teachers at the Venetian institute, Gellner greatly admired Guido Cirilli, considered a master of stone building. But it was the school's new rector, Giuseppe Samonà, who was to be the greatest influence on him, especially as the supervisor of his final dissertation. The esteem was evidently mutual, for Samonà was to offer his protégé the opportunity to pursue an academic career, a chance that Gellner declined, preferring to set up a new professional practice of his own in Cortina d'Ampezzo in 1947. Despite this, he remained in touch with Venice and the intellectual ferment that characterised the city from the 1950s onwards.

With the APAO group (Association for Organic Architecture) Gellner took an active part in the debate on the future of Italian architecture, a debate that focussed on the lessons of Frank Lloyd Wright, whose memorable stay in Venice in 1951 was an important moment. He also took a deep interest in urban and territorial planning, both as a member of the Veneto section of the INU (National Institute of Town Planning) and as the author of the town plan for Cortina (1950 – 55). This interest in urban-scale issues was also evident in his study of housing models in multi-purpose buildings. The solutions he developed in the 1960s were in many ways similar to the experiments of architects such as Jacob Berend Bakema and Aldo van Eyck in Holland.

An Italian by adoption, Gellner divided his time and his affections between Cortina and Venice. He remained in close touch with friends from his student days, especially with Mario De Luigi and Carlo Scarpa, with whom he also collaborated professionally. He was particularly close

OVERVIEW OF THE PROPERTY

VIEW FROM THE TERRACE

DETAIL OF THE TERRACE

to Scarpa, with whom he shared a love of the materials and the details of building, as well as a common architectonic language. Together they would design the church of Corte di Cadore (Belluno). Many anecdotes survive testifying to the lively encounter of minds during the drafting and realisation of the project.

From the 1960s Gellner's contacts with Venice became more sporadic, being dictated mainly by reasons of work, until the thread that tied him to the city was finally broken in the 1970s. Cortina, on the other hand, claimed him ever more completely, becoming the place of both his family life and professional practice. It was here, for example, that he would meet up with Enrico Mattei, who came to see how work was progressing on the village of Corte di Cadore, a commission that the ENI chairman had entrusted to Gellner.

Assisted by Alessandro Apollonio, who collaborated with the architect since 1959, Gellner worked, among other projects, on the organisation of his archive, which was to be housed at the Institute of Architecture in Venice. In 2000 Gellner returned to his old institute to attend the inauguration of an exhibition of his work for the ENI village church, thus re-establishing a relationship that had been interrupted for far too long.

The apartment-cum-studio building which Gellner built for himself (1951–53) at via Menardi 6, Cortina d'Ampezzo, Belluno, and in which he continued to live, has a dual significance. First, it symbolised the architect's deep attachment both to Cortina and, more generally, to the landscape of the Dolomites, and, second, it testified to a whole life devoted exclusively to architecture. Gellner's love of Cortina, which went back over half a century to 1947, only deepened with time, although the region was not the sole focus of his work, as his professional biography shows. The architect's affinity with the place stemmed especially from its characteristic 'rural' and also 'anonymous' architecture, which intrigued him, and whose rules he sought to explore.

But the building, of course, amounts to more than a token of a geographical love affair and of a long career in architecture. Gellner's private apartment in the building was a peaceful space, shared for years with his wife, Licia, who in the role of office secretary acted as his trusty 'right arm'. His studio, which is directly linked with the living area, was the venue of the architect's legendary busy working schedules and strict organisation. Despite this, it was a warm welcoming place, in which some 60 assistants worked over a period of 50 years, and which meanwhile housed a vast quantity of material. It was not just the studio which was thus crammed. The garage, originally fitted out and used as a workshop for constructing models, became a repository for wooden maquettes, some of them large in size, and the private apartment, too, was literally overflowed with books and journals, and especially drawings and other papers. For although the practice had a modest PC in one corner, it remained essentially a place of pencil and paper, rather than computer files.

The Gellner building, which is situated near the centre of Cortina d'Ampezzo, is based around a three-part structure, while the elevation consists of staggered floors. With the exception of the attic, the entrance and the garage area, each floor has two apartments with three outward-facing sides. The heart of the complex is the stairs, whose position allows the inhabited spaces on the north front to be reduced, cleverly exploiting the most favourable climatic exposure. The same principle also underlies the composition of the fronts, whose windows are measured in number and size in relation to the heliothermic axis.

Gellner's house is spread over three levels. The private apartment lies on the top floor, while the studio is on the lowest level, linked to the apartment via the architect's own rooms. The way from the public space

THE FIREPLACE IN THE LIVING ROOM

THE LIVING ROOM

to the private space ends in the bedroom, situated in the attic, which opens onto a large terrace with the stone pine symbolising the building. Despite the fact that the three parts of the house are at different heights, the internal space remains fluid and uninterrupted due to the important role played by the furnishing, designed to suit the overall building project. A fireplace acts as a vertical link between the library, living room and bedrooms, while a long bookshelf provides an element of horizontal continuity.

A characteristic feature not only of the Gellner apartment but of the whole complex is the use of wood. Externally it is used on the galleries and simply as cladding, while inside it also defines the communal spaces, as can be seen, for example, in the mahogany parapet of the staircase, which was designed by the architect and produced by means of a special milling technique.

The Gellner building was built both at an important moment in the architect's career and, generally, during a highly creative phase of Italian culture. It was part of the series of seven projects realised by the architect in Cortina between 1951 and 1956 that led to Gellner being considered one of the few genuine interpreters in Italy of the lessons of Frank Lloyd Wright. During the 1950s the Italian architectural debate was almost entirely dominated by the battle — ideological as well as linguistic — for organic architecture, and also against the tendency towards a banal recovery of vernacular elements typical of the extremely varied Italian panorama. The opposition to 'rustic' architecture, i.e. to buildings which continued to imitate the exterior forms of a supposed 'Ampezzo style', was part of this climate. Gellner's projects responded to these tendencies with a new language, at times explosive, born of a careful reading of the compositional and structural rules of local architecture and based on a use of materials belonging to this tradition.

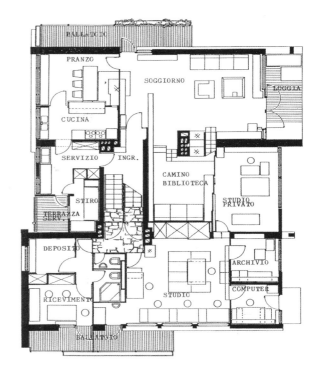

FLOOR PLAN

In these projects of the architect, therefore, the regional landscape is the protagonist, the fundamental condition of the work. Sometimes the ground plan and volumes are fragmented in order to suit the form of the terrain and to attenuate their visual impact, but the sensibility towards place is also evident in Gellner's more compact Cortina buildings. The system of staggered floors used at via Menardi 6 is designed to suit the sharply sloping terrain, while the windows and doors are no less sensitive to the surrounding panorama. The bedroom window, despite its location on the north front of the building, is large enough to afford a fine view of Cortina, with the Tofana di Rozes in the background.

MARTINA CARRARO

THE BOOKCASE IN THE LIVING ROOM

BIBLIOGRAPHY:
1950 Zevi B., 'Un architetto colto: Edoardo Gellner', in Metron, no. 39
1956 Cereghini M., *Costruire in montagna – Architettura e storia. Costruzioni e arredamenti di Edoardo Gellner a Cortina d'Ampezzo*, Milan
1959 Ronchi L., 'Opere dell'architetto Edoardo Gellner: cinque edifici nel centro di Cortina d'Ampezzo, il villaggio ENI a Corte di Cadore', in *L'architettura. Cronache e storia*, no. 44
1988 Gellner E., *Architettura rurale nelle Dolomiti Venete*, Cortina d'Ampezzo
1996 Mancuso F., Edoardo Gellner. *Il mestiere di architetto*, Milan
2001 Cornoldi A., *Le case degli architetti. Dizionario privato dal Rinascimento ad oggi*, Venice, pp. 164, 165

Herman Gesellius, Armas Lindgren, Eliel Saarinen
1874–1916, 1874–1929, 1873–1950

1901–03, NEW CONSTRUCTION, NOW MUSEUM
KIRKKONUMMI (FIN)

MAIN WORKS AND PROJECTS

1898–1900	Finnish pavilion at the 1900 Paris World Fair (F)
1899–1901	Pohjola fire insurance company office and apartment block, Helsinki (FIN)
1900–01	Apartment block, Fabianinkatu 17, Helsinki (FIN)
1900–02	Olofsborg, apartment block, Katajanokka, Helsinki (FIN)
1901–03	Suur-Merijoki manor, Viipuri, Karelia (FIN)
1901–04	Hvittorp villa, Kirkkonummi (FIN)
1902–12	Finnish National Museum, Helsinki (FIN)
1904–19	Railway station, Helsinki (FIN), designed by Saarinen
1905–07	Remer house, Mark Brandenburg (D), designed by Gesellius and Saarinen

GESELLIUS, LINDGREN AND SAARINEN studied together in Helsinki at the School of Architecture of the University of Technology, all graduating as qualified architects in the same year, 1897. Even before they graduated, they had opened an architects' office in partnership (1896), which was successful in architectural competitions. In their first year of practice, 1897, the trio won a competition to design the Tallberg house, but their breakthrough came in 1898, when they won the competition for the Finnish pavilion at the 1900 Paris World Fair. Their dynamic office was housed in Hvitträsk, Kirkkonummi, which the three architects designed in 1901–03. The building contained not just the partnership's studio, but also the private apartments of Gesellius, Lindgren and Saarinen. In the early 1900s the trio's practice was one of the leading offices on the Finnish architectural scene, designing major projects at a hectic pace. However, the three-way partnership ended as early as 1905, when Lindgren gave up his home in Hvitträsk and moved to Helsinki to open his own office. Gesellius and Saarinen still continued to collaborate in Hvitträsk for a few more years.

After Gesellius' death in 1916 (Hvitträsk), Hvitträsk became the property of Saarinen alone. He lived there with his family until he moved to the United States in 1923, after which the place remained the Saarinen family's summer house until the architect died in 1950 (Bloomfield Hills, Michigan). Saarinen's son, Eero, also an architect, who worked in the United States, spent his childhood at the Hvitträsk house. During the house's heyday, in the first few years of the 20th century, Hvitträsk was a cultural focal point, frequented by the likes of the composers Jean Sibelius and Gustav Mahler, the artists Pekka Halonen and Akseli Gallen-Kallela, the author Maxim Gorki, the art historian Julius Meier-Graefe, and the art critic Ugo Ojetti.

In designing their Hvitträsk villa and in opting for its location, Gesellius, Lindgren and Saarinen were following a trend of the times. At the turn of the century many Finnish artists sought relief from the noise of the city and built wilderness studios in untouched nature. In the 1890s artists searched for inspiration in vernacular architecture by travelling especially to Karelia. Akseli Gallen-Kallela, inspired by the Karelian architectural heritage, designed a log house, Kalela, in the Ruovesi wilderness, while Jean Sibelius built Ainola in Tuusula. The three architects proceeded similarly and looked for a peaceful site near Helsinki. They found an attractive sloping plot on the shore of Lake Vitträsk, where they built a wilderness studio and house, naming it Hvitträsk after the lake.

The style of Hvitträsk likewise followed contemporary trends. At the turn of the century Finland's architecture was generally so-called National Romantic, hinting at Finnish national features, and the bold personal design of Hvitträsk combines national with international features. The national component is clear from the use of debarked round logs, while the international element can be seen in a base made of blocks of stone, in powerful roof forms, and in the interior layout.

The main building consisted of two flats, separated by the architects' office. The north wing, which was dominated by a log tower, designed by Lindgren, was entirely destroyed in 1922 by a fire and was not rebuilt to the original design.

Eliel Saarinen's flat was in the south wing, which has been restored and now serves as a museum. The ground floor is dominated by a high wide living room, which opens onto a vaulted dining room. From the living room, stairs lead to the upper floor. The general layout of the living room, stairs and fireplace point to the English architectural tradition, with which Saarinen was familiar through such publications as *Studio* maga-

SOUTH TERRACE AND TERRACE WALL

ENTRANCE SIDE

LIVING ROOM

CHILDREN'S ROOM

GROUND PLANS

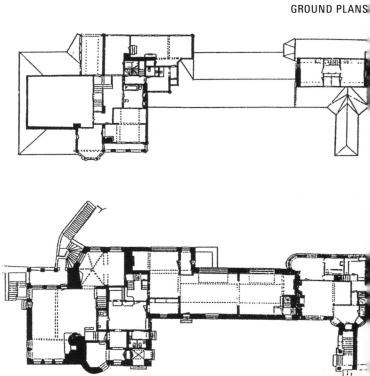

BEDROOM

SITTING AREA

FIREPLACE

THE STUDIO

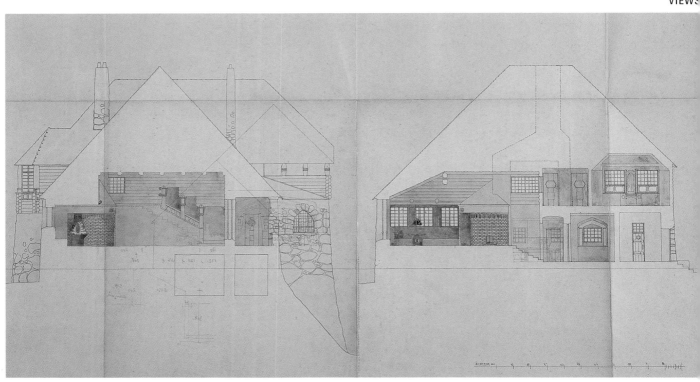

NORTH WING

TOWER BY THE ENTRANCE

zine, while the vaults and paintings of the dining room were inspired by medieval church arches.

Hvitträsk embodies the idea of the English Arts and Crafts movement that the home is a complete work of art, where all the objects must be designed to suit the whole. This is reflected, for example, in the furniture in Saarinen's apartment, which like some of the textiles and ornaments was the handiwork of Saarinen and his wife Loja. The dominant object in the living room, a wall hanging entitled *Flame*, was given to Saarinen by Akseli Gallen-Kallela. Initially, Gesellius lived in a separate house across the yard, but when Lindgren moved out of his apartment at the northern end of the main building, Gesellius settled into it, furnishing the flat with items he had designed himself.   TIMO KEINÄNEN

BIBLIOGRAPHY:
1966   Richards J. M., 'Hvitträsk', in *Architectural Review*, no. 828, February, pp. 152–154
1971   Vuorio A., *Kaksikymmentä vuotta Hvitträskin tähden*, Helsinki
1979   Tuomi R., *Erämaa ateljeet – Studios in the Wilds*, Helsinki
1987   Pallasmaa J. (ed.), *Hvitträsk, the Home as a Work of Art*, Helsinki
2001   Cornoldi A., *Le case degli architetti. Dizionario privato dal Rinascimento ad oggi*, Venice, pp. 165–166, 230 and 344–345

Eileen Gray
1878–1976

1926–29, NEW CONSTRUCTION, WITH JEAN BADOVICI, NOW MUSEUM PROMENADE LE CORBUSIER, ROQUEBRUNE-CAP MARTIN (F)

MAIN WORKS AND PROJECTS

1926–31   Battachon/Renaudin house, Vézelay (F), with Jean Badovici
          Badovici house, Vézelay (F), with Jean Badovici
1930–31   Badovici apartment, Paris (F)
1932–34   Own house, Tempe à Pailla, Castellar (F)
1936–37   Holiday and leisure centre (hypothetical project)

1946–47   Cultural and social centre (hypothetical project)
1954–61   Own house, Lou Pérou, outside Saint-Tropez (F)

THE DAUGHTER OF Lady Eveleen Pounden and the painter James Maclaren Smith, Kathleen Eileen Moray Smith was born in 1878 in Enniscorthy, County Wexford, Republic of Ireland. The family changed its name to Gray in 1893, after Eileen's mother inherited a peerage from an uncle in Scotland and claimed her title, Baroness Gray. Eileen Gray studied drawing at the Slade School of Fine Arts in London and at the Ecole Colarossi as well as Académie Julian, both in Paris. In 1906 she settled for good in Paris, where she earned her reputation initially as a designer of lavish furniture and interiors, in which she adapted traditional Asian lacquer techniques to modern European tastes.

Gray's encounter in 1922 with Jean Badovici (1893–1956), a Romanian who had come to Paris to study architecture at the Ecole des Beaux-Arts, was decisive for her career. As editor of the influential periodical *L'Architecture Vivante* (1923–33), Badovici was an enthusiastic agent for the modern movement. He encouraged Gray to take up architecture, introduced her to the work of the major European designers, and collaborated with her on several buildings. The early issues of *L'Architecture Vivante* were Gray's textbooks, providing fertile territory for her architectonic speculations. In 1926 Gray began a six-year collaboration with Badovici, during which they renovated several houses in Vézelay and completed what has become her best-known work, the villa that she designed (1926–29) both for and with Badovici on the Promenade Le Corbusier, in Roquebrune-Cap Martin, in the South of France. She named the house E.1027, a numerical cipher corresponding to the authors' intertwined initials (E.G. and J.B. to form E.J.B.G), indicating the collaborative nature of the undertaking.

On an exhibition panel relating to the E.1027 home for Badovici at Roquebrune-Cap Martin, Gray articulated her objectives: "House envisaged from a social point of view: minimum of space, maximum of comfort." With this goal in mind, she initiated certain spatial principles that she used throughout her career. She oriented the main living space to the southern exposure and view, and oriented the bedrooms to the rising sun. She segregated private areas from the more public zones of the house, and isolated the service spaces. The spatial hierarchy reflects Badovici's penchant for entertaining. On the main level there is an open living/dining room capable of accommodating extra guests, and a separate zone for sleeping, dressing and work. Near the main entrance an independent kitchen adjoins an outdoor cooking space. On the lower level there is a guest room and minimal servants' quarters. She ensured the occupants' freedom by providing each sleeping area with independent access to the garden.

Gray integrated furniture and architecture to facilitate multiple uses in each space. She conceived of the living room opening onto a narrow balcony as a loggia, equipped with screenlike vertical windows capable of opening fully to admit sunlight and view. A partition, incorporating shelves, coat rack and umbrella stand, blocks this space from view upon entry. A sleeping alcove, adjoining the shower/dressing area, and a dining alcove contribute to the room's plurality of use. Gray invoked the senses directly and indirectly in both architecture and furniture, for example in the tile flooring underfoot, which radiates heat from the sun, or in the cork-covered tea and dining tables, which muffle sound. Her furniture suggests analogies with the body. A flexible table extends to meet the occupant of a bed, drawers pivot horizontally, and a hinged mirror affords oblique views of the head. In the areas of the house where contact with the body is most intimate – the bedroom and bathroom – Gray strove to heighten bodily awareness. She provided the bathroom with a profusion of shimmering materials, including tiled walls, folding mirrors, and a polished aluminium tub enclosure, whose cool surfaces provided a soothing respite from the relentless Mediterranean sun. Gray's focus on the kinaesthetic, tactile and sensual potential of architecture and furniture in E.1027 derives from her interest in merging an aspiration for

VIEW FROM THE SEAWARD SIDE

ROOM WITH MIRROR WARDROBE, BED AND E.1027 TABLE

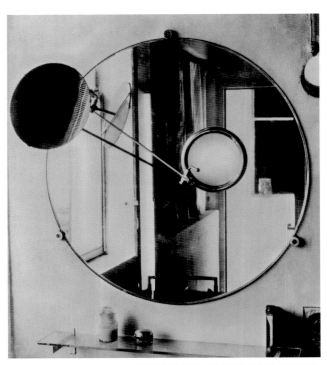

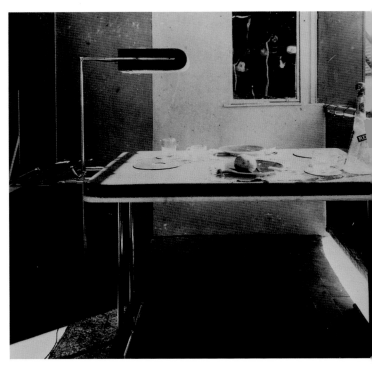

"SATELLITE" MIRROR MADE OF CHROME-PLATED STEEL TUBING   TABLE ON THE TERRACE

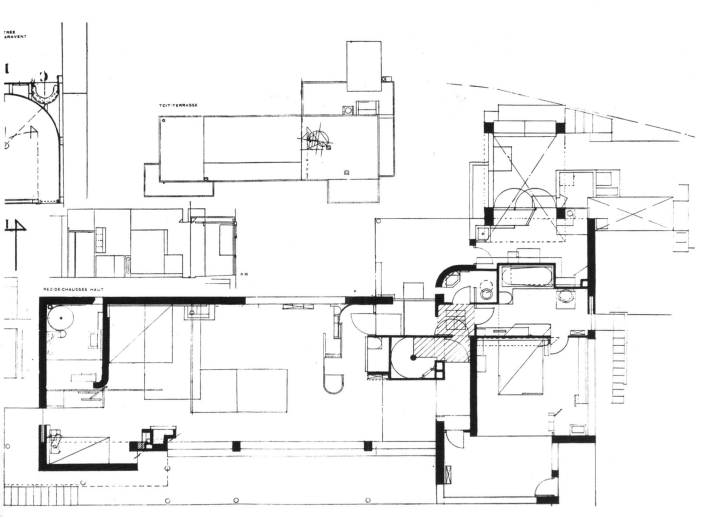

FLOOR PLAN

luxury, typical of the French decorative arts tradition, with the liberal social aims of the architectural avant-garde.

Gray avoided self-promotion. Thus, aside from the special issue of *L'Architecture Vivante* (winter 1929) that Badovici devoted to E.1027, the house has received little critical attention in the annals of modern architecture. However, Joseph Rykwert initiated a re-examination of Gray's architectural contributions in a series of articles beginning in 1968, and, more recently, the series of murals that Le Corbusier painted on the villa's walls at Badovici's invitation in 1937–38 prompted a series of essays by Rykwert on Gray's attitude towards the Swiss architect. Although these murals departed from Gray's constructive integration of furniture and architecture, she objected only to the remarks he made about the house when he published the paintings ten years later. Indeed, her admiration for Le Corbusier's architecture was undiminished.

Rather than begin her designs from a set of theoretical precepts declared in a manifesto, an approach adopted by her more polemical colleagues, Gray challenged the all-encompassing claims of contemporary theorising by adapting a selective combination of modern movement precepts to address the occupants' physical, psychological and spiritual needs. By referring to and expanding on certain spatial devices of the modern movement, such as Le Corbusier's 'five points of a new architecture', in her early buildings and projects, Gray sought to overcome the dehumanising qualities often associated with abstraction by engaging the subjective qualities of experience. "The poverty of modern architecture," she wrote during the 1940s, "stems from an atrophy of sensuality. Everything is dominated by reason in order to create amazement without proper research." Through a relatively small number of buildings and conjectural projects, Eileen Gray offered a significant challenge to the heroic ideals of the modern movement.   CAROLINE CONSTANT

BIBLIOGRAPHY:
1929 Gray E. and Badovici J., 'Maison en Bord de Mer', in *L'Architecture Vivante*, special winter issue devoted to E.1027 house, Paris
1987 Adam P., *Eileen Gray Architect/Designer*, New York
1988 Dessauce M., 'Eileen Gray, villa E.1027: une contribution à l'histoire de l'architecture organique en France', in *Bulletin de la Sociéte de l'Histoire de l'Art Français*, Paris, pp. 233–244
2000 Constant C., *Eileen Gray*, London/New York
2001 Cornoldi A., *Le case degli architetti. Dizionario privato dal Rinascimento ad oggi*, Venice, pp. 172–174

Walter Gropius
1883–1969

1925–26, NEW CONSTRUCTION, DEMOLISHED IN 1945
BURGKÜHNAUER ALLEE, DESSAU (D)

MAIN WORKS AND PROJECTS

1911–21	Fagus shoe factory, Alfeld an der Leine (D), with Adolf Meyer
1914	Office and factory building, Deutscher Werkbund exhibition, Cologne (D), with Adolf Meyer
1920–21	Sommerfeld house, Berlin (D), with Adolf Meyer
1922	Project for Chicago Tribune Tower competition (USA), with Adolf Meyer
1925–26	Bauhaus building, Dessau (D) Own Bauhaus Director's house, Burgkühnauer Allee, Dessau (D), destroyed in 1945

1927–29	Dessau employment office (D)
1929–30	Building at Siemensstadt housing development, Berlin (D)
1936–39	Impington Village College, Cambridgeshire (GB), with Maxwell Fry
1948–50	Graduate Centre at Harvard University, Cambridge, Massachusetts (USA), with TAC
1958–63	Pan American Airways building, New York City (USA), with Emery Roth & Sons, TAC and Pietro Belluschi

WALTER GROPIUS was born in Berlin on 18 May 1883, the son of Walter Gropius, who was a building advisor for the police headquarters in Berlin, and his wife Manon Scharnweber. From 1903 to 1907 the young Gropius studied in the Schools of Architecture of the Technical Universities of both Munich and Berlin. From 1907–08 he undertook a study trip in Spain, and between 1908 and 1910 he worked with Prof. Peter Behrens, after which he opened his own architectural practice in Berlin together with Adolf Meyer. In the same year, 1910, he went on study visits to Italy, France, England and Denmark. A year later Gropius became a member of the Deutscher Werkbund (German Crafts Association), acting as author and editor of the association's yearbooks for 1912, 1913 and 1914. Also in 1911, at the World Fair in Ghent, he was awarded the Gold Medal for interior decoration. Between 1914 and 1918 Gropius fought in the First World War, and in 1915 he married Alma-Maria Mahler, with whom he had a daughter, Alma Manon, who was born in 1916. The couple divorced in 1920, leaving Gropius free to get remarried in 1923 to Ilse Frank.

In 1916 Henry van de Velde, director of the Grand Ducal Schools of Arts and Crafts and of Fine Arts in Weimar, proposed Walter Gropius as his successor, as a result of which Gropius was called to Weimar in 1918 to succeed van der Velde as head of the two schools. In 1919 the two institutions merged to become the Staatliches Bauhaus, Weimar, holding a first extensive Bauhaus exhibition week in 1923. Two years later, in 1925, the State Bauhaus relocated to Dessau, taking virtually all its teachers and students with it. The school acquired the new name of Dessau Bauhaus Academy of Design and was housed initially in provi-

sional accommodation, until the Adademy moved into the new Bauhaus building in September/October 1926, inaugurated on 1 December.

In 1925 Gropius' partnership with Adolf Meyer came to an end, and on 1 April 1928 he resigned as Director of the Bauhaus in order to concentrate on his own architectural work. From 1934 to 1937 he had a practice in London in partnership with the architect Maxwell Fry, after which he held a professorship in architecture at the Graduate School of Design of Harvard University in the United Sates of America, and acted as director of the School of Architecture at Harvard from 1938 to 1952. During these tenures, the *Bauhaus* 1919–1928 exhibition was held in New York in 1938. Between 1938 and 1941 Gropius ran a private architectural practice in partnership with Marcel Breuer in Cambridge, Mass., and in 1946 he formed The Architects Collaborative in Cambridge, Mass. Gropius was awarded the Royal Gold Medal of the Royal Institute of British Architects (RIBA) in 1956, the Grand Cross and Star of Merit of the Federal Republic of Germany in 1958, and the Gold Medal of the American Institute of Architects (AIA) in 1959.

On 31 March 1925 it was decided to construct not only a new building for the Bauhaus, but also a house for its director (Gropius) and six semi-detached houses for the Bauhaus masters Lyonel Feininger, Vassily Kandinsky, Paul Klee, László Moholy-Nagy, Georg Muche and Oskar Schlemmer, each house comprising an apartment and a studio. Ernst Neufert oversaw the planning of the houses in the office of Gropius and Meyer. They are situated in a secluded avenue, separated from the Bauhaus itself by a large area of Dessau city. Houses were only provided for the

AST FRONT

LIVING AND DINING ROOM WITH DOUBLE WRITING DESK

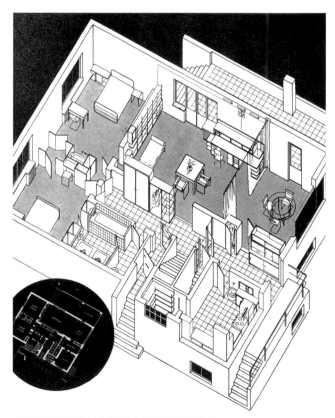

AXONOMETRICAL VIEW OF THE INTERIOR

CORNER OF THE DINING ROOM WITH BUILT-IN CUPBOARD

KITCHEN

SINK ROOM

'old masters', which angered the 'young masters' such as Marcel Breuer, Hinnerk Scheper and Josef Albers. The dwellings were criticised by the Bauhaus students as being antisocial and formalistic. The buildings were quite generously designed, but were so expensive that the rents were 60% higher than what was legally allowed for official residences. Schlemmer wrote to his wife: "I was shocked when I saw… the houses! I imagined that some day people without apartments would stand here, while the artist-gentlemen sunbathed on the roofs of their houses." The Director's house, for example, had a guest flat, rooms for the janitor on the ground level, a maid's room, and a garage! As regard the floor plans and the interrelation of spaces, this house in particular largely reflected the social structures prevalent at the start of the 20th century. Neverthe-less, Winfried Nerdinger (1985) has written of the buildings: "The cubic, three-dimensional exterior appearance of the houses is Gropius' highest achievement in the design of private houses."

Just as the Dessau Bauhaus building was to be the architectural manifestation of the Bauhaus concept, the master houses served as demonstrations of modern life and a new aesthetic for living. In an open calm way, the rooms represented the standardisation of day-to-day ac-tivities in the machine age. The furnishings, as in all Gropius' projects, came from Bauhaus workshops. Many small details demonstrate the effi-cient and practical organisation of daily life in the house: a disc cupboard that opens from both sides, a ventilated linen closet, and a walk-in clo-set. In a short film about this new way of living, Richard Paulick's *Neues Wohnen – Haus Gropius, Dessau* (Humboldt Film, Berlin, 1926), the wives of the Bauhaus masters demonstrate various fine points of the furnish-ings.

Walter Gropius' house was the only one of the masters' houses to be conceived as purely residential. His ideas were implemented with great rigour, right down to the smallest detail. His apartment may be considered as the first to use Marcel Breuer's steel-tube furniture. From the existing photos, it would seem that there were no pictures on the walls, with the exception of a picture niche in the dining room, with frames intended for photos, paintings or prints. It may be, however, that the pictures, and all other 'superfluous' objects, were removed from view

PLAN OF THE GROUND FLOOR

during the photo session – this was the case, for example, with Ilse Gro-pius' extensive cactus collection and the 'old' furniture. During the short period in which Gropius lived in the house (1926–28) many parties were held, and celebrated guests, such as the composer Béla Bartók, were entertained. No opportunity was missed to promote the architectonic and aesthetic concept!

JUDITH WEINSTOCK-MONTAG

BIBLIOGRAPHY:

1930   Giedeon S., *Walter Gropius*, Paris
1962   Wingler H., *Das Bauhaus*, Bramsche
1985   Nerdinger W., *Der Architekt Walter Gropius*, Berlin
1986/87 Probst H. and Schädlich C., 1: Der Architekt und Theoretiker, Werkverzeichnis Teil 1; 2: Der Architekt und Pädagoge, Werkverzeichnis Teil 2; 3: Ausgewählte Schriften. Berlin.
2001   Cornoldi A., *Le case degli architetti. Dizionario privato dal Rinascimento ad oggi*, Venice, pp. 178–182

Jakob Halldor Gunnløgsson
1918–1985

1958, NEW CONSTRUCTION
68 RUNGSTED STRANDVEJ, RUNGSTED (DK)

MAIN WORKS AND PROJECTS

1957–59 Tårnby City Hall, Amager Landevej 76 (DK)
1963–65 Fredericia City Hall, Gothersgade 20 (DK)
1964–66 Tårnby Secondary School, Tejn Allé, Tårnby (DK)
1966–68 Fisheries Museum and Maritime Museum, Tarphagevej, Esbjerg (DK)
1972–74 Uglegård School, Vestre Grænsevej 32, Solrød Strand (DK)

1977–78 Gammel Holte Church (DK)
 Bov City Hall, Kirkestien 1 (DK)
1977–80 Ministry of Foreign Affairs, Asiatisk Plads 2, Copenhagen (DK)
1980–81 Tønder City Hall, Kongevejen 57 (DK)

HALLDOR GUNNLØGSSON was born on 23 January 1918 in Frederiksberg, the son of the merchant Halldor Johannes Gunnløgsson and the actress Else Sten. He completed his secondary schooling in 1937 and then enrolled in the School of Architecture at the Royal Danish Academy of Fine Arts in Copenhagen, from which he graduated in 1942. His teachers at the Academy included Kay Fisker and Steen Eiler Rasmussen.Just after his final examinations, in the depths of the Second World War, Gunnløgsson left Denmark to stay in Sweden 1942–44. During his career he travelled to North and South America, Japan, and the Middle East. The inspiration that he found on these trips he delicately applied to the Scandinavian design fundamental to his buildings. Gunnløgsson combined his architectural design work with a regular teaching career spent almost exclusively at his old college, the School of Architecture at Copenhagen's Royal Danish Academy of Fine Arts. Here he was employed initially as an assistant, then as a lecturer from 1956, and finally as professor of architecture from 1959, before being appointed dean of the School in 1969. Between 1961 and 1962 he was a visiting professor at the Massachusetts Institute of Technology (MIT), Cambridge, Mass., in the United States.

Halldor Gunnløgsson was one of the leading figures of Danish modernist architecture, especially in the field of detached houses. His personal interpretations of the Western modernist and Japanese traditional architectural traditions were shaped by a consciousness of specific local qualities and demands. Using simple materials such as wood and stone, combined with a limited range of colours, he created works that were both minimalist and exquisite.

Gunnløgsson designed and built (in 1958) his own home at 68 Rungsted Strandvej, Rungsted, to house only himself and his wife, Lillemor Gunnløgsson. Because they had no children, the house consists of just two rooms, plus a bathroom and kitchen. The building typifies the individualistic modern lifestyle of the 1950s, is characterised by simplicity and functionality, and is ideally placed in the middle of beautiful natural surroundings, overlooking Øresund. Its secluded and undisturbed location makes outer shielding walls unnecessary, and the outside is left to penetrate the rooms through 'glass walls'.

The feeling of being inside the Rungsted Strandvej house is thus intimately bound up with the feeling of being outside, or rather with the feeling of being on a protected terrace, since it is possible to get a glimpse of the Sound from almost every spot in the building. The floating impression that the house creates, caused by its large windows and the simple wooden construction between its end walls, underlines the floating atmosphere of the interior, with its open and continuous rooms.

The building is erected as a wooden framework between two end walls. The end walls are made of stone and are whitewashed, while the wooden construction is stained in dark shades. In front of the house, on the eastern side, facing the Sound, is a terrace made of salt-impregnated boards. The 'glass walls' on this side have two sliding doors, also in glass, which form the entrance to the terrace.

The interiors are typical of Gunnløgsson's work, designed with simple materials and very few colours. The ceilings are constructed using untreated deal battens. The visible beams are stained in dark shades in the same manner as the supporting timber described above. The interior walls are made of wood, varnished black, and have a polished surface. The sliding doors, which separate the main room from the kitchen and the bedroom, are painted in a light grey, while the chimney brickwork is treated in the same way as the outer walls and whitewashed. To preserve the simplicity and minimalist impression, even the heating pipes are invisible, embedded in the floor and covered by heat-conducting Swedish marble, also light grey in tone. For extra heating, the living room

THE WEST FRONT ON RUNGSTED STRANDVEJ

NIGHT VIEW OF THE EAST FAÇADE

VIEW OF THE LIVING AREA TOWARDS THE SEA

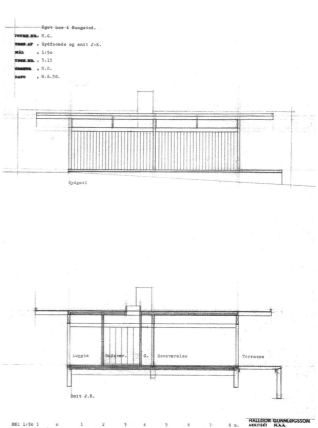

Eget hus i Rungsted.
TEGN.NR. : H.G.
TEGN.AF : Sydfacade og snit J-K.
MÅL : 1:50
TEGN.NR. : 3.13
TEGNET : H.O.
DATO : 8.6.58.

Sydgavl

Loggia   Badeværelse   G.   Soveværelse   Terrasse

Snit J.K.

Mål 1:50 1   0   1   2   3   4   5   6   7   8 m.   HALLDOR GUNNLØGSSON ARKITEKT M.A.A.

SIDE ELEVATION AND SECTION

SITTING AREA IN THE LIVING ROOM

is supplied with a chimney and a fireplace, situated in the middle of the room. The windows can be covered by Venetian blinds in the same light colour as the untreated wood of the ceiling.

Approaching the house from the main road, you need to walk along the garden, following the sloping terrain. The difference in altitude between the road level and house level is almost two metres. The garage is situated in the northern part of the building, while the living facilities are placed towards the south. Entering from the western side of the building through a door leading to a narrow part of the main room behind the kitchen, you continue directly into the main room with its central free-standing chimney. The bathroom and the kitchen lie parallel to the façades, and can be entered either from the bedroom or the main room.

Gunnløgsson's own house on Rungsted Strandvej is a brilliant example of the new style characteristic of the modernist movement in Denmark in the 1950s and 1960s. Traditionally the whole area along the coast of Øresund north of Copenhagen was characterised by large prestigious villas with many rooms, sited in parks and surrounded by garages, barns, etc. Gunnløgsson's home is modest in comparison with these. The old parks were divided up into smaller plots of 1000 – 1500 m² consistent with the new ideal of a more functional and individual way of living, without the staff required to maintain the large villas and their grounds. In the case of Gunnløgsson's home, the maintained gardens are replaced by the natural flora of the coast, while the house itself is limited to the specific needs of a couple. Gunnløgsson's own house thus resembles Farnsworth House by Ludwig Mies van der Rohe or Philip Johnson's Glass House, and in its overall impression the building clearly shows an

THE LIVING AREA

original Japanese inspiration. However, its Nordic materials – bricks, wood and Swedish marble – turn the house into an indisputably Scandinavian interpretation of these styles. Gunnløgsson's detached houses in general, and his own house in particular, inspired many architects of the period.

The same attitude towards materials and simplicity also characterises the architect's other major works. In the case of Tårnby or Fredericia City Halls, the costly materials and the severe and rhythmic structure of the façades are remarkable. Working in the southern part of Jutland, he used the local red brick so that the new buildings could match the existing traditional ones. He often underlined the function and importance of a building, making large steps lead up to official buildings such as city halls or museums. Likewise, in his project for the Ministry of Foreign Affairs in Copenhagen, he tried to make the new buildings correspond to the old monumental warehouses dating back to the 18th century.

Halldor Gunnløgsson's oeuvre is characterised by an overall aesthetic close to that of Gunnar Asplund, defined by the idea of an architectural whole, functionality, regard for the surroundings, thorough construction, and a delicate attention to detail.

KIRA PEDERSEN

BIBLIOGRAPHY:
1959   Skriver P. E., 'Eget hus i Rungsted', in *Arkitektur*, no. 4, pp. 92–99
1970   Langkilde H. E., Kollektivhuset: En boligforms udvikling i dansk arkitektur, Copenaghen
1974   *A school without corridors*, in *L'Architecture d'Aujourd'hui*, no. 175, pp. 106–109
1977   Mackay D., *Multiple Family Housing*, London
1980   Lund H. and Balslev Jørgensen L., Halldor Gunnløgsson, in *Magtens Bolig*, Copenaghen, pp. 150–159

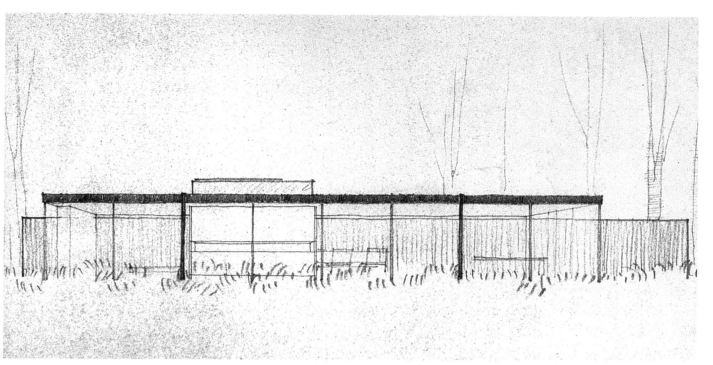

PERSPECTIVE OF THE EAST FAÇADE

FLOOR PLAN

Herman Petrus Coenraad Haan
1914 – 1996

1953, NEW CONSTRUCTION, NOW ALTERED
KRALINGSEWEG 187, ROTTERDAM (NL)

MAIN WORKS AND PROJECTS

1952   Exhibition about the Sahara, Volksuniversiteit Rotterdam, Rotterdam (NL)

1956   Uitenbroek house, Rotterdam (NL)
            Vervat house, Capelle aan den Ijssel (NL)

1964   Exhibition about the Tellem, Museum voor Land- en Volkenkunde, Rotterdam (NL)

1965   Student housing, Twente (NL)

1982   Project for Sangra Museum and Cultural Centre, Bandiagara, Mali

ALTHOUGH HE WAS born in 1914 in Amsterdam, Herman Haan grew up in Winschoten, a small village in the north of the Netherlands. In 1920 his father became director of the Verenigde Oost-Groningse Steenfabrieken, a brick factory. Haan's wayward temperament emerged in secondary school, when he attended a series of different institutions, but without ever finishing one. For two years he also attended the MTS School in Groningen, a famous example of Het Nieuwe Bouwen architecture by the architects van der Vlugt and Wiebengen. His father often took him on business trips to Scandinavia and Germany, and from childhood on he collected stones and prehistoric artefacts. At the age of 15, he set off for a three-month desert journey in Morocco, where he met and lived with the Berber nomads.

Haan embarked on his professional life as an architect in 1932. His first job involved drawing in Egbert Reitsma's office in Groningen, after which he worked as a technical draughtsman for British Petroleum. In 1935, not even armed with a degree in architecture, he opened his own architectural practice in Winschoten! He moved to Rotterdam in 1940, and a year later, at the age of 27, enrolled in Amsterdam's Academy of Architecture, where he met Willem van Tijen, who acted as a kind of mentor throughout Haan's entire studies. Despite this tutelage, the aspiring architect never passed his final exams and abandoned his degree course.

During the Second World War Haan was very active. He used to live in the famous bridgeman's house on the Maas, in Rotterdam, where he was able to provide much assistance to the resistance. In 1948 he married designer Hansje Fischer and moved to a flat on De Boompjes Avenue, still near the Maas, where the couple designed their own interior.

During the post-war years, Haan became involved with many of the Dutch modernists and future members of the COBRA group. Corneille, Gerrit Rietveld, Aldo and Henny van Eyck and Mart Stam became close friends, with whom he shared the unique experience of his annual expeditions through the Sahara, to the Tellem and the Dogon tribes, as well as to Algeria and Morocco. During the same years he worked as a tutor at the Hochschule für Gestaltung (College of Design) in Ulm, Germany, and also lectured in Oslo, London, Bristol and other universities about his discoveries in Africa. Haan was also invited to present his experiences at the Academy of Architecture in Amsterdam, where he had a great influence on the students, including Piet Blom. He participated actively in the meetings of Team X and showed his work at the CIAM congress in Otterlo.

In 1967 Haan founded "Atelier Aa". This was his first serious attempt at running a proper architectural office of his own, as before he had always worked out of a small studio in his private Kralingseweg house either alone or with his friend Piet de Hoog. In the mid-1970s Haan dissolved "Atelier Aa" so that he could retire, but he continued to design some small projects after that date, although these were never realised.

Haan built his private home at Kralingseweg 187, Rotterdam, which was a new construction, in 1953. He designed it mindful of the vastness and oppressive heat of the Sahara Desert. The architect did not want to live in "a space that is limited to the few square metres and which has to be protected because of the climate". The house occupied a dream position. Both near to the centre of Rotterdam and yet close to the countryside, it lay between the lake and woods of Kralingseplas and the Ringvaart Canal and its surrounding polders.

At that time if a house was to attract a subsidy, it could not exceed volume of 375 cubic metres. Haan built his home within these restrictions, but thanks to the building's openness and because of the vast surrounding landscape it looked much larger. Huge glass walls could be fully slid open, minimising the distinction between inside and outside. The house was totally open to the street and had no secrets – privacy did not exist for Haan.

THE STUDIO FOR HERMAN HAAN AND HIS WIFE

VIEW FROM THE MAIN STREET

THE SPLIT LEVEL BETWEEN LIVING ROOM AND STUDIO

The higher position of the canal made Haan decide to elevate the living room to obtain a wider view. A large suspended terrace served as a perfect transition between living room and landscape. Partly under the living room, a small architecture studio was located, which was directly connected with the covered terrace, a garden and a pond. Studio, living room, kitchen and entrance formed one flowing space, with only the bedrooms, bathroom and garage forming a separate unity. The minor rooms were as small as possible. The dimensions of the bedrooms, in particular, were minimal – Haan considered sleeping to be a state of unconsciousness. As much space as possible was given to the house's living rooms.

Haan's house was an intersection of two main prisms with one connecting element. This simple uncomplicated composition was the most important concept behind the home. One prism was a closed box consisting of a garage, two small bedrooms and a minimal bathroom. The other, elevated prism had a totally open view and contained the living room. The connecting element was a one-and-a-half-level-high studio, giving access to the half basement under the living room, where Haan had his small architecture office. More precisely, the open prism was nothing more than a concrete floor and roof, supported only by one wall and one huge column.

There was no enclosed porch or corridors, which were replaced by the large hall functioning as a studio. This hall was the spine of the house. It was the link between the rooms on different levels, the entrance and studio with a panoramic view. The space between the two main volumes opened up a view to the pond, the terrace and the landscape behind, and continued under the elevated living room. The fronts of the house were chosen either as totally closed surfaces, or as floor-to-ceiling glass panels. The glass fronts to the south were withdrawn from the roof for reasons of indoor temperature, but this intermediate space also created the possibility of long terraces and of opening the living room to the landscape.

The materials used in the house were concrete structures, walls of reused cobblestone, wooden windows, glass sliding doors and stone pavements. Steel, too, was deployed for the structure of the building, but in an almost invisible way. The girders were hidden, and the columns were round and as thin as possible. This almost invisible use of steel was in strong contrast with the tactile presence of the wood and stone. In general, Haan liked to use materials with a radical tactile character: rough wood, scraggy stone, and smooth glass, although always very refined in their application. His architecture was shameless in its expression, but human in its simplicity.

Much of Haan's oeuvre consisted of private detached houses, and his private Kralingseweg home can be considered as a prototype of them. Its realisation coincided with a rapid acceleration in his career. In the years after 1953 the architect built several other villas around Rotterdam, taught at Ulm's Hochschule für Gestaltung (College of Design) in 1957

VIEW OF THE LIVING ROOM TOWARDS THE KITCHEN

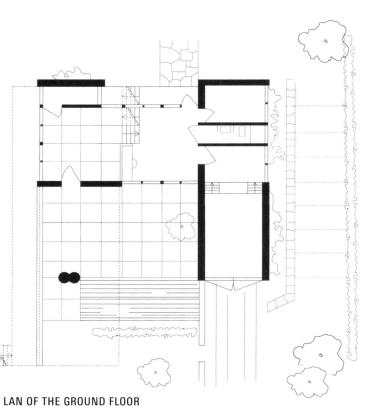

PLAN OF THE GROUND FLOOR

and 1958, and participated in several Team X meetings. He organised exhibitions and trips to Africa, produced television programs, and gave lectures throughout Europe. Allison and Peter Smithson visited Haan's house on one of their Team X trips, and called it "their first experience of living in a glass house as a tourist attraction with buses stopping in front".

Haan's own home was the first of a whole series of houses all based on the same principle of two or three interlocking volumes, creating one flowing space. The use of materials could also be considered as an experiment for his later houses. The influence of his African travels was clearly recognisable in the way of living, in the tactile approach to architecture, and in the vision of space, although it was not present in the form and the materials. Haan's discoveries in the Sahara were, however, extremely important for younger architects such as Aldo van Eyck and Piet Blom, who did interpret African architecture in a literal way.

SILVIA DE NOLF

BIBLIOGRAPHY:
1956   'H. P. C. Haan, Architect's own house', in *Architectural Design*, no. 3, pp. 73–74
       H. P. C. Haan, Huis aan de Kralingseweg', in *Forum*, Rotterdam, pp. 127–129
1958   'Habitation de l'architecte Haan à Rotterdam', in *l'Architecture d'Aujourd'hui*, no. 75, p. 13
1995   Vollaard P., *Herman Haan architect*, Uitgeverij 010, Rotterdam
1996   Vollaard P., 'Het huis van Haan', in *Avenue*, no. 8, pp. 82–87

**1924, NEW CONSTRUCTION, NOW ALTERED
EBELSTRASSE 27, DOLDERTAL, ZURICH (CH)**

MAIN WORKS AND PROJECTS

1897	Zur Trülle commercial building, Zurich (CH)
1899–1900	Schatzalp Sanatorium, Davos (CH)
1902	Protestant Kreuzkirche, Zurich (CH)
1906–11	Queen Alexandra Sanatorium, Davos (CH)
1908	Allerheiligen Lung Sanatorium near Olten (CH)
1909–24	Extension to the Jelmoli department store, Zurich (CH)

1910	Own house Im Guggi, Zurich (CH)
1912	Red Cross surgical clinic, nurses' accommodation building, Zurich (CH)
1914–16	Regional administration building, Zurich (CH)
1923–24	Dermatological clinic of Zurich Cantonal Hospital (CH)

MAX HAEFELI grew up on the Giseli country estate near Lucerne, where his father owned the Hotel Schwanen. After attending primary and secondary school in Lucerne, he enrolled in the School of Architecture of the Eidgenössisches Polytechnikum or Federal Polytechnic in Zurich (later the Swiss Federal Institute of Technology or ETH). His most important teacher was Alfred Friedrich Bluntschli, himself a pupil and successor of Gottfried Semper. After graduating in 1893, Haefeli went with his college friend and future work partner Otto Pfleghard to Wiesbaden to work for two years in the office of the architect Alfred Schellenberg, after which they spent two more years in Berlin and Leipzig. Upon their return to Switzerland, Haefeli and Pfleghard established a partnership that would last until 1927.

Pfleghard & Haefeli's architectural practice was one of the most successful in Switzerland during the first quarter of the 20th century. It went through the development typical of its generation, from the late historicist architecture of Semper and Bluntschli, via Art Nouveau and Heimatstil, to Neoclassicism around 1920. The firm realised a wide range of public and private buildings, but their real speciality was sanatorium buildings, in which they incorporated some innovative structural and technical solutions. The best known building of this group, the Schatzalp Sanatorium in Davos, has a reinforced concrete construction, steam floor heating and a flat roof with inside-situated drainage. It is not surprising that the pioneers of modern architecture, namely Le Corbusier and Sigfried Giedion, referred to this building as a proof of the validity of their claims.

Max Haefeli's house in the Doldertal, Zurich, is, chronologically speaking, the second of three homes that he built for himself and lived in. He designed the first one, Im Guggi, also in Zurich, as early as 1910, and in the 1930s he purchased an old Ticinese house (Campo d'oro) in Barbegna on Lake Lugano, which he gradually developed into his home for his later years. As different as Haefeli's three homes may seem at first glance, they do in fact reveal some common principles, which lead to conjectures both about his architectural approach and his own way of life. All the houses are carefully integrated into their existing surroundings, and they are all oriented towards the south-west. Particular attention was paid in each case to the relationship between the house and the garden. The interior organisation takes little account of the need for prestige, and monumental effects – such as impressive halls and suites – are entirely lacking.

Although Haefeli was by nature an artistic architect, he also possessed an aptitude for engineering, a double talent that is clearly visible in the Doldertal house. The logic of the design, based on practical aspects, is combined with a fine feeling for proportions, materials and colours. Since the house was designed for the needs of a specific individual, Peter Meyer regarded it as the "most representative example of modern Swiss residential architecture" of its time.

The house occupies the north-eastern corner of a large triangular site on the Zürichberg mountain, which slopes steeply down towards the Wolfbach valley. The building is arranged in two dissimilar volumes, a three-storey section emphasising the vertical on the valley side, and a two-storey part emphasising the horizontal on the hill side. Concerning the exterior, various features create a homogeneous overall impression. The windows on the bedroom floor, for example, although they are placed at different distances, have a uniform design and are arranged in a line. There is a studio in the basement, the living rooms are placed on the ground floor, and the first floor accommodates the sleeping quarters. On both the living and the sleeping floors, the rooms are concentrated into functional groups. A staggering of the building volumes creates a wind-protected terrace, which is cleverly integrated, spatially and visually, with

VIEW OF THE SOUTH-WEST FAÇADE

HAEFELI WITH HIS FAMILY AND SOME FRIENDS OUT ON THE TERRACE

THE TERRACE ON THE SOUTH-WEST FAÇADE

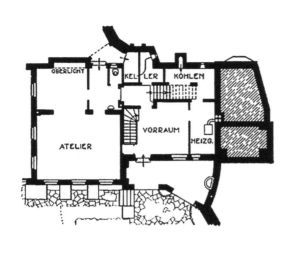

PLAN OF THE LOWER FLOOR

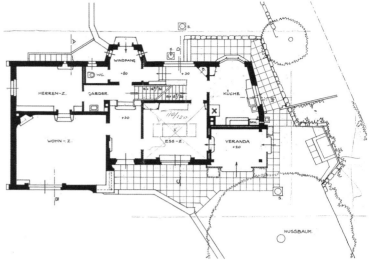

PLAN OF THE GROUND FLOOR

SKETCHES OF THE FURNISHINGS

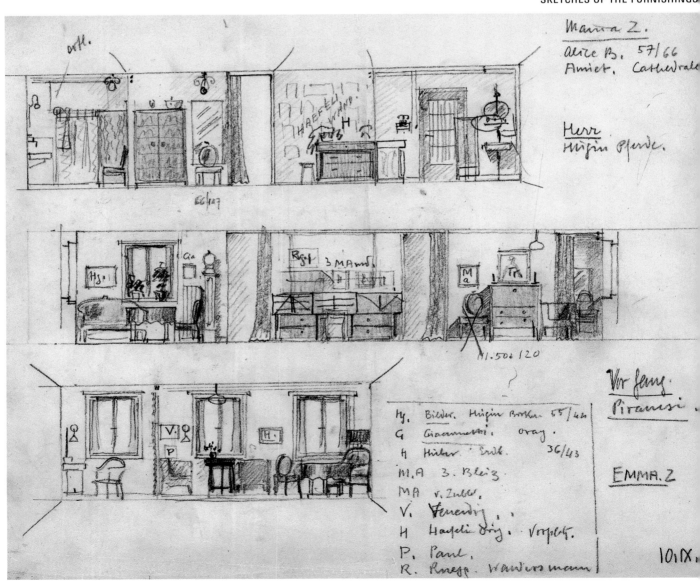

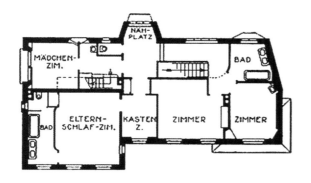

PLAN OF THE UPPER FLOOR

SOUTH-WEST FAÇADE

SITTING AREA IN THE LIVING ROOM

BIBLIOGRAPHY:
1925   Meyer P., 'Wohnhaus des Architekten M. Haefeli, im Doldertal, Zürich', in *Schweizerische Bauzeitung*, no. 85, pp. 111–115
1928   Meyer P., *Moderne Schweizer Wohnhäuser*, Zurich, pp. 15–22
1939   Jegher C., 'Campo d'oro – Tusculum eines Architekten', in *Schweizerische Bauzeitung*, no. 114, pp. 266–274
1941   *Schweizerische Bauzeitung*, no. 117, pp. 261–264
1998   *Swiss Architectural Lexicon of the 19th and 20th Centuries*, Basel / Boston / Berlin, pp. 418–419

the house. The visual connection between the living room and the terrace is achieved by means of a stanchion-free (!) corner window.

The building is also divided into two parts on the horizontal plane. Since the house is oriented towards the sun and the view, the living and sleeping areas are located on the south-west front, whereas the kitchen and bathrooms are situated on the entrance side. As in English country residences, the size of the rooms is adapted to their individual purposes, which means that axes and symmetry are entirely lacking. Unlike the English model, however, there is no grand entrance hall. The imposing house is intended entirely for private use and is not designed for any representative purposes.

The house in the Doldertal was constructed at a time when the first examples of modern architecture were emerging in Switzerland. Despite the traditional disposition (reminiscent of old gabled Zurich lake houses), the steep pitched roofs, punched window openings and firm anchorage to the ground, the building is more than a mere harbinger of this movement. In terms of form, there is evidence of the influence of the model of the then highly esteemed Dutch architecture, and in its interior organisation it pre-empts the functionalist Neues Bauen. In his book on modern Swiss residential buildings, the Swiss architect and art historian Peter Meyer describes Haefeli's house at the very beginning in order to "point out the latent modernity of historic architecture".

Although Haefeli was an attentive observer of contemporary trends in architecture, as is shown by his second home, he never again took any consistent steps towards Neues Bauen, unlike his colleague Karl Moser, the "father of modern Swiss architecture", who was older by nine years. His role as mentor was limited to his influence on his son Max Ernst, whom Haefeli introduced to the architectural métier in his own office. Under the benevolent influence of his father, Ernst developed into one of the leading protagonists of the Swiss architectural avant-garde.

Max Haefeli's home is now privately owned and is currently under dire threat from a conversion project.

BRUNO MAURER

Gunnar Hansson
1925–1989

1957–59, NEW CONSTRUCTION
SÓLHEIMAR 5, REYKJAVÍK (IS)

MAIN WORKS AND PROJECTS

1951–54   *Morgunbladid* newspaper building, Adalstraeti 6, Reykjavík (IS)

1957–59   Church of the Independent Parish, Háteigsvegur, Reykjavík (IS)

1959   Terraced houses, Hvassaleiti 101–113, Reykjavík (IS)

1961   Ísólfsskáli holiday house, near Stokkseyri (IS)

1962–65   O. Johnson and Kaaber coffee factory, Tunguháls, Reykjavík (IS)

1967   Agricultural Bank of Iceland, Hlemmur, Reykjavík (IS)

1973–84   Hólabrekkuskóli elementary school, Sudurhólar, Reykjavík (IS)

1976   Central bus station, Hlemmur, Reykjavík (IS)

1986   Holiday Inn Hotel, Sigtún, Reykjavík (IS)

AFTER GRADUATING from the Commercial College of Iceland in 1943, Gunnar Hansson was determined to study architecture. Since no training was offered in that discipline in Iceland, and Europe was off limits due to the Second World War, he decided to go to America. After three semesters of architectural studies at Berkeley University in California, Hansson returned to Iceland in 1945 to work in the office of Reykjavík's municipal architect, Einar Sveinsson. From 1946 to 1947 he worked in an architect's office in Copenhagen, and in 1950 moved to Trondheim, Norway, resuming his architectural studies at the Norwegian University of Technology (NTH) until 1953. Parallel to his studies, Hansson was engaged 1951–54 in the design of his first major commission, the *Morgunbladid* newspaper office building, located at Adalstraeti 6 in Reykjavík. From 1953 to 1958, Hansson worked for the City of Reykjavík, both with the municipal architect and in the Planning Department. In 1958, he opened his own architectural practice, which he directed for over 30 years, until his death in 1989 (Reykjavík). During that time he designed many prominent buildings in Reykjavík.

In 1946 Gunnar Hansson married journalist Hulda Valtysdóttir, whose father was the chief editor of the national newspaper *Morgunbladid*, and whose mother was a well-known painter. The family lived at Laufásvegur 69, in a house designed in 1928 by the architect Sigurdur Gudmundsson and influenced by 1920s Nordic Classicism. A few years later Gudmundsson added a painting studio at the back of the Laufásvegur house, creating a south-facing courtlike space in the garden. It became the family's favourite spot during warm summer days and provided Hansson with inspiration for his new home.

One of Gunnar Hansson's commissions during his time at Reykjavík's Planning Department was the district plan for Reykjavík's Heimar suburb,

drawn up between 1955 and 1956 in collaboration with Planning Director Gunnar H. Ólafsson. It was the first residential district in Reykjavík planned in the light of modern theories of urbanism. For the first time, high-rise apartment buildings became a prominent feature in the city skyline. Another new type of housing was terraced houses with access from pedestrian walkways. One of the few plots set aside for single-family houses was allocated to the Hanssons late 1956. In March 1957, Hansson's plans for the new house, located at Sólheimar 5 and realised in 1959, were complete.

Unlike his next-door neighbours, Hansson chose to adapt the form of his home to the natural slope of the site, rather than excavate the ground to suit a predetermined house type. In principle, the building is L-shaped on split levels. The living room is raised half a level above the middle platform, which consists of bedrooms, family room, kitchen, dining room and service spaces. The living room, partially elevated from the ground on pillars, forms one side of a semi-enclosed south-facing garden space, which is directly connected with the family room by a large sliding door. Underneath the living-room wing is an open carport and the main entrance to the house. The open carport was an unusual feature in an Icelandic house, since most suburban houses had a built-in garage, disconnected from the main entrance.

The strength of Hansson's design is evident in the way the house relates to the site and in the quality of the spaces created with the disposition of the different functions. The relationship of approach, carport and entry has strong similarities to Le Corbusier's famous driveway at Villa Savoye. The garden court, half a level above, is partially enclosed and sheltered from cold northerly winds by the two wings of the house, rem-

GARDEN COURT

STREET VIEW

STAIRCASE LEADING TO THE LIVING ROOM (ABOVE)

PLAN OF THE UPPER FLOOR

KITCHEN

DINING ROOM

HALL

iniscent of the 'outdoor rooms' commonly found in the work of Alvar Aalto. The elevated living room has a large sliding door, which opens onto a balcony facing the street. On the side wall next to it is a square window facing west, framing a view of the ocean and Snaefellsjokull Glacier on the distant horizon.

Like most houses in Iceland at that time, the Hanssons' house at Sólheimar is built of reinforced concrete. The exterior walls were cast in situ with the insulation on the inside, cemented and painted on the outside. The original drawings show the base walls next to the entrance covered with slabs of natural stone, which in the actual house were painted in a dark blue colour. The roof construction is made of wood, clad externally with corrugated metal and internally with panels of pine. The house's central heating system was connected to a boiler in the basement until the street was connected to Reykjavík's geothermal heating system.

The plan of Hansson's house included a studio room on the ground floor, next to the entrance. This room was originally intended to be his architectural office, but was only used as such for about one year. Hansson preferred to work in a downtown office, and the room on the ground floor became his private study. The house at Sólheimar was a good place to live for Gunnar, Hulda and their three daughters. It still belongs to the family and has been perfectly maintained from the beginning.

Several of Hansson's buildings may be regarded as great works of their period in Iceland: the terraced houses at Hvassaleiti 101–113 in Reykjavík, the Church of the Independent Parish in Reykjavík, the O. Johnson and Kaaber coffee factory in Reykjavík, the office building of the Agricultural Bank at Hlemmur in Reykjavík, Ísólfsskáli (the summer house of composer Páll Ísólfsson, near Stokkseyri), and last but not least his own house at Sólheimar 5. In Hansson's buildings from the 1950s, the formal vocabulary of the architecture has a lot in common with the work of the other modern architects of the time, in particular Sigvaldi Thordarson, Skarphédinn Jóhannsson and Gudmundur Kr. Kristinsson. This can be seen in many aspects, such as the simplicity of form, clear-cut windows and the articulation of walls into clearly defined surfaces, rendered in either contrasting primary colours or natural materials with different textures. This tendency within 20th-century Icelandic architecture can be referred to as the 'purist' period of the 1950s. There is an obvious connection between the abstract geometric paintings of Icelandic painters at that time and the works of the modern architects. In this regard, the Sólheimar house is a product of a local school of thought based on the interpretation of the universal language of modern architecture. The masterful application of these ideas to solve a particular project on a specific site is the main strength of Hansson's design. PÉTUR ÁRMANNSSON

BIBLIOGRAPHY:
1989   Obituaries for Gunnar Hansson, in *Morgunbladid*, 17 January
1997   Ármannsson P. H., *A City District is Born*, Reykjavik Art Museum
1998   Ármannsson P. H., 'Purism in 1950s architecture', in *Dream of Pure Form, Icelandic Abstract Art 1950–1960*, National Gallery of Iceland
2000   *A Guide to Icelandic Architecture*, The Association of Icelandic Architects, Reykjavík, pp. 104, 113 and 117
2001   *Interview with Gunnar Hansson* conducted by Pétur H. Ármannsson with Hulda Valtysdóttir and Helga Gunnarsdóttir, Reykjavík

Clemens Holzmeister
1886–1983

**1929–30, NEW CONSTRUCTION
HAHNENKAMM 20, KITZBÜHEL (A)**

MAIN WORKS AND PROJECTS

1913–14	School, Marbach an der Donau, Niederösterreich (A)
1921–23	Crematorium of Vienna (A)
1927–28	Eichmann country house on Lake Attersee (A), with Max Fellerer
1927–32	First construction phase of Turkish War Ministry, and other government buildings in Ankara (TR)
1931–32	Atatürk Palace, Ankara (TR), with Max Fellerer
1938–61	Parliament building, Ankara (TR)
1956–60	New Festspielhaus, Salzburg (A)
1962	Own house at Brunnhausgasse 14a, Nonntal, Salzburg (A)
1966–71	Elementary School, Grafstein (A)
1978–83	Extension to the Branch Church St. Nikolaus, Lamprechtshausen-Holzhausen (A)

CLEMENS HOLZMEISTER was born on 27 March 1886 in Fulpmes, in the Stubai valley (near Innsbruck), Tyrol, Austria, the son of Johann Holzmeister and his second wife, Maria Kirchstätter. His father, who was originally from the same Tyrolean valley, had emigrated from Austria to Brazil, where between 1859 and 1876 he had made a fortune in the import and export business. But, following domestic misfortunes, he had returned to Fulpmes in the Stubaital, where he had remarried, having four children, including Clemens, by Maria Kirchstätter. Not wanting to have his sons liable for military service later in life, Johann Holzmeister registered these children as Brazilian citizens.

Clemens Holzmeister went to elementary and secondary school in Innsbruck, and then, between 1906 and 1913, studied architecture at the Technical University in Vienna. From 1911 he was the head of a building advice centre of the association Deutsche Heimat in Vienna, and between 1913 and 1919 he was an assistant professor back at his Alma Mater, the Technical University in Vienna, where he gained a doctorate in 1919 for a thesis in the history of architecture on the Cistercian diocese of Stams. In the same year Holzmeister moved from Vienna to Innsbruck, where he lived until 1924. In Innsbruck he began both to teach at the Staatsgewerbeschule (trade school) and to work as a freelance architect, opening a practice in the town. In the early 1920s he generated commissions in North and East Tyrol (Austria), in South Tyrol (Italy), in Austria's Vorarlberg and in Vienna. Subsequently, in the late 1920s and during the 1930s, he was awarded projects in Turkey, Germany, Italy, Yugoslavia and the United Kingdom.

In 1924 Holzmeister was appointed to a chair at the Academy of Fine Arts in Vienna, which he held until 1938, directing at the Academy an architecture masterclass. As a result of the appointment he moved his practice from Innsbruck to Vienna. During this professorship in Vienna, Holzmeister also held 1928–33 a second chair at the Academy of Art in Düsseldorf. For a while he commuted between the two cities, and during his absences from Vienna his teaching was covered by his assistant, Max Fellerer, who was also a friend and partner. In collaboration with Max Fellerer, Holzmeister completed some important projects, including the Eichmann country house on Austria's Lake Attersee (1927–28) and Atatürk Palace in Ankara, Turkey (1931–32). In 1938, the year of Hitler's annexation of Austria, the architect went into exile in Turkey, where he held a chair at the Technical University in Istanbul from 1940 to 1949, after which he returned to Vienna to lead once more a masterclass at the Academy of Fine Arts between 1949 and 1961. In the early 1960s Holzmeister moved to Salzburg, where he built a second private house for himself, which was not far away from his first private house at Hahnenkamm, in the Kitzbühel Alps, finished back in 1930. The architecture office that had followed him from Innsbruck to Vienna now moved with him to Salzburg.

If this was how things developed in Holzmeister's life on the academic and professional front, on the domestic and private front they unfolded as follows. In 1913, the year of his graduation from the Technical University in Vienna, he married Judith Bridarolli, who came from Innsbruck and was acquainted with Gio Ponti. At the Bridarolli family home in Innsbruck, Holzmeister met Luis Trenker, who later, in the early 1920s, became his partner in his Innsbruck architectural practice as well as a lifelong friend. Clemens and Judith had two children, a son Guido, who was born in Vienna in 1914, and a daughter Judith, who was born in

THE SOUTH-EAST CORNER WITH TERRACE

THE SOUTH-WEST CORNER

"THE LORD'S PARLOUR"

HOLZMEISTER'S STUDENTS FROM THE ACADEMY

Innsbruck in 1920. In 1932, at his Hahnenkamm mountain house, Holz-meister met the photographer Gunda Lexer, who was to become his second wife, and with whom he had another daughter, Barbara, who was born in Athens in 1939. Although Holzmeister separated from Judith and remarried Gunda, he always maintained a good relationship with both Judith and his first family.

During his life Holzmeister was closely involved with the Catholic Church in both Austria and the Rhineland, and in 1933 he was President of the Allgemeiner Deutscher Katholikentag (General Conference of Ger-man-Speaking Catholics) in Vienna. Over the years he made several study trips and also gave numerous lectures. As an architect he was particu-larly impressed by modern Scandinavian design. In 1936 he said: "I have always made an effort to keep abreast of current innovations, and to keep up to date, but I have also been concerned to defend valuable trad-itional architectural art against the extreme excesses of the modern movement." Clemens Holzmeister died on 12 June 1983 in Salzburg.

Clemens Holzmeister built two private homes for himself. The second, completed in 1962, was at Brunnhausgasse 14a, Nonntal, Salzburg. Situ-ated beneath Salzburg's 'Festung' or fortress, it was the house in which the architect spent the last 20 years of his life, from 1962 to 1983. The first, the one that concerns us here, was a new construction, designed and realised some 30 years earlier (1929–30). This was Holzmeister's so-called Berghaus or 'House in the Mountains', located at Hahnenkamm 20 in Kitzbühel, not so far away from Salzburg. Today this home, which perhaps has more the nature of a holiday house, remains in its original condition and is still used by the Holzmeister family.

Although the house is located very high up (at 1800 m) on the Hahnenkamm mountain, where it is exposed to the storms and snow of alpine weather, it is not obscure, enjoying good connections with the outside world. The refuge is easily reachable first by the international express trains that stop in Kitzbühel and then by the Hahnenkamm funicular railway, which was inaugurated in 1928, an arrangement well suited to a busy professor and architect who had many national and international commitments.

Holzmeister's Berghaus was at its busiest in the 1930s, up to the architect's emigration to Turkey in 1938. Christmas was celebrated there for the first time in 1930, and in the following years the House in the Mountains saw much conviviality, with relatives and friends often coming to stay. For a while it was the centre of Holzmeister's socialising, although the architect, who was an extremely communicative and mobile person, also liked to reflect and work in peace there. Among the guests were artists, writers and politicians, some of whom left their mark in the guest book in the form of drawings and poems. Visitors included Holzmeister's friend and collaborator Max Fellerer, the architect Herbert Eichholzer, the painter Alfons Walde, the ceramic artist Gudrun Baudisch, the Swiss sculptor Walter Rupp, and the Austrian Minister of Foreign Affairs Guido Schmid. During the Nazi period the house was empty.

In 1937 the architect wrote of his Hahnenkamm home that, because it was sited at such a high altitude and was so exposed to the weather, he built it bearing in mind key factors such as sun, snow, wind, type of construction and construction materials. "Masonry was used sparingly due to high costs, and the basement – not really habitable owing to snowdrifts – was retracted, creating a projection of the wooden house. This resulted in a strange, most agreeable phenomenon. The retracted basement caused the wind to blow around the house, but because of this the snow never reached it, but instead created an almost circular snow cornice." Seen from the west, the house resembles a tower. Much-published photographs, taken by Julius Scherb in the 1930s, show a striking view from the Berghaus, which today, however, is compromised by a mountain forest that has meanwhile grown up.

From the outset the house was fitted with all modern conveniences. It had two bathrooms, electricity, a telephone line, and an intelligent heating system with a stove situated at the centre of the house, in the parlour. For Holzmeister, the Tyrolean farmhouse parlour represented the very essence of homeliness, although his wife Judith did not quite see things this way. She had a say in the design of the House in the Mountains, insisting that the kitchen be separated from the living room and that her room on the first floor should be elegantly fitted out.

Holzmeister's Berghaus is brilliant in conception, with a unique economy of space, a fascinating variable sequence of rooms that are precisely defined in function yet flexible in use, and climatic zoning, which runs from the heatable living room via the covered veranda to the sun-oriented terrace. The veranda, which has large windows that can be lowered, was used by the architect as a working area. The 37-m²-large living area can be divided up into three smaller areas or reconnected into one single space by means of sliding walls. The house's bedrooms can sleep five people. Additional guests are put up in the living area and/or attic.

Some of the interior fixtures of the Hahnenkamm house – the wooden ceiling and wall lining with windows and fitted furniture – had already been produced by a Viennese carpenter in 1929, prior to the building's actual construction. They were even shown at the Christmas exhibition of the Künstlerhaus in Vienna under the title of 'Ski House for the Hahnenkamm'. The Berghaus was, therefore, featured even before it was built, a sign perhaps of the importance that was attached to the project. Today the considerable artistic, historical and cultural value of Holzmeister's Berghaus is confirmed by the fact that it has been listed, with its original interior, since 1994. The Austrian Federal Authority for the Preservation of Historic Monuments draws the following conclusion: "Although formally the building makes no historical references, the style of construction is related to landscape and tradition (retracted concrete socle, wooden shingling). From a historical point of view, the house represents a milestone in modern Alpine architecture, where functional room planning and proximity to nature are combined with modified elements of the local building tradition."

GEORG RIGELE

PLAN OF THE GROUND FLOOR

BIBLIOGRAPHY:

1932   Vetter H. A. (ed.), *Kleine Einfamilienhäuser mit 50 bis 100 Quadratmeter Wohnfläche*, Vienna, pp. 42–45

1976   Holzmeister C., *Clemens Holzmeister: Architekt in der Zeitenwende. Selbstbiographie*, Salzburg

1980   Achleitner F., *Österreichische Architektur im 20. Jahrhundert*, vol. 1, Salzburg/Vienna, p. 314,

1982   *Clemens Holzmeister*, exhibition catalogue with contributions by F. Achleitner, W. Holzbauer and H. Muck, Academy of Fine Arts, Vienna

2000   Rigele G. and Loewit G. (eds.), *Clemens Holzmeister*, Innsbruck

Victor Horta
1861 – 1947

**1898, NEW CONSTRUCTION, CONVERTED TO THE HORTA MUSEUM
RUE AMÉRICAINE 23 – 25, BRUSSELS (B)**

MAIN WORKS AND PROJECTS

1893	Maison Tassel, 6 rue Paul-Emile Janson, Brussels (B)	**1901**	'A l'Innovation' Department Store, rue Neuve, Brussels (B)
1894	Hôtel Solvay, 1894, 224 avenue Louise, Brussels (B)	**1903 – 28**	Musée des Beaux-Arts, Tournai (B)
1895	Maison du Peuple, place Emile Vandervelde, Brussels (B)	**1906 – 23**	Hôpital Brugmann, place Van Gehuchten, Jette, Brussels (B)
	Hôtel Van Eetvelde (now FIGAZ), 4 avenue Palmerston, Brussels (B)	**1919 – 28**	Palais des Beaux-Arts, rue Ravenstein, Brussels (B
1899	Hôtel Aubecq, 520 avenue Louise, Brussels (B)		

VICTOR HORTA was the son of a Ghent cobbler. Having studied architectural drawing at the Fine Arts Academy of his native city, he worked for a Parisian decorator (1878 – 80) before continuing his studies at the Académie des Beaux–Arts in Brussels (1881 – 84). He turned Free-mason in 1881, becoming a member of the 'Philanthropic Friends', a lodge associated with the progressive intelligentsia. Horta's devotion to the Left was reflected in his teaching career: he gave courses at the Maison du Peuple (Art Section) and in 1893 took up a Professorship at Brussels' Université Libre. It was in this milieu that he met his first clients, the engineers Eugène Autrique and Emile Tassel; in 1893, they commissioned a private house for themselves. The Hôtel Tassel marks a clear break with the Eclectic style: Horta openly used industrial materials, and prioritised fluidity of movement, multiplication of internal perspectives and the circulation of light. The cohesion of architecture and decoration was effected by an ornamental language based on arabesques.

During the last decade of the 19th century, Horta achieved a style that could accommodate both the luxury and refinement required by the industrial bourgeoisie and the aesthetic aspirations of the Belgian Parti Ouvrier (Workers' Party). The Party was antagonistic to tradition in all areas, not least architecture, and in 1895 it commissioned the Maison du Peuple (House of the People). Two years later, Horta's talent as interior designer was revealed to the wider public when he exhibited a collection of furniture at the Salon de la Libre Esthétique. Designed for the Hôtel Solvay and Hôtel Van Eetvelde, it immediately elicited an extensive article in the French journal *Art et Décoration*. Note that, throughout his very fertile 'Art nouveau' period, Horta showed a reluctance to publish his own work in marked contrast with the attitude of contemporaries such as Hector Guimard or Henry van de Velde. His career is therefore inadequately documented. Moreover, he himself burnt almost his entire archives in 1939 and 1945. By the turn of the century, managers of major

Belgian department stores (L'Innovation, les Galeries Anspach) were beginning to compete for his services. His style was now fashionable and had lost its ideological overtones. A period of official acknowledgement followed, marked by commissions for the Musée des Beaux-Arts in Tournai, the Brugmann Hospital and Brussels Central Station. In 1911, Horta resigned from the Université Libre, and in 1912 he accepted a Professorship at the Académie des Beaux-Arts in Brussels, where he envisaged an overhaul of the teaching system. But in 1915, having made a clandestine trip to London to attend a conference, he found he could not return to Belgium. As a result, he spent the next four years in the United States, where earned his living by lecture tours. On his return to Belgium, he set about designing the Brussels Palais des Beaux-Arts. The building's classicizing Art Deco style is unspectacular, but the quality of the distribution and interconnected spaces is exceptional. Horta had hoped that his Palais des Beaux-Arts and Central Station were the first stages in a large-scale development plan for central Brussels, and looked forward to this commission. It never came. His disappointment is recorded in the *Memoirs* that he began in 1939.

Horta built his house and studio at what he considered the culminating point of his career: "That was the high watermark of my happiness," (*Memoirs*). After five years of intense activity, he purchased two plots of land in the Saint-Gilles *commune*, near that most fashionable of Brussels arteries, the avenue Louise. There he built four large private houses. He chose to respect the existing layout in his design, which comprised different facades for house and studio; behind the scene, he 'bent' the party wall in order to allow greater space for the main stairwell.

His main goal in this rather narrow site (6.5 metres) was to create an impression of space for the receptions that he so enjoyed giving. The *étage-noble* originally consisted of a music room looking onto the street

OOF GLASSWORK ABOVE THE STAIRS

STREET VIEW

STAIRS WITH RIBBED HEATING (LEFT)

PAGES 178–179: THE HALL

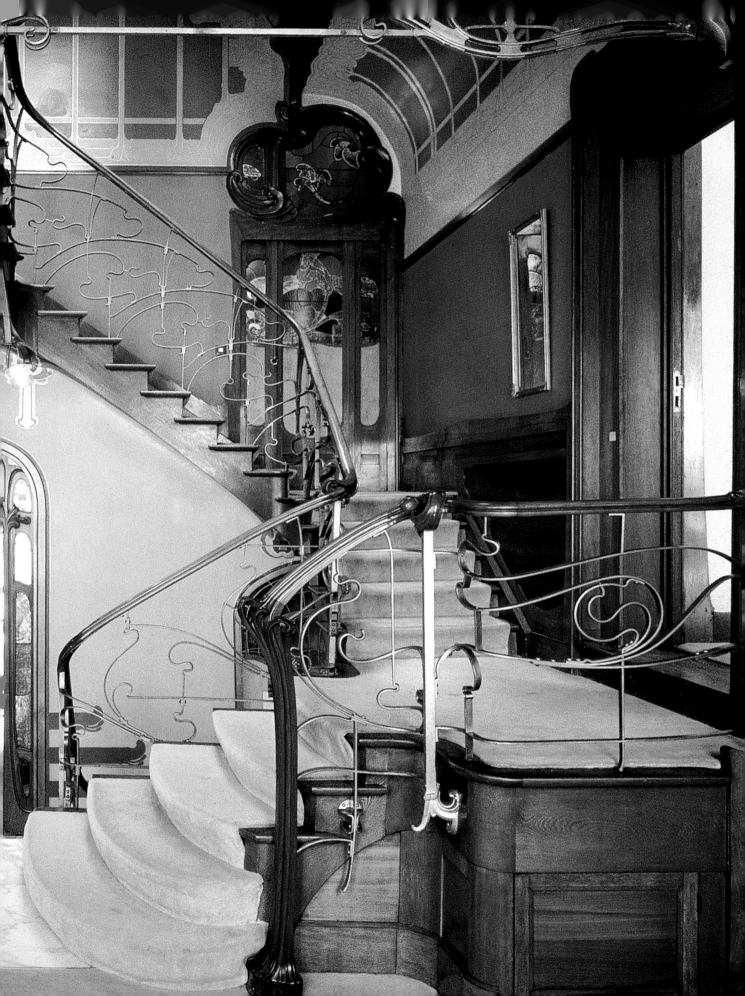

DINING ROOM

and a dining room flanked by an office on the garden side. At this level, the stairwell, surmounted by a lantern, occupies half the width of the house, and its steps could become a tier of seats for musical evenings. At the first landing, a door opens onto the first floor of the studio, where Horta's working life was spent. The front room, marked out on the façade by elegant wrought-iron work and a subtle division of bays and sashes, also served as a salon and smoking room.

The three independent stairwells of the house and studio enabled Horta to keep his professional, social and private life apart. The first floor of the house was given over to the family living room, the main bedroom and a bathroom, the second to a guest room (on the street side) and to his daughter's room overlooking the garden.

Soon afterwards, in 1906, Horta reshaped his house, extending it by one bay on the garden side. His main concern was probably to create a nicer room for his daughter, who had found her parents' acrimonious divorce very painful. Simone gained a broad south-facing terrace with a winter garden. In 1908, Horta extended the basement sculpture studio by digging up the garden, covering the new space with a double-pitched roof pierced by a large lantern and several skylights; the latter stand sixty centimetres above ground-level. Three years later, he bought a car, and converted the ground-floor office (street-side) into a garage. This involved removing the large sash-window shared between basement and ground-floor, along with the grille and the columns holding it. They were restored by Barbara van der Wee in 1993. In 1919, when he returned from the States, Horta decided to sell his property on rue Américaine. He signalled

his social ascension by moving onto the avenue Louise, to a block that he himself converted. The rue Américaine house and studio led a separate existence till 1971, when the Commune de Saint-Gilles bought the studio. The house had been bought in 1963, when it was the first Brussels Art Nouveau building to be classified a historic monument. Designated as the Horta Museum, the double building was restored and converted by Jean Delhaye, one of Horta's former collaborators. It opened to the public in 1969.

A second restoration was undertaken in 1992 by architect Barbara van der Wee. These works revealed the use Horta had made of the party wall in lighting the house from the studio side (the house was deeper than the studio). Windows were pierced in the party wall at every level, a practice normally forbidden by planning regulations and only authorised in this case because Horta was sole proprietor of both buildings. Light therefore enters in equal parts from façade, party wall and roof, a feat of great originality in the Brussels context.

Another surprise in the house is the daring choice of white-enamelled brick in the dining room, which consequently resembles the interior of a shell; this impression is enhanced by the vaulted roof. Within this white-wrapped space, Horta makes play with contrasting materials: rich and poor, warm and cool (gilded laminated iron, gilded tin, copper, oak, American ash, Italian marble, American glass, and mirrors). The addition of Pierre Braecke's plaster low-reliefs makes the room into a work of 'total' art. The bare white walls originally reflected the play of light and shade from the garden, but this effect was lost when the extra bay was

DETAIL OF THE BANISTER

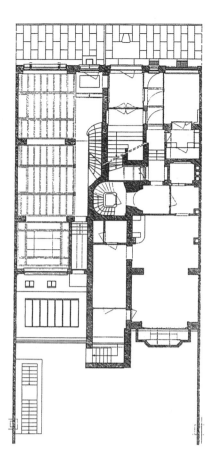

PLAN OF THE GROUND FLOOR

CROSS-SECTION

built to accommodate a new salon. Not that the general impression was one of austerity: Horta, like many of his contemporaries, was an avid collector of Chinese and Japanese antiques, and these were displayed throughout the house.

Horta's studio-house testified to his artistic, professional and social success. But it was also an intimate witness of his private life. The coincidence of his divorce with the death of Art Nouveau made sale of the property inevitable.

FRANÇOISE AUBRY

BIBLIOGRAPHY:
1970   Borsi F. and Portoghesi P., *Victor Horta*, Brussels
1972   Hoppenbrouwers A., Jos Vandenbreeden J., Somers B., *Het Hortamuseum*,
       in *Sint-Lukaskahiers*, pp. 74–84
1976   Portoghesi P., Victor Horta. *Hôtel Van Eetvelde. Bruxelles, Belgium, 1894–1901.*
       Maison et atelier Horta. Bruxelles, 1898–1900, in *Global Architecture*, no. 42 (Tokyo)
1990   Dierkensy-Aubry F., *Musée Horta. Bruxelles Saint-Gilles*, Brussels
2001   Aubry F., *Le Musée Horta, Saint-Gilles, Bruxelles*, Ghent, Amsterdam

Francine Houben
*1955

1990 – 91, NEW CONSTRUCTION, DESIGNED AND BUILT BY MECANOO,
STILL INHABITED BY THE ARCHITECT
KRALINGSE PLASLAAN, ROTTERDAM (NL)

MAIN WORKS AND PROJECTS BY MECANOO

1984 – 87	Residence, Rotterdam-Bospolder (NL)
1989 – 91	Boompjes Pavillon, Rotterdam (NL)
1993 – 95	Isala College, Silvolde (NL)
1993 – 98	Library for the Technical University in Delft (NL)
1995 – 2000	Entrance building for the Dutch open air exhibition Arnheim (NL)
1998 – 2000	De Landjes Residence, Nieuw Terbregge, Rotterdam (NL)
1999 – 2000	Cultural Centre Canadaplein, Alkmaar (NL)
	Residence, Hilversum, (NL)
2000 – 01	Chapel of St Mary of the Angels, Rotterdam (NL)
2001 – 03	The Toneelschuur theatre and concert building, Haarlem (NL)

AFTER GRADUATING from the Technical Academy in Delft, Francine Houben (born 1955) founded the group Mecanoo, together with her colleagues Chris de Weijer, Erick van Egeraat und Henk Döll (all born in 1956). The name Mecanoo is suggestive of a well-known toy in Holland: a metal erector set. From its start in Delft during the height of architectural Postmodernism, the group developed a highly individual profile with its anti-cyclical references to the concepts and formal language of Modernism, above all Dutch Modernism. Mecanoo mainly worked on social housing projects in the 1980s where the challenge to achieve maximum stylistic quality with minimum financial means matched their architectural-aesthetic orientation. In their earlier work, the link to Modernism is expressed in a relaxed manner, neither dogmatic nor nostalgic but rather with pragmatic overtones. The work does not lose sight of the extensive aesthetic possibilities developed by the "Neues Bauen" movement, yet also succeeds in forging new directions. These progressive developments affect not only construction materials and techniques, but also the social arena, which is manifested through changed ways of thinking and lifestyles. The private family residence that Houben and van Egeraat built for themselves and their children exceptionally exemplifies this casual and creative contact with the Modernist vocabulary.

Since the 1990s, public and large-scale buildings have become an essential part of these architects' work. This is true for the remaining three partners of Mecanoo as well as for van Egeraat, who founded his own successful Rotterdam office, Erick van Egeraat Architects (EEA), in 1995. Not least due to social and economic shifts (for instance, the increased competition between cities for tourists and investors), the recent projects of both offices demonstrate a tendency towards spectacular effects. This is evident, for example, in the organic shapes used by Mecanoo for their Arnheim open-air museum and by EEA for the ING bank extension in Budapest. Van Egeraat has described this style as "modern baroque".

Von Houben's and van Egeraat's residence, completed in 1991, lies northeast of the centre of Rotterdam, not far from the Kralingse Plas, an artificial lake created in the 1920s. On the west side, the structure is linked to an existing terraced house complex separated only by a narrow path. On the east side, future buildings can also be erected close to the house. The north side offers a panoramic view of the lake, while a small East Asian-inspired garden ending in a little pond borders the south side. The interior rooms are designed based on the characteristic qualities of the site – the panoramic lake view and the intimate garden. In order to re-stage this panoramic view in the interior, the main living area is situated on the first floor which has the highest ceiling. From the street side, the house's entrance is behind a vertical wooden wall that stands freely in front of the extensive glass facade of the house. The wall reduces the contrast to the historical neighboring house and introduces a play of layers typical for the entire house. Through minimal projections and overlays, the façade becomes a thrilling site for staging the exchange between

EATING AREA

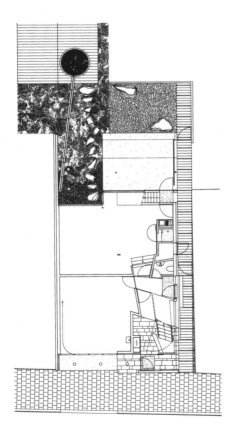

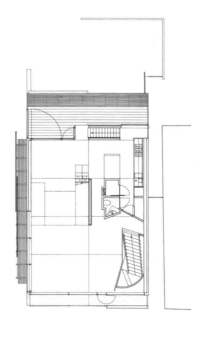

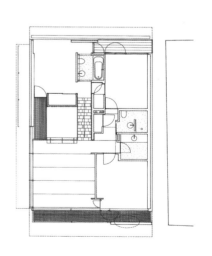

PLAN OF THE GROUND FLOOR

PLAN OF THE FIRST FLOOR

PLAN OF THE SECOND FLOOR

VIEW INTO THE KITCHEN

VIEW OF THE GARDEN FROM THE STUDIO

interior and exterior. On the main floor, which is reached from the entrance by a slightly angled staircase, one's view is directed towards the centre of the room. The central element is a wood-covered wall that divides the large space into a kitchen (which can be further separated), eating area and living room. On the eating area side of the wall, an ornately constructed staircase positioned in the opposite direction of the entrance staircase leads to the upper-most floor containing three bedrooms and the library. The library is visually linked to the main living room by a recess in the floor. On the northeast corner, the glass front on the street side wraps around almost half of the building so that the living area and library appear as the transparent centre of the house. In order to filter the light streaming in from the sides, Mecanoo utilizes a curtain made of bamboo on the exterior of the house and adjusted by a motor-driven chain. The curtain fundamentally defines the lighting quality of the interior space; through the irregularity of its material it produces a pleasant contrast to the sharp-edged, exacting qualities of the rest of the house.

In other details, Mecanoo uses clever accents or breaks the rational by playful aspects: for instance, the oval opening in the roof projection that emphasizes the free standing element of the wooden wall at the entrance, or the angled wall in the garden front. This wall copies the contour of the staircase that leads from the eating area to a studio below. The studio provides direct access to the terrace and garden and can also be accessed from the small path in between the buildings, the entrance or the garage positioned on the street side. This variety of access possibilities applies to the rest of the main rooms in the house as well. Even the

LIBRARY ON THE UPPER FLOOR

EXPLODED VIEW

children's rooms have two doors. Thus, the inhabitants can experience numerous spatial short cuts and paths. With its superior combination of pragmatism, flexibility and surprising detail, the house can be compared to Gerrit Rietveld's Schröder House in Utrecht, an icon of Modernist architecture whose influence reaches far beyond the Netherlands.

EBERHARD SYRING

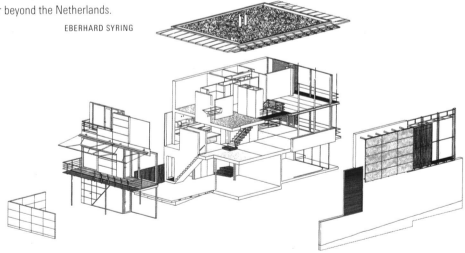

BIBLIOGRAPHY:
1985   Meyhöfer D., *Contemporary European Architects*, Vol. II, Cologne
1992   Confurius G., 'Clair-Obscur. Wohnhaus Mecanoo in Rotterdam', in *Bauwelt* 23 / 1992, pp. 1266–1275
1997   Buch J., *Ein Jahrhundert niederländische Architektur 1880–1990*, Munich
1999   Jodidio Ph., *Building a New Millennium. Bauen im neuen Jahrtausend*, Cologne
2000   Ibelings H. (ed.), *Die gebaute Landschaft. Zeitgenössische Architektur, Landschaftsarchitektur und Städtebau in den Niederlanden*, Munich

Arne Emil Jacobsen
1901–1971

1946 – 51, NEW CONSTRUCTION, NOW ALTERED
STRANDVEJEN 413, SØHOLM I, KLAMPENBORG (DK)

MAIN WORKS AND PROJECTS

1929	Model of Fremtidens Hus (House of the Future) for an exhibition in Copenhagen (DK), with Flemming Lassen
	Own home, Gotfred Rodesvej 2, Charlottenlund (DK)
1934	Bellavista, Klampenborg (DK)
1935	Bellevue Theatre, Klampenborg (DK)
1937 – 38	A. Stellings building, Gammel Torv, Copenhagen (DK)
1939	Own summer house, Gudminderup Lyng, Sejrø Bay (DK)
1940 – 42	Århus City Hall (DK), with Erik Møller

1946 – 51	Søholm I (small housing development), Klampenborg (DK)
1953 – 55	Søholm 2 (small housing development), Klampenborg (DK)
1959	SAS Royal Hotel, Vesterbro, Copenhagen (DK)
1961 – 69	Head office of the Hamburg Electricity Supply Company, Hamburg (D), with Otto Weitling
1963	St Catherine's College, Oxford (GB)
1964	Project for Belvedere, Herrenhausen, Hanover (D)

ARNE JACOBSEN was born in Copenhagen, the son of Johan Jacobsen, a wholesaler, and Pouline Salmonsen. He went to boarding school in Nærum, where he met the future architects Mogens Lassen and Hans Bretton-Meyer. Jacobsen soon showed great aptitude for painting and drawing, and for many years he wanted to become a painter. However, Mogens Lassen convinced him to become an architect instead – a happy circumstance, as Jacobsen went on to become one of the 20th century's greatest architects.

The elements and chronology of Jacobsen's career are typical of those of 20th-century Danish architects. Having passed the final exams of Copenhagen's Institute of Technology in 1924, he enrolled in the Royal Danish Academy of Fine Arts, also in Copenhagen, to study architecture under Kay Fisker, Ivar Bentsen and Kaj Gottlob. During his education at the Institute, he spent his holidays doing practical training as a bricklayer's apprentice, while at the Academy he was very successful owing to his abilities in drawing, already sitting his leaving examination in 1927. In 1928 Jacobsen was awarded the Minor Gold Medal by the Royal Danish Academy of Fine Arts for a National Museum project.

Between 1927 and 1929 Jacobsen was employed by Poul Holsøe, city architect for Copenhagen, and in 1929 he opened his own studio. In 1955 he became a Fellow of the Royal Academy, and in 1956 he was appointed professor at the School of Architecture of the Royal Danish Academy of Fine Arts, where he worked until 1965. He received many awards, for example the Grand Prix Internationale d'Architecture et d'Art (1960) and the Prins Eugen Medal (1962), and adjudicated at several exhibitions in Denmark and around the world.

In 1929, in collaboration with Mogens Lassen's brother, the architect Flemming Lassen, Jacobsen made a model for the Fremtidens Hus

(House of the Future) for an exhibition in Copenhagen. The house was his first modernist manifesto, built to match the needs of the modern population, who preferred a healthy outdoor life with cars, boats and helicopters to fulfil their individual transport and communication needs. The rooms in the circular house were positioned in such a way as to catch the sun throughout the day, starting with an eastern bedroom, and ending with a western dining room. Domestic appliances took over the hard work of the housewife, leaving her free to sunbathe on the roof!

Jacobsen was a great designer as well as an architect. While in Sweden during the Second World War, he designed tapestries in collaboration with his wife Jonna Jacobsen, inspired by his interest in plants and drawing. His furniture, designed individually or as part of an overall interior decoration scheme that included cutlery, chairs, etc., is known all over the world. The idea of the *Gesamtkunstwerk* or total work of art is altogether characteristic of Jacobsen's work both as an architect and as a designer. He attended not just to the overall impression and functionality of a building, but also to the smallest details of the projects in which he was involved.

From the mid-1940s, Jacobsen constructed two groups of semi-detached houses, called Søholm I and II, in Klampenborg north of Copenhagen. The homes were built on a site to the south of another project of his, the Bellavista buildings at Bellevue, which he had built 1932 – 34. The Søholm houses, which were all constructed in yellow brick and had sloped non-symmetrical roofs made of asbestos cement, are of a chain and terrace type. The problems created by the seaside view, which is to the east, while the buildings face south-east, were solved by a displacement of the houses, allowing all of them to overlook the Sound. Their architectural

STREET VIEW

THE FIREPLACE IN THE LIVING ROOM

VIEW FROM THE GARDEN

THE LIVING ROOM ON THE FIRST FLOOR
THE DINING ROOM ON THE GROUND FLOOR

expression was seen as a 'relaxed Modernism', and Søholm I (1946–51) in particular won international acclaim. Jacobsen chose to live in the last of the five houses, at the south-eastern end, towards the road and the Sound. Linked to the main house, an extra building was erected, which contained the architect's studio, a meeting room, and a work room. The gardens are closely related to the houses, and the terraces are protected from both the wind and the eyes of the neighbours.

The garden of Jacobsen's house was a little bigger (300 m²) than the other gardens, and was to play an important role in the architect's life as part of his great interest in plants. He grew more than 300 different species in his garden, and created a spacious arrangement by cutting the hedges at different heights. The species were mainly chosen for their colour, form and structure, as well as for the way they harmonised with the surrounding species.

The buildings of Søholm I are two storeys high and were erected during a period of restrictions, when only 110 m² was allowed per house. Jacobsen managed to plan the houses in such a way that they seemed much bigger than this. He did so by creating spatial interaction both between the outside and the inside, and between the rooms themselves. At ground level the houses contain a bedroom, three smaller rooms, and a dining room directly connected to the outdoor terrace and to the first-floor living room. The terrace can be included in the dining room if wished, as the width of the dining room towards the terrace is the same as the

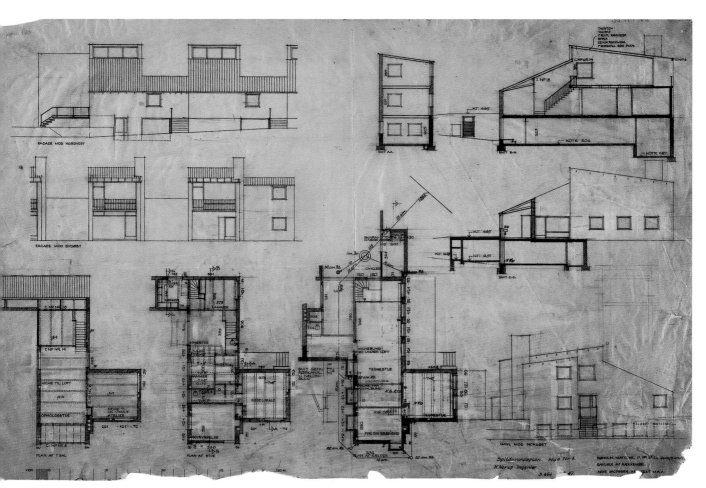

PLANS, SECTIONS AND ELEVATIONS

width of the terrace towards the garden. In this way the windows and the wall can easily be moved. The living room he located on the first floor partly because of the splendid view to the Sound, and partly because the room then ceases to be a place of passage, as is normally the case. The stairway connecting the ground floor and the first floor is illuminated by a row of windows pointing south-west just below the top point of the sloping roof. The open space created by the free connection between the two floors and the interior balcony as part of the living room makes the plan very fluid and airy.

Jacobsen saw exhibitions of the works of Le Corbusier, Walter Gropius, and Ludwig Mies van der Rohe in Paris as early as 1925. The influence of international Modernism was obvious in the House of the Future (1929), where the flat roof was one of the very first introduced into Danish architecture. The roofs of Søholm I are unusual in a Danish context. The way of dealing with the 'shared view' of the Sound is similar to the solution of Bellavista, which belongs to the period of Jacobsen's white modernism. Søholm I is the first example of a very personal interpretation of international Modernism, and seen in an overall perspective Søholm sums up Jacobsen's experiences during the 1930s and 1940s. The sense of the specific qualities of materials – in this case the soft kinds of bricks meant quickly to attain a greyish look, the wooden doors and windows, the roofs of asbestos cement – is typical both of his own way of building and of Nordic Functionalism in general.

The Søholm way of linking the dining room with the living room is also seen in Jacobsen's summer house at Gudminderup Lyng (1939), but here the windows are wider and the connection between the interior rooms and the outside terrace and balcony is sharpened. In Søholm the single buildings are repeated by displacement into groups of buildings in a way that makes them seem like three-dimensional patterns similar to textiles or prints. Impressions of the same repetitive kind can be seen at Bellavista or at Søllerød City Hall.

KIRA PEDERSEN

BIBLIOGRAPHY:

1954   Pedersen J., *Arkitekten Arne Jacobsen*, Copenhagen
1964   Faber T., *Arne Jacobsen*, Stuttgart
1989   Solaguren-Beascoa de Corral, *Arne Jacobsen, Works and Projects*, Barcelona
1998   Thau C. and Vindum K., *Arne Jacobsen*, Copenhagen
2001   Cornoldi A., *Le case degli architetti. Dizionario privato dal Rinascimento ad oggi*, Venice, pp. 200–201

Knut Knutsen
1903–1969

1946–49, NEW CONSTRUCTION
PORTØR, OSLO FJORD (N)

MAIN WORKS AND PROJECTS

1936	Nøkle house, Oberst Angellsveien 5, Oslo (N)	**1949**	Viking Hotel, Oslo (N)
1939	Own house, Lillevannsveien 8, Oslo (N)	**1952**	The Norwegian Embassy, Stockholm (S)
	Office building, Youngstorget, Oslo (N)	**1960**	Bergendahl summer house, Tjøme (N)
1945	Natvig house, Østhornv. 13, Oslo (N)	**1961**	Thorkelsen summer house, Portør (N)
1949	Block of flats, Helgesensgate, Tøyen, Oslo (N)		

KNUT KNUTSEN was born on 4 December 1903 in Oslo, where he grew up in a middle-class home. His father worked as an accountant and deputy head of Centralbanken. His mother, Adelheid Sitt, came from Cologne in Germany. The young Knut was influenced and inspired by two architect uncles of his, Finn and Sverre Knutsen. In 1920 Knutsen enrolled in the National College of Art and Design (SHKS), Oslo. During the morning he worked as an unpaid assistant at his uncle Sverre's office, and in the afternoons and evenings he studied drawing, painting, design and construction at the SHKS. His thorough studies of sketching can easily be seen in his later sketches, which, despite their simplicity, resemble small works of art. Knutsen graduated from the SHKS in 1925 and continued as an assistant in his uncle's firm. Together they executed many successful projects. In 1928 Knutsen worked in the office of Ole Øvergaard, who had a considerable impact on the development of both his professional practice and his personality, and in 1930 he married Hjørdis Christiansen.

In 1936 Knutsen opened his own practice and from 1934 Knutsen taught at the SHKS in Oslo, where his exercises and experiments with form were clearly influenced by the Bauhaus school. This period allowed him to fully develop his talent as an architect. After a while he developed his own style, in which he adopted the idea of an organic architecture suited to Norwegian conditions. His ability to place buildings into their surroundings and his way of respecting both man and nature, seemed to have a favourable appeal in Norway's post-war society, leading to Knutsen becoming a central figure in Norwegian architecture of that period. In 1959 Knutsen won – together with his son Bengt Espen Knutsen – the Sundt Prize for Lyder Sagensgatan 6 in Oslo, and in 1961 he won both the first Timber Award and the Houen Foundation Prize. In 1966 he was appointed Professor of Architectural Composition at the Oslo School of Architecture (AHO), where he taught until his sudden and unexpected death in the summer of 1969, at the age of only 66.

Knutsen expressed a core tenet of his architecture as follows: "We must free ourselves from the straitjacket we have got used to wearing, and begin to express our true nature. This search for freedom is the basis of the project for my holiday home in Portør. In our projects we should try to use ideas that are more timeless in order to obtain greater unity and harmony in the art of building. We must also manage to find a reciprocal harmony both between individual houses and between houses and landscape."

Knutsen's summer house in Portør, Oslo, a new construction designed and built 1946–49, is considered the climax of the architect's career. It constitutes a synthesis of his work and reflects his ability to build in harmony with the environment. Knutsen had a strong public commitment. A social tendency towards disintegration was, so he believed, reflected in the architecture of the time. He was critical of contemporary architecture's tendency both to threaten the environment and to disturb and dominate the existing landscape. He was concerned to create meaningful houses. He sought an architecture free from solemnity, an architecture that should convey a natural and relaxed atmosphere.

Knutsen perhaps achieved this ideal most successfully in his own Portør summer house, which both avoids any encroachment on the landscape and has an atmosphere of well-being. It is a place in which to rest and seek inspiration, and it reflects a congenial architecture subordinated to nature. The building lies almost invisible, hidden among rocky hillocks and pine trees. It slides into the landscape, creating a harmonious whole with the surroundings, and responds well to the climatic and topographical conditions of the site. It seeks shelter from the wind, and adapts nicely to the light, sun and panorama.

The house consists of two parts: a living-room section with a bedroom wing, and between these a covered terrace with a window wall on one side. A continuous roof binds the two parts together. The terrace

THE PORTICO CONNECTING BEDROOMS

THE COVERED VERANDA

DESK IN THE LIVING ROOM

THE LIVING ROOM

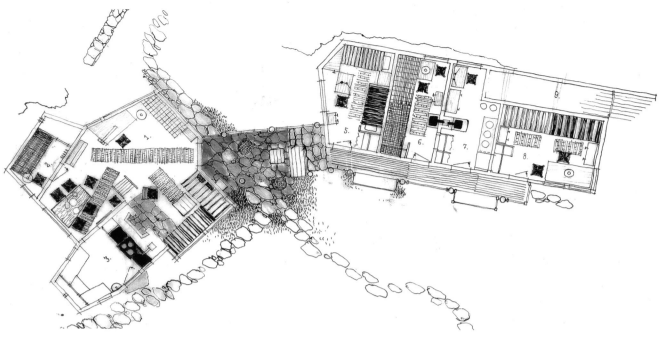

combines the natural topography with the artificial landscape, causing nature to become an integral part of the interior.

Gennaro Postiglione has described his first encounter with Knutsen's summer house as follows: "The living room is organised as a single continuous space in wood, where only the stone block of the fireplace, imposing in its physicality, separates the sitting area from the dining area. Apart from this, our gaze seems to be directed towards the outside, always in perspectives that are never closed, due to the way in which the architect designed the corners, which are all obtuse – the only right-angle corners are 'annulled' by the presence of the windows. This gives the space a continuous sense of openness, since there are no categorical closures of perspective. It also gives the composition a dynamic sense, characterised by a powerful centrifugal force."

Postiglione continues: "Everything seems natural and organic, and the irregular but rigorous geometry of the composition hides the 'secret' of the search for appropriate form (appropriate to the aims, the place and the meanings) according to methods and typologies that tradition hands down and modifies, perfecting them through tiny variations. This wisdom is hidden between the lines of the project and is incorporated in its construction. However, we should not be misled, for the house is not of a traditional 'type' in the sense of the simple transposition of forms. Apart from the wood, there is little – almost nothing – that maintains the link with tradition in a direct manner. At the same time, however, the house is in keeping with traditional architecture in the sensibility and appropriateness of the use of materials, in the way it gives form to necessity, in the way it offers itself as a place for people, and in the way it establishes a balanced and harmonious relationship with the surrounding nature."

Knutsen's summer house is often regarded as part of the new wave of anti-rational tendencies flooding international architecture in the years following the Second World War. In this context the architect be-

comes a pioneer in the revolt against the simplified and unemotional version of functionalism. The Norwegian architectural theorist Christian Norberg-Schulz evaluated Knutsen's work as follows: "Freed from architectonic styles, architecture could make the art of building a language of more lasting value… Everyone can learn the techniques of construction, the use of materials, the function and economy of the building sector, but very few have the talent to 'make music', to ensure that the materials and the dimensions sing, live and convey universal values."

Norberg-Schulz's assessment helps to explain Knutsen's originality and distinctive expression. Despite the fact that Knutsen was undoubtedly inspired by both Alvar Aalto and Frank Lloyd Wright, as well as traditional Norwegian and far eastern architecture, his oeuvre stands out as something which paved the way for a renewal in Norwegian architecture. The Portør summer house constitutes a climax of his output and in many ways reflects Knutsen both as a man and as an architect. Here he fulfilled his overall task to "give expression to a 'human content'". Through his buildings and his teaching, Knutsen inspired and influenced many colleagues and contemporaries, especially younger architects, and continues to do so even 30 years after his death.   SILJE SKRONDAL

BIBLIOGRAPHY:

1982   Tvedten A. S. and Knutsen B. E., *Knut Knutsen* 1903 – 1969, Oslo

1996   Grønvold U., 'Knut Knutsen. A Summer House', in *The Architectural Review*, no. 8, pp. 73 – 77

1999   Flora N., Giardiello P. and Postiglione G. (eds), *Arne Korsmo – Knut Knutsen due Maestri del Nord*, Rome

2001   Cornoldi A., *Le case degli architetti. Dizionario privato dal Rinascimento ad oggi*, Venice, pp. 211 – 212

Toivo Korhonen
*1926

1960, NEW CONSTRUCTION, STILL INHABITED BY THE ARCHITECT
TAKANIEMENTIE 5, LAUTTASAARI, HELSINKI (FIN)

MAIN WORKS AND PROJECTS

1958–69	Lauritsala Church (FIN), with Jaakko Laapotti
1959	Tonttukallio, estate of terraced houses, Matinkylä, Espoo (FIN), with Jaakko Laapotti
1960	Residential building, Pohjoiskaari 29, Lauttasaari, Helsinki (FIN)
	Munkkivuori Secondary School, Helsinki (FIN)
	Main building, University of Tampere, Tampere (FIN)
1961	Kotka Savings Bank business centre, Kotka (FIN)

1963	Mäntykallio, residential development, Matinkylä, Espoo (FIN)
1964–65	Pellos, industrial and residential development (FIN)
1972	Finnstadt, experimental low-rise residential development, Wulfen (D)
	Experimental low-rise housing development project, Lima, Peru

TOIVO KORHONEN'S career unfolded at a time when architecture was characterised by rationalisation and standardisation of construction, as well as by the use of concrete and structural elements. The Finnish architect was one of the late modernists who applied Le Corbusier's methods and deployed the developing (prefabricated) modular building technique.

Korhonen, born in 1926 in Kuopio, graduated from the School of Architecture at Helsinki's University of Technology in 1952. From 1952 to 1953 he worked in Alvar Aalto's office, and in 1955 opened his own architectural practice. He specialised in designing residential buildings, ranging from single-family houses to 10-storey residential towers. Even though he designed numerous blocks of flats, he favoured terraced housing, considering it the best dwelling type for the metropolitan area.

Korhonen's significant works include the main building of the University of Tampere (1960), and he is particularly well known for Lauritsala Church (1958–69), whose dynamic sculptural form and use of concrete surfaces as an architectural element were brave new concepts in Finnish architecture at the time. Korhonen designed the church together with Jaakko Laapotti, who also helped Korhonen design his own house.

Korhonen's own home at Takaniementie 5, Lauttasaari, Helsinki (1960), was an experimental new construction that disregarded traditional rules. It had a courtyard and flat roof that were considered unsuitable for Finland's wintry climate. Nevertheless Korhonen and Laapotti went ahead and realised their Finnish courtyard house, which was closed to the outside and open to the inside. They had already tested the idea in the Tonttukallio terraced houses of 1959.

The living space of Korhonen's house is grouped around the courtyard. Not being limited by partition walls, the space also has no room hierarchy. Looked at the other way round, the common areas, such as the kitchen, dining and living areas, create a series of spaces without walls and open to the courtyard through large windows. The bedrooms, by contrast, are separated by light partition walls. The idea of the courtyard house, which is based on the residential architecture of the ancient Romans, was rediscovered in the early 1960s.

In the *Finnish Architectural Review* (4 / 5, 1961), Korhonen described his own house as follows: "My office is in Helsinki city centre, and we don't have a holiday home. We enjoy the summer, the sun, swimming and the sauna, and we want our privacy, so the courtyard house seemed like a functional solution for us. The rather restless site also supported the courtyard idea. The slope makes it possible to remove snow from the courtyard to the lower terrace."

The architect described the materials and structures of the house as follows: "The actual habitable floor consists of a wood-element frame. The external wall cladding is partly of concealed fixed Minerit board, while the internal walls are lined with veneered chipboard. The partition walls comprise chipboard, glass and sliding walls. All the windows are of insulation glass, mostly triple glazed. The floors are mainly covered with dry-pressed mosaic, part of the living space is covered with a Metsovaara carpet, the bedroom floors are laid with bouclé carpet, and there is underfloor heating."

The house's simple furnishing is made up of modern classics: Alvar Aalto furniture in the kitchen, and Ludwig Mies van der Rohe Barcelona chairs, Pablo Picasso prints, and Paolo Venini as well as Timo Sarpaneva

STREET VIEW

VIEW FROM THE GARDEN

THE LIVING AREA

200

SITTING AREA IN THE LIVING ROOM

PLAN OF THE GROUND FLOOR

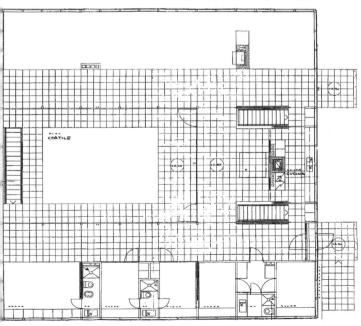

art glass elsewhere. Korhonen himself did not design furniture, but for his home he used some of the pieces that interior designer Esko Pajamies had created for the University of Tampere, including the fibreglass chairs in the dining area and the chairs in the library space. TIMO KEINÄNEN

BIBLIOGRAPHY:

1961 Korhonen T., 'Oma talo' (My own house), in *Finnish Architectural Review*, nos 4/5, pp. 77–83
Benson J., 'The Work of Young Architects in Finland, Private House, Lauttasaari, Helsinki', in *Architectural Design*, May, pp. 188–189

1964 'Finlande Actualités, Habitation de l'Architecte Korhonen à Lauttasaari', in *L'Architecture d'Aujourd'hui*, 113–114, p. 123

1967 Weidert W., *International Private Houses, Einfamilienhäuser – international*, Stuttgart, pp. 134–139

Arne Korsmo
1900–1968

1952–55, NEW CONSTRUCTION, WITH CHRISTIAN NORBERG-SCHULZ
PLANETVEIEN 12, OSLO (N)

MAIN WORKS AND PROJECTS

1929 Frøen housing development (ten single-family houses), Lille Frøens vei 10–16, and Apalveien 16–18, Oslo (N)

1930 Apartment block, Pavelsgatan 6, Oslo (N)
Damman house, Havna Allé, Oslo (N)

1930–35 Havna housing development (14 single-family detached houses, Havna Allé 1–14, Oslo (N), with Sverre Aasland

1933–36 Christians and Møller grain store, Kristiansand (N)

1935 Three detached houses, Slemdalsveien 33 a, b and c, Oslo (N)

1937 Stenersen house, Tuengen Allé 10c, Oslo (N)

1954 Norwegian pavilion at Milan Triennale, Milan (I)

1961–63 Interior remodelling of Britannia Hotel, Trondheim (N)

ARNE KORSMO was born in Oslo on 14 August 1900, the son of Emil Korsmo, who was a professor of botany, and Aagot Jacobine Wiger. After completing a basic training in civil engineering, Korsmo graduated from the School of Architecture at the Norwegian University of Technology (NTH) in Trondheim in 1926. From 1926–27 he worked in Bryn and Ellefsen's architectural practice, where he first came into contact with European Modernism, especially in the form of the Weissenhof housing development in Stuttgart. Korsmo would also have read at that time *What is Modern Architecture?*, an essay published by his employer Ellefsen, which was the first Norwegian essay on modern architecture.

Korsmo was undoubtedly influenced by these new ideas, and in 1928, funded by a grant from the Henrichsen Foundation, he travelled to continental Europe to view the innovative architecture. His impressions during the trip unleashed his artistic talent. "As I travelled about, I felt like a child leafing through a lovely picture book and delighted in all the new sights. But my eyes learned to see with discrimination, for I sorted the sights, discarding many, until not much remained – perhaps my mind was influenced by the modernist minimalism I saw." Korsmo's European journey brought him into contact with many leading contemporary architects, including Erich Mendelsohn, Le Corbusier, Louis Kahn and Willem Marinus Dudok.

In 1928 Korsmo married his first wife Åse Thiis, and in 1929 he opened his own architectural practice in partnership with Sverre Aasland. They mostly designed detached houses, but also exhibitions and interiors. Korsmo developed an architecture with a strong sense of the site with all its qualities, such as light, space, colour, form and material – in short, everything man must take into consideration in order to be able to dwell in the true sense of the word. According to the great Norwegian

theorist of architecture Christian Norberg-Schulz, this was Korsmo's ultimate goal: to help people to dwell.

From 1936 to 1941 Arne Korsmo taught at the National College of Art and Design (SHKS) in Oslo. It was here that he met his second wife Grete Prytz. They married in 1945 and built up a fruitful cooperation that was to last for several years. Together they later developed their 'work home' at Planetveien 12, where Grete Prytz Kittelsen still lives and which she has carefully preserved. In 1949 Arne and Grete went to the USA on a Fulbright scholarship. Here Korsmo met and became friendly with more great architects of the time, including Mies van der Rohe, Charles Eames, Frank Lloyd Wright and Walter Gropius.

In 1950, Siegfried Giedeon, a pioneer of modern architecture, suggested to Christian Norberg-Schulz that he should form an independent Norwegian delegation to the CIAM (International Congress of Modern Architecture). Norberg-Schulz took up the idea and in turn asked Korsmo to head the group, which Korsmo accepted with alacrity. The group was called PAGON (Progressive Architects Group Oslo Norway) and consisted of Christian Norberg-Schulz, Peter Andreas Munch Mellbye, Sverre Fehn, Geir Grung, Odd Østbye, Håkon Mjelva, Robert Esdaile and Korsmo himself. On several occasions PAGON, which remained active until 1956, was also joined by Jørn Utzon. Their natural meeting place was Arne and Grete Korsmo's home in Løkenveien on Bygdøy, Oslo.

During his career Korsmo was awarded many honours and prizes, including the Sundt Prize (in 1933) and the Grand Prix at the Milan Triennale (1954). Between 1956 and 1968 Korsmo worked as a professor at his old college, the NTH in Trondheim, where he met his third wife, the young architect Hanne Refsdal, whom he married in 1965, and with whom he had two daughters. In 1968 Korsmo participated in a conference for

VIEW FROM THE GARDEN

GRETE KORSMO IN THE LIVING ROOM

ENTRANCE

designers in Huampani, near Cuzco in Peru. He travelled to it in the company of his second wife, Grete. He had always dreamt of seeing the ruins of the monumental megalithic architecture of the Incas. But having struggled with poor health for several years, Arne Korsmo died on an arduous trip to Machu Picchu in Peru on 29 August 1968.

Korsmo's main goal, to create a meaningful way of dwelling, is perhaps expressed most clearly in his own home at Planetveien 12, Oslo, a new construction. This is one of a small terrace of three houses, jointly designed with Christian Norberg-Schulz between 1952 and 1955, and situated on a hill in the north-western outskirts of Oslo, in one of the most attractive residential areas of the city.

The layout of the houses is based on a modern skeleton construction of steel. These modular structures using frames allow the plans and the elevations of the houses to be organised with great freedom. The two architects based their design on a project method perfected by Korsmo, called 'Hjemmets mekkano' (the Meccano house). This is an analytic method which Korsmo defined as a "working method and analysis of man, the home and the house, the aim of which is to give the individual, the family and the environment a chance to free themselves from passivity and become consciously active in dwelling and building." The possibility to change the layout of the rooms and the treatment of the

façades was intended by Korsmo to stimulate the users' participation in dwelling and building, as well as underlining the possibility of adapting the house to the constantly changing needs of a family.

Korsmo's idea of a 'work home' reflected his conception of human life. Here dwelling and working were combined in a whole, as an expression of living. Work was not just a way to earn money, it should reflect a way of living. In this sense, Planetveien served as a framework for the interaction between the natural surroundings, which are clearly an integral part of the architecture, and the family life and activities going on within the three-house terrace.

The composition and geometry of the design of the Planetveien terrace, upon which the system of construction is based, is quite simple: the small terrace forms a long low compact body, onto which the three volumes constituting the sleeping areas are grafted, allowing the individual properties to be identified from the outside.

In Byggekunst, Norberg-Schulz presents Planetveien as follows: "From the forest, these houses look like three independent cubes, with a living room on the ground floor and the bedrooms upstairs. The house in the middle, Korsmo's home, was without doubt the most exciting, but it was also the most vulnerable from an architectural point of view. In order to get a living room with no pillars, Korsmo had to abandon the structural

THE FIREPLACE CORNER IN THE LIVING ROOM

rhythm of 12-foot spans, such as was adopted in the other two houses, and increase the dimension of the steel skeleton. As a result, the construction became five times more expensive than the other two houses..."

Norberg-Schulz continues: "The skeleton frame made it possible to have both a free floor plan and a free façade. The building elements as well as their accessories were modular, so that a standard compositional system would be used. In this way, the Meccano houses enabled the new modern and free human being to shape his domestic space and his life. Human beings should always be active and creative, and Korsmo tried to realise this ideal in his own house."

"Planetveien represented the first introduction of the characteristically Mies van der Rohean steel-and-glass architecture in Norway. It also represented a new and visionary way of looking at the dwelling. Korsmo was in his own time regarded as somewhat avant-garde. However, his ideas of dwelling and his architecture have been of great significance for subsequent generations, and for the evolution of dwelling. Planetveien was an important base in his teaching. Here friends, students and colleagues met, visionary designs were drawn up, and the improvement of dwelling was the subject of lively debate. The house is a manifestation of Korsmo's theory of architecture and practice."

Christian Norberg-Schulz characterises Planetveien as both an interpretation of traditional vernacular architecture and as modern architecture. By avoiding means of superficial imitation, and instead going to the source of the means, a 'natural' atmosphere emerged. At the same time, Planetveien is modern, this being expressed in the interior as a place that comprises the essence of the modern conception of space. For Arne Korsmo, building was much more than a problem related to square metres. For him architecture was poetry.

SILJE SKRONDAL

PLAN OF THE GROUND FLOOR

BIBLIOGRAPHY:
1985   Grønvold U. (ed.), *Aasland/Korsmo*, monographic issue of "Byggekunst" no. 6
1986   Norberg-Schulz C., *Arne Korsmo*, Oslo
1996   Postiglione G. (ed.), *Oslo Funkis 1927–1940*, Rome, pp. 73–89
1999   Flora N., Giardiello P. and Postiglione G. (eds.), *Arne Korsmo – Knut Knutsen due Maestri del Nord*, Rome
2001   Cornoldi A., *Le case degli architetti. Dizionario privato dal Rinascimento ad oggi*, Venice, pp. 213–215

Adolf Krischanitz
*1946

1995–98, NEW CONSTRUCTION, STILL INHABITED BY THE ARCHITECT
STEINAWEG, LOWER AUSTRIA (A)

MAIN WORKS AND PROJECTS

1980	Austrian New Wave exhibition, New York (USA), with Otto Kapfinger
1983	Renovation of the Werkbundsiedlung, Vienna (A), with Otto Kapfinger
1985	Renovation and conversion of the Secession building, Vienna (A), with Otto Kapfinger
1987–92	Pilotengasse housing development, Vienna (A)
1990–93	Steirerhof office and commercial building, Graz (A)

1991–92	Kunsthalle, Karlsplatz, Vienna (A)
1992–94	Neue Welt Schule (New World School), Vienna (A)
1992–95	Kunsthalle, Krems (A)
1994	Austrian pavilion at the Book Fair, Frankfurt (D)
1996–99	Lauder Chabad School, Vienna (A)

ADOLF KRISCHANITZ was born 1946 in Schwarzach/Pongau in the Austrian federal province of Salzburg, the son of an electrical engineer and a housewife. His father worked for Austrian Federal Railways on the construction of power stations and transformers, and because he had very good technical skills, he climbed progressively up the railway hierarchy. Due to the father's career, the Krischanitz family often had to move from one place to another. After his childhood in Schwarzach/Pongau, Adolf Krischanitz spent his schooldays in Linz, where he attended secondary school from the age of 10 to 14, and subsequently received a solid education in engineering at the local technical school. After his school-leaving exams in 1965, Krischanitz studied architecture at the Technical University in Vienna, where his teachers included Karl Schwanzer and Günther Feuerstein. This was a place where various experimental tendencies had developed in the wake of the events of 1968. A post-68 group that was to become legendary was Krischanitz's Missing Link partnership, founded together with Otto Kapfinger and Angela Hareiter in 1970. The group has had a lasting influence on the Austrian architectural scene.

Since 1979 Krischanitz has worked as a self-employed architect in Vienna, moving between Vienna, Berlin and Steinaweg. He is married to the journalist Elisabeth Schnürer and has a brother, Helmut, who is a teacher and who has also inherited their father's technical skills. As an architect, Krischanitz maintains a close connection with modern art. His interest in the works of contemporary artists was initiated by Edelbert Köb, formerly an assistant at the Technical University in Vienna, who introduced Krischanitz to the contemporary art scene. Apart from theoretical works in the magazine UM BAU, Krischanitz has realised projects together with Oskar Putz, whose Neo-Geo colour has given Krischanitz's

buildings a specific tension. In the early 1980s Krischanitz spent time in the USA organising the important Austrian New Wave exhibition.

Krischanitz's magnum opus so far has been the Pilotengasse housing development in Vienna (1987–92), a project carried out in collaboration with Otto Steidle from Munich and Herzog & de Meuron from Basle, both of whom he invited to join him in this key work. During the cooperation he came into contact with Helmut Federle, with whom he formed a successful partnership for many further projects. Over the years Adolf Krischanitz has also established many personal contacts abroad, probably more than any other Austrian architect apart from Hans Hollein, and especially in Germany and Switzerland. He is in contact with and undertakes joint projects with Hans Kollhoff, Herzog & de Meuron, Diener & Diener, Snozzi, and Peter Meili.

Krischanitz has twice been the President of the Vienna Secession, has worked as a guest professor at various European summer academies, and has acted as an international juror on several occasions. His works have been exhibited three times in a row in the Austrian pavilion at the Architectural Biennale in Venice. Meanwhile the name Adolf Krischanitz has become a European trademark at the interface of contemporary art and avant-garde architecture.

Krischanitz lives in three different places: Vienna, Berlin and Steinaweg. While his apartment in the centre of Vienna is no more than a pied-à-terre, somewhere to stay overnight between two working days, Berlin, where he teaches Design at the Hochschule der Künste (Academy of Fine Arts), is a place for living. If Krischanitz's exhibition in America and his cooperation with the Basle-based firm of Herzog & de Meuron on the Pilotengasse project in Vienna have been two significant turning points in his career, his professorship in Berlin represents a third. Because his

VIEW FROM THE SOUTH-WEST

VIEW FROM THE NORTH-WEST

THE STUDIO

207

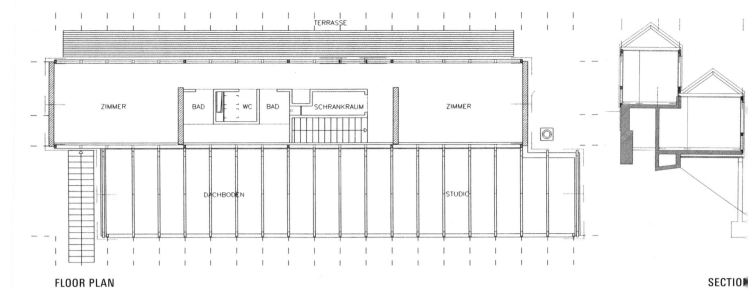

FLOOR PLAN   SECTIO▌

DINING ROOM IN THE STUDIO

STAIRS

DETAIL OF THE BATHROOM

practice in Vienna is extremely busy, his stays in Berlin are necessarily limited, taken up with lecturing, teaching, correcting and research. But for Krischanitz, Berlin has an important regulating effect on Vienna, for it is a place where he has a social life with colleagues, other architects, contemporary artists, students and politicians. And since he has not yet built anything in Berlin, it is obviously much easier for him to get to know other professors and architects there without being seen as a rival. If Berlin is very different from Vienna, Krischanitz's private house-cum-studio in Steinaweg is in complete contrast to both.

Krischanitz built his own private house for himself and his wife in Steinaweg. This tiny municipality lies in the heart of Lower Austria, well over an hour by car from Vienna, and enjoys a view of the massive Baroque monastery of Göttweig. From the outside it is already clear that the house is not meant to be just a residential building. The lower part has been conceived as a place to receive guests, but above all it is a studio for the architect and his journalist wife, Elisabeth Schnürer. Unlike him, she lives and works in the house-cum-studio almost all the year round. The upper part of the double building includes the couple's two apartments. This sequence of rooms, organised like hotel suites and interacting with the

garden, forms the real living space. The connection between the two parts of the house is ambivalent, as is the architect's relation to his house in general, as he can only be there at the weekend. His stays are thus more like guest visits, while Elisabeth Schnürer uses the house as a permanent base. She is very attached to nature, and the house represents a lifestyle choice, whereas Krischanitz enjoys the benefits of this lifestyle only at the weekends, when time in the country is a compensation for his life in the metropolises of Berlin and Vienna.

The house nestles against a steep 38-degree slope of ancient rock in one of the valleys of the Danube. In response to the slope, the building is articulated into two identical elements, each 19 m long by 3.70 m wide, which are positioned directly one behind the other. By staggering the heights of the two elements, it was possible to avoid excavating a large volume of rock. The pitched roof and the main access via a steel staircase connecting the blocks have the same slope as the terrain. Standing in front of the building, the dramatic underface of the lower unit becomes visible. A reinforced concrete foundation slab with no downbeams rests on four high slender reinforced concrete columns. The accesses and adjoining rooms are part of a stratification of massive walls linking the two blocks. The rest of the house has been erected as a timber frame

THE KITCHEN

construction. The exterior surfacing of the house is also made of wood. With an architect like Krischanitz, even such a simple statement leads to radical realisation. In fact everything about this house is made of wood, even the roof has been covered with the same homogeneous material as the walls. These circumstances led to long discussions with the local planning authorities and the neighbourhood. And it is true: the residents of Steinaweg today still have to contend with the odd architectural tourist as well as with the unusual sight of the famous architect roping himself up in his steep garden!

Krischanitz puts his house to the test. An architect's professional work consists among other things in 'prescribing' existential stages to unknown human beings, a three-dimensional set usually considered as architecture. But the architect rarely experiences everyday life himself via his architecture. It is only with his own house that the architect realises that construction sites are not completed after they have been handed over. Thousands of details still have to be taken into account, although the architect now no longer plays the main role, whereas the resident lives in his house and observes it.

Adolf Krischanitz has been influenced by Viennese architecture. This is where his main roots as an architect lie. The language of his archi-

tecture has developed from a knowledge of this tradition, which includes Loos, Frank and Wittgenstein, and must therefore be considered as Viennese. It is a culture more of furniture, music, and art theory, rather than of architectural theory. Small wonder, then, that Krischanitz's creations are mainly to be found in smaller forms: in furniture, pavilions and private houses. The house in Steinaweg may be the country home of an architect, but it is also a jewel of the finest Viennese building culture, with a place in the history of Viennese architecture. Similarly, it may be the house of an architect, yet it is still architecture – something that is by no means always the case.

KLAUS-JÜRGEN BAUER

BIBLIOGRAPHY:
1997   *Adolf Krischanitz*, with articles by Jos Bosman, Adolf Krischanitz and Dietmar Steiner, Barcelona
1998   Krischanitz A., *Adolf Krischanitz, architect, buildings and projects 1986–1998*, Basel/Boston/Berlin
1999   Steiner D., 'Casa-atelier Steinaweg, Austria', in *Domus*, no. 821, December, pp. 44–47
2000   Pozsogar W., 'Auf Qualität reduziert', in *Die Presse – Schaufenster*, 28 January
       Graf A., *Wohnen und Arbeiten unter einem Dach*, Munich , pp. 40–43

Mogens Lassen
1901–1987

1936, NEW CONSTRUCTION, 2000 SOME ALTERATIONS, NOW LISTED
SØLYSTVEJ 5, KLAMPENBORG (DK)

MAIN WORKS AND PROJECTS

1933	Project for Copenhagen's Kastrup Airport (DK), with Erhard Lorenz
1935	House, Anchersvej 6, Klampenborg (DK)
1936	Own house, Sølystvej 5, Klampenborg (DK)
	Gentofte badminton hall, Gentofte (DK)
1937	Project for Århus City Hall (DK), with Erhard Lorenz
1941	Project for Museum of Contemporary Art at Statens Art Museum, Copenhagen (DK)
1941–42	Sorgenfrihusene, Hummeltoftevej, Sorgenfri (DK)
1943–44	Maglemosevej, Vedbæk (DK)
1944	Hvidørevej 24, Klampenborg (DK)
1966	Ordrupdalsvej, Julsø, Silkeborg (DK)

MOGENS LASSEN was born as the first of two sons of Hans Vilhelm Lassen, a decorative painter and later the owner of a coffee-roasting business, and the painter Ingeborg Winding. Both his parents were educated as painters at the Royal Danish Academy of Fine Arts in Copenhagen. When still children, Mogens Lassen and his brother Flemming started to do surveys, drawings and photographs of buildings in their neighbourhood. Mogens Lassen went to boarding school in both Nærum and Hørsholm on the island of Zealand (Sjaelland). At school in Nærum he met the future architects Hans Bretton-Meyer and Arne Jacobsen, and was able to convince them of the advantages of architecture. The basis of his career as an architect was partly formed at the Institute of Technology at Ahlefeldtsgade in Copenhagen in 1919–23, partly by practical work as a bricklayer's apprentice in the summertime, and partly for a short period at the Royal Danish Academy of Fine Arts. Lassen enrolled in the academy in the summer of 1923, but due to the family's financial problems he was unable to continue his education. His practical education as an architect was therefore mainly obtained by working at several studios, for the longest period (1925–34) with Tyge Hvass. In 1935 he opened his own architectural practice.

In 1927–28 Mogens Lassen was employed by Christiani & Nielsen in Paris. During this stay he learnt about Le Corbusier and the new architectural ideals of European Modernism. He was even offered a chance to work for Le Corbusier at 35 Rue de Sèvres, but decided not to do so because of his lack of competence in the French language and his fear of being artistically overwhelmed by the great master. Instead he wanted to return to Denmark to work independently. By introducing the new ideas back home, he became one of the pioneers of Danish Modernism. He applied the new architectural forms in his own works, for instance directly modelling the construction of his house at Anchersvej 6 (1935) on Le Corbusier's Weissenhof house (1927) in Stuttgart, which in turn was based on the master's L'Esprit-Nouveau exhibition house of 1925.

Subsequently, however, Lassen replaced his strict application of specific models from Le Corbusier's architecture, as seen in Anchersvej 6, with a freer and more personal interpretation of Modernism. In the early years of his career he built many single-family houses or detached houses using concrete and climbing forms of steel plates. The method was developed by the civil engineer Ernst Ishøy, who owned the house at Anchersvej 6, and with whom Lassen was to collaborate for many years. It was an architecture characterised by room-wide windows on a fillet, two-storey rooms, and big roof terraces protected by tall walls, while as a whole the rather severe structural vocabulary was softened by vivid green vegetation. The symmetries in the fronts recall Lassen's starting point as a classicist, educated in the tradition of national Romanticism and Neoclassicism.

Lassen was a member of several juries for architectural exhibitions. For a considerable period (1939–67) he was the chief architect of the Den Permanente exhibition, which was a sales window for Danish arts and crafts, and from 1939–46 he was an adjudicator at the same exhibition. Especially early on he designed furniture and other applied art, creating for example furniture objects in steel and wood that have become classics in the history of Danish design. Although Lassen was mainly involved in constructing detached houses, he sometimes jointly entered competitions for larger projects, such as those for the new main building of Copenhagen's Kastrup Airport, or Århus City Hall, won by Arne Jacobsen and Erik Møller.

However, detached houses were Lassen's real forte. He demonstrated a Le Corbusier-inspired but very individual style that combined the needs for functionality and changes within the house with an extraordinary sense of space both inside and outside the building. The houses

THE ROOF TERRACE

VIEW FROM THE GARDEN

VIEW FROM THE ROAD

LASSEN IN HIS OFFICE

THE LIVING AREA

he designed – including his own – for the old Christiansholmsfortet site clearly show his ability to make the buildings follow from and interact with the surroundings, which in this case were a valley and a hill. The modelling of the surroundings was just as important for him as the interior of the house, and it was his wish that the final impression of the building should match the specific brief in a natural way.

Lassen's own home, a new construction at Sølystvej 5, Klampenborg (1936), was one of the first houses to be erected on the old Christiansholmsfortet fortress site north of Copenhagen. The buildings were all inspired by the remains of the old fortification and sited in the terrain with as much respect as possible for the existing trees. Lassen's four-storey house stands on a slope and is built in reinforced concrete. The simplicity of spaces and materials allows the mixture of different furni-

ture and other items in the often over-furnished rooms to become very pleasant. The architect's way of living, compared to his cubic and often austere construction, is thus far from the minimalist style of other modernists. In a similar vein Lassen allowed his garden to luxuriate like tropical vegetation, which turned the house and its surroundings into an oasis among Copenhagen's more conventional northern quarters.

Sølystvej 5 is built in accordance with Ishøy's method, using concrete and climbing forms of steel plates, and the house as a whole is a variation on the Corbusian house at Anchersvej 6. It is constructed with carrying floors and façades of reinforced concrete, and oriented on a north-east/south-west axis, with the main entrance on the north-eastern side. Originally the shape of the building was rectangular, with two storeys, a roof terrace and a lower floor. Situated as it is in the old moat and on the slope of the rampart, access from the street on the northern side is made possible by means of a gangway leading from the street to the small house containing the stairways of the building. This part of the house has been advanced from the building itself and has a small row of windows where the buildings meet. The situation in the moat makes the house seem small and quite modest when viewed from the road. In this way the difficult building terrain has been turned into a strong point, resulting in an exciting interaction between the house and the surrounding nature. The main entrance from the road is on the first floor, while the ground floor offers direct access to the garden on the other side of the house. The upper floor is made as an open roof terrace, protected by a tall wall and with a view to the garden and Christiansholmsfortet's many trees. On the ground floor are some ancillary premises and a garden room. The first floor contains a kitchen, a dining area, and a lounge. On the third floor there are two bedrooms, a bathroom, and Lassen's first studio.

Over the years the house at Sølystvej 5 has undergone alterations. Its interior has been modified many times, the ground-floor façade has been advanced beyond the formerly free-standing columns so as to correspond to the upper floors, and a self-contained flat has been designed on the lower floor. A separate studio building has been erected (1963) in the garden, replacing the studio inside the house. The house has been able to cope with all these changes due to its flexible plan, allowing partitions to be moved, for example. The austere impression of the exterior forms conceals a vivid space for living, which is hard to imagine from the outside.

KIRA PEDERSEN

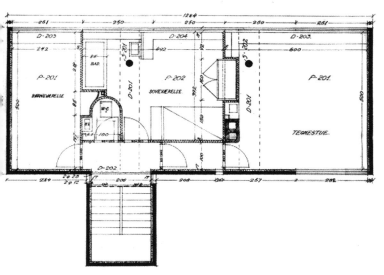

PLAN OF THE GROUND FLOOR

SECTION

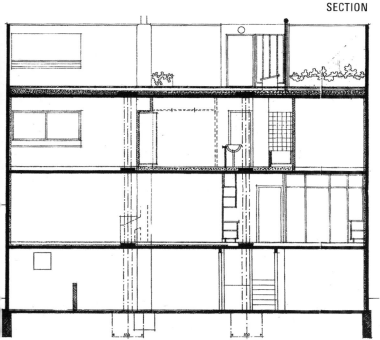

BIBLIOGRAPHY:

1947   'Immeuble à Charlottenlund' in *L'architecture d'aujourd'hui*, no. 16, Dec., p. 43
1948   'House in Copenhagen' in *Architectural Design* (GB), vol. XVIII, December, p. 241
1963   Faber T., 'Mogens Lassen', in *Dansk arkitektur*, Copenhagen, pp. 163–167
1972   Skriver P. E., 'Arbejder af Mogens Lassen', in *Arkitektur*, no. 3, pp. 49–92
1989   Balslev Jørgensen L., *Arkitekten Mogens Lassen*, Copenhagen
       'Mogens Lassen: System-House, Charlottenlund, Denmark' in *The Architect and Building News* (GB), vol. 194, no. 4161, Sept. 17, pp. 24–43

Le Corbusier
1887 – 1965

1931 – 33, NEW CONSTRUCTION, WITH PIERRE JEANNERET, NOW OWNED BY THE FONDATION LE CORBUSIER
24 RUE NUNGESSER ET COLI, PARIS (F)

MAIN WORKS AND PROJECTS

1925	Esprit Nouveau pavilion at the Paris International Fair of Arts and Crafts (F)
1929	Ville Savoye, Poissy (F)
	Centrosoysus Palace, Moscow (USSR)
1936 – 43	National Welfare Palace, Rio de Janeiro (Brazil), with Lúcio Costa, Oscar Niemeyer, A.E. Reidy, Jorge M. Moreira, Ermani Vasconces
1946	'Unité d'habitation', Marseille (F)
1950	Pilgrimage chapel in Notre-Dame-du-Haut, Ronchamp (F)
1950 – 64	Punjab government buildings, Chandigarh (India)
1952	Jaoul houses, Neuilly-sur-Seine (F)
	Own summer cottage, Cap Martin (F)
1957 – 60	Convent de Sainte-Marie-de-la-Tourette, Eveux-sur-Arbresle (F)
1961	Carpenter Center for the Visual Arts, Harvard University, Cambridge (USA)
1963	La Maison de l'Homme, Zurich (CH)

IN THE BOOK *Le case degli architetti* (2001), Monica Galvan writes: "Charles-Edouard Jeanneret [i.e. Le Corbusier] was born on 6 October 1887 in La Chaux-de-Fonds, Switzerland, the son of Marie Perret, a piano teacher, and Georges-Edouard Jeanneret, a clockface enameller. Intent on following in his father's footsteps, he enrolled in art school (the École des Arts Décoratifs), but his final choice of profession was determined both by serious problems with his eyesight and by the ardent encouragement of one of his teachers, Charles L'Eplattenier." The latter was one of the most highly regarded teachers in the school, and Le Corbusier came to work on several projects with him during the years of his college education. It was in his home town of La Chaux-de-Fonds that Le Corbusier designed his first architectural works, several villas for local jewellers and one for his own family.

After graduating from art school, Le Corbusier undertook his first study trip, making short visits to several Central European cities and a longer stay in Italy. The trip allowed him not only to visit works by illustrious architects from the past, but also to find out about the latest developments in contemporary architecture, as manifest in the work of figures such as Josef Hoffmann and Otto Wagner in Vienna, Peter Behrens in Berlin, and Auguste Perret in Paris. Le Corbusier was to meet Behrens and Perret personally, first through the Wiener Werkstätte, and later through the Deutscher Werkbund, and to work as an apprentice in their studios, where he had the chance to meet two other young architects destined to play an important role on the architectural scene for the next 40 years: Ludwig Mies van der Rohe and Walter Gropius.

Le Corbusier's travels, his work experience and his encounter with leading international architects and with contemporaries seeking new forms of expression in all the arts were to be the real school for the young Swiss apprentice, the only one he would never repudiate. Always defining himself as self-taught, Le Corbusier in fact tended to downplay the importance of the time he spent at art college and of the teachings of L'Eplattenier in favour of his education 'in the field', his apprenticeship in workshops, and above all his frequent journeys. These trips he recorded by means of photos, notes, drawings, books, postcards and reflections, which conserved the memory of the places he visited and also their atmospheres. The records and mementos were materials that became an integral part of his projects, both in his architecture and his painting, as well as in his lectures and his writings.

After returning for a few years to La Chaux-de-Fonds, where he taught at his old art school, in 1917 Le Corbusier moved to Paris for good. In the French capital he frequented the world of the literary and artistic avant-garde and met the painter Amédée Ozenfant. Ozenfant ran an exhibition space in the dressmaker's shop of Ghislain Grégoire, the sister of the celebrated Paul Poiret. Here Le Corbusier met the woman who would later become his wife, Yvonne Gallis, a model at the shop.

It was Ozenfant who invited Le Corbusier to take part in the exhibition *Après le cubisme*, held in Paris in 1918, and to contribute to the theoretical text on painting that accompanied the exhibition. An appendix to this text contained what is considered to be the manifesto of Purism, the new current inaugurated by the work and theoretical reflections of Ozenfant and Le Corbusier. After this collaboration the two friends joined forces again in 1919, when they founded with Paul Dermée the review *L'Esprit Nouveau*. The journal was to have a powerful influence for several decades on the world of the visual arts and architecture, publishing theo-

WINDING STAIRCASE TO ROOF TERRACE >

THE KITCHEN

retical texts accompanied by images of the new style and, above all, the striking slogans for which Le Corbusier became renowned: 'la machine à habiter', 'lois du ripolin', etc. As in his architectural works, Le Corbusier tended to cut things down to a bare minimum in order to bring about more effective understanding and communication.

The review survived a relatively long time, until 1925, ending with the presentation in Paris of the *L'Esprit Nouveau* pavilion at the Exposition Internationale des Arts Décoratifs et Industriels Modernes, at the very moment when its ideas, partly through the pavilion itself, began to spread rapidly around the world. Apart from Le Corbusier's pavilion, in fact, only Kostantin Melnikov presented a work that did not use formal languages borrowed from the past, recent or otherwise, attempting to experiment with new forms and languages.

In 1920 Ozenfant and Le Corbusier were joined by the latter's cousin, Pierre Jeanneret, who later became the architect's partner, sharing a studio in rue de Sèvres for many years. It was here, during the 1920s, that many of the masterpieces of 20th-century architecture were created, including the Stein villa in Garches (1927) and the Savoye villa in Poissy (1929), as well as the houses designed for the Weissenhof residential quarters in Stuttgart, an event organised on the occasion of the exhibition of the Deutscher Werkbund in 1927, where Le Corbusier was invited by Ludwig Mies van der Rohe to present a project for two dwellings.

Le Corbusier's participation in the 1922 Salon d'Automne in Paris marked the beginning of an extremely prolific and remarkably creative professional career in a variety of fields, from design to furnishings (in collaboration with Charlotte Perriand), urban design projects for the great South American capitals, abstract painting and architecture. The 1920s were also years of intense theoretical reflection for the architect, which saw him establish himself not only as a writer and publicist, but also as a participant in important architectural meetings such as the CIAM (*Congrès International d'Architecture Moderne*). At the first CIAM, held in 1928 in La Sarraz, Switzerland, Le Corbusier was already one of the leading figures in the debate, influencing the subsequent editions until they finally came to a close in 1956, in Dubrovnik.

Le Corbusier assigned to architecture a symbolic and subversive role, which translated into spaces suggesting a sense of freedom from dogmas and habits of living. The pursuit in all his projects of a spatial continuity between the various environments is realised through the application of his legendary 'five points': the pilotis, roof gardens, open plan, ribbon windows and free façades (1926). These five points derive from a programmatic text, entitled *Cinq points d'une architecture nou-*

THE BEDROOM AND THE WASH AREA

velle, which Le Corbusier wrote to accompany the exhibition of the Weissenhof housing developments. The work was to be another of the architect's publishing and marketing successes, like his earlier *Vers une architecture* (1923).

In collaboration with Charlotte Perriand, who had already begun to work in his studio from 1927, Le Corbusier carried out an analysis of the theme of furnishing, eventually leading the pair to develop prototypes that were to enjoy lasting success. The process of reduction, applied previously to architecture and to language, was now also applied to the design of objects of everyday use, such as tables and chairs. Conceived for industrial production and mass distribution, the designs embody the principles of the standardisation of needs and activities, in keeping with the ideas of Taylor that had previously influenced only the processes and places of production. In 1929, at the *Salon d'Automne* in Paris, Le Corbusier and Perriand presented their collection of household objects, termed 'L'Equipement de l'habitation' or habitation equipment.

Le Corbusier's work in the 1930s, by contrast, was more oriented to town planning, partly as a result of political developments in Europe and America. This interest led the architect to undertake numerous journeys, in the hope of convincing one of the political leaders of the time, such as Hitler or Mussolini, to commission him to design new cities, develop historic urban centres, or create important monuments and public buildings capable of representing the new powers. Although generally unsuccessful, this intense activity of self-promotion allowed Le Corbusier to obtain commissions elsewhere, in North Africa and South America.

In 1933, on the occasion of the IV CIAM (held on a ship that took the participants from Marseille to Athens), Le Corbusier made a significant contribution to the Athens Charter, a document which for the first time set out guidelines for those who intended to practise in the field of town planning on the basis of the dictates of the new style. The charter, edited by the architect himself, was not published until much later, in 1941. It outlined for a wide audience the four functions to which the main activities of human life had been reduced: inhabit, work, enjoy oneself and move about.

After the pause imposed by the Second World War, Le Corbusier introduced major changes in his office in rue de Sèvres, which now became a partnership. He wanted to be ready to take advantage of the great prospects offered by post-war reconstruction. He appointed Jacques-Louis Lefèvre as the studio's administrative director and Marcel Py as director of works, while Vladimir Bodiansky was made responsible for technical studies, and André Wogenscky for architectural planning. Le Corbusier's cousin, Pierre Jeanneret, with whom he had worked for so

VIEW OF THE FIREPLACE IN THE BEDROOM   THE LIVING ROOM AND THE DINING ROOM

many years, left the practice. On Saturday afternoons, the master's collaborators would take turns giving public lectures on his work.

During the same period, the architect also developed his own system of proportions, which he called 'Le Modulor' or 'The Modulor' (1942 onwards). This new system allowed Le Corbusier to integrate the decimal system and the dimensions of the body, re-establishing human character in the abstract world of numbers, something that had been lost when the Anglo-Saxon systems of measurement (feet and inches) had been abandoned and the decimal system took their place.

Finally, in the 1950s and 1960s, Le Corbusier was more active than ever, taking part in conferences and giving lectures all over the world, and ceaselessly promoting his professional studio. These were the years of the major commission for Chandigarh (1950–64), in India, projects in the United States, and the *unité d'habitation* in Marseille (1946), which was the first in a series of housing complexes built around Europe. It was also a period of great changes in his language: from rigorous stereometric abstractionism, which was the fruit of his experience with Purism and then with *L'Esprit Nouveau*, to the chapel of Notre-Dame-du-Haut in Ronchamp (1950) and the Dominican convent of La Tourette in Eveux-sur-Arbresle (1957), near Lyon. In all his subsequent works Le Corbusier moved on to a new formal and figurative season. Construction materials exposed without any further finishing touches, the addition of curved figures to stereometric lines, the search for the symbolic and metaphorical value of form, and the use of colour as form and light were the elements of the new language, which would be defined by some observers as brutalist.

Le Corbusier was a tireless worker, which is reflected in the bare statistics of his life and work: he completed 100 buildings, 170 projects, 65 urban-design projects, 400 paintings, 7 murals, 200 lithographs, 40 tapestries, 50 sculptures, 20 models and prototypes of furnishings, 50 books, and 7 art books; and he took part in any number of conferences and lectures around the world. It may be said, quite simply, that Le Cor-

busier was the most brilliant and most influential figure in 20th-century architecture.

The architect's intense activity during these late years led him to build a small wooden refuge, the legendary *cabanon*, in Cap Martin, in the South of France, where he used to stay at the home of Jean Badovici and Eileen Gray, who had designed a stupendous villa in the 1920s right here on the Côte d'Azur. With the little summer cabin (1952), Le Corbusier intensely exploited just a few square metres in line with the principle of economy that he had employed throughout his career without losing either identity or the poetic power of form. During his brief stays in the *cabanon*, the mature architect recovered the energy and concentration that he needed for his work.

It was at Cap Martin that on 27 August 1965 Le Corbusier died as the result of drowning following a heart attack while swimming in the Mediterranean Sea. He was buried in the cemetery at Roquebrune next to his wife Yvonne, whom he had married many years earlier, in 1934, and with whom he had lived on the top floors of a building he had designed at 24 rue Nungesser et Coli, in Paris.

Le Corbusier's apartment block at 24 rue Nungesser-et-Coli, Paris, in which he had his own home, was designed and built between 1931 and 1933 in collaboration with Pierre Jeanneret, who was his architectural partner from 1922 to 1940. Until recent years the building was not considered one of the major products of their partnership, even though it was an important test of their theories in the field of both architecture and urbanism. Yet '24 N.C.', as Le Corbusier liked to call the block, was not just a showpiece of these theories, but was also the place in which the master chose to live. On the top two floors of the block he designed an apartment and studio, which was his home together with his wife Yvonne Gallis from 1934 until his death in 1965.

The main façade of 24 N.C. comprises seven levels. The top two, housing Le Corbusier's own apartment and studio, are slightly set back, while a large bow window juts out in the central part of the building. The

THE STUDIO WITH RUBBLE STONE WALL AND ARCH

THE ROOF GARDEN KIOSK

façade is characterised by a glass wall, partly built using glass brick and virtually lying on the concrete basement, where a circular column draws the main axis of the building and the entrance to the block. When the block was completed, Le Corbusier recalled that: "A great event occurred this morning: we carried up the large fireside sofa… and installed it in the apartment. And suddenly the whole place looked snug, just like a real home." (Petit 1970, p. 32)

"My apartment," Le Corbusier observed in an interview, "is 24 m long, including the balcony, and light floods in from both sides. It is extremely narrow, only 4 m wide… Yet everything is in proportion. The standard height is 2.50 m, which means that we don't have to stoop anywhere – this height in fact forms part of the dimensions stipulated by the local authorities. …When I open my doors, I can see from one end of the apartment to the other. But do not imagine that this creates an austere atmosphere. On the contrary, it is very homely, thanks to my research into all the ways of opening a large door. It is normal practice for a large wall opening to have two or three folding doors. I remember once in Majorca I visited a house somewhere… and there was a fairly wide door, which opened outwards on its left pin… Anyway, it stayed in my mind for a long time, and so instead of hanging my doors on a pin, I positioned them on two non-symmetrical pivots, at the top and at the bottom, around 50 cm one side and 1.80 on the other. This means that I did not need to use any metalwork at all because there was no strain on the hinges. Even after 17 years, these doors have remained intact, despite the poor conditions that they were exposed to for a period of seven years,

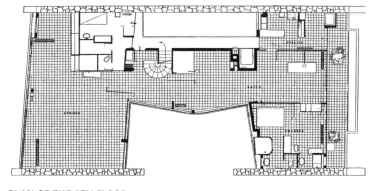

PLAN OF THE 7TH FLOOR

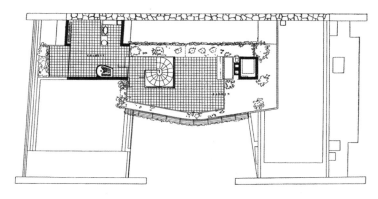

PLAN OF THE 8TH FLOOR WITH ROOF GARDEN

B 2869

DRAWING OF THE FAÇADE

STREET VIEW

caused by the German occupation and lack of adequate heating. They are made out of wood, are light, and can be opened with one's little finger." (Sbriglio 1992, p. 75)

The apartment is entered through a gallery served by a lift and a staircase. The bathroom and toilet open directly onto the gallery, as do the kitchen and the hall, situated in a barycentric position with respect to the living area and the studio, where Le Corbusier left the structure of the back wall exposed, anticipating the brutalist aesthetic that would characterise his later period. The horizontally pivoted doors, the fixed furnishings richly decorated with purist paintings, and the enormous glass front are the most characteristic features of the space. To this we should add Le Corbusier's decision – rather unusual in contemporary buildings – to use vaulted ceilings in many of the rooms, giving them remarkable expressive power. Lowered areas alternate with more spacious rooms, creating the rhythmic use of space that was typical of the architect's composition. A small helicoidal staircase, completely exposed, leads to a roof garden, a sort of pavilion on the roof of the apartment which in itself already seems to be an extraneous body placed on top of the building – a house on a house. Destined exclusively to be used as guest quarters, and with hardly any internal division, the pavilion's continuous space is immersed in the dazzling light of the eighth floor and in the plants covering some of the external terraces.

The apartment is decorated with paintings by Le Corbusier himself but otherwise is completely furnished according to the dictates that had led him, together with Charlotte Perriand, to produce the 'habitation

equipment' presented at the *Salon d'Automne* in Paris in 1929. There are also, however, some specially made furnishings, such as the dining table and several containers for the kitchen. Apart from these, everything conforms to the needs of standardisation and mass production, the new principles that inspired the modern aesthetic.

The main elements of Le Corbusier's expressive language are light, colour and form, and it is these that structure the composition of his own Paris apartment just as they do the composition of his much more demanding works, irrespective of scale, from the single object to the city.

GENNARO POSTIGLIONE

BIBLIOGRAPHY:

1971 Von Moos S., *Le Corbusier*, Paris
1972 Boesiger W., *Le Corbusier*, Zurich
1987 *Le Corbusier. Une Encyclopédie*, Paris
1996 Sbriglio J., *Apartment Block 24 N.C. and Le Corbusier's Home*, Basle/Boston/Berlin
2001 Cornoldi A. (ed.), *Le case degli architetti. Dizionario privato dal Rinascimento ad oggi*, Venice

Arno Lederer, Jórunn Ragnarsdóttir, Marc Oei

*1947, *1957, *1962

2001–02, NEW CONSTRUCTION,
STILL INHABITED BY THE ARCHITECTS
GUNTERSTRASSE, STUTTGART (D)

MAIN WORKS AND PROJECTS

1983–87	City centre renovation, Fellbach (D)
1988–91	Extension of the city tax offices, Reutlingen (D)
1992–94	Warehouse and office building, Reutlingen (D)
1993–97	Central administrative offices for the Schwabian energy utility, Stuttgart (D)
1999	Catholic seminary, Stuttgart-Hohenheim (D)
1999–2002	School and gym, Ostfildern (D)
2000	Salem International College, Überlingen (D)

ARNO LEDERER was born in 1947 in Stuttgart and Jórunn Ragnarsdóttir, with whom he lives and works, was born in 1957 in the Icelandic city of Akureyri. Lederer's junior partner Marc Oei was born in 1962 in Stuttgart. Lederer began his studies at the University of Stuttgart in 1968 at the peak of the student revolts. His time as a student was marked by his growing political awareness as well as the wish to not jeopardize his chances for a career as a practicing architect. If one recalls Dieter Hoffman-Axthelm's conclusion that the rebellious students of 1968 saw "not building" as the ideal of architecture, then Lederer can be seen as an exception to this rule. He developed his architectural signature mainly after graduation while working in the Zurich office of Ernst Gisel in 1977. The general political climate of his student years is expressed in the relentless reflection and public discussions of contemporary architectural issues, above all, by the editorial board of the magazine *Der Architekt*.

In 1979, Lederer opened his own office in Stuttgart. His first important project was the renovation of the city centre of Fellbach. Here, directly next to the city hall designed by Ernst Gisel, he built an apartment and office building (1983–87) that also housed the city library. The signature of Jórunn Ragnarsdóttir, who joined the office in 1985, is already recognizable. In the same year, Lederer became Professor for Construction and Design at the University of Applied Sciences in Stuttgart and since 1990, has taught at the University of Karlsruhe. In 1992, Marc Oei joined Lederer's office as a junior partner.

Although their earliest works show a slight affinity to the postmodernist *Zeitgeist*, LRO (Lederer, Ragnarsdóttir, Oei) soon developed a characteristic architectural language and style. The key word to describe this style is simplicity, yet this should not be confused with the exquisite aesthetic of materials prevalent in New Swiss Minimalism or with the design

dogma of Berlin's city planning. For LRO, simplicity means concentration on the basics. The basics of an architectonic project are always comprised of different factors – site, existing architecture, light, social function, construction, atmosphere, etc. – factors which must be synthesized to create an overall successful design. "Good architecture always takes a holistic approach," Lederer said in a recent interview (Interview with Haila Ochs, in: Bachmann, Wolfgang (ed.), p. 79). Here, the old functionalist method applies where form is not fixed from the start but rather arises out of the process of dealing with a given set of conditions.

Buildings such as the tax office expansion in Reutlingen, the central administration of the Schwabian energy utility in Stuttgart or the school and gym in Ostfildern are distinguished mainly through their structural succinctness and their atmospheric interior, achieved through finely orchestrated lighting. LRO is consistently engaged in building residences. For Lederer, quality of life should be the main factor for architecture. He regrets the backwardness of Germany in this area, in contrast to Scandinavia, for example. LRO's particular affinity for this subject is not least of all demonstrated by their own homes. In 1993–94, LRO built the "Haus Buben" (boy's house) in Karlsruhe for the Lederer / Ragnarsdóttir family; a residence that also houses the architects' office on the top floor. The name is a word play on the husband and wife partners' four sons, whose first floor rooms connect directly to the garden. The building skilfully takes advantage of the property's hillside location.

A hillside location is also a chief characteristic of their second residence in Stuttgart, a double house for both the families of Lederer / Ragnarsdóttir and Oei. Since Stuttgart is topographically situated in a basin, much-coveted sites for homes with a view over the city are rare. The narrow

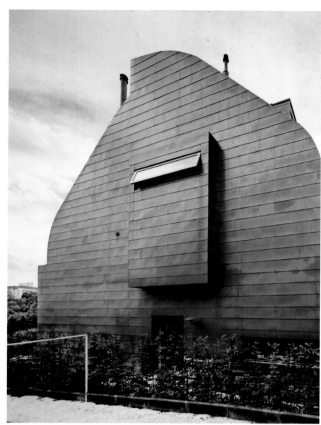

VIEW FROM THE ENTRANCE YARD ON THE STREET SIDE

ENTRANCE ON THE LONG SIDE

ENTRANCE YARD

VIEW FROM THE INTERMEDIARY FLOOR

COMBINED KITCHEN AND LIVING AREA

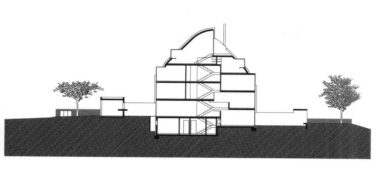

SECTION AND VIEW

plot of land between existing structures that could be acquired was not simple to develop for the families' envisioned use. The double house, which is hardly recognizable as such from the outside, is no more than eight metres wide. Only the street-side enclosed porch – a portal building of exposed concrete – has two separate entrances on the right and left sides. In between are rust-coloured, gate-like areas, which at first glance appear to be garage doors. For the architects, however, this garage area was too valuable for cars. Instead, two multi-use rooms used for hobbies, parties or storage have been developed. These rooms are linked with the intimate entrance courtyards in front of the house. Both the house halves can be entered through the middle of the long side.

The kitchen and eating area are in the front facing the street and are connected to the courtyard by a glass wall. The rooms on the valley side are split-level. The living room area is divided over two floors and visually unified by a floor recess and a vertical bookcase that runs along the entire wall, opening onto a lower level garden area. A 2-m-high concrete wall separates both of the double house halves in the front and back courtyard areas, while the garden, positioned at the furthest end of the site, takes up the entire width of the property. Continuing the split-level structure, the individual bedrooms for the architects' large families are located on the upper floors. In order to prevent a claustrophobic feeling which could arise in the narrow, 4 m width of the individual residences, the architects have created a maximum of transparency: suspended steps on narrow steel stringers forming a white staircase, or the possibility of keeping open the tall, two-wing bedroom doors in order to maximize light and spatial flow. Finally, under the freely curved roof, the top

VIEW FROM THE KITCHEN WINDOW

PASSAGE BESIDE THE HOUSE

225

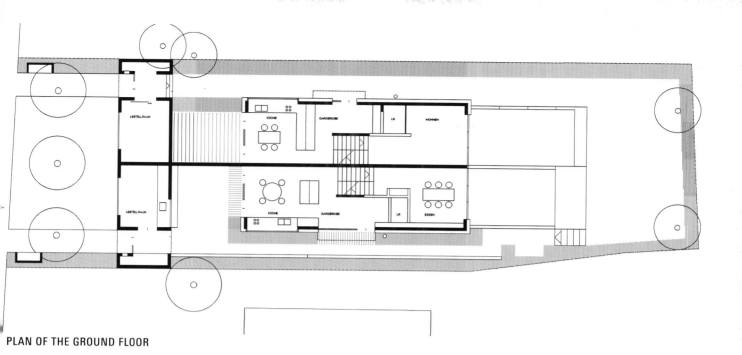

PLAN OF THE GROUND FLOOR

GROUND PLAN OF THE ATTIC

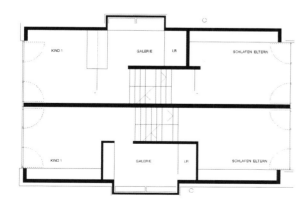

PLAN OF THE UPPER FLOOR

floor room offers a gallery-like terrace along with the best view of the city. Rectangular panes of glass with rust-coloured borders dominate both of the main façades. In the background, a copper covering allows the curved roof to merge with the sides of the building. The entrances on the side façades are accented by oriels directly positioned above.

EBERHARD SYRING

BIBLIOGRAPHY:

1992   Lederer A. and J. Ragnarsdóttir, *Wohnen heute*, Stuttgart

1995   Bachmann W. (ed.), *Lederer, Ragnardóttir, Oei*, Munich

1998   Lederer A., 'Gibt es noch Werk- und Materialgerechtigkeit?', in *Der Architekt* 7/98, pp. 415–417

2002   Schwarz U. (ed.), *Neue Deutsche Architektur. Eine reflexive Moderne*, Ostfildern-Ruit, pp. 112–119

2003   'Im Doppelpack. Doppelhaus in Stuttgart', in *Deutsche Bauzeitung*, no. 9/03, pp. 57–62

< STAIRCASE TO THE ROOF TERRACE

Roger Le Flanchec
1915–1986

1969–80, NEW CONSTRUCTION
TRÉBEURDEN, CÔTES D'ARMOR (F)

MAIN WORKS AND PROJECTS

1936–38	Strniste house on the Île Grande (close to Trébeurden) (F)
1949	Project for a youth hostel on the Île Grande (F)
1950–62	Hélios building, Trébeurden (F)
1952	Project for a 'cité radieuse', Trébeurden (F)
1954	Projects for the Beauvir house in Larmor Plage (Morbihan) and club house in Trébeurden (F)
1954–65	Orain house, Brélévenez (F)

1961	Tower project comprising 254 flats, Guingamp (F), with Ernest Novello and Georges Beck
1965–66	Kerautem house, Locquénolé (F)
1969–73	Quéré house, Ploumoguer (F)

ROGER LE FLANCHEC was born in Guingamp on 6 November 1915. After the death of his father in 1918 he grew up with his mother and grandfather until the latter's death in 1924. 1931–33 he attended the local architecture school (École Régionale des Beaux-Arts), Rennes, and 1933–37 he worked for Jean Fauny, an architect in St Brieuc. An inheritance from his father allowed him to set up his own practice in 1937. Before he obtained professional architect's permit in 1947, he lived as an aristocrat and gentleman on his boat (1944–47).

Le Flanchec's Hélios project at Trébeurden, Côtes d'Armor, grew out of a commission by the Naëder family. The plan was to realise on a coastal site in Trébeurden an apartment tower and later a Corbusian 'unité d'habitation' or housing complex called Cité Hélios, which would be conceived in accordance with Le Corbusier's principles: 30 split-level flats with loggia. The first design for the project dates back to 1950, and work proper on Hélios, which was interrupted several times, started in 1952. In the end only the tower was built, its structure completed in 1962. During the long construction of the Hélios building, the architect lived for many years (1956–70) on site in a shack. But in 1970 Le Flanchec moved into the tower's show flat on the 13th floor, in which he lived and worked until 1980, the year in which all the apartments in the Hélios building were completed. Now that the block was finished, the architect set in the flat he had planned for himself in it. This was the Inis Gwirin (Glass Island) apartment, which was located at the top of the building, and which was executed at length between 1969 and 1980. Finally, on 9 July 1980, Le Flanchec moved out of the show flat and into Inis Gwirin, living there until his death in 1986.

It took Le Flanchec's fully 30 years to achieve his dream of the Hélios tower. Progress was slow for a number of reasons. He had great difficulty obtaining planning permission for the project, which was only gained because the architect fought tooth and nail for permission, even making a trip to Paris and threatening to go on hunger strike under the windows of the Président du Conseil. Le Flanchec was a painstaking architect, who worked slowly. This meticulousness caused him to decide to demolish a first version of the block and revise the plans.

Shortly before his death, Le Flanchec wrote copious notes on the architectural detailing of his Inis Gwirin penthouse, ranging from its orientation and dimensions to the colours of the lining and plexiglas. "From north to south, the precinct of the apartment is made entirely of curved lines, which in the blueprint resemble the contour of ample breasts… A circular study desk… skirts the round bed, 2.5 m in diameter, covered with black skai… In the east, a huge chimney with a 3-metre opening is preceded by a circular windowsill that evokes the shape of butterfly wings… Three doors lead out to the lawn, access to which is barred by a high concrete balustrade." According to Daniel Le Couédic, Le Flanchec used to receive guests here, dressed in a yellow or red blazer in the manner of his yachting days. Armed with photos, modified blueprints and models, he spoke eloquently about his work, providing "a text which could never have tolerated any sort of improvisation".

Constructed on a footprint of some 300 m², the Inis Gwirin apartment was conceived on the basis of a bean-shaped plan. The plan, which Le Flanchec had already used for his Orain house (1954–65), lays out the living rooms following the Corbusian principles of the *plan libre*. In the apartment, the hearth is given a central position, as in the houses of Frank Lloyd Wright. An initial project, dated 1957, comprised a huge main room, designed according to the open plan. The subordinate rooms were partitioned and closed by sliding doors. Modifications to the structure resulted in a bean-shaped construction, implanted at the eastern edge of the flat roof. A staircase from the 13th floor, which leads to a long and

THE ARCHITECT IN THE LIVING AREA

THE FIREPLACE AREA IN THE LIVING AREA

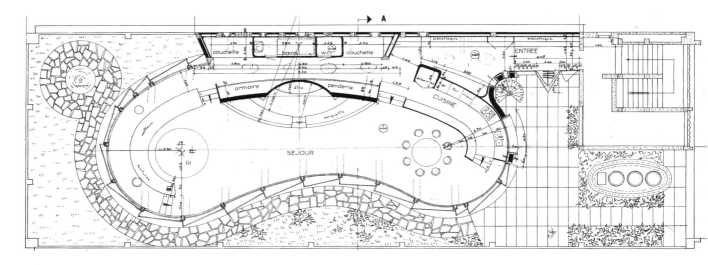

FLOOR PLAN

THE CIRCULAR BED IN THE LIVING AREA

dimly lit entrance, accesses the roof. A flight of three steps leads to the living area. The main façade is composed of double glasswork 35 m in length and fully exposed to the west. The panorama, exceptional in itself, is further improved by the view from the terrace above, reached by an exterior helicoidal staircase. "[The terrace], serving as a garden, has a 360° view of the sea and the countryside." The apartment's location on the flat roof of the Hélios building made it into "a lofty and solitary look-out post", since the architect used to contemplate his work from the roof top.

Le Flanchec's Inis Gwirin apartment is the culmination and synthesis of an exceptional career. The architect created open living areas, which he decorated and furnished with a meticulous choice of objects paying homage to the modern masters: a Mies van der Rohe bench, a set of Saarinen chairs, a Charlotte Perriand-Le Corbusier armchair, and the complete works of Paul Valéry in the library. Le Flanchec was rarely published in reviews (although there were references to him in *L'Architecture d'Aujourd'hui* and *Maisons de l'Ouest*), and – with the exception of a project for 254 apartments in Guingamp – he worked alone. Nor was his influence very great, being limited, according to Daniel Le Couédic, to

two cases among young architects from the Trégorrois region. Le Couédic felt that this "Breton penn kalet" or obstinate Breton was strangely connected with Paul Valéry, being an "unsubjugated man" and an indefatigable worker, who was always at war with the authorities responsible for granting permits.

CATHERINE LE TEUFF

BIBLIOGRAPHY:

1957   'Immeuble haut à Trébeurden', in *L'Architecture d'aujourd'hui*, no. 74, November, p. 44
1965   'La cité radieuse Hélios', in *Maisons de l'Ouest*, no. 7, October 7, pp. 56–59
1972   Goulet P. and Emery M., *Guide architecture en France: 1945–1983*, Paris, pp. 344, 349, 360, 371
1995   Le Couédic D., *Roger Le Flanchec, les manoirs futuristes*, exhibition leaflet IFA / Château de Kerjean, Paris
2001   Dieudonné P., Bonnet P. and Le Couédic D., *Bretagne XXe, un Siècle d'Architectures*, Rennes, pp. 198–199

Henry-Jacques Le Même
1897–1997

1928–29, NEW CONSTRUCTION
CHEMIN DU CALVAIRE, MEGÈVE (F)

MAIN WORKS AND PROJECTS

1927	Angèle de Bourbon's chalet, Mont d'Arbois, Megève (F)	**1942–44**	Interior design of the Mont-Blanc, Soleil d'or and Hostellerie hotels, Megève (F)
1928	Hôtel Albert Ier, Megève (F)	**1957**	Savoy pavilion, Brussels International Exhibition (B)
1929	Roc-des-Fiz Sanatorium, on Plateau d'Assy (F), with Pol Abraham	**1958–81**	Projects for numerous schools, including *lycées* in Briançon (1958–60), Cluses (1966–68), and Annemasse (1974–75) (F)
1932	Guébriant Sanatorium, on Plateau d'Assy (F), with Pol Abraham	**1964–67**	Administrative building in Annecy (F)
1936–37	Savoy pavilion and Timber pavilion at the 1937 International Exhibition in Paris (F)	**1979–81**	Le Talisman chalet for Michel Dassault, Megève (F)

HENRY-JACQUES LE MÊME'S father was from Brittany and his mother from Anjou, but he chose to settle in another region of France, Savoy. He grew up and went to school in Nantes, and shortly after the First World War discovered the pleasures that Paris had to offer, particularly the antique bookshops of the 6th *arrondissement*. He began to collect rare editions, such as *Eupalinos et l'Architecte* by Paul Valéry and *Le Cortège d'Orphée* by Apollinaire (with Raoul Dufy woodcuts). As well as an avid reader of literature, Le Même was also a theatre lover, enjoying especially the modern productions of Jacques Copeau or Louis Jouvet. Between his admission to the Ecole Nationale des Beaux-Arts in 1917, where he entered Pascal-Recoura's studio and later that of Emmanuel Pontremoli, and his subsequent move to Megève (1925), he studied with the greatest designers of the time, Pierre Patout and Emile-Jacques Ruhlmann. Le Même exhibited at the Salon d'automne in Paris, and designed theatre sets and shop fronts. Prior to obtaining his degree (for Angèle de Bourbon chalet in Megève in 1929), he received several commissions for modern farms and sanatoriums. In 1928 he began a friendship and collaboration with an old school friend, Pol Abraham, with whom he built several sanatoriums in the Alps.

Despite his multiple professional activities (Ordre des Architectes, Commission des Constructions Scolaires, Chief Architect of Reconstruction, Habitat Commission of the IUA, Franco-British Association of Architects, etc.), Le Même preferred to live and work in Megève. In the early 1930s this village became the most famous French winter sports resort, mainly thanks to Le Même and his architecture. In 1938, while working on a project for the Olympe fashion boutique, he met the young Czech clothes designer Théa Nowitzka, whom he would later marry. Their Megève home would become a place of meeting and retreat in the mountains of Savoy.

With his own home, constructed new in Megève's chemin du Calvaire between 1928 and 1929, Henry-Jacques Le Même built what some people have called "a manifesto of modern architecture", as if he wanted to affirm for all time his commitment to the modern movement. In fact, this home-cum-studio, built on a plot of land belonging to his mother and his aunt, seems like a variety of dwellings rolled into one: a refuge for a skier light-headed from mountain air, a home for an architect dreaming of travel, and a house for an extended family including many friends. But this is what Le Même rather wanted for the house, which should bring all these functions under one and the same roof: a studio and apartment for his wife and himself on the ground floor, an apartment for his mother and his aunt on the first floor, and two rooms for guests also on the first floor.

Erected on a footpath to a Calvary (representing Christ's passion), the home is situated on the border of Megève village and a forest, between civilisation and nature. Further demonstration of Le Même's love of contrast can be found in the fabric of the house itself. While the façade appears rather reserved, the interior is animated with decorative motifs of Wiener Werkstätte wallpapers and paved floors. Careful to unite modernity and regional tradition, the architect conceived interiors which were as warm as the red roughcast of the exterior walls. Le Même's sketches of the village church and his numerous photos of the local countryside indicate the architect's deep interest both in shadows cast by trees on snow and in high-altitude colour. The interest is reflected elsewhere in the

SUMMER VIEW OF THE ENTRANCE

WINTER VIEW OF THE HOUSE AND THE CALVARY

THE STUDIO ALCOVE

house's interior furnishings. The warm tints of the Okoumé furniture in Le Même's office are highlighted by the Pompeii red of the alcove linoleum. Henry-Jacques Le Même never imposed the modern aesthetic demonstrated in his own home on clients in search of a picturesque mountain chalet. Nevertheless, all the elements that he developed through those commissions, which launched his career, are present in his home: a compact plan, open airy rooms from which to enjoy the view, large south-facing balconies, entry doors and steps with original motifs, and long windows and fences.

The Megève house has a roof terrace, and Le Même spoke of his reasons for choosing one: "When I arrived in Megève, I was obviously under the influence of Le Corbusier, having just read his famous new book *Vers une Architecture*." However, the architect did not follow Le Corbusier's ideas such as flat roofs to the letter. He arranged a series of gargoyles on the flat-fronted façades to assist the drainage of rainwater. He also decided not to use a guard rail on the terrace, erecting a simple parapet instead. Moulding of the parapet resolved a stonework problem

and added elegance to the façades. The long window on the front of the building brought light to the living room, as well as to the kitchen, toilets and bathroom. Different styles of window and door revealed the function of the respective rooms: for example, circular for the dining room and a porthole for the company secretary. The interior, no less than the exterior, also reflects the artistic qualities of the architect. It was here, at 28 years of age, that Le Même created a style that was to become his trademark: "a mountain art", as Maurice Culot wrote, "that through the subtle play of simple materials brings modernity and tradition together".

The Megève building is a point of departure in the life and work of Henry-Jacques Le Même. Nevertheless, this one structure far from does adequate justice to the architect's diverse and profuse career. Any idea of a manifested architecture is rejected by his constructions or extensions of mountain chalets. For these new holiday places, with their familiar and reassuring shadows, are, on the contrary, inventions formed of their environment. Other projects similar to Le Même's Megève home-cum-studio include his famous Hôtel Albert Ier, built in Megève in 1928.

THE DESK DESIGNED BY GILLES ADNET, 1928–29

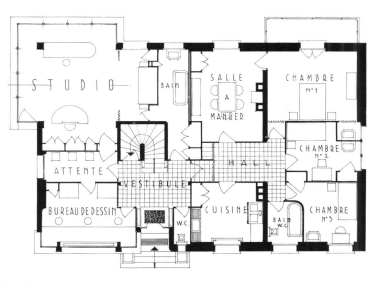

PLAN OF THE GROUND FLOOR

With this building, he began to develop the modern vocabulary that he would use in new hospital spaces. In all his interior designs and furnishings, he would remain faithful to the influence of Pierre Patout and Emile-Jacques Ruhlmann, as well as to the decor of De Stijl. Le Même's constructions drew on French tradition and Nordic influences, often bringing to mind the designs of Natalia Goncharova's Russian ballets and the architect's first theatre designs.

AYMONE NICOLAS

BIBLIOGRAPHY:

1933   Laprade A., 'L'œuvre de H.-J. Le Même à Megève', in *L'Architecture*, vol. XLVVI,
         no. 2, pp. 53–62
1934   'Le Même Henry-Jacques, Villa Privée à Megève', in *Le Linoleum*, no. 22, February, pp. 13–14
1950   Gereghini M., *Costruire in Montagna*, Milan
1988   Véry F. and Saddy P., *Henry-Jacques Le Même, or the Invention of Winter Sports Resort
         Architecture in France*, Liège, pp. 36–39
1999   Culot M. and Lambrichs A., photographs by Delaunay D., *Megève 1925–1950.
         Architectures de Henry-Jacques Le Même*, Paris, pp. 91–99

Sigurd Lewerentz
1885–1975

**1970, ALTERATION WITH A STUDIO EXTENSION BY KLAS ANSELM
KÄVLINGEVÄGEN 26, LUND (S)**

MAIN WORKS AND PROJECTS

1911–18	Project for housing developments in Eneborg and Pålsjö, Helsingborg (S), with Torsten Stubelius
1914	Project for a crematorium in Bergaliden, Helsingborg (S), with Torsten Stubelius
1915–61	Extension of South Stockholm Cemetery in Enskede, Stockholm (S), competition, with Gunnar Asplund
1916–71	East Malmö Cemetery, Malmö (S), competition, First Prize
1929–30	Pavilions, buildings and objects for the Universal Exhibition in Stockholm (S)
1930–32	Headquarters of the National Insurance Company, Stockholm (S), competition, First Prize
1933	Competition for Johannesberg church, Gothenburg (S)
1943	Own apartment-cum-studio in a converted attic over a fittings company, Bruksgatan 14, Eskilstuna (S)
1956–64	St Mark's parish church, Björkhagen, Stockholm (S), competition, First Prize
1962	St Peter's parish church, Klippan (S)
1968–71	Project and realisation of flower stall and caretaker's house in East Malmö Cemetery, Malmö (S)

SIGURD LEWERENTZ was born in 1885 in Bjärtrå, in northern Sweden. Initially he studied engineering at Göteborg (Gothenburg) Polytechnic, only later switching to architecture, which he studied at the Academy of Fine Arts in Stockholm. Following his studies, Lewerentz went to Germany (1908–10) to undertake a period of apprenticeship – first in Berlin, then in Munich – at the studios of some of the country's most prestigious architects, such as Bruno Möhring, Theodor Fisher and Richard Rimerschmid. Here he came into contact with the ideas that were developing at the beginning of the 20th century in continental Europe. On his return to Sweden in 1910 he attended the Klara Skola. This free institution was set up at the instigation of Gunnar Asplund and Osvald Almqvist as well as of Lewerentz himself.

In 1911 Lewerentz opened a professional practice of his own in partnership with Torsten Stubelius. The arrangement lasted until 1917, when the two architects went their separate ways. While it lasted, the collaboration proved extremely fruitful, sowing the seeds of architectural ideas that would accompany Lewerentz throughout his career. After this time he mainly worked alone, except for a number of competition entries and specific projects, on which he collaborated with architect colleagues or artists.

A man of few words, and reluctant to provide explanations of his work or to seek theories that might justify his choices, Lewerentz said everything he had to say exclusively through his projects and realised buildings. This silent retiring nature of his accounts for the fact that his oeuvre is relatively unknown. The fact that his comparatively modest out-

put is unknown is perhaps surprising, given that Lewerentz's architectural experience was one of the most significant of the 20th century, evolving as it did on the margins of Modernism. He was a colleague, for example, of Asplund, with whom he entered and won the competition for the South Stockholm Cemetery extension, the famous Woodland Cemetery. However, due to events surrounding the brief's implementation, Lewerentz's decisive role in the development of the project was never acknowledged by the critics, most of whom saw the extension as the work of Asplund alone.

Lewerentz quickly earned a reputation as a 'bad manager'. This is explained partly by his rather awkward character and partly by his inability to honour commitments, but also by his natural tendency to continue to modify his projects even when they could be considered to be definitive. His work bears witness to the questing activity of a man who was always ready to set himself new questions, with a capacity to seek answers beyond the bounds of existing knowledge. This was the attitude with which the architect worked right from the outset of his career, when his debt to the trend of the time, Neoclassicism, is stronger and more recognisable.

Lewerentz's oeuvre is also characterised by a certain 'obliquity' of form that demonstrates the tetchy architect's reluctance to accept preconceived formulas. Again, the attitude is visible from the start, witness three works all developed during the first few years of his career: the project for Helsinborg Cemetery, the competition for the extension of South Stockholm Cemetery, and the project for East Malmö Cemetery.

ABOVE AND BELOW: VIEW OF THE "BLACK BOX"

THE ARCHITECT'S DESK

238

VIEW OF THE MAIN ENTRANCE

in the south of Sweden. He was able to do this thanks to the affection and esteem of a younger colleague, the architect Klas Anselm, who not only gave him free use of a house he owned, but also converted and extended it to meet Lewerentz's needs. The most important alteration was the construction of a studio in the garden. The new room was rather unusual in that it had no windows, and was lit only by three evenly spaced skylights in the roof. In line with Lewerentz's character and choices, the room was painted black, with an aluminium covering on the ceiling to exploit the natural light from above. This design explains the name by which the studio was known: 'The Black Box'.

The new house was also chosen by Anselm for its proximity to the public hospital which the ageing architect was forced to visit more and more frequently during the last years of his life. Towards the end Lewerentz devoted most of his time to creating an archive of his drawings. He died in Lund at the venerable age of 90, a few years after the realisation of the flower kiosk at East Malmö Cemetery.　　　GENNARO POSTIGLIONE

Lewerentz always sought highly personal solutions, outside the customary parameters and extremely pertinent to the demands of the project and construction in question. But it was during the final years of his activity, from the project for the St Mark's parish complex in Stockholm (1956) up to his death in 1975, that his 'oblique' thought is most powerfully evident. In the realisation of the St Mark's project, and in an even more conscious way in St Peter's church at Klippan, there is both a deliberate evasion of rules, i.e. of predetermined rules lying outside the demands of the construction, and the emergence of a new anarchic and aristocratic way of conceiving and implementing architecture.

During his long career, Lewerentz was concerned not just with the classic themes of architecture, but also with city and cityscape design (as can be seen in many of his urban projects) as well as the design of industrial objects, even including advertising graphics. For example, he designed the posters and logos for the Stockholm Universal Exhibition of 1930, and was also responsible for numerous patents for the construction and correct operation of metal fittings – for a long time Lewerentz owned a company and was in charge of its production. During this period he moved from Stockholm to Eskilstuna, turning the disused attic of the fittings company he had bought into his home and studio, in line with the medieval custom of having one's home and workplace not only in the same building, but also intercommunicating.

After the period in Eskilstuna managing his metal fittings factory, Lewerentz moved to Skanör, a small exclusive holiday resort in the south of Sweden that enjoyed mild winters. The move had been made necessary by the poor health of his wife. Being wheelchair-bound, she was unable to leave the attic in the factory. They thus decided together to move to a bungalow in an area where the climate was more suited to an ageing couple. In Skanör Lewerentz continued to work. Indeed, these were the years of his most revolutionary projects, which would once again fill the pages of the architectural press in Scandinavia and beyond. On the death of his wife, Lewerentz left the house in Skanör, which was too isolated and too far from his friends and relatives for an old man whose health was failing, and moved to the small university city of Lund,

FLOOR PLAN

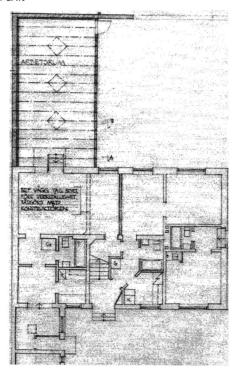

BIBLIOGRAPHY:

1976　Nyberg B., 'Sigurd Lewerentz's last house', in *Arkitektur*, no. 2, May, p. 2

1985　Ahlin J., *Sigurd Lewerentz Arckitekt*, Stockholm

1994　Constant C., *Towards a Spiritual Landscape*, Stockholm, pp. 133–135

2001　Flora N., Giardiello P. and Postiglione G. (eds.), *Sigurd Lewerentz. Opera Completa*, Milan
　　　Cornoldi A., *Le case degli architetti. Dizionario privato dal Rinascimento ad oggi*, Venice,
　　　pp. 226–227

Eugeen Liebaut
*1952

1993–96, NEW CONSTRUCTION, STILL INHABITED BY THE ARCHITECT
GUCHTERSTRAAT 12A, SINT-ANTELINKS (B)

MAIN WORKS AND PROJECTS

1979–83	Own house and studio, Binnenstraat 24, Aalst (B)
1987	Own weekend 'capsule', near Aalst (B)
1988–90	Plateau dance theatre, Herderstraat, Brussels (B)
1989–91	Vanderpooten house, Levoldlaan 16, Dilbeek (B)
1992–94	Seynaeve house, Slachthuisstraat 2, Ghent (B)
1993–96	Van Damme house, Landries, Aaigem (B)
1994–98	Police station, Beekveldstraat, Aalst (B)

1996–98	Bolle house, Kapellestraat, Herne (B)
1997–99	Van Kersschaever house, Kouterstraat, Destelbergen (B)
1998–2002	Auditorium building of Charlemagne Academy, Brusselstraat, Antwerp (B)

EUGEEN LIEBAUT was born and grew up in Aalst, a Flemish town deeply marked by the Industrial Revolution, its historical centre scattered with numerous old factories and remnants of working-class housing. He stems from a family that was closely linked with this industrial past. His father and his grandfather were supervisors in a cotton mill, where they distinguished themselves with their technological inventiveness. After secondary school in his home town, Liebaut studied architecture at Saint Luke's Institute in Brussels (1971–76), where he was taught by Pieter de Bruyne, Jean-Paul Laenen and Alfons Hoppenbrouwers. During an apprenticeship with Achiel Hutsebaut in Aalst, he also engaged in the participation movement which developed in his home town. He was an active member of a workshop for urban rehabilitation which fought against the dilapidation of the urban heritage, and advocated a revaluation of the city as a dwelling place. In 1979 he opened his own practice in Aalst.

In 1980 Liebaut settled in an old workman's house at Binnenstraat 24, Aalst, which he transformed with his own hands into his first home and studio (1979–83). He cleared the interior space and made it into an almost suprematist composition of separate elements. This was characteristic of his craving for experiment at the beginning of his practice. His early development showed a restless testing of contemporary architectural languages, from Le Corbusier to James Stirling, from Rob Krier to Frank Gehry, from Aldo Rossi to the New York Five – mainly in projects on paper. At that time Liebaut also started teaching at his old college, St Luke's Institute, which was an establishment where conceptual originality used to be held in high regard. He toured France, Ticino in Switzerland, Italy and Portugal to study both contemporary architecture and elementary forms of vernacular building. In his designs he initially went through a short period of Neo-Rationalism, experimenting with the archetypes of the traditional Flemish house, which can be seen, for example, in his

design of a studio-house for Paul Gees, a conceptual artist friend. Later, stimulated by the work of Alvaro Siza, he evolved a personal approach.

Liebaut came up with an architecture of a refreshing simplicity, an idiom that linked up with the purity of the 20th-century avant-garde, but which was at the same time attuned to its specific situation. Its simplicity was inspired by both economic and ecological considerations. On the assumption that natural resources are not inexhaustible and have to be used sparingly, the aim was to achieve the maximum result with the minimum resources: on the one hand, the deliberate choice of a limited number of materials, and on the other, the ambition to create as much space as possible with as little material as possible. And although at first sight this architecture might seem completely autonomous, it is in several respects attuned to its context. For each project Liebaut interpreted the whole of the required functions and relationships as a single organic entity, as an organism that reacts to its environment, to the ambient space and energy, and assumes a particular form consistent with them. At the same time, the immaterial weightless character of his architecture is also intended as a response to its environment, notably the unplanned proliferation of the built environment in Belgium. Liebaut deliberately sets out "to burden the already overfull landscape as little as possible". He wants to create houses that do not really occupy the land, but appear to float, giving the impression of being mobile installations which, if so desired, can be moved or removed, so that "the landscape can be restored at any time".

This was almost literally the case in the little weekend house the architect made for himself near Aalst in 1987. He conceived it as a white box raised on steel legs in a meadow, looking like a capsule from outer space, landed to investigate the terrestrial landscape. The need for this weekend

SOUTH AND EAST FAÇADES FROM THE STREET

NORTH FAÇADE

THE CORRIDOR ON THE FIRST FLOOR

PAGES 242–243: VIEW OF THE LANDSCAPE FROM THE LIVING ROOM

THE LIVING ROOM WITH THE STRIP-WINDOWS

retreat arose from the constant industrial pollution that was annoying the young Liebaut family in Aalst town centre. And it was, in fact, a prelude to the construction of a new house of their own in the countryside, where the architect later moved while maintaining his office in the old house.

In the late 1980s Liebaut acquired a building lot at Guchterstraat 12a on the edge of the quiet village of Sint-Antelinks, overlooking a valley of the Flemish Ardennes. After exploring the possibilities of the site with different plans, he opted for a concept very similar to his weekend capsule: a sheltered dwelling platform, lifted off the ground and enjoying a view of nature on all sides. The house was given a most elementary form, a pure rectangular prism opened up with oblong Corbusian strip windows.

SKETCH OF THE VOLUME

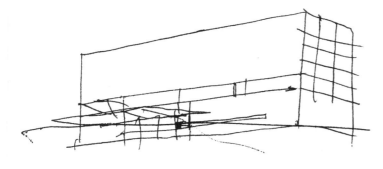

This white prism seems to be a striking realisation of Le Corbusier's view of "a marvellous sign of clarity in the middle of the confusion of nature", an expression of "geometrical will", "a gesture of optimism". But despite this apparent purism, the geometrical body does not adopt a commanding attitude towards its built context. The edge of the roof barely extends beyond the eaves of the surrounding saddle roofs. Hidden behind a hedge, it is not raised on pilotis but sits a little sunken in the slope. The prism only shows its crystalline form to its immediate surroundings in the garden.

The living area, which covers the whole first floor (a rectangle of 14.70 by 4.30 m), has a completely open plan with a free-standing utility cluster of kitchen, stairs and toilet. Space does not expand upward to double height, but develops horizontally on all sides through the continuous strip windows, which offer a panoramic view of the surrounding landscape. Sight and light are intensified at both ends of the prism, where the strip windows turn into a glass wall reaching the ceiling: on the east side it draws the morning sun into the kitchen, and on the west it opens up a larger view of the valley.

In spite of its somewhat limited width (4.30 m), this living area evokes a pronounced feeling of space. It is as if space flows steadily through the continuous windows. The family lives in the middle of the landscape, in constant contact with the changing rhythms of climate and vegetation. The necessary sense of security is provided by a continuous 80-cm-high parapet – a situation the architect likes to compare with the

WEST FAÇADE WITH THE BIG SQUARE WINDOW

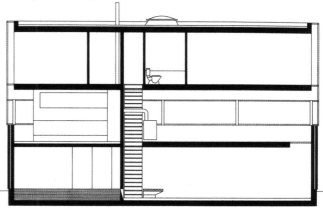

LONGITUDINAL SECTION

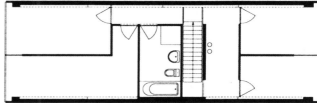

PLAN OF THE SECOND FLOOR

PLAN OF THE FIRST FLOOR

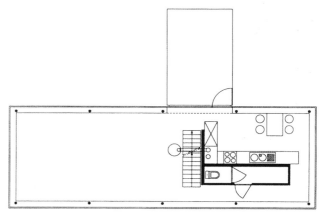

sides of a ship: "When you lie on the bottom, you see only the play of clouds and sun in the infinite sky."

The slender immaterial look of the building also stems from its unusually light construction. Contrary to what one might think, it is not made of concrete. The bearing soil, which lies 2 m deep, proved not to be strong enough for a massive construction with normal wall foundations, but instead of adopting an expensive pile foundation, the architect decided to lighten the construction as much as possible and to base the whole thing on a 2-m-thick layer of clay granules. The bearing surface of the house that rests on the clay layer is a 25-cm-thick slab stiffened with upright edge beams. The latter supports a bearing structure of five steel portals, the lower half of which is bricked up with solid walls, which ensure the necessary rigidity to counteract the wind. The upper half is filled with a wooden frame, clad in a 2-cm-thick stone slab and the necessary insulation. Both halves are finished with the same white plaster. The steel portals at both ends were stiffened with a pair of steel wind beams. Far from harming the view, these judiciously placed oblique elements, which evoke the memory of industrial constructions, are conducive to the dynamic of the interior space.

Eugeen Liebaut's own house can be seen as exemplary of the approach he adopts in most of his house designs. Not that they all turn out as pure prisms. Depending on the impediments of the built context, the geometrical bodies assume individual character with intriguing bends, bevels and curves. They become latently biomorphous bodies that respond to their surroundings with a particular attitude, a specific expression.

Eugeen Liebaut is one of the protagonists of the new generation that initiated a new spring in Flemish architecture in the mid-1980s. His work consists mainly of individual houses built in the area between Aalst and Brussels. Public buildings he has designed include the Plateau Theatre in Brussels and Aalst police station.   FRANCIS STRAUVEN

BIBLIOGRAPHY:
1997   Dubois M., 'Woning Liebaut in Sint-Antelinks', in *De Architect*, no. 9, pp. 78–82
1998   'Eigen woning Eugeen Liebaut – Maison personelle Eugeen Liebaut', in *Jaarboek Architectuur Vlaanderen/Annales de l'Architecture en Flandre/Flanders Architectural Yearbook 1996–1997*, Brussels, pp. 126–129
1999   Salazar J. and Gausa M., *Single-Family Housing – the Private Domain*, Basel, pp. 24–26
        Taborini S., *Living in a Small Space*, Stuttgart/London, pp. 76–79
2000   Strauven F., *Eugeen Liebaut, Architect*, Ghent, pp. 65–72

Kjell Lund
*1927

1964, NEW CONSTRUCTION
NILS COLLETT VOGTSVEIEN 17, OSLO (N)

MAIN WORKS AND PROJECTS

1958	Asker Town Hall, Asker (N)		**1980**	Cultural Centre, Sølvberget, Stavanger (N)
1968	Nic. Waals Institute, Spångbergveien 25, Oslo (N)		**1982**	St Hallvard Church and Monastery, Enerhauggatan 4, Oslo (N)
1969–72	The Ål cabin, a prefabricated building system, Ål county (N)		**1988**	St Magnus Church, Lillestrøm (N)
1970	Chateau Neuf, student hostel, Oslo (N)		**1997**	Protective enclosure for the Hamar Cathedral ruins (N)
1973	Bank of Norway, Bankplassen 2, Oslo (N)			
1976	The Norwegian Veritas, Veritasveien 1, Høvik (N)			

KJELL LUND was born in Lillehammer on 18 August 1927. His father, Arve Lund, was an assistant tax inspector, while his mother, Margit Hornes, came from Oslo. He grew up in the central part of inland Norway. As a young boy he wandered around at Maihaugen, an open-air museum consisting of many different types of old wooden farm buildings. His natural inheritance was a close relationship with Norwegian wood architecture, and this he brought with him into his profession.

In 1950 Lund graduated from the School of Architecture of the Norwegian University of Technology (NTH) at Trondheim. At the NTH he was a member of the executive committee and a theatre director in the Students' Union as well as an editorial assistant on the university newspaper, *Under Dusken*. For one year, from 1951 until 1952, Lund was employed by architect Nils Holter in his office in Oslo. In 1952 he opened his own practice, but his many talents made him uncertain as to what he wanted to do. His different abilities were demonstrated in a children's book published in 1955, which he both wrote and illustrated. In 1958 Lund was invited by the Norwegian Broadcasting Corporation to produce Children's Hour for a period of three weeks during that spring. The songs from these radio programmes ensured his place in many songbooks and in the minds of two generations of Norwegian children.

In 1954 Lund married Tove Berg from Oslo. In 1956, while employed in the Farmers' Building Office for Architectural Planning, he met Nils Slaatto, a friend from his childhood in Lillehammer and from his student days at the NTH. Together they established the firm of Lund & Slaatto Architects in 1958, which later became one of Norway's foremost architectural offices. Their partnership has led to many important and productive results, and there is no doubt that their different personal qualities were mutually complementary.

The work of Lund and Slaatto bears evidence of a deeply rooted knowledge of traditional Norwegian building techniques. This knowledge was given a contemporary expression, in clear harmony with present-day demands of functionality and rational production. They designed dynamic and vital buildings that were timeless and yet belonged to our times. An essential feature in Lund & Slaatto's production has been, and still is, their ability to combine systematic order, often based on primary geometrical forms, with architectural quality.

During his career Lund has received, together with Slaatto, the Sundt Prize (1972), the Houen Foundation Prize (1972, 1988, 1991, 1994 and 2000), and the 'Concrete Panel' award (1964, 1977, 1987 and 1988). In 1966 they won the Timber Award, and in 1985 both partners were made Knights 1st class of the Royal Norwegian Order of St Olav.

Lund is still active and creative. His last building, a protective enclosure for the Hamar Cathedral ruins, has attracted international attention for its dramatic and audacious expression. Sadly, in 2001 Nils Slaatto died, Lund's closest friend and his colleague for over 40 years.

Kjell Lund has compared his own private home, a new construction at Nils Collett Vogtsveien 17, Oslo, to a nest in the pine trees – a very apt description. The house is designed with the closest consideration of nature, as it almost seems to grow out of the tree trunks. Wherever you move in it, the presence of nature is clearly felt through the building's many windows. The house consists of three concrete towers, combined in a simple tree-like construction. In conjunction with the surrounding landscape, this construction draws attention to the components of the tree – with its vertical solid trunk, surrounded by horizontal light branches. The contrast is also maintained in the choice of materials, concrete and wood respectively.

We enter the house at one of the split levels and then, as in a spiral, climb all the way to the top level, like a squirrel wandering in a tree. This spiral-like movement helps give the house a unique flexibility. The build-

ONE OF THE CONCRETE TOWERS

WOODEN STRUCTURE WITH COVERED VERANDA

THE COVERED OUTDOOR AREA

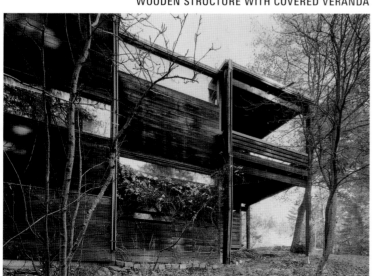

DETAIL OF THE LIVING ROOM

ing's flexibility is also taken into careful consideration in relation to the family's constantly changing needs. Thus, the house is designed as a building system capable of being developed. Completing elements can easily be added to the existing 'trunk'. Like a growing tree, this home is a living organism subject to constant change. In summary, one could say that Lund's own house becomes an architectural expression for the state of dwelling in the woods. Sitting on the veranda or even in the living room is almost like sitting in the treetops.

The Lund house is situated in Liaskogen, a hillside in the woodland overlooking the lake at Bogstad, on the outskirts of Oslo. It represents something new in the Lund & Slaatto repertoire. The building is a combination of three core areas (concrete towers) and an airy post construction. One of the towers is three-storeys high and contains the kitchen and laundry room and a food storage area in the basement (food). The second tower, with two storeys, contains bathroom facilities (water). The third tower is the chimney shaft with an oil heater in the basement and a fireplace in the living room (fire). There are four different levels in the wooden structure. The bedrooms are on the ground floor and the living room above. The entrance and the dining room are placed at different inter-

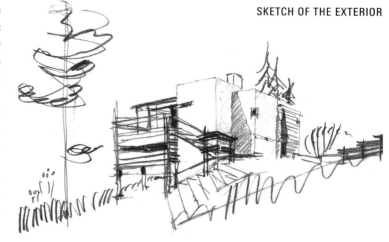

SKETCH OF THE EXTERIOR

THE STAIRCASE LEADING TO THE LIVING ROOM

SKETCH OF THE INTERIOR

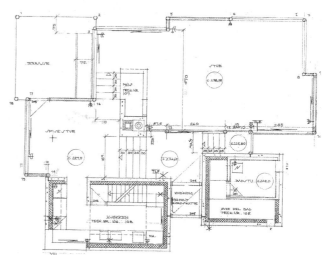

PLAN OF THE MAIN FLOOR

mediate levels. Because of the building's construction, another bedroom has been added without any problem of integration, creating a fifth level. These split levels convey vertical motion. The main stairs wind around the chimney shaft, while in the kitchen core the ladder in the wetroom core leads to the sauna above. In addition, there is an exterior staircase giving direct access to the balcony.

Lund's house clearly contains elements of what later became a strong presence in Lund & Slaatto's architecture. The construction, consisting of two separate parts – the concrete towers and the light wooden framework – contains elements of an additive architecture which was to preoccupy Lund and Slaatto in the 1970s and 1980s.

The two partners which are considered to be the leading exponents of the structuralist style gradually developed an architectual method that was able to deal with the dilemmas of postmodern society. In a postmodern climate with strong materialistic growth and rapid changes, a demand for a more flexible architecture gradually developed. It became necessary to find architectural solutions that could correspond to the rapid changes in society in general. Buildings should consist of basic modules with additional elements, allowing the user to influence the final layout in accordance with his or her own ideas.

For more than two decades Lund and Slaatto have been among Norway's leading architects. In an uncertain and complex architectonic landscape, they have been the pathfinders in whose steps many have followed. Their course has become the mainstream. Others have equalled or even exceeded them artistically, but none have made important contributions in so many different fields. The magnitude and high quality of their production is unsurpassed.

SILJE SKRONDAL

BIBLIOGRAPHY:

1977   Lund K. (ed.), *Kjell Lund, Nils Slaatto: Oslo buildings 1958–76*, Oslo
1988   Grønvold U., *Lund & Slaatto*, Oslo
1990   Skriver P. E., 'Lund & Slaatto, Lin Utzon', in *Arkitektur DK*, no. 5, pp. 221–268

Charles Rennie Mackintosh

1868–1928

1906–14, INTERIOR ALTERATION AND FURNISHING, WITH MARGARET MACDONALD, DEMOLISHED 1963, PARTLY RECONSTRUCTED IN THE HUNTERIAN GALLERY (1973–81)
6 FLORENTINE TERRACE, GLASGOW (GB)

MAIN WORKS AND PROJECTS

1896–97	Miss Cranston's Tearooms, Glasgow (GB), with Margaret Macdonald
1896–99	Competition project (First Prize) for completion of Glasgow School of Art (GB), with Honeyman and Keppie
1898–99	Miss Cranston's Argyle Tearoom, Glasgow (GB)
1899–1901	Windyhill, Kilmacolm (GB)
1900–06	Interior alteration in an existing building (own home) at 120 Main Street, Glasgow (GB)
1901	The 'House for an Art Lover', competition project, with Margaret Macdonald

1902–04	Hill House, Helensburgh (GB)
1907–09	Extension to Glasgow School of Art (GB), with Honeyman and Keppie
1919	Interior of the guest bedroom, 78 Derngate, Northampton (GB)
1920	Project for three 'studio-flats', Chelsea, London (GB)

THE SCOTTISH ARCHITECT and designer Charles Rennie Mackintosh, who was prominent in the Arts and Crafts movement in Great Britain, was born in Glasgow on 7 June 1868. From early on he studied drawing and art, partly because he suffered from a disabled foot, which often prevented him from playing with other children. In 1884, at the age of 16, he joined the studio of local architect John Hutchinson as an apprentice, at the same time attending evening classes at the Glasgow School of Art.

At the Glasgow School of Art, Mackintosh became close friends with Herbert McNair. The two in turn befriended the artist sisters Margaret and Frances Macdonald, who were also studying at the school and who later became their wives – Charles Mackintosh and Margaret Macdonald married in 1900. The four of them formed an artistic group destined for international renown, although they were scoffed at by their fellow countrymen due to their similarities with the abstract aestheticism of continental Art Nouveau. In 1889 Mackintosh joined the architectural firm of Honeyman and Keppie, becoming a partner in 1904, and in 1894 – together with Herbert McNair and the Macdonald sisters – he set up a collaborative artistic group named 'The Spook School'. The period 1900–14 was enriched by friendships with Anna and Hermann Muthesius (Hermann was an architect and cultural attaché at the German Embassy in London), with Fritz Waerndorfer and his wife (Fritz was the patron of the Wiener Werkstätte), and with important Glaswegian cultural figures, such as Francis Newberry (who was the principal of the Glasgow School of Art) and members of the McLehose family (publishers by profession, for whom Mackintosh worked).

Against this stimulating background Charles Mackintosh and also Margaret Macdonald embarked on their brilliant joint professional career. Collaborating with her as well as with the other two, Mackintosh designed unorthodox furniture, craftwork and posters, which brought him international acclaim in the 1890s. Further resounding successes followed during the first decade of the new century. These included four remarkable tearooms he designed in Glasgow (1896–1904), including Miss Cranston's Tearooms (1896–97), Miss Cranston's Argyle Tearoom (1898–99) and the Willow Tearooms (1904), as well as other domestic interiors of the early 1900s. The same period saw the completion of Mackintosh masterpieces such as Windyhill in Kilmacolm (1899–1901), the unrealised project for the 'Haus eines Kunstfreundes' or House for an Art Lover (1901), Hill House in Helensburgh (1902–04), Scotland Street School (1904–06), the Glasgow School of Art (1907–09), which is considered to be the first original example of Art Nouveau architecture in Great Britain, and the interior alteration and furnishing of his own house at 6 Florentine Terrace, Glasgow (1906–14).

As a student Mackintosh found his inspiration on the one hand in the careful study of nature, and on the other especially in the vernacular buildings both of the Scottish countryside and of Italian architecture, from which he took a powerful sense of rationality and detail. These interests led the young architect to develop an increasingly personal language, nearer to the Viennese school than to the English architecture of the time. A brilliant student, he would never become a theorist like William Morris or Charles Voysey, but would design interiors of exemplary rigour, to the extent that Ludwig Mies van der Rohe called him "a

DESK IN THE LIVING ROOM

BEDROOM

DRAWING ROOM

LIVING ROOM >

THE DINING ROOM

purifier in the field of architecture". His work at the turn of the century, exemplified in the tearooms, is original, elegant and light, unlike contemporary fashion, while his mature designs of the early 1900s show a mind of exceptional inventiveness and aesthetic perception, even if they still evince traditional characteristics.

Throughout this time Mackintosh exhibited extensively at numerous venues: in 1895 at the Arts and Crafts exhibition, Glasgow; in 1900 at the Secession, Vienna; in 1902 in Turin; in 1903 in Moscow; in 1904 in Dresden; and in 1905 in Berlin, which was his last major exhibition in continental Europe. Nevertheless, in 1909 and 1914 he continued to show objects respectively in Vienna and Paris. In 1913 Mackintosh split up with Keppie, his partner since the beginning of his career, and opened a small studio on his own. The year 1914 witnessed the start of the decline of Charles Mackintosh and Margaret Macdonald. By this time he had virtually stopped practising as an architect-designer and henceforth devoted himself mainly to painting watercolours. In the same year the Scottish couple moved away from their Glasgow house in Florentine Terrace and went to live in the small Suffolk seaside town of Walberswick (1914–15), where they rented rooms. However, after just one year there they then moved on to Chelsea, London, where they remained for eight years

(1915–23), living in bed-and-breakfast accommodation in Oakley Street, and where they had a studio at 43a Geble Place.

When the Mackintoshes relocated from Glasgow to Walberswick and London, they simply left their Florentine Terrace home completely abandoned – they eventually sold it in 1920. Because they took only a few of their furnishings with them from Glasgow to London, this meant that most of them were, unfortunately, lost. The loss of the Mackintoshes' own furnishings and a general lack of surviving examples from their homes was compounded by the fact that the couple habitually lived in rented accommodation, in flats that were already furnished.

From Chelsea, Charles Mackintosh and Margaret Macdonald moved to Port-Vendres in the South of France, where they lived from 1923 until 1927 in the Hôtel du Commerce. In the latter year they returned to London, where just a year later, in 1928, he died from cancer on 10 December. She continued to divide her time between France and England, where she died in Chelsea, London, on 7 January 1933. Following his death, Mackintosh was largely forgotten for decades, until there was a revival of interest in his work towards the end of the 20th century. Contemporary taste warmed to the stark simplicity of design of some of his furniture, which then began to be manufactured.

On marrying in 1900, the Mackintoshes move in a new rented flat at 120 Main Street, Glasgow, altering its interior. Hermann Muthesius devoted several pages of his *Das Englische Haus* (1904) to the couple's Main Street home: "Mackintosh's rooms are refined to degree which the lives of even the artistically educated are still a long away from matching. The delicacy and austerity of their artistic atmosphere would tolerate no admixture of the ordinariness which fills our lives." Charles and Margaret remained in this home until 1906, when they finally found a more valid and spacious alternative – a terraced house at 6 Florentine Terrace, on the edge of Glasgow's West End. With three floors, an attic and a terrace, the property lent itself to alteration to suit the needs of the young artists and the circle of intellectuals they frequented, and the couple set about modifying and furnishing it.

As had been the case with the Main Street flat, the Mackintoshes' Florentine Terrace home was furnished mainly with duplicates of objects designed by the couple for their customers, although there were also some new furnishings designed specifically for the property, such as the kitchen dresser and the bedroom chest of drawers (and, in the case of Main Street, the dark-stained writing cabinet and the pair of white-painted display cabinets). In short, the furnishings at Florentine Terrace, like those at Main Street, can be imagined as the personal collection of the Mackintoshes' favourite objects, to the extent that many of the pieces were used for display at the numerous exhibitions in which the couple were invited to take part, including the Secession in Vienna (1900) and the International Exhibition of Industry in Turin (1902). The dominant colours were black and white, although their love of Japanese art and Margaret's work brought a powerful note of colour.

The alterations to the house in Florentine Terrace mainly involved the first floor, where three bedrooms were sacrificed to make way for a spacious drawing room and a study, while on the top floor another two rooms were turned into the main bedroom and bathroom. The ground floor, on the other hand, comprised the hall, the dining room, kitchen and bathroom. Although the Mackintoshes had produced true masterpieces during this period, such as Hill House or Willow Tearooms, there was no trace in their own new home of the sophisticated decoration of those interiors. The only exception was the stencil design reproduced in the dining room, an almost exact copy of the one in the hall of Hill House.

If only minor alterations were made to the interior at Florentine Terrace, the exterior was subjected to large-scale changes. New windows were built on the south side of the hall, in the drawing room and the first-floor landing so as to let in warm sunlight. In particular, a bow window was built in the main facade, altering the character of the house substantially compared to the rest of the row of terraces. Inside, too, the windows were decorated with careful attention. The frames and brackets join or separate the windows markedly, giving rise to the interior design typical of the Mackintoshes.

The Mackintoshes' own Florentine Terrace home in Glasgow was abandoned by the couple, as said, in 1914, after which they finally sold it in 1920. In 1963, however, the house at 6 Florentine Terrace was demolished altogether, and meanwhile its address has been changed to 78 South Park Avenue. Nevertheless, in the 1970s an ambitious proposal was made at least partly to reconstruct this important cultural-architectural testimony, a project that came to fruition. However, the recreation (1973–81) was not done on the original site, but actually inside Glasgow's Hunterian Gallery, sponsored by the Gallery itself and also by the University of Glasgow. Work on the reconstruction was seriously hampered not just because the original no longer existed, but also because the property's furnishings had been dispersed and there was a lack of iconographic material (drawings or photos). In the end the interiors and objects were recreated mainly from written descriptions, and indirectly from photographic records of the Main Street apartment, from which most of the Florentine Terrace furnishings came. In addition, the projects and works produced by Mackintosh and Macdonald during the relevant years were studied thoroughly in order to draw clues for the reconstruction of those parts of the house that remained undescribed or unrecorded. Against the odds the Mackintosh House Museum opened to the public in the early 1980s within the Hunterian Gallery, which also keeps the archive of drawings by the couple. The trouble in recreating the Mackintoshes' home has been worthwhile, as the Museum has enjoyed success and popularity since its completion.   GENNARO POSTIGLIONE

FLOOR PLANS

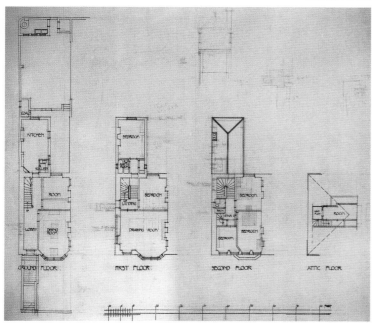

BIBLIOGRAPHY:
1977   Howarth T., *Charles Rennie Mackintosh and the Modern Movement*, 2nd ed., London
1979   Muthesius H., *The English House*, London (orig.: Das Englische Haus, Berlin, 1905)
       Billcliffe R., *C. R. Mackintosh: The Complete Furniture, Furniture Drawings and Interior Designs*, New York
1989   Moffat A. and Baxter C., *Remembering C. R. Mackintosh: An Illustrated Biography*, Lanark
1995   Crawford A., *C. R. Mackintosh*, London
1997   Robertson P., *The Mackintosh House*, Glasgow

Robert Mallet-Stevens
1886–1945

1926–27, NEW CONSTRUCTION, SUBSTANTIALLY ALTERED IN 1951
RUE MALLET-STEVENS, PARIS (F)

MAIN WORKS AND PROJECTS

1923	de Noailles villa, Hyères (F)
1924	Doucet villa, Marly (F)
1925	Embassy hall, Tourism pavilion, garden with concrete trees, and Syndicat d'Initiative pavilion at the Exposition Internationale des Arts Décoratifs et Industriels Modernes, Paris (F)
1926	Collinet house, Boulogne-sur-Seine, Paris (F)
1926–27	Allatini, Dreyfus, Martel, Reifenberg and Mallet-Stevens houses, Paris (F)

1929	Apartment building, rue Méchain, Paris (F)
1930	Distillery, Istanbul (TR)
1932	Cavroix villa, Croix (F)
1934	Ship's cabin, Salon d'Automne, Paris (F)
1937	Pavilions for the Exposition des arts décoratifs, Paris (F): Palais d'électricité et de la lumière, de l'hygiène, des tabacs, de la solidarité nationale, des Cafés Franco-Brésil

ROBERT MALLET-STEVENS was a French architect known primarily for his modernistic works in France during the 1920s and 1930s. After the First World War he emerged as a fashionable and even somewhat avant-garde designer, who drew other innovative artists and composers into his projects. He was born in Paris in 1886 into a wealthy family of Belgian origin, which provided him with his early education in art – his father, Maurice Mallet, and his maternal grandfather, Arthur Stevens, were both art experts. In 1905 Mallet-Stevens enrolled in the Ecole Spéciale d'Architecture in Paris, where he was a pupil of Josef Hoffmann, and to which he was to return in 1924 as a teacher. During his study years, between 1905 and 1910, he made frequent visits to Palais Stoclet, the home of his uncle Adolf Stoclet.

Mallet-Stevens worked on numerous projects influenced by the ideas of Modernism, and in 1911 published articles and drawings in two Belgian journals (*Le Home and Tekhnè*). In 1912 he took part with 20 interior design and architecture projects in the Salon d'Automne, the annual Parisian exhibition that gathered together the most 'innovative' architects. Between 1913 and 1915 he participated in exhibitions in Ghent, London, Lyon, Brussels and San Francisco.

From the early 1920s Mallet-Stevens wrote for the journal *L'Architecture Vivante* and worked on projects in which he involved many exponents of the international avant-garde based in Paris, including Fernand Léger, Robert Delaunay, Francis Poulenc, Arthur Honegger and the De Stijl group. In 1924, at the exhibition of the final-year projects of the students of the Ecole Spéciale d'Architecture, where he was now lecturing, Mallet-Stevens also invited the De Stijl group to take part. The decision, considered too extreme, led to protests and eventually to his exclusion from the teaching staff.

One of Mallet-Stevens' first commissions was for the villa of the Vicomte de Noailles (1923). The house was used by Man Ray as the set for his film Les Mystères du Château d'Dé. The Doucet villa designed by Mallet-Stevens and also used as a film set dates to the following year. Done in collaboration with the painter Fernand Léger and others, it featured in Marcel Lherbier's film L'Inhumaine. Both these houses are representative of the architect's sophisticated synthesis of Cubist painting, Art Deco details, and other contemporary artistic modes. In 1925 Mallet-Stevens took part in Paris in the important Exposition Internationale des Arts Décoratifs et Industriels Modernes, the exhibition from which the 'Art Deco' style drew its name. Here, helped again by artists and musicians, he designed five projects of various types, including the so-called French embassy and the Tourism pavilion.

In 1929 Mallet-Stevens founded and chaired the *Union des Artistes Modernes* (UAM) and also became a member of the executive board of the new journal *L'Architecture d'Aujourd'hui*. In 1935 he led the UAM team at the Brussels Exposition Internationale and designed seven pavilions at the Paris Exposition of 1937. During the Nazi occupation of France, the architect and his Jewish wife were forced to take refuge in the South of France. Mallet-Stevens died in Paris in 1945 after a serious illness.

Mallet-Stevens' own house-cum-studio, located in Paris' rue Mallet-Stevens, so named in honour of the architect, is part of a set of studio-houses and a caretaker's lodge that was constructed new (1926–27) in the street for the sculptors Joël and Jan Martel, the musician Mme Reifenberg, the film-maker Allatini, and M. Dreyfus, as well as Mallet-Stevens himself. On its completion, the street project, which has been described as a "manifesto of modern architecture", was formally opened by a min-

RUE MALLET-STEVENS

STREET FRONT

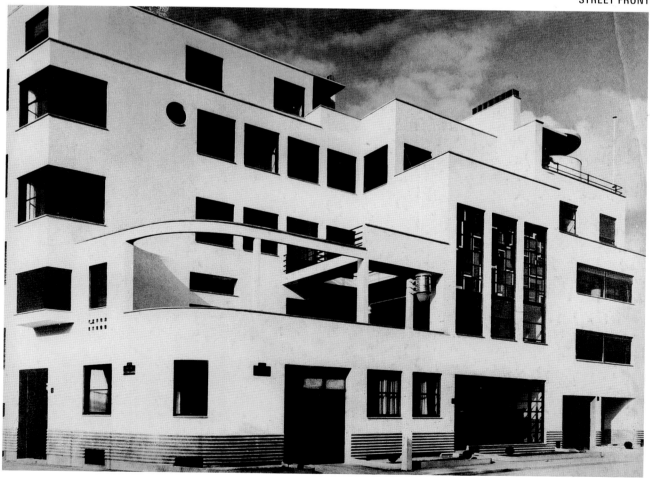

THE MAIN LIVING ROOM

ister and two prefects, in the presence of the whole of the Parisian literary and artistic world.

In the street project with its five houses, Mallet-Stevens aimed to make each building different, but at the same time to give the street an urban character. In order to build homes with the best possible fittings and furnishings, he called on other architects and artists, such as Gabriel Guevrekian (responsible for the whole quarter), Pierre Chareau and Francis Jourdain (for the furnishings), Hélène Henry (for the fabrics), and Louis Barillet (for the windows). Opposed to the rigour of formalism, Mallet-Stevens made shrewd use of detail in the group of houses.

The architect expressed his aims as a designer, which were applied in particular in the creation of his own house-cum-studio, very clearly: "The role of the modern architect now consists in organising space in a practical clean comfortable way, a space where air and light reign in profusion, where the corridors and passages are easily accessed, and the distribution carefully planned, and where to achieve this aim the architect is able to use materials that meet his needs admirably. The art of the house is thus changed – in the decoration, in the general plan, in the composition of the façades, in the furnishing of the various rooms, in the furniture, in the colours... The art is simplified, admitting only elements treated with sincerity, banishing minute decorative detail." (*Le Home,* no. 6, 1911)

In Mallet-Stevens' own studio-home, the external volume, reduced at certain points by the presence of terraces and corner windows, is characterised by the intersection of sharp angular forms (parallelepipeds) with circular forms (the volume of the terrace). The white exterior, which is clean, compact and devoid of decoration, is cut across by ribbon win-

dows or by vertical windows. In an article published in *Casabella* in 1929, Enrico Paulucci praised the project, underlining "a certain very modern lyricism, a clean pleasant and, I would say, optimistic sense of freshness and of life". Unlike the sober exterior, the interior is rich in decorative detail.

The house and the studio are divided over five floors. On the ground floor is the garage, the studio, and the laundry. The first floor comprises the 'public area', with the living room and the dining room, which opens onto the kitchen. On the second and third floors we find the 'private areas', including the bedrooms. And on the top floor there are guest rooms and other utility rooms.

The living room, two floors high, is characterised by tall windows decorated with geometrical motifs, and contrasts with the lower corner with the fireplace, furnished with aluminium shelves that mark the edge of the cowl, covered with polyhedral mirrors. The whole composition is embellished by the design of the floor, made up of grey, brown and black tiles, and by the lively yellow and purple fabrics that cover the furniture. The base of the armchairs and the sofa, the supports of the four lamps, and the rail of the staircase leading to the bedroom are in aluminium. The rigorously square-shaped furniture is reminiscent of cubist and neo-plastic art, while the overall decor of the rooms and many of the details have much in common with Art Deco interiors of the same period.

Mallet-Stevens was expert in the uses of reinforced concrete and also metal framing, and the five houses are among the structures in which he applied such modern techniques and amenities. Built using reinforced concrete, they also contain lifts and all the appliances made possible by the use of electric power and new technologies. Like his con-

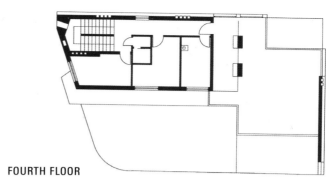

FOURTH FLOOR

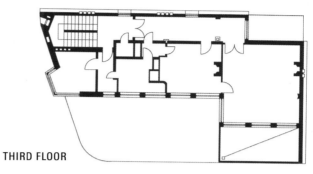

THIRD FLOOR

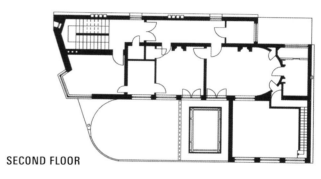

SECOND FLOOR

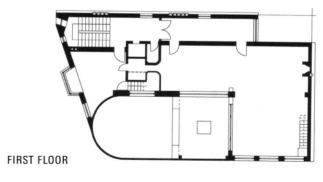

FIRST FLOOR

THE WORK SPACE

temporaries Le Corbusier and Lurçat, Mallet-Stevens believed that technology and materials make formal transformations possible. "A thousand
forms become possible, unforeseen forms emerge, sometimes strange,
but rational and honest. Reinforced concrete allowed projecting structures, the elimination of many supports and the reduction to a bare minimum of the various elements of construction." (*Bulletin de la vie artist-
ique,* no. 23, 1924)

In this approach to design, defined by Le Corbusier as "eminently
orthogonal art" and close to the analytic method of De Stijl, the volumes
are organised around a vertical block, from which the horizontal lines of
the terraces and roofs stand out. In an article published in 1929, Gio Ponti
noted: "Those simple square forms, which appear in some elements of
the furnishing to be dictated by real constructive needs, by concepts of
hygiene or by practical arrangements, are used again to form the decoration as such, in the floor, the mirror, and the windows."   LUISA GATTI

BIBLIOGRAPHY:

1931   Moussinac L., *Mallet-Stevens*, Paris
1979   Vago P., *Robert Mallet-Stevens: L'architetto cubista*, Bari
1980   Jeannot H. and Deshoulières D. (eds.), *Robert Mallet-Stevens architecte*, Archive d'Architec-
       ture moderne, Brussels
1994   Gatti L., *La figura dell'architetto arredatore tra innovazione e tradizione in Francia e Austria
       1920–1939*, Ph.D. thesis, Politecnico di Milano, Milan
1996   Ottolini G., Gatti L., Nufrio A., Rizzi R. and Salvadè E. (eds), *Civiltà dell'abitare. Evoluzione
       dell'arredamento domestico attraverso i modelli d'interni dall'antichità ai giorni nostri*,
       Galleria del Design e dell'Arredamento, Cantù

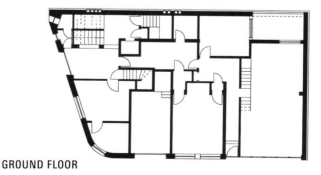

GROUND FLOOR

Sven Markelius
1889–1972

1942–45, NEW CONSTRUCTION
KEVINGESTRAND 5, DANDERYD, STOCKHOLM (S)

MAIN WORKS AND PROJECTS

1918–44	Several town plans as a consulting architect
1925	The Lidingö Building and Living (Bygge och Bo) exhibition, town plan and single-family houses, Lidingö (S)
1930	Student hostel at the Royal Institute of Technology, Stockholm (S), with Uno Åhrén
	Own house at Nockeby, Stockholm (S)
1932	Engkvist villa, Eldtomta (S), also 1952–53
	Helsingborg Concert Hall (S)
1935	Collective apartment house, John Ericssonsgatan 6, Stockholm (S)

1937	House for The Builder's Society, Stockholm (S)
1942–45	The 'systemhuset' (system house) at several sites, including his own house at Kevingestrand 5, Danderyd, Stockholm (S)
1945–60	Folkets hus (People's House), with congress hall, theatre and offices, Stockholm (S)

SVEN MARKELIUS was born as Sven Jonsson in Stockholm on 25 October 1889. He grew up at Södermalm, in the southern part Stockholm, where his father was a master house painter. The family lived in an old craftsman's house with workshops on the ground floor. As a young boy Markelius already had a keen interest in painting, drawing, music, singing as well as engineering and science. In 1909 he enrolled in the School of Architecture of Stockholm's Kungl. Tekniska Högskolan or Royal Institute of Technology (RIT). Among his teachers were Lars Israel Wahlman, Ivar Tengbom, Erik Lallerstedt and Carl Bergsten. Markelius graduated as a qualified architect from the RIT in 1913, but extended his studies to include two years at the Royal Academy of Arts, also in Stockholm. He was a good singer, and after finishing his studies at the Academy he was accepted at the Opera School, but decided not to abandon his career as an architect. Later, during a trip to Italy in 1921, he took lessons with Mattia Battistino in Rome. That same year he changed his surname from Jonsson to Markelius. At the time many Swedes with common names were adopting instead Latinised names. Sven's grandfather had been a crofter on a small farm called 'Mark', and from this he took his new surname.

Markelius involved himself in the social democratic movement and participated in some radical intellectual groups such as Kulturfront, becoming one of the leading architects in the social democratic welfare program. He also had a hand in the standardisation and prefabrication of building elements. Through participating – with five projects – in the 1930 Stockholm Exhibition, and through buildings such as his own Nockeby house (1930) and his Helsingborg Concert Hall (1932), Markelius was

one of the architects who introduced modern architecture to Sweden. His main work, however, concerned urban planning and housing, and from 1944–54 he was head of Stockholm's town planning department. He became known around the world as an architect who embodied the Swedish way of building a welfare society. From 1929 Markelius was a member of CIAM, and in 1947 also a member of the FN consulting group in Paris. Between 1952 and 1958 he was, further, a member of the UNESCO Advisory Committee, and from 1954–1972 also a member of UNESCO's Art Committee. He was a visiting professor at Yale University in 1949, at the Massachusetts Institute of Technology in 1961, and at Berkeley in 1962.

Between 1920 and 1966 Markelius wrote almost 200 articles, some of them published in renowned international journals and reviews. The subjects ranged from discussions about the need for standardisation of building components, new kitchen models, and the ventilation of dwellings, to town planning and housing, professional ethics, and the rational production of prefabricated elements. He also took part in many wider debates.

One of the most important objectives of the Swedish state welfare program was good housing for everyone, and during the 1940s there was a debate about how to achieve this goal. Markelius was against high-rise apartment blocks. He believed that the best for children and family life was one- or two-storey houses with some kind of garden. He thus worked on the development of standardised building elements for small houses. The industrialisation of the building process, with a view to minimising building costs, had already been on the agenda in the early modernist

VIEW FROM THE GARDEN

THE LIVING ROOM WITH THE PIANO

movement. Now this had to be realised, and Markelius developed the so-called 'systemhuset' or system house. Sweden had long had a tradition of prefabrication, which started with Fredrik Blom in the 19th century and developed on a large scale at Enskede in Stockholm in the late 1920s. Several small factories also produced prefabricated wooden houses for the market. At that time Walter Gropius was grappling with the same problem and had probably inspired Markelius to develop elements capable of being used in many different ways. The idea was to avoid standardised house types and instead to allow different kinds of plans and house sizes.

Between 1942 and 1945 four houses were built using these elements, of which Markelius' own house at Kevingestrand was the last of these experiments. The ambition was to achieve a highly systematised type of construction with elements based on the measurement of 600 mm that could easily be combined with other components, and the aspiration of the system was that it should be possible to construct such a house in a short time on site: "It should be possible for a man to put up his house in a few hours together with his wife."

Early modernist buildings were criticised for being more avant-garde and intentional than practical and useful, more rationalist than human. During the 1940s Modernism slowly moved to a softer, more graceful and useful architecture, more in keeping with Nordic culture and traditions. Asplund and Aalto are well-known exponents of this trend.

At the same time, another movement became very influential, which was characterised by pragmatic, political, social, scientific and economic thinking, and was closely bound up with the social democratic political program. Markelius came to be one of the leaders of this kind of pragmatism or, as it was called, New Empiricism. The thinking influenced the Swedish attitude to architecture, housing and building until quite recently. In spite of Markelius' plans for flexible elements allowing different house-types, the market developed in a different way, and cheap standardised wooden house-types have blotted the Swedish landscape for 50 years.

Markelius' own home at Kevingestrand 5, Danderyd, Stockholm, was – as we have said – the last of four houses that he built (1942–45) experimenting with the systematised type of house developed by him. Its exterior design is simple, almost anonymous. The impression is light and elegant, based on traditional architecture, but has no unnecessary dimensions or expressive decoration, as often happens in traditional Swedish wooden architecture. The window surroundings are thin and straight, put together at right angles. The panel is plain with thin matching.

The plan of the house is sophisticated and has a carefully studied function. It is rather closed towards the road, and the entrance area contains not only the main door but also parking space for a car and bicycles. Near the main entrance there is in addition a kitchen garden. The house opens up towards the inner garden with large windows and terrace doors from the drawing room, the library and the bedrooms. The garden was important and showed Markelius' interest in garden planning. The integration of house and garden was essential, and it was not just the house, but also the garden that attracted great interest when the building was published in international magazines.

SITE PLAN

The organisation of the rooms is both practical and refined. The drawing room is connected at a right angle to the library in a way that allows both the simultaneous use of the two rooms and also clear separation. Where these two rooms meet, and in connection with the garden, there is a big open fire. The study behind the library allowed the creation of a separate working area, not disturbed by the rest of the family. There is a sauna connected to the study and also with the garden. The kitchen is closely linked to the public parts of the house, and can be reached directly both from the entrance and from the maid's room. The bedrooms create a private area with bathroom and generous wardrobes.

Markelius experimented not only with the overall planning, but also – closely liaising with the building industry – with technical equipment, such as a dishwasher and an air-born heating system, which freed the house from radiators. The whole house is very well designed and carefully throught out, with separate zones for work, social life and privacy, although these different zones also overlap. The house's artistic functional plan is clearly a result of the debate in Sweden about good planning and everyday life. Much research into 'the good home' had been carried out since the 1930s, with considerable political and social significance for the Social Democratic Party. It related to healthier living, women's liberation and the ambitions of a state that wanted to take responsibility for its citizens.

In some ways it is remarkable and ironic that Markelius, who was one of the most important representatives of the modern movement in Sweden, designed a house so strongly related to Swedish tradition, a house that garnered for him international fame and repute. His Kevinge home is very far from the more heroic modernist buildings he designed in the 1930s. On the other hand, this kind of architecture and construction was more appropriate to prefabrication and rationality than the functionalist houses, even though they were firmly based on the dream of industrialised construction. So what Markelius actually realised here was the functionalist dream of industrial construction, but in a more traditional and pragmatic guise.

GUNILLA SVENSSON, FINN WERNE

BIBLIOGRAPHY:

1974   Volny O., *Markelius och bostadsfrågan*, Stockholm
1985   Fowelius J., *Helsingborgs konserthus*, Stockholm
1987   Jadelius L., Folk, *form och funktionalism*, dissertation, Chalmers Technical University, Gothenburg
1989   Rudberg E., *Sven Markelius, arkitekt*, Stockholm
2001   Cornoldi A., *Le case degli architetti. Dizionario privato dal Rinascimento ad oggi*, Venice, pp. 244–245

Erich Mendelsohn
1887–1953

1929–30, NEW CONSTRUCTION
AM RUPENHORN 6, BERLIN (D)

MAIN WORKS AND PROJECTS

1915	Project for The Large House, a private home for the architect		1929–30	Columbushaus, Potsdamer Platz, Berlin (D)
1917	Project for another home for himself		1935–36	de la Warr pavilion, Bexhill, London (GB)
1919–20	Einstein Tower, Potsdam (D)		1936	House at 64 Old Church Street, Chelsea, London (GB), with Serge Chermayeff
1921	Mosse building, Berlin (D), with Richard Neutra and Rudolf Henning		1936–38	Medical Centre of the Hadassah University on Mount Scopus, Jerusalem (Israel)
1923	Factory, Luckenwalde (D)		1946–50	Maimonides Hospital, San Francisco (USA)
1928	Schocken department store, Chemnitz (D)			
1929	Headquarters of the Metal Workers' Union, Berlin (D)			

ERICH MENDELSOHN was born on 21 March 1887 into a family of humble origins in Allenstein (now Olsztyn), in East Prussia (now Poland). The future protagonist of architectural Expressionism came into the world not just on the first day of spring, but also on the birthday of Johann Sebastian Bach – a coincidence that was to become significant later in his life. Mendelsohn considered himself a born architect, a fact confirmed by the recollections of his family, who described him as a child obsessed with building things, using whatever materials came to hand.

As a student, Mendelsohn initially studied economics for a year, enrolling in 1907 – to satisfy his father's wishes – in the School of Economics in Munich. But he soon turned to architecture, studying first, from 1908, at the Technische Hochschule (Technical University) Berlin-Charlottenburg and then in Munich, likewise at the Technical University (School of Architecture). In the latter city he met Paul Klee, Vassily Kandinsky, Franz Marc and the Dada group. These artists and Munich's stimulating atmosphere were to have an enormous influence on the young Mendelsohn, who graduated as a qualified architect from Munich's Technische Hochschule in 1912.

In 1910 Mendelsohn met Louise Maas, a music student, marrying her in 1915. She recalled that: "This meeting was the beginning of a life devoted – by both of us – to architecture, to his work. [It was the start of] 43 years in his peculiar world [until his death in 1953], entirely structured around his creative impulse." Mendelsohn felt entirely dominated by this force, which expressed itself best in the quiet of the evening, when he would draw, listening to music, especially to Bach, amid an ambience that served to isolate him from the world. In this solitary private sphere he would produce a first sketch of whatever building was to be designed, a continuous line defining its volume.

During the First World War Mendelsohn served as a soldier from 1917 to 1918. In 1923 the Jewish architect visited Palestine, where he became enthusiastic about Judaean villages. The years 1928–33, which were to prove his last five years in Germany, were a period of intense work. They were also an especially happy time in his life, when he was at the peak of his career.

In 1933, following Hitler's seizure of power, Mendelsohn as a Jew was forced to flee Nazi Germany. He went first to The Netherlands and Belgium, and then moved to London, where he started a partnership with Serge Chermayeff. In 1941 he moved on to the USA, where he died on 15 September 1953 in San Francisco.

During his architectural career Erich Mendelsohn built numerous large-scale buildings, including theatres, cinemas, department stores, synagogues, factories, hospitals, and his famous Einstein Tower in Potsdam (1919–20). However, he also happily designed single houses, including his own at Berlin-Charlottenburg. Before he came to realise this private home for himself, he had earlier made two attempts at designing his own house. But these designs, conceived when he and his wife Louise were young newly-weds living in a small flat in Berlin's Westend, remained projects, essentially unrealisable dreams. The first, dating to 1915 and describing a building known as 'The Large House', is fairly detailed, while the second, from 1917, is little more than a sketched 'idea for a house'.

The home that Mendelsohn did finally manage to design and build for himself and his family, fulfilling his dreams, was a new construction, erected 1929–30 at Rupenhorn 6, in Berlin-Charlottenburg. Built during a particularly happy period of the architect's life, when he was at the

PATH TO THE ENTRANCE

VIEW FROM THE SOUTH-WEST

MUSIC ROOM

height of his fame and professional success, the Rupenhorn house is one of the most significant works in his oeuvre. Rupenhorn is a hilly area between Grunewald Forest and Lake Stössen, to the west of Berlin, in an open landscape reminiscent of that of Mendelsohn's childhood. The house, in steel and brick, covers almost the whole plot, a long strip of land running from east to west and expanding in the direction of Lake Stössen.

With his Rupenhorn home, the architect abandoned the tension of enveloping forms and aggressive volumes typical both of his public buildings and of his earlier Sternefeld Villa, in order to express the private character of the dwelling, defined by Zevi as an "architecture of silence". Mendelsohn's desire to create a place of peace was confirmed by his own words: "In order to live, I need a certain degree of comfort, a home in which I can take shelter after being pushed aside by everything that surrounds me outside." Nevertheless, the house does share certain elements with those he constructed for other people: a vitality of the interior spaces and a harmonious relationship with the site itself.

The carefully studied composure of the building's volume is achieved through an asymmetrical composition of rooms, which in turn are themselves asymmetrical. Wide and not very deep, and surrounded by large terraces, the house has an unusual front, based on the dynamic balance between the closed avant-corps of the entrance hall and the ribbon windows on the upper floor. Although contained in size, the house is conceived in such a way as to be able to satisfy the occupants' various domestic needs. A rational use of space is ensured by the careful design of the interiors, characterised by niches and fitted wardrobes instead of free-standing furniture. The most 'lived-in' room is the music room. The sense of 'happiness' that emanates from the whole building lies in its simple but intense spatiality, which can be felt both in the direct intimate relations between the rooms and in the relations between the rooms and the surrounding area.

Unfortunately, Mendelsohn was unable to enjoy the house he had so long and so carefully planned for himself, for after just a couple of years of living in it he was obliged to flee Germany when the Nazis came to power in 1933.

MARIAROMANA QUENDOLO

BIBLIOGRAPHY:
1932   Mendelsohn E., *Neues Haus – Neue Welt*, Berlin
1961   von Eckardt W., *Eric Mendelsohn*, Milan
1970   Zevi B., *Eric Mendelsohn. Opera completa*, Turin
1987   Achenbach S., *Eric Mendelsohn 1889–1953. Ideen Bauten Projekte*, Berlin
1999   Stephan R. (ed.), *Eric Mendelsohn: Architect 1889–1953*, New York

STUDY ON THE FIRST FLOOR

SITTING AREA IN THE MUSIC ROOM

PLAN OF THE GROUND FLOOR

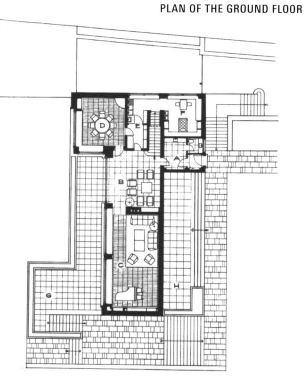

Carlo Mollino
1905–1973

1938, ALTERATION AND FURNISHING, NOW DEMOLISHED
VIA TALUCCHI, TURIN (I)

MAIN WORKS AND PROJECTS

1933–34	Federazione Agricoltori head office, Cuneo (I)
1937–40	Società Ippica Torinese building, Turin (I)
1939–40	Interior design and furnishing of Giorgio Devalle apartment, via delle Alpi 3, Turin (I)
1946–47	Station Hotel, Lago Nero, Sauze d'Oulx (I)
1948	Furnishing for Reale Mutua Assicurazioni head office, Turin (I)
1950–53	Conversion of Vittorio Emanuele Theatre into an RAI auditorium, Turin (I)

1959	Interior design and furnishing of Lutrario dance hall, via Stradella 3, Turin (I)
1961–70	Own apartment, via Napione 2, Turin (I)
1963–65	Garelli house, Champoluc (I)
1965–72	Chamber of Commerce, Turin (I)
1965–73	Structure and furnishings of Regio Theatre, Turin (I)

CARLO MOLLINO was born in Turin in 1905. In 1931 he graduated in Architecture at the Politecnico of Turin, and began to work with the father Eugenio, an engineer, who instilled in him technical and building skills and an extremely professional approach. He also inherited his father's love of the mountains and interest in local architecture. 1950–52 Mollino taught interior architecture, furnishing and decoration in the School of Architecture of Turin Polytechnic and in 1953 he was appointed professor of architectonic composition.

Mollino was an extravagant architect, and besides architecture he also cultivated a series of interests such as photography, cinema and literature, as well as sporting disciplines from skiing to motor racing and flying. He created a brilliant circle of friends, including talented painters, writers and photographers like Mino Maccari, Albino Galvano, Piero Martina, and Carol Rama. A central figure in Mollino's cultural development was the painter Italo Cremona, who introduced him to Surrealist aesthetics.

One of the main assumptions behind Mollino's poetics is that architecture is a synthesis of art and technique. In his designs and building projects he drew on his various interests. His re-reading of the rationalist aesthetic was based on a personal interpretation of the all-inclusiveness of art and the fact that art is not autonomous. He embodied a sort of resistance to social uniformity, which led him in 1959 to design a provocative mirror floor in the Black and White Lutrario dance-hall.

Throughout his career he continued his research into mountain architecture, begun in 1930 when he carried out a survey of the architecture of the Valle d'Aosta. As well as producing critical essays and photographs on the subject, he also incorporated this line of research into his projects, where the history, the materials and the building tech-

niques of the mountain tradition created a repertoire to be used with an ironic, contradictory spirit. He was interested in the problems of large public spaces and in the theme of the distribution of space in multifunctional complexes; above all, however, he developed the psychological theme of the home and home furnishing.

In 1938 Mollino turned a two-room flat in via Talucchi, Turin, into his Casa Miller, a private drawing room, a place for conversation with his friends. In the design for the house Mollino began to experiment with the Surrealist features that he would develop in his interior designs. Casa Miller became the material translation, in terms of space, colour and light, of a novel. He created fantastic sets to live in, for his meetings, his photos, and his fantasies. The result was a multiple reflection of images and meanings. All the things are equally close and each implies an infinite number of others, the vision of things does not assume the hierarchical order of perspective. He was able to break the hierarchy of perspective by using mirrors and illusions. In this way he made clear his cultural links with Italo Cremona and Piero Martina. In 1938 Carlo Levi wrote: "This is a closed world: we are on the stage, or inside a chapter. The threshold is locked: what is outside is totally arbitrary." During the same period Mollino himself wrote the novel entitled *L'Amante del Duca*, in which the description of the architect's house reminds us of Casa Miller.

In the limited space of Casa Miller Mollino concentrated dozens of different colours and materials, from the most traditional to the most modern, managing to dissolve the banal space of an anonymous apartment formed of just two rooms. He destroyed the conventional distribution and constructed spaces that open one inside the other like a play of reflected mirrors. Panels in coloured velvet and perforated drapes hide

LIVING ROOM AND PHOTOGRAPHIC STUDIO

VIEW OF THE LIVING ROOM

VIEW TOWARDS THE BED NICHE

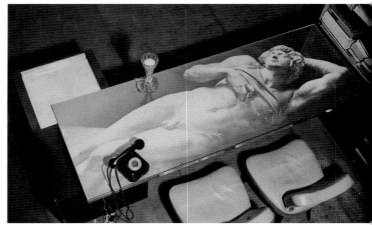

MOLLINO'S DESK

the walls, cover the ceiling, and divide up the spaces. Mirrors and transparent surfaces deform the perception, creating the sensation of a space dissolved in the infinite fragments of a fantastic vision.

Carlo Levi concluded: "Anyone looking for new solutions to problems of the construction of household appliances, the arrangement of objects in an environment for living in, or decorative details (like how to frame a Japanese print, or how to hide unsightly radiators, or a radio, etc.), will undoubtedly find brilliant suggestions that very few other Italian interior designers would be able to give."

The furnishing is composed of unique pieces, whose role is more symbolic than functional, part of the overall composition. The space is reminiscent of a set, conceived as an extension of the walls, the ceilings and the floors, like the mirror in the form of the Venus de Milo, which reflects the objects mirrored and cut out erotically, the shelves of various shapes moulded in Securit crystal that jut out of the walls, the black piece in the bedroom which balances on one leg. Others pieces of furniture seem to rise up out of the floor, like the desk with the glass top on which there is a life-size photo of a sculpture by Michaelangelo. The lighting in the main room consists of a lamp anchored to a rail that describes a wide curve on the ceiling. The display case in the living room is a glass parallelepiped anchored at one end with a single support, which can turn round on itself. The leading player on the stage is the adjustable seat, "the curved form of that embroidered bed is raised, it is tempting and precious: but preciosity loved for itself hides rather than reveals, and in a sense betrays the meaning of the house". The whole volume of the apartment can be manipulated to obtain a space artificially constructed by the mind for its own needs. The only things that remain of Casa Miller are photos, descriptions in the magazines of the time, and a few drawings of the plans.

LORENZA COMINO

BIBLIOGRAPHY:
1938   Levi C., 'Casa Miller', in *Domus*, no. 129, September, pp. 1–11
1941   Pica A., *Architettura moderna in Italia*, Milan, pp. 8, 72, 116, 328–32
        Galvano A., 'Un arredamento di Carlo Mollino', in *Stile*, nos. 5/6, May/June, pp. 31–42
1983   Montuori M., *L'insegnamento di Carlo Mollino*, Venice
1985   Brino G., *Carlo Mollino – architettura come autobiografia, architettura mobili, ambientazioni 1928–1973*, Milan
1989   Irace F., *Carlo Mollino 1905–1973*, Milan
2001   Cornoldi A., *Le case degli architetti. Dizionario privato dal Rinascimento ad oggi*, Venice, pp. 263–264

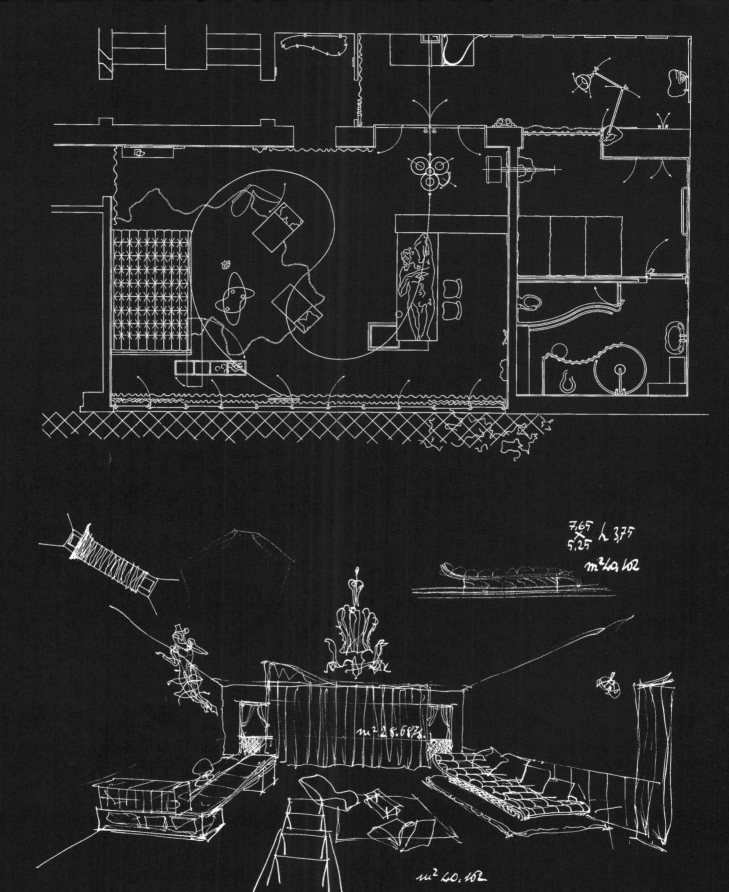

7,65 λ 3,75
× 5,25
m² 40,102

m² 28,58½

m² 40,102

William Morris
1834–1896

1859, NEW CONSTRUCTION, IN COLLABORATION WITH PHILIP SPEAKMAN WEBB, OWNED SINCE 2003 BY THE NATIONAL TRUST UPTON, BEXLEYHEATH, KENT (GB)

MAIN WORKS AND PROJECTS

1857	Ceiling decorations in the Oxford Union Library (GB)
1862	Furniture by the firm of Morris, Marshall, Faulkner & Company is presented at the International Exhibition in South Kensington, London (GB)
1863–64	Decorative work in Queen's College Hall, Cambridge (GB)
1866	Furniture and interior design for St James' Palace, South Kensington, London (GB)

Furniture for the Green Dining Room of the South Kensington Museum, London (GB)

1867	*The Life and Death of Jason*, London
1868–70	*The Earthly Paradise*, London

THE ENGLISH DESIGNER, craftsman, poet, and early Socialist William Morris, whose designs for furniture, wallpaper, stained glass, fabrics, and other decorative products gave rise to the Arts and Crafts Movement in England, revolutionising Victorian taste, was born on 24 March 1834 into a large affluent family in the Essex village of Walthamstow, on the southern edge of Epping Forest, not far from London. After preparatory school, Morris went at the age of 14 to Marlborough College, where he did not shine, but learned – as in later life – only what he wanted to learn.

In 1853 Morris went up to Exeter College at Oxford University. Here he met Edward Coley Burne Jones, who was to become the renowned painter and designer Edward Burne-Jones, and with whom he formed a lifelong friendship. For a while the students Morris and Burne-Jones were profoundly affected by the High Church (Anglo-Catholic) movement of the Church of England, and they looked set to become clergymen. But then they joined the Brotherhood, a group of young writers and poets influenced by the work of Carlyle, Ruskin and Tennyson. Particularly the writings of John Ruskin on the social and moral basis of architecture (notably in his *The Stones of Venice*), which hit Morris "with the force of a revelation", ousted his churchy sentiments and leanings. In this climate Morris began to write poetry and to study mediaeval architecture.

In 1856, accompanied by Burne-Jones and also another friend, William Fulford, Morris went on holiday to northern France, where the trio visited the region's mediaeval cathedrals. During this trip they also met the Pre-Raphaelite painter and poet Dante Gabriel Rossetti, whose powerful influence would lead Morris to deepen his interest in architecture and lead Burne-Jones to devote himself to painting. In the same year, the year of his graduation from Oxford University, Morris joined the Oxford office of the architect George Edmund Street, an exponent of the

Neo-Gothic movement. Here he met Philip Speakman Webb, the 'senior' assistant in the practice, and between the two young men, despite the fact that their characters were very different, a deep, lasting and fruitful friendship was born. However, after just one year with Street, Morris decided to give up architecture, and in 1857 began to paint under the guidance of Rossetti, sharing a studio from 1856 to 1859 with Burne-Jones in London's Red Lion Square. But this, in turn, he also abandoned, being unsure of his talent as a painter. Nevertheless, Rossetti enrolled Morris among the band of friends who in 1857 were decorating the walls of the Oxford Union, in Oxford, with scenes from Arthurian legend. It was through Rossetti and the Union painting project that Morris met his wife, Jane Burden. The beautiful enigmatic daughter of an Oxford groom, she had modelled for Rossetti and then also posed for Morris. They married in 1859, but the liaison was ultimately to prove a source of unhappiness for both of them. Together they had two daughters, Jenny and May, who were born in 1861 and 1862.

In 1858 Morris went with Charles Faulkner and also Philip Webb (from Street's architectural studio, which Webb left the same year to set upon his own) on a long journey along the River Seine in France. During the trip Morris spoke with Webb about his plans to build a house for himself. At this time, perhaps wanting to repeat the experience of the Brotherhood in Oxford, he also decided to set up an association of artists, painters and craftsmen. The two projects could come together in the house. An association of 'fine art workmen', consisting of Morris and his friends, could furnish and decorate the house, attempting to bring together and harmonise the work of the mind, the eye and the hand. The house would be an opportunity to put the planned new association to the test, and in the building the members would be able to try out their ideas on art, architecture, and arts and crafts.

GARDEN VIEW

VIEW OF THE EAST FAÇADE

FIREPLACE IN THE FIRST FLOOR DRAWING ROOM

DRESSER (BY PHILIP WEBB) IN THE DINING ROOM

In April 1861 the association of friends mutated into the firm of Morris, Marshall, Faulkner & Company, with premises in Red Lion Square. Other members of the firm were Ford Madox Brown, Rossetti, Webb, and Burne-Jones. In 1862 Morris' company exhibited stained glass, furniture and embroideries at the International Exhibition in South Kensington, which led to a series of important commissions, including decorations for new churches, notably St Martin's-on-the-Hill in Scarborough, and stained-glass windows, for example for Jesus College Chapel, Cambridge (done by Burne-Jones).

The plot for Morris' home, in the village of Upton, at Bexleyheath, Kent, was chosen in 1858, and work on the house, called the Red House, started in 1859. Morris commissioned his friend the architect Philip Webb to design it. In 1860, at the end of the summer, William and Jane Morris moved into the Red House, staying there for five years. Between 1860 and 1864 the garden was set out and the house decorated. In 1864 Webb drew up plans for an extension to the Red House, in which Burne-Jones and his wife might live. However, in the same year the plan for the two friends and their respective families to live together was abandoned, and Burne-Jones moved to Kensington. Nevertheless, the five years that Morris spent at the Red House were the happiest in his life. At the end of November 1865, following a serious attack of rheumatic fever, brought on by overwork, Morris and his family left and sold the Red House to move to Bloomsbury in London.

The greater part of Morris' new house at Upton was given over to his firm's workshops, an arrangement which, incidentally, combined with other factors, reduced Jane to a state of neurotic invalidism. At the Red House, between 1862 and 1864, Morris made his first wallpaper designs, including 'Trellis', 'Daisy', and 'Fruit' or 'Pomegranate', although he did not arrive at his mature style until ten years later, with the famous 'Jasmine' and 'Marigold' papers.

Morris was involved in many other activities besides painting and interior decoration. He was a poet, who found success in his day with works such as the romantic narrative *The Life and Death of Jason* (1867), a series of narrative poems *The Earthly Paradise* (1868–70), and his principal poetic achievement, the epic story of *Sigurd the Volsung and the Fall of the Niblungs* (1876). He was a traveller and travel writer, who in 1871 and 1873 went to Iceland. He was a public speaker, who gave his first lecture, *The Decorative Arts* (later called *The Lesser Arts*), in 1877, and whose collection of lectures, *Hopes and Fears for Art*, appeared in 1882. He was the founder in 1877 of the Society for the Protection of Ancient Buildings, which sought to counter drastic restoration methods being carried out on Great Britain's cathedrals and parish churches. He was an evangelising socialist, who in 1883 joined Henry Mayers Hyndman's Democratic (later Social Democratic) Federation, who toured industrial areas to spread the gospel of Socialism, and who marched alongside George Bernard Shaw on demonstrations in London. He founded the Kelmscott Press in 1891, and up to 1898 produced some 50 titles, also designing three type styles for the press.

In 1871 Morris tried to live together with Rossetti at Kelmscott, an Elizabethan manor house in Oxfordshire. The attempt, recalling the earlier failed joint tenancy with Burne-Jones at the Red House, was never a success, and in 1874 Rossetti moved out. At this time the firm of Morris, Marshall, Faulkner & Co. was reorganized under Morris' sole proprietorship as Morris & Co. In 1875 Morris began his revolutionary experiments at the firm with vegetable dyes, which, after the company's move in 1881 to more spacious premises at Merton Abbey in Surrey, resulted in

STAIRS, SEEN FROM ACROSS THE FIRST FLOOR LANDING >

SETTLE IN THE FIRST-FLOOR DRAWING ROOM

their finest printed and woven fabrics, carpets, and tapestries. In 1878 Morris and his family moved into Kelmscott House (named after their Oxfordshire country house), in Hammersmith, London. By the mid-1890s Morris was worn out by his multiple activities. A sea trip to Norway in the summer of 1896 failed to revive his flagging energies, and William Morris died after returning home, in Hammersmith, on 3 October. He was buried at Kelmscott beneath a simple gravestone designed by his old friend Philip Webb.

William Morris' home, the Red House, at Upton, Bexleyheath, Kent, which was a new construction (1859), was so called because it was built of red brick when the fashion was for stucco villas. It was designed by Morris' architect friend Philip Webb, who became known for the unconventional country houses (relatively few in number) that he did between 1859 and 1900, and who was a pioneer figure in the English domestic revival movement. Morris' famous Red House was Webb's first commission and is characteristically informal and unpretentious. Webb, who also designed household furnishings and decorative accessories in metal, glass and wood, and embroidery for Morris' firm, followed a basically practical approach, and his original designs, although influenced by vernacular medieval styles, pointed toward 20th-century Functionalism in their bold use of materials and exposure of structural elements.

The search for a suitable site for Morris' home took Morris and Webb to the village of Upton in Kent, where they settled on a plot near an orchard. Webb quickly drew up the plans, and building began in 1859. Morris and Webb naturally worked in close collaboration, and it is difficult to tell where the contribution of the one starts and that of the other ends. The house was, in fact, a collective work, where the talents and ideas of the whole group of artists and intellectuals around Morris came together. It could be argued that the Red House is a synthesis of Morris' romanticism and Webb's pragmatism. During construction Morris and his wife moved to Aberleigh Lodge, close to the orchard, so they could supervise the work day by day. Both Morris and Webb were firmly convinced that a house, the place of home life, should have the same dignity and value as public architecture, but that at the same time it should aim at stylistic simplicity, devoid of monumentality.

The house has an L-shaped plan, with a tower containing the stairs at the juncture and two wings looking onto the garden. Near the tower stairs, on the garden side, is a well with a tall conical roof, supported by massive oak pillars. This picturesque corner seems to have been the place where philosopher and poet friends of Morris' gathered to discuss political and social issues. The entrance to the house, on the north side, consists of a deep arch, which is the main feature of the front. Inside, in the background, is the staircase, the dominant feature both of the plani-

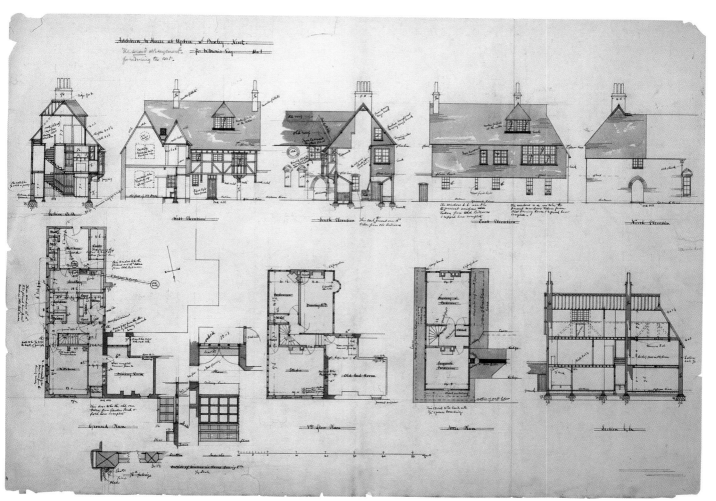

ELEVATIONS, PLANS AND SECTION

metric composition and of the internal arrangement of the two floors. The staircase is in ash, with tall, slender, tapering newel posts that underline the vertical development of space. The ceiling over the staircase is decorated with a clear, geometric, curvilinear pattern. The motifs are abstract, but obviously inspired by nature, showing how the role of nature is predominant even in the definition of the internal spaces, as if to underline the 'rural' character of the whole building, the fact that it is a 'country house'. Edward Hollanby states that the house and the garden were designed as a single whole, and that there is a special relationship between the house, solid and romantic, and its surroundings. The house and the garden were designed to conserve as many trees as possible in the orchard, and two of the old apple trees are still present on the lawn to the south-east, beyond the well court.

On the right of the hall is a wardrobe, designed by Morris himself, with scenes from the *Nibelungenlied*, while on the left is the entrance to the gallery that leads to the portico in the garden. On the ground floor of this wing is the dining room, the living room and the fireplace room, while upstairs, together with the bedrooms and bathrooms, is the study and the drawing room. The latter is characterised by a large piece of furniture designed by Morris for his flat in Red Lion Square, placed in the studio and later modified by Webb, who added a platform with banisters reached by a ladder.

When William and Jane Morris moved into the Red House in 1860, it soon, as they had wished, became a meeting place for their friends. So as to pick up these friends from the nearby railway station, the Morrises had built a sort of carriage, almost in the style of an ancient chariot. The weekends at the Red House were times of relaxation and amusement, but also of creativity and art. In the special atmosphere created by the hosts, everyone made their own intellectual or practical contribution, by decorating or planning furnishings and ornaments for everyday life. Even the mathematician Faulkner contributed by developing the geometrical patterns for the decoration of the ceilings.

PAOLO GIARDIELLO

BIBLIOGRAPHY:
1947   De Carlo G., *William Morris*, Milan
1968   Henderson P., *William Morris: His life, Work, and Friends*, London
1970   Zevi B., 'William Morris – La Casa del riformatore', in *Cronache di architettura*, vol. V, no. 486, Bari, pp. 252–260
1983   Gorjux R., *La Red House*, Bari
1999   Hollanby E., *Red House* in 'Arts & Crafts Houses', pp. 5–34

Hermann Muthesius
1861–1927

1906–09, NEW CONSTRUCTION, SOME ALTERATIONS DURING THE 1960S
POTSDAMER CHAUSSEE 49, BERLIN (D)

MAIN WORKS AND PROJECTS

1904–05	Bernhard house, Berlin-Grunewald (D)
1907–08	Freudenberg house, Berlin-Nikolassee (D)
1910	Dwellings in Hellerau Garden City, near Dresden (D)
1911–12	Cramer house, Berlin Dahlem (D)
1912	Michels Silk Weaver's, Nowawes, near Potsdam (D)

1917–20	Radio station, Nauen (D)
1923–24	Tuteur house, Berlin-Charlottenburg (D)

FEW ARCHITECTS have focused their attention on the theme of the single house as much as Hermann Muthesius. In the last century his theoretical and critical work, even more than his constructions, represented a turning point in the approach to private housing. And no other architect after him has dealt in such an explicit way with the subject of how to build one's own house.

Muthesius was born in 1861 in Gross-Neuhausen, a modest village near Weimar. His father owned a small building firm there, in which the young Hermann worked during the school holidays, acquiring considerable mastery of manual skills and ultimately completing a two-year apprenticeship with his father. From a very young age Muthesius proved to be a remarkably quick learner. He was taught Latin and French, as well as German, by the parish priest. He learned to play the piano and the organ, developing a special liking for Bach. He was also interested in literature, art and the applied arts, building up a substantial library.

Following his apprenticeship with his master builder father, Muthesius initially enrolled in 1881 in the Faculty of Philosophy at the Friedrich-Wilhelm-Universität in Berlin, but a couple of years later, now aged 22, he switched to architecture, studying 1883–87 at the Technische Hochschule (University of Technology) in Berlin-Charlottenburg. After graduating in 1887, he worked first in Berlin, and then for four years in the Ende-Böckmann studio in Tokyo, where he assembled a rich collection of Japanese woodcuts and works of art. From 1895–96 Muthesius travelled around Asia, and also – thanks to a travel grant – in Italy. In the latter year he married the well-known opera singer Anna Trippenbach, with whom he had two children. She abandoned her singing career to work with her husband on interior designs.

In 1896 the Muthesiuses moved to London, where they lived in a house on the Thames in Hammersmith. In the English capital Hermann worked until 1903 as the cultural attaché at the German Embassy. He was particularly attracted to the developments of English residential architecture linked to the Domestic Revival, and drew up extremely detailed reports on various aspects of building and engineering in England, to such an extent that he was charged by William R. Lethaby with industrial espionage. In fact, Muthesius was driven by his deep interest in innovative technical solutions as a response to changing human needs.

Back in Germany, Muthesius published from 1904–05 his seminal three-volume study *Das Englische Haus*, which remains today a key study of English residential architecture of the period, which combined the Arts and Crafts movement and the Romantic movement. In the work, which went on to influence residential architecture on the European continent, Muthesius presented the houses designed by the main contemporary British architects, including William Morris, Richard N. Shaw, Charles Francis Annesley Voysey, William R. Lethaby, and Mackay H. Baillie Scott, amply illustrating his study with drawings and photos. His interest focused on the pragmatic and inventive method of planning, as well as on the underlying objectives of simplicity and domesticity, with the aim of creating the conditions for a higher quality of living in perfect harmony between aesthetics and ethics. Distancing himself from monumentalism, symmetry, and a *priori* choices of language, Muthesius was an advocate of convenience, comfort, the integration of architecture and the craft industry, the importance of the interior compared to the exterior, and the harmony of house and garden.

Muthesius advocated a new style of life, and introduced a new form of architecture based on the developments in England. Appointed as a government adviser on education (1904–26), he promoted an innovative reform of the Prussian schools of applied art based on the English model. In 1907 he was one of the co-founders of the important Deutscher Werkbund (German Association of Craftsmen), which, aiming to combine quality and quantity, encouraged collaboration between industry and artists, including Behrens, Taut, Gropius, Tessenow and Muthesius himself. In many ways the Werkbund can be seen as the forerunner of the

VIEW FROM THE MEADOW

VIEW FROM THE ORCHARD

STUDY

Bauhaus. Here, too, Muthesius proved his ability to interpret the spirit of a new era.

From 1904 onwards Muthesius designed a large number of single-family houses, most of the them in the residential suburbs to the southeast of Berlin, near the Grünewald, in the pleasant countryside that slopes down to the lakes formed by the Havel. The characteristic feature of these houses is an attempt to combine the traditions of the English house with those of the Central European house, between the mixtilinear geometry of the former and the compact stereometric layout of the latter. The result was a hybrid use of volumes, with a formally eclectic, not always uniform exterior appearance and a rather complex, concentrated and at the same time elaborate interior plan. The various rooms, arranged around a large welcoming hall (often two floors high), are all very different in their forms and proportions as well as in their fittings, with the aim of practicality and of satisfying the requirements of the various aspects of domestic life, yet at the same time they follow a highly controlled overall composition. Among the most original and coherent of Muthesius' designs are the Bernhard house (1904–05), the Neuhaus house in Berlin (1906), and the Stave house in Lübeck (1909).

During the First World War Muthesius wrote numerous books and articles, including *Wie baue ich mein Haus?*, an important essay on how to build the most suitable house for one's own needs. In the course of his life the architect divided his time between an intense web of institution-al commitments, his theoretical studies and his professional work. He died in Berlin on 26 October 1927, in a road accident while on his way to a building site.

Muthesius' work continues to grow in stature and relevance, witness the large number of publications and cultural events organised in the last 20 years in the context of the rediscovery of the 'private' and of the specific nature of private house design. His architecture was not rigorous in terms of style, to which he admitted his indifference. Although some of his works display essential unified compositions, the main point of interest in Muthesius' houses is the quality of the interiors, their scale, the use of natural light, the fittings and furnishings, and the overall use of space.

Muthesius built his own house-cum-studio between 1906 and 1909 at Postdammer Chaussee 49, Berlin-Nikolassee, on a large sloping plot near the Grunewald. He erected the new construction next to the Freudenberg villa, which he designed at around the same time, adapting the 'butterfly' plan of Victorian residences. His own home, even more so than those he designed for other people, represents a *summa* of the principles advocated in his books and essays.

The building comprises two bodies. There is the house, with a rectangular plan and four floors, and then there is the study, with an L-shaped plan and two floors, facing a square, fenced courtyard. Together they form

FIREPLACE IN THE MUSIC ROOM

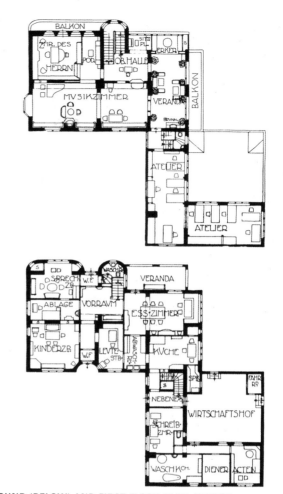

GROUND (BELOW) AND FIRST FLOOR PLAN (ABOVE)

an asymmetric but geometrically precise construction, covered with wide-pitched roofs.

The first floor of the house, which enjoys a fine view over the valley, is devoted entirely to the family's leisure and cultural life. From an intermediate floor reserved for smokers, several steps lead down to the architect's comfortable study, where the light from three large windows falls on the desk and the 'English-style' bookcase that covers two walls, while the oak floor is embellished with an inlay pattern. Next to the study is the music room, where the use of rich materials and the lowered-vault ceiling are designed to make the room warmer and to improve the acoustics. Next to the grand piano are wall niches for scores, the fireplace corner, and attractive window seats. The music room extends through two sliding doors into the lady's drawing room, which opens onto the garden through large windows. Although only to a limited extent, the presence of architectural elements in the garden recalls Muthesius' susceptibility to Mediterranean traditions.

Compared to the houses he had built for other clients, the spaces in his own home are more intimate. The niches, slight bow windows and varying levels create more opportunities for privacy, showing the architect's attention to this aspect of family life. Other details, such as the rectification of the volumes and the simplification of the plan by means of a square-based modular grid, make this the least 'English' of the houses designed by Muthesius. After substantial modifications during the 1960s

– the study wing of the house was partially demolished, and a six-floor building was constructed close to the road – there are now plans to restore the house.

ADRIANO CORNOLDI

BIBLIOGRAPHY:

1904–05 Muthesius H., *Das englische Haus*, Berlin
1917 Muthesius H., *Wie baue ich mein Haus?*, Munich
1985 Bucci F., 'La casa a Nikolassee di Herman Muthesius', in *Casa Vogue*, no. 165, pp. 84–89
1986 'Casa Muthesius a Berlino', in *Domus*, no. 676, p. 186
2001 Cornoldi A. (ed.), *Le case degli architetti. Dizionario privato dal Rinascimento ad oggi*, Venice, pp. 271–273

Christian Norberg-Schulz
1926–2000

1953–55, NEW CONSTRUCTION, WITH ARNE KORSMO, ALTERED
PLANETVEIEN 14, OSLO (N)

MAIN WORKS AND PROJECTS

1951–52	Alfredheim, Oslo (N), with Arne Korsmo
1956	Trade Fair building, Oslo (N), with J. I. Hovig
1963	*Intentions in Architecture*, Cambridge (Mass.)
1975	*Architektur des Barock*, Stuttgart
	Meaning in Western Architecture, New York
1979	*Genius loci: paesaggio, ambiente, architettura*, Milan

1979	Digerud J. G., Fjeld P. O. and Norberg-Schulz Chr., *Louis I. Kahn*, Oslo
1986	*L'Abitare*, Milan
1993	*Nattlandene: om byggekunst i Norden*, Oslo
1997	Postiglione G. and Norberg-Schulz C., *Sverre Fehn: Complete works*, New York

CHRISTIAN NORBERG-SCHULZ was born in Oslo, Norway on 23 May 1926. He studied architecture at the Swiss Federal Polytechnic (now the famous Federal Institute of Technology or ETH) in Zurich, graduating in 1949. At this institution, one of his teachers was Sigfried Giedion, and as a young student, Norberg-Schulz was among a select circle invited to regular meetings held at the home of the illustrious professor and pioneer of modern architecture. Following graduation, Norberg-Schulz returned to Norway intending to open his own architectural practice, but instead laid the foundations for a career as an eminent academic, as a world-renowned critic and theorist of architecture, author of influential books on the subject, and as an editor.

In 1950, as a direct result of Giedion's call to form an independent Norwegian delegation for the CIAM congresses, Norberg-Schulz co-founded the PAGON group (Progressive Architects Group Oslo Norway), which also comprised the fellow founding Norwegian architects Arne Korsmo, Sverre Fehn, Odd Østbye, Geir Grung, Peter Andreas Munch Melbye, Håkon Mjelva, Robert Esdaile and Norberg-Schulz himself, who were sometimes joined by Jørn Utzon. The group met at Korsmo's home at Planetveien 12, Oslo, in a house in a terrace that Norberg-Schulz and Korsmo designed together, and which also contained Norberg-Schulz's house, Planetveien 14. In 1951 Norberg-Schulz went with the PAGON group and delegation to the CIAM congress in Hoddesson, England. In the 1950s he designed with other members of PAGON many modernist projects for Oslo and Bergen, unfortunately never realised.

Norberg-Schulz also embarked during the same period on the academic side of his career. He assisted Arne Korsmo in his architecture course at the National College of Art and Design in Oslo (SHKS). The intellectual collaboration spilled over from the confines of the SHKS into the practical sphere, and they began jointly designing and building archi-

tectural projects, including the terrace at Planetveien which contained their own two houses. Norberg-Schulz also cooperated fruitfully during these years with the Danish architect Jørn Utzon, jointly entering numerous international competitions with projects ranging from urban design to furnishing products, none of which, however, were successful.

In the early 1960s, Norberg-Schulz's career as an architect seemed to be at an end, even though he was still only in his thirties. But in 1963, he was appointed as a lecturer at the School of Architecture (AHO) in Oslo, which properly launched him on his academic career. In 1964 Norberg-Schulz was awarded a Ph.D. in architecture, in 1965 he was a visiting professor at Yale University, New Haven, Connecticut, USA, and in 1966 he was a visiting professor at MIT, Cambridge, Massachusetts, USA. He would lecture at the AHO in Oslo until 1994, when illness forced him to retire.

His 1964 Ph.D. thesis grew out of a book that he had published in 1963, *Intentions in Architecture*, which brought him world-renown and marked the start of Norberg-Schulz's career as a theorist. Also in 1963 he was invited to become the editor of the Norwegian architecture journal *Byggekunst*, a post that he would hold until 1978. By the mid-1960s, therefore, Norberg-Schulz had embarked upon what were to turn out to be his true vocations: working as a teacher, as a theorist, and especially as an editor. Norberg-Schulz's publications have been translated into many languages, garnering him acclaim around the world and also bringing him during his lifetime numerous invitations to give lectures and take part in conferences in many countries. His first milestone, *Intentions in Architecture* (1963), was based on studies he made during his stay at Harvard University between 1952 and 1953. The book's aim, he said, "was to give architecture a humanistic basis, and I defined this intention as an integrated theory of architecture, meaning a theory capable of involving

VIEW OF THE PROPERTY

THE DOOR LEADING TO THE VERANDA

THE LIVING ROOM FROM OUTSIDE

THE DOUBLE HEIGHT LIVING ROOM

not only all the Vitruvian categories, but also their interrelations." Norberg-Schulz lamented the fact that the general public was no longer able to understand the built environment in which it lived, while architects had no desire to communicate the contents of their work.

The second milestone in Norberg-Schulz's critical output was *Genius loci* (1979), written as a result of his stay as a visiting professor at Yale University in 1965. At Yale he encountered the work of Louis Kahn and was introduced both to the phenomenological theories of Edmund Husserl, Gaston Bachelard and to the philosophy of Martin Heidegger. By introducing the role of personal experience in the comprehension and perception of built form within the natural and/or artificial context in which it is realised, Norberg-Schulz now shifted the focus of his interests from the universalism that pervaded *Intentions in Architecture* to a theory centred more specifically on Heideggerian 'being in the world' and on 'space' as the 'locus' of life. He developed these themes further in the 1990s in his *Nattlandene: om byggekunst i Norden* (1993) and also *Stedkunst* (1995), in which he showed how an architectural tradition can both have roots and be modern, can both belong to a place and have a universal value. He also explored the same lines of research in *L'Abitare* (1996), which combines in a more radical manner the research undertaken in *Genius loci* with the thought and philosophy of Heidegger, aiming at a revaluation of the existential dimension of being and its needs. Dwelling, claimed Norberg-Schulz, was more than the realisation of a shelter, of a roof over our heads. It was an existential dimension and need, a need that allowed man to find his way in the world.

During the 1980s, Norberg-Schulz's interest in the issues raised by Postmodernism led him to overvalue certain works and authors. This was the period of his partnership with Charles Jencks, whose *The Language of Postmodern Architecture* excited the Norwegian. Fascinated by a theory that returned built form to the centre of the project, Norberg-Schulz adhered enthusiastically to the new fashion, but was quick to realise that the value of postmodern ideas could not be expressed adequately in works of architecture. He paid for this postmodern 'interlude' with a certain isolation that marked his work from the late 1980s to the end of the 1990s, when at 70 years of age and despite failing health he continued to work every day, sitting at his desk in his office in St Olavs gate 9, in Oslo, in a room made available by the School of Architecture (AHO) during his final years of teaching. Christian Norberg-Schulz died in Oslo on 28 March 2000 after a long battle with cancer.

Norberg-Schulz's own home at Planetveien 14 is one of a terrace of three houses that he designed and built with Arne Korsmo between 1953 and 1955. Korsmo moved as his neighbour into Planetveien 12, while the third dwelling went to the owner of the plot of land on which the terrace is built. The three houses are situated on a hill to the north-west of Oslo, in one of the most attractive residential areas of the city, and both introduced the international principles of glass and steel architecture to Norway, and also constituted a sort of manifesto of a new way of living.

The floorplan of the houses is based on the use of a square grid, four feet per side, which informs all the elements of the construction, including the steel frames used as the structural system. The compositive and geometric design is extremely simple, and the small terrace forms a low long compact body, onto which the three volumes containing the

bedrooms are grafted. This also makes it possible to identify the single properties from the outside.

The modular structure allowed the floorplans and elevations of the three houses to be organised with a considerable degree of freedom, since the two architects used an analytical project method developed a few years earlier by Korsmo. The system, called 'Hjemmets mekkano' (the Meccano house), is used as a regulating plan which informs the realisation of every part of the construction. Both Korsmo and Norberg-Schulz were fascinated by the ideas that were being developed at the time in American architecture. When he had been a visiting professor at MIT in 1966, Norberg-Schulz had attended a course run by Ludwig Mies van der Rohe, and had published a long interview with the master in *Byggekunst*. Similarly, it was Korsmo's visit to Charles Eames' house in Pasadena that influenced both his subsequent architectural research and to a certain extent the design of the terrace in Planetveien.

In *Byggekunst* Norberg-Schulz wrote of the individual houses in the terrace: "…on the upper level we needed a double bedroom which would overlook the living room, and a smaller bedroom that would be entirely separate. We also left a space to create a small guest room, this too looking down onto the living room. On the ground floor, by contrast, all the rooms form a continuous whole, with the exclusion of the kitchen and bathroom, although they are partially screened by teak panels hanging from the ceiling, and by curtains that can further divide up the space. …The steel skeleton acts as an ordering element and is visible in its entirety throughout the house, partly because it is painted a soft shade of red." It is precisely this apparently insignificant detail that on the one hand demonstrates the distance separating Norberg-Schulz and his Norwegian colleague Korsmo, who in his own house had painted the metal frame white, and on the other shows Norberg-Schulz's close links with the architecture of Mies van der Rohe on the other side of Atlantic.

GENNARO POSTIGLIONE

FLOOR PLAN

BIBLIOGRAPHY:
1955 Norberg-Schulz C., 'Hos arkitekt Christian Norberg-Schulz', in *Byggekunst*, no. 7, pp. 184–189
1962 Norberg-Schulz C., 'Italiesin', in *Byggekunst*, no. 6, pp. 164–168
1986 Grønvold U., 'En søken etter mening', in *Byggekunst*, no. 6, pp. 321–328
1996 Various authors, *Christian Norberg-Schulz. En fest utskrift*, Oslo
2001 Cornoldi A., *Le case degli architetti. Dizionario privato dal Rinascimento ad oggi*, Venice, pp. 281–282

Francisco Javier Sáenz de Oíza
1918–2000

1985, RENOVATION
POLLENÇA, MAJORCA (E)

MAIN WORKS AND PROJECTS

1949–55	Aránzazu Basílica, Oñate, Guipúzcoa (E), with L. Laorga
1956	Apartments, Entrevías, Madrid (E), with M. Sierra
1959	House, Durana, Álava (E)
1960	Lucas Prieto house, Talavera de la Reina, Toledo (E)
1962–69	Torres Blancas (high-rise apartment block), Madrid (E)
1965	Oíza's summer house, Colonya, Majorca (E), renovated stone house
1968	Juan Huarte house, Formentera, Balearic Islands (E)
1972–81	Banco de Bilbao office tower, Madrid (E)

1985	Museo Atlántico de Arte Contemporáneo, Las Palmas de Gran Canaria (E)
1986	Apartment block on the M30 motorway, Madrid (E)
1989	Palacio de Festivales de Santander (festival centre), Santander (E)
1992	Torre Triana, office block for the Junta de Andalucía (regional government), Seville (E)

FRANCISCO JAVIER SÁENZ DE OÍZA was born on 12 October 1918 in the small town of Cáseda, in the northern Spanish region of Navarra. However, he spent most of his childhood and adolescence in Seville, where his father worked as a state architect. In 1934, intending to study architecture, he moved to Madrid, where he enrolled in the School of Exact Sciences, studying there until 1936. At the time this was a preliminary step that had to be taken before entering the Madrid School of Architecture, which Oíza joined in 1936.

Almost immediately his architectural studies were interrupted by the outbreak of the Spanish Civil War (1936–39), and it was not until 1946 that Oíza was finally able to graduate from the School as a qualified architect. At his graduation he was awarded the prize for best student of his year.

In 1946, after college, Oíza started working in Madrid's City Planning Department and in the same year won the National Architecture Prize for a project to remodel Segovia's Plaza de Azoguejo, situated next to the Roman aqueduct. Around this time he also won a scholarship which enabled him to go to the United States for two years, an option that he took up. Oíza has said of this decision that – either in Spain or in America – he could have done a Master's degree or some other course of further study to obtain more paper qualifications and impress people, but instead he wanted to spend time travelling in the US and studying the American way of life. He was fascinated by how American architecture utilised technology and turned it to society's advantage. "In America I discovered that it was actually modern technology that interested me more than modern art. American traffic lights and concrete blocks… make you realise what the American spirit is – inventions all around. In

the States, the patents office is as important as the Prado Art Gallery here in Madrid."

Back in Spain, Oíza built his first apartment block in Madrid in 1949 and worked 1949–55 on a project connected with the Aránzazu Basílica in the Basque region, through which he met the sculptor Jorge Orteiza. Also in 1949 he began a long career (over 30 years) as a lecturer at his old college, the Madrid School of Architecture, initially teaching the subject of health and hygiene, and then (1952–83) architectural design. His activities as a teacher were a fundamental aspect of his life, making him quite a public figure over generations of students, and also grounding a man given to grand aspirations and dreams. In 1954 Oíza met the builder Juan Huarte, who later becomes a generous patron of his, and for whom he designed a house in 1968 on Formentera, one of the Balearic Islands. And in 1972 he won a competition to design the head office of the Bank of Bilbao, considered by many architects to be Spain's finest 20th-century building. As his academic career unfolded, he progressed up the hierarchy, being appointed Professor of architectural design at the Madrid School of Architecture in 1970 and then Director of the School (1981–83).

Sáenz de Oíza was far from being a dry academic, but was a passionate, highly active, rather theatrical and even controversial man, as well as a brilliant speaker. Even though he died in 2000, his colourful person and sayings are far from forgotten, especially because he became almost a mythical figure amongst Spain's youngest architects. He could be a contrary and argumentative figure, who once said: "I am a quibbler. I would love to write a book in which I affirm one thing on one page and contend exactly the opposite on the next, leaving the reader to choose which thesis he prefers."

GENERAL VIEW FROM THE SOUTH

PARTIAL VIEW OF THE ADDED FAÇADE
THE OUTER HALL

THE OUTER DINING ROOM

In 1960 Oíza arrived on Majorca to work on the Alcudia White City Project, involving 100 apartments. From that moment he established a link with the island which was to last until his death 40 years later. For four decades he spent his summers there, at first staying in different houses and apartments. But in 1965 he bought a house in the Colonya valley, situated near the old town of Pollença. The house, built around 1900 by Guillem Cifre, said to be Colonya's 'last gentleman', stood next to the old residence of his family, and in its day was innovative, evincing an aspiration to a more cosmopolitan culture. This appealed to Oíza, who – at least during the summers – moved into the house, taking the old gentleman's place. Here the architect carried out minor alterations to the building, adapting it to the needs of his large family. He made a terrace on the roof, from which a wonderful view could be enjoyed of the whole Colonya valley and the sea, and installed a skylight in the roof, giving the house its most distinctive feature, and making it easily recognisable by day or night.

Twenty years later Oíza bought Les Rotes, another house near Pollença, in the Colonya valley, at the foot of the Sierra de la Coma mountains, on the island of Majorca. Built in 1913, it was a simple rustic dwelling that the architect set about renovating to make his second private summer house (1985). It lies obscurely at the end of a narrow side road and then a path, and even today, when you arrive at its entrance, marked by a green-blue iron gate with floral decorations, the place seems to have stood still in time. Again, Oíza acquired the property because he was attracted to its spirit. But where his first Colonya house represented a certain sophisticated cosmopolitan culture, Les Rotes symbolised the land, and was a place where the architect could come into contact with rural tradition and the purity of the old. The name of the house derives

from the word 'rota', meaning poor-quality land that belonged to some large estate. Such land would be cultivated for a time by a farmer known as a 'roter', who would pay part of his crops to the estate owner. Often, for the duration of his contract with the landlord, this farmer would build a simple house on the land, using whatever materials were available locally, and constructing a place like Les Rotes.

The small rectangular house has two floors, and – like Oíza's first Colonya home – its main façade faces south-east. Its walls, constructed with stone rubblework, enclose a small space divided in two by the staircase, which leads to the first floor. The height of the two floors is minimal, and the composition of the main façade, with three windows on each floor, is symmetrical in relation to the central axis. Oíza found these minimal dimensions and spaces congenial and familiar. They reminded him of the sparing plans for his early social housing projects, in which

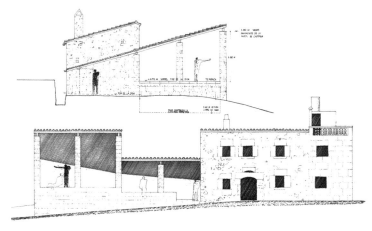

FRONT AND SIDE ELEVATIONS

every measurement had to justify itself down to the last centimetre, and in which the basic necessities had to be provided for with few resources.

Oíza enlarged Les Rotes by adding an extension to its eastern side, which also had two floors. However, where the original building had an inclined roof, the new part had a flat roof, which acted as a terrace and viewpoint. As in his previous Colonya summer house, the architect and his family could go up onto the roof terrace to contemplate the landscape, the horizon and the sky. The terrace introduced a new spatial dimension, allowing one to go up and look outwards, which followed Gastón Bachelard's text *The Poetics of Space*, which Oíza constantly consulted, and a reading of which is necessary to comprehend Oíza's intentions in his houses. On the terrace he built a very light aluminium structure to mitigate the effects of the sun on the roof.

But the most significant intervention was the construction of another extension to the south-west. Oíza lengthened the back wall, following the lie of the land, and enclosing an open terrace. In front of the terrace he constructed a porch or canopy, made up of nine square stone columns, which support a large roof with the same inclination as the roof on the original house. Under the roof he placed a large rain tank, partly dug into the ground. A system on the roof collects rainwater, which runs into the tank, where it is stored. The roof shades the stored rainwater, helping to conserve it. The whole facility generously extends the house outwards, affording many additional uses in the summer.

The new canopy provides the house with shade and water, supplying it with the conditions needed to live in such a hot remote place. But Oíza's essential addition also represents, as is the case in all his projects, a desire to invest the whole building with a plastic intention. Here, as in his Huarte house (1968), the addition is achieved by extending the existing roof. However, the plastic effect comes more from the creation of the large façade. The effect is highlighted through the creation of a horizontal platform on the ground, enabling the exterior area of the house to be defined, and serving as a base for the whole building. The roof of the new canopy projects forward, rising to the top of the original façade. The extension also respects this alignment. This is how the façade is extended, achieving an almost monumental scale.

Little has been published about Les Rotes, perhaps because it was Oíza's summer house. It was his refuge, a place largely tucked away from scrutinising evaluative gaze. Yet it was a home slowly adapted in all tran-

THE OUTER CANOPY

quillity as it was lived in, and the product of a whole life of architectural knowledge. As an elderly Sáenz de Oíza said in one of his last public appearances: "I would have liked to use my time building my own house, but instead I have spent it constructing other people's homes."

FEDERICO CLIMENT GUIMERÁ

BIBLIOGRAPHY:
1988   'Sáenz de Oíza: 1947–1988', monograph issue of *El Croquis*, nos. 32/33, February/April
1991   Fullaondo J., *La bicicleta aproximativa: conversaciones en torno a Sáenz de Oíza*, Madrid
2000   Special monograph issue of *Arquitectura*, devoted to Sáenz de Oíza, September
        Cánovas A., (ed.): *Banco de Bilbao. Sáenz de Oíza*, Madrid
2001   Climent Guimerá F., *J. Sáenz de Oíza. Mallorca 1960–2000. Proyectos y obras*, Palma de Mallorca, pp. 96–105

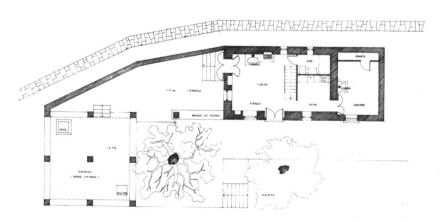

PLAN OF THE GROUND FLOOR

Joseph Maria Olbrich
1867–1908

1901, NEW CONSTRUCTION, REBUILT WITH ALTERATIONS AFTER THE SECOND WORLD WAR
MATHILDENHÖHE, ALEXANDRAWEG, DARMSTADT (D)

MAIN WORKS AND PROJECTS

1897–98	Secession pavilion, Vienna (A)
1899	Residence for Dr. Hermann Stöhr, St. Pölten (A)
	Interior conversion for Alfred Stifft, Hohe Warte 48, Vienna (A)
	House Ernst Ludwig, Darmstadt (D)
1900	Residential buildings for the Darmstadt artists' colony: Christiansen house, Habich house, Glückert houses, Keller

	house, Deiters house, group of buildings for Wilhelm Ganss, Darmstadt (D)
1902	House for Princess Elizabeth of Hesse in Park Schloss Wolfsgarten, Langen (D)
1906–09	Tietz department store, Düsseldorf (D)
1907	New design of Louisenplatz, Darmstadt (D)
1907–08	The Nuptial Tower (Hochzeitsturm) in Darmstadt (D)

INITIALLY, between the ages of 15 and 19, Joseph Maria Olbrich, who was to become one of the founders of the modern architecture movement in Europe, attended the State Industrial School in Vienna, returning to his hometown of Troppau (now Opava in the Czech Republic) in 1886, where he worked as an architect and director of works for a building firm. But in 1890, aged 23, he enrolled in Vienna's Akademie der Bildenden Künste (Academy of Fine Arts), where he studied architecture under Carl von Hasenauer. At the Academy he won in 1893 the Rome Prize, which allowed him to make an extended study trip to Italy and North Africa (1893–94).

On his return to Vienna and the Academy, Olbrich joined Otto Wagner's studio, in which he worked as an assistant for four years (1894–98). In 1897 he was a co-founder of the Wiener Sezession (Viennese Secession group), which brought together Gustav Klimt, Kolomon Moser, Josef Hoffmann and Otto Wagner. In this context Olbrich, who was an expert draughtsman and watercolourist, began designing graphic motifs, and also organised annual exhibitions, mainly of the work of British artists, including Charles Rennie Mackintosh and the Glasgow group, who exerted a considerable influence on the contemporary Austrian arts and crafts scene. Olbrich designed the building in Vienna to house the exhibitions of the Secession (1897–98). It has a blocklike simplicity, though it has floral Art Nouveau decoration on the metal cupola.

In 1899 Olbrich was invited by Ernst Ludwig Grand Duke of Hesse to join the Artists' Colony that the grand duke had established in Darmstadt. The 32-year-old architect took up the offer, moving to Darmstadt the same year and joining the Colony as a founder member (along with Peter Behrens). Subsequently directing construction of the artists' colony for eight years, until his death from leukaemia in 1908, Olbrich designed six of the houses there, including his own, as well as a central hall for

meetings and studios, which manifests the influence of the Scottish architect-designer Mackintosh. The group of houses and exhibition areas of the Colony was opened in 1901, extended in 1904, and completed by the Exhibition Palace and the Nuptial Tower in 1908. The idea informing the artists' collective was that of the *Gesamtkunstwerk* or total work of art. Aspiring to the integration of all the arts, the colony strove ambitiously, supported by Grand Duke Ernst Ludwig, to create a 'new city', including both interiors and urban design, as a synthesis of art, life and nature. As part of their initiative, the group's members focussed on the simplest things, such as the pattern of everyday life, furnishings and housing.

Olbrich's versatile talent, his passion for the idea of the total work of art, and his keen desire to include everyone in the longed-for harmony of a new way of life, launched him on a brilliant but short-lived career. He rapidly acquired fame on the European continent, in Great Britain and in the United States. He participated in 1900 in the Paris International Exhibition with the *Darmstadt Room project*. In 1902 he presented a number of interiors at the International Exhibition of Modern and Decorative Art in Turin. And in 1904 he took part in the International Exhibition of St Louis with *Summer Residence* of an Art Lover. Olbrich was a co-founder of both the Bund Deutscher Architekten (1903), and of the Deutscher Werkbund in Munich (1907). In the summer of 1907 the architect moved with most of his collaborators to Düsseldorf.

Besides the Secession pavilion and the buildings for the Darmstadt colony and its exhibitions, Olbrich also constructed residential accommodation for Grand Duke Ernst Ludwig and Princess Elizabeth of Hesse. He, further, designed the Hochzeitsturm or Marriage Tower in Darmstadt (1907), which had rounded fingerlike projections on its roof suggestive of Art Nouveau, but which also featured bands of windows evincing a distinctly modern trend. Among Olbrich's last works were Tietz depart-

THE LIVING ROOM

HALL WITH FIREPLACE

ment store in Düsseldorf (designed in 1906 and completed 1907–08 after his death) and a house at Cologne-Marienburg (1908–09).

The single-family house that Olbrich built for himself on Darmstadt's Mathildenhöhe was part of the Artists' Colony at Alexandraweg. Constructed new in 1901 on the occasion of the Colony's first exhibition, it formed part of the exhibition of that same year and manifests the collective's aspiration to the *Gesamtkunstwerk*. Like the home that Behrens also erected for himself at the Künstlerkolonie, it is designed down to the last detail. Olbrich planned the entire dwelling with individual life in mind. In an article he wrote entitled 'Unsere nächste Arbeit', he described it as a place of peace, where art must be represented in the surfaces and in the form, where "it is possible to listen to music, talk, receive guests, and pass the time pleasantly". Each room in the house must contain "the golden threads of perfect happiness", and even the humblest ornaments should be designed with the same intensity and the same lines as the architectural project. The plan of the house is clearly influenced by English country homes, where an almost enchanted atmosphere is created by rooms furnished and decorated in lively colours. Shortly before his death, Olbrich wrote the following words to his wife: "I am always cheered by our little house and the fullness of our happiness."

Built on a triangular sloping plot, the house is composed of a basement, containing the kitchen and utility rooms, and three floors above ground. A south-facing veranda, characterised by a blue ceiling and chessboard-style floor in black-and-white marble, leads into the hall on the mezzanine floor. This leads in turn to the dining room, which has white walls decorated with a pattern of golden triangles, and also to the hall, which is the fulcrum of the house. Lit by a large window and destined for

entertaining and conversation, the room is two floors high. The lower part of the walls is covered with oak panels, the ceiling is dark green, and a large lilac carpet with a geometrical pattern covers the floor. From a high wooden balcony comes the music of a piano, while the benches at the sides of the hearth within the large wall fireplace volume provides a more cosy area. The ample hall is separated from the study, a quiet space decorated in grey tones, by a drape embroidered with a polychrome pattern, which was created like other pieces in the house in collaboration with Claire Morawe, who was to become Olbrich's wife.

The attic, the most private and isolated part of the house, contains two guest rooms as well as staff quarters. The blue guest room, located on the first floor, and the pink and green guest rooms take their names from the colour of the lacquered furniture. The green room is divided into two areas. One area, open towards the visitor, is characterised by a window niche for conversation, and the other, which is a more intimate bedroom area, is separated simply by a drape.

Olbrich's home at Alexandraweg can be considered an example of modernist artistic tendencies around the turn of the 19th and 20th centuries and, more specifically, as representative both of Jugendstil and of total art. As said, the architect was involved in the design of every part of the house, just as he was in every detail of the Colony as a whole. Concerning the overall project, he attended to the plan of the whole colony, to the architecture, to the design of the gardens, to furnishings, and even to the publicity graphics for the exhibitions. The ambitious title of the Colony's first exhibition, in 1901, of which Olbrich's private house was a part, was "A Record of German Art", and among the architect's notes we read that "no square inch [of the Colony and exhibition] must have forms and colours that are not pervaded by artistic spirit".

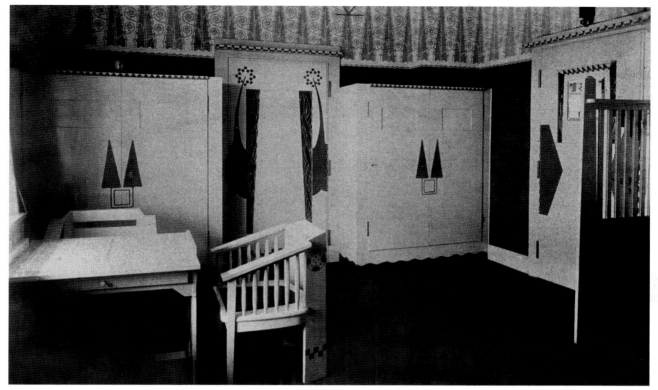

THE LIVING ROOM

ELEVATION AND PLAN

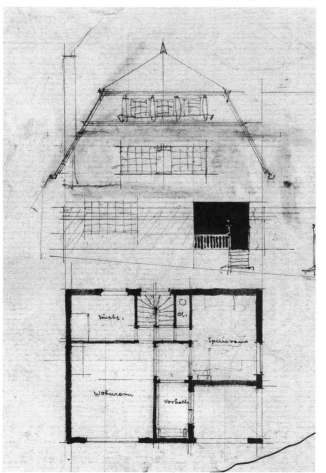

Olbrich's home, like the Exhibition in general, caused a considerable stir not just in Germany but abroad as well. But its model furnishing, like that of the other houses, also provoked considerable criticism from other contemporary artists. The creators of the furnishings at the Colony may have spoken continually of 'popular art' and of art for life, but their over-individualistic designs were in reality the expression of an upper middle-class way of life. Moreover, Olbrich's aim to 'crystallise' a new form of social life was condemned by many of his contemporaries. In *Die Fackel* Karl Kraus railed: "No one would refuse to acknowledge Mr Olbrich's notable decorative ability, an ability that he still retains from his father's art as a confectioner. But the astonishing originality is no longer recognisable when Mr Olbrich applies to objects and furniture square-shaped wooden ornaments that are generally used for furnishing fabrics. And we are also firmly opposed to the fact that some people want to glorify the art of the confectioner as the apex of artistic creation, as the Austrian style." Nevertheless, it can be said, more charitably, that Olbrich's interiors and his sketches of applied art actually embody a more classical artistic attitude, which would later influence and mark the work of J. Hoffmann, P. Behrens and other architects and designers.

LUISA GATTI

BIBLIOGRAPHY:

1978   Messina M. G., *Darmstadt 1901 – 1908: Olbrich e la colonia degli artisti*, Rome
1980   Latham I., *Joseph Maria Olbrich*, New York
1983   *Joseph M. Olbrich: 1867 – 1908. Mathildenhöhe Darmstadt*, catalogue of the exhibition, Darmstadt
1988   Ulmer R. (ed.), *Joseph Maria Olbrich. Architettura: riproduzione completa dei tre volumi originali 1901 – 1914*, Milan
1992   Olbrich J. M., *Ideen von Olbrich*, Stuttgart (orig. ed. Leipzig, 1904)

Alexander Nisbet Paterson

1862–1947

1900–02, NEW CONSTRUCTION
ROSSDHU DRIVE, HELENSBURGH (GB)

MAIN WORKS AND PROJECTS

1892	Arngask Library, Glenfarg (GB)
1906	The National Bank of Scotland, 22–24 St Enoch Square, Glasgow (GB)
1909	Liberal Club, 54 West George Street, Glasgow (GB)
	Colquhoun Arms Hotel, Arrochar (GB)
1910–12	Drum Millig, Woodend, and Courtallan, all Helensburgh (GB)

1911	Scalescleuch, Cumberland (GB)
1916	Municipal buildings and Council Chamber, Gourock (GB)
1920s	War memorials, including Helensburgh, Douglas and Campbelltown; the National Bank, Edinburgh (GB)
1926–27	Gleddoch House, Renfrewshire (GB)

ALEXANDER NISBET PATERSON was born in 1862, the son of Andrew Paterson, who was a successful manufacturer and prominent churchman, and of Margaret Hunter. His parents hoped that he might choose the Church as a career, but as a talented draughtsman and watercolourist he aspired to become an artist. However, with his brother James already a painter, his parents were unwilling to support another artist in the family, so he turned to architecture instead. Paterson's brother James had trained at the Ecole des Beaux-Arts in Paris from 1877–83, while another brother of his, William Bell Paterson (1859–1952), was an art dealer.

Paterson was educated at Glasgow Academy and the University of Glasgow, where he graduated with an MA in 1882. From 1883–86 he continued his studies in Paris at the Ecole des Beaux-Arts, attending the studios of Jean-Louis Pascal (architecture) and Maurice Galland (decoration). Subsequently, from 1886–89, he was an assistant at Burnet Son & Campbell, before working in the offices of Sir Robert Edis (1889–91) and then with Aston Webb and Ingress Bell. In 1889 Paterson travelled in Italy, sketching Santa Chiara, the tomb of Maria di Valois in Naples and San Clemente in Rome. He is known also to have toured in France and Holland. Paterson commenced independent practice in Glasgow in 1892. Three years later, in 1895, he gave an address to the Glasgow Association of Architects, entitled 'Style, Individuality and Tradition', which debated the issue of a Scottish national style. His conclusion was later to be represented in the design for his Long Croft home. Nationality was a subject Paterson returned to in February 1911, when he presented a lecture entitled 'Scottish Architecture from the 15th to the 17th Centuries' at a joint meeting of the Edinburgh Architectural Association and the Franco-Scottish Society.

In 1896 Paterson was awarded the Royal Institute of British Architects' (RIBA) Godwin Bursary, which enabled him to visit America's

eastern states, a study trip that was to influence the interior planning of the Long Croft. Two years later, on 18 April 1898, he presented the findings of his trip to the RIBA. The presentation, entitled 'A study of domestic architecture in the eastern states of America in the year 1896, with special reference to questions of plans, construction, heating, drainage etc.', generated lively debate in the Institute on the relative merits and practicalities of British and American domestic architecture.

In 1897 Paterson married Maggie Hamilton (1867–1952), a talented embroideress and also painter of still-life subjects, who exhibited at the International Exhibition in Glasgow in 1901. She was much involved in the Arts and Crafts Movement of the time. They had two children, a daughter Mary Viola, and a son Alastair Hamilton. From 1899–1935 Paterson exhibited regularly at the Royal Scottish Academy, becoming an Associate in 1911. In 1906 he served as President of the Royal Incorporation of Architects in Scotland, while from 1912–13 he was President of the Glasgow Institute of Architects.

Paterson started out as an architect working in other people's practices, before opening, as said, his own office in 1892. In 1904 he went into partnership for two years, until 1906, with Campbell Douglas, and then, from 1918–30, with Donald McKay Stoddart. At the height of his architectural career Paterson developed throat cancer, leaving him with a speech impediment, although the disease did not stop him from continuing a long and fruitful life.

When in 1900 Paterson began planning his private Long Croft home in Helensburgh at Rossdhu Drive, Helensburgh was a fashionable location for Glasgow's middle classes who wished to move away from the city and build their own small-scale estates overlooking the mouth of the River Clyde, serviced by the railway. The Long Croft (1900–02), a new construction, was not built simply as a family home, but also as a setting for

VIEW FROM THE SOUTH-WEST, 1981

THE DRAWING ROOM, 1981

ALEXANDER NISBET PATERSON SEATED AT HIS DRAWING BOARD

the artistic creations of Paterson, his wife Maggie Hamilton, and their circle of artistic friends. In addition, it was to embody Paterson's ideas on a Scottish national architecture, while embracing the practical aspects of planning that he had learnt from American domestic architecture. Within the house, but with independent access, Paterson designed a studio in order to work, away from his Glasgow practice, for his burgeoning number of Helensburgh clients.

The photographs of the house, with the family in residence, were probably taken in 1908 by Paterson's brother James. They provide an unusually intimate portrait of the family's life in the house. The image of Paterson at his drawing board in his studio shows the desk and chimney piece (with ornamentation by George Walton) that he designed himself.

Paterson and his family lived at the Long Croft all their lives. In 1977, a few years before Mary Viola's death, an exhibition on the Paterson family stated that the house "embodies much of the last 100 years of Scottish Art", and that "the atmosphere of the place is completely of its time". The two-storey, asymmetrical, L-plan house is sited to have spectacular views over the Firth of Clyde, with a picturesque drop down to the Glenan Burn. The walls are of local stone and, in places, brick, harled with Portland cement roughcast, with grey freestone dressings. The roofs are covered with a random mixture of purplish-blue Ballachulish and dark green Aberfoyle slates, finished with a cast cement ridge. Five turrets give drama to the skyline. Ornament, as befits the parsimonious Scot, is rationed and used to greatest effect in the stylised hood-mould over the

main entrance, with its charming carved portraits of Paterson's children. Also over the door are carved Paterson's and his wife's initials as well as the symbols of their occupations, namely architecture, painting and embroidery. In addition, there is an inscription which reads: "A house that God doth oversee – is grounded and watched as well can be – Salve Bene Dicite". Almost all other decoration is found in functional details: in the Dutch gable, the mock dovecot in the chimney flues, and the dormer heads, one with the carved date of 1901.

The internal planning, with rooms opening on to each other, a lack of corridors, a high provision of bathrooms, a basement to provide underfloor heating, and the use of the hall with balcony as a sitting area, are all reminiscent of the American planning Paterson had described in his lecture to the RIBA in 1898. The interiors provide spacious living areas, a studio, day and night nurseries, and room for two resident domestic staff. The main reception rooms are placed to the south to enjoy the views, while the studio is placed furthest from family activity.

Paterson designed the Long Croft at a relatively early stage of his career, and it provides a vivid demonstration of his beliefs about a national Scottish style, beliefs that were to preoccupy him throughout his career. In his search for a national style, he looked for his inspiration to the Scottish Renaissance Heriot's Hospital, Drumlanrig and Falkland Palace, admiring their "breadth and dignity, largeness of scale, simplicity of composition, and interesting skyline, concentration of ornament", and stating: "I would have the spirit of such work translated and made use of

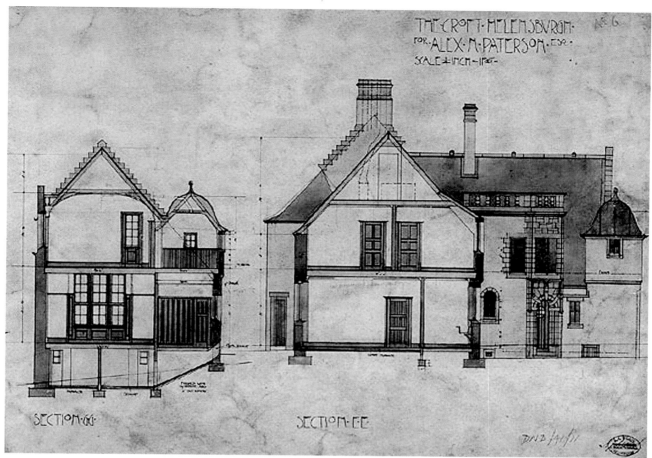

SECTIONS

PLAN OF THE GROUND FLOOR

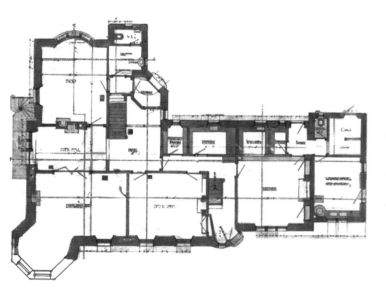

in carrying out, with all modern resources, the different architectural problems of our day." Paterson believed this national style grew from the inherent Scottish character, which he described as "cautious yet pushing; logical, humorous and imaginative, yet parsimonious or at least averse to lavish display; enthusiastic especially in its [Scottish] hero-worship, yet in matters in everyday life undemonstrative". These characteristics he believed "did and still should find an echo in its architecture".

This logic, humour, parsimony and restrained character are all found in Paterson's Long Croft, echoing the lifestyle of a comfortable, middle-class family of discerning and artistic taste. As Ian Gow has observed, the Long Croft is "a representative example of the 'House Beautiful', and the perfection of these small British villas was admired by the German critic Hermann Muthesius during his visit to Britain."

REBECCA M. BAILEY

BIBLIOGRAPHY:

1903   *Academy Architecture*, vol. 1, p. 68
1908   Nicoll J. (ed.), *Domestic Architecture in Scotland*, Daily Journal Offices, Aberdeen, plate 57
1977   *The Paterson Family – One Hundred Years of Scottish painting: 1877–1977*, exhibition catalogue, Belgrave Gallery Ltd., London
1992   Gow I., *The Scottish Interior*, Edinburgh, pp. 52–53
1995   Riches A., 'The Architect's House and the Search for a "National Style"', in Gow and Rowan (eds.), *Scottish Country Houses 1600–1914*, Edinburgh

John Pawson
*1949

1994–96, CONVERSION AND ALTERATION, STILL INHABITED BY THE ARCHITECT
NOTTING HILL, LONDON (GB)

MAIN WORKS AND PROJECTS

1982	Apartment for Bruce Chatwin, London (GB)	1996	Jigsaw store, London (GB)
1985	Waddington Galleries, London (GB)	1998	Cathay Pacific lounge, Chek Lap Kok Airport, Hong Kong (China)
1988	Cannelle cake shop, London (GB)		
1989	Neuendorf villa, Majorca (E)	2002	Architectural design of the Venice Architecture Biennale (I)
1995	Tilty Barn, Essex (GB)		
	Calvin Klein store, New York (USA)		
	Tunish house, Tunis (Tunisia)		

BORN IN 1949 in Halifax, in the English county of Yorkshire, John Pawson comes from an affluent family, which owns a textile mill. Despite this, the family home is not so much luxurious as solid and dignified. Not far from it lie the ruins of Fountain's Abbey, and it may well have been the essential charm of the Cistercian abbey and its site that struck the young John's receptive mind, propelling him at an early age to the desire to eliminate all unnecessary ornamentation that subsequently came to characterise his architecture.

This propensity was to inform not just Pawson's architecture but his life also, although in the early years it emerged more as an everyday need than as an aesthetic quality. Thus we learn, for example, that as a schoolboy at Eton College (1963–67), Pawson refused categorically to sleep in his bed, preferring a hammock made out of a simple white sheet. And that in the family home, when his brothers moved out, he had the walls separating his room from his brothers' rooms knocked down because, so he claimed, he needed the space for his drawing boards, although in the end the resulting enormous room was occupied only by a single bed. Later Pawson moved into a cottage that his father had designed and built on the family estate. Here, too, although aware of his father's displeasure, he could not resist the temptation to simplify the internal space, eventually even removing the fireplace.

For several years (1967–74) Pawson worked in the family textile firm. He also began travelling throughout the world, which ultimately led him to live from 1974 to 1978 in Japan, where he taught English at the University of Nagoya. Pawson's four-year stay in the Far Eastern country played a crucial role in his development. Especially important was his meeting with the Japanese architect Shiro Kuramata. The two men became very close, although their relationship was never that of master and pupil. Pawson often visited Kuramata's office, and followed the

design and realisation of the latter's projects, although he never contributed in any way to the Japanese architect's work. Some time later, after Pawson had returned to England in 1978, the Englishman received a surprise phone call from Kuramata, who now urged him to study architecture. A few hours later, Pawson found himself for other reasons near the Architectural Association in London and, still shaken by his friend's words, suddenly decided to enter and enrol. Such was the decisive role that Kuramata played in Pawson's life.

The would-be architect's time at the school, perhaps partly due to the fact that Pawson was now already over 30, was not particularly enjoyable. At that time the curriculum, under the influence of Bernard Tschumi, was centred on a technological engineering-based approach, which left the mature student indifferent, even hostile. And so, despite Pawson's deep respect for the Association's chairman, Alvin Boyarsky, his attendance of the school turned out to be largely a waste of time. However, during the three years of his studies (1979–82) he did learn one thing that would be useful in the future – a determination to defend his own style and planning decisions even when no one else seemed to understand or appreciate them.

Opening his own office in 1983 in London, Pawson began his first projects, and his architectural style soon took clear shape. It was a powerful individual style, influenced by his experiences as a young man, by Japanese architecture, and also by celebrated masters such as Ludwig Mies van der Rohe and Luis Barragán. But above all his style was and is the expression of a sort of self-discipline, far from the whimsical self-referential style typical of the 1980s.

Pawson has never worked in the offices of other architects, and this adds to the difficulty in classifying his work. He himself does not codify his style, except through an appeal to austerity as one of the fun-

REAR OF HOUSE FROM THE GARDEN

THE KITCHEN

TERRACE AND LIVING ROOM

damental souls of architecture, nor does he put forward a real architectural manifesto.

In his definition of spaces each detail is essential: the choice of how a door opens, of how the floor meets a wall, the presence or absence of a lintel. In a kind of aesthetics of absence each element assumes much greater weight, and contributes through its specific physicality to the creation of a particular atmosphere. Nothing must distract the eye from the whole. What emerges is a sort of personal ability, although the hand of the artist, restrained by a certain reticence, is never visible.

Pawson's minimalism does not prejudice the careful choice of materials (white marble, stone, cedar, oak, etc.), whose physical natures play a significant part in the creation of a feeling of calm, light and freedom, which admirers of his work appreciate. His minimalism is the deliberate exclusion of everything that is not necessary, of everything that could disturb the minds of those who inhabit his spaces.

Sometimes it is said that there is no space in Pawson's houses for objects. But this is not true. There is space for objects, but somehow the space has simply become invisible, rendering the potential intrusiveness of the objects innocuous. The same goes for the prevalence of emptiness, which actually is often confuted, with even the decision to juxtapose different shades of white helping to give a sense of fullness and warmth. The result is a calm sense of order that contrasts sharply with the chaos of city life and its superfluity of visual stimuli.

Success was not long in coming to Pawson. Wealthy clients allowed the architect to build prestigious works, including houses for many famous figures. Among them was the writer Bruce Chatwin, who on the subject of Pawson's houses has written: "To live in one of his interiors is not for the lazy-minded; it requires a certain act of will."

The home that John Pawson built for himself (1994–96) in Notting Hill, London, in which he still lives, is the result of a restoration so radical that the project might better be called a reconstruction. The building restored by the architect was chosen by himself and his wife Catherine when they were forced to vacate the home they had previously been inhabiting with their two sons. The family moved into their new home very quickly, but initially made few changes (the walls and fittings were painted white, and white carpets were fitted in all the rooms) so that they could take their time planning the final alterations.

The house is part of a rectangular block of Victorian terraces, whose four sides are formed by the fronts, all facing a park, thus reversing the typical geometry of London housing. At the back of each house is a small private garden bordering the neighbouring gardens, so that from the inside the main view in every direction is of trees and the sky, giving the impression of being in a detached house rather than in a terrace.

Pawson made a long study of the history and evolution of London housing, of its main features, and of the differences that make one house distinguished and another more humble. The Pawsons' house was originally rather simple, comprising two rooms on each of the four floors, and enjoying a total floorspace of no more than 150 square metres.

After 'restoration' only the façade of the original structure remained, which was completely preserved except for the cornice of the door. The rest of the house was razed to the ground and rebuilt according to strict criteria concerning the use of space and materials. Pawson's aim was to exploit as fully as possible the features of the house and to respect its forms by redesigning them in such a way as to make the spaces usable – in other words, new needs but with sensitivity to the original features.

In arranging the spaces, the architect carefully considered the requirements and relationships of each member of the family, both currently and in the future, when the two boys would be grown up. He gave thought to the orientation of the windows, the morphology of the ground, the characteristics of the houses in the area seen from above, and even the hydrogeological conditions of the terrain, for one aim of his

STAIRS FROM ENTRANCE AND LIVING ROOM

FIRST FLOOR (LEFT) AND GROUND FLOOR PLAN (RIGHT)

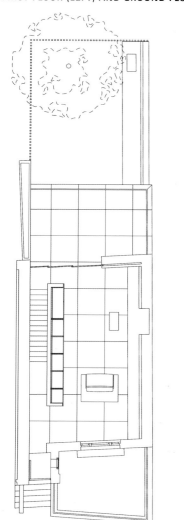
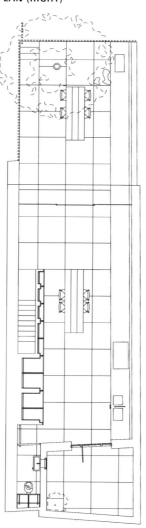

was to dig down and tap into natural heat of geothermal origin. Overall Pawson's principal objective was to create not a beautiful house, but a house that would be beautiful to live in.

On the mezzanine floor the two original entrances are joined together to make a single area, with two fireplaces. Along the whole length of the wall is a bench. In the dining room the wooden table and two benches are the same colour as the flooring. In the kitchen the marble top is not only a work space, but also a piece of architecture. It is so thick and long that a crane was needed to place it in position. The large glass wall in the kitchen leads to the garden, which is like an extension of the room. Here the stone paving, the bar, the table and the benches are a mirror image of those inside. The bathroom is all in brown stone, with the flooring designed to allow the water to drain below. On the top floor, on the other hand, right under the roof, is a shower with a glass ceiling, permitting a view of the sky. The glass can even be opened when the weather permits.

For Pawson the family home is not just a good house, but must necessarily be the best. This is because architecture is the inevitable reflection of the life of the architect, in the sense of what he is and what he wishes to be in the future.

LUISA CORNOLDI

BIBLIOGRAPHY:

1992   *John Pawson*, Barcelona
2000   Sudjic D., *John Pawson Works*, London
2001   Cornoldi A., *Le case degli architetti. Dizionario privato dal Rinascimento ad oggi*, Venice, pp. 52–54
2002   Pawson J., *Themes and Projects*, London

Auguste Perret
1874 – 1954

1929 – 32, NEW CONSTRUCTION, NOW SEAT OF THE INTERNATIONAL UNION OF ARCHITECTS (UIA)
51 – 55 RUE RAYNOUARD, PARIS (F)

MAIN WORKS AND PROJECTS

1904	Apartments in Rue Franklin, Paris (F)
1907	Garage, Rue de Ponthieu, Paris (F)
1912	Paul Guadet's house, boulevard Murat, Paris (F)
1913	Théâtre des Champs Elysées, Paris (F)
1923	Church, Le Raincy, near Paris (F)
1933	Algerian government building, Algiers, Algeria
1937	Museum of Public Works, Paris (F)

1942 – 58	Tower building, Amiens (F)
1948 – 53	Nuclear research facility, Saclay, near Paris (F)
1948 – 58	General plan for the reconstruction of Le Havre (F), with a number of collaborators, including Jacques Tournant and André Hermant

AUGUSTE PERRET was born in Brussels in 1874 as one of five children. His father, Claude-Marie Perret, a Burgundian stonecutter, had been exiled to the Belgian capital in 1870. In 1881 the family relocated to the centre of Paris, where Auguste's father started up a construction firm, and Auguste and his two brothers quickly became familiar with building work. This early exposure to construction sites and the entire building process resulted in Auguste designing plans at only 15 years of age for a pavilion, built for the World Fair. At 17 he was admitted to the Ecole Nationale des Beaux-Arts in Paris, entering the studio of the architect-theoretician Julien Guadet, who urged Perret to develop his critical and theoretical skills in conjunction with his prodigious building talents. In spite of his brilliant studies, Auguste Perret never proceeded to a degree. But this did not prevent him from winning acclaim with his favourite material, reinforced concrete, or from being recognised as an exceptionally talented architect. By a twist of fate, he became the first President of the Society of French Architects (1942), was even elected to the French Academy (1943) and became President of the International Union of Architects (1948).

Perret was as single-minded and unique in his approach to the structure of his business as he was to the structure of his buildings. In 1905, with the assistance of his two brothers, he founded a novel commercial operation, which comprised an architectural agency (A. G. Perret) and a construction development company (Perret Frères), the whole outfit being named 'Perret frères, architectes, constructeurs, béton armé'. The structure led to the creation of some of Perret's most famous buildings, of which the Ponthieu garage (1907), the Théâtre des Champs-Elysées (1913) and Raincy Church (1923) mark only the beginning of an impressive career. The latter constructions reveal Perret's deep interest in the arts and artists, and he was familiar with writers such as Paul Valéry

and André Gide, with the sculptor Antoine Bourdelle, and with painters such as Maurice Denis, Mela Muter and Henri Matisse. His love of poetry showed through in his thoughts and in his teaching. He created numerous aphorisms, with which he loved to impress his students and colleagues, who numbered even Le Corbusier for a short time around 1908 as well as Ernö Goldfinger and Jacques Tournant. One of the best-known of these sayings was: "The architect is a poet who thinks and speaks through the art of constructing." 1924 – 26 Perret taught in the first 'free studio' and 1942 – 54 at the second 'free studio' at the Ecole Nationale des Beaux-Arts, as well as 1930 – 37 at the Ecole Spéciale d'Architecture in Paris.

Auguste Perret built the apartment block at 51 – 55 rue Raynouard, Paris, in which he had his own residence and architectural office, between 1929 and 1932. Position and light seem to have been the watchwords both for the building as a whole and for the Perrets' flat in particular. In 1930 the architect wrote: "Thanks to the favourable situation of the building, which is filled with sunlight from dawn to dusk, and to the heat-retaining precautionary tanks, a single source of energy is used: electricity, which runs the heaters (through storage), the kitchens, the hot water." This list reveals the care taken by Perret to preserve comfort and the rhythm of life. The apartment has certain similarities to a lofty perch, from which, thanks to terraces and two external elevators, he was able to look down upon the city. It could also be seen to represent the social ascent of the builder-architect. Before 1930, the Perrets lived at the same address, 51 rue Raynouard, in the 16th *arrondissement*. But following his public recognition, the architect wished to 'move up' several floors, thus bringing together his home, his work and his reception area. Dominating rue Berton and situated one level below the rue Raynouard entrance was

VIEW OF THE SIDE FAÇADE

THE LIVING ROOM

THE BEDROOM   VIEW FROM THE SITTING ROOM   VIEW TOWARDS THE BATHROOM

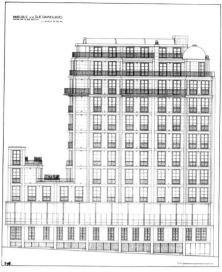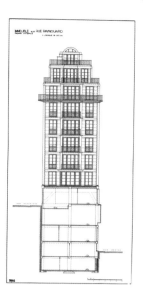

VIEWS OF THE FAÇADES

the architect, and representative of what the historian Joseph Abram would call 'structural classicism'. From the exterior, the block is perfectly integrated into the building line of rue Raynouard, while from the interior, the building acts as a figurehead. Thus, it can be seen that Auguste Perret did not try to change the typology of the residential building, as did Henri Sauvage with his hygienist convictions, nor did he wish to introduce the formal rupture pursued by modernists such as André Lurçat and Michel Roux-Spitz. Nevertheless, the frankness of the block's constructive vocabulary and the refinement of its materials make the building a landmark of modern French architecture.   AYMONE NICOLAS

his agency with its elegant flight of stairs, which 'le patron' walked down every morning to go to work.

The main interest of Perret's apartment block lies in the architecture and construction of its eight floors. In a description of the building, the architect highlighted the procedures used in its construction: "The building is constructed with reinforced concrete, and the fillings of the façade are triple-partitioned. Outside the concrete panels (linked with lime) are two plaster panes, separated by 0.04 m. The floors are made of reinforced concrete beams and fillets, and covered with parquet flooring. […] the windows, which are made of red pinewood with double-glazing, separated by a space of 0.03 m, are rendered waterproof by means of aluminium bronze strips." This long citation contains no less than twelve references to materials and textures, all of them evocative of different colours and smells. Nonetheless, Perret continues, "it is the reinforced concrete frame, designed in such a way as to remain noticeable from the interior and the exterior, which adorns the house."

The subtlety of detail allowed the architect to temper the structural rigour of the frame, the vertical windows and the rough concrete columns. Four of these free columns frame the central circle of the living room, which is marked at the floor and the ceiling. This design reveals Perret's attempts to develop a modern architectural order derived from the architectural orders of Antiquity. His architecture is centred on mastery of proportion. Thanks to his detailed studies of interior circulation, Auguste Perret is able to offer different users complete access to this fluid space. The couple living in the apartment would be able to enjoy the sunrise in a number of different rooms, from the original octagonal bathroom to the living room. A guest, amazed by the elevator ascent with its view of the Eiffel Tower, would be able to discover another panoramic view – this time horizontal – through the numerous vertical bay windows of the large living room. The domestic staff had access to two large rooms overlooking the terrace and the street.

1928 – 1929 Auguste Perret worked on two major public commissions, both in Paris. In critical discourse, these large-scale projects have somewhat overshadowed the importance of his residential buildings. The apartment block in rue Raynouard could be considered a mature work of

PLAN OF THE 7TH FLOOR

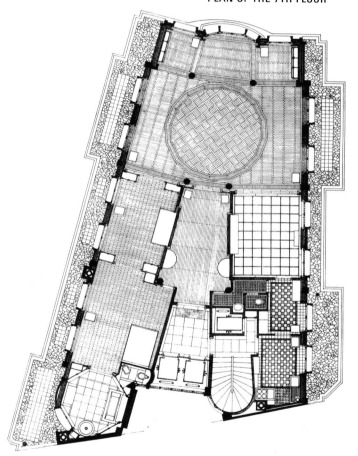

BIBLIOGRAPHY:
1934   De Thubert E., 'Un immeuble 51–55 rue Raynouard, Paris 16e, Perret arch.', in *La Construction Moderne*, no. 10, pp. 224–232
       'Immeuble et hôtel particulier, Perret arch.', in *L'Architecte*, June/July, pp. 57–60
1938   Dormoy M., *L'Architecture française*, Boulogne sur Seine
1993   Gargiani R., *Auguste Perret*, Milan
2000   Culot M., Ragot G. and Peyceré D., *Les frères Perret, l'œuvre complète*, Paris, pp. 192–194
2002   Abram J., Lambert G. (eds.), *Encyclopédie Perret*, Paris, p. 508

Charlotte Perriand
1903 – 1999

1960 – 61, NEW CONSTRUCTION
MÉRIBEL LES ALLUES, SAVOY (F)

MAIN WORKS AND PROJECTS

1926	Bar Sous le Toit, a roof-top bar, Paris (F)
1927 – 37	Co-designs with Le Corbusier and Pierre Jeanneret numerous items of furnishing and fittings, including tubular steel furniture and the Grand Confort armchair
1939	Hotel extension, Saint-Nicolas-de-Véroce (F)
1940 – 41	Oversees production of Japanese industrial art for the Japanese Ministry of Commerce, Tokyo (Japan)
1946 – 49	Research work for mountain resort at Méribel les Allues, Savoy (F)
1950	Prototype of an integrated kitchen for Le Corbusier's 'Unité d'habitation' in Marseille (F)
1951	French pavilion at the IX Triennale in Milan (I)
1957	Air France office, London (GB), with Peter Bradok
1959	Air France office, Tokyo (Japan), with Junzo Sakakura and K. Suzuki
1959 – 70	Collaborates on modernisation of ONU building, Geneva (CH)
1962	Apartment, Rio de Janeiro (Brazil), with Manuel E. Costa
1967 – 82	Directs and coordinates a team of architects and engineers involved in the construction of a massive winter resort, comprising the three buildings Arcs 1600, 1800 and 2000, at Les Arcs, Savoy (F)
1970	Refurbishment of an apartment for herself, Paris (F)
1975	Installation of the showroom of Shiki firm house, Paris (F)
1993	Pavilion tea house in the gardens of UNESCO, Paris (F)

CHARLOTTE PERRIAND was born in Paris on 24 October 1903. In 1920 she enrolled in the Ecole de l'Union Centrale des Arts Décoratifs in Paris, where she studied for five years, until 1925, under the designer Henri Rapin. She also attended decorative arts courses with Paul Follot and Maurice Dufrène. During this period she read Le Corbusier's books *Vers une Architecture* (1923) and *L'Art Décoratif d'Aujourd'hui* (1925), which encouraged her to search for a style relevant to the 'machine age'. In 1926 she took part in the *Un coin de salon* exhibition, mounted at the Salon des Artistes Décorateurs. At this time she also designed a roof-top bar, the Bar Sous le Toit, which was exhibited in 1927 at the Salon d'Automne.

By good fortune, Perriand's bar caught the attention of the legendary Le Corbusier. Admiring the anodised aluminium and chromed steel furniture that she had designed for it, he invited her to join his studio. Thus from 1927 she came to work with the master and with his cousin Pierre Jeanneret in their Paris studio, designing furniture and in 1928 jointly taking part in the *Salle à manger* exhibition at the Salon des Artistes Décorateurs. For the next ten years Perriand was responsible for most of the furniture designs that issued from Le Corbusier's studio, including the first tubular steel designs for systematised furnishings, known as 'habitation equipment' (1928–29). These were exhibited by Le Corbusier, Jeanneret and Perriand under the title of *L'Equipement de l'habitation: des casiers, des sièges, des tables* at the Salon d'Automne in

1929. Another design on which Perriand collaborated with Le Corbusier and Jeanneret was that for the 'Grand Confort' armchair (1928), the very epitome of the International Style. She, further, supervised the installation of interior fittings for Le Corbusier's Villa La Roche, his Pavillon Suisse and his Cité de Refuge (Salvation Army hostel), all in Paris, in 1928, 1930–32 and 1932 respectively. And in 1930 she co-founded with Jeanneret the Union des Artistes Modernes (UAM), at which she began to exhibit under her own name in 1931. In 1930 Perriand had her first solo exhibition at the Musée des Arts Décoratifs.

From 1927 to 1930 Perriand had a studio in Saint-Sulpice, Paris, but in the latter year she moved to Montparnasse, where she lived in a flat until 1940. During the 1930s she travelled extensively in Germany, and in 1931 she exhibited in Cologne with Le Corbusier and Pierre Jeanneret. At the same time she joined the Association des étudiants et artistes révolutionnaires (AEAR), and in 1933 she took part in the IV CIAM congress, titled 'The Functional City'. In 1935 Perriand participated together with Louis Sognot and René Herbst in *La maison du jeune homme*, an international exhibition in Brussels, and in 1937 she showed at the Paris international exhibition *Le refuge bivouac* along with Pierre Jeanneret and André Tournon. She produced her first 'sculptured' tables in 1938.

Charlotte Perriand's partnership with Le Corbusier came to an end in 1937. Three years later, in 1940, she established an architectural office with Pierre Jeanneret, Jean Prouvé and George Blanchon, in which they

THE SOUTH AND THE WEST STONE WALLS

LOWER FLOOR WITH STAIRCASE

THE CORNER WITH THE DINING TABLE ON THE UPPER FLOOR >

researched and designed temporary prefabricated buildings in aluminium. In June of the same year her life took a dramatic and unexpected turn. Invited by the Japanese architect Junzo Sakakura, one of Le Corbusier's former aides, to visit Japan and work for the Japanese Ministry of Industry and Commerce, she ended up staying in the Far East for fully six years, stranded as a result of the Second World War. For two years (1940–41), fulfilling this commission, Perriand oriented and supervised the production of Japanese industrial art, living in Tokyo. With her sponsor Sakakura she wrote *Contact avec le Japon* in 1942. Then, however, she moved to Indochina, where she lived for three years, from 1943–46. Here she married Jacques Martin, a navy purser, and together they had a daughter, Pernette, who herself later became an architect. Charlotte Perriand's stay in Asia, especially in Japan, became a major source of inspiration for her and played a crucial role in the development of the designer-architect's aesthetic. Wood became her material of choice, and space was increasingly defined by the Japanese dynamics of 'the void'. It was a sensitivity to 'local conditions' that also affected work she did during the 1960s in Brazil, where she incorporated indigenous materials and vernacular approaches in her designs, and which, closer to home, related to her sustained interest in Alpine architecture and furniture design.

Following the long interlude in the Far East, Perriand returned to Paris in 1946, resuming work with Jeanneret, Prouvé and Blanchon in their joint office, work that was to go on for a further two and a half decades. Within the partnership she continued to design buildings, interiors and furniture, such as the London office of Air France (1957) and conference rooms for the United Nations in Geneva. The group's interest in the mechanics of daily life culminated in Perriand's prototype of an integrated kitchen for Le Corbusier's 'Unité d'habitation' (vertical housing community) in Marseille (1950).

Between 1946 and 1949 she conducted research for a mountain resort at Méribel-les-Allues, in 1950 she wrote 'Art d'habiter', which appeared in *Techniques et Architecture*, in 1951 she was responsible for the French pavilion at the "IX Triennale di Milano", entitled 'Useful Shapes and Furniture', and in 1955 she took part in the *Synthèse des arts* exhibition in Tokyo, collaborating with Sakakura and Martha Villiger. During the 1960s Perriand travelled in Brazil and other parts of Latin America (1962–68), lectured in the School of Fine Arts in Besançon (1966–68), and began a major long-term project (1967–82) in which she headed a team of architects and engineers involved in the building of a vast winter resort at Les Arcs, in the French region of Savoy. She was responsible

for coordinating the construction of three buildings – Arcs 1600, 1800 and 2000.

From 1983 to 1984 Perriand presided over the jury of an international competition for office furniture organised by the French Ministry of Culture, and in 1985 a retrospective exhibition of her works was staged at the Musée des Arts Décoratifs, Paris. In 1993 she created a tea house in the form of a bamboo pavilion topped by a navy sail in the gardens of the UNESCO in Paris at the request of the Japanese ambassador to that international organisation. The work was in keeping with many of her pieces, which were much in tune with Japanese style. Fittingly, the year 1998 saw a major exhibition, celebrating Perriand's long career, held in Tokyo, where she is considered a 'living treasure'. Another retrospective exhibition of her oeuvre was mounted in 1996 at the Design Museum, London. Finally, in 1999 she oversaw the installation of the monographic exhibition *Charlotte Perriand, Fernand Léger: une Connivence*, which focussed on the architect's collaboration with the French painter Fernand Léger, and which was mounted at the Musée National Fernand Léger in Biot. Charlotte Perriand died in October 1999 at the age of 96.

Charlotte Perriand is one of the most remarkable figures in the development of modernist design. She is best remembered for her elegant modernist tubular steel furniture, done in the 1920s and 1930s in collaboration with Le Corbusier. But she also produced craft-based designs, such as the diminutive Synthese des Arts chair (1955). Perriand collaborated not just with Le Corbusier, but also with the architect Jean Prouvé and the painter Fernand Léger, who initially trained as an architectural designer. She was an independent woman with a strong sense of self at a time when this was rare. She had an unwavering adoration of the modern and admired work created by multidisciplinary design teams headed by humanist architects. She was fond of saying that she found a life in the 20th century and was working to invent the 21st.

Perriand did not consider herself either a true architect or designer. She was primarily concerned to improve living conditions in apartments, which she sought to achieve by reinventing the notion of inhabitable space. In an interview she once said: "I'm not an architect; I'm for teamwork. I'm very interested in the life in houses. Everything is created from within – needs, gestures, a harmony, a euphoric arrangement, if possible in relation to an environment. In that respect I side with architecture, I project myself outside, and I admit that there is a to-and-fro between the environment and the horizon. After all, we are part of the universe. So perhaps, as Confucius said (I think), man is in the universe. That is, there are no barriers. I'm not even a designer. I don't know. I'd say first

PLAN OF THE UPPER FLOOR

PLAN OF THE GROUND FLOOR

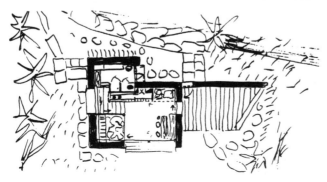

THE FIREPLACE

of all that I'm nothing. For the following reason: I have never designed an object, a form, a piece of furniture that I didn't need to relate to a whole. If you asked me today to design you a chair, I would say: 'To go where?' I have no imagination. I could do it in relation to my skeleton, but I still need to know how it fits into a whole. There is the purely functional side, and there is the functional side in relation to the human being. After all, design is about responding to the gestures of the human being. Then there is a side even beyond this, which has to do with a sort of harmony with oneself, with one's environment. This kind of awareness affects everything. At that moment, it gives me imagination. Otherwise I don't have any."

Between 1960 and 1961 Charlotte Perriand designed and built for herself a small chalet in Méribel les Allues, in France's Savoy region. Even at first glance it is apparent that the building is a private intimate place, almost a place of refuge for the spirit. Nestling on the side of a mountain and overlooking a valley, it has two floors, both of which are accessible from the outside, thanks to the natural slope of the ground.

On the lower floor of the chalet, the main feature is the living room, in which a large fireplace stands opposite two windows that look out over the valley. Next to the living room is a small room, accessible only from the outside, known as the *tanière*, meaning den or lair, perhaps because of its size, or perhaps because it is wedged into the ground. A fold-up bed gives more space during the day, making the small room more practical, while an ingenious device allows a single pipe to serve three water points (a sink, a bath-cum-shower, and a toilet).

On the upper floor of the chalet, on the other hand, there is a large room reminiscent of traditional buildings, which has an exposed ceiling and another large double window also enjoying fine views over the surrounding landscape. The beds are sunken and closed so as to leave the space completely free. The various walls, curtains and double doors mean that the space can be divided up in different ways, creating numerous separate corners and modulating the areas of light and darkness according to different living requirements.

A large east-facing terrace forms one of the accesses to the garden, and during the summer becomes an invaluable outside living space. The chalet's interior is very simple, with either wood or exposed stone, in line with the brutalist aesthetic that had also characterised much of Perriand's work with Le Corbusier. Its small dimensions, the attention to comfort, and the simplicity of the materials and the solutions call to mind the *cabanon* that Le Corbusier himself had built on the Côte d'Azur, although Perriand's chalet in Méribel is more spacious.

In her chalet Perriand cleverly combines oriental influences with materials and techniques typical of mountain buildings, creating refined, functional and above all extremely intimate spaces.

GENNARO POSTIGLIONE, KRISTELL WEISS

BIBLIOGRAPHY:
1976   Di Puolo M., Fagiolo M. and Madonna M. (eds.), *La machine à s'asseoir*, exhibition catalogue, Rome
1985   *Un art de vivre*, Paris
1998   Perriand C., *Une vie de création*, Paris
1999   *Charlotte Perriand – Fernand Leger, une connivence*, exhibition catalogue, Musée National Fernand Léger at Blot, Paris

Gio Ponti
1891–1979

**1957, NEW CONSTRUCTION
VIA DEZZA 49, MILAN (I)**

MAIN WORKS AND PROJECTS

1925	Own house, via Randaccio 9, Milan
1933	Rasini house, Milan (I)
1934	Faculty of Mathematics, Città Universitaria, Rome (I)
1935–38	First Montecatini building (I)
1950	Harrar-Dessiè housing development, Milan (I), with Luigi Figini and Gino Pollini

1956	Pirelli Tower, Milan (I), with Giovanni Vertolina and Emilio Dell'Orto; structure: Pier Luigi Nervi and Arturo Danussi
1958	Carmelo di Bonmoschetto (I)
1970	Taranto Cathedral (I)
1971	Denver Art Museum, Denver (USA)

WHAT THE ITALIAN ARCHITECT Gio Ponti managed to achieve in a single lifetime was phenomenal. During 60 years of work, he constructed buildings in 13 countries, worked on projects for 120 companies, made 20,000 architectural drawings, attended conferences in 24 countries, taught for 50 years, published 560 articles, and dictated 2,500 letters. Architecturally, his work is impossible to label, not belonging to any one single trend, and as a result he is somewhat marginalised in the official histories of the modern movement. On the other hand, Ponti's work was so individual and his personality so strong, that he can stand alone as a unique one-off. As Edoardo Persico wrote in 1933: "Gio Ponti is an isolated inventor, for whom the history of art is not a single line of progress, but a succession of different strands."

Gio Ponti was born in 1891 in Milan, in via Meravigli, the son of Enrico Ponti and Giovanna Rigone. In 1921, at the age of 30, he graduated from the Politecnico or Polytechnic of Milan as a qualified architect, and in the same year married Giulia Vimercati, with whom he subsequently had four children: Lisa, Giovanna, Letizia and Giulio. In the lively environment of Milan, he began a long series of architectural and also artistic partnerships with Giovanni Muzio, Giuseppe De Finetti and Emilio Lancia. It was with Lancia that he realised his first buildings in 1925, which were based on the Neoclassical style.

Ponti was not just an architect, but also a practitioner of the applied arts. From 1923 to 1930 he was artistic director of the Richard Ginori ceramics factory, whose entire product range he renewed. Ponti's aim was to create quality objects that could be mass-produced. A man of great sensibility, he was the first to feel the need to promote Italian design, founding the journal *Domus* at the suggestion of the journalist Ugo Ometti. In *Domus* Ponti began his battles "against the fake antique and ugly modern" styles that characterised contemporary Italian domestic culture. *Domus* was followed later (1941) by *Stile*, which has been acclaimed as one of the the 20th century's most beautiful magazines. Despite the war, *Stile* published works by architects and artists, writings by Giorgio De Chirico, the poetry of Filippo De Pisis, and the thoughts of Pier Luigi Nervi. As Lisa Licitra Ponti has observed: "The magazines were born out of a combination of love, play and chance. Gio Ponti never ceased to think of them as a kind of diary. Together with the great exhibitions, they were his favourite place."

With his many commitments, Ponti lived a busy life. He would already be in his studio, located within his house, at 5 o'clock in the morning and spend a couple of hours writing letters to friends and colleagues even before he started work on his architecture and periodicals. He also wrote letters while travelling, both by air and by car. Towards the end of his life, Ponti undertook what he called "art journeys", trips in a twelve-seater minibus accompanied by his daughters, his friend Filippo Neri and his colleagues.

Gio Ponti's large house-cum-studio in Milan's via Dezza, a new construction designed and realised in 1957, encompassed both the architect's life and work. In her fine book about her father, Lisa Licitra Ponti wrote of their multi-purpose home: "Very few doors and very few stairs separated the house and the studio, so that there was hardly any distance between Gio's night-time and daytime projects. …He worked in his studio in via Dezza from seven o'clock in the morning until eight o'clock in the evening. It was an enormous vaulted hangar-like space, and the draughtsmen used to ride into the hangar-cum-garage on their Vespas and Lambrettas, pulling up right beside their desks. Under the vaults there were more tables than walls, and in the middle stood the little room for private conversations. Then night came, the fine nights in the house where we slept, with the lights still on, and Gio drawing in silence in the company of other lights in other houses."

THE BEDROOM

In 1933 Ponti published *La casa all'italiana*, in which he defined the characteristics that a house should typically have. As a 'vase', a home was more than simply a matter of comfort. It must be "as beautiful as a crystal, but perforated like a grotto full of stalactites". A house was a built inhabited space that contained life's gestures, activities and emotions. "A house should be a simple thing, to be judged by the degree of enchantment one feels both when looking at it from the outside and when living inside."

Most importantly, a house needed luminosity, modernity, colour and large rooms. Ponti's via Dezza home, which he designed from top to bottom, embodies these requisite characteristics as well as his inventions on the theme of living and his whole architectural vision.

After being planned for years, the house was built in a very short time. Especially the floorplan and furniture show Ponti's architectonic inventiveness. The unbroken wall of the façade is a single glass window, and like a 'decorated window' it bears projecting shelves. In the building Ponti and his family occupied a 160-m² apartment. Here, the space was organised as a single environment, broken up by moveable walls. Only three 'modernfold' walls allow the different areas, divided on the façade, to be joined together in an enfilade. Only the north-facing kitchen

THE SELF-LIGHTING LIBRARY

and bathroom are closed. The façade/window, understood as a 'human diaphragm' between inside and outside, allows a wide view over the tree-lined via Dezzi avenue. The continuous design expands in the interior, in the wall panels, the shelves for books and ornaments, the drawers and the lamps.

Some of the furniture uses concealed lighting. All the beds, chairs and tables are the same. All the wall furniture and the wooden panels are in elmwood. The flooring, too, is continuous, with a ceramic pattern of diagonal lines, like the ceiling of white stucco, with glossy and matt diagonal lines.

The focal point of Ponti's work was always the study of space in relation to the home. The question of space is the thread that runs through and links all the houses he designed, and his own via Dezza home exemplifies this key interest, as we have seen. Ponti was fascinated by the idea of open fluid space and how it relates to people's needs and to the changes that take place in buildings during any one day in line with the rhythm of everyday life. However, the lavish use of space required by Ponti and seen in many of his houses runs counter to architectural economy and was especially at odds with the building requirements of the planning authorities at the time. This was particularly the case between the wars,

THE LIVING ROOM

"SUPERLEGGERA"-CHAIRS

when the authorities sought to standardise and minimise the space that a building or apartment might take up, and when the laws of the market in any case tended to reduce the surface area of a dwelling.

Nevertheless, Ponti did not give up on his ideal of plenty of (open) space in his housing or on his aspirations to make homes as interesting and comfortable as possible for their inhabitants. His Harrar-Dessiè housing development, a subsidised building project realised with Luigi Figini and Gino Pollini in 1950, evidences this, showing no departure from the Ponti philosophy. Here are 'horizontal skyscrapers' and housing units enhanced with colours and gardens, which seek to prove that suburbs can also be a pleasant place in which to live. It is no coincidence that Ponti is loved above all by the people who have actually lived in his houses, by the inhabitants of the Borletti house in Milan's via S. Vittore or of the Ina housing development in the city's via Dessiè.

All the houses that Ponti realised, from his own open-plan via Dezza house to his Laporte and Marmont houses, have been criticised for being essentially bourgeois in conception. Ponti would counter that his houses are designed based on a principle of comfort, which for him was a moral issue. "The design of an Italian house, which is uncomplicated both inside and outside, ...is not determined solely by the material requirements of living – it is not just a Corbusian 'machine à habiter'." This is not to say that Ponti was not influenced by the likes of Le Corbusier. His refer-

VIEW OF THE INTERIOR WITH "FURNISHED WINDOWS"

FLOOR PLAN

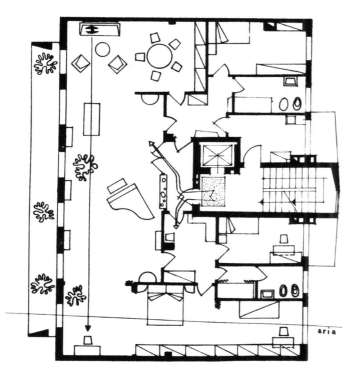

ences are just as much to the modernists Le Corbusier, Walter Gropius and Frank Lloyd Wright as they are to classicists such as Francesco Borromini and Andrea Palladio. But Ponti's views on house design are more widely related to a general reformulation of design philosophy, to an artistic type of designing with architectural, decorative, artistic and writerly influences. Departing from a Neoclassical starting point, Gio Ponti's is an individualised unpredictable multi-faceted and aestheticised architecture.

FRANCESCA ACERBONI, PAOLA ATTARDO

BIBLIOGRAPHY:

1933   Ponti G., 'La casa all'italiana', in *Domus*, Milan
1945   Ponti G., *L'architettura è un cristallo*, Milan
1957   Ponti G., *Amate l'architettura*, Genoa
1988   Irace F., *Gio Ponti. La casa all'italiana*, Milan
        Ponti L. L., *Gio Ponti, L'opera*, Milan
1994   Arditi G. and Serrato C., *Gio Ponti Venti Cristalli di Architettura*, Venice
2001   Cornoldi A., *Le case degli architetti. Dizionario privato dal Rinascimento ad oggi*, Venice, pp. 310–312

Jean Prouvé
1901–1984

1953, NEW CONSTRUCTION, LISTED AS A HISTORIC BUILDING IN 1987, PURCHASED BY THE CITY OF NANCY IN 1990
4–6 RUE AUGUSTIN-HACQUARD, NANCY (F)

MAIN WORKS AND PROJECTS

1938	Covered market, Clichy, Hauts-de-Seine (F)
1946	Study for prefabricated housing for the Unité d'habitation at Marseilles (F), with Le Corbusier
1949–50	School and teacher's accommodation, Vartoux (F), with Henri Prouvé
1951	Shell house, housing exhibition, Salon des arts ménagers, Paris (F), with Henri Prouvé
1953	Lopez house, Guerrevielle (F), with Henri Prouvé
1954	Pavilion for the centenary of aluminium, Paris (F), with Michel Hugonet

1956	Maison de l'Abbé Pierre or 'House of Better Days', Paris (F)
	Buvette de la Source Cachat, Evian-les-Bains (F), with Maurice Novarina and Serge Skétoff
1970	Headquarters of the French Communist Party, Paris (F), with Oscar Niemeyer
1972	Gauthier house, Saint-Dié (F), with Bauman and Remondino

BORN IN Paris on 8 April 1901, Jean Prouvé was the son of Victor Prouvé and Emile Gallé, who were among the founders of the Ecole de Nancy. At an early age Jean began to absorb the ideals debated at the school, one of which was to promote 'total art' as the expression of a different way of understanding the organisation of labour through a new alliance between craftsmanship, industry and art. In an interview filmed in 1982 Prouvé said of this vital formative period of his education: "I would run from the school to my father's workshop. And it was there that I would meet all the members of the Ecole de Nancy (...). They were revolutionaries in every way, but above all in the idea of the industrial revolution destined for the masses. Their idea was that all objects should be quality objects, and that all architecture should be of its age."

In 1916 Prouvé left school without completing his schooling and became an apprentice metal craftsman in Emile Robert's workshop in Enghien-les-Bains. In 1919 he moved to Paris to continue his training until 1921 under Adalbert Szabo. At Robert's and Szabo's workshops Prouvé learned the art of working metal, gradually developing his skills and using the most advanced techniques, until he became one of the masters of the use of bent, welded sheet metal. He soon began to produce metal elements for architecture, often commissioned by other architects, such as the grilles for the Reifenberg villa and the gates for the Gompel house in Paris, both for Robert Mallet-Stevens.

By now an expert in the use of metal, in 1924 Jean Prouvé opened his first workshop in rue du Général Custine in Nancy, where he went on to develop a whole series of prototypes, exploiting the possibilities of sheet metal (especially aluminium), bent and then electrically welded.

During the 1920s and 30s Prouvé's circle of connections grew. In 1926 he met in Paris the architects Le Corbusier, the latter's cousin Pierre Jeanneret, and Paul Herbé. In 1930 Prouvé was a founder member of the Union des Artistes Modernes (UAM), and in 1932–33 he met the architect Tony Garnier, and also Eugéné Beaudouin and Marcel Lods.

In 1931 Prouvé opened another, much larger metal workshop in Nancy's rue des Jardiniers. He also founded Ateliers Jean Prouvé, into which he introduced collective working methods in 1941. During the Second World War Prouvé was in the Resistance (1939–44), and for a few months (1944–45) he was mayor of Nancy and a delegate to the Assemblée Consultative à la Libération. In the war years he began to work with Pierre Jeanneret and Jeanneret's cousin and partner Le Corbusier, as a result of which he studied industrialised building.

After the war Prouvé returned to his work at the Ateliers Jean Prouvé, continuing his collaboration with studios such as the joint Pierre Jeanneret/Le Corbusier office. In 1947 he built a factory in Maxéville and began collaborating with a number of French industrial companies producing aluminium. These wanted to open up new markets in the housing sector, which in the post-war years was expanding rapidly due to the need for reconstruction. In the same year the Pechiney aluminium company used Ateliers Jean Prouvé to make prototypes. But Prouvé's main contract, concluded in 1949, was with Aluminium Français (STUDAL) for the study of aluminium prototypes for buildings.

However, after four years the relationship went sour. In 1953 disagreements arose with Aluminium Français about the organisation of labour at the Ateliers, which then employed some 150 workers. The rift

320

SOUTH FAÇADE

LIVING ROOM

BATHROOM

LIVING ROOM

led Prouvé to vacate his offices in Maxéville, resign as chairman to become a technical consultant, and leave the Ateliers that he himself had created. It was a turning point. The 1953 debacle seemed to Prouvé like the end of a hope and in some way the defeat of the industrial model he had sought. But the dark clouds had something of a silver lining, for his departure from the Ateliers led him to construct his private house in rue Augustin-Hacquard, Nancy, in the same year.

Also in 1953 Prouvé took part in the CIAM in Aix-en-Provence. In 1954 he moved to Paris, winning in the same year a Silver Medal at the IX Milan Triennial. From 1955 to 1956, he co-founded another company with Michel Bataille, which he named Les Constructions Jean Prouvé,

SKETCH OF THE HILLSIDE LOCATION

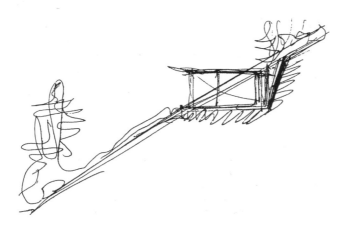

and despite their being taken over in 1957 by the Compagnie Industrielle de Matériel de Transport (CIMT), he continued working for this venture until 1966. From 1957 to 1970 he taught at the Conservatoire National des Arts et Métiers (CNAM), and in 1971 he was jury chairman in the competition to design the George Pompidou Centre in Paris. Accolades bestowed on Prouvé include the Auguste Perret Prize of the International Union of Architects (1963), being made a Chevalier de l'Ordre des Arts et des Lettres (1965), and being created an Officer of the Légion d'Honneur (1976). Jean Prouvé died in Nancy on 23 March 1984.

Prouvé's embracing of innovation and the idea of architectural modernity goes right back to his early experience of his parents' Ecole de Nancy. Rejecting any form of historicism, he subsequently participated in the CIAM and collaborated on some of the most important projects of the masters of the European modern movement. These included the project for Le Corbusier's unité d'habitation (housing community) at Marseilles, which was initially planned to be built according to a system designed by Prouvé with prefabricated metal housing cells, but which ultimately used a much less ingenious system in reinforced concrete.

In the same 1982 interview mentioned earlier Prouvé said of innovation that it "is a collective work… Nothing can be done alone in life. Work is collective." This pithy observation expresses some of the fundamental themes that marked all his activity as a furniture designer and architect. Especially during and after the Second World War Prouvé believed in technological innovation, notably in the field of prefabricated elements for housing. Technology really could contribute, he was convinced, to the improvement of the quality of life of society as a whole, ensuring better and more modern standards of housing for everyone.

LIVING ROOM WINDOW AND ENTRY

SHELVING IN THE LIVING ROOM

FLOOR PLAN

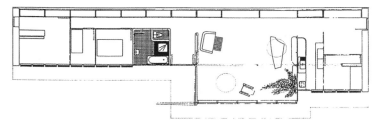

And to achieve this lofty laudable goal, new forms of labour organisation had to be sought through a commitment to collective collaboration, which Prouvé put into practice in concrete form in his own studios. Such collaboration would involve an open process of project development, the sharing of knowledge and techniques, and the overcoming of the established divisions between architect, engineer, builder and craftsman.

Jean Prouvé's private home was partly a response to the debacle in the same year when he left his own company, Jean Prouvé Ateliers, as a result of disagreement with Aluminium Français about the organisation of labour. Wounded by the contretemps, Prouvé felt that there had been some kind of historic defeat of his innovative idea of architecture and industry, and ultimately of the reforms dreamed of by the cream of the modern movement. Building his own house himself would be a symbolic undermining of this defeat and a reaffirmation of his model. He erected the house with his family and with the help of a few workers from the Ateliers over a single summer, reusing some of the materials recovered from his Maxéville offices.

The south-facing building rests on a terrace which, besides providing a safe foundation for the whole house on rather unstable terrain, also affords a view over the city of Nancy. The north façade, which backs onto a wood, is blind, while to the south the home faces the city. Inside, a 27-metre-long corridor serves all the rooms. At the centre is the living area, marked off by the two blocks placed at the ends of the kitchen and the bathroom, the only walls in the house apart from the two outer walls on the two short sides of the building. At the two ends of the house are the three bedrooms and a workshop area. The corridor, the north side of which is completely lined with wall cupboards, is the backbone of the house, and of an ingenious structural system. The cupboards, in fact, are divided by a system of metal sheets, which provide support for the wooden panels of the roof. These sheets are connected in turn to metal beams sunk in the concrete slab which forms the base of the house. The slab simply rests on the earth, with a hole in which seeds were planted. One of his most beautiful works, characterised by a sense of lightness, an ingenious construction, a total lack of redundancy, and a formal coherence, Prouvé's Nancy home today remains a model in the use of technology in architecture and in the harmony between the system of construction and the planimetric layout. The house is still capable of evoking what was ultimately at the basis of Prouvé's research: an ethic of architecture that is at the same time concern for man's needs, a new ethic of work, and a wide complex concept of economy in construction.

GIULIO PADOVANI

BIBLIOGRAPHY:
1971   Huber B. and Steinegger J.-C., *Jean Prouvé, une architecture par l'industrie*, Zurich
1983   Clayssen D., *Jean Prouvé, l'idée constructive*, Paris
1998   Prat N., *Jean Prouvé*, Galerie Jousse Seguin/Galerie Enrico Navarra, Paris
1990   Archieri J.-F. and Levasseur J.-P., *Prouvé, cours du CNAM 1957–1970*, Sprimont
2001   Chavanne B., Coley C. et al., *Jean Prouvé constructeur, 1901–1984*, Paris

Josep Puig i Cadafalch
1867–1956

**1917–19, CONVERSION, NOW DEMOLISHED
CARRER PROVENÇA 239, BARCELONA (E)**

MAIN WORKS AND PROJECTS

1897–1905	Own summer house, Argentona (E), integration and conversion of two existing houses (E)
1900	The Cros Garí, Argentona (E)
1904–06	Terradas house, Avenida Diagonal 416–420, Barcelona (E)
1909–11	Pere company house, Barcelona (E)
1911	Casarramona factory, Calle Mexico, Montjuich, Barcelona (E)
	International Electrical Industries Exhibition project, Montjuich, Barcelona (E)

1919–21	Pic i Pon house, Plaça de Catalunya 9, Barcelona (E)
1923	Plaça de Catalunya project, Barcelona (E)
1923–28	Monastery of Montserrat (E)
1923–29	Alfonso XII and Maria Cristina pavilions, Montjuich, Barcelona (E)

JOSEP PUIG I CADAFALCH'S origins lie in the mid-19th-century textile society of the industrial town of Mataró, near Barcelona. Here he received a primary and secondary education typical of that enjoyed by the well-to-do, Catholic, conservative and nationalistic middle classes of the time. From his native town he then moved to Barcelona, where he embarked on a degree course in the exact sciences and architecture, in the process earning himself a reputation as a brilliant student.

Puig's biography is closely bound up with his professional undertakings. He was politically and socially active as a representative and leading member of the Catalan Regionalist League party, president of the Mancomunitat de Catalunya from 1917 to 1923, a renowned architect and key exponent of Noucentisme, an art historian, and an archaeologist. An erudite and cultivated man, he was awarded an honorary doctorate by several universities, such as the Sorbonne, Harvard and Istanbul. Biographers of Puig i Cadafalch and people who knew him say that he was a distant person, frenetically absorbed throughout his life in his work, vocation and many different scholarly interests. He was passionate about music, regularly sitting among the cream of contemporary society at the Liceu opera house, and also about painting, which he cultivated in the final years of his life.

During his life, Puig i Cadafalch built or, more precisely, remodelled and extended two houses for himself. The first was his summer residence in Argentona (1897–1905), the product of joining together two traditional family farmhouses on a triangular site, clearly inspired by Modernism. The second was his house-cum-office in Carrer Provença, Barcelona (1917–1919). His purchase of the Carrer Provença house came at the height of his career as a politician and man of influence of his time. He

succeeded Prat de la Riba as President of the Mancomunitat de Catalunya, in which role he was to govern Spain's destiny between 1917 and 1923. Initially at least, this home attracted a whole entourage of adulators and people seeking the favours that emanate from power. Bankers, industrialists and members of his own party attended musical and poetry soirées around the fireplace on the house's principal floor.

But in 1923, with the dictatorship of Primo de Ribera and Puig i Cadafalch's removal from office as the country's principal authority, the Carrer Provença house ceased to be frequented quite so assiduously and became the architect's office and studio, shared only by Puig's few collaborators and those in his confidence. Now he alternated his time there with frequent trips abroad, before the periods of his forced political exile and his responsibilities as a speaker and lecturer. In the final years of his life, between 1941 and 1956, Puig i Cadafalch's Carrer Provença house became the clandestine meeting place for the Catalan nationalist resistance, hosting readings of poetry and nationalist texts and other acts of patriotic affirmation.

Barcelona and Puig i Cadafalch enjoyed a shared history for almost half a century. The architect was involved in the transformation of the mountain of Montjuïc in the form of the project which he initially drafted and then presented as the basis for the Universal Exhibition of 1929; in the construction of Via Laietana, cutting through the old part of the city down to the sea; in the project for Plaça de Catalunya; and in other lesser projects.

Puig's opposition to the Cerdà Plan, which was to produce Barcelona's Eixample, was public and well known. He referred to it as "that vulgar, standardising grid" which clashed with his topographic, monu-

STREET VIEW

THE LIVING ROOM

mental view of a Haussmann-style, capital, radial, concentric city. It is, then, paradoxical that the architect should have built his own house in the Eixample that he so detested, on a plot with party walls, over an existing house. This studied rehabilitation is a recurring characteristic of Puig's work, which, unlike the conservative recipe in vogue at the time, radically transformed what was there into something modern and up to date. Other examples in this vein include the Amatller house, the Pic i Pon house in Plaça Catalunya, and the Términus Hotel.

The Carrer Provença house comprises a ground floor with two upper storeys. Its initial separation from its party walls was preserved, giving it the appearance of a detached building, which complied with neither the height nor the volume permitted by municipal regulations. The ground floor continued to be used for commercial purposes and, by manipulating the construction span based on three orders of bearing walls, Puig built the first floor as his own home, in the form of a principal space, arranged in the façade by a central axis resting on a base of columns, with the entrance to one side. For the second floor, he designed a great hall and the secondary bedrooms, along with his office, which is where most of the documents and plans for his later works were kept.

As Jordi Romeu has argued (1988), Puig i Cadafalch may originally have cultivated a modernist style, but he was actually in the end the supreme eclectic of his time. His Carrer Provença house shows this very clearly. Over a conventional structure of bearing walls, the architect proposed Doric and Corinthian pillars. His passion for the Viennese Sezession can be seen in the Olbrichian composition of the façade, the clearly Borrominian lines of the tribunes and balconies, and the Italianate crowning

THE DRAWING ROOM

PLAN OF THE FIRST FLOOR

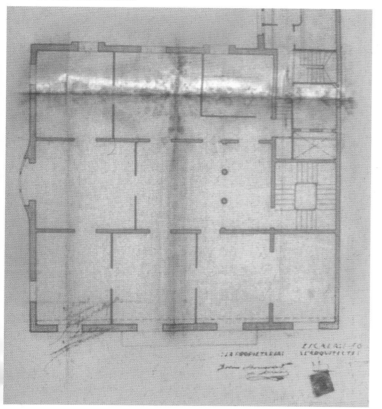

in the form of a pergola. The building's furnishings and central fireplace as well as aspects of its ornamentation were inspired by the palaces of Trianon, particularly the smaller one, while the rest of its elements – the ceramics, the dividing up of the floors, the joinery, etc. – can be traced to the architect's love of archaeology. Like other of Puig i Cadafalch's works, the Carrer Provença house is currently in a lamentable state of preservation.

JORDI ROMEU

BIBLIOGRAPHY:

1966   Cirici i Pellicer A., *Puig i Cadafalch's Architecture*, Barcelona

1975   Jardí E., *Puig i Cadafalch: Architect, Politician and Art Historian*, Barcelona

1980   De Solá-Morales I., *Palace and Pavilions: The 1929 Universal Exhibition Architecture*, Barcelona

1988   Romeu i Costa J., *Josep Puig i Cadafalch: Works and Projects since 1911*, Ph.D. thesis submitted at ETSAB (Escuela Tecnica Superior de Arquitectura), Barcelona

1989   De Solá-Morales I. and Rhorer J., *Puig i Cadafalch: Architecture Between House and City*, Barcelona

Roland Rainer
1910 – 2004

1965 – 66, NEW CONSTRUCTION
WEIDLICHGASSE, VIENNA (A)

MAIN WORKS AND PROJECTS

1950 – 54	Own house in Engelbrechtweg, XIII district, Vienna (A)
1952 – 58	City Hall, Vienna (A)
1955 – 58	City Hall, Bremen (D)
1957 – 58	Böhlerhaus office block, Vienna (A)
1958	Own summer house in St Margarethen, Burgenland (A)
1958 – 61	Planning concept for Vienna (A)
1960 – 65	City Hall, Ludwigshafen (D)

1965 – 95	Puchenau garden city, Linz, Upper Austria (A)
1968 – 80	ORF (Austrian Broadcasting Company) Centre, Küniglberg, Vienna (A)
1971 – 74	Indoor swimming pool, Vienna (A)
1985 – 92	Tamariskengasse urban housing development, Vienna (A)

ROLAND RAINER has been the most significant figure in Austrian architecture since 1945. During the 1950s and 1960s he built city halls in Vienna, Bremen and Ludwigshafen, and from 1968 to 1980 he designed the Austrian Broadcasting Corporation Centre in Vienna. Between 1958 and 1963 he was Vienna's chief architect, developing within three years a planning concept for the city that is still relevant today. From 1953 – 54 he held a professorship at the Technical University in Hanover, Germany, and in 1955 he was appointed professor at the Technical University in Graz, Austria.

For a quarter of a century (1956 – 80), Rainer was a highly influential head of the architecture masterclass at Vienna's Academy of Fine Arts. In 1950 he was a member of the Austrian section of the CIAM (International Congress of Modern Architecture), and in 1982 he participated in the documenta urbana in Kassel. Rainer has been an author, a persistent polemicist and an environmentalist. The main theme of his work has been living, and his *magnum opus* may be said to be Puchenau garden city (1965 – 95), located near Linz in Upper Austria.

Rainer's upbringing was far from conventional, and during his formative years in unusual family and cultural surroundings he was exposed to experiences that had a lasting influence on his life and work. He was born in 1910 in Klagenfurt, in the Austrian province of Carinthia. His parents were educated people, interested in the arts. His father, who had Social Democratic convictions, was an art teacher, who had studied in Vienna under Josef Strzygovski. It was Strzygovski who was the first to integrate the Middle and Far East into art-historical research in Austria. "If my father hadn't studied under Strzygovski," Rainer says, "I would probably never have travelled to Persia and China." And in that case his work might never have felt the impact of those cultures. Rainer's parents were also pedagogically enlightened, sending their son in the 1920s to a

progressive school in Vienna, which focussed on autonomous creative work and self-expression, which was very unusual at the time.

Also during the 1920s the young Rainer was sent with other undernourished post-war children in need of recuperation to the Netherlands. By good fortune his group was looked after by architect Margarete Schütte-Lihotzky. His contact with her led to a long-standing personal relationship and was another formative influence. In 1928 Rainer enrolled in the Technical University of Vienna, where he studied architecture, graduating in 1933. The architect says impishly that it was not university that taught him what was essential in life, but his parents.

Over the years Rainer did not seek to glitter as a brilliant innovative individual architectural star. Rather he developed a radically social practice following a general concept. Designing anonymous functionalist buildings oriented to the basic needs of life, he and his office were far from contemporary architectural stardom. Rainer smoothly applied the ideas of Modernism to his architectural projects, enriching them with elements of nature conservation, historic monument protection and ecological awareness long before these became the latest buzzwords. At the same time, however, his work was linked with the Dutch (De Stijl) and English building traditions on the one hand, and with Eastern culture from places like the Balkans, Turkey, Persia and China on the other.

During his professional life Roland Rainer always lived in houses designed by himself. Altogether he built three private homes. During the 1950s he constructed his house in Engelbrechtweg in Vienna's XIII district for himself, his first wife and their two children; in 1958 he built his summer house in St Margarethen, Burgenland; and 1965 – 66 he created his 'Residential Building among the Trees' in Weidlichgasse, also in Vienna's XIII district, a new construction in which he and and his family lived.

VIEW FROM THE STREET

VIEW FROM THE GARDEN

THE POND

THE LIVING ROOM

The site of his first house in Vienna's Engelbrechtweg in many ways typifies Rainer's work. It lies within Vienna's celebrated Werkbundsiedlung or Werkbund housing development, realised in 1932. Specifically, Rainer's house replaces a house by Hugo Häring that was destroyed by bombing. It is characterised by modernist architecture of the 1920s and 1930s, the period of Rainer's formative years. In particular, the house is informed with the Viennese Modernism of Josef Frank, who both initiated the Vienna Werkbundsiedlung and its concept of living, and personally instructed Rainer during the 1930s. At the same time Rainer's building also draws closely on the concept underlying Häring's destroyed house. Thus Rainer retained and elaborated Häring's notions of reducing everything to essentials, of keeping the house compact on the smallest possible site, and of passively utilising the sun's energy. In line with the latter, the building is oriented to the south, where it has a completely open glass façade, while the north façade is largely closed and is the location of the secondary rooms. The most significant difference in Rainer's home from Häring's original building lies in a garden wall, covered with plants, which replaces Häring's fence. The change is a simple measure, but one that incorporates a key Rainer concept, of being able to live with a garden or atrium in total privacy. Rainer's Engelbrechtweg house is a prototype of the houses that the architect subsequently built in his residential estates. And, indeed, he saw the home as containing an important message, as representing an exemplary solution for the urban dweller, whereas he described his later Weidlichgasse house as a purely private and special solution.

Interesting about Rainer's summer house in St Margarethen, Burgenland, which was constructed in 1958 not far from a quarry, is the exemplary integration of architecture and landscape. Strictly speaking, the 'quarry house' is not a conventional house, for its walls are of unplastered limestone bricks from the nearby quarry, and its plot is divided into various open and closed (yard) areas in line with the sun, the wind and the lie of the land. In one respect the holiday house is not a conventional home at all – it no has electricity and thus provides an experience of living stripped down to the core.

Rainer's third private home, newly built in Vienna's Weidlichgasse, may not be a prototype like his first house in Engelbrechtweg, but it illustrates further qualities of Rainer's architecture, especially the way he dealt with exterior space. This is more than just a house. The main theme here is both the garden, which the architect laid out together with his wife, and the integration of the house into the garden, as well as the proximity of the house to the garden's trees. For the plot contains venerable old trees that once belonged to a palace – a feature that persuaded Rainer to purchase the site. The house, with a rectangular footprint and a green flat roof, is situated on a hillside and has been integrated into the tree population. To the north it is protected from the wind by conifers, while to the south it is protected from the summer sun by deciduous trees. According to Rainer, deciduous trees not only regulate the climate, but are also a source of 'energy' – the building was planned bearing in mind the principles of *feng shui*, which had meanwhile become almost a craze. He set the house so close to the trees that one can touch their

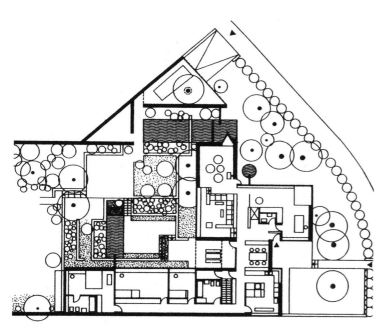

FLOOR PLAN

before finally reaching the large living, cooking and dining area, via an anteroom. These further 'obstacles' further evidence the premium Rainer placed on introverted privacy. However, the living, dining, cooking and working space has no traditional room divides, although it is organised into different areas.

The dining area leads directly to a further covered open-air dining space, which is protected on three sides, and which also doubles up as an alternative sleeping place on warm summer nights. The living area, which is somewhat dark owing to the black wooden-beam ceiling and the low room height, is terraced down to a lower seating space. This lower area, with a bench all around, which is typical of Turkish living culture, is open to the large glass façade, which fills the entire height and width, and which is oriented towards the southern part of the garden.

Rainer designed the garden of the house as 'room outside'. Using the same second-hand bricks as in the house and the garden walls, he terraced the plot's meadow hillside, a terracing in the garden that echoes the terracing in the lower area of the living space. The terracing features a basin, fed with rainwater from water tanks. In the rear south-facing part of the densely landscaped garden, which is planted such that from February to November there is always something in bloom, water, flora and fauna form a symbiotic whole. A bench positioned in the lower seating area allows one to enjoy the garden and experience the rotation of the seasons. At Rainer's Weidlichgasse house it is really possible to understand the meaning of 'garden habitat'.

In the northern part of the house, the living area opens onto a working space, which can be partitioned off by a sliding door. Between the work space and the kitchen there is a see-through connection through the forecourt, and from both rooms there is also a view towards the entrance of the house. In keeping with the American way of living, the bedrooms, children's rooms and bathrooms are situated in a separate wing, accessible via a separate corridor.

MARIA WELZIG

huge trunks while sitting in the living room. And an oriel window with flowers protrudes between the trunks of two old lime trees. Many feared that the proximity of the house and the trees would lead to structural damage, but even after 40 years they continued to coexist without a mishap.

Rainer never built either ostentatious villas or prestigious housing developments. On the contrary, his residential buildings are totally introverted. Accordingly they differ completely from the traditional Viennese villa. With its garden and also an enclosed forecourt, the Weidlichgasse house maintains this introversion. At the front, on the street side, the house and forecourt are protected from Weidlichgasse by a 60-metre-long wall, made of second-hand bricks and building masonry. For Rainer, living meant above all protected privacy. In addition, only one side of the plot, the street side, is oriented to the public, a layout reminiscent of Oriental and Chinese housing culture.

The materials used to build the house are rough and simple: unplastered second-hand bricks for the walls, black-stained wood for the roof, doors and windows, and pale ashwood for the floors and furniture. Inside there are black wooden-beam ceilings and white walls.

The entrance to the house lies on its north side, the side facing Weidlichgasse. To reach it, you pass from the street, through the masonry wall and across the forecourt, before walking along a brick path, which brings you to the closed wall of the northern front. Here the narrow entrance to the house lies hidden to the right. After stepping into the house, you are again confronted with a closed wall and are diverted,

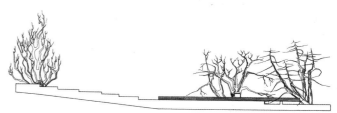

SIDE ELEVATION

BIBLIOGRAPHY:
1948   Rainer R., *Städtebauliche Prosa*, Tübingen
1990   Rainer R., *Arbeiten aus 65 Jahren*, Vienna/Salzburg
        Rainer R., *Dekorationen ersetzen Konzepte nicht*, Vienna/Cologne
1995   *Roland Rainer. Vitale Urbanität*, exhibition catalogue, Museum für Angewandte Kunst (MAK), Vienna
2000   Rainer R., *An den Rand geschrieben. Wohnkultur – Stadtkultur*, Vienna/Cologne/Weimar

Umberto Riva
*1928

1966 – 67, NEW CONSTRUCTION
45 VIA PARAVIA, MILAN (I)

MAIN WORKS AND PROJECTS

1956 – 60	Summer houses, Stintino (I), with Fredi Drugman
1965 – 66	Cooperative housing, 45 via Paravia, Milan (I)
1968 – 69	Berrini house, Taino (I)
1974 – 75	Ferrario house, Osmate (I)
1977 – 79	Primary and secondary schools, Faedis (I)
1983 – 84	Frea house, Milan (I)
1990 – 96	Miggiano house, Otranto (I)

1994 – 98	Restoration of Caffè Pedrocchi, Padua (I)
1997 – 98	Restoration of Palazzo Barbaran, Fondazione Andrea Palladio, Vicenza (I)
1999 – 2002	Shipyard, Castellamare di Stabia, Naples (I)

FOR MANY years the work of Umberto Riva, an Italian architect belonging to the third generation of the modern movement, was ignored by most specialist critics, who only recently seem to have decided to accord him the recognition he was due – in 2003 the Milan Triennial awarded Riva the Gold Medal for Architecture. After years of hard work seeking to resolve the problems posed by a random variety of clients and at the same time to identify a personal path within the poetics of architectural Modernism, Riva has managed to find public patrons interested in commissioning projects of considerable interest.

Umberto Riva was born on 16 June 1928 in Milan. As a boy he spent the long school holidays at the home of his paternal grandfather in northern Sardinia. This, together with his frequent subsequent visits to that island, left a deep impression on the architect, who often speaks nostalgically of the south, with its light, its nature and its architecture, vital and full of contrasts.

After attending a technical school, Riva enrolled in the School of Architecture of the Polytechnic of Milan, upsetting his parents' plans for his future. However, the conservative atmosphere of the Polytechnic, as well as his difficulties with his studies, led him to transfer to the Institute of Architecture of the University of Venice (IUAV). Here, in Venice, Riva finally found a cultural climate more suited to his temperament. He was an introverted student, extremely slow in learning scientific subjects, but with a marked sensibility for materials.

At the IUAV Riva discovered the work of Carlo Scarpa and other masters of the Italian tradition. Above all, however, he learned both the value of craftsmanship in relation to materials, techniques and technologies, and also the capacity of materials to communicate. His time in Venice was extremely important, although – as he likes to point out – he only completed his studies thanks to the determination of his wife, who

encouraged him continuously and prevented him from dropping out due to the burden of the competitive demands of university exams. Riva finally graduated from the IUAV in 1959. Much later he returned to the Institute of Architecture in Venice as a visiting professor (1987–98), while from 2000 to 2003 he was a visiting professor at the School of Architecture in Rome.

With a profound knowledge of the work of the modern masters, especially Louis Kahn and Le Corbusier, Riva passed through 50 years of Italian architecture almost on tiptoes. Without creating a stir, shunning fashions and flattery, he worked with such rigour that he soon acquired a reputation for being slow, and also exclusive. In actual fact, his character prevents him from seeking glory in the architectural marketplace, and he simply devotes however much time is necessary to each commission, causing considerable problems for his clients, and also for himself, since he has often remained unemployed for long periods – to the benefit of his pictorial output.

Despite this, during all these years house design has been Riva's main occupation, to the extent that he can be defined as an architect of domestic spaces, or, more precisely, of 'domestic places'. Since the early years of his career he has planned residences, single-family homes, condominium apartments and, above all, renovations and restorations, bringing new life to the (wholly Italian) tradition of interior design, and often providing qualitative depth to a branch of architecture often relegated to mere exercise. It is a tradition whose roots lie in the work of masters such as Carlo Scarpa, Franco Albini, and Ignazio Gardella, who managed to combine local craftsmanship with the needs of the building process.

Whether they are realised in existing buildings or new constructions, Riva's works are characterised by a clear methodological homogeneity. His poetics never substantively changes the place or the type of

ENTRANCE

STREET VIEW

CEILING WINDOW IN THE STUDIO

COLOURED CEILING IN THE LIVING AREA

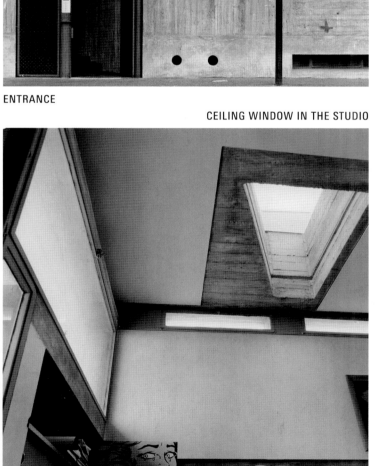

THE KITCHEN SEEN FROM THE DINING AREA

building to be realised, whatever the conditions. His is a poetics which, although based on sophisticated formal design, is not deaf to the demands of each single plan, but actually grows out of these demands.

Riva's method of work involves a number of constants. One of the first elements to emerge from an analysis of his drawings, or from visits to his works, is the great strain to which he subjects the architectural space through the manipulation of built form and the elaboration of the materials of which it is constructed. Through this analytical effort, performed especially by using the drawing as a means of research, places are organised according to new and unusual configurations. The final solutions may sometimes seem excessive, but a careful study shows that it is precisely his concern to interpret activities in relation to the users, the space and the context, that determines the nature of his projects.

The graphic elaboration of the form proceeds hand in hand with the investigation of the expressive potential of the material, which explains the care over detail typical of Riva's work. Riva rejects codified answers, and searches for new answers, or rather truer answers, by asking himself concrete questions. This gives rise to one of the fundamental features of his poetics, which is his rejection of the pre-constituted and his desire to seek small answers to simple questions, and to seek them on his own.

All these considerations can be seen at play in the home that Riva designed for himself and his wife, Maria Bottero, in Milan's via Paravia

(1966–67). It is an apartment on the top floor of a cooperative housing block, likewise designed by the architect (1965–66). More precisely, the project was sponsored by a cooperative in the early 1960s and involved friends and relatives of Riva as well as his wife. The new construction turned into something of a laboratory experiment to see if it is possible to live in the city without resigning oneself to the poverty of multi-storey buildings.

The themes and elements of Riva's poetics are already contained in essential form in the entrance hall of the building, and are then fully developed in his apartment itself: the transgression of orthogonality, the use of wide bands of colour, the design of light through the arrangement

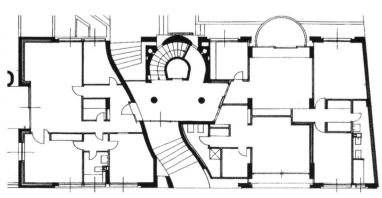

FLOOR PLAN OF THE FIRST FLOOR

THE DINING AREA SEEN FROM THE LIBRARY

and form of openings, and the contrast between the exposed (load-bearing) concrete structure and several (supported) volumes that are independent in form and colour.

The Riva apartment is organised around a single open space, where various independent volumes, with different heights, materials and formal treatments, are placed between three load-bearing columns: the bathroom, the kitchen, the cloakroom, the library, etc. The plan is underscored by the treatment of the single ceiling, which becomes a great tapestry on which wide bands of colour are painted, thus helping to give a sense of dynamic acceleration to the perception of the space. As in an urban fragment, the various volumes present in the apartment mark out main routes, secondary axes, rest places or large domestic 'squares' where people can stop to talk – separate areas whose privacy is asserted through the geometry of the plan and the choice of materials, without forgetting the attention devoted to the modulation of natural and artificial light.

The living area, centred around a large concrete table, is separated from the space that contains the alcoves for the beds by an axis made up of the bathroom areas and finally Riva's little study, the true hinge of the composition. There are no bedrooms as such because the spatial continuity characterising the whole apartment does not admit interruptions, which means that only the form and the distribution of the space give these areas the necessary privacy.

Riva's apartment also shows the architect's clear interest in the design of natural light and in the resulting relationship between interior and exterior. Openings in the walls and in the ceiling, high and low, large and small, of various forms, express his desire to govern light and shade in every corner of the home, in a constant search for the right atmosphere and the right relationship with the materials. The surfaces, in fact, change with the light. The exposed concrete of the structure and the stone of the floors, the Masonite of the doors and the asbestos of some of the furnishings assume a role in the project, just as the colours of the easel become light on the canvas.

In the design of this domestic space, every effect is carefully and artfully sought after, nothing is left to chance, and the frequent use of industrial materials is combined with elements made to measure, as if handicraft and industry had finally achieved a profitable relationship through a dialectics made up of differences and distances.

NICOLA FLORA, GENNARO POSTIGLIONE

BIBLIOGRAPHY:
1989 Nicolin P. (ed.), 'Umberto Riva – Album of drawings', in *Quaderni di Lotus*, no. 10
1990 'Umberto Riva', in *Bauwelt*, no. 2 (monographic issue)
1993 Nicolin P. et al., *Umberto Riva*, Barcelona
2001 Cornoldi A. (ed.), *Le case degli architetti. Dizionario privato dal Rinascimento ad oggi*, Venice, pp. 333–335

Ernesto Nathan Rogers
1909–1969

1956, ALTERATION, NOW DEMOLISHED
VIA BIGLI, MILAN (I)

MAIN WORKS AND PROJECTS

1932	Competition project (First Prize) for the Typical Fascist House in the *Littoriali di Architettura* (I)
1936	Urban plan for the Valle d'Aosta (I), with the architects Piero Bottoni, Luigi Figini and Gino Pollini and also in collaboration with Adriano Olivetti, Renato Zveteremich and Italo Lauro
1938	Sun treatment camp, Legnano (I), demolished in 1956
1945	'AR' plan, with the Italian CIAM group (I)

1946	War memorial in concentration camps, war cemetery, Milan (I)
1953	Ina-Casa buildings, Lombardy and Piedmont (I)
1956	Restoration and museum design of the Castello Sforzesco, Milan (I)
1959	Torre Velasca, Milan (I)
1965	Olivetti office building, Barcelona (E)

ERNESTO NATHAN ROGERS is undoubtedly one of the most significant figures in the history of Italian architecture. He was born in Trieste in 1909 into a wealthy cultured family. His mother was Italian, while his father, whose friends included men of letters such as the Irish writer James Joyce, was English. In 1914 his family left Trieste, moving first to Rome, then to Zurich, and finally settling in Milan in 1921. Here the future architect attended grammar school and then, after resolving the dilemma that had been tormenting him – whether to embark on a literary or a practical career – he enrolled in 1927 in the School of Architecture at Milan Polytechnic.

During his studies at the polytechnic, Rogers met Gian Luigi Banfi, Lodovico Belgiojoso and Enrico Peressutti, with whom he founded the famous BBPR architectural practice immediately after graduating in 1932. Meanwhile he had also begun his prolific activity as an essayist and critic, an activity he would pursue to the end of his life. Between 1930 and 1932 he was editor of the journal *Arti plastiche*, and from 1933 to 1936 he co-edited *Quadrante*.

The 1930s brought many problems for Rogers. He was estranged from his family and plagued by financial worries. He had no house of his own but lived, as he did for much of his life, in a hotel. In 1938, at the height of the 'political difficulties' that beset Italian architecture, he was compelled by the Fascist regime and Italy's race laws to embrace professional anonymity. In 1942, at the invitation of the journal *Domus*, Rogers set out his plan for his 'House of the Anonymous': "My house is a body, and like my body it contains my joy and my grief … Against the ruthless voracity of time, give me this place with my own roots, which contains a space of my own." In this unhappy awkward incognito position, the Anglo-Italian architect remained in Milan until 1943, when he was forced

to go into exile in Switzerland, where he taught at the Champ Universitaire Italien in Lausanne.

In 1945, with the war at an end, Rogers returned from Switzerland to Milan, where he rejoined his two surviving architectural partners. Between 1946 and 1947 he was editor-in-chief of *Domus*. It was in the pages of this journal that Rogers proposed commencing the moral and material reconstruction of post-war Italy by starting out from the 'house of man'. His words were a warning addressed to all architects, whom he called upon to play a social as well as a planning role, and to contribute through their work to the creation of a civil conscience. Rogers' passionate intellectual and cultural commitment animated the contemporary international architectural debate, and was thus invaluable in the School of Architecture at Milan Polytechnic, where he played a vital role.

Rogers continued to contribute to the theoretical debate especially from 1953 to 1964, when he was editor of *Casabella-continuità*, addressing important issues such as the relation between utility and beauty, responsibility versus tradition, and building in 'pre-existing environments'. These were fundamental matters that took concrete form in his projects, in particular in the Velasca Tower in Milan (1958). Alongside his architectural, editing and also authoring work – his book *Esperienza dell'architettura* was published in 1958 – Rogers also came to have an academic career. Starting out as a temporary lecturer in the School of Architecture at his old college, Milan Polytechnic, in 1952, he was appointed to a chair in architectonic composition at the school in 1964. Ernesto Rogers died on 7 November 1969 in Gardone after a long illness.

Finally, in 1956, after years of living in hotels, Rogers acquired a home of his own. This was an apartment in Via Bigli in the centre of Milan, which

HE LIVING ROOM

THE LIVING ROOM

DETAIL OF A BOOKCASE

DINING ROOM

he renovated. In the pages of *Domus*, now edited by Gio Ponti, the architect himself provided an admirable moving description of this home, which represented a concrete and symbolic point of arrival after his long years of wandering:

"My house, the house of a bachelor, is somewhat incomplete, like the bachelor's life, though there are some advantages deriving precisely from this condition, i.e. a certain nonchalance, the development of a coherent discourse (perhaps a monologue?) uninterrupted by the tastes of other people. For 20 years I have moved from one hotel to another, and everyone has told me that sooner or later, not least because I am an architect, I should have my own home. The one I finally have is not mine, but it is for me. Nor can I understand how I managed for so long to live a roving life, outside this shell, which is now as necessary for me as clothes or shoes.

"I am lucky enough to live in an area dear to Stendhal, who is an author particularly dear to me. Thus when I re-read his books, I seem to be moving around my own rooms. If he describes the parks of Milan (which can still be glimpsed from my windows), it seems as if he has come to visit me and confirms, in a wonderful manner, my own daily impressions.

"It might seem strange at first that it is more difficult for an architect to design his own house than to build one for strangers, but in actual fact it is a matter of giving concrete form to the *cognosce te ipsum* (know

yourself) which, as we know, is the most tormenting irresolvable problem an individual can pose himself.

"There are no ideal houses other than those we can realise historically – the others are utopias. Therefore I have tried to take advantage as far as possible of the objective data that presented themselves, to interpret them in my own way so as not to suffer them passively but to possess them and transform them, according to the practical needs of my life and its spiritual requirements.

"When a building is constructed, the essential problem is to set it in the pre-existing natural and historical environments. The same is true when one arranges furnishing, which must always bear in mind both the character of the building and – where it exists – the natural landscape that surrounds it. The modernity, the relevance, of a work lies in the personal values of this operation. And one must ask enough of one's self to be sure of interpreting life in every way.

"If I had had to design the rooms of my house *ex novo*, I would have tried to create something similar to what I found in this old building in the heart of Milan. It goes without saying that the first negative limitation (of a situation that, as a whole, is quite positive) was dictated by the economy I had to impose on myself if I wanted to prevent my desires from running wild and making me do something foolish. I do not, in fact, own any objects of real financial value. From my parents' home, destroyed partly by the sad circumstances of penury and partly by the

THE LIVING ROOM

barbaric actions of the Nazis, I only managed to save very few things, which now set the sentimental key in my apartment. Apart from that there are only objects bought during my many journeys to far-off lands or in the back rooms of antique dealers, where I am led both by curiosity and by professional duty.

"I do not love technique, except as a means to express poetic feelings, but I cannot bear things done shoddily. Although they are simple – perhaps because they are simple – the few pieces of furniture I have designed require great skill in those who make them, which is why I entrusted them to Piero Frigerio of Cantù, who works with the loving care and mastery of an ancient Italian artisan. I am grateful to him on this occasion, too, for having realised with precision the things I have designed.

"The paintings are all presents from artists, a sign of their affection over the years. One day, observing a shelf with Peruvian, Greek and Brazilian ceramics, a colleague of mine said jokingly: 'It looks like the house of an explorer.' I have never discovered anything, not even myself so far, but I took this definition as a flattering compliment. It seems to me to match at least the secret aspirations of my dreams – though in my dreams, of course, I am a much better architect!"

FEDERICO BUCCI, ANNETTE TOSTO

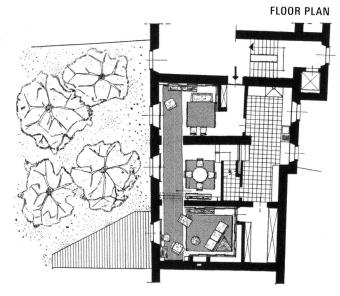

FLOOR PLAN

BIBLIOGRAPHY:

1957 'Un architetto per sé. L'appartamento di Ernesto N. Rogers a Milano', in *Domus*, no. 326, January, pp. 21–29
1958 Rogers E. N., *Esperienza dell'Architettura*, Turin
1961 Rogers E. N., *Gli elementi del fenomeno architettonico*, Bari
1967 De Carli C., 'Ernesto N. Rogers nella sua casa', in *Interni*, no. 3, March, pp. 3–12
1968 Rogers E. N., *Editoriali di architettura*, Turin

Alfred Roth
1903–1998

1960–61, NEW CONSTRUCTION
BERGSTRASSE 71, ZURICH (CH)

MAIN WORKS AND PROJECTS

1928	Roth & Co. warehouse, Wangen an der Aare (CH)
1929–30	H.S.B. Society apartments, Gothenburg, Sweden (S)
1935–36	Two houses in the Doldertal, Zurich (CH), with Emil Roth and Marcel Breuer
1943–44	Hélène de Mandrot house, Zurich (CH)
1951–52	Primary school, Berkeley, St Louis (USA)

1961–63	Riedhof Primary School, Zurich (CH)
1966–69	Heinrich Pestalozzi Secondary School, Skopje, Macedonia
1967–70	Girls' secondary school, Rumaithiya, Kuwait Sabbag commercial building, Beirut, Lebanon

ALFRED ROTH was born 21 May 1903 in Wangen an der Aare, in the Swiss canton of Berne. His father, Adolf Roth, owned a horsehair spinning mill in Wangen, and it was his wish that his son should study mechanical engineering at the Federal Polytechnic in Zurich (now the renowned Swiss Federal Institute of Technology or ETH). Alfred enrolled in the Polytechnic in 1922, but during his first semester changed from the institute's School of Mechanical Engineering to its School of Architecture. Here he studied under Karl Moser, a pioneer of modern Swiss architecture, graduating from the School as a qualified architect in 1926. Karl Moser proved most helpful to Roth on his graduation, for first he employed the fledgling architect in his own private practice, and then he was instrumental in getting Roth a job in Paris with Le Corbusier and Pierre Jeanneret.

It was here, in 1927, that Roth collaborated on the visionary competition design for the League of Nations building in Geneva and subsequently supervised the construction of the two residential buildings in the Stuttgart Weissenhofsiedlung (the Werkbund Weissenhof housing development). The experience not only enabled Roth to be in at the very beginning of the Neues Bauen, but also brought him into contact with the international architectural and artistic avant-garde. Also at this time he became friends with Piet Mondrian. A year later, in 1928, Roth moved to Gothenburg (Göteborg) in Sweden, where for two years he ran an architectural office of his own in partnership with Ingrid Wallberg.

In 1931 Roth returned to Switzerland, settling in Zurich, where he worked in the office of the Neubühl Werkbundsiedlung, before opening another private practice in 1932. From this office, and collaborating with his cousin Emil Roth as well as Marcel Breuer, Roth realised the legendary Doldertal houses between 1935 and 1936 for the art historian and journalist Sigfried Giedion. In addition to his building commitments, Roth was actively involved in the propagation of the modern movement. He

promoted the achievements of the Neues Bauen both as the editor of *Das Werk* between 1943 and 1957 and as the author of the programmatic book *Die Neue Architektur*, a collection of 20 exemplary buildings from the 1930s.

His 1950 study on contemporary school buildings, Das Neue Schulhaus (The New School), earned him a reputation as an expert on the subject and brought him commissions for schools both at home and abroad. From the mid-1960s onwards, his expertise was particularly in demand in Arab countries, where he realised not only schools but also projects for commercial buildings and town planning. Another aspect of his professional activities was his commitment as a teacher, which began at the George Washington University in St Louis in 1949 and finally took him, via Harvard University, back to the Federal Institute of Technology – ETH in Zurich, where he lectured from 1957 to 1971. In his later years Roth devoted an increasing amount of time to painting, which had already occupied him before he started his career as an architect, creating a constructivist oeuvre towards the end of his life.

The house that Roth built for himself in 1960–61, the so-called Fellowship Home, is situated on the mountainous Zürichberg, one of Zurich's most prestigious and desirable residential locations. The site lies just a stone's throw from the Doldertal apartment buildings, which Roth had constructed with great success 25 years earlier. Another outstanding example of modern architecture, the home of the architects Rudolf and Flora Steiger-Crawford, is located immediately to the south-west of Roth's house. The last of this unique ensemble of buildings on the mountainside site is Max Haefeli's house, which is also featured in this book.

As a bachelor university lecturer who was well aware of the difficulty experienced by students trying to find living accommodation, Roth decided to design a house not only for himself and his frequent guests,

VIEW WITH THE ENTRANCES TO THE STUDIOS AND THE ARCHITECT'S FLAT

THE WEST FAÇADE AND ROOF TERRACE

VIEW FROM THE SOUTH

THE LIVING AREA SEEN FROM THE STUDIO ON THE UPPER FLOOR

but also to provide a number of students' rooms. The topography of the site, sloping steeply down towards the south, and his desire to preserve privacy and independence both for himself and for the students, led to a storey-based organisation of the rooms. The ground floor comprises the students' entrance, the house-owner's private office (originally used by the students as living and dining premises), and the cellars. The floor above contains five students' rooms with sanitary facilities and working niches integrated into the bay windows of the west façade, a small kitchen with a dining recess, wet cells accessible over a common landing, and the outer entrance to the architect's apartment. The architect's flat consists of a 20-metre-long open space, structured by the cubes of the

kitchen and bathroom and the zigzag-shaped picture walls. The high-ceilinged living room with seating accommodation round an open fireplace forms the central spatial focus. A bridge leads from the back entrance to a garden sitting area, and a narrow staircase to a roof terrace.

The structure of the building consists of reinforced concrete and plastered cork-insulated brickwork. Round concrete-filled steel columns made it possible to use a wood construction for the projecting zigzag-shaped west façade, clad on the outside with asbestos cement slabs, with wood panelling on the inside of the student's rooms, and light grey fabric on the picture walls. The non-loadbearing partitioning walls on the students' floor allow easy changes in the scheme. All the windows, fitted

THE FIREPLACE AREA ON THE UPPER FLOOR

furniture and door frames are executed in natural varnished wood, and the other woodwork is left white. The ceilings are painted white, and the walls a very light grey so as not to detract from the effect of the numerous pictures. The floors consist of clay tiles on the ground floor, plastic covering on the students' floor, bathrooms and kitchen, with white cast stone in the architect's apartment on the staircase and landing, and a dark grey fitted carpet in the living area. The lack of colour did justice to the architect's own furniture from the Wohnbedarf collection, chairs by Alvar Aalto, and paintings by Mondrian, Baumeister, Le Corbusier, van de Velde and others, all of which combined to turn the whole interior decoration into an integral work of art.

The well-proportioned overall composition is founded on a modular system that developed during the design process and is based on the axis dimensions of a student's room. The resulting modular sequence consists of fragments of the basic dimension of 3 metres and its multiples. This procedure facilitated the establishment of the dimensions during planning and finally resulted in a harmonious overall design.

Seen from a typological point of view, the house is reminiscent of the strictly ordered volumes of Le Corbusier's 1922 Citrohan House, open towards the south and accessible by a lateral staircase. But its plastic design goes beyond the volumes of the abstract white cube that Roth realised for his master in Stuttgart in 1927. The building has a sculptural

THE LIVING ROOM ON THE UPPER FLOOR

presence created by the zigzag-shaped west façade and the triple staggering of the south wall, expressive elements of design intended by Roth both in a functionalist sense as a precise solution to the lighting of the students' rooms and picture walls, and as sun protection for the exposed valley side façade. This established Roth as an 'architect of continuity' who, despite his concern for design, never ceased to be mistrustful of all formalism in post-war modern architecture.

In contrast with the calm and static outer impression, the interior of the architect's apartment presents an organic spatial landscape reminiscent of Wright and Aalto, both of whom had a crucial influence on Swiss post-war modern architecture. Incidentally, Aalto and Roth were united by a close friendship that led, among other things, to architectural collaboration on the Schönbühl ensemble in Lucerne between 1964 and 1967.

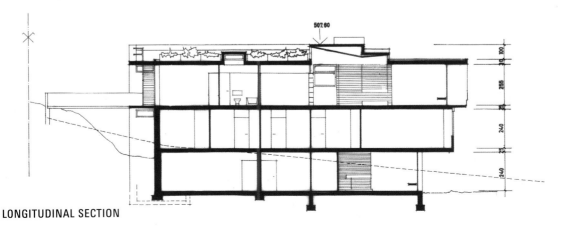

LONGITUDINAL SECTION

THE LIVING ROOM ON THE GROUND FLOOR

PLAN OF THE UPPER FLOOR

With his programmatic Fellowship Home, Alfred Roth generated an architectural type from the synthesis of domestic and social life that corresponded with both his professional intentions and his universal nature. A tireless ambassador of modern architecture, he ran his house as a venue for students, architects and artists until late in his life. His guests included personalities such as Alvar Aalto, Aldo van Eyck, Sigfried Giedion and Max Bill. His essentially well-preserved house has been privately owned since his death in 1998.

DAVID WYSS

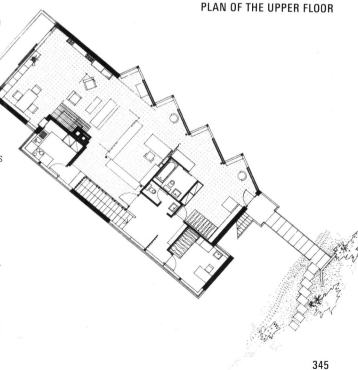

BIBLIOGRAPHY:

1962   'Architect's own house, Zurich', in *Architectural Design*, no. 9, pp. 421ff
        Roth A., 'Eigenheim eines Architekten in Zürich', in *Das Werk*, no. 5, pp. 161ff
1963   Roth A., 'Eigenheim eines Architekten in Zürich', in *Architektur und Wohnform/Innendekoration*, no. 5, pp. 217ff
1988   Roth A., *Amüsante Erlebnisse eines Architekten*, Zurich
1995   von Westersheim K., 'Alfred Roth: Fellowship Home', in *Abitare*, no. 339, pp. 164ff
1996   Rüegg A. (ed.), *Die Doldertalhäuser. Ein Hauptwerk des Neuen Bauens in Zürich*, Zurich
2001   Cornoldi A., *Le case degli architetti. Dizionario privato dal Rinascimento ad oggi*, Venice, p. 341

Otto Ernst Schweizer
1890–1965

1935–39, NEW CONSTRUCTION, 1985 DEMOLISHED
KRONPRINZENSTRASSE, BADEN-BADEN (D)

MAIN WORKS AND PROJECTS

1922–23	Extension to Pfaff and Schlauder coil spring factory, Schramberg (D)
1926–27	Nuremberg Planetarium (D)
1926–29	Employment office, Nuremberg (D)
1927–29	Sports complex, Nuremberg (D)
1928–31	Creamery, Nuremberg (D)
	Stadium, Vienna (A)

1929–31	Urban design project (development of the Prater area), Vienna (A)
1932	Urban design project (remodelling of the Normalm district), Stockholm (S)
1948–54	New plan for city centre, Stuttgart (D)
1955–61	Lecture hall at University of Freiburg im Breisgau (D)

OTTO SCHWEIZER was born on 27 April 1890 in Schramberg, in the Black Forest area of Germany, as the son of Rudolf Schweizer, who was a master furrier, and Anna King. Between 1906 and 1913 he served an apprenticeship and worked as a surveyor in Schramberg and Stuttgart. In 1914 he enrolled in Stuttgart's Technischen Hochschule, but a year later switched to the Technischen Hochschule in Munich in order to study under the architect Theodor Fischer. In the summer of 1917, after just two years of study there, he graduated with honours as a qualified architect.

From 1917 to 1919 Schweizer worked under Theodor Fischer's guidance in the architectural department of the Krupp company. In 1921 he married Gertrud Schlauder, and their first son, Hanspeter, was born in 1922. For ten years, from 1919 onwards, Schweizer headed the Departments of Municipal Architecture and Town Planning in Schramberg, Stuttgart and – for four years – Nuremberg, before he opened an architectural office of his own in 1929.

A year later, in 1930, he was appointed to a professorship at Karlsruhe Institute of Technology. Back in 1928, when he had entered the Art Competition at the Amsterdam Olympic Games, Schweizer won the Gold Medal in the architecture category for his design of a sports complex in Nuremberg (1927–29). Four years later, in 1932, he participated in two similar events: the V Milan Triennale and the Architecture Exhibition at the Los Angeles Olympic Games.

After the war Schweizer was appointed a member both of the Advisory Council on the Reconstruction of Germany and in 1949 of the Council for the Establishment of Bonn, working together with Herman Mattern, Hans Schwippert and others. He participated in the 1951 CIAM congress, held in Hoddesson, England. In 1955 he was elected Fellow of Berlin's Academy of Arts, and five years later, in 1960, he was awarded the Order

of Achievement of the Federal Republic of Germany. Otto Ernst Schweizer died on 14 November 1965 in Baden-Baden.

Schweizer had a fully formed philosophy of his own both of architecture and of urban design, which he always described in a most precise way. He visualises the modern city as reflecting the old spatial parameters and at the same time opening up to nature. He proposes monumental structures when they contribute to the readability of the city and to its functional coherence. It was very important to him to unify the town centre with nature, and to integrate recreational and cultural amenities with residential use. A constant development process can be seen in his urban design projects for Vienna (development of the Prater area, 1929–31), Stockholm (the urban redesign of the Normalm district, 1932), Karlsruhe and Baden-Baden, as well as later for Stuttgart (new plan for the city centre, 1948–54) and Bonn.

His buildings for the sports complex in Nuremberg (1927–29) and the stadium in Vienna (1928–31) led the architectural historian Arnold Tschira to regard him as the unrivalled master of reinforced concrete in Germany. The German historian Paul Zucker, writing after his emigration to the USA, singles Schweizer out – above the elite of German architects such as Otto Bartning, Hans Scharoun, Hugo Häring or Egon Eiermann – as being the only one who, after a long period of inactivity during Hitler's government, was able to continue the development of his own style from the point where it had been interrupted in 1933. During his lifetime Schweizer's work was discussed in many German and international journals, although after his death he has received little or no attention.

Schweizer's own house in Kronprinzenstrasse, Baden-Baden seems to be characteristic of his understanding of architecture: design in the sense of a search for simplicity in the solution to a given building task. Alfons Leitl

VIEW FROM THE GARDEN

VIEW FROM THE GARDEN

LIVING ROOM

SECTION AND ELEVATION OF THE GARDEN SIDE

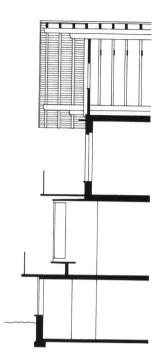

ELEVATION OF MAIN FAÇADE

PLAN OF THE GROUND FLOOR

wrote that the house responds to the qualities of the landscape and the typical features of the traditional Black Forest house, although it was a new interpretation, using modern building techniques. The house was situated on a slope above Baden-Baden's spa buildings, surrounded by large trees, with a wide view over the valley to the south-east. Visitors did not enter directly, but had to walk three-quarters of the way around the house before finding the entrance! The building opened out towards the valley, with the main rooms facing in that direction (the upper-floor bedrooms, the dining and living rooms on the main floor, and the work rooms in the basement). Terraces and deep projecting balconies extended the interior space to the outside, providing sufficient shade for the glazed areas in the summer. The walls were rendered and painted in earth colours, a sort of framed construction clearly distinguishing the roof floor from the base.

JUDITH WEINSTOCK-MONTAG

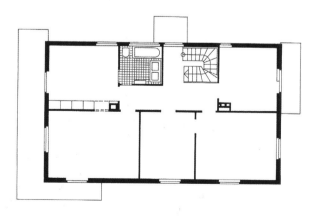

BIBLIOGRAPHY:

1940 Leitl A., 'Ein Wohnhaus und ein Buch von Otto Ernst Schweizer', in *Monatshefte für Baukunst und Städtebau*, no. 10, p. 269
1950 Tschira A., 'Otto Ernst Schweizer, der Architekt', in *Bauen und Wohnen*, no. 4, p. 197
1956 Schweizer O. E., *Die Architektonische Grossform. Gebautes und Gedachtes*, Karlsruhe
      Zucker P., 'Serene Spatial Balance' (critique of Schweizer's book *Die Architektonische Grossform*), in *Progressive Architecture*, no. 2, p. 190

Michael Scott
1905 – 1989

1937 – 38, NEW CONSTRUCTION
SANDYCOVE, COUNTY DUBLIN (IRL)

MAIN WORKS AND PROJECTS

1933 – 36	County Hospital, Portlaoise, County Laois (IRL)
1934 – 37	County Hospital, Tullamore, County Offaly (IRL)
1938 – 39	Irish pavilion for World Fair, New York, US
	Ritz Cinema, Athlone, County Westmeath (IRL)
1946 – 48	Chassis factory, Inchicore, Dublin (IRL)
1946 – 51	Donnybrook bus garage, Dublin (IRL)

1946 – 53	Busáras (Áras Mhic Diarmada), Store Street, Dublin (IRL)
1958 – 66	Abbey Theatre, Dublin (IRL)
1959 – 61	Radio Telefís Éireann studios, Donnybrook, Dublin (IRL)

MICHAEL SCOTT, who was elected in 1972 Honorary Fellow of the American Institute of Architects and received in 1975 the RIBA Royal Gold Medal for Architecture, is considered Ireland's most important 20th-century architect. Apart from Busáras, his most important buildings include his own home, 'Geragh', at Sandycove, and Donnybrook bus garage. He was born on 24 June 1905 in Drogheda, County Louth, in what is now the Republic of Ireland. His family originated in County Kerry, and he was educated at Belvedere College, Dublin. Here he first demonstrated his skills at painting and acting, and initially he wanted to pursue a career as a painter. But his father pointed out that it might make more financial sense to become an architect, which he duly did. Of his father's advice Scott said later in life: "I think he was right because I've always been interested in shaping materials since the day – at the age of six – when to my delight I caught a glimpse beneath my teacher's skirts of a well-formed wooden leg."

Like most other Irish architects of his period, Scott did not study architecture at the various schools of architecture, but was articled as an apprentice for the sum of £375 per annum to the Dublin firm of Jones and Kelly. In this practice, which at the time was conservative, he studied between 1923 and 1926 under Alfred E. Jones. Jones and Kelly were responsible for housing estates at Mount Merrion, Dublin, which were based on the garden city ideal, and for the last major public classical building to be constructed in Ireland, Cork City Hall, which was finished in 1935, and on which Scott worked for a while. Scott later claimed that it was not until he left Jones and Kelly that he became aware of the trends of modern architecture, but in fact the firm had a great architectural library with many books on contemporary European architecture and design.

During his apprenticeship, Scott joined Sarah Allgood's School of Acting at the Abbey Theatre, appearing there until 1927 in many plays,

including the first productions of Sean O'Casey's *Juno and the Paycock* and *The Plough and The Stars*. Between 1923 and 1926, under the tutelage of Sean Keating, who was professor of painting, he also studied art at the Dublin Metropolitan School of Art in the evenings, alongside such people as Maurice MacGonigal and Nano Reid. His relationships with these artists were to prove important, as Scott was to commission work from them in later years. In 1926 he was elected head of the Students Union and organised an Arts Week with lectures, plays and exhibitions. During this Arts Week he took the lead role in a play, *King Argimenes and the Unknown Warrior*, the set of which was designed by MacGonigal. Scott's total immersion through his acting and painting in the arts and Dublin artistic society was to provide important contacts in future years and be the source of valuable commissions for his firm.

In 1926 Scott left Jones & Kelly for the office of Charles J. Dunlop Architect, before moving on to the Board of Works as an assistant architect. He opened his own architectural practice in 1928, and since 1931 he practised in partnership with Norman Good which he left in 1937 to set up his own practice, Michael Scott Architect.

That same year he also designed his house 'Geragh', at Sandycove, County Dublin. He had bought the site by a Martello tower some years earlier, and originally intended it as a plot on which to build a home for his father, who was a keen fisherman. But his father rejected the idea, and so Scott built a house on the plot for himself. He named the building after the valley in County Kerry where his father had been born. Scott never had much money, but in 1933 he had – in the parlance of the day – 'married well', and his wife Patricia had inherited a small sum of money. This amounted to about £5-6000 and was used to buy the site and construct the house. He became so enthusiastic about the site that he claimed to have designed the house in one day: "I started one morn-

VIEW OF THE PROPERTY

FAÇADE

THE DINING AREA

THE LIVING ROOM

PERSPECTIVE SKETCH

ing at eight o'clock and by 4 o'clock the following morning had finished the initial sketch plans. I was a quick boy in my day." Actually, his haste probably had another, more mundane cause. Scott bought the site from an eccentric old lady, Mrs Chisholm Cameron, who sold it to him on condition that construction should start within three years. But, due to other commitments, the architect forgot about the stipulation. Then, one day, he received a letter in the post reminding him of the clause, and so had to rush out a design, hence the above claim.

The house is sited in an old quarry, next to the Forty Foot bathing place and Martello tower, and seems to rise out of the rock. A public pathway winds its way around the seaward side of the site, and so for privacy as well as protection from the prevailing wind, the building faces towards Dun Laoghaire, rather than out to sea. It was one of the first houses built in Ireland using mass concrete throughout. The concrete is rendered externally and painted white. Using the maritime imagery of the international style, the building is made up of a series of decks, railings and portholes – indeed, one end resembles the stern of an ocean liner with a descending series of circular bays and crescent balconies – a motif which also reflects the nearby Martello tower and naval defences at the Forty Foot. Scott said: "I thought of the house as a series of descending circles, each one wider than the other. It's my tribute to the Martello tower and also to James Joyce."

FLOOR PLANS

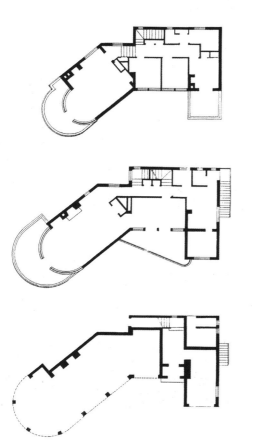

The house's curved bay feature was much used by Scott in this period, being deployed both in his home for Arthur Shields (1934), where the living room is projected out with a curved bay, and also at the hospital at Tullamore, where a series of curved bays are placed above one another. The flat roof and balconies all command great views over Dublin Bay. Original to the aesthetic of its day, Scott's house at Sandycove was originally sited on stilts, but over the years the spaces underneath were filled as the family's needs expanded. Apart from this, however, it remains intact.

CLAUDIA ZANLUNGO

BIBLIOGRAPHY:

1986   Pidgeon M., *Michael Scott – Your Mother Éire is always Young*, slide/tape set, London
1989   Doyle P., obituary of Michael Scott, in *RIAI Yearbook 1990*, Royal Institute of the Architects of Ireland, Dublin
1993   O'Regan J. (ed.), *Works 10 – Michael Scott 1905–1989*, Kinsale
1995   O'Regan J. and Deary N. (eds), *Michael Scott Architect in (Casual) Conversation with Dorothy Walker*, Kinsale

Wenche Selmer

1920–1998

**1963, NEW CONSTRUCTION, WITH JENS SELMER
TROSTERUDSTIEN 1, OSLO (N)**

MAIN WORKS AND PROJECTS

1955	House, Eiksstubben 9, Bærum (N)	**1973**	House, Stjerneveien 8c, Oslo (N)
	House, Sondreveien 30, Oslo (N)	**1974–76**	House and studio, Gråkamvn. 7c, Oslo (N)
1957	Own cottage, Brekkestø (N), as well as other summer	**1976**	Twin houses, Skådalen, Oslo (N)
	cottages in the same area, with Jens Selmer	**1978**	House, Heierstuveien 3, Oslo (N)
1968	House, Vettaliveien 8b, Oslo (N)		
1969	Summer house, Brunlanes, Oslo (N)		

WENCHE SELMER was born in Paris to Herman Foss Reimers (1874–1961) who was a barrister and Bibbi Næss (1881–1945). In 1941 she enrolled in the National College of Art and Design (SHKS) in Oslo, where she studied for four years in the School of Civil Engineering, graduating in 1945. She complemented her studies practically by working for a year on building sites and in various workshops. At that time, following four years of study in the School of Civil Engineering, graduates could only work as drafting assistants in architects' offices. To try to remedy the anomoly, Wenche and other students initiated a course called the Course for War-Affected Students of Architecture. It was implemented with the help of a group of well-established and renowned architects, including Arnstein Arneberg, Herman Munthe-Kaas, Gudolf Blakstad, Georg Eliassen, Knut Knutsen and Are Vesterlid. The course later gave rise to the Oslo School of Architecture (AHO). She obtained her diploma in Architecture in 1946.

1946–47 Wenche Selmer was employed in the office of Arnstein Arneberg in Oslo, and 1947–48 she worked in Marcel Lod's practice in Paris. Between 1948 and 1954, back in Oslo, she worked in the studio of Arne Pedersen and Reidar Lund, where she was responsible for planning and executing the Norwegian student hostel at the Cité Universitaire in Paris.

In 1954 Wenche married architect Jens Andreas Selmer, opening her own practice the same year. The private house which she designed for herself (Trosterudstien 1, Oslo) was done in collaboration with her husband and won the Sundt Prize for outstanding architecture in 1963. In 1969 the Selmers won the Timber Award for their wooden architecture in general. Wenche Selmer designed some of the most distinguished Norwegian timber architecture and small-scale houses of her day. Her houses remain manifestations of life, unpretentious and low-key. Within a limited budget, she was able to create practical and harmonious spaces.

From 1976 to 1987 Wenche Selmer taught as a senior lecturer at the Oslo School of Architecture. Her philosophy of teaching was not based on an authoritarian approach, but on empathy, as she was concerned to be in contact with her students and foster their talents. She once said: "I think that as a teacher you should be interested in people. You have to be open and aware... It is a joy to see a student who has talent, but you should appreciate that such things are not always immediately apparent." Wenche Selmer herself was a student of the architect Knut Knutsen, whom she credited with having had the greatest influence on her work. In 1993 she was awarded a state scholarship by her country for mature artists.

Wenche Selmer mostly built detached houses or summer houses. As a mother of small children in the 1950s, she chose to turn down larger-scale projects. However, this gave her a deeper insight into the problem of the dwelling and its basic requirements, implemented within a limited financial budget. In its refined simplicity, her own home clearly reflects these insights, manifesting her architectural philosophy, which has been characterised by Elisabeth Tostrup as "architectural thoughtfulness". Selmer's architecture is thoughtful both in its technical elaboration and precision, and in its artistic refinement, both aspects being enhanced by a particular empathy and skill with regard to what can be called social and environmental factors.

Wenche Selmer is well-known for her respectful sensitivity to place and surroundings. Her houses are not 'invisible', but scrupulously designed so as to cultivate the relationship between building and terrain, manifesting a modesty in terms of limiting the extent of construction in and encroachment on the landscape. In an interview she explained: "The positioning of a house in the surrounding terrain is a key factor for me. I almost always experience a form in relation to its location. The placing can be in relation to a rock or a field, but there has to be something at the site that gets the project going."

VIEW FROM THE GARDEN

THE LIVING ROOM AND DINING AREA

THE LIVING ROOM TOWARDS THE FIREPLACE

Sometimes Selmer's preoccupation with the formal aspect of a site, be it in relation to some rocky feature or to a small plain, even led her to spend a night in a sleeping bag on the plot in order to experience sunrise there. She was especially concerned with spatial coherence or continuity as a strategy to achieve favourable spatial quality. A typical architectural means to achieve this was her ability to create an intimate relationship between the building and the outdoor space.

Besides environmental 'thoughtfulness', another essential feature of Selmer's architecture was her awareness of the people who would live in and use the house. Together with her client she would analyse the site, the idea of the house, primary and secondary needs, and functional as well as aesthetic aspects, the aim being to create a well-founded project. Many of her clients later told her that they had experienced this planning time as a very stimulating and instructive period. Most of her houses had low-cost budgets, making it necessary to take full advantage of the space available. She explained: "Because of this, I try never to lose a single square metre to something that isn't attractive or useful."

Another core concern of Selmer, possibly connected with the fact that she was a female architect, was with finding good solutions for the rooms in the house that are often neglected by architects, such as the kitchen, bathroom and utility rooms. She had some success in positively influencing matters in this area, enhancing the quality of everyday life.

In general it can be said that Wenche Selmer followed in the footsteps of influential architects such as Magnus Poulsson, Fredrik Konow Lund and especially Knut Knutsen. Like them, she practised the difficult art of making tradition contemporary. She also had the distinction of being one of the few women to rank among Norway's most renowned 20th-century architects.

Trosterudstien 1, the home that Wenche Selmer and her husband designed for themselves in 1963, is a small-scale construction. The house is organised as a long rectangular space and faces the trees and the garden

outside, well adapted to the site's terrain. As in most of Wenche Selmer's buildings, wood is the predominant material. Our gaze is consciously drawn towards the garden through the large windows at the front. These windows also function as sliding doors, allowing a close contact between inside and outside.

Elisabeth Tostrup has written the following about Wenche Selmer's private house: "Trosterudstien 1 in Oslo is an outstanding example of the delicate way in which Selmer reduces and selects measures of architectural articulation. The relationship between the size of the windows and openings and the space inside is effectively balanced so that the actual dimensions of the rooms can be decreased. The dining area or niche, only 2.4 m. wide, takes advantage of a large window placed at a height that enables people seated at the table to have a panoramic view of the garden. Further, the entire dining table can be wheeled a few feet to the kitchen area, where it can serve as an auxiliary surface for kitchen work.

"The windows in the bedrooms are placed and shaped in such a way that you do not notice that the rooms are in fact narrow. Another key factor is the combined spaces for living and working, in which the large sliding doors cause the garden, which is sheltered from the road by an evergreen spruce hedge, to become part of the interior.

"A look at the interior confirms how the use of wood as a structural principle constitutes the main architectural, and even ornamental, component, as in the system of double main beams and secondary beams. Pinewood is used in panel boarding on the walls and other fittings throughout the house. The overall idea is that the material itself should constitute a major architectural means, a source of beauty, and surfaces are only treated if they need protecting.

"The house is rare both in its denial of a bourgeois lifestyle and in its minimalism. However, the intricate and refined measures of architectural composition that bring about the apparent simplicity make it all the more interesting. This particular attitude, this skill, is something that Selmer cultivated and displayed in all her works, using wood as the primary instrument."

SILJE SKRONDAL

BIBLIOGRAPHY:
1980   Seip E., 'Profil 6. Interview: Wenche Selmer', in *Byggekunst*, 3/1980, pp. 46–52
1986   *Norsk Kunstlerleksikon 3*, Oslo
1988   Rognlien D. (ed.), *Treprisen, Thirteen Norwegian Prize-Winning Architects*, Oslo
1989   Sjølie M., *Sosial Boligbygging i Norge: 1945–1980: en studie av arkitekt Jens Selmers arbeider*, Oslo
2001   Tostrup E., *Architect Wenche Selmer*, Oslo

< PLAN OF THE GROUND FLOOR AND PERSPECTIVE SKETCH

Alison & Peter Smithson
1928 – 1993, 1923 – 2003

1959 – 61, ALTERATION
FONTHILL, WILTSHIRE (GB)

MAIN WORKS AND PROJECTS

BOTH BORN in England, in Stockton-on-Tees and Sheffield respectively, Peter Smithson and Alison Gill met after the Second World War at the School of Architecture of the University of Durham. They married in 1949, after Peter had finished his studies at the Royal Academy of London, and began a long and fruitful partnership. In 1950 they won the competition for a school in Hunstanton, Norfolk, one of the most controversial buildings in Britain at the time: openly opposed to the more widespread practice of neo-traditionalist reconstruction, the Smithsons designed a building with an exposed structure in which the symmetry of the group, inspired by the work of Ludwig Mies Van der Rohe, is countered by the use of exposed fixtures and pipes. The school brought the Smithsons very much to the forefront of contemporary British architecture: their influence on the debate in the 1950s and the 1960s was based not so much on buildings that were actually constructed, a relatively small number due partly to the undeserved failure of many of their competition projects, but on a series of urban designs and projects that were never realised, as well as on a significant body of theoretical writings. At an international level, especially in the context of the CIAM meetings, the Smithsons set up Team X (1953) together with other promising young architects like Aldo van Eyck, Jacob Bakema, Georges Candilis, and Shadrac Woods: the group, which was to dominate the Otterlo Congress in 1959, developed a critical revision of the principles of functionalism, advocating a closer correlation between urban form and psychological needs. In England the Smithsons worked in close collaboration with other artists (including the sculptor Eduardo Paolozzi and the photographer Nigel Henderson) and intellectuals. In 1951 they set up the Independent Group, organising a series of important cultural events, including the exhibitions Parallel of Life and Art (1953) and This is Tomorrow (1956), both in London. With the considerable support of the critic Reyner Banham, who defined their work within the newly-established category of "New Brutalism", they promoted a new aesthetics for the masses.

The term Brutalism alludes to a rough, at times violent style, founded also on the deliberate display of techniques and materials, beginning with exposed concrete, following the poetics of béton brut typical of the mature works of Le Corbusier. Their own house in Soho, built in 1952, develops a poetics based on the use of rough material surfaces to divide up the space, in line with the contemporary experiments of other English architects like James Stirling and Denys Lasdun. The work of Le Corbusier had a substantial influence on the Smithsons in many of their projects – beginning with the facade screens that characterise buildings such as the hall of residence at St. Hilda's College, Oxford (1967 – 70) – and is especially clear in their large-scale urban projects. In the light of a new sensibility, they designed large-scale residential structures seen as relatively autonomous parts of the city, often with pedestrian routes quite distinct from vehicle routes, as in the unrealised plans for Golden Lane Housing (1951 – 52) and Manisty Street (1963) in London.

As well as their many experiments on the house and housing – either on a small scale as a flexible structure open onto the landscape (Upper Lawn, 1959 – 62), or as a concentrate of technology (the House of the Future at the Daily Mail exhibition in London, 1955 – 56; The Appliance House, 1957 – 58), or on a large scale as a group of large high-rise structures as in Robin Hood Gardens, built between 1966 and 1970 – they also explored the relationship between modern architectural idioms and the historical context in the Economist building in London (1959 – 64).

Upper Lawn Pavilion is a holiday house which the Smithsons designed for themselves at Fonthill, deep in the Wiltshire countryside. They took a pre-existing structure and converted it between 1959 and 1961. The pavilion, which is characterised by the poetics of the objet trouvé as well as a radical formal research, exemplifies the working method of the couple. Starting with the ruins that they found, the Smithsons meticulously measured them up, before interpreting and adding to them. Thus the chimney on one of the outside walls of the old building became the

VIEW ACROSS THE GARDEN WALL WITH SOUTH AND EAST FAÇADES

NORTH FAÇADE WITH NEIGHBOURS' GARAGES

WESTERN GARDEN FAÇADE

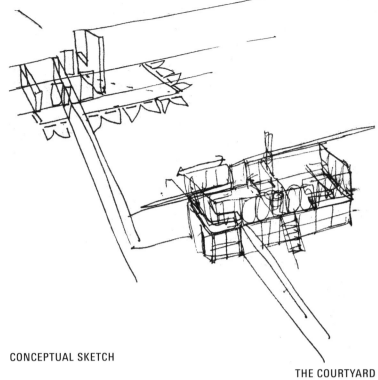

CONCEPTUAL SKETCH

THE COURTYARD

the living area — a continuation, thanks to the sliding doors, of the outside terrace. A steep ship-style staircase leads to the upper level, where the intrusive presence of the pre-existing wall divides the space into two rooms.

The constant oscillation between austere rational organisation and the poetic sensibility in the additions, between artifice and integration with the pre-existing, form the picturesque elements that tame the building's brutalist character, making it an unrivalled example of the synthesis between thought and action.   FABIO MANGONE, GENNARO POSTIGLIONE

VIEW FROM THE FIRST FLOOR

BIBLIOGRAPHY:
1982   Smithson A. and Smithson P., 'The Shift', in *Architectural Monographs*, London
1986   Smithson A., *Upper Lawn. Solar Pavilion Folly*, Barcelona
1991   Vidotto M. and Smithson A. and P., *Pensieri, progetti e rammenti fino al 1990*, Genoa
1997   Vidotto M., *A+P Smithson*, Barcelona

centrepiece of the new composition, turning the former inside floor into a remarkable open-air terrace adjacent to the pavilion.

Maintaining their typical approach, the couple carefully selected what they wanted to keep of the extant structure. Beside the chimney, they conserved the inside floor, two windows, several fragments of the walls, as well as the wall surrounding the property, whose proportions they altered to great effect. One of the windows on the outer wall is used inside the pavilion, while the other is placed at the far end of the terrace, creating a link between the Wiltshire countryside and the Smithsons' little court, and also giving the outside space a private homely atmosphere. The stone placed on the outer wall next to the main gate also serves to link the pavilion with the landscape.

The conserved wall is completely exposed so as to highlight its stone ashlar structure. No other walls have been added. The diaphragms between the interior and the exterior are made of plugged wood, glass panels, or sandwich wood panels, insulation panels and aluminium. Inside, on the other hand, the only closed space is made entirely using wood panels, as if it were a vast piece of furnishing.

The whole house rather resembles a large cage placed around the old chimney, where only the wall resting on the outer wall is partially shielded. A window with large panes provides a link between the new volume and the pre-existing structure. Although the whole structure is in wood and glass, the Smithsons — wishing to highlight their way of working through contrasts — rested the wooden first-level floor on a beam made of reinforced concrete, which in turn rests on two square pillars. The anomalous presence of the concrete structure is further reinforced by the fact that the pillars are turned 45° relative to the general plan of the house, so that they seem to be out of scale and out of place.

At garden level we find the entrance hall, behind the chimney, the furnishing that serves as a kitchen and to separate the bathroom, and

SITE PLAN

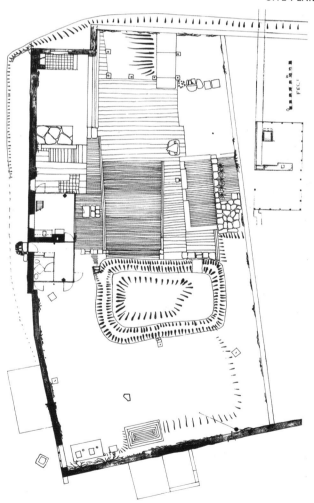

361

Werner Sobek
*1953

1999–2000, NEW CONSTRUCTION, STILL INHABITED BY THE ARCHITECT
RÖMER STRASSE 128, STUTTGART (D)

MAIN WORKS AND PROJECTS

1991–93	Ecole Nationale d'Art Décoratif, Limoges (F), with LAB.F.AC.
1992–97	Rothenbaum Stadium, Hamburg (D), with Schweger + Partner
1995–2000	Sony-Centre, Berlin (D), with Murphy & Jahn
1995–2004	New Bangkok International Airport, Bangkok (Thailand), with Murphy & Jahn
1996–2000	Interbank in Lima (Peru), with Hans Hollein

2001	Neues Kranzler-Eck office building, Berlin (D), with Murphy & Jahn
	Highrise for Deutsche Post AG, Bonn (D), with Murphy & Jahn

WERNER SOBEK was born in Aalen, Württemberg (Germany), in 1953. From 1974–80 he studied structural engineering and architecture at the University of Stuttgart. He became a research assistant at the same university from 1980–86 and gained further experience working for the office of Skidmore, Owings and Merrill in Chicago. Sobek received his doctorate at Stuttgart in 1987. He then worked for the renowned engineering firm of Schlaich, Bergermann und Partner in Stuttgart. In 1991 he became a professor at the University of Hanover. Sobek founded his own engineering firm in 1992. In 1995 he took a professorship in Stuttgart. Following in the footsteps of Frei Otto, the pioneer of lightweight construction techniques, he became director of the Institute for Lightweight Structures and of the Central Laboratory Structural Engineering. In 2000 he succeeded Jörg Schlaich to the Chair of the Institute for Design and Construction II. His plans for a merger of these two renowned institutes led to the creation of the Institute for Lightweight Structures and Construction (ILEK). Sobek thus consolidated the continuity of a long research tradition in the field of innovative structural engineering at Stuttgart University. He quickly succeeded in moulding a distinctive profile of his own. One focal point of his research is applying the knowhow and products from such high-tech fields as space travel, aviation, automobile construction and textile production to the field of building construction.

The engineering firm of Werner Sobek Ingenieure (WSI) based in Stuttgart and Frankfurt/Main operates worldwide and now employs a 90-strong staff. The firm works with many internationally renowned architects. The fact that the input of engineers need not be seen as secondary in such collaborative projects, but can actually become the main attraction of a building, is clearly illustrated by such works as, for example, the new glass foyer of the University of Bremen (architects:

Störmer und Partner) with its impressive glass facade suspended on steel cables, their tension held by tilting spring mechanism that allows the glass skin to billow out like a sail by as much as 35 cm in a storm. WSI works closely with the Chicago-based architectural practice of Murphy & Jahn. Werner Sobek and Helmut Jahn even coined the term "archi-neering" to describe their cooperative endeavours. Their joint projects include the Sony Center in Berlin as well as airport buildings in Bangkok, Cologne-Bonn and Munich.

However, it was a relatively modest building that first made Sobek famous. House R128, built in 2000 for the Sobeks and their son, unleashed a debate that defined contemporary architectural discourse in Germany. The main reason for this was the unusual overall concept of the building which combines three components: the use of cutting edge building technology and equipment, the insistence on ecological sustainability and the creation of an extraordinary sense of architectural space. The debate was also fuelled by the fact that Sobek adopted a key motif of modern architecture: the glass house. Joseph Paxton's 1851 Crystal Palace was a seminal structure in the history of modern architecture. It prompted Paul Scheerbart to quip that "Glass heralds a new dawn – redbrick merely makes us yawn" and inspired Bruno Taut to create his famous 1914 glass pavilion in Cologne. A few years later, Ludwig Mies van der Rohe designed glass highrises for Berlin. On a smaller scale, he went on to create the Tugendhat House in Brünn in 1930 and, most notably, in 1950, the Farnsworth House in Plano, Illinois, both of which are widely regarded as the most important examples of glass architecture in Classical Modernism. The latter building, however, in spite of the aesthetic virtuosity of its design, also demonstrated the difficulty of actually

NIGHT VIEW >

HORIZONTAL AND VERTICAL VISUAL LINKS IN THE ENTRANCE AREA

putting the idea into practice, for it proved unsatisfactory in everyday use – mainly because the transparent shell was unable to compensate for changing weather conditions. Farnsworth House is sweltering in summer and chilly in winter.

The evident contradiction between aesthetic fascination and technical or functional problems may well have prompted Werner Sobek to design a state of the art glass house without the shortcomings of its predecessors by drawing upon the findings of half a century of technical progress and development. The result is House R128. It is a four-storey cube with a ground area of about 8 x 9 m and 11 m in height. All four sides are fully glazed. The 104 identical panes consist of a special treble glazing; some can be opened as doors or ventilation wings. A metal-coated film reduces the thermal flow. Inert gases between the panes of the treble glazing provide extremely high levels of thermal insulation. Power required for heating and regulation is generated by a rooftop solar energy unit. An innovative computer-controlled energy concept ensures that the solar energy entering the house is absorbed by waterflow ceiling elements and stored. In winter, the thermal exchange process is inverted, so that the ceiling elements become heaters. With this sophisticated system, Sobek has not only solved the problems that burdened the glass house of the classical modern era, but has actually created a zero-energy house. The construction itself is based on criteria of sustainability. The steel frame, erected in just four days, can be dismantled with ease, as can the facade elements, and is completely recyclable.

Visitors to the house tend to be flummoxed by the absence of such familiar functional elements as door handles, light switches and water

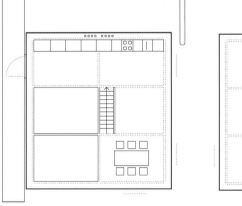

PLAN OF THE THIRD FLOOR

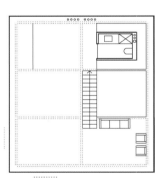

PLAN OF THE SECOND FLOOR

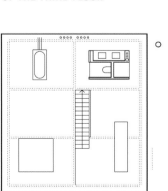

PLAN OF THE FIRST FLOOR

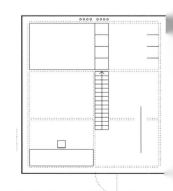

PLAN OF THE GROUND FLOOR

VIEW OF THE STAIRCASE TO THE GARDEN

LIVING AND DINING AREA

taps. These functions are in fact carried out by sensor technology: motion sensors, voice control, or touch screens. With this radical approach, Sobek is merely applying to architecture some forms of technology that are already widely accepted in other areas of life. Yet it is this aspect, in particular, that has been the focus of much of the controversy surrounding the Sobek house. Critics have decried the loss of a tactile quality in this kind of architecture, an increasing abstraction of spatial perception and the one-sidedness of a technological approach that does not take into account the fallibility of technology and simple human error.

Sobek stresses that the aesthetic concept is even more important than the technical aspect. This aesthetic concept, he maintains, is aimed at creating "spatial fluidity and transparency, which is also developed in the vertical" (*Arch+*, 157, 9/2001, p. 24). The concept brooks neither partitions (with the exception of the toilets) nor curtains. The glass outer skin not only integrates the natural surroundings into the fluid space, but also the urban setting seen from this house, placed high above the Stuttgart valley. Its hillside location also prevents the construction of any directly adjacent buildings, so that the house is sheltered from curious onlookers. The entrance to the house is on the top floor, accessed by a walkway at the side which juts out with a pulpit-like viewing balcony over the façade, that looks towards the valley. The kitchen and dining area are located on the top floor. A central stairway leads to the lower floors, first to the living area and then to the bedroom level, where even the mobile bath is placed openly within the room. On the ground floor is the nursery and the water tank. All the rooms are elegantly minimalist – only the bookshelf provides a splash of colour. Transparency in the verti-

cal is achieved by three open floor spaces in the steel frame: two in the upper floor and one on the floor below. With House R128 Sobek has undeniably shown that the idea of the glass house is still an exciting aesthetic project for the modern age. What is more, he has also shown that it is possible to build an ecologically sound glass house. It is hardly surprising that such an extraordinary house is not to everyone's taste, given that home-making is still one of the most conservative areas of human life. As an experiment – even such a heroically isolated experiment as this one – this house could prove to be an important point of reference for the architecture and the homes of the future. EBERHARD SYRING

BIBLIOGRAPHY:

1999 Anna S. (ed.), *ARCHI-NEERING. Helmut Jahn, Werner Sobek*, Ostfildern-Ruit
2001 'Experiment Wohnen', in *db – Deutsche Bauzeitung*, no. 7/2001, pp. 27–71
      'Sobeks Sensor', in *Arch+*, no. 157, pp. 24–69
2002 Blaser W. and Heinlein F., *R 128 by Werner Sobek. Architektur für das 21. Jahrhundert*, Basle
      Schwarz U. (ed.), *Neue Deutsche Architektur. Eine reflexive Moderne*, Ostfildern-Ruit,
      pp. 182–189

Eduardo Souto de Moura
*1952

1993, NEW CONSTRUCTION
RUA CARTELAS VIEIRA, MATOSINHOS (P)

MAIN WORKS AND PROJECTS

1980–84,	
1997–2001	Municipal market, Bairro di Carandà, Braga (P)
1981–91	Casa das artes cultural centre, Oporto (P)
1982–88	Houses 1 and 2 , Nevogilde, Oporto (P)
1984–89	House, Quinta do Lago, Almasil, Algarve (P)
1989–94	House 1, Bom Jesus, Braga (P)
1989–97	Restoration and conversion of the Convent of Sta. Maria do Bouro into a pousada, Amarès, Braga (P)

1991–98	House, Caminha, Moledo (P)
1992–95	Housing block, Rua do Teatro, Oporto (P)
1993–2002	Conversion of the Alfandega into the Museum of Transport and Communication, Oporto (P)
2000–03	Municipal stadium, Braga (P)

EDUARDO SOUTO DE MOURA was born in Oporto on 25 July 1952. He attended an Italian school in that Portuguese port city before enrolling in its School of Fine Arts (ESBAP). Here his teachers included Fernando Távora and Alberto Carneiro, who first introduced him to contemporary art, a major influence on his work with its constant references to artists including Antoni Tàpies, Donald Judd, Richard Serra and Joseph Beuys, and to movements such as Land Art and American Minimalism.

At the ESBAP Souto de Moura experienced the period of the revolution against the Salazar regime, and was a member of the Brigate Saal, a group of architects and students of architecture which, working together with skilled craftsmen, was awarded a commission to build new social housing. With the SAAL housing complex at São Vitor (Oporto, 1974–79), Souto de Moura had the opportunity to work for five years with Alvaro Siza. On the basis of their professional collaboration, they soon developed a close friendship, although the master-pupil character of the relationship remains apparent even to this day.

Together with Siza, Souto de Moura took part – still a student at the ESBAP – in the SIAC seminars (Seminario Internacional de Arquitectura Contemporanea) organised by Aldo Rossi in the Spanish cities of Santiago de Compostela and Seville, an experience that would consolidate the influence of Rossi's ideas on him, often acknowledged by the Portuguese architect. During the seminars he was able to meet numerous architects from various European countries, establishing solid relations based on intellectual exchange.

In 1980 Souto de Moura graduated in architecture from Oporto School of Fine Arts, following which he began to lecture as an assistant professor at the ESBAP, which in 1986 became the Faculty of Architec-

ture of the University of Oporto (FAUP). At the same time he opened his own architectural practice. Souto de Moura taught for ten years (1981–91) at the ESBAP/FAUP, after which lectured 1991–2002 as a visiting professor in various schools of architecture around the world, including those at the Universities of Paris-Belville, Harvard, Dublin, Zurich and Lausanne.

Particularly important in his development was his time at the Harvard School of Architecture, which was directed by Rafael Moneo, whose lessons Souto de Moura made a special point of following. At Harvard the Portuguese architect also met Jacques Herzog, with whom he established a close friendship, marked by reciprocal influence.

The house that Eduardo Souto de Moura designed and built for himself and his family is a new construction (1993), located in Rua Cartelas Vieira, in the town of Matosinhos, slightly north of Oporto. It is part of a small site in the gardens of a historic residence, situated on the slopes of the hill overlooking the port of Leixões. The site consists of a terrace of patio houses, in two slightly different variants, plus a detached house that constitutes the exception to the rule. The detached house was intended for Souto de Moura's own family, but in fact it remained empty until it was sold a few years later.

"The individual plots at the site," writes Souto de Moura, "are divided by parallel walls, with three long strips of concrete forming the roofs. Between these strips are the patios, where the plants will eventually merge into the gardens and the surrounding fields. From the outside it will only be possible to see the stone walls of the side elevation, and the walls on the new road will be plastered and painted ochre … The patio houses are based directly on a reading of the morphology of the area:

VIEW OF THE HOUSE IN THE RURAL LANDSCAPE

THE ENFILADE TOWARDS THE HOUSE

DETAIL OF THE STAIRCASE AT THE ENTRANCE

STREET VIEW

THE KITCHEN

THE ENTRANCE

THE LIVING ROOM

narrow roads lined by granite walls … We wanted to create a low-density complex, which will allow a certain 'anonymity' and a certain 'naturalness', although this is an ambitious aim."

"The idea, which takes up the project of the house," he continues, "is to build walls, a characteristic feature of this area. The Portuguese house is the continuation of the wall around it, and sometimes the only sign from the road of the presence of the house is a window. There is a similarity with the structure of some Chinese villages, but I only realised this when the project was completed. Nor was I aware of the patio houses designed by Sert, which I saw later, and which are very similar. I wanted to build stone walls parallel with the sides of the plot, and to cover them with a single concrete layer covered with earth, but since we didn't have enough money to build in stone, the walls were made of concrete."

"The plan for the site, drawn up by Távora, had included a road that cuts it in two, more or less diagonally. The lower part of the site, which is a triangular plot, was not for sale, so it became my payment. At the time I was building the pousada in Bouro, so I asked the bricklayer who was working on that plot to build the outer walls in stone, then the house inside. The central idea was a design exercise intended to hide the triangular form of the plot. The short side of the triangle leads into a trapezoidal space, with a corridor cutting through the whole space on the fourth side. Then there is the strip of the bedrooms and the living room. After that comes the patio, also trapezoidal, with a garden and some trees, the swimming pool, once again a trapezium, and the garage – all

gradually diminishing in size, to force the perspective. Inside, too, all the stone and wood elements, such as those making up the floor, use a triangular pattern."

In the houses in Matosinhos, the theme of the patio, already widely explored in Souto de Moura's work as part of complex distributional structures, became an extreme solution, allowing him to give up the advantages of a house open to the world without giving up a free homogenous space, using complete introversion to eliminate the awkward question of the figuration of an elevation. In this and in other cases, the model of Ludwig Mies van der Rohe and the apparent reference to Lluís Sert is denied by the architect, who seems to be driven rather by his own exigencies.

The triangular house, which stands out – as said – as the exception to the rule, actually contains the principles that lie behind the whole project: the house as a concretion of the perimeter wall, as a space of shelter growing out of the line of the granite perimeter, open to the outside through very few small windows, arranged strategically with respect to the surrounding space. As the basic framework of the project, the triangular house cannot display the impurity of its non-orthogonal geometry, so the definition of the spaces and the elements is obsessively constructed by faking orthogonality by means of optical artifices – even the trapezoidal outline of the battens of the wooden floor – which accentuate the perspective of the space.

As is often the case with Souto de Moura, the space is constructed through the juxtaposition of elements following a 'negative' procedure of

INNER COURTYARD WITH POOL

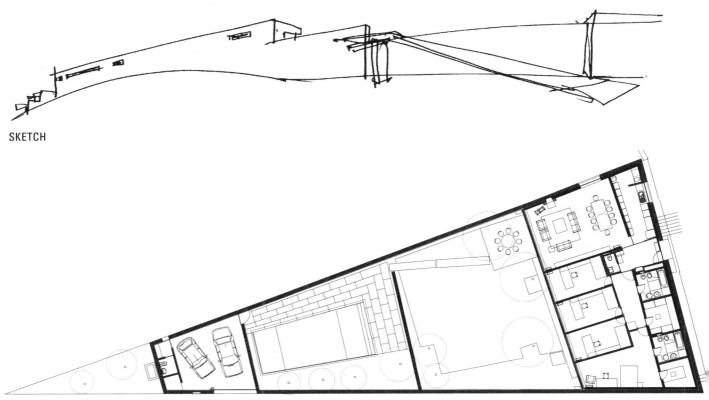

SKETCH

PLAN

THE LIVING ROOM

BATHROOM

definition, in which the qualities of the space and the light constitute a discovery that springs from the tensions between the parts and between the materials. This is in contrast to what occurs in other houses designed by the architect in the south of Portugal, where the soul of the project stems from the desire to define a space by a 'positive' procedure, building the box – the walls – which contains it and which becomes its material imprint, its mould.

ANTONIO ESPOSITO, GIOVANNI LEONI

BIBLIOGRAPHY:
1999 'Patio housing estate in Matosinhos', in *Architècti*, no. 47, July/September, pp. 80–85
2000 Baglione C., 'Case a patio, Matosinhos', in *Casabella*, no. 678, May, pp. 38–43
      Fernandez-Galiano L., 'Domicilios. El paisaje privado: doce casos de casas', in *Arquitectura Viva*, no. 73, July/August, pp. 46–49
      Cohn D., 'Hofhäuser in Hafennähe. Wohnanlage, Matosinhos, Portugal', in *Bauwelt*, vol. 91, no. 33, September, pp. 36–39
2003 Esposito A. and Leoni G., *Eduardo Souto de Moura*, Milan, pp. 150–155

Rino Tami
1908–1994

1961, NEW CONSTRUCTION
SORENGO (CH)

MAIN WORKS AND PROJECTS

1935	Il Torchio own holiday home, Lisora di Monteggio (CH)
1940	Cantonal Library, Lugano (CH)
1946	Lucendro Hydroelectric Power Station, Airolo (CH)
1956	Corso Cinema, Lugano (CH)

1957	La Torre apartment block, Lugano (CH)
	Own holiday home, Maroggia (CH)
1963–83	Aesthetic consultancy work for N2 motorway (CH)

RINO TAMI was born in Lisora di Monteggio on 7 August 1908, the son of Giuseppe, a hotelier, and Giacinta Bordonzotti. His grammar school studies in Lugano left him with a love of poetry that would continue throughout his life. As a young man he devoted himself to wood engraving, from which he took the form of graphic representation of his first architectural designs. After secondary school he attended the Scuola Reale Superiore di Architettura (Royal School of Architecture) in Rome for two years.

Having abandoned his studies for health reasons, Tami began to work – together with his older brother Carlo, who had graduated in architecture from the Accademia di Belle Arti in Bologna in 1922 – in the well-established Lugano practice of his uncle, Giuseppe Bordonzotti, a leading figure in Ticino's late-eclectic movement. After their uncle's death, the two brothers took over the office, but Rino chose to follow the courses held by Otto Rudolf Salvisberg at the Federal Polytechnic (now Swiss Federal Institute of Technology or ETH) in Zurich.

In 1934, Rino Tami won his first important competition with his design for the Institute for the Blind in Lugano, leaving his studies and returning to Lugano to supervise its construction. In the following years he won many more competitions, including in particular the competition in 1937 for the new Cantonal Library in Lugano, his most renowned building, which was immediately published by important architecture journals, beginning with *Casabella*. Tami's Cantonal Library is considered the first 'modern' public building in Ticino. Initially viewed with scepticism by the public, it marked the definitive affirmation of modern architecture in the Swiss canton of Ticino. For Tami, the building was the start of a successful career in both the public sector and private sectors, during which he constructed many single-family houses. The architect was invited to represent Ticino at the National Exhibition in Zurich in 1939.

From 1957 to 1960 Tami was Professor of Architecture at the Federal Polytechnic in Zurich. He was a member both of the Federal Committee for Historic Monuments, on which he showed great concern for the problems

of restoration, and of the St Luke's Committee for modern sacred art. During the 1960s, Tami was employed by the cantonal government as an aesthetic consultant for the Ticino stretch of Switzerland's N2 motorway, an activity that he undertook until his death in 1994.

In his work Tami was always open to the experiments of both Modernism and organic architecture, which he grafted onto various elements deriving from his cultural background. Describing his Ticinese Grotto, built for the National Exhibition in Zurich in 1939, the architect defined it as "our local construction in the modern spirit" and underlined the harmony between the traditional buildings of Ticinese villages and the spirit of modern architecture, evident in the harmonious collocation in the landscape, the use of materials according to their particular characteristics, and an internal distribution in keeping with the affective needs of the inhabitants. In the Ticinese Grotto the roof was of fundamental importance, while the reference to popular architecture in the bare plastered façades was reduced to mere allusions.

A marked local component reappears years later in Rino Tami's Erreti house, which he built for his family and himself in 1961 in Sorengo. The home is situated in a quiet residential area near Lugano, where it is the last in a road of single-family houses designed by Tami. Its plot is slightly sloping, with the house lying at the highest point, in the north-west corner. Located thus, the plot's short side borders the access road, and the whole garden to the south-east overlooks Lake Lugano. The design of the house has a powerful impact. This stems from the volume of the roof, which dominates and even crushes the volume of the house proper. The roof's two slopes rise from the level of the first floor, while the ground floor consists mainly of windows. Only two full vertical elements interrupt the windows, acting as columns to support the massive upper façade, which becomes an exploded gable. There is a clear reference here to the large roofs of old Ticino farm buildings used to protect hay and farm equipment. The traditional appearance created by the roof prevails

GARDEN VIEW

THE LIVING ROOM

over the modern appearance of the reinforced concrete walls, and is underlined by the powerful presence both of the chimney and, in front of the house, of a rustic stone column, which surmounted by a bronze sculpture depicting a crowing cockerel, a typical symbol of rural life.

The structure of the house is of reinforced concrete, while one of the roof's two slopes is split and clad in tiles. The plan is more or less rectangular. There is a clear dichotomy between the volume of the house, which suggests a personal interpretation of organic architecture, and the plan, which is strictly geometric and seems to rest on a rectangular platform, just as all the elements of the garden, from the flower beds to the perimeter walls and the swimming pool, are linked by a geometric hierarchy.

Inside, the distribution of space is planned so as to have the main rooms on the garden side, while the hall, bathrooms and stairs are at the back. The ground floor is occupied by the daytime rooms, the first floor by the bedrooms, and the small attic by a studio. The garage is placed beneath the living room, an arrangement made possible by the drop in level between the house and the road. The daytime floor is characterised by a fluidity of the spaces, both between one room and the next, and between the interior and the exterior, thanks to the large windows. A covered veranda facing both the dining area and the kitchen is designed as a patio, with one side open to the garden.

With his Erreti house, Tami returned to the sloping roofs he had often used before, but which he had given up after 1957 with his holiday home in Maroggia, and which he would abandon for good after this project. The form of the Erreti house's roof resembles both that of the Park-

theater in Grenchen, a building designed by Ernst Gisel in 1953, which Tami certainly knew, if only from the journal *Werk*, and also the roof of the grammar school of Bellinzona, designed by Alberto Camenzind in 1958. However, while in the latter two cases the geometric aspect predominates in the composition due to the use of materials, which allow a clear separation between the walls and the roof, in the Erreti house the traditional construction of the roof accentuates the contrast with the reinforced concrete walls. The monochrome façades do not present the typical differentiation of materials according to their function that had characterised Tami's previous work with villas, namely stone or plaster for the walls, and wood for the padding. Tami returned to reinforced concrete, which would characterise his subsequent projects, from the Church of the Risen Christ in Lugano (1974) to his motorway work, both a prelude to the widespread use of the material in Switzerland in the 1970s.

RICCARDO BERGOSSI

BIBLIOGRAPHY:

1983 Disch P. (ed.), *50 anni di architettura in Ticino*, Lugano
1984 Carloni T. (ed.), *Rino Tami: 50 anni di architettura*, Lugano
1992 Carrard P., Oechslin W. and Ruchat Roncati F. (eds.), *Rino Tami. Segmenti di una biografia architettonica, exhibition catalogue*, Zurich
1998 Tedeschi L., 'Rino Tami', in *Archivi e Architetture. Presenze nel Cantone Ticino*, Mendrisio, pp. 262–264
2001 Tedeschi L., 'Rino Tami e l'autostrada come opera d'arte', in *Progetto e territorio*, ed. by Galfetti A. and Tedeschi L., Mendrisio, pp. 49–62

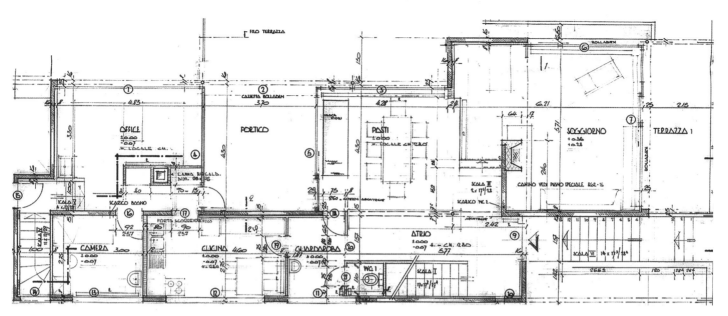

PLAN OF THE GROUND FLOOR

VIEW OF THE DINING AREA

Bruno Taut
1880–1938

1926–27, NEW CONSTRUCTION
WIESENSTRASSE, DAHLEWITZ (D)

MAIN WORKS AND PROJECTS

1911	Office building, Linkstrasse, Berlin-Mitte (D)
1913–15	Garden city, Falkenberg, Berlin-Grünau (D)
1921–23	Urban planning, Magdeburg (D)
1925–28	Residential building Leinestrasse, Berlin-Neukölln (D)
1925–31	Hufeisensiedlung, Berlin-Britz (D))
1926–31	Onkel Toms Hütte residential quarter, Berlin-Zehlendorf (D)

1927–32	Deutscher Verkehrsbund building, Fritz-Heckert-Strasse, Berlin-Mitte (D)
1932	Okura villa, Azabu, Tokyo (Japan)
1936–40	Faculty of Language and History, Ankara (TR)
1937–38	Own house, Istanbul-Ortaköy (TR)
1938	Catafalque for Kermal Atatürk (TR)

BORN ON 4 MAY 1880 in Königsberg, Bruno Taut was the second of the five children of the wealthy merchant Julius Taut (like himself, his brother Max also became an important architect). From his father Bruno inherited a natural bent for mathematics and also an indifference towards money. He studied in Königsberg, where he developed a precocious passion both for social themes, which would lead him at an early age to stand up against all forms of authoritarianism, and for great philosophical problems – he studied his fellow townsman Kant, who was buried in the nearby cathedral.

After graduating in 1902, Taut moved from Königsberg to Berlin, where he worked for and learned from Bruno Möhring. Subsequently (1904–08) he worked for Professor Theodor Fischer in Stuttgart. In 1906 Taut won his first commission, the restoration of a church in the village of Unterriexingen. In 1908 he settled in Berlin, where he began to study art history and town planning at the Technical University in Charlottenburg. It was in Berlin that Taut opened his first professional practice in 1909 (with Franz Hoffmann).

With some important first projects under his belt, including an office building in Berlin-Mitte (1911), Taut felt a growing desire to work 'for the people'. Between 1913 and 1914 he was engaged on the design of the Falkenberg garden city residential quarter in Berlin-Grünau. Later he became a leading figure in the great project for such 'Siedlungen' or social housing developments that were built in Berlin in the 1920s, including Berlin-Britz (1925–31).

However, Taut was not concerned exclusively with residential districts. In 1914 he designed the highly colourful glass pavilion for the Werkbund exhibition in Cologne, and, following his artistic interests, he illustrated 1918–19 his utopia of a harmonious combination between architecture and nature in two great painting cycles, published in *Ein*

Architekturprogramm (1918) and *Alpine Architecture* (1919). Similarly, he published his visions of a city conceived in "the social spirit" in the successful satirical pamphlet *Die Stadtkrone* (1919), and in 1920 designed the stage set for Schiller's play *The Maid of Orléans*, which was staged at the National Theatre in Berlin.

For three years (1921–24) Taut worked as Director of Building in Magdeburg, during which time he chose to have public and private buildings decorated in bright colours. Back in Berlin, he turned his attention again to large-scale housing complexes, designing (1924–31) several such estates with a total of 12,000 apartments in the capital. During the 1920s and early 1930s Taut won the highest recognition both at home and abroad. In 1930 he was, for example, nominated honorary member of Japan's International Order of Architects, and in the same year he was appointed to a chair at the Technical University in Berlin.

However, the contemporary political and historical storm clouds that were gathering now began to impact on the architect's life. In Germany the economic crisis blocked building activity, causing Taut in 1932 to accept an invitation to work in Moscow, where he was attracted by the challenge of the enormous problems of housing in the USSR. Moving to the Soviet capital, he set up the City Council Office for New Building in 1932. But his stay was short-lived, and after just a year he returned to Berlin in 1933. The atmosphere in the communist Soviet Union was too uncongenial for a sceptical enlightened intellectual such as Taut. But in exchanging Moscow for the Berlin of 1933, Taut was jumping out of the frying pan into the fire, and after just two weeks, which he spent in hiding, he was forced traumatically to flee from Germany first to Switzerland and then to Japan in order to escape from the Nazis. Unbeknownst to himself, he was wanted in his homeland as a 'Bolshevik cultural leader'. Japan was a country that had always attracted the architect's interest,

GARDEN VIEW

THE LIVING ROOM

but his spell there proved largely fruitless, although he did create the interior conversion of the Hyuga villa in Atami in 1935.

In 1936, at the age of 56, Taut moved to Ataturk's Turkey, which was experiencing a period of turbulent modernisation. Settling in Istanbul, he was appointed Director of the Institute of Fine Arts and Director of the architectural office of the ministry of education in Ankara. His poor health, which had already worsened in Japan, began to fail him in Turkey, allowing him only two more years of life – he died in Istanbul on 24 December 1938. Nevertheless, during this final period Taut managed to make some sketches for the Opera Theatre in Istanbul, as well as several school buildings, and also a second house for himself in Ortaköy, perched high above the sea. Alluding to the first house he had built for himself in Berlin-Dahlewitz back in 1926–27, Taut said of his Turkish home: "A new Dahlewitz is rising over the dark blue Bosphorus, supported by a re-inforced concrete pillar 15 metres tall, a 900-year-old Noah's dovecote." The building represents a suspended platform with a beautiful view, and is a homage to traditional Turkish architecture. Its rectangular plan with a central corridor ends with a large semi-octagonal living room, opening onto the landscape.

The first home that Bruno Taut designed for himself, a new construction (1926–27) which has been restored by architect Winfried Brenne in 1992–94, lies in Dahlewitz, a suburb of Berlin. The design and construction of the dwelling were an opportunity for Taut to illustrate the research he had carried out up to that time. His thinking is contained in *Ein Wohnhaus*, which he wrote in 1927, and which describes the Dahlewitz building in minute detail. The text contains an analytic account of the develop-

ment of the project, from the choice of form – a quarter circle, which is "at the same time also an expression of a life in society" – to the search for full integration between the domestic space and the physical presence of the people who would occupy it. "The appearance of the rooms without people does not matter; what counts is the appearance of people in the rooms." It is no coincidence that the photos illustrating the text are animated by the presence of members of the architect's family. "It follows that the size of every door, of every window – of everything, in fact – must be in relation to man… Absolutely flat surfaces, which exclude plasticity and reflections, uniformity created by a limited range of colours, rejection of any kind of symmetry, the absolute dominance of the triangle and the square in a plan… all this, hardened in a thesis, does not mean progress in building, but a new condition of tiredness."

The house is a plastered two-floor volume in the unusual shape of a quarter of a cylinder, with the convex side, painted black, towards the entrance. This figure, which Alexander Klein defined scornfully as "a piece of Swiss cheese", and which Taut compared more cheerfully to a slice of cake, reflects the architect's desire to apply the geometry of the circle to a domestic project, searching for a less straightforward dialogue with the surrounding landscape. The building, also likened by Taut to a meridian that measures the sun, seems almost to move "towards the lawn like the prow of a ship", its oblique walls seeking to achieve as much contact as possible with the greenery. Next to the main building, at one end of the large circular wall, Taut placed a single-floor rectangular volume in exposed brick, destined to house the washhouse, pantries, coal depot, boiler room and garage. The most important rooms, the living room on the ground floor and the bedrooms on the upper floor, confirm

STUDY BEDROOM ON THE FIRST FLOOR

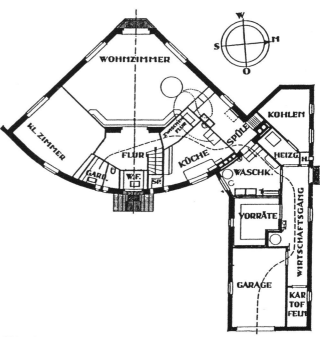

PLAN OF THE GROUND FLOOR

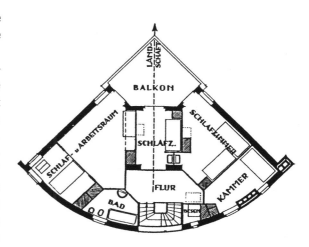

PLAN OF THE FIRST FLOOR

the radial geometry of the plan. The walls, which converge towards the geometric centre of the house, are arranged so as to favour an oblique rather than frontal approach to the interior space.

Taut paid great attention to the functionality of the furniture and fittings and to the use of colours and materials. This may have been in line with the latest experiments – Margarete Schütte-Lihotzsky's 'Frankfurt Kitchen' was from the same period – but was also characterised by a highly personal style, largely independent of the most radical ideologies. On this subject Taut wrote that: "Every dogma must be absorbed by single forms. Ultimately churning out the same old yarn about 'modern' form is just as outdated and retrograde as every stylistic canon of the past." Taut designed the living room area as an elaborate system of spaces. By exploiting the radial geometry of the plan, he linked the dining room niche with the kitchen and with the sink through a large piece of furniture acting as a wall, thus ensuring great versatility of use in a relatively small area, and mediating between continuity of space and privacy. The bedroom-cum-study upstairs was designed with the same approach: "The alcove resulting from the angular form of the plan contains the bed, behind a hand-woven drape with black and white stripes. In the opposite corner a sort of bow window receives light from the door to the balcony…Here there is a work table that forms part of a wardrobe-cum-archive… It is possible to concentrate in one's own space." Not least, the Dahlewitz house exemplifies Taut's keen interest in colour and its use in architecture.

LUCIANO PIROTTI

BIBLIOGRAPHY:
1927   Taut B., *Ein Wohnhaus*, Stuttgart (new edition with an afterword by Roland Jaeger, Berlin, 1955)
1978   Junghanns K., *Bruno Taut 1880–1938*, Milan
1981   Capaccioli L., *Bruno Taut: visione e progetto*, Bari
1990   Salotti G. D. (ed.), *Bruno Taut: la figura e l'opera*, Milan
2001   Cornoldi A., *Le case degli architetti. Dizionario privato dal Rinascimento ad oggi*, Venice, pp. 387–389
       Nerdinger W., Hartmann K., Schirren M., Speidel M., *Bruno Taut: 1880–1938; Architekt zwischen Tradition und Avantgarde*, Stuttgart/Munich

Fernando Távora
1923–2005

1973–76, CONVERSION
GUIMARÃES (P)

MAIN WORKS AND PROJECTS

1958–60	Cedro primary school, Vila Nova de Gaia (P)
	Restaurant and fuel station, Seia (P)
1964–71	Chapel and pavilion of Nun'Alvres Institute, Santo Tirso (P)
1968–73	Apartment block, Oporto (P)
1975	Project for the renovation of block QIII, Barredo district, Oporto (P)
1983	Urban intervention project, Avenida Almeida Ribeiro, Macau (P)

1987–93	Polytechnic Institute of Viana Do Castello, Ponte De Lima (P)
1988–93	Renovation and extension of the Soares Dos Reis National Museum, Oporto (P)
1991–99	Coimbra University, Coimbra (P)
1993–97	Renovation of Plaza 8 De Maio, Coimbra (P)

FERNANDO TÁVORA was born in the Portuguese city of Oporto on 25 August 1923. His father was José Ferrão, who was a member of the Lusitanian fundamentalist movement, the political expression of the Miguelist line. Despite his family's doubts, the young Távora became involved early on with the arts. He became friends with Santos Simões, the future scholar of azulejos, studied art history under Arode Lacerda, took private lessons in watercolour painting with Joaquim Lopes, and discovered the work of the architect Raul Lino, the main exponent of the Casa Portuguesa movement.

Távora's education, which he once described as 'classical', was soon further enriched by a knowledge of contemporary art, including the latest international developments, which was unusual in Portugal at the time. Particularly important in this respect was his relationship with Carlos Ramos, who was both a teacher at the Escola de Belas Artes de Porto or ESBAP (Oporto School of Fine Arts) from 1940 to 1969 and the founder of the National Organisation of Modern Architects (ODAM). Távora enrolled at the ESBAP, graduating in architecture in 1952, and through Ramos began to discover contemporary international architecture, especially Le Corbusier and the Brazilian architecture of Lucio Costa and Oscar Niemeyer. This happened in a climate described by Távora himself as a moment of great intellectual confusion, still dominated by traditional values, but ready to question the moribund, pseudo-authentic 'tradition' of Portuguese architecture supported by the Salazar regime, which culminated in the Universal Exposition of Lisbon in 1940.

Távora's immersion in and burgeoning contribution to both Portuguese and international architecture was precocious. At the age of 21 he began a study of the traditional Portuguese house, intended not as a styl-

istic re-reading or as a confirmation of the eclectic positions expressed by Cassiano Branco in the manifesto-like Portogallo dei Piccoli, but as a recognition of the values of functionality and coherence, in line with the positions of Keil do Amaral or Raul Lino, and more indirectly of Gabriel Pereira, Fialho de Almeida and Dom José. Távora's study led to the publication in 1947 of his celebrated essay *O problema da casa portuguesa* (in *Cadernos de Arquitectura*, no. 1, 1947). In the same year *Cadernos de Arquitectura* also published an article by Keil do Amaral, suggesting the need for a scientific study of the Portuguese architectural tradition. The idea was only turned into reality in 1955, with the survey *Inquerito da arquitectura popular portuguesa*. Led by Amaral himself, the survey was extremely varied in terms of methodology and ideology. Távora's role in the project, which had the direct backing of Salazar, was as the director of the group responsible for the Minho region. For Távora, the research into Portuguese tradition merged with his continuing experience of international architecture and with highly original experiments, giving rise to what he defined as the 'third way' – an architecture that transcended both local tradition and internationalist abstraction and formalism.

From 1951 up to the Otterlo meeting, Távora took part as Portugal's representative in the meetings of the CIAM, during which he discovered affinities outside his own country: the Le Corbusier of Chandigar, undoubtedly different from the Le Corbusier he had discovered through Ramos and Viana de Lima, the research into the Catalan house of Coderch, Rogers' Velasca Tower, the architecture of Gardella, the writings of Zevi, and TEAM X.

Another important stage in Távora's development was the long study trip he undertook in 1960 thanks to grants from the Calouste

THE INNER GARDEN

VIEW TOWARDS THE ENTRANCE FROM THE SOUTH TERRACE

THE MAIN LIVING ROOM AT THE GROUND FLOOR

Gulbenkian Foundation and from the Portuguese Institute for Culture. The scholarships enabled him to visit Japan and the United States, where he had an opportunity to experience the works of architects such as Frank Lloyd Wright and Louis Kahn.

Over the years Távora was involved in many other projects, areas and positions. In 1950, with other exponents of the ODAM, the architect was invited by Ramos to teach at the ESPAB, the school where he had graduated two years earlier with the project Casa sobre o Mar. This was to be the beginning of a long career as a teacher, first at the ESBAP and then in the School of Architecture of the University of Oporto, where he was chairman of the Founding Committee and later emeritus professor. Távora was also a guest professor in the School of Architecture at the University of Coimbra, which awarded him an honorary doctorate. He was architect for the Oporto city council, a consultant to Gaia town council, a consultant in the Technical Bureau of the Portuguese Northern Planning Commission, a consultant for the Ribeira/Barredo urban renovation project, and a member of the EU Advisory Committee for architectural training. Távora participated in the Survey on Portuguese Architecture and exhibited at the São Paulo Biennial. He was a member of the CIAM, took part in the first UNESCO International Conference of Artists in Venice, and was awarded First Prize for architecture by the Gulbenkian Foundation. He also won the Europa Nostra Prize, the Gold Medal of the city of Oporto, the Tourism and Heritage Award (1985), and the National Award for Architecture (1987).

An overview of Távora's development as an architect shows him early on abandoning the use of perspective, which is limited almost ex-clusively to his earliest, most scholastic projects, where he experimented with the forms of the modern movement. His architectural research developed by drawing plan and section, or rather by imagining the plan of a space and gradually making it more complex. He did this through a process of gemmation, after a careful analysis of the possible movements within the space, designed according to considerations relating to time, place, and experience. The space becomes increasingly complex and changes its identity as the project proceeds, controlled by means of the section and constantly assessed, thanks to the simultaneous presence of different scales of representation on the same sheet, also in terms of the overall construction and of details. There was no desire to describe and plan the architecture in a single design. Many aspects of the project were entrusted to other means, such as oral accounts, or above all left in latent form as they await a voice and a body at the moment of realisation and also subsequently, during the life of the building.

This also explains the difficulty of representing the salient qualities of Távora's architecture *a posteriori*, through photography. His work was a radical departure from the formal attractions of Modernism, the abandonment not only of a linguistic repertoire but also of a method of work based on prefiguration, which peaks in several buildings constructed or restored without any pre-drawn plans, with every decision made as work was in progress. The restoration of the Casa da Covilhã, for which there is only one drawing, is a fine example of his method.

Describing his relationship with the Casa da Covilhã Guimarães, which Fernando Távora converted for his own use mainly between 1973 and

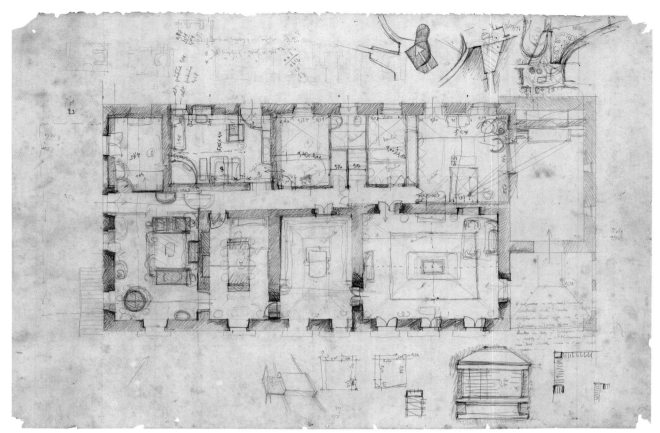

PLAN

1976, the architect wrote romantically: "We had known each other a long time. I knew something about her soul and her body. I knew that she had been begun by João, a schoolmaster and ambassador who died of nostalgia and sadness, had been enriched by Francisca from Baia, and had been ennobled by the descendent of Bernardo, the Secretary of the Infante who did not manage to die at Alcácer. She was born again thanks to the money that Luis Antonio had brought from S. João de Rei, was re-awoken by the ire of the other Antonio, the Miguelist canon who would be defeated, was conserved by the austere Adelino, and was much loved by José. I knew her to be strong and safe in her thick granite walls and with her chestnut structures, but I discovered scars, the fruit of successive growths or of wrongs inflicted by time which, like her, I am unable to forgive. … We had known each other for a long time, but we only began to understand each other better when we set off, together, on the romance of her – or our – transformation. I had to touch her, and touching her was an act of love, long and slow, insistent and cautious, guided by doubts and certainties."

According to legend and some documents, the house dates back to the 16th century. A clear origination identifies the main building with 1642. Until the 18th century the Casa da Covilhã enjoyed a certain notoriety, after which it fell into decline until Távora gained ownership of it, renovating and improving the whole property.

The house is entered by a 150-m-long walkway, which leads through an 18th-century gate, emblazoned with the coats of arms of four families, to a yard. Here a few steps bring the visitor up to a porch, which leads on the right to an 18th-century chapel and also an entrance hall.

Originally the house covered two floors, with one partially underground and opening to the south, and the other opening on all sides. A third floor, with several bedrooms, was added later. The house abuts not only the yard but also gardens, one of which has a swimming pool, another of which provisions the kitchen, and the third of which contains camellias.

Távora's renovation, starting in 1973, brought radical changes, although he preserved the existing spatial arrangement. The ground floor of the three-storey house comprises a storage area and a room. The first floor has a large reception room, a library, a dining room, a large sitting room, which leads to the gardens, the kitchen, and the master bedroom, which overlooks the main altar of the chapel. From this floor a 19th-century staircase leads to the second floor, which has three more bedrooms.

The renovation, including additional restoration of furnishings and of the chapel, was completed in 1980, but further alterations for the purposes of conservation have continued subsequently. The gardens, designed by the owner, would need time in order to become established. The property also includes a farm, which belongs to a group of four farms, traversed by the River Selho and its mills, and covering an area totalling some 100,000 acres.

ANTONIO ESPOSITO, GIOVANNI LEONI

BIBLIOGRAPHY:
1988 *Arquitectura Popular em Portugal*, Associação dos Arquitectos Portugueses, Lisbon
       Fernandez S., *O Percurso de Arquitectura Portuguesa 1930–1974*, Oporto
1991 Borella G., *Guida di architettura – La scuola di Porto*, Milan
       Portas N. and Mendes M., *Portogallo in Architettura, gli ultimi vent'anni*, Milan
1993 Távora F. and Costa A., *Fernando Távora*, Oporto

Leslie Grahame Thomson
1896–1974

1934–35, NEW CONSTRUCTION
THE LOAN, WEST LINTON (GB)

MAIN WORKS AND PROJECTS

1929–33	Reid Memorial Church, Edinburgh (GB)		1953	Longstone Church, Edinburgh (GB)
1932	Ardnasaid, 6 Easter Belmont Road, Edinburgh (GB)		1954	Moncur Memorial Church, Orkney (GB)
1936–42	National Bank of Scotland head office, Edinburgh (GB), with Mewes & Davis of London		1954–57	Christ's Church, Oban (GB)
1937	Fairmilehead Church, Edinburgh (GB)		1968	Housing development, Ganavan, Oban (GB)
1938–40	Caledonian Insurance company offices, Edinburgh (GB)			

SON OF PATRICK William Thomson, the founder of a successful merchandising business in Edinburgh, Leslie Grahame Thomson came from a wealthy family. He was educated at Edinburgh's fee-paying Merchiston Castle School, where his future career was confirmed when as a schoolboy he saw his father commission a new house in 1905. His schooling was terminated by the outbreak of the First World War, during which he served in the Middle East with the Egyptian Expeditionary Forces.

Thomson started his architectural training in 1920 at Edinburgh College of Art, from which he graduated in 1925 as the first to complete – along with another student – the full Royal Institute of British Architects (RIBA) 'Recognised' Diploma course awarded by the College. During his studies he served an apprenticeship with Sir Robert Lorimer in 1921, and the experience he gained at this office proved to be the greatest influence on his work throughout his career. Thomson commenced private practice in 1926, and worked independently throughout his career except during 1936–39, when he went into partnership with Frank J. Connell.

In 1933 Leslie Grahame Thomson married Barbara Mary Henderson, designing a year later, in 1934, Srongarbh as their marital home. It was, however, an unhappy marriage, and they divorced in 1943. In 1948 he remarried Coline Helen Elizabeth MacDougall, daughter of Colonel A. J. MacDougall of MacDougall, at one time one of the most powerful clans in Scotland. When Coline MacDougall's father died, she herself became clan chief. In recognition of this, Thomson assumed the name of MacDougall in 1953, now calling himself Leslie Grahame MacDougall. Thomson had no children from either marriage. He died in 1974 after a long illness and is buried at the family burial ground near Oban, next to his second wife.

As a young architect, when many of his contemporaries were seeking work in England, Thomson chose to stay in Edinburgh. A true Scots architect, he worked almost exclusively in Scotland. He had the same office throughout almost all of his career at 6 Ainslie Place, Edinburgh, and a second office at 2 Shore Street, Oban, in the mid-1950s. Most of Thomson's buildings are found in the city of Edinburgh itself as well as in the Lothian and Argyll regions. He did, however, enter architectural competitions abroad, including the one for Sydney Opera House in Australia. Thomson, who was a fluent French speaker, travelled extensively throughout his life, visiting much of Europe, including Scandinavia, as well as Japan and Hong Kong. Whilst residing at Barcaldine Castle, Oban, he and his second wife played host to clan members from abroad, and often travelled to clan conventions around the world.

Described by Mark Glendinning as the "polemical weathervane of traditionalist opinion", Thomson was one of the leading 20th-century architects of the traditionalist movement. The traditionalists were concerned with the concepts of national identity and with continuing the development of Scottish stone or harled buildings, and like them Thomson was a great advocate of the use of local materials. In 1932 he stated that "nothing could be better than the true Scots tradition – I do not mean tripe à la Bruce … but that same line of work refounded and continually practised by the late Sir Robert Lorimer". Thomson's reputation as a traditionalist was further enhanced by his Highland dress. He always wore a kilt, an attire that apparently well suited his six-foot figure.

Thomson had an extensive knowledge of Scottish architectural history, with a specialist interest in church symbolism. In 1953 he represented the Royal Incorporation of Architects in Scotland (RIAS) at the National Trust for Scotland, using his role to raise awareness of the need to preserve Scotland's heritage. He was also Joint Honorary Secretary with Sir Frank Mears of the Association for the Preservation of Rural Scotland in 1932. He exhibited regularly at the Royal Scottish Academy, becoming an Associate in 1937.

GARDEN VIEW FROM THE SOUTH-WEST

VIEW FROM THE SOUTH-EAST

THE LOUNGE

During his career, Thomson designed several churches, insurance offices and hotels, but the majority of his commissions were single private houses. During the 1930s, he designed and built twelve houses of varying sizes, at a time when, in Scotland, very few houses in the private sector were being constructed. In Scotland during the 1950s and 60s, Thomson was probably the most active traditionalist architect in the country house field.

In keeping with his traditionalism, Thomson sought to construct buildings that were 'recognisably Scottish' and rooted in tradition. In 1955 he wrote: "We think with pride of the men who built Melrose Abbey and Glasgow Cathedral … Heriot's Hospital and Drumlanrig … none of which could be anything else but Scots. Let us, therefore, remember our

tradition of original design and fine building, and go forward into the new age with … a will to produce an architecture worthy of our past and second to that of no other nation in the world today." Many of his smaller houses show a debt to Sir Robert Lorimer's 'Colinton-style' cottages, with shaped gables, low-slung roofs and white walls.

Thomson's private house Srongarbh, The Loan, West Linton, was built as his first marital home, after he married Barbara Mary Henderson in 1933. Above the front door, a plaque depicts his own coat of arms and a carved monogram of his and his wife's initials, 'LGT' and 'BMH.' Srongarbh was designed to be a grand house with an impressive sweeping entrance, yet it is relatively small in size. For a house of modest proportions, the inter-

PLAN OF THE GROUND FLOOR

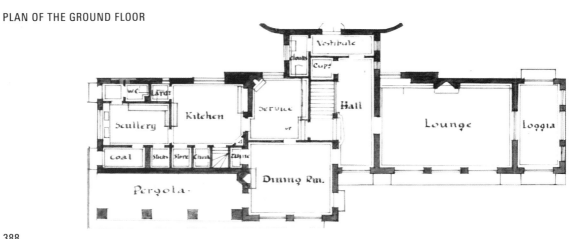

THE MOVEABLE BOOKCASE

THE ENTRANCE HALL WITH MAIN STAIRCASE

ior planning is rather ostentatious. There is a clear divide between the servants' quarters to the north-west, and the family apartments to the south-east. The handles on the doors that separate the family from the servants are of a better quality on the family side. In addition, the letter-box is situated in the back door, accessed only by the servants.

Srongarbh was designed with no specific office or workplace. When Thomson occupied it, he continued to travel daily to his practice at 6 Ainslie Place, Edinburgh. The house was, therefore, essentially for living and entertaining in, with the garden an integral part of the scheme. The extensive terraced gardens, with the 11-foot-deep swimming pool, are accessed directly from the lounge and dining room through the large arched and glazed doorways. Thomson designed the house to be both impressive to visitors and convenient as a family home. However, he only lived in the house for the length of his first marriage and sold the property in April 1944.

With its steel-frame construction, Srongarbh utilises the finest materials and workmanship. The walls are harled white, and the roof is finished with large stone slates. The two-storey house is well positioned within its site, with picturesque views of the Pentland Hills. The gardens to the south-west are bound by a retaining wall, behind which the land drops steeply to the dramatic Lyne Water valley. The narrow plan of Srongarbh has a horizontal aspect. This horizontality is emphasised by the band of windows running almost unbroken the length of the façade on the first floor, the low-slung roof, the balconies at each extremity, and the

projecting side wall. Thomson was obsessed with symmetry in his treatment of the elevations. Two of the windows are positioned to provide this symmetry, without serving an internal function. One window on the first floor lights only a cupboard. In the lounge, where a bookcase lies behind one window, the bookcase is hinged to swing into the room and reveal the window. In addition, there are two balconies at either end of the house, yet one – in the servants' quarters – is completely inaccessible. They are positioned simply to balance the composition of the elevation.

The entrance hall has an air of grandeur, with its double-height space and curving staircase. Similarly, the lounge is a step down from the hall, facilitating a greater ceiling height. Beautifully detailed, the interior features oak flooring, carved skirtings and underfloor heating, while the exterior boasts intricate wrought iron at the entrance railings and on the windows. Particularly in its prominent chimney breasts, Srongarbh has several characteristics of a Scottish Arts and Crafts house, although with its pergola, loggia, balconies and swimming pool it also demonstrates evidence of a Mediterranean influence.　　KIRSTEEN WILKINSON

BIBLIOGRAPHY:
1929　Thomson L. G., 'The Late Sir Robert Lorimer and His Work', in *Quarterly of RIAS*, no. 31, pp. 63–76
1932　Thomson L. G., 'Concerning This Heritage', in *Quarterly of RIAS*, no. 38, pp. 42–46
1955　MacDougall L. G., 'Centurial Message', in *Quarterly of RIAS*, February, no. 99, p. 4
1996　Glendinning M. et al, A *History of Scottish Architecture*, Edinburgh
2001　Wilkinson K., *The Life and Work of Leslie Grahame MacDougall* (1896–1974), M.Sc. dissertation, Robert Gordon University

Oswald Mathias Ungers
1926–2007

1958, NEW CONSTRUCTION, EXTENDED AND ALTERED 1989
BELVEDERESTRASSE 60, COLOGNE (D)

MAIN WORKS AND PROJECTS

1953–58	Institut zur Erlangung der Hochschulreife (Institute for Admission to Higher Education), Oberhausen (D)
1979–84	Museum of German Architecture, Frankfurt am Main (D)
1980–83	Trade Fair Pavilion 9 and Galeria, Frankfurt am Main (D)
1986–96	Kunsthalle Hamburg, Hamburg (D)
1987–95	German Embassy, Washington (USA)
1988–94	Family court, Berlin (D)
1990–99	Exhibition centre and pavilions, Berlin (D)
1991–95	Friedrichstadtpassagen (Friedrichstadt Arcade), Berlin (D)
1996–99	Wallraf-Richartz-Museum, Cologne (D)

OSWALD MATHIAS UNGERS was born in 1926 in Kaisers-esch in the Eifel region of Germany, and between 1932 and 1947 attended school in Mayen. In the latter year he enrolled in the Institute of Technology in Karlsruhe, where he studied architecture under Egon Eiermann, graduating in 1950. In the same year he opened in Cologne a practice of his own, which he still directs today. In 1956 he married Liselotte Ungers, with whom he had three children. The house presented here has been the long-standing refuge and first home of the Ungers family.

When Ungers embarked on his architectural career in the twilight of the German post-war era, the prevailing mass housing was character-ised by a grid-designed and monofunctional pragmatism devoid of any architectural content or pretensions. He immediately created a number of meticulously planned buildings evidencing his architectural ideas and concepts. Here was an architect who refused to think in predetermined categories, and who was and still is a questing intellectual.

Ungers designed considered buildings that were spatially and tech-nically precise, and which embodied the most useful and durable motifs and concepts of Modernism, at the same time transforming them. He created both expressive brick textures and sleek white membranes with sharply incised window openings reminiscent of 1920s architecture. He experimented with the basic elements of architecture, with elements that are typically its own: with plinth, cornice and jamb, with heaviness and lightness, with open and closed spaces, with the principle of similarity and difference, and ever and again with the wall as a membrane between inside and outside, i.e. with the wall as a surface for regulating architec-tonic meaning and appearance. But it was not the motifs resulting from the use of the elements as such that interested Ungers, but – and this is what has constituted the dynamite of his thinking up to the present day – the 'ideas on architecture' underpinning these images, whose results they function as, so to speak as architectonic codings of social-cultural and intellectual effect. Ever since, Ungers researched this 'thematisa-tion of architecture', to use a title that he gave to a book about his work in 1983.

In this sense Ungers' first years of architectural practice were a second course of study with experimental arrangements under emer-gency conditions, marked by a search for an idea of architecture beyond construction as fulfilment of duty or the serving of a purpose. Ungers wanted more than others. He wanted to create not just a physical corpus of works, but also an intellectual oeuvre reflected in the built works. His studio was a laboratory for these processes, his drawing board as it were a test tube above the intellectual flame, in which the fund of ideas of architectural history was mixed anew. Structural volumes, physiogno-mies of façades, floor plan configurations and textures were in each case the results of coolly calculated and rationally answered questions. They were conclusions, manifesto-like concisions in urban space. But in reach-ing these conclusions, Ungers took into account the immediate context and the materials as well as motifs found there, just as he pondered how he could make more out of them than banal houses, coaxing out of them so to speak aesthetic-conceptual value added, with which to ennoble the locality.

This thinking runs through the entire creative oeuvre of the architect. Above all it was also Ungers' credo when he began his activity as a univer-sity lecturer, teaching for example as a professor from 1963 at the Univer-sity of Technology (TU) in Berlin and from 1969 in New York at Cornell Uni-versity. The theoretical studies and teaching concepts that he continued here, his contacts and lectures as well as his involvement in competitions paved the way for an international reputation, which after his return to Germany in the mid-1970s rapidly translated into a string of large-scale commissions. Without doubt Ungers was – seen also from an international perspective – the most important German architect of his time.

STREET VIEW

THE LIBRARY EXTENSION OR CUBE

PAGES 392–393: THE LIBRARY

Oswald Mathias Ungers' own house-cum-studio at Belvederestrasse 60 in Cologne-Müngersdorf was built new by the architect in 1958. It played a special part both in Ungers' biography and in the history of German architecture. For almost half a century it served its owner as a monk's hermitage, a thought factory, and as a treasure store for his book collection. But above all it is an architectonic manifesto that has so far withstood all changes in taste and in social custom. Built in the first instance as a home for Ungers and his family, with a separate flat to "pay off the mortgage" and a small office section on the ground floor, the house marks a turning point both in construction and in German architecture.

Where the architect was his own client, he naturally had an ideal opportunity to realise a building into which he could infuse the sum of his experiences and insights. And that is the case with the studio-house presented here. As Ungers wrote, "The house is living space, a laboratory, a world view and a test case all at the same time… It is a reflection of an idea of the world, of life, of existence. It is an existential world piece." A world piece and piece of work on the one hand, and a piece or play in the sense of a theatrical performance on the other, for it is at the same time a theatrical piece and stage for the actors appearing here. Architects, children, clients, dogs, cats and employees have been going in and out of the house for years, and testing so to speak the emergency – usage. They are all part of this trial arrangement, of the experiment of architecture.

Located at the end of a conventional terraced housing development in a suburb of Cologne, the house appears as a sculptural figure composed of positively and negatively formed spatial volumes. It is a monolith modulated in a relief-like way, and characterised by a tough but – and this is no contradiction – on the inside elastic structure. The classic question of the façade is radically addressed, and interpreted as the result of a spatial principle operating in the interior of the building. Here Ungers created a labyrinth which makes the basically small house large, expanding it. Room sequences, wide, narrow, open and closed spatial compartments alternate, stairways interpenetrate the building at nodal points, and visual relations between the individual spatial sections nullify the time-honoured sequence of individual rooms.

The result is remarkable. A continuum of spatial elements arises, which projects onto the exterior skin, becoming visible here in negative and positive imprints. Built of fired bricks and concrete, the house is characterised by their materiality and surface structure. It is interesting to note just how elastic even these materials can basically be when they find the hands of a master who knows how to shape them intelligently. They lay their surfaces around the spaces almost supply and sleekly, simultaneously demarcating the limits of these spaces. The window openings meanwhile follow no conventional composition, but correspond to the internal spatial structuring and the necessity prevailing there, whereby lighting considerations and views are decisive.

The English architectural critic Reyner Banham, who recognised immediately that Ungers' house was something special, described it in detail in his book *The New Brutalism*. Nothing comparable – not with regard to quality, but in terms of the radicality underlying this programmatic idea of architecture – was built in Germany at the time, because nobody thought as radically as Ungers. This radicality was continued in 1989, when Ungers extended his labyrinthine residence-cum-

LIVING ROOM

LIBRARY

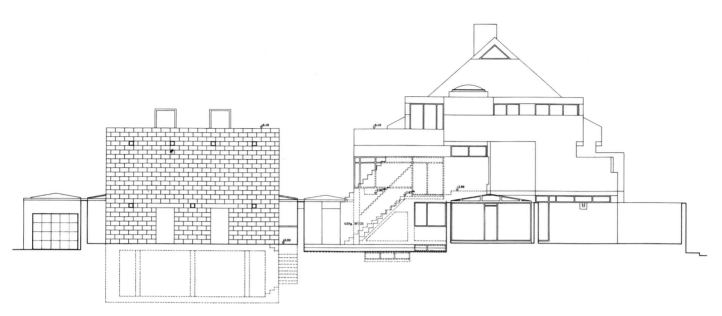

CROSS-SECTION OF THE HOUSE AND LIBRARY EXTENSION

GROUND PLAN WITH LIBRARY EXTENSION

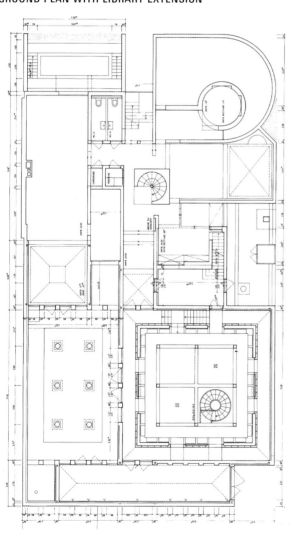

research laboratory, at the same time renovating, altering and consolidating it. The original floor plan was replaced by the extended structure of a more complex spatial configuration supplemented by a black stone cube which, in the eyes of the architect, "looks like a mini town of squares, courtyards, side streets and cubes". The black cube housed Ungers' unique private library of books on architectural history and on the theory of architecture, mostly rare first editions. And in structural-spatial terms, as the architect said, it is "a white ideal framework measuring 6 x 6 x 6 metres, a fundamental element of architecture, cube and framework, block and struts, ark and chest, cave and tent, the two basic modules united in one concept. A little pantheon." Given this stance, it is not difficult to imagine the lasting and powerful response that such an oeuvre and way of thinking triggered for 40 years. Needless to say, such a keenly intellectual position and such an intensification of questions about contemporary architecture drew critics to Ungers' plan — but also a considerable cohort of followers and admirors. The latter see in his project an avenue that takes the debate about architecture beyond what we call taste, about which — as is well known — there is no argument. Along this avenue Ungers' house in Cologne's Belvedere-strasse marks an important direction, a direction which is well worth following.

MARTIN KIEREN

BIBLIOGRAPHY:

1960   Rossi A., 'Un giovane architetto tedesco: Oswald Mathias Ungers', in *Casabella*, no. 244, pp. 22–35

Ungers O. M., 'The Architect's Own House, Cologne-Müngersdorf', in *Architectural Design*, no. 11, pp. 455–457

1966   Banham R., *The New Brutalism – Ethic or Aesthetic?*, New York, pp. 125, 144

1991   Ungers O. M., *Architektur 1951–1990*, Stuttgart, pp. 38–41

Kieren M., *Oswald Mathias Ungers*, Zurich, pp. 54–57, 200–203

1999   Ungers O. M., *Aphorismen zum Häuserbauen*, Wiesbaden / Cologne, pp. 5–27

Jørn Oberg Utzon
1918 – 2008

1971, NEW CONSTRUCTION
PORTO PETRO, MAJORCA (E)

MAIN WORKS AND PROJECTS

1956–60	Kingohusene, house, Helsingør (DK)
1956–66	Sydney Opera House, Australia
1959	Melhi Bank, Teheran, Iran
1960	Project for Silkeborg Museum of Art (DK)
1967	Project for a stadium in Jeddah, Saudi Arabia
1973–82	Houses of Parliament, Kuwait

1974–76	Bagsværd Church, Bagsværd (DK)
1979	Project for a swimming pool in Copenhagen (DK), with his son Jan Utzon
1992	Own house Can Feliz, Majorca (E)

JØRN OBERG UTZON was born in Copenhagen, the son of the naval architect Aage Oberg Utzon and Estrid Maren Valeska Halina Olsen. He grew up in Ålborg, in the northern part of Jutland, in a family whose members and friends included many artists. As a child, Utzon sailed in the area around Ålborg and often visited the workshops of the local shipyard, admiring the detailed work of the boatbuilders. He went to secondary school at Ålborg Katedralskole and, shortly after completing his studies there in 1937, enrolled in the School of Architecture of the Royal Danish Academy of Fine Arts in Copenhagen, from which he graduated in 1942. As a student he quickly showed a talent and special feeling for the specific qualities of each kind of building material.

During the Second World War, Utzon left Denmark, as did many architects of the period, for Sweden, staying in Stockholm from 1942 to 1945, after which he went to Finland in 1945, to Morocco in 1948, to the USA and Mexico in 1949, and to China, Japan and India in 1957. In that same year, Utzon also visited Australia, to which he was to return frequently and for long periods during the following nine years.

During his stay in Stockholm Utzon worked for Hakon Ahlberg, while in 1945, when he was in Finland, he was employed by Alvar Aalto. Later that year, when he was back in Denmark, he established his own architectural practice, in the same year winning a Gold Medal for a project for a crematorium. In 1973 he was a visiting professor at the University of Honolulu, Hawaii. Over the years Utzon won a number of prizes and medals from both Danish and foreign institutions as well as in competitions. In 1980 he was awarded a grant for life by the Danish Arts Foundation. Utzon published numerous articles on architecture, as well as a volume on the design of his world-famous Sydney Opera House.

During his wartime stay in Sweden, when he was working for Hakon Ahlberg in Stockholm, Utzon began to admire the ideas and architecture of Gunnar Asplund, who was an important figure for many

Danish architects, especially because of Swede's view that all details should be subordinated to a superior idea. This early Swedish inspiration was later carried over into Utzon's oeuvre. Other influences on his architecture were also the result of his travels. In America he was able to study at first hand the buildings of Frank Lloyd Wright, while in Morocco the houses had an impact on him, and in Mexico the pyramids. The Chinese sense of harmony obtained through contrasting elements, and the Japanese interaction of outdoor and indoor likewise left their mark on Utzon's architecture. However, his work was not so much directly inspired by these sources; rather, it metamorphoses their ideas. Utzon always succeeded in giving foreign impressions a unique, individual, and very visionary touch.

Utzon's legendary Sydney Opera House, which has become the landmark for a whole continent, is a classic example of this visionary aspect of his architecture. It was also the work that brought him an international reputation, and it is much to be regretted that Utzon never had a chance to finish the interiors of the Opera House. The visionary aspect of his architecture may also explain the modest number of projects actually realised by Utzon, another cause for regret. The individualistic side of his architecture, where local traditions and materials are combined with a personal idea, can be seen in the two houses that he built on the Spanish island of Majorca, one of them Can Lis, both being typical of his design style.

In Utzon's thinking, place and the human being were key elements. Place is to be understood as a geographical point together with the vegetation, light and atmosphere there, while human beings are the people who live at the geographical point or place. He believed that our human identity depends on the identity of the place in which we live. Utzon's own house Can Lis, constructed 1971 on Majorca, can be seen as an interpretation

VIEW OF THE LIVING ROOM

VIEW OF THE SQUARE TERRACE

THE LARGE TERRACE SURROUNDED BY LODGING

PAGES 398–399: THE SOUTH-EAST FAÇADE

THE LIVING AREA

of these thoughts. On the island, he studied the local architecture, the mode of building, the materials used, and the light, interpreting everything in his own personal way. The result was so astonishing that a colleague from Majorca gave Utzon a book on local architecture, dedicating it to him with the words: "To Jørn Utzon, who showed us our own local stone. Thank you."

Utzon's family described the feeling of living in the house as similar to living on a boat or in a friendly fortress, due to the many walls separating the courtyards from surrounding nature. Can Lis is situated on a natural stony terrace, overlooking the Mediterranean. Seen from the road, it looks very modest, like a wall with only one opening. On opening the front door, the visitor sees through the entrance a tiled lunar motif, which alludes to the name of the street: Cala media luna.

Actually, Can Lis is not one house but four individual homes, including a separate guest house, which are linked by walls and courtyards. Even though the buildings all face the sea, they are individually oriented, creating an overall rhythm that is closer to organic nature than to mathematics.

The building material is a local stone from the island, a special kind of pinkish-yellow sandstone, which changes colour depending on the

light. This has been cut to form building blocks measuring either 40 x 40 cm or 40 x 20 cm, while the columns are 40 x 40 cm wide.

The rooms are built with high ceilings made of white, closely spaced concrete beams with slight barrel vaults between them. The roofing is made of yellow tile, and the stepped end walls are shaped according to a Chinese system, which Utzon also used in his houses in Fredensborg. The chimneys are inspired by a local tradition. The walls are constructed by placing local stone on top of two concrete beams, while the roofing is constructed by inserting a shallow terracotta vault between two concrete beams. On top of this is a slab and then mission tiles.

The reflection of the light from the Mediterranean is extremely strong and would normally be unbearable to the eye if allowed to penetrate the house too freely. Utzon solved the problem by creating several zones between the darkness inside and the light outside. These zones were constructed by means of both columns and wall fragments, which are short and in places even oblique. The window frames are mounted on the outside surface of the walls in order to be invisible from within the house, and to avoid dark shadows on the inside. As a central idea of the buildings, Utzon emphasised the interplay between light and shadow, inside and outside, combined with the extraordinary coloured glazed

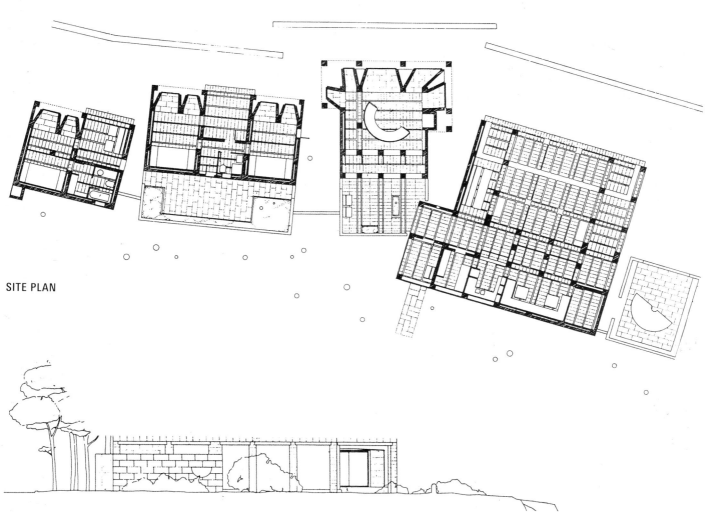

SITE PLAN

ELEVATION

COLUMNED PASSAGE

tiles, which are used both in the furniture and as decoration. The tiles of the table in the courtyard point to the north, and the walls surrounding the courtyard leave views open to watch the sunset and the sea. Whatever the weather, there is always a room or a courtyard at Can Lis in which to seek shelter or to enjoy the warmth of the sun. The buildings' diversity of rooms is interspersed with sunny patios and shady courtyards, meaning that overall the mini complex is carefully adaped to the specific place, climate and light.

KIRA PEDERSEN

BIBLIOGRAPHY:

1982   Inyesta N. G., 'Jørn Utzon's house', in *Quaderns*, Sep. no. 153, pp. 23–29
1989   Moller H. S., 'Can Lis: Jørn Utzon's own house', in *Living Architecture,* no. 8, pp. 146–173
1996   Norberg-Schulz C., 'Jørn Utzon's houses on Mallorca', in *Arkitektur DK*, vol. 40, no. 2, pp. 73–115.
2000   Fromonot F., *Jørn Utzon: architect of the Sydney Opera House*, Milan
2001   Cornoldi A., *Le case degli architetti. Dizionario privato dal Rinascimento ad oggi*, Venice, pp. 400–402

Nicos Valsamakis
*1924

1960–63, NEW CONSTRUCTION, STILL INHABITED BY THE ARCHITECT
NIOVIS 22, PHILOTHEI, ATHENS (GR)

MAIN WORKS AND PROJECTS

1957–58 Apartment block, odos Semitelou, Athens (GR)
1961–63 Summer houses in Anavyssos, Attica (GR)
1963–65 Amalia Hotel, Delphi (GR)
1977–79 Amalia Hotel, Olympia (GR)
1981–90 Alpha Bank head office, Athens (GR)
1988–91 Daedalos tourist complex, Kos (GR)

1990–97 Commercial Bank of Greece data-processing centre,
         Holargos, Athens (GR)
1993–95 Athens College, primary school Attica (GR)
1994–95 House in Vouliagmeni (GR)

NICOS VALSAMAKIS was born in Athens on 17 July 1924, the son of Andreas Valsamakis, who came from a shipping family on the island of Cephalonia, and Penelope Lazarides. He grew up in the centre of Athens, and as a youngster loved to draw. In 1945 he enrolled in the School of Architecture at Metsovio Polytechnic in Athens, but had to interrupt his studies in 1947, when he was called up to fight in the Greek Civil War, during which he served on the front line in Macedonia as a wireless operator. While he was a soldier, Valsamakis carried with him a book on Le Corbusier's architecture and tried to keep up with his studies. In 1949 he was awarded a medal for bravery in the conflict, which essentially ended in the same year with the defeat of the insurgent communist forces. After the Civil War he was able to resume his studies in 1950.

In 1953 Valsamakis opened his own architectural office in the centre of Athens, out of which he has practised right up to the present day. An early project of his was an apartment block in odos Semitelou (1957–58), which had a significant impact on the prevailing architectural style in Athens. Other commissions followed, including summer houses, hotels and a head office for a bank, and between 1960 and 1963 he designed and built a highly innovative house for himself at Philothei, near Athens. In 1961 he was elected Vice-President of the Greek Architectural Association, and a year later he became President of the architectural department of the Greek Chamber of Technology. Following the end of his first marriage to Martha Deligiannis, Valsamakis married in 1965 his second wife, the architect Maria Serdaris, with whom he still lives, sharing with her a common interest in architecture.

In 1977 Valsamakis became a member of the Greek Architectural Society, and in 1991 he was awarded an honorary doctorate by the Aristotelian University of Salonica (Thessaloniki). Between 1988 and 1991 the architect designed and constructed for the Robinson Club his much-acclaimed Daedalos tourist complex on Cos (a Greek island in the Aegean

Sea), which in 1992 was shortlisted for the Mies van der Rohe Pavilion Award for European Architecture. In 1994 Valsamakis' public buildings were presented at the Fifth Venice Architectural Biennale, while in June 1997 the architect was represented at Belgrade's Fifth Architecture Triennial, entitled *Revival of Light: Twelve Leading Architects from Twelve Countries*. In 1995 Valsamakis was a founding member of the Greek Institute of Architecture, and in March 1999 he was awarded a Distinction in Letters and Arts by the Greek Academy for his architectural work. In February 1999 his work was included in an exhibition of 1960s and 1990s Greek architecture entitled *Landscapes of Modernization*, which was held at the Netherlands Institute of Architecture (NAI) in Rotterdam, and in June of the same year the architect was represented in the exhibition *20th-Century Greek Architecture*, mounted at the Deutsches Architekturmuseum in Frankfurt in association with the Hellenic Institute of Architecture. Valsamakis was awarded an honorary doctorate by the School of Architecture of Athens' Metsovio Polytechnic in October 2001.

During his career Nicos Valsamakis has lectured in Greece and also England, where he has exhibited a number of projects at the Architectural Association in London. He has been chosen to serve on juries in a number of architectural competitions, and much of his work has been featured in both the Greek and international architectural literature. He has always been interested in architectural photography, and either himself takes or personally organises the photos for all his works.

Valsamakis leads a quiet life. Having no children, he can devote almost all his time to his architecture. His practice is just a small office and only undertakes as much work as he can personally handle, enabling him to look after every planning detail himself. Valsamakis keenly follows all major architectural projects and events around the world, and from his early years has travelled frequently to many countries to study their architecture.

NIGHT VIEW FROM THE GARDEN

VIEW OF THE STRUCTURE

PAGES 404–405: VIEW FROM THE ENTRANCE TOWARDS THE GARDEN

VIEW TOWARDS THE LIVING ROOM

Nicos Valsamakis' own home is a new construction, designed and built at Niovis 22, Philothei (near Athens), between 1960 and 1963, at a time when there was no modern architecture in Greece. The architect decided to build the house as an experiment in contemporary design and techniques, applying the theory and ideas of the modern movement, and implementing a 'total design' which was expressed throughout the house, including the furniture. The dominant notion was to be continuity of space both internally and externally, achieved using a free plan executed with clarity of planning, detailing and elevation. The absence of a client other than himself presented Valsamakis with a unique opportun-

ity to translate his design principles down to the minutest detail. Prior to the Philothei house, he had attempted to apply modernist 'total design' and other ideas of his to previous houses, but they had never been fully carried out. The Niovis 22 house is one of the very few examples of 'total design' in Greece, as clients are mostly unwilling to support the modernist concept.

The interior and exterior spaces are totally unified by open views to the gardens, which make the inside and the outside a single entity the whole year round. Even the bathroom overlooks a small private garden. Although open to the secluded gardens, the house is nevertheless closed

PERSPECTIVE SKETCH

to the public eye and is warm, comfortable and pleasant to live in. The plan of the building is a rectangle measuring 10 x 16 m on the ground floor, with a basement for an office and other ancillary spaces. Throughout the house, a 0.93 x 1.00 m module has been adhered to, which is reflected in every component, internally and externally. Due to the location of the site, with its long west elevation facing the road, which is protected by greenery from the setting sun, Niovis 22 has an east-west orientation. There are only three main walls, in exposed yellow brick. The remaining area of the elevations is glazed.

The roof is a thin 30-cm double concrete slab including the beams, supported on steel columns with a cantilever of 3.5 m on one side and shorter cantilevers on the other sides. This protects the windows from the sun and the rain. All the other walls are free-standing, insulated, specially designed partitions, veneered in rosewood. The Oregon pine windows are all sliding, and those in the living room are single pane, 5 metres long. Sliding timber shutters further protect the glazing. All the windows and doors are floor to ceiling. The internal height is 2.53 m, and the floor is in teak. Thus the house is constructed out of just three materials: concrete, brick and timber. When building Niovis 22, Valsamakis used some materials and construction methods that had never been tested before. The bricks were specially designed, the partitions were specifically manufactured according to designs by the architect, and the very large sliding windows may well be unique. Likewise all the fixed furniture was specially designed, and, where this was not the case, classic pieces were imported for the movable items.

Valsamakis's private home at Niovis 22 has been the subject of many visits and studies by architecture students from Greek and European schools of architecture and continues to be so, evidencing the timeless aspect of the project and justifying the effort that went into its making. Similarly, the house continues to feature in design magazines as a prime example of 1960s modernist architecture. The home has maintained its original furniture, designed – as said – by the architect himself and supplemented by pieces from modern designers such as Charles Eames, Le Corbusier and Hans Wegner.   MARIA VALSAMAKIS

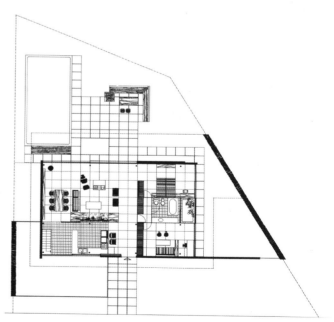

PLAN

BIBLIOGRAPHY:
1976   Constandopoulos E. (ed.), *Nicos Valsamakis*, in *Zygos*, no. 22, Athens
1984   Constandopoulos E. (ed.), *Nicos Valsamakis 1950–1983*, London
1992   Constandopoulos E. (ed.), *Nicos Valsamakis*, in *Architecture in Greece*, no. 26, pp. 59–138
2000   Philippides D. (ed), *Nicos Valsamakis*, in *Architecture in Greece*, no. 34, pp. 43–86
2001   Cornoldi A., *Le case degli architetti. Dizionario privato dal Rinascimento ad oggi*, Venice, pp. 404–405

Charles Vandenhove

*1927

1961–63, NEW CONSTRUCTION, EXTENDED IN 1974 AND AGAIN IN 1989, STILL INHABITED BY THE ARCHITECT
RUE CHAUVE SOURIS, LIÈGE (B)

MAIN WORKS AND PROJECTS

1962	Lucien Brull student hostel, Liège (B)
1962–85	Centre Hospitalier Universitaire, Sart Tilman campus, Liège (B)
1963–66	Institut Universitaire d'Education Physique, Sart Tilman campus, Liège (B)
1978–85	Hors-Château housing complex, Liège (B)
1979–81	Rehabilitation of Torrentius Hotel, Liège (B)
1987–96	Théâtre des Abbesses, apartments and day-care centre, Paris (F)

1987–98	Het Zieken housing complex, the Hague (NL)
1988–95	Le Balloir, Liège (B)
1992–98	Palace of Justice, 's-Hertogenbosch (NL)
1999–2000	Bonne Fortune house, Liège (B)

CHARLES VANDENHOVE was born on 3 July 1927 in Teuven, Belgium. In 1945 he enrolled in Liège's Ecole d'Architecture (School of Architecture), studying both there and at La Cambre in Brussels until 1951. For a while he worked with Lucien Kroll, before opening his own practice in 1958. In 1957 Vandenhove married Jeanne Belvaux, who was to have a significant impact on his life. During this period the architect assimilated various influences, from the Brutalism of Le Corbusier's Jaoul houses to the power of the wall in the work of Louis Kahn. It was especially Kahn's tectonic approach which determined the direction of Vandenhove's work in the early 1960s, as can clearly be seen in his Lucien Brull student hostel (1962) in Liège and in his university sports complex (1963–66) likewise in Liège.

Vandenhove's large-scale university hospital in Liège, constructed over many years (1962–85), is considered his *magnus opus*. The strict symmetry of its plan shows a strong Palladian influence. But even as he was building the hospital, he still had time during the 1960s and 1970s to design a number of fascinating individual country houses. A milestone in the evolution of Vandenhove's work are two projects: his Hors-Château housing complex (1978–85) and his restoration and renovation of the Torrentius Hotel (1979–81), both in Liège. Three major retrospective exhibitions in Paris (1985), Amsterdam (1986) and Antwerp (1986) were instrumental in bringing him from 1986 onwards various larger commissions in the Netherlands, mainly in the housing sector.

Back in the 1970s Vandenhove drew on the work of both Belgian and foreign architects in his public buildings as well as in his residential houses. His more recent buildings evidence a control of a classical vocabulary, in which recurring building elements determine his language.

Given that his language of forms reveals classical elements, his architecture is often considered to be postmodern. Vandenhove's own house-cum-studio might be said to represent a synthesis of these leanings.

Charles Vandenhove's own house-cum-studio was constructed new from 1961 to 1963 in the rue Chauve Souris, Liège. Subsequently he twice extended the building, in 1974 and 1989. The architect chose an unusual location for his home: the plot occupies part of some abandoned coal workings and has a steep slope. The elongated cubage of the flat-roofed house has been carefully integrated into the site, almost amounting to a camouflage exercise. But this is no neutral approach. On the contrary, the language of forms that Vandenhove applies is intended to possess the plot powerfully. While the house itself is oriented to the south and the city of Liège, the windows of Vandenhove's studio behind it face north. The outside stairs to the house's hallway are flanked by parallel brick walls, giving rise to an intriguing promenade leading up to the entrance door. Once inside the entrance hall, we discover a stairway descending from the hall floor to the living area below. Vandenhove's drawings show his passion for stairways, a part of his designs that he lavishes attention on. Both the exterior and interior are dark-bricked, while all the ceilings are made of visible concrete. This material selection resulted in an interior with a sense of intimacy and a tempered incidence of light. The character of the massive walls is strengthened by the fact that the wooden inner doors are on top of the wall surface. It is a house that serves as a shelter, as a safe place to retire to.

In 1974 Vandenhove decided to extend his home. On top of the existing house he added a volume quite at odds with the first building

GARAGE WITH EXTENSION (1989)

ORIGINAL BUILDING (1963)

DETAIL OF THE STAIRS

DETAIL OF THE FAÇADE

VIEW OF THE LIVING ROOM

LIVING ROOM IN THE UPPER EXTENSION (1974) WITH GLASS ROOF

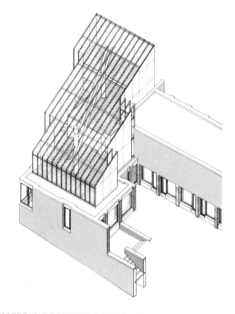

AXONOMETRIC DRAWING OF THE 1974 EXTENSION

PLAN

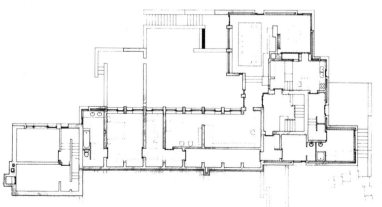

stage, both in terms of form and material. The pitched glazed roof surface is supported by two cylinder columns, which clearly relate to other works of the architect, especially to the impressive glass roof of the hall area in his university hospital, which also deploys a combination of cylinder columns and beams. A few years after 1974 Vandenhove closed part of the glass roof and gave the façade, which had originally been done with Eternit plates, a zinc covering. He also installed three circular skylights in the roof surface.

Anyone who analyses the 1974 extension will find that its seeds were actually already present in the first stage. For Vandenhove's rue Chauve Souris home has been a "house in the process of formation" from the outset, allowing the introduction of new spaces wherever existing ones can be enlarged – a stance far from the notion of flexibility prevalent in the 1960s. The extremity of these two poles of growing possibilities is clearly visible in a *Casabella* cover of 1969, where Vandenhove's walls were combined with a project by Archigram. Bekaert has termed the architect's attitude towards the extension as "synchronic plurality". There is no question of denying what was previously constructed, but of applying the simultaneity of the opposites.

In the 1980s Vandenhove moved his office out of his home into the centre of Liège, installing it in the Torrentius Hotel, which he had himself rehabilitated 1979–81. His old studio in the rue Chauve Souris was converted (1989) into a house for Prudent De Wispelaere, who had been Vandenhove's most important collaborator for more than 20 years. On top of the garage he added a semi-cylindrical volume, covered with zinc. The roof shape of this further extension, which had two bedrooms for De Wispelaere's children, alluded to large-scale housing projects that Vandenhove had implemented in the Netherlands. In order to obtain more light in the original 1963 part of the building, the architect recently plastered the concrete ceiling with white marmorino.

Vandenhove has always regarded his home and studio as an integral part of life, as a living organism in the making. The building is not a static manifesto to be left untouched, no abstract theoretical attitude. It is intimately bound up with his and his family's lives and is in constant transformation, not least in relation to the architect's oeuvre as it unfolds. Vandenhove's conception of his home resembles that of a contemporary of his, the German architect Oswald Mathias Ungers, who several times adapted and extended his house in Cologne, originally built in 1959. Not content with his own house, Vandenhove has also applied his conception to the Wuidar house, which was first realised in 1974 and then extended 1993–95. Here, too, there is no dissociation from the 'old' work, but a desire to emphasise and strengthen the simultaneity of the elements by making judicious additions. It is the acceptance of a continuity, not the elimination of the dimension of time in order to freeze a particular phase.

MARC DUBOIS

BIBLIOGRAPHY:

1974   Bekaert G., 'Charles Vandenhove: l'architecte et sa maison', in *Art Press*, February, pp. 26–29
1975   Bekaert G., 'L'architecte et sa maison', in *A+*, no. 17
1976   Bekaert G., *Architectuur en Architect / L'architecture et L'Architecte / Architecture and Architect*, Liège
1985   Chaslin F., Lascault G. and Bekaert G., *Charles Vandenhove: une architecture de la densité*, Liège
1998   Bekaert G., Verschaffel B. and Dercon C., *Charles Vandenhove: Art and architecture / Kunst en architectuur*, Tournai

Marie-José Van Hee
*1950

1990–97, NEW CONSTRUCTION, STILL INHABITED BY THE ARCHITECT
VARKENSSTRAAT 7, GHENT (B)

MAIN WORKS AND PROJECTS

1983–86	Derks-Lowie house, Ghent (B)
1988–91	Pay house with showroom and storage, Laken (B)
1990–92	Hufkens gallery and apartment, Brussels (B), with Paul Robbrecht and Hilde Daem
1990–93	Van Hee-Coppens house, office and storehouse, Deinze (B)
1991–93	Van Backlé-De Feu house, Wemmel (B)
	Braet-De Paepe house, Ghent (B)

1997–99	Reconstruction of Museumplein, Antwerp (B), with Paul Robbrecht and Hilde Daem
1999–2001	Fashion Museum (ModeNatie), Antwerp (B)

MARIE-JOSÉ VAN HEE is one of the few women to have come to prominence in Belgian architecture in recent years. She started to study architecture in 1968 at the Hoger Architectuurinstituut Sint-Lucas (St Luke's Institute of Architecture) in Ghent, graduating in 1974. After working for a period both as a freelance and as an associate, she only opened her own practice in 1990. A number of her projects have been designed in collaboration with Paul Robbrecht and Hilde Daem, with whom she won the biennial Flemish Culture Prize for Architecture in 1997.

Van Hee's modest corpus of works built to date comprises mainly houses and conversions. The architect prefers a small-scale approach, which allows her to work intensively on housing projects. She is not interested in abstract considerations in architecture. Architecture is not a matter of abstraction, but is bound up with concrete human experiences and emotions. According to her, the home is a place of protection and intimacy, and is not a venue suitable for a designer's formal experiments. Van Hee's work consists of a quest for authentic simplicity and austerity, connoted with a strong sensual element. She regards architecture as a medium in which slowness plays a part, and which enables us to go beyond the casual. She gives priority to seeking a timeless dimension. In order to rediscover the essential joys of life that we have lost, she pursues sensuality in her work, rather than adopting a purist or ascetic attitude. She gives the house a new intensity, even a necessary sensuality. She seeks these experiences in all her houses, and stands worlds apart from fashionable architectural tendencies.

In her architecture Van Hee does not strive for transparency or for the visual neutralisation of gravity. Her careful approach to the dimensions by which she creates a wall's solidity shows an affinity to the work of Luis Barragán and Dom van der Laan, two architects she greatly ad-

mires. According to her, space originates in the vicinity of walls, static walls being necessary as a frame of reference for human movement in space. Designing is a patient search for the serenity of things and the removal of what is redundant. For her, it is important to give silence a place in architecture, which may be understood as a deliberate and fundamental reaction to the abundance of images flooding our world. Her pursuit of austerity is by no means a plea for minimalism. Rather it is a quest to find the richness that lies in the authenticity of things. In a time of visual overconsumption, Van Hee draws our attention to the 'richness of austerity'.

Van Hee's private home at Varkensstraat 7, which was constructed new between 1990 and 1997, is situated in Prinsenhof, in an old quarter of the city of Ghent. In choosing this location, the architect wanted to take a personal stand against urban decay. The house has an L-shaped ground plan and is oriented towards a private patio – an intimate 'outside room'. The patio type of housing is found not only in Ludwig Mies van der Rohe's work, but also in various Belgian "béguinages". In these exceptional urban configurations, the plan of the houses unfolds in their breadth, and they also have a walled garden. In selecting such a configuration, Van Hee embraces a housing type with both historical and modernist traditions. Between the garden and the interior there is a covered arcade, a transitional area that is at once both outside and sheltered.

On the street side, the new house behaves scrupulously in the built urban context. The bricks have been given a light cement coating so that their pattern remains visible. There is no hard plastering to stress the building's newness, but a classic treatment of the façade, so that the house fits in almost invisibly without lapsing into formal associations. In contrast to the solidity of the surface of the façade, the edge of the roof

LIVING ROOM WITH WINDOWS ONTO THE STREET

VIEW OF THE COURTYARD

table

PLAN OF THE GROUND FLOOR

has a fragile line. The façade's five high vertical windows already hint at the special interior concept.

The central space is a large, five-metre-high rectangular living room with a ceiling of wooden beams. The way daylight penetrates into this high space, with sunlight from morning to evening, evidences Van Hee's great mastery in making the orientation an essential part of the design. Architecture is used to make light visible. The large rectangular space evokes the image of the cleanly constructed rooms in old rural Tuscan houses, spaces with an impressive brightness and exactly the right proportions.

A stone stairway leads to the library on the first floor, and next to it there is the bedroom. This bedroom is connected to the garden by means of a covered outside stairway, which introduces a fascinating additional route. The large generous space, which does not separate the sitting room and dining room, incorporates a large table in the centre. By locating the table in this way, Van Hee dissociates herself from the stereotypical image of a cosy sitting area forming the core of the house. The kitchen and bathroom are in the shortest arm of the L-shape. She deliberately relativises the concept of comfort in order to intensify the physical

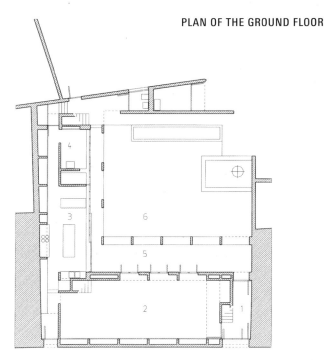

414

THE GALLERY IN THE COURTYARD

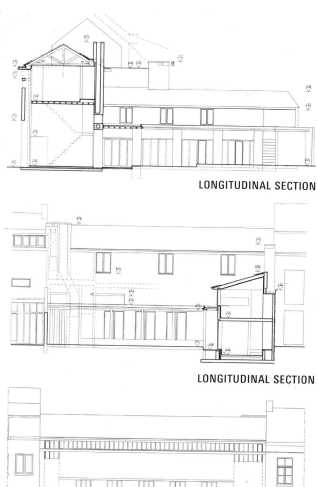

LONGITUDINAL SECTION

LONGITUDINAL SECTION

STREET FAÇADE

experience. In order not to escape the daily physical experience of the difference between interior and exterior, the toilet has even been placed outside. On the first floor there are consultation rooms for her husband's practice, a room which can be reached by means of a separate stairway from the hall. Van Hee's architectural office is not combined with the private house.

The house developed slowly, over some seven years, taking time for any inessential parts to be removed so that what was already present from the outset would have time to develop. As Le Corbusier said when he spoke of 'travail patient', designing houses requires patient and intense work to penetrate to an essence, a labour far removed from the serial approach. Van Hee's private house is a genuine mirror of her way of living and thinking, an autobiographical house. When it was finally finished, she gained a mention in the 6th Mies Van der Rohe Award for European Architecture in Barcelona in 1997.

MARC DUBOIS

BIBLIOGRAPHY:

1997 Dubois M., 'Resisting the Ethereal: Van Hee-Adriaens House', in *A+U*, Tokyo
       Wortmann A., 'Posities – Positions: Marie-José Van Hee', in *Archis*, no. 2, pp. 28–33

1998 'Woning – Maison Van Hee-Adriaens / Van Hee-Adriaens House', in *Jaarboek Architectuur
       Vlaanderen / Annales de l'architecture en Flandre / Flanders Architectural Yearbook
       1996–1997*, Brussels, pp. 142–145

1999 'Van Hee-Adriaens House', in *6th Mies van der Rohe Award for European Architecture*,
       Barcelona, pp. 150–153

2000 Dubois M., 'Woning Marie-José Van Hee reflecteert autobiografisch referentiekader', in
       de Architect, November, pp. 58–61

Bob Van Reeth
*1943

1969 – 70, CONVERSION
BOGAERD 6, MECHELEN (B)

MAIN WORKS AND PROJECTS

1969 – 71	Botte house, Battel, Mechelen (B)
1973 – 78	Onze-Lieve-Vrouwe College, Antwerp (B)
1982 – 89	Own house-cum-studio, Paardenmarkt, Antwerp (B)
1985 – 88	Van Roosmalen house, Antwerp (B)
1988 – 89	Competition project for maritime trading centre, Zeebrugge (B)
1990 – 93	Office building for Editions GP Averbode and Editions Altiora, Averbode (B)

1993	Competition project to extend the casino and spa hall, Ostend (B)
1994 – 97	Seppenshuis reception and garden pavilion, Zoersel (B)
1994 – 98	Mariaplaats urban-development project, Utrecht (NL)

BOB VAN REETH grew up as the youngest of six children. His classical education at the Jesuit College in Antwerp seems to have been a torment for him and might have helped form his disaffected nature. The future 'rebel' of Belgian architecture studied the discipline from 1963 to 1968 at the Hoger Architectuurinstituut Sint-Lucas (St Luke's Institute of Architecture) in Schaarbeek, Brussels. His decision to pursue an 'artistic' profession was not encouraged by his parents, even though Van Reeth likes to talk about his father's carpentry workshop and his passion for making furniture. Van Reeth himself is passionately fond of modern design, and in the 1990s he successfully took into production a remarkable series of tables and chairs.

During the 1960s St Luke's Institute in Brussels probably provided the most adventurous architectural training available in Belgium, with teachers such as Willy Van Der Meeren and – more importantly for Bob van Reeth – Alfons Hoppenbrouwers, who called himself the theorist of modern architecture. Here, where there was room for a personal undogmatic discovery of the history of modern architecture, Van Reeth thrived, developing a precocious talent. Halfway through his studies, he carried out his first commission, a jewellery shop in Antwerp, and immediately after graduating he designed a publishing house in Kalmthout. These projects brought Van Reeth much publicity from the start. When, fresh out of college, he built his Botte house (1969 – 71) and also his own house in Mechelen (1969 – 70), he was even profiled in *TA/BK*, an influential Belgian-Dutch architecture and visual arts magazine.

All Van Reeth's early projects subsequently became part of Belgium's post-war architectural canon. Especially his Botte house demonstrates a desire to endow architecture with the vitality of popular building and with a liberty and unrestrained quality that stands out amid the Belgian architectural chaos of the time. In his first writings Van Reeth

dealt with the poetry of 'Belgium's backside', whose buildings had often been put up without an architect or precise rules. "The crackin shakin breakin sounds're the only beauty I understand," wrote Bob Dylan, the poet who taught Van Reeth, by his own account, everything about architecture. Pilgrimages to Van Reeth's buildings were organised, and the Low Countries were flooded with generations of followers and imitators.

From the start of his career Van Reeth has been a popular speaker. Even though he claimed no central role in local architecture debates, he was recognised as the mouthpiece and figurehead of a new generation of architects and students. Like his buildings, his texts also represent a quest for the concrete possibilities of architecture. In the anti-authoritarian climate of those years they were written as a response to the need to find a social justification of his own activities. With their trenchant straightforwardness, they are – together with the texts and pamphlets of Luc Deleu, another veteran of St Luke's in Schaarbeek and a contemporary of Van Reeth – the most coherent 'self-analysis' by a Belgian architect in the 1960s and 1970s. In the early 1980s these texts were collected and published by the Faculty of Applied Sciences at the University of Ghent (RUG). The discussion book *Architecture is not interesting*, a similar volume, in which Van Reeth's ideas are questioned by his philosopher friend from Amsterdam Willem Koerse, was published in 1995.

Fairly quickly Van Reeth gravitated to architecture education. He worked for various institutes in Belgium and the Netherlands, but his activities were mainly focussed on the Henry Van de Velde Institute in Antwerp, where he became the college's most influential studio supervisor. He is, however, not interested in formal schooling, but in training designers who will think for themselves, who will pay attention to the materiality of architecture and to its social implications. Van Reeth's commitment was not restricted to a particular institute, and when, in the late

VIEW TOWARDS THE STAIRCASE

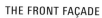
THE FRONT FAÇADE

THE FIREPLACE

VIEW FROM THE STAIRCASE

1980s, he seized the opportunity to reform the training of civil engineering architects at the University of Ghent (RUG), he and Charles Vermeersch, an urban development specialist and President of the Architecture and Urban Development Department, sided with this movement for renewal.

In architectural-historical terms, during the 1960s and 1970s Van Reeth occupied a key position in Belgian architecture, although official bodies were utterly indifferent to the meaning of his work at the time. Full recognition of his achievements did not come until 1983, when he

PLAN OF THE GROUND FLOOR

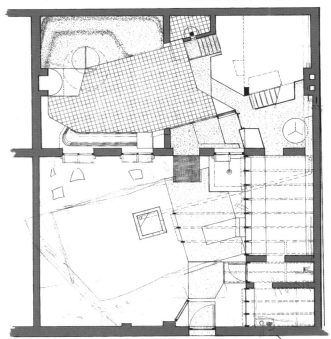

won the Eugène Baie award for architecture. True, along with the sculptor Jean-Paul Laenen and the urban-development specialist Marcel Smets, he was selected for the Venice Biennale as early as 1976 to show a Krokus group urban-development study, yet no exhibition dedicated to his architecture would be organised until 1985 at the University of Ghent, although thereafter exhibitions of his work were organised in quick succession in places such as the Netherlands, Berlin and Moscow as well as, at the turn of the millennium, Buenos Aires, São Paulo and Prague.

Similarly, Van Reeth had to wait a long time before he got his first public commission. Not until the late 1980s, when his Van Roosmalen house caused a furore, and in 1990, when Van Reeth, together with Geert Bekaert and a multitude of poets, artists and other sympathisers, opposed the demolition of the magisterial Royal Storehouses in Antwerp, were his talent and commitment taken seriously in wider circles. But even then there was a storm of protest when Van Reeth submitted a proposal to extend Ostend's casino and spa facilities out on the open sea, a refined design that Hugo Claus had assisted, and which had been adopted unanimously by the jury of an international competition. During those heady days, his work captured the attention not only of architecture critics, but also of poets and essayists, such as Herman De Coninck and Cyrille Offermans. And from then on it was all plain sailing. In the mid-1990s, Bob Van Reeth's Architecten Werk Groep (AWG) received one large-scale housing commission after another in the Netherlands. He became a household name after his official appointment in 1999 as Flemish State Architect, the 'guardian of quality' in public architecture. Since then Van Reeth has put forward a series of proposals, creating opportunities for young and even newly qualified architects.

Van Reeth had only just graduated in 1968 when he acquired an old house at Bogaerd 6, in Mechelen's Little "Béguinage" an attractive but dilapidated city quarter that had been left to building speculators for years. He was attracted to the property not only because it was beautifully situated in the bend of a narrow alley with an underpass, but also and especially because he wanted to live in a city. The houses he later occupied in Antwerp are also located in quarters that have a definite historical stratification. Van Reeth needed this stratification more and more in order to build, as De Coninck observed, a remembrance of something that had never existed. A new classroom wing at the Jesuit College in Antwerp also exemplifies this inclination. In the late 1960s, the architect's decision to live in the historic city centre was a statement, especially in Belgium.

After purchasing the house, Van Reeth set about converting it (1969–70). The lot is completely walled, and measures about ten by twelve meters. The existing house had three blind walls and one façade on the forecourt side, where the house could be entered. There was a corridor with stairs in the centre, a room on both the left and right-hand sides, and bedrooms and an attic upstairs under a saddle roof. This arrangement and the static notion of living was thrown open completely by means of a series of overlapping spaces, confirming the entire interior and reorganising it into one dynamic course. The stairway was moved to one side of the plan and put into a sloping position in a zone opening

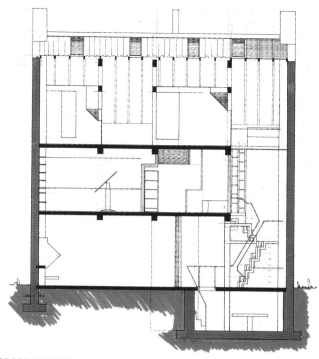

CROSS-SECTION

VIEW TOWARDS THE CEILING

along the entire height, where the light fell in through the open roof. This may remind one of Piranesi, and even more so of Horta, whose work was rehabilitated in those years and was known to as well as admired by Van Reeth.

Construction and finishing of the house were fundamental. Downstairs the floor was done with 'aggregate exposure' concrete, on the other levels in wood. Some remnants of former dividing walls still fulfil a constructive function. The stairway starts in concrete, ascends to a mezzanine floor, and then leads as straight wooden stairs to numerous subtly defined landings, which serve as transitional zones, a feature reminiscent once again of Horta, but also of Aldo Van Eyck's 'between'. Elsewhere, an affinity with Rudolf Schindler is evident – it was Van Reeth who organised a Schindler exhibition in Brussels in 1969 – as well as with the work of Atelier 5, in which Van Reeth had once served a holiday apprenticeship.

Van Reeth's own home and also his Botte house represent a pivotal moment in Belgian contemporary architecture, a moment when new perspectives came into being, and when a new generation was able to express its vision in some exemplary pieces of work.　　MIL DE KOONING

BIBLIOGRAPHY:

1985　De Kooning M., 'Bob Van Reeth. Marc Van Bortel. Herhalen wat nooit gezegd is', in *Vlees en Beton*, no. 3

1987　De Kooning M., *AWG Antwerp*, exhibition catalogue, deSingel International Arts Centre, Antwerp

1995　Bekaert G., 'Bob Van Reeth and the Demands of Architecture', in *The Low Countries 1995–96*, Rekkem

1998　De Kooning M., 'Bob Van Reeth Revisited. Mechelen 1965–1975', in *Vlees en Beton*, no. 38

1999　T'Jonck P., 'Bob Van Reeth/AWG', in *Horta and After. 25 Masters of Modern Architecture in Belgium*, ed. M. De Kooning, Ghent

2000　Bekaert G., *AWG Bob Van Reeth Architecten*, Ghent

Henry van de Velde
1863 – 1957

1927–28, NEW CONSTRUCTION
1 AVENUE ALBERT I, TERVUREN (B)

MAIN WORKS AND PROJECTS

1895	Own Bloemenwerf (Flower Wharf) house, near Brussels (B)	**1921**	The Tent, own wooden house, Wassenaar (NL)
1902	Folkwang Museum, Hagen (D)	**1932–36**	University Library, Ghent (B)
1903	Nietzsche Archives, Weimar (D)	**1936–57**	Kröller-Müller Museum, Otterlo (NL)
1904–11	Kunstschule (School of Art), Weimar (D)	**1937**	Belgian pavilion, World Exhibition, Paris (F)
1905–06	Kunstgewerbeschule (School of Applied Arts), Weimar (D)	**1939**	Belgian pavilion, World Exhibition, New York (USA)
1907–08	Hohenhof villa, Hagen (D)		
1908	Own Hohe Pappeln (High Poplars) house, Weimar (D)		
1914	Werkbund theatre, Cologne (D)		

IN HIS LONG CAREER Henry van de Velde designed no fewer than four homes for himself and his family. The series began in 1895 with his Bloemenwerf (Flower Wharf) house, built near Brussels, which the architect explicitly wanted to present as a *Gesamtkunstwerk* or total work of art. The building was not only filled with works of art, but was also decorated by the designer down to the last detail. First and foremost the house had to be an intimate place in which art could find a place within life. Flower Wharf embodies precisely the kind of ideology that Adolf Loos criticised in various texts. "There will come a time," he wrote, "when the design of a prison cell by Professor Van de Velde will be regarded by the prisoner as an aggravation of his sentence."

The four houses that Van de Velde built for himself are representative examples of both his stylistic development and his multifaceted life. If Flower Wharf marked his switch from a career in painting to one in applied art and architecture, his Hohe Pappeln (High Poplars) house in Weimar (1908) combines his predilection for intimacy with the classically inspired austerity of his German period. His wooden house The Tent (1921), which attempts to reconcile individual creativity with standardisation, is representative of his subsequent Dutch period. Finally, Van de Velde's La Nouvelle Maison (New House), done after his return to Belgium, shows the architect applying his principles for the first time to post-war Modernism.

Van de Velde's quartet of private dwellings perfectly illustrate the fact that he considered himself not just an architect, but also – as from the beginning – an artist. He defines a line as a deposit of "the power and energy of the person who drew it", and by the same token a house for him reflects its designer and its inhabitant. A Van de Velde house is, as Walter Benjamin pointed out, an expression of personality, and its ornamentation rather resembles a painter's signature. This proto-expressionist conception of the private house is consistent with the private utopia of Art Nouveau or Jugendstil. Besides advocating this personalised individualised artistic type of architecture, Van de Velde was also one of the first designers to wax lyrical about industrial technology and to propagate a radical break with 19th-century neo-styles. This meant that he had little interest in standardised mass-produced public housing and urban-development problems. His architectural output comprises primarily houses for progressive aesthetes or larger projects embodying cultural values, such as museums, libraries, theatres and monuments.

Van de Velde's La Nouvelle Maison or New House was built on a triangular plot of land in Tervuren, near Brussels, between 1927 and 1928, shortly after his return to his native Belgium, following spells in Germany, Switzerland and the Netherlands. Far from evincing the architect's explicit pre-war ritualism of creating a *Gesamtkunstwerk*, as seen in his Flower Wharf, the New House shows him addressing Modernism. Now the intimate atmosphere of his own private house became the venue for an experimentation with a new simplified language, which would subsequently be applied in other projects.

La Nouvelle Maison draws its power first and foremost from the subtle play of volumes. For instance, the entry side shows an intense contrast between the underground garage entrance and the rhythm of the doorway and the windows in the brick wall. The protruding balcony on the second floor is not only an awning over the entrance, but also a juxtaposition with the garage's indentation. Also on the garden side, the wall, which at first sight seems to be flat, contrasts with the cubical volume of the studio. Moreover, the façade surface is also complemented

THE NORTH-WEST FAÇADE TOWARDS THE STREET

THE NORTH-EAST AND NORTH-WEST FAÇADES

SOUTH-WEST VIEW

THE LIVING AREA

THE LIBRARY

by the volumetric play of the terrace, edged with a low brick wall and by the stairway, which attach the whole to the garden.

Van de Velde was clearly not satisfied with the purity of the forms. Volumes must be sculpted in a plastic way, and the material must be revived. Instead of a white introverted cube, the architect preferred the dynamics of an organic continuum. In the New House, as in many other Van de Velde projects of this period, the notion of movement is suggested by protruding elements, such as terraces and balconies, and by rounded corners. According to the architect, rounded corners represent the modernist equivalent of the dynamic line principles of his Art Nouveau period, which is why the cubic content is moulded to a plastic mass. His expressive brick treatment contributes to this. Cornices, bases and the masonry of the belvedere bricks break through the monotony of the plain wall surfaces. (Belvedere bricks are a kind of bricks often used in Belgian architecture from the 1930s up until the late 1950s, originally from Holland, with darker color than the usual red.)

The contrast between the modernist preference for clearly defined volumes and the expressive treatment of the whole also creates ambiguity as far as the ground plan is concerned. Here, too, we are struck by the simplicity of the systematic organisation and the functional transparency. Unlike the exceptionally irregular design of Van de Velde's previous houses, the plan of La Nouvelle Maison consists of an oblong with rounded angles. The organisation of the second floor is particularly striking because of its simplicity: the corridor is an axis of symmetry around which the more or less identical rooms are grouped. Despite the simpli-

city of the ground-floor drawing, there are still signs of the architect's earlier tendency to individualise each and every room, which is also proved by the fact that the four façades are composed in absolutely different ways. Moreover, there is a compactness and an organic connection between the different rooms.

In the New House, despite the presence of typically modernist solutions, such as a flat roof and the replacement of theatrical monumentality by a functional programme, Van de Velde's modernism still shows traces of Art Nouveau. Instead of the dematerialised surfaces of the clearly defined volumes of the avant-garde, the materiality of the building has to be revived by the artist's hand. When Van de Velde spoke of "dematerialisation of the material" as a sine qua non for good architecture, he never treated this in practice as a pursuit of intangibility in the sense of Paul Scheerbart's 'Glasarchitektur' or the elementarism of Theo van Doesburg and Ludwig Mies van der Rohe. Van de Velde does not abstract architecture, but the building's materiality must be taken apart into dynamics experienced in a personal way. The cubical volume must be marked with the artist's self. The building represents a plastic equivalent of the nervous arabesques of Van de Velde's late paintings.

Van de Velde may have written extensively in his memoirs about his first private house, Flower Wharf, but he does not say much about the last home he built for himself, the New House. Nevertheless, it is clear that in this house the 'modernist' Van de Velde was not aspiring to a Corbusian *machine à habiter*, but clung on to an introverted quality, a feeling of shelter. A link between inside and outside, between the private and the public, is merely created by means of the terrace, the garden and the treatment of the exterior.

Van de Velde lived in his Nouvelle Maison for fully 20 years, during which time he was constantly active and also gained international recognition. In this period he not only designed various other houses, but also executed some large commissions, such as the University Library in Ghent, the Kröller-Müller Museum in Otterlo and the Belgian pavilions of the Paris and New York World Exhibitions. At the same time he also lectured at the University of Ghent (RUG) and became the director of the newly founded Institut Supérieur des Arts Décoratifs (ISAD) in Brussels. In 1947, four years after the death of his wife and during the aftermath of the war, the architect left Belgium once more. Despite being asked by Queen Elizabeth to stay in Belgium – she paid a visit to the architect in Tervuren – he moved with his daughter Nele to Switzerland. For the last ten years of his life, until his death in 1957, he lived in Oberägeri in a bungalow renovated by Alfred Roth.   STEVEN JACOBS

PLAN OF THE GROUND FLOOR

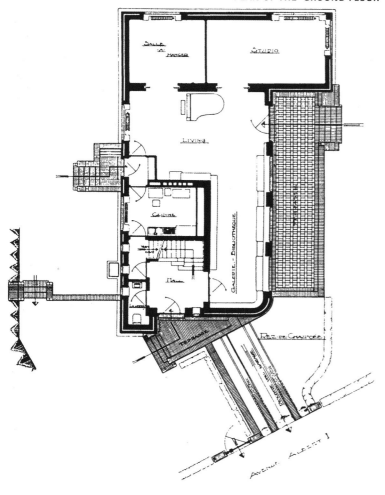

BIBLIOGRAPHY:

1987   Ploegaerts L. and Puttemans P., *L'oeuvre architecturale de Henry Van de Velde*, Brussels/Quebec

1989   Sembach K.-J., *Henry Van de Velde*, New York

1993   Sembach K.-J. and Schulte B. (eds.), *Henry Van de Velde: Een Europees kunstenaar in zijn tijd*, Brussels

1996   Jacobs S., *Henry van de Velde: Wonen als kunstwerk, een woonplaats voor de kunst*, Leuven

2001   Cornoldi A., *Le case degli architetti. Dizionario privato dal Rinascimento ad oggi*, Venice, pp. 407–409

Vittoriano Viganò
1919 – 1996

1956 – 58, ALTERATION AND FURNISHING
MILAN (I)

MAIN WORKS AND PROJECTS

1947 – 68 Exhibition designs at the VIII, IX, X, XII and XIV Milan Triennale; design of the Fiore, Schettini, Apollinaire, Grattacielo, and Levi art galleries, and of the Tom Boy and Arteluce shops in Milan (I)

1953 – 57 Istituto Marchiondi Spagliardi, Baggio, Milan (I)

1953 – 58 La Scala house (André Bloc's villa), Portese del Garda (I)

1965 – 67 Colorificio Attiva factory, Pozzolo Formigaro, Novi Ligure (I)

1965 – 87 Extension of the School of Architecture at Milan Polytechnic (I)

1967 – 68 Mollificio Bresciano factory, San Felice del Benaco, Bergamo (I)

1967 – 86 Landscaping of Marecchia Park and of the Murri and Bellariva districts in Rimini (I)

1980 – 87 Urban design of Milan's Corso and Piazza Sempione (I), the partial outcome of a long series of plans (1953 – 96) to improve the Parco Sempione and its monuments

1981 – 84 Competition project for the reconstruction of the Teatro Carlo Felice, Genoa (I)

1983 – 88 Urban design of the lakeside and historic centre of Salò (I)

VITTORIANO VIGANÒ was born in Milan on 14 December 1919, the son of Vico Viganò (1874 – 1967) and Eugenia Riccardi. His father was a versatile Milanese artist, who painted, engraved, wrote poetry and designed architecture, authoring in 1926, for example, a famous project for a campanile (a free-standing bell tower) near Milan Cathedral. Especially given Vico Viganò's multifaceted métier, Vittoriano grew up in a family atmosphere characterised by a deep love of forms and colours. Originally Vittoriano had wanted to study medicine, but his family encouraged him to take up architecture instead. He attended Milan's Beccaria Grammar School, passing his leaving exams in 1939. In the same year he enrolled in the School of Architecture of the Politecnico of Milan, from which he graduated on 21 December 1944.

In March 1945 Viganò took first place in the state examinations for qualification as an architect, and in the same year undertook a brief apprenticeship in the BBPR studio. From 1946 to 1947 he took part in Arturo Danusso's masterclass on reinforced concrete construction, an experience he would later put to good use in works that were labelled 'Brutalist' by international critics. Then, in 1947, Viganò opened his own practice in the family home, where he was to work for fully 50 years. Between 1945 and 1969 he also taught furnishing and decoration in Milan Polytechnic's School of Architecture, which was directed at the time by Gio Ponti, rising up the academic hierarchy until he himself was eventually appointed to a chair at the School in the Department of Interior Design, Decoration and Furnishing. Viganò's university commitments would con-

tinue throughout his life. Besides being involved in lecturing and academic research, he also participated in syllabus reform.

From 1947 to 1960 Viganò designed and built single pieces of furniture and lamps for various companies. He worked as a technical and artistic consultant for Arteluce, Pozzi and Ideal Standard. From 1947 to 1963 he also was the Italian correspondent for *L'Architecture d'Aujourd'hui*, in 1952 – 53 editing two special issues devoted to Italian architecture. During the same period he contributed to *Aujourd'hui*, the journal founded in 1955 by André Bloc, with whom he developed an intense intellectual relationship, and for whom he built one of his most celebrated works, the La Scala house in Portese del Garda (1953 – 58). But besides being in touch with cultural life and groups in Milan and Paris, Viganò was also in close contact with faculties of architecture in Mexico and the United States, as well as with the Hochschule für Gestaltung (College of Design) in Ulm and the Swiss Werkbund in Zurich. In search of new ideas and forms, he made frequent trips within Italy and Western Europe as well as to North Africa, North America and Mexico, travels that are recorded in an original photographic archive. Viganò was always involved in the theoretical debate, especially in Milan, and corresponded regularly with many leading protagonists of the architectural and artistic world in Italy and Europe, as well as with environmentalists.

In 1981, for an article in *Domus*, Viganò gave Bruno Zevi some typewritten notes about his own home in Milan, built more than 20 years earlier

THE LIVING AREA

CHILDREN'S ROOM

THE FIREPLACE IN THE MIDDLE OF THE LIVING ROOM

THE LIVING AREA

(1956–58). The architect was at pains to point out that this was not a house built in keeping with the dictates of fashion, such as might please the rising Italian bourgeoisie of the boom years, but was a house of the reconstruction period, constituting "neither realism nor revival, but a moment of experiment, understood as the provocative exposition of both a discipline and an individual". And, in fact, with his sense of belonging to an intellectual and aesthetic aristocracy, Viganò had already stated as

PLAN

early as 1960 that in the matter of furnishing and decoration he followed "a direction contrary to bourgeois mannerism".

The house is ambiguous in nature. Its difficult complex interior, designed by the architect down to the last detail, challenges the intelligence, like the Minoan labyrinth. But, as a Viganò self-portrait and as a representation of his family's history, it is almost disarmingly intimate. At the same time the building was conceived as a magnificent art gallery, to be filled with its owner's many ancient and modern works. Viganò wanted to implement the idea of a dynamic home, continuous and at the same time unified throughout, an environment that would lead visitors to try out for themselves the various perceptions of proportions created by the low tables and "seating surfaces". He intended the house to be "a space in which to learn by testing, even on one's own self".

Viganò pursued his intention of creating spatial unity and continuity by starting out exclusively from the external walls of the apartment, an attic surrounded on three sides by a terrace. The height of the spaces destined to become the kitchen, the main bathroom and the fitted wardrobes was lowered, so that the ceiling forms an uninterrupted level, where the refined alternation of black and white areas leads to changing perceptions of space. The rooms are, therefore, small volumes contained within a large volume, creating accessible mezzanines and a visual con-

DETAIL

AXONOMETRIC DRAWING

tinuity. While the volumes of the rooms emerge from below, the hood of the fireplace in the living room is suspended from the ceiling around an existing pillar. Where possible, the architect eliminated doors and diaphragms. However, the area destined for day and night use is separated clearly by a nucleus formed by the children's bedroom and by a large room used for housework, where the maid's bed was originally hidden from view during the day underneath a built-in wardrobe. Two extremely narrow corridors lead to the bathroom and to the main bedroom. At the top of the walls, some of which are plastered in rustic style, there is a metal beam, used to hang works of art. The colours are predominantly black but also white and red, which are supplemented by the grey sections of the walls in rustic plaster, framed by plaster pilasters painted red or black. The few doors are clad in cork and have iron jambs, while the large windows that overlook the city are screened by metal Venetian blinds, either white or red. The wardrobes are all built-in, and the furnishing consists of a single system of low-slung modular pieces in wood and iron.

Viganò's own Milan home and his Istituto Marchiondi (1953–57) are somewhat two peas from the same pod. Designed almost at the same time, the violence of their message must have seemed like a desecration, which perhaps explains the criticism that Ernesto Nathan Rogers levelled at them. In Viganò's oeuvre, his private house looks both forwards and backwards. Its play of volumes and planes anticipates other interiors that the architect subsequently designed, while many of its details are reminiscent of the decoration in art galleries that he had already executed in previous years. Thus, we find, for example, walls plastered in rustic style in his Galleria Apollinaire (1954–58), and wall-top metal beams used for suspending paintings in his Galleria del Fiore (1953–54). References in the house to the modern movement are to be seen mainly in Viganò's use of the open plan typical of rationalist architecture. However, his deployment of this plan has an original twist, for Viganò made the continuum more explicit on the upper level, at the level of the ceilings, a fact that was pointed out in 1981 by Bruno Zevi of *Domus*, who considered the house a provocative erotic act for its time.

VALERIA FARINATI

BIBLIOGRAPHY:

1959   'Unità e continuità negli spazi interni', in *Domus*, no. 359, October, pp. 13–28

1960   'La pianta libera nei soffitti di una casa milanese', in *L'Architettura*. Cronache e storia, no. 11, March, pp. 752–753

         'Appartement d'un architecte à Milan', in *Aujourd'hui. Art et architecture*, no. 26, April, pp. 88–92

1981   Zevi B., '23 anni dopo', in *Domus*, no. 617, May, pp. 33–35

1992   *A come architettura. Vittoriano Viganò*, exhibition catalogue, 21–31 May 1991, School of Architecture of Milan Polytechnic, Milan

Manfred Vilhjálmsson
*1928

1959–62, NEW CONSTRUCTION, WITH GUDMUNDUR KR. KRISTINSSON,
STILL INHABITED BY THE ARCHITECT
ÁLFTANES (IS)

MAIN WORKS AND PROJECTS

1956	Car service station, Ellidaár, Nesti, Reykjavík (IS), since demolished	1986	Epal furniture showroom, Faxafen 7, Reykjavík (IS)
1964	House, Mávanes 4, Gardabaer, near Reykjavík (IS)	1987–89	Campsite service building, Laugardalur, Reykjavík (IS)
1967	House and studio, Bardavogur 13, Reykjavík (IS)	1987–91	Renovation of Ásmundur Sveinsson Museum, Sigtún, Reykjavík (IS)
1971	College at Skálholt, Árnessysla (IS), with Thorvaldur Thorvaldsson		
1972–96	National and University Library at Birkimelur, Reykjavík (IS), with Thorvaldur Thorvaldsson		

AFTER COMPLETING his architectural studies in 1954 at Chalmers Technical University in Gothenburg (Göteborg), Sweden, Manfred Vilhjálmsson worked for architects Brolid and Wallinder in Gothenburg (1954–55) and in Skarphédinn Jóhannsson's architectural practice in Reykjavík, before opening his own office in 1959. Together with Gudmundur Kr. Kristinsson, he was instrumental in introducing new spatial and structural concepts in Icelandic architecture, based on the use of lightweight construction and open planning. An early example is his design for two car service stations in Reykjavík (Nesti), where materials and details common in the automobile industry were used in the construction. In Vilhjálmsson's most frequently published work, the house at Mávanes 4 (1964), a clear distinction is made between the enclosing rough-textured concrete wall and the skeletal wood-frame structure supporting the roof. In later projects, Vilhjálmsson has continued to work with modern concepts of space and construction, and with their adaptation to Iceland's cultural and environmental conditions.

Gudmundur Kr. Kristinsson was born in 1925 in Reykjavík and educated at the Federal Polytechnic (now Swiss Federal Institute of Technology or ETH) in Zurich, Switzerland. He graduated as an architect in 1953, moved to Reykjavík, and began collaborating with Gunnlaugur Halldórsson (1909–86), a key architect in Iceland's modern movement. While working with Halldórsson, Kristinsson gradually built up his own architectural practice. His work includes banks, office buildings and power stations as well as the design of many private houses in and around Reykjavík, which are noted for their progressive design, innovative use of building technology, and close attention to detail.

Vilhjálmsson and Kristinsson came to work as architects in Iceland at about the same time, in the mid-1950s. Although educated in different countries, they shared a strong interest in the latest developments in modern architecture. Like many architects of their generation, they were fascinated by the spatial concepts of traditional Japanese architecture, by open planning and flexible walls, by modular construction, and by the idea of the building as a system of prefabricated components. These ideas were new at the time in Iceland, where the convention was to build houses with massive cast-in-place concrete walls.

For some time Vilhjálmsson and Kristinsson had both been seeking building lots in the city of Reykjavík, on which they might construct their own houses, when Kristinsson's partner, architect Gunnlaugur Halldórsson, offered to let them build on land he owned on the Álftanes peninsula, outside the city limits. They fell in with the idea and in 1959 bought from him two adjacent plots near the south coast of the peninsula. On a site nearby was Halldórsson own house, which he had built in the early 1940s. At the time Vilhjálmsson and Kristinsson acquired their land, Álftanes was a sparsely settled farming community. Their two plots were situated on a ridge with a south-facing panoramic view towards the mountains and dark lava fields across Hafnarfjördur Bay.

Vilhjálmsson and Kristinsson regarded the building of their private houses as an opportunity to carry out radical experiments in design and building technology, which they were not in a position to do in regular commissions. On that basis, they opted to collaborate on a single design concept. Their decision to use the same design for both houses made it possible to rationalise the building process and keep construction costs down by sharing purchases of materials and components.

The houses consist of two parts: a lightweight building of steel and wood with an open living space, and a service core with massive walls.

VIEW OF THE HOUSES OF KRISTINSSON (LEFT) AND VILHJÁLMSSON (RIGHT)

THE ENTRANCE COURT

THE SOUTH FACING WINDOW AND SUN TERRACE

THE LIVING ROOM

In Vilhjálmsson's house, the main living space has a structural system of wooden beams resting on delicate steel columns, placed on a modular grid of 360 x 360 cm. Exterior walls and windows are made of modular components that fit into the structural frame system. Inside, the living space is divided up with canvas-clad partitions and sliding doors. The open kitchen in the centre divides the living space into a sitting room and a less formal family, dining and play room. The private rooms are at either end of the open space, a parents' room and study on the living-room side, and children's rooms on the other. By removing a light wall, two small children's rooms can be combined into one. In place of conventional window openings there are air slots with inside shutters. The rooms are heated through air ducts built into the floor, the first system of its kind in an Icelandic house.

The service core with entrances, bathrooms and other service spaces runs along the north side of the houses. Its massive walls are made of blocks of volcanic pumice, left exposed and painted white. The walls of the core provide structural stability for the frame construction of the main house. The north elevation has a seemingly random pattern of windows, placed in outward-projecting steel boxes that are fitted into openings in the masonry. Both houses follow the same basic design, but with some variations in construction and detailing.

The Vilhjálmssons named their home 'Smidshús' (Carpenter's House) in honour of Manfred's father and the builder of the house, master carpenter Vilhjálmur Jónsson. The building, which looks almost too delicate for Iceland's harsh climate, has actually stood the test of time very well. The flexibility of the living space has allowed the family to adapt the house to the changing needs of a family with five children. The interior has a feeling of warmth and personality, which is enhanced by Vilhjálmsson's collection of paintings, furniture and personal objects. On the living room wall there is a work by the Swiss artist Dieter Roth, who became a friend of the family during a stay in Iceland. In the 1970s the Vilhjálmssons built a garage annex beside the house with a small studio apartment.

The design of the two houses at Álftanes was revolutionary at the time in every respect. But the radical thinking of Vilhjálmsson and Kristinsson is above all reflected in their notion that an architect's own house should be a testing ground for advancing new concepts of architecture, lifestyle and building technology. The buildings' realisation was also an

CENTRAL LIVING AREA WITH OPEN-PLAN KITCHEN

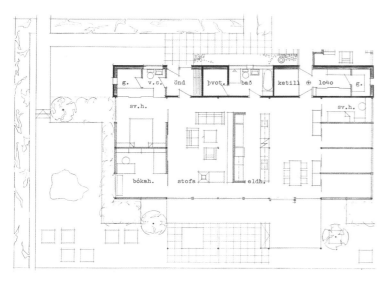

PLAN

achievement, given the undeveloped state of the construction industry in Iceland and the limited range of materials available. Compared to what went before and what came after, the houses are of great significance for the development of modern architecture in Iceland. For the architects themselves, the artistic and technical experiments carried out in the process became a basis for their subsequent architectural work in the 1960s and 1970s.

PÉTUR ÁRMANNSSON

BIBLIOGRAPHY:

1985   Ingólfsson A., 'Thjódarbókhladan og byggingarlist Manfreds Vilhjálmssonar', in *Stord*, no. 1, pp. 8–15

1996   *Dictionnaire de L'Architecture du XXe Siécle*, Paris, p. 935

1997   Helgason H., *Arkitektatal*, Reykjavik, pp. 452–453

1998   Ármannsson P. H., 'Purism in 1950s Architecture', in *Dream of Pure Form, Icelandic Abstract Art 1950–1960*, Reykjavik

2000   *A Guide to Icelandic Architecture*, Reykjavík, pp. 50, 109, 111, 114, 147 and 185

Charles Francis Annesley Voysey
1857–1941

1900, NEW CONSTRUCTION
SHIRE LANE, CHORLEY WOOD, HERTFORDSHIRE (GB)

MAIN WORKS AND PROJECTS

1888	Cottage, Bishop's Itchington, Warwickshire (GB)
1890	Walnut Tree Farm, Castlemorton, Worcestershire (GB)
1891	Forster house, 14 South Parade, Bedford Park, Chiswick, London (GB)
1892	Hans Road house, Knightsbridge, London (GB)
1893–94	Perrycroft, Colwall, Herefordshire (GB)
1895	Annesley Lodge, Platt's Lane, Hampstead, London (GB)
1897	New Place, Haslemere, Surrey (GB)

1897	Norney house, near Shakleford, Surrey (GB)
1898	Broadleys, Lake Windermere, Cumbria (GB)
	Moor Crag, Lake Windermere, Cumbria (GB)
1902	Wallpaper factory, Chiswick, London (GB)

AN ARCHITECT AND THEORIST, Charles Voysey was above all a man of resolute character and iron convictions. While these characteristics led him to play an important role as a moraliser in late 19th-century England, it was his search for a new essentiality that underlay his contribution to the birth of the modern movement. Although his activity as an architect was concentrated in relatively few years and comprised almost exclusively country houses, Voysey's influence was enormous. Even Edwin Landseer Lutyens, the most highly regarded architect of public commissions at the time and the advocate of a different direction, observed that "No detail was too small for Voysey ... He was a revolutionary, and it is not difficult to understand to what extent he was so because we are surrounded by houses that are indirect descendants of the ones he designed. Falsified almost beyond what is acceptable, they nevertheless represent – albeit inadequately – a way of living that is infinitely more human than that which he helped to leave behind." Voysey's influence extended beyond the shores of Britain to continental Europe, where from 1890 to 1910 his work was a source of inspiration for Art Nouveau.

Born in 1857 in Hessle, Yorkshire, as the first son of a numerous family, Voysey had two sisters, who were to have considerable influence on him, and three brothers, who were so much younger than him that he could never play with them. This solitude, and the loss of the family estate in 1871, led Charles at an early age to assume a precociously mature role by the side of his father, the Reverend Charles Voysey. An Anglican vicar, Reverend Voysey soon left the Church of England, losing his property and facing long trials in order to found his own doctrine and the Theistic Church. He invested all his resources in this stubborn undertaking, establishing friendships with famous intellectuals and scientists such as Charles Darwin, and taking his family along with him to remote poor parts of the world, as far away as Jamaica. His father's strong personality, his isolation, and that fact that he was not able to experience the fantastic world of childhood helped to forge Voysey's character according to austere iron principles that would influence his architecture and, even more clearly, his critical writings.

Introverted and marked by such a difficult childhood, the young Voysey was judged by Dulwich College to be too shy, slow in learning, and thus unsuited to study – it seems, in fact, that at the age of 14 he still had difficulty reading, which explains why he was so prone to spelling mistakes in later life. Accordingly, he was assigned to a tutor, who advised him to study architecture, a profession held at the time to be fairly undemanding, and which was also in line with the family tradition – his grandfather, in fact, had been a well-known builder. Thus it was that in 1874 Voysey was articled to J. P. Seddon, who seemed to take no account of the opinion expressed by the school, entrusting the young Voysey with important decorative tasks. Then, in 1880, Voysey became the assistant of George Devey, the eminent country house designer, who was also a follower and friend of his father. It was to be a generous legacy from Devey that would later allow Voysey to build in 1895 the Voysey family home, Annesley Lodge, at Hampstead in London.

In 1880, during his year working with Devey, Voysey developed an interest in the small scale of rural buildings, a field to which he would devote himself from 1881, when he set up on his own with the aim of winning competitions and developing his career. Among his first works was a plan for a cottage for himself in 1885, the year of his marriage to Mary Maria Evans, a teacher he had met during a rare holiday. The preponderance of areas in the dwelling devoted to Voysey's professional

VOYSEY AND HIS DAUGHTER PRISCILLA IN FRONT OF THE HOUSE

PAGES 434–435: GARDEN VIEW

activity compared to the domestic spaces makes the cottage seem more like the residence of a bachelor than a family house. Nevertheless, the publication of the project won the fledgling architect his first actual commission: the M.H. Lakin Cottage in Bishop's Itchington, Warwickshire (1888), which, despite a few significant similarities with the cottage designed for himself, aims at a much greater sense of intimacy in the carefully studied arrangement of the passages.

Voysey was a man of almost maniacal rectitude, both in his work and in his life, and came to identify architectural qualities with moral qualities. Various sources – including Hermann Muthesius – report that he would turn down commissions from clients who did not appreciate his personal ethics. Voysey himself wrote that his attitude led him to have many Quaker clients, due to their propensity to simplicity and frankness. A convinced individualist, he tended to want control over every little detail, to the extent that when he built his own house he moved with his family to be as near as possible to the building site. His individualism may be the reason why his studio would never reach the colossal size of those of his rivals. It consisted of just two communicating rooms, so that his assistants could always know everything that was happening. The rooms were almost bare, and contained very little of the technological equipment, such as telephones or typewriters, typical of commercial activities.

Voysey was part of the fertile tradition of the English country house, to which he brought innovative solutions in the general appearance, in the distribution of spaces, and in the details, solutions that favoured a new simplicity and essentiality. In this context The Orchard, the house designed for himself and his family and completed in 1900, was especially significant.

In 1917, in dire financial straits as a result of a lack of work caused both by the war and by his own choices, Voysey left his family at The Orchard and went to live on his own in a small flat at 73 St James's Street, London. He was to remain there until 1940, when his son, who was also an architect, took him away, almost by force, to his home in Winchester, where Voysey stayed until his death in 1941.

Voysey chose the site of his own house, The Orchard, in Shire Lane, Chorley Wood, Hertfordshire (1900) primarily for two reasons. There was an old orchard on the plot, which could shelter the house from the wind, and the site lay close to the London underground, which allowed the architect to keep his studio in Baker Street in central London. In the eyes of the Victorian middle classes, it was a sign of success to have a residence in the country and an office in the city, although Voysey himself was never able to adapt to this situation.

The cuspidate façade of the new construction reflects the three-part layout of the interior. The hall passes through the house towards the garden. The rooms are oriented and arranged according to the degree of privacy required. The overall plan shows Voysey's predilection for the horizontal – even in the doors the width exceeds the height, which is just enough to pass under. The only exception is the baluster of the staircase, with its dense vertical lines stretching to the ceiling, alluding in Cartesian manner to ascent. The elimination of the banister, necessarily oblique, underlines the absolute dominion of right angles.

The carpets, the chairs, the clock, the door hinges, everything is designed by Voysey himself. The walls are covered in gay floral wallpaper (Voysey stated that wallpaper should only be used where there is no

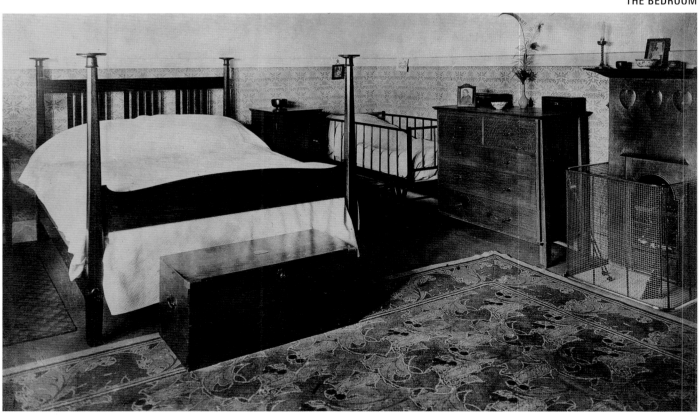

THE HALL

PLAN OF THE FIRST FLOOR

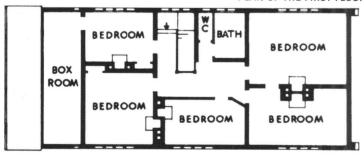

PLAN OF THE GROUND FLOOR

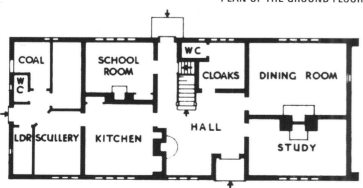

valuable furniture). An innocent brightness, combined with an almost expressionistic alteration of the elements, contrasts sharply with the education, the character and even the austere physical appearance of the architect as well as with his idiosyncratic attitude towards useless details, even in clothes.

The most important family space in the house, the dining room, has a cosy atmosphere, created by the low ceiling, underlined by the long low window. This quiet informality is countered by the beam jutting from the ceiling, while the table and the imposing high-backed chairs at the heads of the table create a longitudinal axis that is also a reflection of the rigid family structure. It is worth pointing out that, although Voysey defined The Orchard in one of his letters as a "house for my wife", there are no rooms for her sole use, nor rooms in which to sleep or entertain guests (such as a drawing room or sitting room), spaces that Voysey normally included in houses designed for other people. RUGGERO RAGAGNIN

BIBLIOGRAPHY:
1975   Gebhard D., *Charles F. A. Voysey, Architect*, Los Angeles
1979   Simpson D., *Voysey, an Architect of Individuality*, London
1992   Durant S., *C. F. A. Voysey*, London

Rudolf Wäger
*1941

1991–92, NEW CONSTRUCTION, STILL INHABITED BY THE ARCHITECT
FÄLLE 26, SATTEINS, VORARLBERG (A)

MAIN WORKS AND PROJECTS

1964–66   Own house ('Cube House'), Götzis, Vorarlberg (A)
1970   Gassner house, Schlins, Vorarlberg (A)
1971–73   Ruhwiesen housing development, Schlins, Vorarlberg (A)
1972–76   Ess house, Düns, Vorarlberg (A)
1978   Hollenstein house, Höchst, Vorarlberg (A)
1982–84   Own R. house (Rüdisser house), Hohenems (A), with
               Elisabeth Rüdisser

1982–85   Maria Königin des Friedens Church, Dornbirn, Vorarlberg
               (A), with Wolfgang Ritsch and Siegfried Wäger
1985–87   Cooperative housing project, Bayreuth, Bavaria (D)
1993   Lindner house, Hohenems, Vorarlberg (A)
1993–94   F. house, Lustenau, Vorarlberg (A)
1998   Concin house, Bludesch, Vorarlberg (A)

EVERYTHING THAT the autodidact Rudolf Wäger knows about architecture he has taught himself. Born in 1941 in Götzis, Vorarlberg, Austria, he served an apprenticeship as a carpenter from 1957 to 1960, and then went as a skilled carpenter to study for a year (1963–64) at the Academy of Fine Arts in Vienna, where he attended Roland Rainer's masterclass. Afterwards, in the early years of his architectural career, he tried twice to work in architecture offices, but soon realised that all this was simply not for him.

This led Wäger to embark on an idiosyncratic course that followed his own idea of architecture, which has brought him success. The first houses he designed were realised in collaboration with his brother Siegfried, a skilled bricklayer. Then, in 1967, he opened an architectural practice of his own in Götzis, Vorarlberg, which he transferred in 1972 to Schlins, also in Vorarlberg, before moving his office in 1978 to Feldkirch, again in Vorarlberg, where he settled until 1992. In this latter year he completed a studio for himself in Satteins, Vorarlberg, where he has run his practice to this day, himself moving into the studio-house in 2001.

During his work, in which he has designed many residential houses, a housing development in Schlins (Ruhwiesen, 1971–73), and a church (Mary Queen of Peace Church, Dornbirn, 1982–85, with Wolfgang Ritsch and Siegfried Wäger), Wäger has won a number of awards, including a prize in 1975 for his Schlins development, and the Grosse Österreichische Wohnbaupreis (Grand Austrian Housing Prize) in 1985 for his R. house (Rüdisser house). In 1984 he co-founded with 15 other architects the Gruppe Vorarlberger Baukünstler (Vorarlberg Group of Architects), which was a response to a prohibition by the Association of Architects and Consulting Engineers, which wanted to prevent craftsmen with no academic degree and young architects who were not qualified civil engineers from officially practising as architects. The Vorarlberg Group countered the objections of the Association by invoking artistic freedom and inveighing against a conservative educational establishment and a generally elitist architectural system. The idealistic rebels drew wide support, especially from writers, painters and other artistic figures, some of whom placed commissions with the young architects.

The Vorarlberg architectural scene had long been rather different from and independent of the mainstream. It started out on its individual route back in the 1960s, when far from the international scene a new young generation of Vorarlberg architects started to search under special local conditions for their own identity and voice. This first generation of Vorarlberg architects positioned themselves, as Friedrich Achleitner has put it, within an "alternative culture", or, as he has also observed: "Theirs is an architectural language based on the dialectics of technical thinking and industrial production, on critical traditionalism and life-related Modernism, against the background of a new sensibility towards lifestyles and cultural definition." What this meant was the young Vorarlberg school of architecture emphasised at one and the same time tradition and innovation, old craft skills and new technology. And, indeed, the regional school is characterised by technical innovation combined with a reflective interest in highly developed traditional local craft skills and rural housing culture, coupled with Alemannic pragmatism. Vorarlberg architects sought to revive and enter into a dialogue with local craft and housing traditions, adapting them in a critical context and in the light of modern architectural developments, to lead to new technical and formal results. Over the years the trend was tempered with a premium on a good aesthetic work, close liaison between architect and client, and ecological awareness.

By the 1980s the young Vorarlberg school of architecture had acquired a considerable aura in Austria, attracting attention nationwide.

THE NORTH-WESTERN CORNER WITH ENTRANCE
VIEW FROM THE KITCHEN TOWARDS THE GARDEN

THE SOUTH-EASTERN CORNER

THE LIVING AREA ON THE FIRST FLOOR

THE DINING AREA ON THE FIRST FLOOR

What had once seemed revolutionary had almost become socially acceptable. And, indeed, the school in Austria's westernmost federal province meanwhile occupies almost a leading position in Austrian architecture, at least in terms of quality, even if the pioneering era is over, the original idealistic conditions of the founding phase no longer exist, and the mantle has been taken over by a third generation of architects. Wäger, of course, belongs to the first generation of Vorarlberg architects, but among the newcomers he still occupies an authentic position, takes an interest in contemporary issues, and represents the principles of the school. These days he especially admires new Swiss architecture, notably in the Ticino area, and also the simplicity of south German architecture.

Wäger built his first private house in his home town of Götzis between 1964 and 1966 (design to completion). Known as the 'Cube House', it is one of the architect's most extraordinary works. A pioneering achievement of recent Vorarlberg architecture, it became a model for many subsequent houses. Friedrich Achleitner described the Cube House as a key building in the quest for rational housing. With its simplicity of form, exemplary use of space and extremely low building cost, it represents a landmark in the evolution of the construction of single-family houses. Actually, the house rather runs counter to Wäger's beliefs about the single-family house. He is ambivalent about the idea, so loved by the people of Vorarlberg, of one house for one family, which leads to problems of overdevelopment of the landscape. It was partly to answer his own criticism of such houses that he designed his Ruhwiesen housing development in Schlins (1971–73), another landmark in his oeuvre. This was the first development in Austria in the 1970s built by an owners' cooperative. Working together with the architect, Wäger and the residents were able to construct Ruhwiesen in wood with a high degree of efficiency and economy.

Between 1982 and 1984 Wäger built his second home in Hohenems together with his partner, Elisabeth Rüdisser, the actual construction work taking only five months. This house, built with a shuttering girder, has a lean-to roof and a glazed veranda with gallery. Some 12 metres from the main house there is a studio building, which is characterised by formal simplicity and reduction. In 1985 the Rüdisser house won the Grosse Österreichische Wohnbaupreis, a major prize for housing awarded for the first time that year.

From 1991–92 Wäger realised his third 'home' at Fälle 26 in Satteins, a small village in Vorarlberg. It was designed as a studio for him to work in. At the time the architect did not need it as a residential building because he already lived in another house nearby, in a development that he had also designed. The Satteins studio is a minimal tower-like building with a ground plan of 6 x 8 m, and was constructed as a wooden post-and-beam structure, with untreated concrete slabs as elements for the façades. Unfortunately, the design process has not been documented, due mainly to the fact that Wäger usually draws his plans on notepads, often throwing existing drawings away, and to the way the architect usually works with the builders orally. Details are developed actually on the construction site, and solutions reached through direct communication.

The two-storey interior is characterised by a tension between vertical and horizontal forces, which becomes apparent on the façade, with the same dialectics also evident in the strip windows. Inside the house,

the two floors are connected by an open stair. The architect's working area, a tiny kitchen and wet rooms are situated on the ground floor. Recently, Wäger has made a few adaptations to the studio, converting it into a studio-cum-house. His work area remains on the ground floor, while the upper floor has become a living and sleeping area. This is because in March 2001 the architect sold his house in the nearby development, which seemed to him superfluous, and moved into his studio.

In Wäger's brilliant and sophisticated Satteins studio-house, dwelling has been reduced and tailored to the inhabitant's specific requirements. Anything that is not absolutely essential has been dispensed with. Living takes place within a very restricted space, although one never feel a sense of confinement. The rooms have a calm natural aura, nothing is overdone, and whatever does exist in the building is housed with a touching simplicity. A few books of Heinrich Heine, whose timeless expressiveness Wäger much appreciates, sit on the bookshelf, and in the living room there are chairs designed by the architect, a system of bars and straps that fulfil their functions in a simple way, and a single large inviting table – what more do we need, asks Wäger. Like his other buildings, and indeed like his whole life itself, the studio-house is reduced, minimal, calm, clear, authentic, independent and autochthonous, a condensate of Wäger's architectural thinking. GABRIELE REITERER

PLAN

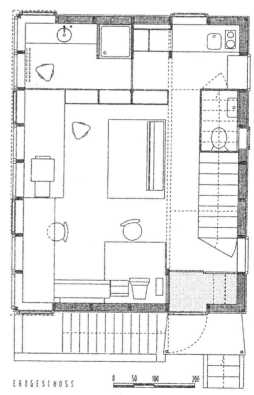

ERDGESCHOSS   0 50 100   200

BIBLIOGRAPHY:
1993   Purin B. (ed.), *Architektur in Vorarlberg seit 1960*, Bregenz
1994   Steiner D., *Architektur / Beispiel Eternit*, pp. 166–167
1995   Becker A., Steiner D. and Wang W., *Architektur im 20. Jahrhundert. Österreich*, Munich / New York, pp. 194–195
1998   Kapfinger O., *Baukunst in Vorarlberg seit 1980*, Stuttgart, p. 8/1

Otto Wagner

1841–1918

1911–12, NEW CONSTRUCTION, RESTORED OUTSIDE AND ALTERED INSIDE HÜTTELBERGSTRASSE 28, VIENNA (A)

MAIN WORKS AND PROJECTS

1882–84	Länderbank, I district, Vienna (A)
1884–95	Ankerhaus, I district, Vienna (A)
1886–88	First Wagner house, Hüttelbergstrasse 26, XIV district (formerly XIII), Vienna (A)
1894–1900	Buildings for the elevated and underground Wiener Stadtbahn (Vienna City Railway) (A)
1898–99	Apartment buildings, Linke Wienzeile 38 and 40, Vienna (A)
1902–04	St Leopold's Church/Steinhof, XIV district, Vienna (A)
1904–06	Postsparkasse (Postal Savings Bank), I district, Vienna (A)
1909–10	Apartment building, Neustiftgasse 40, VII district, Vienna (A)
1911–12	Apartment building, Döblergasse 4, VII district, Vienna (A)

THE HIGHLY INFLUENTIAL Austrian architect and teacher Otto Wagner, closely identified with Art Nouveau, was born on 13 July 1841 in Penzing, on the outskirts of Vienna. His father was a notary, while his mother, Susanne, was the daughter of a well-to-do court and war archivist. He had one brother. When at the age of five Otto lost his father, his mother became the guiding figure in his and his brother's lives, financing their education partly from the rent generated by three properties that she owned in Göttweihergasse. Her philosophy of life was based on the premises of 'education and property', and she brought her sons up training them to become personally and economically independent, for that in her view was the foundation of social success. Berta Zuckerkandl describes Wagner as an "epicurean, optimist, revolutionary, sceptic, man of the world and diplomat", but also as an "ill-mannered madcap".

Until the age of nine Wagner was educated by private tutors and French governesses, after which he attended grammar school and the Benedictine seminary in Kremsmünster, Upper Austria. Wagner's interest in architecture may have been awakened at an early age by a meeting with Theophil Hansen. Between 1857 and 1859 the future architect studied at Vienna's Technical University, in 1860 at the Academy of Architecture in Berlin, and from 1861 to 1863 at the Vienna Academy of Fine Arts under August Siccard von Siccardsburg and Eduard van der Null.

In 1863 Wagner married Josefine Domhard, from whom he separated in 1880, and together they had one daughter, Susanne. In addition he had two illegitimate sons, Otto and Robert, by Sophie von Paupie. Wagner's second wife, Louise Stiffel, was the governess of his daughter. This happy relationship produced three children: Stefan, Louise and Christine. Louise Stiffel died relatively young in 1915, and until his own death on 11 April 1918 in Vienna Otto Wagner wrote letters to her in his diary and also mourned her at an altar in his house specially erected for that purpose.

Otto Wagner was Vienna's most outstanding architectural personality of the late 19th and early 20th century, and is widely regarded as being one of the founders of European modernist architecture. In 1894 he was appointed to a professorship, succeeding Karl Hasenauer, at Vienna's Academy of Fine Arts, where he directed one of the two schools of architecture until 1913. As a lecturer at the Academy, he shaped almost two generations of architects in the outgoing Austro-Hungarian empire and its succession states. His most important pupils included Joseph Olbrich, Josef Hoffmann, Jan Kotêra, Josef Plecnik, Max Fabiani and Rudolf M. Schindler. Some of Wagner's buildings, such as his blocks of rented apartments on the Linke Wienzeile (1898–99), his St Leopold's Church at the Steinhof nursing home (1902–07), and his Postsparkasse or Postal Savings Bank (1904–12), have long since become icons in the history of 20th-century architecture. Especially the Postal Savings Bank, sparingly decorated and with a curving glass roof over its central hall, is acclaimed as a milestone in the history of modern architecture. As 'the best constructor of apartment palaces', Otto Wagner realised roughly 50 houses and blocks of rented flats, living in some of them himself.

The first house that Otto Wagner designed exclusively for his own private use was built 1886–88 at Hüttelbergstrasse 26 in Vienna's XIV (formerly XIII) district. Originally it served as the family's summer residence, but became their main home in 1895, when the city palace on Rennweg where the family had previously been living was sold. The villa, which is symmetrically structured and has a portico situated at the front, shows the architect referring to stylistic models from the Renaissance. This is in keeping with the rest of his early work, which is in the already-established Neo-Renaissance style. Especially the house's ground plan – a central space flanked by two pergolas – recalls Andrea Palladio. On a marble slab above the right-hand arched niche on the external façade

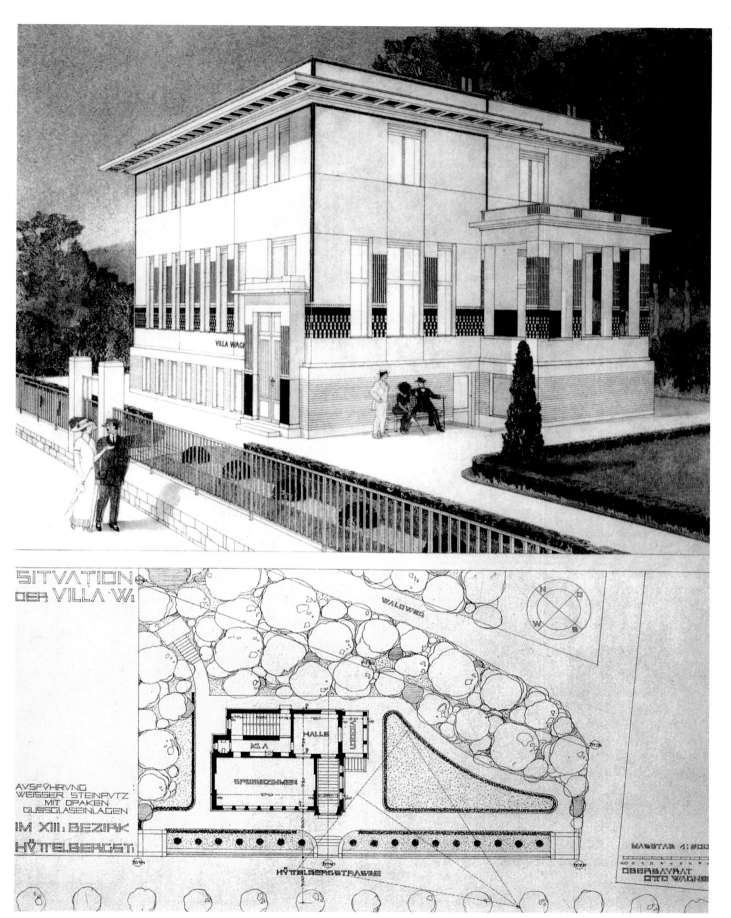

PERSPECTIVE VIEW AND SITE PLAN

Wagner inscribed his motto *artis sola domina necessitas*. The architect may initially have drawn on historical principles in the design of his buildings, as is the case here, but nevertheless he always remained true to his doctrine of structure, rationality and expediency.

From 1864 onwards Wagner worked as a freelance architect, at the same time financing in an entrepreneurial capacity a series of projects, including the three blocks of rented apartments on Vienna's Linke Wienzeile (1898–99). The buildings, especially the Majolikahaus with its weather-resistant tile cladding, were constructed in accordance with the design principles of the Vienna Sezession, which Wagner joined in 1899, remaining a member until the departure of the Klimt group in 1905. Wagner moved into a small apartment on the upper ground floor of the block at Köstlergasse 3. The flat's bedroom, with its almost exclusively vegetable ornamentation, as well as its celebrated glass bath were presented in the rotunda at the jubilee exhibition of 1898.

This furnishing became the prototype of an interior for the city dweller living a modern lifestyle, a clientele for which Wagner designed almost exclusively. The interior decoration manifested progressiveness in the social and technological sphere while the furnishings clearly evinced the rooms' functions. At the same time the façade was executed uniformly, giving each apartment equal weighting. This anonymisation of an individual lifstyle became the basic requirement of a modern way of living. The apartment block with mixed use, as a new, functionally and economically qualified type of building, sequenced additively along a straight street, corresponded completely to Wagner's conception of a dynamic expansion of the historical town into a limitless city. An enthusiastic advocate of the dense conurbation, Wagner opposed the decentralisation and deurbanisation propagated by the garden-city movement.

STREET VIEW

His publication *Die Groszstadt. Eine Studie über diese* (Vienna, 1911) advanced a convincing argument in favour of the metropolis.

Wagner created his last apartment block as client or property developer in 1911–12 at Döblergasse 4, in Vienna's VII district. Here, in December 1911 he moved with his family into the 250-m^2, street-facing apartment on the first floor. His studio was on the same floor in the courtyard wing. Many of the interiors used by himself Wagner exploited in published form. His multi-volume work *Einige Skizzen, Projekte und Ausgeführte Bauwerke* (1889–1922) shows him turning, among other things, living and dining rooms, gentleman's and lady's rooms, and bathrooms into public spaces that represent an ideal setting for a bourgeois reception. With his portrait, which hung originally in the billiard room of the first Wagner house and then in the drawing room of the Döblergasse apartment, Wagner declared himself to be a member of upper-class society. Striking an impressive pose in festive attire, his top hat in his hand and decorations around his neck, which would stimulate plenty of conversation, he presented himself with an architect's gravitas. As he put it: "The appearance and offices of the inhabitant should be one with the look of his rooms." This requirement was expressed in the appearance of the second Wagner house, which corresponded to the type of the apartment block *en miniature*. In addition, 'modern', fashionably dressed people supported the idea of Wagner's cityscape: "After all, it is simply ridiculous to design certain houses for city dwellers like farmhouses and to allow these houses to be inhabited by drawing-room farmers and city lasses."

The second home that Wagner designed exclusively for his private use was built 1911–12 at Hüttelbergstrasse 28. Likewise a new construction, the house was envisaged as a summer residence and also eventually as a widow's home for his much younger second wife, Louise. Unlike his first villa, located immediately next door, which formally opens to the outside, the second house is imbued with the strict closed self-containedness of the cube. The three-storey reinforced-concrete structure,

LOGGIA

ELEVATION DETAILS

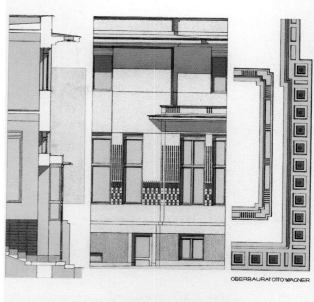

VILLA ~~FÜR HERRN~~ ~~UND FRAU~~ WAGNER HÜTTELBERGST. 28.

OBERBAURAT OTTO WAGNER

ELEVATION DETAILS

which has a walk-on flat roof and built-on loggia, is perforated by three rows of windows that concatenate almost serially. The entrance is no longer located in the middle axis, but is placed – due to the interior use of space – on the right side of the building, where it stands out boldly on account of its decorative design. The glass windows were designed by Leopold Forstner and made by the Viennese mosaic workshops.

The service rooms and a staff flat are housed on the lower ground floor, which can be accessed by a second (staff) entrance at the rear of the building. Steps lead from the main entrance area into a hall on the upper ground floor. This in turn leads into the loggia and also into the dining room, which as the largest room in the house extends the entire length of the street-facing window façade. Parallel to the dining room lies the staircase. On the top (third) floor, facing the street, are a bedroom, a dressing room, guest room and studio, while on the garden side there is a bathroom adjoining the bedroom as well as a small room for the servant. The toilet is at the end of the corridor accessing these rooms.

The only furniture in the house of which there is any record is that in the hall and dining room, which was documented by photos in Wagner's *Die Baukunst Unserer Zeit* (1914). Nothing is known about the remaining furnishings in the other rooms. The hall has a double function, serving also as the living room. It is furnished with a square table, four easy chairs designed by Marcel Kammerer, and a cabinet with a projecting base, beside which an occasional table is placed. Except for the cabinet, which is an Otto Wagner design, these are all pieces of bentwood furniture, produced in serial form by Thonet. The dining room is furnished with a pull-out dining table, 18 arm chairs, a sideboard and four side tables as well as a small group of seats in front of the fireplace. The furniture in the horizontally divided room, underscored by the chromatic composition in red and white, is predominantly characterised by 'practical arrangement' as well as 'simplicity and durability'. The furnishing reflects a hierarchisation and differentiation among the rooms. Thus the furniture

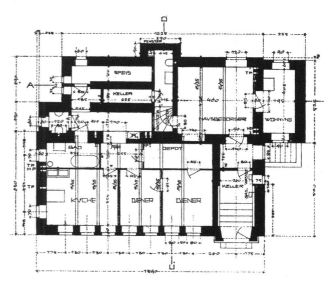

PLAN

in the dining room is varnished unlike that in the hall. There is even differentiation among the colours.

Otto Wagner's designs, his 'functional decor' and his personal lifestyle are not shaped by any desire to reform life, but by an upper-class aspiration to self-portrayal and by a constant proclamation of the contemporaneous beyond a historical hotchpotch.   MONICA PLATZER

BIBLIOGRAPHY:
1922 Tietze H., *Otto Wagner*, Vienna / Berlin / Munich / Leipzig
1984 *Otto Wagner: Möbel und Innenräume*, Museum Moderner Kunst, Stiftung Ludwig, Vienna, Salzburg / Vienna
1985 Graf O. A., *Otto Wagner. Das Werk des Architekten*, 2 vols., Vienna / Cologne / Graz
1993 Mallgrave H. F. (ed.), *Otto Wagner. Reflections on the Raiment of Modernity*, Santa Monica
2001 Cornoldi A., *Le case degli architetti. Dizionario privato dal Rinascimento ad oggi*, Venice, pp. 421–423

Sarah Wigglesworth & Jeremy Till
*1957, *1957

1998–2001, NEW CONSTRUCTION, STILL INHABITED BY THE ARCHITECTS LONDON (GB)

MAIN WORKS AND PROJECTS

1999	Writer's retreat, London (GB)
2000–02	Chelsea Flower Show Garden and Pavilion, London (GB)
2001–03	Classroom for the Future: Mossbrook Special Primary School (GB)
2002–	Siobhan Davies Dance Company Sudio and Headquarters, London (GB)

SARAH WIGGLESWORTH, born in 1957, graduated in architecture from the University of Cambridge in 1983. After gaining experience working in a number of architectural firms, she received a Fulbright scholarship in 1991 for further studies in the USA. In 1993 she founded her own architectural practice in London: Sarah Wigglesworth Architects. Two years later, Jeremy Till (1957) entered the firm as partner. They had met as students in Cambridge and had also studied together in the USA. Given their experience in the USA, these two architects found their key theme – an intense interest in the ecological aspects of architecture – at a relatively late stage. For Wigglesworth, however, another important factor is the gender issue. The fact that women – whether they design, commission or use a building – are still unable to exert enough influence on shaping the environment is a social problem that she has addressed in many lectures and essays. She fervently believes that improvement of this situation would promote new approaches to the built environment and would enhance its quality on a permanent basis. Wigglesworth and Till both teach architecture at the University of Sheffield. As a result, they have, until now, built relatively few actual projects. A "writer's retreat" in the north of London may be regarded as the first built manifesto of their architectural practice. The complex relationship between inside and outside, the changing light in the course of the day and the seasons, and the blend of concentration and relaxation in this cabin bear witness to an architectural approach that respects what Gaston Bachelard has described as the "poetry of space" without subordinating the functional to the aesthetic.

The most important project to date by Wigglesworth and Till is also in north London. It is their own home and office. The ecological core of the concept applied in its design has earned it the epithet "Straw House". In actual fact, the building is far more than just a straw house. Indeed, it

would be more fitting to describe it as a collage of various experiments in form and material that cannot be reduced in this case to purely formal effects. In terms of form alone, the composition could even be described as over-orchestrated to the point of cacophany: wood, steel, concrete, rubble, corrugated metal, sandbags and plastic alternate seemingly at random, overgrowing the L-shaped building. This is reminiscent of such architectural outsiders as Bruce Goff, Lucien Kroll or the early Frank O. Gehry. And something of their protest against the perfectionism of established architecture may also have determined the Straw House. Above all, however, it is a built experiment in the sustainable use of building materials and the creation of a pleasant spatial atmosphere in an extremely urban context. The building is right beside a railway line. Every quarter of an hour, a train hurtles past – the noise and the vibrations demanded special structural measures, such as steel springs under the building tract nearest the railway line to absorb the vibrations. For Wigglesworth and Till, acquiring this site gave them an opportunity of building in the centre of London on a shoestring budget. At the same time, the building was intended to demonstrate that, with a little imagination, it is possible to create an urban home and workplace with real atmosphere even on such an unappealing site.

The angle of the building frames a courtyard and garden. The shorter wing, nearer the railway line, shelters the courtyard and also insulates the longer wing, which houses the living quarters, against the noise of the trains. Both wings are elevated, leaving the floor level more or less free. The tract nearest the railway line – housing the two-storey office – is set on huge concrete pillars whose voluminosity is further emphasised by a cladding of wire mesh gabions filled with concrete rubble. In stark contrast to this are the slender steel pilotis under the accomodation tract, which has a southfacing glass facade that opens towards the courtyard. Apart from a small area of wood and little windows in front of the kit-

BOOK TOWER >

VIEW OF THE STRAW BALE WALL FROM THE GARDEN

NOISE INSULATION FAÇADE MADE OF SANDBAGS

chen, reminiscent of a garden shed, this facade is the most conventional part of the entire building. The side of the office tract facing the railway line closes with a wall of stacked sandbags, containing not only sand but also a lime-cement mixture, which will absorb moisture and harden as time passes. This wall insulates most of the sound of the passing trains. The windows here, appropriately enough, are framed by old railway sleepers. At the courtyard side of the office tract, the architects have experimented with a textile outer skin made of plastic material. This certainly flies in the face of most conventional notions of ecological building. The same is true of the bales of straw used as cladding, from which the house takes its name. This wall of bales is situated on the north side of the accommodation tract and continues round the western end where the bedrooms are situated, as far as the courtyard side. There is a smooth lime finish on the inside, and an industrial-style cladding of corrugated metal panels on the outside. Nothing of the economic ecological building material would have been visible, had not the architects replaced some of the corrugated metal panels with identically profiled transparent polycarbonate panels. Sarah Wigglesworth intends to study the long-term behaviour of this building material, which is still barely tested in the UK.

One might surmise whether the aesthetic statement or the spectacular media impact are foremost considerations here. After all, what would be the point, in media terms at least, of a straw wall that nobody can see? This might explain the scepticism felt by some dyed-in-the-wool adherents of ecological building towards this hybrid structure. Wigglesworth and Till counter that the ecological balance of a building involves a number of highly divergent factors that are too complex to treat in terms of the superficial judgment of individual materials. At any rate, with their provocative collage, the architects have succeeded in liberating the key issues of ecological building from its conservative and esoteric connotations to create a sense of contemporary urban living. This

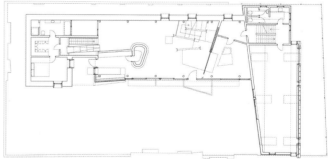

PLAN OF THE UPPER FLOOR

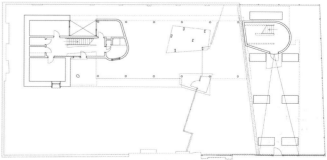

PLAN OF THE GROUND FLOOR

KITCHEN

VIEW BETWEEN PANTRY AND YARD FAÇADE

SLIDING WALL

DINING ROOM

latter effect can be felt in the openness, complexity and versatility of the interior.

The centre of the house is the spacious living area under a pitched roof that rises towards the office tract. Here, the pale hues of rendered surfaces and plywood cladding are predominant. At the higher side is a dining area separated by a sliding partition which can be transformed into a meeting room for office work. The kitchen is at the other end. Sitting at the kitchen table, the logic of the little windows in the wooden wall becomes clear: they focus details of the surroundings. The transition from kitchen to living room is accentuated by the conically upward tapering shape of the pantry. Based on a traditional North African construction technique, it acts as a natural refrigerator. The distinctive tower that rises three storeys high out of the living area also has a natural air conditioning function. Its main purpose is to store books, and there is a reading

area right at the top with views of the city. From the tower, there is access to the roof – a grass roof with wildflowers, which is watered in dry weather by a rainwater cistern, and which also enhances the quality of the air inside the building. The ventilation and light shafts jut up from the grass like surreal objects. The architects have invested a great deal of time and energy in the creation of this remarkable experimental house. Planning began in 1994, construction in 1998, and the house was finally completed in 2000. Because of their concentration on this private project, Wigglesworth even had to reduce her staff. She now shares her two office floors with another firm of architects. But the effort has been worth it in more than one sense: on the one hand, Wigglesworth now has a highly distinctive home in a central location and, on the other hand, the building has drawn considerable attention to Sarah Wigglesworth Architects.

EBERHARD SYRING

SECTION

BIBLIOGRAPHY

1998   Till J. and Wigglesworth S. (eds.), *The Everyday and Architecture*, special edition of *Architectural Design*

2001   Toy M. (ed.), *The Architect. Women in Contemporary Architecture*, Chichester, pp. 174–179

2002   'Vom Glatten und Haarigen', in *Deutsche Bauzeitung*, no. 4

2003   'Wie Sarah Wigglesworth den Öko-Bau neu erfand', in *Häuser*, no. 1

Michael Wilford

*1938

2000, NEW CONSTRUCTION, IN COLLABORATION WITH SUZANNE GARRETT AND DAVID GUY, STILL INHABITED BY THE ARCHITECT CHUCK HATCH, HARTFIELD, EAST SUSSEX (GB)

MAIN WORKS AND PROJECTS

1967–76	Residence Complex in Runcorn New Town (GB), James Stirling and Partner
1977–84	National Gallery Extension, Stuttgart (D), James Stirling and Partner
1983–88	Center for Performing Arts, Cornell University, Ithaca, New York (USA), James Stirling, Michael Wilford and Associates
1986–92	Braun Manufacturing Plant, Melsungen (D), James Stirling, Michael Wilford and Associates with Walter Nägeli
1991–96	Temasek Polytechnic, Singapore (Malaysia), James Stirling, Michael Wilford and Associates

1994–97	Sto AG, Weizen, Baden-Württemberg (D), Michael Wilford and Partners
1995–2000	British Embassy, Berlin (D), Michael Wilford and Partners
1997–2000	The Lowry, Performing and Visual Arts Centre, Salford (GB), Michael Wilford and Partners

MICHAEL WILFORD was born in 1938 in Surbiton, Surrey. He was educated in London at the Kingston Technical School, the Northern Polytechnic School of Architecture and the Regent Street Polytechnic Planning School. Before graduating, he worked in the office of James Stirling (born 1926). During this period in the early 1960s, Stirling and James Gowan, his partner at the time, built the Engineering Building at Lancaster University – a work that established their reputation across England. The building makes reference to 1920s Russian Constructivism, without a feeling of revolutionary pathos. The attempt to unify cultural heritage with contemporary forms of expression through ironic and playful means (a characteristic that would mark the office's later endeavours) is already apparent in this early work and rightfully demonstrates the influence exerted on Stirling by the architectural historian and theoretician Colin Rowe. In 1963, Stirling and Gowan separated and Michael Wilford became an associate partner in 1965.

The growing significance of Wilford's participation in the partnership with Stirling lead to the office being renamed James Stirling, Michael Wilford and Associates in 1980 until Stirling's death in 1992. In the mid 1970s, as work slowed down and the office entered many competitions, it began a crucial phase of development, placing an increasing emphasis on architectural history in its designs. This approach corresponded with the growing public unease with the autism of late modernist architecture. The consequences of this, a return to sites of cultural identity, was reflected in the museum building boom which took place at the same time and in which Germany played a pivotal role. It is no surprise that this

new phase of development manifested itself in the designs for three museum building competitions in Germany. Finally, Stirling was able to realize his ideas in the extension of the National Gallery in Stuttgart. The Stuttgart museum unleashed a vehement and controversial architectural debate. The National Gallery was the first example of Postmodernism in Germany. Even though one can distinguish the formal language of Stirling and Wilford through its spatial and sculptural complexity from the main currents of Postmodernist architecture, it clearly demonstrates one of the movement's key precepts: the "double coding" that Charles Jencks, the inventor of the term Postmodern architecture, speaks of. This term signifies on the one hand, that architecture should be popular, and on the other that it should have a higher cultural significance. In the same vein, the Stuttgart museum is full of historical references that can only be read by those who have the corresponding educational background. This cultural-historical "baggage", however, does not inhibit the popular acceptance of the building. As examples of servicing the public's taste, one only needs to think of the colourful details or the powerfully oversized handrails on the ramp balustrades.

The complex collage techniques displayed for the first time in Stuttgart significantly determined the style of the numerous buildings that Stirling and Wilford would consequently design and build, even though the allusions in these subsequent works were not on the same flamboyant scale. The key works of this phase included the W.Z.B. Research Centre in Berlin, the Clore gallery in London, the State Music School in Stuttgart, the Center for Performing Arts at Cornell University in Ithaca, New

NIGHT VIEW OF THE ENTRANCE SIDE >

SIDE VIEW, ENTRANCE ON THE RIGHT

York, and the National Gallery extension in London. In buildings such as the Braun manufacturing plant in Melsungen (with Walter Nägeli) and the Temasek Polytechnic in Singapore, the earlier postmodern flamboyance is further reduced in favour of clear construction dimensions, however, the characteristic ironic and playful features remain. These "trademarks" also characterize the buildings that Michael Wilford continued to design at an uninterrupted pace after the sudden death of Stirling in 1992. The most important works of Michael Wilford and Partners, the name of the office after 1993, include The Lowry Performing and Visual Arts Centre in Salford, the British Embassy in Berlin and the multifunctional Esplanade National Performing Arts Centre in Singapore. In 2001, the office of Michael Wilford and Partners was fused with MUMA (McInnes, Usher, McKnight Architects) in London and Wilford Schupp in Stuttgart.

In 2000, Michael Wilford built a villa for himself and his wife in a forested, scenic region south of London. The two-story house is half-situated on a hillside. Coming from the street above, one enters the long extended building over a bridge directly in the middle of the first floor. This path continues in a straight line, connecting a shorter cross wing on the middle axis housing the living area, while on the left hand side the kitchen and eating area are oriented towards the south. The spacious bedroom is situated opposite on the north side. From the entrance hall, one staircase leads below to the ground floor, while a second leads above to Wilford's home office in an open gallery in the main living area.

Two guest rooms are housed on the north side of the ground floor, while on the west is a small living area connecting to the lower terrace. The main attraction on this floor, however, is the pool oriented towards the south, with a large circular window on the front offering a view of the adjacent forest.

Observed from the exterior, the house shifts between regional style and pop collage. The very rustic exterior wall of the base consists of sandstone blocks. The windows are small and deeply inlaid. The upper floor, constructed from wood with ample panes of glass, offers a striking contrast. Primarily through the dominance of the horizontal structure of the beams, the rows of windows and the flat, widely hipped roof with a projecting gargoyle, the above floor demonstrates a dynamic reminiscent of Frank Lloyd Wright's Prairie House, and is effectively visually grounded through the weight of the base.

The cohesive effect of the entire design is thwarted by three structures that jut out from the contour: on the west side, through the acute-angled steel construction of the upper terrace painted in strong colours that ends in a spiral staircase; on the east side, through two metal sculptural forms set back from the façade which whimsically flank the entrance bridge. The right form is organically curved and contains the bathroom; the left one, a deconstructivist tipped cube, is the food pantry. In contrast to such postmodern ideas – the telescopic lookout under the west gable also belongs to this category – the interior rooms, on the main floor, extending up into the space under the roof, appear as classical modern. The chimney wall and protruding bedstead structure the space

THE FIREPLACE IN THE LIVING ROOM

BEDROOM

KITCHEN

DRESSING TABLE

LIVING ROOM

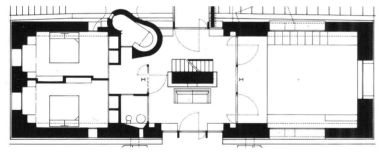

GROUND PLAN

SECTION

as a white sculptural form; a space, which by way of the extended rows of windows, forms a unity with the surrounding landscape.

EBERHARD SYRING

BIBLIOGRAPHY:
1984 Arnell P. (ed.), Blickford T. (ed.), *James Stirling – Bauten und Projekte 1950–1983*, Stuttgart
1998 Maxwell R., *James Stirling, Michael Wilford*, Basle
2000 Steinberger P., 'Eine sehr komplizierte Torte', in *Süddeutsche Zeitung*, May 2
       Wefing H., 'Tony Blairs Gesandte wohnen nicht im Herrenclub,' in *Frankfurter Allgemeine Zeitung*, July 15
2002 Pietsch H., 'Stadtflucht auf die feine englische Art', in *Häuser*, no. 1/02, pp. 42–49

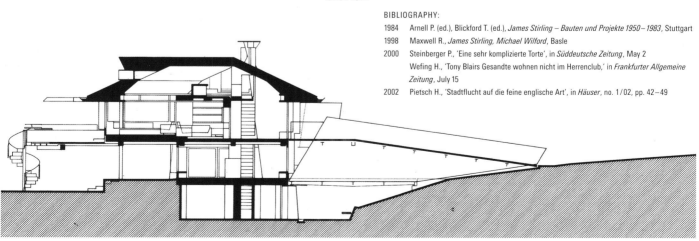

Colin St. John Wilson
1922–2007

**1961–64, NEW CONSTRUCTION, NOW HOUSES THE WITTGENSTEIN ARCHIVE
2 GRANTCHESTER ROAD, CAMBRIDGE (GB)**

MAIN WORKS AND PROJECTS

1953–56 Bentham Road Estate, Hackney, London (GB), for London
County Council

1957–59 Extension to School of Architecture, University of Cambridge (GB)

1957–62 Harvey Court, Gonville and Caius College, Cambridge (GB),
with Sir Leslie Martin

1957–64 Library group, Oxford University (GB), with Sir Leslie Martin

1960–64 The Stone Building, Peterhouse College, Cambridge (GB),
with Sir Leslie Martin

1962–98 Entrance hall and reading room, The British Library,
St Pancras, London (GB)

1965–69 Cornford House, Cambridge (GB)
Liverpool Civic and Social Centre (GB)

1973 Own house, 31 Grove End Road, London NW8 (GB)

1973–80 Restaurant, extension to The British Museum, London (GB)

1985–88 Library for Queen Mary's College, University of London (GB)

COLIN ST. JOHN WILSON was born in Cheltenham on 14
March 1922. In 1940 he went up Corpus Christi College at the University
of Cambridge to study architecture as part of a two-year 'War degree'
course. At the time he took a great interest in painting and poetry. On
finishing the course in 1942, he joined the Royal Navy. During his time in
the Navy (1942–46), Wilson became attached to an Air Arm Communication Squadron at the time of the invasion of Europe, and subsequently
served in India until the end of the war. Far from interrupting or spoiling
his studies, these war experiences actually formed a very important part
of his education. Between 1946 and 1949 Wilson continued his studies at
the University of London, graduating as a qualified architect from University College in 1949.

In 1950 Wilson joined the Architects' Department of London County
Council, which was overrun by ex-servicemen and women determined to
build a 'Brave New World' out of a London devastated by the war.
Among his contemporaries here were James Stirling, Peter and Alison
Smithson, Alan Colquhoun and Peter Carter. This was the time of the
'Angry Young Men', and Wilson was a leading activist in the Independent Group, which among other things launched the collaborative *This is
Tomorrow* exhibition of architects and artists, mounted in 1956 in London's Whitechapel Gallery. The show led to friendships with many artists,
an upshot of which was Wilson's major private collection of British art
from 1950 on, which he had built up over nearly half a century and which
would be housed in the building on which the architect was then working,
the extension to Pallant House Gallery in Chichester.

In the same year as the exhibition, 1956, Wilson was invited to join
Sir Leslie Martin, the newly elected Professor of Architecture at Cam-

bridge University, both to lecture there and also to work in association
with him in a joint architectural practice (1956–64). Together they produced the first project for the enlargement of the British Museum Library
and a number of important developments and buildings at the Universities of Oxford and Cambridge, such as the three libraries complex at
Oxford (1957–64), and Gonville and Caius College's Harvey Court (1957–
62) as well as Peterhouse's Stone Building (1960–64), both in Cambridge.

In 1960 Wilson decided to build his own house and studio (1961–
64), enabling him in 1964 to found his own independent practice. Within
a short time he received a number of important commissions, including
a development plan for the British Museum and a Civic Centre for Liverpool (1965–69). During this period he also formed close teaching ties
with the USA, lecturing as a visiting professor at Yale University (1960,
1964, 1983 and 2000) and at MIT (1970–72). It was at Yale that he met
Mary Jane Long, a student of his, who became one of his first assistants
back in his Cambridge office, subsequently becoming a partner in the
practice. In the course of time (in 1972) they got married and had a
daughter and a son. Wilson continued teaching at Cambridge until 1970,
when he moved his architectural practice to London. He did, however,
return to Cambridge in 1975, heading the School of Architecture until
1989.

The project that marked Wilson's practice from beginning to end is
the British Library in London, for which he produced two designs opposite the British Museum in Bloomsbury (1962–64 and 1969–73) and a
final design at St Pancras (1975–99). The new British Library is the major
monument built by government in the 20th century and was the subject

FAÇADE TO GRANTCHESTER ROAD

MAIN STAIRCASE

THE OFFICE

THE LIVING ROOM

ST. JOHN WILSON TALKING WITH STUDENTS IN THE LIVING ROOM

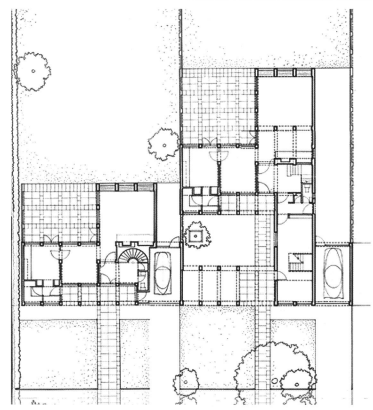

of an unprecedented political and procurement campaign, lasting 36 years – even longer than the construction of St Paul's Cathedral by Christopher Wren!

In addition to his commitment to practice and teaching, Wilson wrote two important theoretical books, *Architectural Reflections* (1992) and *The Other Tradition* (1995). He was also a trustee of the National Gallery and the Tate Gallery. In 1997 a touring retrospective exhibition of his work was accompanied by a booklet with texts by Kenneth Frampton, Martin Richardson and the artist R. B. Kitaj. Wilson was made a Commander of the Order of the Lion of Finland, and in Britain he was knighted in 1998.

Wilson built his own house-cum-studio at 2 Grantchester Road, Cambridge between 1961 and 1964 primarily, of course, as a building in which to live and run his practice. But the new construction also served other purposes. Many jibes had been made in the popular press about modern architects who did not actually live in the houses they themselves had designed, and Wilson wanted to repudiate such scoffing. Moving into the house was a gesture of confidence in modern design. Things got off to a good start in his new home when, as said, his office there – which was his first independent practice – was quickly awarded commissions for three projects. Soon he gathered a design team around him in Grantchester Road. But the house was not just a place of residence and work. It also fulfilled an academic as well as social function. Wilson supervised

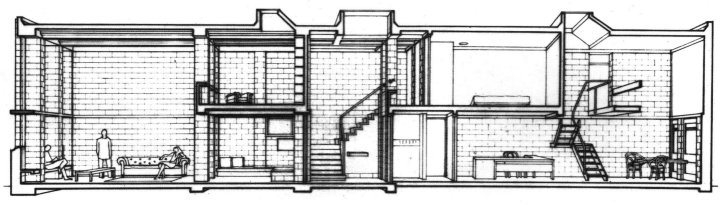

PERSPECTIVE CROSS-SECTION

his Cambridge students there, giving them singly or in small groups week-ly one-hour tutorials, in the traditional Cambridge University teaching style. He preferred to teach architecture both in the intimate setting of his own house with its natural light, rather in the impersonal neon-lit rooms of the School of Architecture, and in a piece of modern "carved space" that he himself had designed, which could serve as an object lesson. From both the office and his tutorials, work would often spill out of the house in the summer into the patio and garden, where a more infor-mal, relaxed and playful atmosphere prevailed.

The site of the house, which lies on the western edge of the city of Cambridge among medium-sized houses 30–50 years old, is formed by the division of an orchard into plots measuring 15.15 m wide by 45.45 m deep. Actually, Wilson designed a pair of houses on the site, and had envisaged constructing a series extending up the street, but in the end only two were built, his and the Squire house. The design of the pair explores the conventional idea of a mixed residential street architecture, and is based on a system of spatial and constructional elements whose combination would have extended the two dwellings up the whole street with many variations. Common to each home is the disposition of the entrance loggia, back entrance and larder on the street side, and kit-chen, dining room and living room facing onto a walled patio on the gar-den side.

With regard to the remaining elements, the two houses differed widely. The Wilson house was advanced along the grid lines into the gar-den with its office and an entry courtyard on the street frontage, and the living room was developed into a double-height space with a roof-lit library gallery at the rear, whereas the Squire house carried its principal bedroom over the single-height living room. Maximum privacy was the aim, attained in relation to the road by the use of glass blocks and trans-lucent glass, and achieved between the houses by orienting the living rooms around walled patios that faced south and west and by enclosing the gardens with walls.

The building system is modular. Each house is set out on a modular planning grid by a regular bay space 1.30 m located on an irregular tar-tan of 300 cm in the east-west grain and 400 cm in the north-south grain. Both houses are constructed of standard 200 x 400 cm concrete blocks made with crushed Abergele limestone and of waterproof white cement, with white aggregate concrete beams exposed. The interior walls are also of fair-faced blockwork except in the bedrooms and the bathroom,

which are plastered. All timber is stained with dark brown preservative. The floors are white rubber tile, the windows are double-glazed, and heat-ing is provided by off-peak electric underfloor panels. The pair of houses represented the first time that concrete block had been used in this coun-try as an 'architectural' material, and they soon became the precedent for buildings all over England, including a Richard Rogers house in Cornwall and a theatre by Peter Moro in Nottingham.

When construction of Wilson's house had reached a height of one metre, a passer-by wandering onto the site enquired: "What is the tem-ple dedicated to?", while Colin Rowe, who was teaching at the School of Architecture at the time, described the building as "the smallest monu-ment in Cambridge". The living room in Wilson's home was the subject of both a major painting by Howard Hodgkin (*Grantchester Road*, 1975) and an unfinished crayon drawing by David Hockney.

Since 1994 Wilson's house has become the home of the Wittgen-stein Archive, directed by Dr Michael Nedo. Nedo, who has been editing the Vienna edition of Wittgenstein's manuscripts, an undertaking descri-bed by Karl Popper as the most important editorial project of our time, has perceived a 'family resemblance' between Wilson's building and the house that Wittgenstein designed in 1926 for his sister Margarete, some-thing that Wilson happily acknowledges, although he did not set eyes on the Wittgenstein house until 1966. In 2000 Wilson's former house in Cambridge was listed by the Department of English Heritage as being of historic importance.   NICOLA FLORA

BIBLIOGRAPHY:
1965   St John Wilson C., 'Two houses in Cambridge', in *Architectural Design*, November, pp. 546–549
1967   Weidert W., *Einfamilienhauser – International*, Stuttgart, pp. 90–93
1970   Aloi R., *Nuove Ville*, Milan, pp. 302–309
1996   Giedion S., 'Quella terza generazione', in *Zodiac*, 2nd series, no. 16, pp. 41, 204–209
1997   Frampton K., Richardson M., and Kitaj R. B., *Colin St John Wilson*, London

Gert Wingårdh

*1951

1990, RENOVATION AND EXTENSION, STILL INHABITED BY THE ARCHITECT
TOFTA 240, LYCKE, KUNGÄLV (S)

MAIN WORKS AND PROJECTS

1989–99 Astra Hässle (Astra Zeneca) pharmaceutical research facilities, Mölndal (S)

1993–95 Ale cultural centre and secondary school, Nödinge, Gothenburg (S)

1994–98 Ericsson ECS office block and research facilities, Lund (S)

1996–99 Swedish Embassy building, Berlin (D)
ARCB Astra Research Centre, Boston, Waltham, Massachusetts (USA), wins First Prize in competition

1997–2001 Auditorium and student union building, Chalmers Technical University, Gothenburg (S)

1998–99 Ericsson office building, St James Square, London (GB)

1998–2001 Universeum science centre and aquarium, Gothenburg (S), wins First Prize in competition

GERT WINGÅRDH was born on 26 April 1951 in the small town of Skövde, which lies to the east of Gothenburg (Göteborg). He was the only child of an affluent family, which lived in a big villa designed by Hans-Erland Heinemann, at the time a well-known architect in Sweden. His father was a production manager in one of the country's largest concrete-producing companies. At the age of 10 Gert moved with his family from Skövde to a suburb of Gothenburg. The relocation left him feeling lonely, which perhaps caused him to immerse himself increasingly in painting, drawing and construction.

After completing his secondary schooling, Wingårdh began to study art history and economics. He envisaged a career in the art world as a gallery owner, but a study trip to Rome, when he encountered baroque architecture, changed all that, kindling a passionate new interest in architecture. Seeing this, his art history teachers encouraged him to start training as an architect, and he enrolled in the School of Architecture of the Chalmers University of Technology, Gothenburg, where his tutors included the architects Jan Wallinder and Johannes Olivegren. Wingårdh quickly proved to be a talented student, and where others were getting embroiled in the social and political issues of the day, he investigated the work of various celebrated architects, seeking to learn from and emulate them. He was fascinated and inspired by a wide range of architecture, from that of the Baroque to that of Frank Lloyd Wright, Vittorio Gregotti, Robert Venturi and Oscar Niemeyer.

In 1975 Wingårdh graduated from Chalmers as a qualified SAR-accredited (Swedish National Association of Architects) architect and began working with Olivegren at FFNS, a large architectural practice in Gothenburg. However, two years later, in 1977, he left to open his own

office in partnership with the architect Lennart Assmundsson and the sociologist Stefan Ostrowski, and not long after that he launched a second new studio in Stockholm with his wife Annika, who worked in the field of advertising. First assignments included projects for architectural competitions and commissions for villas, one of which, his Nordh house, was featured in *Arkitektur* as early as 1981.

During the early 1980s Wingårdh developed an interest in interior design and a skill for detailing that has remained with him ever since. At the time it led to a series of interior designs for shops, restaurants and hotels, which he implemented with his wife. In the mid-1980s the husband-and-wife duo, now joined by Anders Wilhelmsson, landed their first large-scale commission, for the Scandic Crown Hotel in the centre of Stockholm. This major brief was a breakthrough, leading to an ability to handle more complex projects and also to further important designs, such as his Öijared country club, for which Wingårdh won in 1988 the Kasper Sahlin Prize (awarded annually by SAR for the best new building).

Since 1990, now working again on his own, Wingårdh has been involved in more large-scale commissions as well as in smaller housing projects, villas and competitions. Notable among them have been his Astra Hässle (later Astra Zeneca) pharmaceutical research centre at Mölndal with its many laboratories, which occupied the architect for a full decade (1989–99); his Ale cultural centre and secondary school (1993–95), which has become such a key public building for the small community of Nödinge, outside Gothenburg; his office block and research facilities for Ericsson ECS in Lund (1994–98); his Swedish Embassy building in Berlin (1996–99); his auditorium and student union building at Chalmers Technical University, Gothenburg (1997–2001); his Universeum

THE KITCHEN

THE LIVING ROOM

DETAIL OF THE STAIRS

science centre and aquarium in Gothenburg (1998–2001); and his Bo-01 housing exhibition in Malmö (1999–2001). After winning the Kasper Sahlin Prize in 1988, Wingårdh won it twice more in 1993 for his Astra Hässle project and in 2001 for his Chalmers student union building.

Wingårdh might be said to be an eclectic architect who is freely influenced by both historical and contemporary architecture. He tries to arrive at a fresh solution for every situation. He is open to persuasion during discussions about an ongoing brief and to making changes while it is being executed, and he can make adjustments in the light of new trends. A feature of almost all his projects is a skilful handling of scale, in which he manages to break down enormous programmes to a meaningful human level. His designs also have both an expressionistic and sensual quality. Wingårdh's interest seems to be directed more towards the object than to its context, although in later works a more contextual focus is evident. By Swedish standards the detailing in his work is outstanding. Ecological concerns provide the architect with a dilemma, for he likes to use in his buildings both state-of-the-art 'green' technology and traditional materials, sometimes combining the two. This can lead to an intriguing paradoxicality and complexity that has been typical of Wingårdh's architecture since the 1970s. Gert Wingårdh is not only one of Sweden's most accomplished and renowned contemporary architects, but has inspired and influenced many fellow architects in the country. He has also done much to raise the profile both of architecture and its practitioners there, and has generally helped promote architectural discussion in Sweden.

In 1990 Gert Wingårdh began building a summer house at Tofta 240, Lycke, Kungälv. They bought an old farmhouse, dating back to 1790, renovated and converted it, and also extended it by adding a new living space as well as a studio for the architect to work in. The modest original house, known as Sandstugan, is secluded and not easy to find, lying at the end of a narrow winding track. It is located in a clearing amid trees, and to one side lies a hillock with fruit trees, while on the other there is a cliff. The sea is not far away. Visitors, as they enter the welcoming courtyard, are struck by the intimate scale of the buildings and site.

The summer house is a three-part complex consisting of the old house and two new wings, one on each side. The wing on the left is a new dwelling part, connected with the original house, and comprises a living room, two bedrooms and a bathroom. At gable there is a traditional outdoor storage room, which is in keeping with the local building culture. The wing on the right is a fairly substantial studio, separate from the old farmhouse, and has six work places. Both the original house and the two wings are built in red-painted wood panels. The interiors of all three buildings are closed from the courtyard, and the main entrance with a traditional porch is in the old farmhouse. The intimacy of the entrance yard could be explained by the slight deviation from the right angle that is created by the placement of the studio house. It is the same way to treat a spatial scale as Michelangelo executed in the Capitoline hill in Rome.

Although the roofs of the two wings are covered with peat and grass on birch bark, they are unquestionably modern. The wood panels

LIVING ROOM WITH LIBRARY

OVERVIEW OF THE OLD FARMHOUSE AND BOTH NEW WINGS

are likewise solved modernistically, while the entrances are executed in a sophisticated way, combining steps and benches in a manner reminiscent of Carlo Scarpa. When you enter the original building, passing through a small entrance hall that is connected with an ultramodern kitchen, you come to the library, with its beautiful view over the sea. In this way, a private exterior place is created towards the sea in the west and the sloping meadow. The two other buildings are connected to the court yard and a big lawn north of the studio.

The new dwelling wing is linked with the original house via a small, almost hidden gangway, an arrangement that alludes to a Venturian notion of complexity, whereby the new part is not simply added in an utterly obvious way. The gangway also leads to a small outdoor space between the south gable of the old house and the cliff. It is a sunny corner covered with wild strawberry plants – perhaps a reference to the Swedish saying that the place where wild strawberries grow is a wonderful spot in which to rest.

When Wingårdh started to design the two wings of his summer house, there were few examples of ecological buildings in Sweden that he could draw on. So he decided to – was almost forced – experiment in this respect. He used ecological insulation, avoided plastic materials, and minimised metals and other non-recyclable building materials. The roofs, as said, were covered with peat. The floors are either of soap-washed limestone or scrubbed pine, and the walls and ceilings are glaze-painted with egg-oil-temper. Water is drained away from the roof in the traditional way with wooden guttering.

Although the original farmhouse is much smaller than the two extensions, it remains the principal component of the complex. Taken together, the different parts refer variously to historical and contemporary modes. Wingårdh's summer 'cottage' is an innovative project experimenting both with ecological solutions and architectural concepts. Its

different parts unite heterogeneous ideas into a single sensual entity, even though different idioms are spoken. The result is a feeling of liberated creativity, pleasure and delight. GUNILLA SVENSSON, FINN WERNE

PLAN OF THE GROUND FLOOR

BIBLIOGRAPHY:

1996   Hellmann H. et al. (eds.), *Northern factor: new generation of the North*, exhibition catalogue, Helsinki, pp. 138–145

1999   Hultin O., *Arkitektur I Sverige, Architecture in Sweden 1995–1999*, Stockholm

2000   Tuukkanen P. (ed.), *Matter and Mind in Architecture*, 7th International Alvar Aalto Symposium, Helsinki, pp. 72–73

André Wogenscky
1916 – 2004

1950 – 52, NEW CONSTRUCTION
SAINT-RÉMY-LES-CHEVREUSE (F)

MAIN WORKS AND PROJECTS

1950 Office, 54 Avenue de la Motte-Piquet, Saint-Rémy-les-Chevreuse (F)

1958 Competition project for master plan of Berlin (D)

1967 Maison de la Culture, Grenoble (F), with Alain Richard

1968 Ministry of Defence, Beirut (Lebanon), with Maurice Hindié
Health facilities at the Necker and Saint-Antoine Hospitals, Paris (F)

1968 – 72 Prefecture and law courts, Nanterre (F)

1975 – 82 Social housing (F), 2,000 Salamandre units, Paris (F)
Hospital and sports complex, Riyadh (Saudi Arabia)

1980 – 84 Takarazuka University of Arts and Design (Japan)

ANDRÉ WOGENSCKY, born in Remiremont, studied 1934 – 44 at the Ecole Nationale des Beaux-Arts, at the Institut d'Urbanisme of the University of Paris, and at the Ecole des Arts et Métiers, all in Paris. 1936 – 39 he worked as draftsman in Le Corbusier's offices in Paris. After the war he continued his work for Le Corbusier as an assistant, later as office head, before he opened in 1956 his own practice.

It is said that André Wogenscky discovered his architectural vocation at only seven years of age. And in spite of the disappointment he experienced during his training at Paris' Ecole Nationale des Beaux-Arts in, he did finally manage to fulfil his ambition to become an architect. In his architecture Wogenscky expressed his interest in music and dance, of which he said, "With the body, with gesture and with movement, we achieve a transcendence of the self. Since it is spatial, and constantly evolving, it is very close to architecture." This comment reveals the architect's knowledge of the Oriental philosophy Zen and of its conception of space: relative, anisotropic, dynamic, and composed of currents of force and energy. Together with his wife, the sculptress Marta Pan, Wogenscky shared many of the interests of their mid-20th-century contemporaries, including French artists from the Groupe Espace, American abstract painters, and composers of serial music. Like many French architects of his generation, Wogenscky spent a large part of his career abroad, living in the Lebanon, Saudi Arabia and the French overseas territories.

Wogenscky's private house-cum-studio, a new construction that he designed and built for himself and his wife Marta Pan between 1950 and 1952 in Saint-Rémy-les-Chevreuse, does not have a name. Annik Pély-

Audran, who has written a book about the architect, described it as made-to-measure, a characterisation that brings to mind the idea of architecture as clothing. This house provides made-to-measure 'clothing' for its two inhabitants, an architect and an artist. In keeping with the architecture-clothing metaphor, Wogenscky was fond of talking about a 'milieu physique', a physical or bodily milieu into which the body is plunged. And, indeed, it is difficult to separate out the house's different constituent rooms from its spatial unity. Using this goal as a starting point, the architect attempted to reveal the continuity between the interior and the exterior, between structure and volume, and between decor and architecture. Thus, "the garden comes into the house, and the house goes into the garden". Not a single door constrains space. Only the massing of the volumes guide the body and eye. The employment of a harmonious system, like colours and geometric forms, is part of the same quest for unity.

The kitchen, the metaphorical stomach, is the point of origin for this three-dimensional spiral. Wogenscky used Le Corbusier's 'Modulor', a system he helped develop for the master. The different functional spaces develop in an uninterrupted fashion over the 150 m² used, with the living room opening over the garden, the sculpture workshop lying to the east, and the concrete stairs with no guard rail to the west. On the first floor, the architect's windowless office opens onto the space of the living room and the workshop, as well as the bedroom and bathroom. Above, the roof is a terrace protected by a parapet. Their organic forms are juxtaposed with pebbles, thus combining open sky with an enclosed landscape. Wooded terrain – man's first shelter – surrounds the house. But the depth of the windows and doors, a conical chimney in stainless steel,

THE SOUTH FAÇADE

VIEW OF THE HOUSE IN THE PARK

THE LIVING AREA

SITE PLAN

FLOOR PLAN

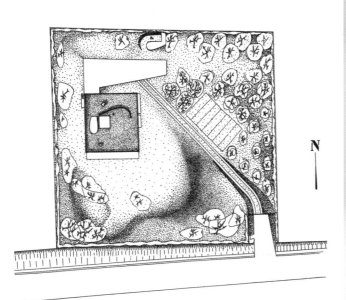

N

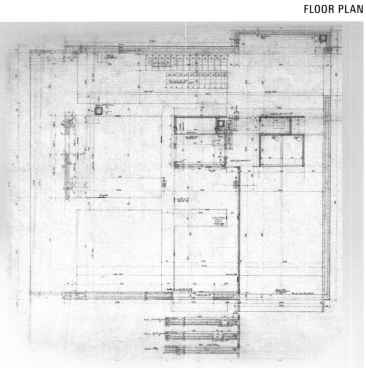

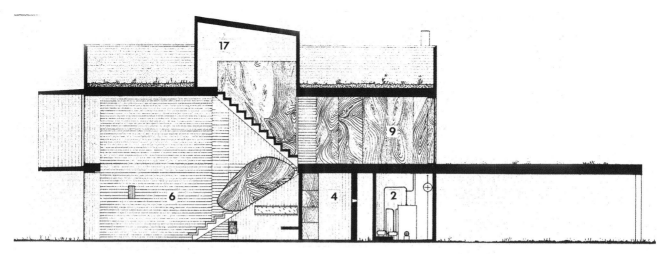

NORTH-SOUTH SECTION ACROSS THE STAIRCASE

NORTH-SOUTH SECTION ACROSS THE ATELIER

a hollow concrete window ledge between the living room and the garden, and the systematic use of red and black all reveal a sophistication of design far beyond the need to create shelter. In the same way, the geometry of the structure and the spaces – stairs or table – was a conscious choice, the fruit of long reflection. In addition, the building's two inhabitants added personal touches. Several of Marta Pan's abstract sculptures are placed in various rooms, on the terrace and in the garden. The house had been inhabited since 1952 but was somewhat transformed over the years, e.g., by the addition of a pond linking the exterior to the interior of the living room.

The house may be André Wogenscky's first personal work, and he may have spent much of his time working on Le Corbusier's apartment blocks, but the building is neither a pale imitation of the master, nor a failed attempt at extremist originality. It is a reflection of the personality of the couple who occupy it. Amazingly, the house was not selected for inclusion in the September 1952 issue of *L'Architecture d'Aujourd'hui*, the magazine devoted to individual dwellings. Yet it bears comparison with the homes of Marcel Breuer and of Richard Neutra in the United States. Like those residences, this building seems to explore the link between interior and exterior, as well as the purity of the materials – glass and concrete. At the end of his career, in 1981, Wogenscky had pushed his

interest in dynamic space, initiated in his home in Saint-Rémy-les-Chevreuse, to its limits. It is unfortunate that his late 'Maison dans le vent' (house in the wind), a project commissioned for the mountains in Faraya, was never built. Nevertheless, the model for that building, and what the architect said about it, enable us to understand the route taken by Wogenscky after 1952: "While studying this project, I always felt the force and the direction of the wind. Sometimes I had the impression I was carried in this direction, into a dynamic and polarised space. My project had to be that as well. The ridges are rounded to allow the wind to slide off them."

AYMONE NICOLAS

BIBLIOGRAPHY:
1955   Winkler R., *Das Haus des Architekten*, Zurich
        'Maison à Saint-Rémy-les-Chevreuse, A. Wogenscky arch.', in *Nouveau Femina*, January
1957   'Maison à Saint-Rémy-les-Chevreuse, A. Wogenscky arch.', in *Domus*, no. 326, January
1972   Wogenscky A., *Architecture Active*, Paris
1993   Pély-Audran A., *André Wogenscky*, Paris

John Young
*1944

**1986–89, NEW CONSTRUCTION, STILL INHABITED BY THE ARCHITECT
HAMMERSMITH, LONDON (GB)**

MAIN WORKS AND PROJECTS

1971–77	Centre Pompidou, Paris (F), Rogers and Piano
1978–86	Lloyd's of London (GB), RRP
1987–92	Reuters Data Centre, London (GB), RRP
1990–94	Channel 4 TV Headquarters, London (GB), RRP
1989–	Terminal 5, Heathrow Airport, London (GB), RRP
1996–2002	Broadwick House, Soho, London (GB), RRP
1997–	Madrid Barajas Airport (E), RRP with Studio Lamela

JOHN YOUNG'S career is intimately intertwined with the history of high-tech architecture. While still a student, he was already working for Team 4, the practice founded in 1962 by Richard and Su Rogers with Norman and Wendy Foster. Young was also part of the international team of architects that realised the Centre Pompidou in Paris. Young describes his role within the Richard Rogers Partnership, formed in 1977, as 'constructor' and he has been closely associated with a number of RRP's most iconic buildings, including Lloyd's of London and the Channel 4 Headquarters.

The Deck House forms part of a residential complex designed by the practice on a site adjacent to the practice's London offices in Hammersmith, West London. Between 1986 and 1989 John Young planned and built this apartment overlooking the River Thames with meticulous attention to detail. The result is spectacular and has won a prestigious RIBA national award. Young's apartment organically supplements the existing structure, topping it with a glass crown. From the exterior the apartment reads as a glass cube housing a dramatic double-height living space surmounted at roof level with two additional spaces housing a bathroom and a glass observatory.

Entering the apartment the eye is drawn to the clarity of the internal space and then to the striking views out over the River Thames and the panorama over the entire London cityscape. The apartment's proximity to the broad expanse of water below means that effects of sunlight, mist or rain-storms create a constantly changing ambience within the space.

Apart from the basic furniture using Modernist classics by Le Corbusier and Eileen Gray, the apartment's interior design is more of an experimental 'essay'. Here, Le Corbusier's metaphor of a 'machine for living' becomes a reality. The staircases, doors and closets are not so much architectural elements as rather a set of apparatus. In his dual role as both architect and client, Young experiments with things that would be impossible with 'normal 'projects. Young has not taken 'off-the-shelf' products but opted to develop a series of technically complex constituent parts, calling on disciplines that fall outside the scope of everyday architecture, i.e. marine technology or specialised machining techniques.

This transformation, or extension, of architectural principles has resulted in a dynamic space prompted by three key 'drivers': Young is obsessive in his continuing evaluation of everyday technical objects – oil refineries, gas holding tanks, light-houses, etc. For Young these are potential 'treasure troves' which he can explore, plunder and adapt for his own purposes. Second, Young is a complete perfectionist, leaving no detail to chance – this apartment is three-dimensional evidence of that ongoing quest. The aesthetic effect of this space is entirely dependent on Young's rigorous exploration and 'fine-tuning' of structure and technology, resulting in an extraordinary impression of all-pervading clarity. Indeed the apartment closely echoes the basic principles of functionalism – where the practical and the aesthetic are fused into an inseparable unity. Third, the actual construction process of this space has demanded highly-skilled craftsmen and technicians with sophisticated technical ability. Here, Young has been able to 'tap into' the English tradition of skilled craftsmanship – he has called upon numerous small specialist firms (boat builders etc) who can create individually crafted elements to the highest technical standards.

The overall impression is, however, anything but 'cold'. Delicate, filigree beams reach into the room like antennae, imbuing the space with an almost 'living' feel. Elsewhere, the use of vertically stacked, highly sculpted circular heating elements (similar to Samurai shields) creates a strictly ordered but nonetheless decorative effect.

ROOF TERRACE

ROUND RADIATORS ON THE WALL OF THE MAIN FLOOR

KITCHEN

VIEW FROM THE WORKING AREA INTO THE KITCHEN

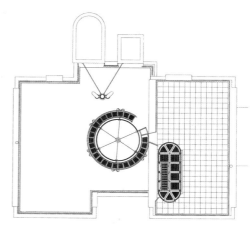

ROOF

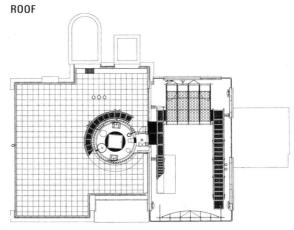

INTERMEDIATE LEVEL

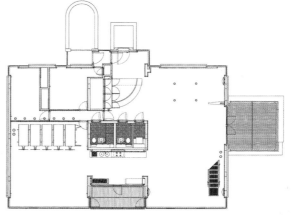

ENTRANCE LEVEL

< STAIRCASE TO THE INTERMEDIARY FLOOR

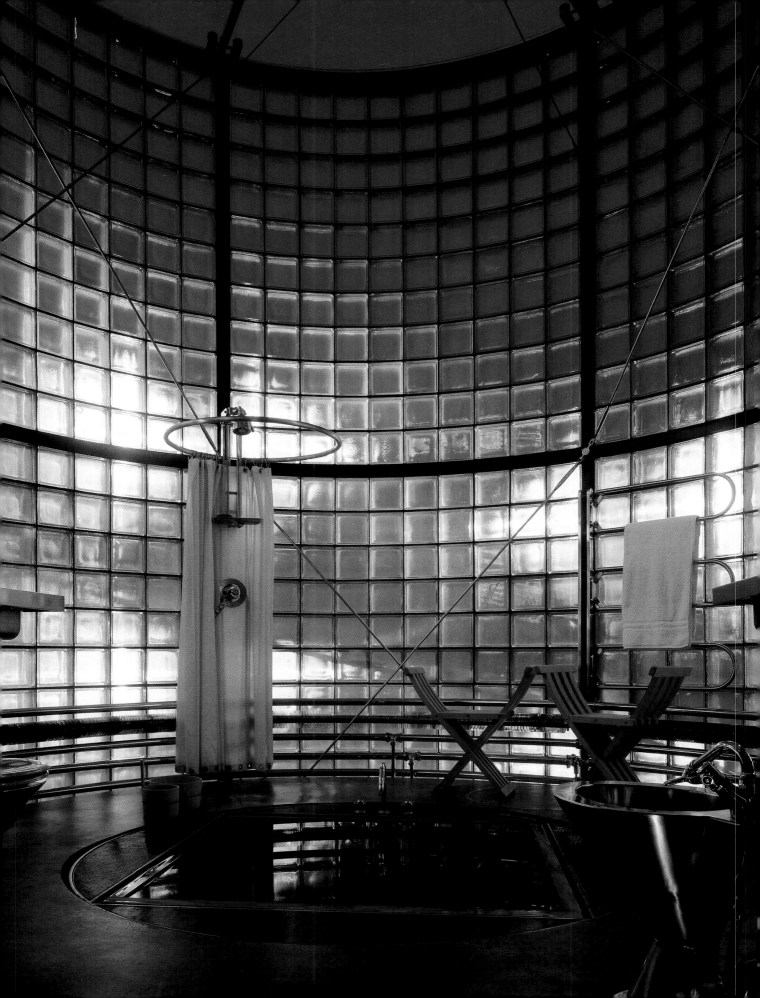

CATWALK FROM THE SUSPENDED INTERMEDIARY LEVEL TO THE BATHROOM

One enters the apartment directly from the stainless-steel lined lift. To the right of the main double-height living space is a single-storey 'wing' containing a study area (facing west) complete with bespoke stainless steel filing cabinets on rolling tracks. The other half of this wing (facing east) contains a separate guest space with two bedrooms and a bathroom. Connecting the main living area and the 'wing' is a kitchen/dining space with an attached loggia overlooking the river.

From the main living space an impressively delicate staircase leads up to a mezzanine bedroom gallery suspended above the living room below. Circular glazed apertures in the concrete flooring increase the sense of delicacy and transparency. A catwalk leading from this sleeping area takes one either to a large roof terrace, or to a set of stairs leading on up to the glass observatory at the upper roof level, or to the bathroom. This room is a visual tour de force – a spacious cylindrical room contained within a translucent wall of glass 'bricks'. A large sunken bathtub of Japanese cedar takes centre stage, with other bathroom fittings arranged around the circumference.

The glazed observatory sited on the upper roof level affords spectacular, panoramic views over the whole city. An elegant external spiral staircase winds around the perimeter of the bathroom, connecting the upper and lower roof terraces.

Young's apartment exemplifies the best aspirations of modern architecture – flowing sequences of space, and the creation of an exquisitely crafted and essentially adaptable environment. Young's extraordinary facility and ingenuity as a designer have demonstrated the sensual possibilities of Modernist architecture.   EBERHARD SYRING

BIBLIOGRAPHY:
1991   'Apartment London Architect John Young', *Blueprint*, Extra 01
1992   'Architektenwohnung in London', in *Baumeister*, no. 1/1992, p. 35
       'Appartement, London', in *Detail*, no. 2/1992, pp. 132–134
1995   'Technischer Ausbau und Architektur. Im Gespräch mit John Young: Entwicklungslinien bei Richard Rogers Partnership', in *Detail*, no. 2/1995, pp. 162–167
1999   Doubilet S., Boles D.: *European house now. Contemporary architectural directions*, New York, pp. 150–161

Álftanes
Reykjavík

Oslo
Portør

Helsinki
Kirkkonummi

Stockholm
Lisön

Helensburgh
Glasgow
West Linton

Lycke

Lund

Rungsted
Klampenborg

Sandycove

Cambridge

Chorleywood
Fonthill
Hartfield

London
Bexleyheath

Den Haag
Nieuwpoort

Amsterdam
Almere
Rotterdam
Sint-Antelinks

Berlin
Dessau

Gent
Bruxelles
Tervuren

Mechelen
Liège

Köln

Trébeurden

Paris
Saint-Rémy

Darmstadt

Baden-Baden
Nancy
Stuttgart
Walddorfhäslach

Wien

Steinaweg

Zürich
Meilen

Satteins
Kitzbühel
Steindorf

Megève
Méribel

Bellinzona
Sorengo

Belluno

Milano

Guimarães
Matosinhos

Torino

Roquebrune-
Cap-Martin

Marina
di Massa

Madrid

Girona
Barcelona

Pollença
Porto Petro

Palermo

Athínai

Acknowledgements

The present volume is a result of the project developed by MEAM Net (Modern European Architecture – Museum Network), a research group at the Department of Architectural Planning of the Polytechnic of Milan, named "One Hundred Houses for One Hundred European Architects of the Twentieth Century". The project was funded by the European Union "Culture 2000" programme, and benefited from the decisive participation of twenty-seven institutions around Europe. The aim of the project was to increase awareness of the common heritage represented by the homes of some of the greatest (though not only the greatest) European architects of the twentieth century, and perhaps also to eventually contribute to their conservation.

The itinerary hereinafter proposed, which the MEAM Net group extended in co-operation with Taschen GmbH, is one of the many possible, and is inspired above all by the desire to create, or rather by the freedom to imagine, an "open-air museum" at European level, providing as wide a public as possible with the traces, sometimes mere remains, of houses that can still be seen intact and those that have been destroyed or completely modified.

A large part of the material is also on the accompanying web-site (www.meamnet.polimi.it), which will remain as a permanent on-line archive of the whole project, and a selection of study-cases forms the core of the travelling exhibition "One Hundred Houses for One Hundred European Architects".

The whole project would never have been realised without the help, contribution, support and co-operation of:
the European programme "Culture 2000"
the project initiator DPA – Politecnico di Milano (Piero Bottoni, Luigi Figini)
the partners:
Architekturstiftung Österreich, Vienna (Günther Domenig, Adolf Krischanitz, Roland Rainer, Rudolf Wäger, Otto Wagner),
Archiv Institut für Geschichte und Theorie der Architektur ETH Zürich, Zurich (Max Haefeli, Alfred Roth)
Archivio del Moderno – Accademia di architettura – Università della Svizzera italiana, Mendrisio (Aurelio Galfetti, Rino Tami, Vittoriano Viganò)
Archivio Progetti – Istituto Universitario di Architettura di Venezia (Edoardo Gellner)
DeSingel Internationaal Kunstcentrum, Antwerp (Peter Callebout, Gaston Eysselinck, Eugeen Liebaut, Henry van de Velde, Marie-José Van Hee, Bob Van Reeth, Charles Vandenhove)
Norsk Arkitekturmuseum, Oslo (Sverre Fehn, Knut Knutsen, Arne Korsmo, Kjell Lund, Christian Norberg-Schulz, Wenche Selmer)
Royal Commission on the Ancient and Historical Monuments of Scotland, Edinburgh (Alexander Nisbet Paterson, Leslie Grahame Thomson)
Suomen Rakennustaiteen Museo, Helsinki (Alvar Aalto, Dag and Kaj Englund, Arne Ervi, Herman Gesellius, Armas Lindgren, Eliel Saarinen, Toivo Korhonen)
the participants:
Arkitekturmuseet, Stockholm (Erik Gunnar Asplund, Ralph Erskine, Sven Markelius, Sigurd Lewerentz)
Bauhaus-Archiv und Museum für Gestaltung, Berlin (Walter Gropius)
Byggingarlistarsafn – Listasafn Reykjavìkur, Reykjavik (Gunnar Hansson, Manfred Vilhjálmsson)
Collegi d'Arquitectes de Catalunya, Barcelona (Antonio Bonet, José Antonio Coderch de Sentmenat, Josep Puig i Cadafalch)
Kunstakademiets-Bibliotek, Copenhagen (Jakob Halldor Gunnløgsson, Arne Emil Jacobsen, Mogens Lassen)
Documentation Centre for Neohellenic Architecture – Benaki Museum, Athens (Nicos Valsamakis)
Hunterian Art Gallery – University of Glasgow (Charles Rennie Mackintosh)
Institut Français d'Architecture, Paris (Roger Le Flanchec, Henry-Jacques Le Même, Auguste Perret, André Wogenscky)
Irish DOCOMOMO, Dublin (Michael Scott)
Nederlands Architectuurinstituut, Rotterdam (Hendrik Petrus Berlage, Herman Petrus Coenraad Haan, Johannes Hendrik van den Broek)
Fondo „Carlo Mollino", Sistema Bibliotecario, Biblioteca Centrale di Architettura, Politecnico di Torino
Südwestdeutsches Archiv für Architektur und Ingenieurbau, Karlsruhe (Egon Eiermann, Otto Ernst Schweizer).

Our thanks are also due to the many private archives, collections and photographers whose efforts enabled us to broaden the scope of the present publication.

Credits

© Alvar Aalto Archives, Helsinki, p. 13, Ph: Maija Holma, pp. 16–19

© Ph: L. F. Alves, Porto, pp. 366–367

© Reinhold Andris Office, Walddorfhäslach, p. 26, 29 below

© Ph: T. & R. Annan & Sons, p. 250

© Architectenbureau Van den Broek en Bakema Archive, pp. 62–63, Ph: V. Cornelius, p. 65 above right

© Archive Famille Prouvé, Paris, p. 322 below, drawing: Isabelle da Costa, p. 323 below

© Archive Museum voor Sierkunst en Vormgeving, Ghent, pp. 116, 118 above, 119 above, 420–423

© Archive Charlotte Perriand, Paris 2003, p. 312, Ph: C. Perriand, pp. 308–311, 313

© Archive Swiss Institute for Art Research, Berne, p. 131 below, Ph: B. Bill, H. Steiner, E. Heinige, p. 130, Ph: Fröhlich, 129 below left, Ph: H. Guggenbühl, p. 128

© Archivio Franco Albini, Milan, pp. 22–25

© Archivio Basile, Dipartimento di Rappresentazione, Facoltà di Architettura di Palermo, pp. 36–39

© Archivio del Moderno – Accademia di architettura, Mendrisio, pp. 132–135, 374–377, 426 below, 427 below, Archivio Vittoriano Viganò, Ph: A. Ballo, p. 426 above, Ph: Studio Casali, pp. 425, 427 above, Ph: E. Valenza, p. 424

© Archivio Alessandro Figini, Milan, pp. 124, 127 below

© Archivio Gio Ponti, Milan, Ph: Salvatore Licitra, pp. 314–319

Area no. 37, 4/5 1998, p. 401

Arkitektur, no. 2, May 1976, p. 239 below

© Arkitekturmuseet, Stockholm, pp. 6, 30, 107 above, 239, 260, Ph: A. Littorinn, pp. 35 below, 263, Ph: M. Plunger, p. 105 above, Ph: S. Sundahl, p. 104, Ph: B. Törngren, pp. 261, 262

© Arxiu Català-Roca, Barcelona, pp. 80, 81 above

© Arxiu José Antonio Coderch, Sant Cugat del Vallès, pp. 81 below, 82–83

© Ph: Paul and Stefan Asenbaum, p. 444 below

© Ph: I. Barbarito, pp. 383, 384

© Bauhaus-Archiv, Berlin, p. 153 below, Ph: Lucia Moholy, pp. 150, 151, 153 above, 152 above and below right, drawing: Lázló Moholy-Nagy, p. 152 below left

© Benthem Crouwel Office, Amsterdam pp. 44, 49

© Ph: P. Berntsen, pp. 355 below, 357

© Bildarchiv, Österreichische Nationalbibliothek, Vienna, p. 442

© Bill Foundation: Ph: B. Bill, pp. 129 above and below right, 131 above

© Winfried Brenne Office, Berlin, pp. 379 below, 380, 381 left

© British Architectural Library (RIBA) London, pp. 272, 432–433, 436, 437 above

© Ph: T. Broekmans, pp. 242–243, 244 above

© Richard Bryant/arcaid, pp. 453–456, 457 above, 471–472, 473 left, 474–475

© Peter Callebout Archive, Brussels, p. 73

© Caruso St John Office, London, pp. 74, 78 below, 79 centre and below, Ph: Hélène Binet, pp. 75–77, 78 above, 79 above

© Ph: Martin Charles: pp. 45, 434–435

© Colegio Oficial de Arquitectos de Baleares, Mallorca, pp. 288 below, 289 below, Ph: T. Ozonas, p. 289 above

© Collection Jean-Louis Cohen, Paris, pp. 257 above, 258, 259 left

© Dipartimento di Progettazione dell'Architettura, Politecnico di Milano, Ph: Topuntoli, pp. 125, 126 above right and above left, 127 above left, Archivio Bottoni, pp. 58–61

© Duccio Malagamba, Barcelona, pp. 368–371, 372 above, 373

© Aldo van Eyck Archive, Amsterdam, pp. 112, 114, Ph: J. Versnel, pp. 113, 115

© Gaston Eysselinck Archive, Ostend, pp. 118 below, 119 centre and below

© Francisco de Asís Cabrero Torres-Quevedo Office, Madrid, pp. 67, 68 left, 69, Ph: Santiago Cabrero, p. 66, Ph: P. Imbault, p. 68 right

© Ph: Federico Climent Guimerá, pp. 286, 287 above left and below, 288 above

© Collegi d'Arquitectes de Catalunya, Barcelona, p. 57

© Ph: Diego Congote, p. 287 above right

© José Antonio Corrales Gutiérrez Office, Madrid, pp. 84, 86 above, 87 below

© Ph: Enrique Delgado, p. 86 below

© Günther Domenig Office, Klagenfurt, pp. 92 below, 93 above

© Ph: J. Donat, p. 459 below centre

© Ph: M. Dubois, p. 117

© Ph: R. Einzig, p. 459 below right and left

© Fondation Le Corbusier, Paris, pp. 214, 216–217, 219–221

© Fondo Carlo Mollino, Biblioteca Centrale di Architettura, Politecnico di Torino, p. 268, Ph: Carlo Mollino, pp. 269–271

© Gandon Archive, Kinsale, pp. 350–353

Philippe Garner, pp. 146–148 above, 149

© Ph: S. Glòmmi, p. 120

© Richard Glover/VIEW, pp. 299–302, 303 above

© Peter Gössel, Bremen, pp. 141, 142 above and below left, 143

© Ph: E. Grønli, p. 354

© Haefeli Family Archive, Zurich, p. 165

© R. Halbe/artur, pp. 223–224, 225 below, 226, 363, 364 above, 365 above

© Hansson Family Archive, Reykjavik, pp. 168, 170 below right

© Ph: Ole Haupt, p. 396

© Ph: D. Held, pp. 417, 418 above, 419 below

© Ph: M. Herrmann, pp. 206, 208 below

© Ph: M. Hetzmannseder, p. 328

Fritz Hoeber: *Peter Behrens*, Georg Müller und Eugen Rentsch, Munich 1913, pp. 41, 42, 43 above left, centre and below

© Clemens Holzmeister Archive, Salzburg, pp. 172, 174 above, Ph: C. Holzmeister, p. 10

Clemens Holzmeister, exhibition catalogue with contributions by F. Achleitner, W. Holzbauer and H. Muck, Academy of Fine Arts, Vienna 1982, p. 175

Clemens Holzmeister: Bauten, Entwürfe und Handzeichnungen, Salzburg/Leipzig 1937, Ph: J. Scherb, p. 173 below right

© Hunterian Art Gallery, University of Glasgow, Mackintosh Collection, Glasgow, pp. 251–255

© Ph: Gudmundur Ingólfsson, 2001, pp. 169, 170 above and below left, 171, 428–431

© Institut Amatller d'Art Hispanic, Archive Puig i Cadafalch, Barcelona, pp. 324–327

© Institut Français d'Architecture, Paris, pp. 229–231, 307, 467–469, Ph: Coumot, p. 304, Ph: Chevojon, pp. 305–306, Ph: D. Le Couédic, p. 228, Ph: M. Pan, p. 466, Fonds Le Même, Archives Départementales de Savoie, Chambéry, pp. 233–234, 235, Ph: Studio S. Holt, p. 232

© Institut für Geschichte und Theorie der Architektur, Zurich, pp. 164, 166–167, 342–343, 344 below, 345 below, Ph: H. Binder, pp. 341 above and below right, 344 above, 345 above, Ph: H. Finsler, p. 341 below left, Ph: D. Quarella, Zollikon, p. 340

© Institut Mathildenhöhe, Darmstadt, pp. 40, 43 above right, 290, 292 left, 293 above

© Istituto Universitario di Architettura di Venezia, Archivio Progetti, p. 336, Fondo E. Gellner, pp. 136–139, Ph: Casali, pp. 337–339

© Ph: E. Katzenstein: p. 54

© Ph: Jan Kempenaers, p. 414 above

© Ph: H. Kessels, pp. 409 below, 410 above right

© Adolf Krischanitz Office, Salzburg, p. 208 above

© Ph: C. Kühne, p. 330

Drawing: Nicole Kuhlmann, Cloppenburg, p. 259 right

© Ph: Soeren Kuhn, pp. 397–400, 401

© Kunstakademiets-Bibliotek, Copenhagen, pp. 154–159, 188–191, 210–213

Drawing: Andreas Längsfeld, Bremen, pp. 65 below, 163 below

© *La maison française*, Paris, p. 71 above

© Ph: Andrée Lawaese, p. 70

© Lederer Ragnarsdóttir Oei Office, Stuttgart, pp. 222, 225 above, 227

© Ph: D. Leistner/artur, pp. 391–394

© Ph: Jannes Linders: pp. 46–48

© Eugeen Liebaut Office, Aalst, pp. 240, 244 below, 245 right

© M. Mannen, Ph: K. Anshelm, p. 239 above, Ph: B. Nyberg, pp. 236, 237, Ph: O. Snogeröd, p. 238

© Mecanoo Office, Delft, pp. 182, 184 below, 187 below, Ph: Daria Scagliola, pp. 183, 186, Ph: Christian Richters, pp. 184 above, 185, 187 above

© Ministère de la Région de Bruxelles-Capitale, Ph: Ch. Bastin and J. Evrard, pp. 177–179, 181 above left

© Ph: José María G. del Monte, pp. 85, 87 above

Walter Müller-Wulckow: *Wohnbauten und Siedlungen aus deutscher Gegenwart*, in: Architektur 1900–1929 in Deutschland, Königstein im Taunus 1999, pp. 379 above, 381 right

© Musée Horta, Brussels, p. 176, drawing: Barbara Van der Wee, p. 181 above left and below

© Musée des Arts décoratifs, Paris, Ph: Marc Vaux, p. 257 below

© Musée Nationale d'Art Moderne – Centre George Pompidou – Bibliothèque Kandinsky, Paris, p. 256, Fonds Cordot Joly, pp. 320, 323 above left, Fonds Eileen Gray, p. 148 below, Fonds Jean Prouvé, pp. 321, 322, 323 above right

Hermann Muthesius: *Landhäuser*, Munich 1912, p. 281 above right

© Nederlands Architectuurinstituut, Rotterdam, pp. 51 below, 53, 64, 160, 161 below, Ph: B. van Beek, Den Haag, pp. 51 above, 52, Ph: V. Cornelius, pp. 65 left above, 162, Ph: E. Deyhle, pp. 161 above, 163 above, Ph: B. Eilers, p. 50

© Neohellenic Architecture Archives of the Benaki Museum, Athens, pp. 402–407

© Ph: Ferdinand Neumüller, p. 88

© F: R. Nikolic/artur, pp. 27–28, 29 above

© Norsk Arkitekturmuseum, Oslo, pp. 121 below, 123 above, 197, 205 below, 248 below, 249 above right and below, 285, 354, © Ph: J. Bengston, p. 122 below, © Ph: P. Berntsen, pp. 199, 247, 248 above, 249 above, © Ph: M. Brun, p. 246, © Ph: R. Gain, p. 196 above left, © Ph: C. Norberg-Schulz, p. 283, © Ph: Teigen Fotoatelier AS, pp.192, 196 above right and below, 202–204, 205 above, 284

© Ph: Anthony Oliver, pp. 273–276

© John Pawson, London, p. 303 below, Ph: Christoph Kicherer, p. 298

© Ph: C. Pfaff, pp. 207, 209

© Ph: Max Plunger, pp. 105 below, 106, 107 below

© Ph: Gennaro Postiglione, p. 282

© Ph: Flora Giardiello Postiglione, pp. 121 above, 122 above

© Roland Rainer Private Archive, Klagenfurt, pp. 329, 331

© Umberto Riva Office, Milan, pp. 332–335

© Richard Rogers Partnership Office, London, p. 473 right, Ph: Dan Stevens, p. 470

© Simone Roose, Ph: P. Joly and V. Cardot, pp. 71 below left and right, 72

© Royal Commission on the Ancient and Historical Monuments of Scotland, Edinburgh, Ph: T. & R. Annan & Sons, p. 294, Ph: Crown, pp. 295–297, 387–389

© Royal Institute of Scottish Architects, Glasgow, Ph: Stephens Orr, p. 386

Alberto Sartoris, Gli Elementi dell'Architettura Funzionale. Sintesi panoramica dell'Architettura Moderna, Milan 1941, p. 125 above right and below

© Ph: J. Scherb, pp. 173 above and below left, 174 below

Ph: Roberto Schezen © Esto, pp. 215, 218

© Ph: Harry Seidler, p. 180

© Wenche Selmer Archive, Oslo, Ph: Teigen Fotoatelier AS, p. 355 above

Klaus-Jürgen Sembach: Jugendstil, Cologne, 1990, pp. 291, 292 right

© Ph: Sendra Archive, Barcelona, pp. 55, 56

© Alison and Peter Smithson Architects Archive, London, pp. 359–361, Ph: Jeremy Baker, p. 358

© Ph: H. Snoek, p. 459 above

© Werner Sobek Office, Stuttgart, pp. 362, 364 below

© Souto de Moura Office, Porto, pp. 372 below

© 2003, Staatliche Museen zu Berlin–Stiftung Preußischer Kulturbesitz, Kunstbibliothek, pp. 264–267, Ph: Knud Petersen, p. 293 below

© Ph: B. Stevens, p. 416

© Stiftung Archiv der Akademie der Künste, Berlin, pp. 278 (SAdK portrait photo no. 4), 279–280 and 281 above left (SAdK Wv 9/3, SAdK Wv 9/5, SAdK Wv 9/10, SAdK Wv 9/11), 378 (SAdK BT Slg 28 147/2)

© Ph: G. Stromberg, p. 458

© Südwestdeutsches Archiv für Architektur und Ingenieurbau, Karlsruhe, pp. 94–99, 346–349

© Ph: S. Sundahl, pp. 31–34

© Suomen Rakennustaiteen Museo, Helsinki, pp. 100, 108, 111 below, 140 left and right, 145 below right, 144 below, 144 above, 198, 201 below, Ph: K. Englund, pp. 13, 101, 102, 103 above, Ph: A. Ervi, pp. 109 above and below left, 110, 111 above, Ph: P. Ingervo, pp. 15 below left and right, 20, 13, Ph: Kolmio, p. 103 below, Ph: Nousiainen/Yhtyneitten Kuvapalvelu, p. 109 below right, Ph: D. Nyblin, p. 140 centre, Ph: E. Mäkinen, pp. 14, 15 above, Ph: Museovirasto, p. 145 above, Ph: S. Rista, pp. 199–200, 201 above

© Fernando Távora Office, Porto, pp. 382, 385

© Oswald Mathias Ungers Office, Cologne, pp. 390, 395

© Victoria & Albert Museum, Picture Library, London, p. 277

© Charles Vandenhove Office, Liège, pp. 408, 411 centre and below

© Ph: P. Vander Maren, p. 409 above

© Ph: S. Vanderstichele, pp. 241, 245 left

© Marie-José Van Hee Office, Ghent, pp. 412, 414 below, 415 right

© Ph: Bart Van Leuven, pp. 413, 415 left

© B. Van Reeth Office, Antwerp, pp. 418 below, 419 above

© Ph: Verb, p. 460 above

© Ph: K. Vermeir, pp. 410 above left and below, 411 above

© Colin Wilson Office, London, pp. 460 below, 461

© G. Wingårdh Office, Göteborg, pp. 462, 465, Ph: Bengt Ericksson, pp. 463–464, Ph: Nils-Olof Sjödén, S. 465 above

© Rudolf Wäger Office, Satteins, pp. 438–441

Otto Wagner: Einige Skizzen, Projekte und ausgeführte Bauwerke, vol. IV, Vienna 1922, pp. 443, 444 above, 445

© Sarah Wigglesworth Office, London, pp. 446, 449 right, 451 below, Ph: Paul Smoothy, pp. 447–448, 449 left, 540, 451 above

© Michael Wilford Office, Stuttgart and London, pp. 452, 457 centre and above

© Gerald Zugmann, pp. 89–91, 92 above, 93 centre and below

Imprint

one hundred houses for one hundred european architects of the 20th century

DPA – Politecnico di Milano with the support of the
EU programme "Culture 2000" – Directorate of Culture

Programme leader: Gennaro Postiglione
Programme committee: Francesca Acerboni, Andrea Canziani, Lorenza Comino, Claudia Zanlungo
Scholarly consultants: Maurizio Boriani, Iain Chambers, Adriano Cornoldi
Coordination: Giulio Padovani, Giulia Pellegrino
Partners:
Barbara Feller, Architekturstiftung Österreich, Vienna
Bruno Maurer, Archiv Institut für Geschichte und Theorie der Architektur ETH Zürich, Zurich
Letizia Tedeschi, Archivio del Moderno – Accademia di architettura – Università della Svizzera italiana, Mendrisio
Roberto Sordina, Archivio Progetti – Istituto Universitario di Architettura di Venezia
Katrien Vandermarliere, DeSingel Internationaal Kunstcentrum, Antwerp
Eva Madshus, Norsk Arkitekturmuseum, Oslo
Rebecca Bailey, Royal Commission on the Ancient and Historical Monuments of Scotland, Edinburgh
Timo Keinänen, Suomen Rakennustaiteen Museo, Helsinki
Participants:
Claus Smidt, Kunstakademiets-Bibliotek, Copenhagen
David Peycere, Institut Français d'Architecture, Paris
Nathalie Boura, Documentation Centre for Neohellenic Architecture – Benaki Museum, Athens
Christian Wolsdorff, Bauhaus-Archiv und Museum für Gestaltung, Berlin
Wulf Schirmer, Südwestdeutsches Archiv für Architektur und Ingenieurbau, Karlsruhe
Shane O'Toole, Irish DOCOMOMO, Dublin
Pétur Ármannsson, Byggingarlistarsafn Listasafn Reykjavikur, Reykjavík
Alfred Marksspain, Nederlands Architectuurinstituut, Rotterdam
Rafael Balanzò, Collegi d'Arquitectes de Catalunya, Barcelona
Bitte Nygreen, Arkitekturmuseet, Stockholm
Pamela Robertson, Hunterian Art Gallery – University of Glasgow
Elena Tamagno, Fondo „Carlo Mollino", Biblioteca Centrale di Architettura, Politecnico di Torino

P.2: House of Herman Petrus Coenraad Haan
© E. Deyle
P. 6: Alvar Aalto with his daughter Johanna on the terrace of their house in Helsinki
P. 10: Clemens Holzmeister's first wife Judith and his daughter Judith sitting on the terrace of their house
P. 13: Living room and dining room in Kaj Englund's apartment

© 2013 TASCHEN GmbH
Hohenzollernring 53, D-50672 Köln
www.taschen.com

Original edition: © 2004 TASCHEN GmbH

© 2013 VG Bild-Kunst, Bonn, for the works of Walter Gropius, Victor Horta, Le Corbusier, Lucia Moholy, Lázló Moholy-Nagy, Robert Mallet-Stevens, Charlotte Perriand, Jean Prouvé, Mies van der Rohe and Henry van de Velde

General editor: Gennaro Postiglione
with: Francesca Acerboni, Andrea Canziani, Lorenza Comino, Claudia Zanlungo

Editor: Peter Gössel
Project manager: Katja Gazey
Design: Florian Brendel, Konstantin Zigmann
Cover design: Sense/Net, Andy Disl & Birgit Eichwede, Cologne

Translation: Mark Eaton, Ishbel Flett (Reinhold Andris, Werner Sobek, Sarah Wigglesworth & Jeremy Till), Christian Goodden (Jan Benthem, Oswald Mathias Ungers, Otto Wagner), Michael Hulse (introduction), Chris Miller (Victor Horta), Christopher Salter (Adam Caruso, Francine Houben, Arno Lederer, Jórunn Ragnarsdóttir, Marc Oei, Michael Wilford, John Young)

Supplementary editing: Christian Goodden

Editorial co-ordination: Susanne Klinkhamels, Christiane Blass

Printed in China
ISBN 978-3-8365-4487-0